# Field Guide to Consulting and Organizational Development with Nonprofits:

## A Collaborative and Systems Approach to Performance, Change and Learning

By Carter McNamara, MBA, PhD

AUTHENTICITY CONSULTING, LLC
MINNEAPOLIS, MN USA

For reprint permission, more information on Authenticity Consulting, LLC, or to order additional copies of this or any of our other publications, please contact:

> Authenticity Consulting, LLC
> 4008 Lake Drive Avenue North
> Minneapolis, MN 55422-1508 USA
>
> 800.971.2250 toll-free
> 763.971.8890 direct
>
> www.authenticityconsulting.com

**Trademarks**

Authenticity Circles, Free Management Library, Free Nonprofit Micro-eMBA and Free Micro-eMBA are service marks of Authenticity Consulting, LLC, Minneapolis, Minnesota. "Leveraging the Power of Peers" is a registered mark of Authenticity Consulting, LLC, Minneapolis, Minnesota.

**Credits**

Cover design by Erin Scott/Wylde Hare Creative, Minneapolis, Minnesota.
Photographs © 2005 JupiterImages Corporation/Comstock.com, primary cover photo;
   © Teri McNamara/ Impressions & Expressions and Erin Scott/Wylde Hare Creative,
   secondary cover photos.
Clip art by Nova Development Corporation Art Explosion 750,000 Images.
Printed by Graphic & Printing Services, Big Lake, Minnesota.

Manufactured in the United States of America
First Edition November 2005
Second Printing September 2010

**Cataloging Data**

McNamara, Carter, 1953 -

   Field Guide to Consulting and Organizational Development with Nonprofits: A Collaborative and Systems Approach to Performance, Change and Learning / by Carter McNamara

   Includes bibliographical references and index.

   ISBN 10 1-933179-00-1 (pbk.)

   ISBN 13 978-1-933719-00-9 (pbk.)

   1. Nonprofit organizations. 2. Consulting. 3. Organizational development.
I. Title

**FSC**
**Mixed Sources**
Product group from well-managed forests, controlled sources and recycled wood or fiber

Cert no. SW-COC-004306
www.fsc.org
©1996 Forest Stewardship Council

# Table of Contents

# Table of Tables

# Introduction

## *For Consultants (External and Internal) and Leaders for Change*

Today, nonprofit leaders must operate as internal change agents if their nonprofits are to show strong performance in meeting the needs of their communities. The best style of leadership to accomplish successful change in organizations is highly collaborative and facilitative in nature – the same style required for external consultants to successfully guide change.

This book is all about working in a collaborative approach with others to facilitate successful and significant change in nonprofits. This book is useful not only to external consultants, but to leaders and managers – change agents working together to guide change in their organizations.

If you are a nonprofit leader, you are encouraged to read and apply this book as if you are an internal consultant using the principles, tools and techniques that make all types of consultants successful in guiding their clients through change.

## *What You Can Do from Using This Field Guide*

1. Understand all about you, the consultant or leader, including how you affect clients and staff members (often without knowing it) and your skills as a change agent.

2. Be able to work *with* others, rather than *at* them.

3. Establish successful working relationships with members of nonprofit organizations that are undergoing major change, including with members who are extremely busy, short of resources or from multicultural organizations.

4. Gain complete participation of others in your projects for change, including Board and staff.

5. Ensure that the organization is really ready for major change.

6. Build and guide powerful teams to collaborate with you as you guide change in their organizations.

7. Conduct highly focused, practical assessments, while using a variety of relevant and realistic tools to examine all aspects of the organization.

8. Use a variety of practical systems tools to carefully analyze and understand the quality of all systems in the organization and their interconnections with each other.

9. Recognize the most common types of problems that occur in all types of nonprofit organizations.

10. Generate specific recommendations to address all issues in the organization – including recommendations based on the strengths of the organization.

11. Develop complete actions plans that are fully aligned and integrated with each other for optimum implementation and effectiveness.

12. Develop a relevant, realistic and flexible Change Management Plan that has the strong ownership and commitment of all members of the organization.

13. Identify what other expertise is needed to implement the Plan and also where and when that expertise should be used.

14. Guide change according to proven principles for successful organizational change.

15. Effectively address resistance from individuals, groups – and from within yourself.

16. Ensure ongoing motivation and momentum during change – not too slow, not too fast.

17. Recognize and capture learning throughout the project, including peer-based learning.

18. Know when to ask for help, if needed.

19. Know when and how to leave a project, if needed.

20. Know how to stay sane and centered during long journeys for change.

### You Can Help Clients in Any of These Situations

Whether you are an external consultant or internal change agent, you can use this book to help nonprofit organizations that, for example:

- Have a variety of complex issues throughout the organization.

- Must ensure a strong, healthy foundation from which to grow.

- Must evolve to the next life cycle.

- Need a complete "turnaround."

- Must address Founder's Syndrome.

- Want to achieve an exciting, overall grand vision.

## Audiences

### This Book Is for You If Any of the Following Are True

- You want to understand and work with the "big picture" in nonprofit organizations.

- You are sometimes intimidated when faced with changing an entire organization.

- You are tired of using just one skill in one part of a nonprofit organization.

- You are tired of handing off projects to others who have stronger skills in organization-wide change.

- You are tired of "winging it" and want to keep more clear and consistent perspective on your work during projects for change.

- You want to be sure that the organization has a healthier foundation from which to use your particular specialty – and you want to help that organization become healthier.

- You are faced with a nonprofit organization that has many recurring issues and you are not sure what to do.

- You suspect that there is a lot that you do not know about organizational change.

- You suspect that traditional approaches to consulting and leading change are not nearly as effective as many people think.

- You have read books that generally suggest *what* you should do to guide change, but you still are not sure *how* to do it.

## *Types of Audiences*

This Field Guide will be useful to:

- Inexperienced consultants who want to start out with a firm foundation of skills for change.

- Internal consultants (nonprofit leaders and managers) who want to learn how to identify and solve complex problems in the workplace.

- Specialists who want to expand their skills for larger and longer impact.

- Generalists who want to ground and integrate their skills.

- Training centers that want to train people how to successfully consult to – and lead change in – nonprofits.

- Nonprofits that hire consultants and want to understand what the consultant is really doing to guide change and also how to ensure that those consultants are indeed very effective.

- Firms that hire consultants and want to be sure that those consultants have strong expertise for guiding change in nonprofits.

# Content of the Field Guide

## *Field Guide – Highly Practical, How-To, Easy-to-Reference*

A field guide can be encyclopedic description of all items in a similar category, for example, field guides for plants and animals. Or, a field guide can be a comprehensive, detailed description of a particular approach to getting something done. In the true style of a field guide, this guidebook provides guidelines for getting things done. There are plenty of models, tools and techniques, all useful in projects for organizational change. Take a quick glance through the Table of Contents and notice how many of the topics start with "How to."

The content is arranged in an easy-to-reference format. Guidelines are organized in a step-by-step, numbered sequence that you can easily follow to accomplish each of the most important activities to guide change. The most important points for you to understand are often in bold type so you can quickly notice them.

You can refer directly to any section of the guidebook that you need at any time during your project. Many sections include cross-references to other useful sections to ensure that you consider all the guidelines, tools and techniques that might be helpful to you at that particular time in your project.

Phase 3: Discovery and Feedback is when you and your client carefully look at the organization to understand its most important issues and what actions need to be taken to address each of the issues. The act of looking around can make a significant positive difference in your client's organization.

Phase 4: Action Planning, Alignment and Integration is when both of you develop a vision for change, then you also develop various action plans by deciding who is going to do what and by when to achieve the vision for your client's organization. The phase finishes with a Change Management Plan that has the commitment and participation of members of your client's organization.

Phase 5: Implementation and Change Management is when your client implements the Change Management Plan. Nonprofits typically do not have a lot of resources. Various crises can occur at any time in the organization. One of the most important challenges will be to help your client sustain motivation and momentum during this phase. Consequently, you should consistently monitor the status of implementation of the Plan and determine how to get things moving again when they stall.

Phase 6: Adoption and Evaluation involves a carefully planned final evaluation to decide if the Change Management Plan has been implemented successfully. Both you and your client reflect on the results and learning from the project.

Phase 7: Project Termination ends the cycle when both of you agree that the project has been completed. Projects can be completed for a variety of reasons and the Field Guide explains them all.

Guidelines are included throughout PART IV to help you and your client sustain motivation and momentum. During any of the phases, if progress seems to get stalled, you and your client might cycle back to an earlier phase in the collaborative consulting cycle.

## PART V

Most of the work in organizations gets done by teams. The same is true during organizational change. Successful consultants for change have learned to build and fully utilize teams in their work. By following the guidelines in PART V, you will be able to facilitate powerful teams for most applications during change. Various challenges can arise during facilitation, for example, groups might pose strong resistance to change, get stuck in their deliberations or struggle to make decisions. Guidelines help groups to consistently and effectively work together. One of the biggest frustrations during projects is when meetings are so poorly designed or implemented that they become a waste of time for participants. PART V provides guidelines to help you design and manage meetings that are productive for you and your client.

## PART VI

One of the biggest fears of new consultants is gathering information to understand issues within their client's organization. Inexperienced consultants sometimes skip the research altogether, which not only is unethical, is also dangerous because the omission of research can damage clients' organizations. PART VI explains the most frequently used methods to collect information during projects for change. There are easy-to-follow, step-by-step guidelines and procedures to use for each of the methods. Via the World Wide Web, there are many publicly available tools that can save you a great deal of time and money. PART VI helps you to carefully select the public tools to use.

## PART VII

One of the most powerful breakthroughs in the field of Organization Development is systems thinking. Systems thinking helps you to see and understand more clearly the many facets of organizations and how those facets work together. As a result, you can more quickly get to the root causes of issues in organizations. You more quickly generate useful recommendations to address those issues. Systems thinking has produced a variety of principles, which can guide people to make changes to systems. PART VII describes the most important principles for changing nonprofit organizations. Systems thinking has also produced a variety of handy tools that can be used to analyze systems. You will find many tools in this part of the guide. The field of Organization Development has produced a great deal of learning about change in organizations. PART VII describes many of those principles, as well.

## Appendices

Appendix A includes an extensive Glossary of the most important terms in conducting organizational development in nonprofit organizations. You can learn a great deal just by reviewing the terms in the Glossary.

Appendix B includes an extensive listing of resources for consultants to nonprofits. Resources include an extensive on-line library of materials about personal, business and organizational development. Organizations and web sites provide more materials that will benefit your practice as a consultant. Many of those resources and materials are free.

Appendix C includes worksheets about important aspects of your projects, including a sample proposal and contract that you might modify with your clients. A complete nonprofit organizational assessment tool is included, which also includes a set of best practices integrated throughout the tool. One of the most important activities in your project is carefully to design research to explore your client's organization.

Appendix D includes an extensive listing of various publications about all aspects of consulting for organizational change in nonprofits. The appendix includes an annotated list of resources, many of which are free articles on the Web.

## *What Is Not Included in This Field Guide*

The Field Guide does not include information about how to set up a consulting business, for example, how to name your company, design your marketing materials, determine what fees to charge, or advertising. Instead, the Field Guide helps you to identify and solve major issues in nonprofit organizations.

See the annotated list of resources about consulting on page 501 in Appendix D for information about setting up a consulting business.

The Field Guide does not include comprehensive, in-depth tools and procedures for any one particular capacity building activity in nonprofits, for example, Board development or strategic planning. Instead, the Field Guide helps you decide which capacity building activities are needed and in which order to accomplish significant change in nonprofits.

See the annotated list of resources on page 497 in Appendix D for resources about conducting specific types of capacity building activities in nonprofits.

# PART I:

# FOUNDATIONS FOR

# COLLABORATIVE

# CONSULTING

# About Consultants

## What Do Consultants Do?

Block, in his seminal book, *Flawless Consulting* (2000), explains that a "consultant" is someone who is trying to change another person, process or organization, but who has no direct control over what they are trying to change. Usually, that change is intended to improve performance – the effective and efficient achievement of goals. One of the greatest frustrations of consulting is the desire to change your client's organization, but not having direct influence to accomplish that change. Experienced consultants have learned to work with – and even appreciate – the indirect nature of effective consulting.

You might argue that a nonprofit leader acting as an internal change agent is not an internal consultant because he or she does have at least some direct control over staff members. However, there is not nearly the extent of direct control that you might assume – especially during long, but successful journeys for change. The highly collaborative and facilitative internal consultant or leader does not always exercise direct control and often is quite successful in guiding change. Thus, a successful leader during change is acting much more like Block's definition of consultant than you might realize.

It might be useful to consider the many perceptions that people have of consultants and the many roles that consultants might play in a project. Consultants often act as:

- Coach – helping individuals clarify and achieve goals and also learn.

- Collaborator/partner – working with people to benefit from the relationship.

- Educator/trainer – helping others develop new knowledge, skills and insights.

- Expert – providing content expertise in certain areas.

- Facilitator – helping a group to decide what it wants to accomplish and then helping the group to achieve those desired results.

- Problem solver – clarifying problems, using various styles and approaches to "solve" them.

- Researcher – collecting, organizing and analyzing information.

- Facilitator – guiding groups or individuals through learning experiences.

Other roles might include analyst, synthesizer, impartial observer, critic, friend and mentor. These are mostly positive roles. Of course, some people have strong negative impressions of consultants, as well. They might view consultants as outsiders, charlatans or even as nerds.

# Reasons Nonprofits Work with Consultants

## Good Reasons to Hire an External Consultant

- The organization has limited or no expertise in the area of need, for example, to develop a new program for clients.

- The time of need is short-term, for example, less than a year, so it may not be worth hiring a full-time, permanent staff member.

- The organization's previous attempts to meet its own needs were not successful, for example, the nonprofit developed a Strategic Plan that was never implemented.

- Organization members continue to disagree about how to meet the need and, thus, bring in a consultant to provide expertise or facilitation skills to come to consensus.

- Leaders want an objective perspective from someone without strong biases about the organization's past and current issues.

- A consultant can do the work that no one else wants to do, for example, historical data entry. (Some would argue that this is not really a consulting project.)

- A funder or other key stakeholder demands that a consultant be brought in to help further develop the nonprofit organization.

## Poor Reasons to Hire an External Consultant

The following reasons are likely open to disagreement – some people would argue that some or all of the following are good reasons to hire a consultant.

- The organization wants a consultant to lend credibility to a decision that has already been made, for example, the Board of Directors has decided to reorganize the nonprofit, but the Chief Executive Officer disagrees – so the Board hires a consultant to lend expert credibility to their decision. Many consultants might consider this reason to hire a consultant unethical.

- A supervisor does not want to directly address a problem of poor performance with one of the employees, so the supervisor hires a consultant to do the job that the employee should be doing. This is an irresponsible action on the part of the supervisor.

- The organization does not want to pay benefits (vacation pay, holiday pay, pension, etc.) or go through the administrative processes to withhold payroll taxes (social security taxes, federal taxes, etc.), so the organization hires a consultant. This reason for hiring a consultant is likely to be illegal and could result in the organization paying fines and penalties to the appropriate government agency.

 See "How to Minimize Legal Liabilities and Risks," on page 35 for guidelines to avoid, or respond to, illegal situations during consulting.

# Major Types of Consultants to Nonprofits

1.  **Technical consultants**
    They usually provide highly specialized content expertise regarding certain specific systems and processes in the organization, for example, computer systems, financial and accounting systems, market research, fundraising, lobbying and advocacy, or facilities management. Many nonprofits hire technical consultants. The types of services provided by these consultants are often referred to as technical assistance.

2.  **Program consultants**
    They usually provide highly specialized "content" expertise that is unique to certain types of program services, for example, expertise about health care, education or childhood development. Their services might also be referred to as technical assistance, depending on how specific and focused their services are.

3.  **Management consultants**
    They help leaders and managers be more productive at planning, organizing, leading and coordinating resources in the organization. Applications for their services might include leadership, management and supervisory development. The types of services provided by these consultants might be referred to as either technical assistance or organizational development activities (see the next paragraph).

4.  **Organizational development consultants**
    This type of consultant helps organizations improve performance, often by focusing on changing a significant portion of the organization or the entire organization itself. These consultants often use a wide variety of approaches, tools and techniques to affect various systems and functions across the organization, for example, technical assistance, coaching, facilitation and training.

    There has been some confusion about the focus of organizational development consultants. Some people assert that these consultants focus mostly on "soft" skills regarding peoples' beliefs, feelings and perceptions, and less on "hard" skills regarding organizational structures, processes and operations. Other people assert that organizational development consultants focus on both the "soft" and "hard" skills. (This author follows the latter assertion.)

    Many people believe there is a difference between the phrases "organizational development consultants" and "Organization Development consultants." These people might use the latter phrase to refer to consultants who adhere to certain working assumptions and values commonly associated with the field of Organization Development.

 See "Field of Organization Development (OD) and Nonprofits" on page 25 for information and various definitions of Organization Development.

## Generalists and Specialists

Some people refer to specialists and generalists as overall, major types of consultants. They might refer to technical consultants as specialists. Many people would consider organizational development consultants to be generalists.

Whether program consultants and management consultants are generalists or specialists depends on the nature of their services. The more specific the nature of their services, the more likely they would be referred to as specialists.

## Functional or Focused Services

Recently, the terms "functional" and "focused" have been used to refer to servicing a specific system, function or process, for example, marketing systems, financial systems or information technology. Functional and focused activities are considered similar or the same as technical assistance.

## Types of Consulting Can Overlap

The distinctions among the types of consultants can be blurry. For example, a management consultant, program consultant or technical consultant might operate as an organizational development consultant if they work in a manner that affects a significant portion or all of the organization.

Also, each type of consultant might be needed at various times in a project. For example, if you are an organizational development consultant, you might work with a client to identify the most important problems in an organization. Later on, you might function as a management consultant to train and coach various leaders and managers during the change effort. You might also bring in various program and technical consultants to contribute their specific expertise to the change effort.

## Focus of This Field Guide – Consulting for Organizational Change

The focus of this Field Guide is on helping all types of consultants to be more effective in accomplishing successful, organizational change, whether that change is focused on a particular portion of the organization or is organization-wide. Note that many experts assert that for any service to be long lasting in an organization, that service should be integrated throughout the organization as much as possible.

# Primary Roles of Consultants

Block (2000) mentions that there are three primary roles for consultants. Any type of consultant might play any or all of these three roles during a project.

1.  **Expert**
    The expert is valued because of their strong content expertise in various areas. The Expert helps clients by conveying or applying their expertise.

2.  **Facilitator**
    The facilitator is valued because of their strong process expertise. Process skills are useful to help group members identify what they want to do as a group and how they want to do it.

3.  **"Pair of hands"**
    The "pair of hands" can probably be used for any set of simple, routine tasks, for example, data entry. Many people, including this author, would disagree that this is a consultant role.

Different types of consultants might fill different roles throughout a project. For example, you might work in a highly facilitative fashion to help clients identify the most important problems in their organization.  Later on, you might function as an expert when training various members of the organization about approaches to organizational change and performance management.

# Most Important Goals for Consultants

Block (2000) suggests that the following goals be primary for people working to help others to accomplish change, particularly change to a significant portion of an organization or to the entire organization itself.  The following overall goals apply to any type of consultant.

1.     **Establish a collaborative relationship with your clients.**
As a consultant, you should work with your clients as if you are peers working as a team. This is in contrast to the consultant who works as an "expert" and directs the client about exactly what to do and when.  Working in a collaborative fashion with your clients helps you ensure that recommendations are accurate, clients follow the recommendations and that they adopt the changes needed.

2.     **Solve problems so your clients can solve them later themselves.**
The approach to problem solving in the project should always involve your client's learning about what is being done and why, so your client can repeat the approaches to problem solving long after you are gone.

3.     **Ensure attention to developing the project and, at the same time, to relationships.**
The quality of the relationship between you and your client is a reliable predictor of the quality of the outcome of the overall project.  Your clients often judge a project, not so much by the outcomes from the project, but by the quality of the working relationship with you.

The guidelines, tools and tips in this Field Guide are intended to help you achieve all of the above-listed goals with your clients.

# Working Assumptions for Consultants

Block (2000) also suggests the following working assumptions for any type of consultant.  The assumptions form the basis for why collaborative consulting is so powerful.

1.     **Problem solving requires information that is as accurate as possible.**
Information is more accurate if it reflects the full range of perspectives and opinions among clients in a project, so involve them as much as possible.

2.     **Effective decision-making requires free and open choice among participants.**  Free and open choice is more likely to produce the full range of opinions necessary for good planning. It also is more likely to ensure that your clients adopt the changes necessary to bring about change.

3.     **Effective implementation requires the internal commitment of your clients.**
If you give participants little choice about what to do, they will likely do what you direct, but only for as long as you are around – and they will not be vested in the outcomes.  They may also blame you if it does not work.  In contrast, if you involve them as much as possible in project planning and implementation, they are much more likely to implement the plans completely and learn at the same time.

# Internal and External Consultants

## What Is an External Consultant?

An external consultant is someone considered not to be an official, ongoing member of the organization. The relationship of the consultant to the organization is determined usually by a project's contract or Letter of Agreement. If the consultant is paid (rather than volunteering), he or she is paid on the basis of a particular project having certain desired results and deliverables from the consultant. Payroll taxes are not withheld from the person's paycheck – the person pays their own payroll taxes.

## What Is an Internal Consultant?

An internal consultant is someone considered to be an official, often ongoing member of the organization. The relationship of the consultant to the organization is determined usually by a job description and various personnel policies. If the person is paid (rather than volunteering), he or she is paid on the basis on their ongoing role in the organization. Payroll taxes are withheld from the person's paychecks.

## Differences Between Internal and External Consultants

The extent of differences between both types of consultants depends on the type of consulting provided by the consultants and how the consultants choose to work. For example, technical and program consultants are often perceived as having highly focused and credible skills that are seldom questioned. They often use similar skills and tools to get the job done. The results of their services are often quickly determined. Thus, members of an organization might perceive little difference between this type of internal and external consultant.

In contrast, consultants focused on organizational and managerial development usually have to establish their credibility over time. Their skills are sometimes highly questioned – members of the organization might even be skeptical of the need for any change in the organization. Results of the consultant's work can take months or years to realize. Consequently, members of an organization might perceive huge differences between these types of consultants.

Official, legal and administrative differences are often easy to distinguish. However, for several reasons, the differences are disappearing between consultants guiding organizations through change. Internal and external consultants are learning similar kinds of best practices and approaches for change. Both types of consultants often focus on highly facilitative approaches to working with clients. Both types of consultants, if they are committed professionals, adopt similar overall goals and working assumptions as consultants.

Traditionally, internal consultants are considered to be members of an organization whose primary job is to assist other people working in other areas of the organization. Often these internal consultants are in large organizations and from training and development or human resource departments. The typical nonprofit organization usually does not have the extensive range of resources that warrants having an internal consultant.

Traditionally, a nonprofit leader would not be considered an internal consultant. However, that perception is changing. With recent emphasis on the importance of using a highly facilitative and collaborative leadership style when guiding change, leaders are beginning to operate more like

members see all sides of a problem and how to resolve it. In addition, the diverse perspectives often cultivate more creativity and innovation than if the members all share the same values, perspectives and opinions.

The collaborative consulting cycle provides a clear structure in which you and your clients continually converse about the actions and learning in the project. Ultimately, collaborative consulting is really a philosophy. It is based on the belief that true change and learning will not take place with your client unless your client shows strong ownership, participation and commitment in that overall process of change and learning.

The design and content of this Field Guide are focused on the philosophy, guidelines, tools and techniques to help you effectively consult collaboratively with your clients.

## *Major Benefits of Collaborative Consulting*

Consultants in organizational change efforts must be able to work comfortably in collaboration with their clients. Often, that starts by explaining collaborative consulting to your client, including why the process is so useful. You might reference the following list when outlining the benefits of working with you in a collaborative approach.

1.   **Ensures you work according to goals and assumptions of effective consultants.**
     Primary goals for any effective consultant are to work collaboratively with clients to ensure current problems are understood, options are identified, problems are solved and that clients can solve problems themselves in the future. A primary working assumption includes that, for projects to be successful, clients must freely provide accurate information and maintain internal commitment to the project.

2.   **Provides powerful means to understanding real causes of problems.**
     Organizations, like people, rarely struggle with a particular problem because of a missing piece of information or specific procedure. Rather, organizations struggle because of misalignment of parts or processes in their organizations, conflicting values or feelings, or the misconceptions of people in the organization. You and your clients have to work together to understand the symptoms and the real causes of problems.

3.   **Ensures your client contributes their full value to the project.**
     A highly collaborative approach to consulting continually considers your client's experiences and learning around the problems in their organization. Your client's value to the success of the consulting project cannot be overstated.

4.   **Ensures that plans remain relevant, realistic and flexible during projects.**
     Plans are rarely implemented exactly as planned. Instead, changes inside and outside of the organization frequently cause plans to be modified. Without the ongoing participation of your clients in changes to the plans, it is not likely that the plans will remain relevant and realistic.

5.   **Ensures learning and continuous improvements in your projects.**
     Learning is a critical outcome for you and your clients, from any of your consulting projects. Adults learn by applying new information to real-world situations and exchanging feedback with others. Breakthroughs in learning for you and your clients come from examining perceptions, assumptions and beliefs, rather than from memorizing new information.

6.     **Ensures the most long-lasting solutions to your client's problems.**
Solutions to complex problems involve changes to structures and systems in your client's organization, not just in inspiring and motivating its people. Changes are not incorporated without the strong, ongoing ownership, commitment and participation of your clients. That commitment requires that they feel ongoing trust and collaboration with you and each other during the consulting project.

# Who is the Client? How to Know Who Your Current Client Is

## *Why Is It So Important to Know Who Your Current Client Is?*

Simply put, a client is the person or group to whom you owe the most allegiance, who directs your work and to whom you are answerable during a project. The client is usually the leverage point, or most important resource, for guiding change in the organization. Therefore, the client is always your most important collaborator or partner in the project. The question, "Who is the current client?" is one of the most important questions for you to be able to answer at any time in your projects. This question is critical whether you are an external or internal consultant. However, if you are an internal consultant, you might actually be your own client.

Usually, there are multiple people who believe that they direct or influence your work and that you are answerable to them during a project. Consequently, you might have several different clients at the same time in a project. Also, you might have different clients at different times during a project. Unless you can recognize these various clients, you can cause great confusion and conflict, thereby damaging your efforts to guide change.

## *Types of Clients and How to Identify Them*

There are three major types of clients during a project for change. The types that you work with and when are determined by the complexity of the project, size and culture of the organization, style of leadership in the organization, and the types of outcomes to achieve from the project. Consequently, specific examples of each of the following types of clients could be endless. However, if you are aware of the following types and can look for them in each project, you can usually identify who your current client is – or, as important, identify which people or groups are of which type of client for now in the project.

## Table I:2 – Types of Clients

| Type | Description | Examples | Your priority |
|------|-------------|----------|---------------|
| Official clients | This is the person or group who hired you (if you are external) or assigned work to you (if you are internal).  They probably interviewed you during your first meeting with them.  They probably sign your paycheck.  Usually, they have positions of authority to make decisions and provide resources during the entire project.  They often define "success" for the project and ultimately decide if the project was successful or not.  Usually, the official client remains the same throughout the project. | In projects for change in small- to medium-sized nonprofit organizations, the official client is often the Board of Directors and/or the Chief Executive Officer.  In larger organizations, the official client might also be a mid-level manager, such as a Program Director. | You need to be sure that the official client is always aware of, and approves, the status of your projects. |
| Direct clients | This is the person or group whom you directly and regularly interact with during a particular time in the project.  They could be different people at different times, depending on the current priorities and focus of your project. | Could be the Board Chair, Board of Directors, Chief Executive Officer, middle manager, Project Team, fundraiser, financial manager, etc. | Direct clients are usually your current priority for strong collaboration with you.  You should always be concerned about using effective communications and interpersonal skills with your direct clients. |
| Indirect clients | This is the person or group who is indirectly and ultimately affected by your work in the organization. | Could include everyone in the organization, such as Board of Directors, CEO, other staff and volunteers.  Could also include people outside the organization directly affected by changes in the organization, for example, clients, funders, community leaders, etc. | Indirect clients need to agree with, or not directly disapprove of, the changes in the organization.  Indirect clients inside the organization often have a major influence on the culture of the organization and often implement the plans for change. |

# How Much Should Your Client Be Involved in Collaborative Consulting?

Block (2000) asserts that, as a consultant, you should not be contributing more than 50% of the effort in a consulting project. Your client should work the remainder. You should never be doing what your client can do in a project. This is especially true for external consultants. Internal consultants might do more than 50% of the work. However, they still should strive to have clients do most of the work if those clients are to learn to solve problems for themselves.

Others might believe that the amount of work each party contributes depends on the nature of services in the consulting project. For example, a technical consultant installing a computer system might do most of the work. However, even in projects where you are an expert consultant, for example, training clients how to conduct a certain procedure, your client must participate substantially in the project. For example, they must actively participate in your training methods, be actively listening to you, thinking about what you are saying to them, and engaging in small group exercises.

Prominent psychologist, Carl Rogers, asserted that you cannot teach anyone anything. People can only learn when they are ready to learn. That is why Block's assumptions about consulting are so valid, particularly that effective decision-making requires free and open choice among participants and that effective implementation requires the internal commitment of your clients.

A challenge, particularly for new organizational consultants, is to cultivate a collaborative relationship with clients so clients are highly involved in all phases of the consulting project. New organizational consultants might fall victim to the myths that they can somehow descend into an organization and "fix" it without the client having to participate. The irony of this situation is that when the organizational consultant follows that approach, the client often reacts positively. However, soon after the consultant leaves the project, both the consultant and client realize that the intended changes to the organization never really occurred. Instead, the client is now in a situation worse than before. Reports from the consultant sit unread on the client's shelves. People are confused about what to do because little or no learning occurred from the project. Perhaps worst of all, members of the organization lose faith in the value of bringing in outside help again in the future.

Organizational change efforts often fail. That is why organizational consultants have to move away from the traditional "outside expert" approach and toward collaborative organizational consulting.

# How to Do Collaborative Consulting with Busy Clients

The typical nonprofit has limited resources of time, energy and money. There are often a variety of unexpected, competing priorities that suddenly demand a lot of time. It can be a challenge to get a client to work continually with you in a highly collaborative fashion.

When your client seems to struggle to actively participate in the project, you are faced with the following dilemma: "Should I just do the client's work now in the project or should the project accommodate the other demands for the client's time?" This is true whether you are an external or internal consultant. If you choose to do your client's work, you and your client assume the high risk that the project will not result in long-lasting changes to the organization. In addition, it is not likely that your client will accomplish any useful learning from the project itself and will not be able to address similar problems in the future.

## *Actions for the Consultant to Take*

The following guidelines pertain to actions that you can take regardless of those taken by your client.

1.  **Be authentic.**
    Notice that your client is not participating in the project, such as not doing what they said they would do, when they said they would do it. Mention your observation to your client.

    See "How to Remain Authentic with Yourself and Others" on page 62 for definition, examples and guidelines about authentic behavior.

2.  **Remind your client of the importance of the collaborative approach.**
    In the midst of the day-to-day challenges of leading a nonprofit organization, your client may have lost perspective on the overall importance of the project. The project may have been replaced by another top priority. Talk with your client to come to a conclusion about importance of the project for now.

    See "Power of Collaborative Consulting with Clients" on page 12 for guidelines about conveying the power of collaborative consulting to others.

3.  **Recognize the other priorities of your client.**
    Collaborative consulting means that both you and your client work together, recognizing the needs of the project, along with your needs and the needs of your client. There will be times during a project when your client suddenly needs to attend to other matters. You will need to recognize those times and, with your client, adjust your plans accordingly.

4.  **Integrate your project plans into your client's current activities.**
    Identify opportunities to include project tasks in activities your client is already doing. For example, use regularly scheduled Board meetings to work with the Board. Use current staff meetings and status reports to communicate about the project. Use current evaluation activities as part of the project's evaluation.

5.  **Realize that your client's lack of participation may be a form of project resistance.**
    If your client is experiencing discomfort about the project, but is not admitting it to themselves or to you, it may lead to resistance. Often, their discomfort shows up, for example, in their lack of participation. It is important for you to effectively recognize and address resistance. Otherwise, your project will lose the momentum necessary for successful change.

    See "How to Recognize Another Individual's Resistance" on page 79 and "How to Respond to Another Individual's Resistance" on page 80 for guidelines about seeing and addressing resistance from others.

6.  **Remind your client that choices about the project affect the entire nonprofit.**
    Many times, clients are so busy reacting to the day-to-day demands that they forget about the importance of their project. They sometimes end up treating the project as if it is a nuisance to be tolerated. It is important for you to remind your client of the difference between working harder and working smarter – working on the project is working smarter. By

avoiding the project, your client is not investing in the overall health of their nonprofit. If they expect to "cut wood all the time, they have to take time to sharpen the saw." Ask them what they want to do about the situation, then be quiet and let them respond. Listen and be authentic.

7.   **Continue to recognize accomplishments in the project so far.**
     Projects are not "all or nothing" events that are either complete successes or failures. If your client gets pulled away to address another priority, the project might have to adjust to a change in plans. Work with your client to keep perspective on what has been accomplished and what remains to be done in the project.

See "How to Help Your Client Appreciate Accomplishments" on page 77 for guidelines about helping clients to recognize their accomplishments .

8.   **Work with a subset of key members.**
     If all key members of your client's organization cannot participate in a particular project activity, consider forming a smaller group of participants to conduct that particular activity. The small group will provide its results, including specific and clear recommendations, back to the larger group when finished.

9.   **Use techniques of personal and professional coaching to move things along.**
     Coaching can be a powerful means to help your client identify obstacles to the project, the real reasons that those obstacles exist, and what can be done to remove the obstacles.

See "How to Coach for Deep Problem-Solving and Learning" on page 68 for guidelines to coach your clients to continued actions and learning.

10.  **Resort to the "Sanity Solution."**
     In situations where project activities seem stalled, especially because of a lack of resources, you and your client can always attempt one or more of three strategies: a) get more resources, b) extend deadlines to get things done, and/or c) decrease the expectations. Present the "sanity solution" to your client and help them decide which alternatives to implement.

11.  **Decide if you should cycle back to Phase 2: Engagement and Agreement.**
     It may be that the activities in the project so far have combined to identify or create another or new priority or problem to address. For example, project activities thus far may have helped the Chief Executive Officer (CEO) to realize that his or her approach to working with the Board of Directors is ineffective. Consequently, the CEO may want Board development to occur as soon as possible. The Engagement and Agreement phase revisits the goals of the project and, thus, is an opportunity to update the direction of the project. It might be useful for you and your client to consider repeating some or all of the activities in that phase.

See "Phase 3: Discovery and Feedback" on page 258 for all guidelines to conduct that important phase of the collaborative consulting cycle.

## Collaborative Consulting for Generalists and Specialists

Based on your particular expertise and the type of consulting that you have done in the past, you might consider yourself to be a specialist or a technical consultant.

See "Major Types of Consultants to Nonprofits" on page 5 to help you identify which type of consultant to nonprofits that you are.

In case you skipped other information in this Field Guide and went directly to this subsection that you are reading now, you might believe that the collaborative approach is not useful to you as a consultant. That belief would be a mistake. Whether you are a specialist or a generalist in your consulting work, the collaborative approach to consulting can be of great benefit to you as you work to ensure that your services are productive and long-lasting for your clients.

See "Problems with Traditional Approaches to Consulting" on page 10 to understand more about how collaborative consulting resolves the many problems with traditional approaches to consulting.

In addition to the benefits mentioned in the two subsections referenced above, as a specialist you can enjoy the additional benefits of using the collaborative and organizational approach to:

1.    Expand your skills to other areas of the nonprofit, to address other systems, functions and practices in the nonprofit organization.

2.    Expand your market for consulting skills as a result of expanding your skills and expertise.

3.    Increase the effectiveness of your consulting by more fully recognizing and addressing problems in your client's organization.

## How to Know What Consultant Role to Play and When

As an organizational consultant, you might provide a variety of types of consulting, such as program consulting, management consulting or technical/specialized consulting. In addition, you might perform a variety of other roles, primarily the roles of facilitator, coach, expert or trainer. This is true whether you are an external or internal consultant.

There are no specific indicators as to when you should fill a certain role. However, there are general guidelines from which you can get an indication as to which roles you might fill based on current conditions in a project. Your proposal or contract may suggest which roles you intend to play during the project.

### When You Might Fill the Facilitator Role

Collaborative organizational consulting is about working, as much as possible, in partnership with your clients to accomplish powerful, long-lasting change in your client's organization. That usually requires a highly facilitative role in your consulting. Facilitating is helping a group of people to decide what results they want to achieve together, how they want to achieve them and then helping the group to achieve them. Styles range from directive to indirectly suggestive. The conditions that often exist in an organizational project and require the consultant to fill the facilitator role include:

1.    **When the project needs ongoing trust, commitment and participation of clients.**
      Ongoing contributions usually do not come from clients during trainings or when receiving advice from experts. Instead, the buy-in of members comes from knowing that their beliefs and opinions are being solicited and valued. This can be especially important when a diverse group will be involved or impacted by the project. The essence of facilitation is to bring out those beliefs and opinions and to help members decide what they want to do and how they want to do it.

2.    **When working to address complex problems or major goals with clients.**
      The most accurate understanding of priorities in an organization often comes from considering the perspectives of as many members as possible. The most relevant, realistic and flexible strategies to address those priorities are developed and implemented from the active participation of members. Facilitation is the most powerful role from which to cultivate that participation.

PART V, starting on page 369, includes extensive guidelines about designing, intervening and helping groups to collect and organize information, and then to make useful decisions about that information.

Also see the list of recommended resources about facilitation on page 502.

## When You Might Fill the Coaching Role

You might choose to fill the coaching role when the following conditions exist.

1.    **An individual in the project seems stalled or troubled.**
      Coaching can be a powerful means to guide and support an individual to clarify current challenges or priorities, identify suitable strategies to address the challenges and then to actually implement the strategies.

2.    **To maximize an individual's learning from experience.**
      Individuals learn differently. Coaching can be a powerful means to guide and support individuals to reflect on their experiences and then use that learning to improve effectiveness in life and work.

See "How to Coach for Deep Problem-Solving and Learning" on page 68 a definition and for guidelines to coach your clients to reflect and learn.

## When You Might Fill the Expert Role

You might choose to fill the expert role when the following conditions exist.

1.    **The project needs general knowledge that would likely be the same in any context.**
      There are certain types of general knowledge that would likely be the same, especially:

      a)  General frameworks from which to develop and/or operate systems, for example, performance management systems, financial systems or marketing systems.

b)  Guidelines for conducting general practices, for example, planning, evaluation, organizational change, addressing ethical dilemmas, use of capacity building approaches or developing learning plans.

2.  **The project needs knowledge that is highly specialized and proceduralized.**
For example, installing computers, conducting market research, conforming to laws and regulations, designing and providing certain program services, financial processes and · procedures, or use of specific tools for problem solving and decision making.

 See Appendix B on page 463 and Appendix D on page 497 for a wide range of resources from which you can gain more expertise about nonprofits, including specialties such as finances, program design and marketing.

## *When You Might Fill the Trainer Role*

Training is activities to help a learner or learners to develop or enhance knowledge, skills and attitudes to improve performance on current or future task or job.  You might choose to fill the trainer role when the following conditions exist.

1.  **Expert knowledge needs to be conveyed in a concise and timely manner.**
There may be times in your project where members need to learn certain expert-based knowledge and need to do so in a highly focused and efficient manner.  The knowledge might be any form of expert-based knowledge as listed in the above topic.

2.  **Knowledge needs to be conveyed to a group of people.**
Training is often most useful when a group of people need to learn expert-based knowledge.  This can be quite common in projects, for example, when training project members about the nature of organizational change, the project's change plans or methods of data collection.

## *How Collaborative Consulting Integrates with Various Roles*

The collaborative approach to consulting is a natural fit with the facilitator role.  The approach integrates nicely with the role of coach, as well, because the essence of the coaching process is the partnership, or collaboration, between the coach and client to work together to meet the client's needs.

Regarding the roles of expert and trainer, the collaborative approach can be used to answer the following questions.

1.  Will the general or technical knowledge (conveyed by the expert or trainer) be used?

2.  How will it be used?

3.  How will any related problems or decisions be addressed in using that knowledge?

## *Guidelines for Switching Roles Between Facilitator and Expert*

1.  **Be clear to your client which "hat" you are wearing, facilitator or expert.**
You might even refer to your various roles as your wearing various "hats."  Otherwise, your

client can become confused about your current priorities, how you are addressing them and how they should participate with you.

2.    **Be clear about the source of your advice.**
Be clear as to whether your advice is based on your expertise (your expert role), general knowledge in the field (other experts) or their own wisdom. Facilitators often count on the wisdom of the participants in their groups.

3.    **Know your own expertise and the limits of that expertise.**
When you realize that you do not have sufficient skills to address a current issue or goal with your client, you are often more effective to adopt a facilitator role. That role more advantageously recruits the skills of others, in addition to your own.

See "How to Inventory Your Consulting Skills" on page 51 for guidelines about inventorying your skills as an organizational development consultant.

4.    **Remember the primary goals and assumptions for any successful consultant.**
Your priorities are to develop the expertise of your clients such that they can solve their own problems in the future. Usually, that means working in an expert role to share your expertise and in a facilitator role to cultivate your client's learning.

See "Most Important Goals for Consultants" on page 7 and "Working Assumptions for Consultants" on page 6 for descriptions of the most important goals and working assumptions for any type of consultant.

5.    **Do not fall in love with one role.**
Consultants who value their own expertise and the need to exhibit that expertise often resort primarily to the expert role. Similarly, consultants who have strong people skills often resort primarily to the facilitator role. Highly effective consultants can switch between roles depending on the needs of the current situation, rather than on their personal comfort levels.

# Overview of the Phases of the Collaborative Consulting Cycle

## Background

Books on consulting usually suggest similar approaches, with five to eight stages, or phases, in the overall consulting process. Authors might use different names and emphasize different terms, but the approaches they suggest are usually quite similar. After all, their approaches are based on the same action research model developed by Kurt Lewin, the founder of social psychology, about 50 years ago.

Collaborative consulting has its roots in several disciplines. For example, Carl Rogers, a humanistic and existential psychologist, developed the practice of client-centered psychology. Rogers stressed that, for real learning and change to occur, the change process has to come from the client. Edgar Schein is widely credited with founding and legitimizing process consultation, which has become the foundation for understanding group dynamics and effective facilitation of groups. Schein (1988) stressed the importance of working *with* clients. Block (2000) was one of the first to mention the phrase "collaborative consulting."

## The Nature of the Cycle and How You Experience It

The organizational change process is often much like that of taking a wide-ranging and wandering journey with your client. Accordingly, the cycle is much like a highly engaging and constructive conversation between you and your client – the cycle and its various phases provide a common frame of reference during that conversation and the consulting relationship.

The phases of the consulting process are highly integrated and often cyclical in nature. It is not uncommon to start in the early phases of the cycle and later on realize that you have to return to an earlier phase because some major aspect of the project or the client's organization has changed, for example, a key leader left the organization or a new issue has arisen in the organization.

There often is no clear-cut distinction between the various phases. The order in which you proceed through the phases and the amount of time that you spend in each depends on a variety of factors:

- The nature of the issues to be addressed by the project, including its focus and the extent of change needed to address the issues.

- Your expertise as a consultant while working with your client to proceed through the phases.

- Whether you are working for a nonprofit service provider who has certain policies and procedures for their consulting projects.

- Whether you are a specialist who focuses primarily on certain nonprofit functions (Boards, programs, marketing, staffing) or a generalist.

- The amount of resistance from your clients and yourself during the project.

- Whether you are contracting to facilitate the change process or to provide recommendations only.

- Whether new issues that affect the project, for example, a more important issue has arisen, a key leader leaves the organization or funds for the project become depleted.

- Your client's resources that are available to commit to the project.

- Any particular model that you might be using to accomplish organizational change, for example, action research or strategic management.

## Phases in Cycle

The phases in this Field Guide include:

1. **Client's Start-Up**
   During this phase, your client first realizes the "presenting priority" in their organization and that they might need help to address that priority. That priority might be a current, major problem or it could be an exciting vision to achieve. Your client begins thinking about how to address the priority. Note that if you are an internal consultant, you might also be the

client who first noticed the need to focus attention on solving the problem or achieving the goal. If you are an external consultant, they might hire you directly or go to a nonprofit service provider, such as a consulting firm, foundation, association or training center. If your client gets you from a provider, the provider may have preferences about how various consulting phases are addressed.

2. **Engagement and Agreement**

This is usually the first time that you and your client meet. The overall goal of this phase is for both of you to understand each other's nature and needs, the intended outcomes from the project, and how you prefer to work together. You also begin exploring the presenting priority in your client's organization, assess the readiness of your client to begin a consulting project, decide if there is a suitable match between you, and then identify next steps, including how an agreement can be established. If you are an external consultant, you might choose to provide a proposal or do a contract.

3. **Discovery and Feedback**

During this phase, you and your client work together in a highly collaborative fashion to further examine the presenting priority, its context and causes, and what can be done to effectively address the priority. Discovery involves carefully collecting information about the priority, how it has been managed, and its effect on the rest of the organization. During this phase, you and your client might review documentation, administer questionnaires and conduct interviews, to get information about the priority. You will use principles of systems thinking and organizational change to identify issues and generate recommendations to address the issues. Then you and your client will share with the rest of the organization the results of your discovery, including issues that you discover and recommendations to address those issues.

4. **Action Planning, Alignment and Integration**

By now, you and your client will have a fairly clear impression of what the issues are and the specific actions needed to address them. Now you will work together to develop those actions into action plans, identifying who will do what and by when. You will ensure that those action plans are relevant, realistic and flexible and that they are fully integrated with each other. Next, you will integrate the action plans into an overall Change Management Plan that will include plans for evaluation and learning, recognition and communications.

5. **Implementation and Change Management**

During this phase, you will guide and support your client in implementing the Change Management Plan, including its various related plans. The focus of your efforts will be on guiding the implementation according to principles of successful organizational change. You will help your client sustain motivation and momentum throughout the implementation. You will inform your client of a variety of tools to track the status of implementation, as well.

6. **Adoption and Evaluation**

This phase is marked by having successfully addressed the presenting priority in your client's organization, as well as addressing any issues found during your discovery activities. You and your client will conduct an evaluation to verify that those accomplishments indeed did occur. Your client will have learned a great deal during the project, including how to successfully manage change efforts in their organization.

7.    **Project Termination**
      You and your client will reflect on what both of you have achieved. If you are an external consultant, you will develop a project termination plan that will address how you will begin moving out of the project . You and your client will further attend to evaluation results and clean up any loose ends in the project. You will likely discuss any future engagements, as well.

# Field of Organization Development (OD) and Nonprofits

The field of OD is focused on the values, theories and models, and tools and techniques to accomplish successful change in organizations. Over the past ten years, experts on nonprofit matters have begun to appreciate the many contributions brought to nonprofits by the field of OD. If you are working with organizations to accomplish successful organizational and management development, you can learn a great deal from the field of OD, as well. Information in this subsection will provide you an overview of the field of OD and describe various perspectives to help you see the "big picture" on the field.

(Portions of the following topics in this subsection are excerpted from the author's writings that are hosted on the Minnesota Organization Development Network's Web site at http://www.mnodn.org .)

## *Definitions of Organization Development*

For many years, the following definition was standard. It was developed in the 1960's, at a time when an organization was considered to be much like a stable machine comprised of interlocking parts.

> *"Organization Development is an effort planned, organization-wide, and managed from the top, to increase organization effectiveness and health through planned interventions in the organization's processes, using behavioral-science knowledge."*
>
> From Beckhard, Richard, *Organization Development: Strategies and Models* (Addison-Wesley, 1969) p. 9

As organizations began to operate in a more rapidly changing environment, one of the most important assets for an organization became the ability to manage change – and for people to remain healthy and authentic. Consider the following definition of OD from the 1980's:

> *"Organization Development is the attempt to influence the members of an organization to expand their candidness with each other about their views of the organization and their experience in it, and to take greater responsibility for their own actions as organization members. The assumption behind OD is that when people pursue both of these objectives simultaneously, they are likely to discover new ways of working together that they experience as more effective for achieving their own and their shared (organizational) goals. And that when this does not happen, such activity helps them to understand why and to make meaningful choices about what to do in light of this understanding."*
>
> From Neilsen, Eric, *Becoming an OD Practitioner* (Prentice-Hall, 1984) pp. 2-3

Many experts agree that the following definition of OD represents the major focus and thrust of today's OD practitioners.

*"Organization development is a system-wide application of behavioral science knowledge to the planned development and reinforcement of organizational strategies, structures, and processes for improving an organization's effectiveness."*

From Cummings, Thomas, and Worley, Chris, *Organization Development and Change*, Sixth Edition (West Publishing, 1997) p.2

## One Perspective – OD Practitioners as "Organizational Physicians"

The system of organizations is similar, if not the same as, the system of human beings. After all, organizations are made up of humans! Therefore, in trying to understand the field of Organization Development, it might be useful to compare aspects of the field of Organization Development to aspects of the field of medicine.

For example, the study of the theories and structures of organizations (often in courses called "organizational theory") is similar to the study of anatomy and physiology of human systems. Similarly, the study of organizational behavior is similar to the study of psychology and sociology in human systems. An OD practitioner might work in the manner of an "organizational physician" intending to improve the effectiveness of people and organizations by:

1.  Establishing relationships with key personnel in the organization (often called "entering" and "contracting" with the organization).

2.  Researching and evaluating systems in the organization to understand dysfunctions and/or goals of the systems in the organization ("diagnosing" the systems in the organization).

3.  Identifying approaches (or "interventions") to improve effectiveness of the organization and its people.

4.  Applying approaches to improve effectiveness (methods of "planned change" in the organization).

5.  Evaluating the ongoing effectiveness of the approaches and their results.

## Another Perspective – Organic, Holistic OD

Physicians rely on empirical forms of research based heavily on the scientific method. They work from a linear model in which the practitioner analyzes a symptom, makes a diagnosis, treats the apparent problem with an intervention of some sort and then waits to see what difference the intervention made. When the symptom goes away, the practitioner concludes that the problem is "fixed." Basically, in the physician/patient relationship, the physician did the treatment *to* the patient, rather than *with* the patient.

Particularly in today's high-stress environment, the patient soon experiences other problems with other symptoms. Too often, the patient tragically assumes that discomfort is what life is all about and accepts a lower quality of life than could otherwise be had.

### Features of Holistic Medicine

Many people now seek remedies in alternative, holistic forms of medicine. Fortunately, a new paradigm seems to be developing in medicine that accommodates and integrates new forms of treatments. Medical schools recognize this new paradigm. Some experts assert that OD practitioners must now do the same.

Holistic medicine works from a systems perspective rather than the linear model of traditional medicine. Service providers in holistic medicine consider the patient to be so dynamic that cause-and-effect perspectives cannot grasp the true nature of the patient "system." Providers consider all aspects of the patient, including physical, mental, emotional and spiritual. Providers harbor no illusions of "fixing" anything. Instead, they work toward wellness, improving the overall quality of life for the patient. Providers believe that the patient's system knows how to take care of itself. The wisdom is there, but the provider and patient must work together to let this wisdom come out.

Holistic services include varied forms of treatment, for example, trainings about time and stress management, programs on spirituality, physical and mental exercises, and support groups. Treatments are integrated into comprehensive treatment programs, including ongoing support to patients as they accomplish necessary life changes. There is concerted effort by service providers to train clients about methods of holistic treatment.

## Beginnings: Holistic OD

Actually, developers have been adopting various forms of holistic development for several years. Many practitioners now take a systems view of organizations. They focus as much on the processes among the parts of an organization as on the parts themselves. They talk of patterns in organizations, rather than events. They talk of paradoxes and polarities, rather than fixing.

Self-organizing systems and self-managed teams are now mainstream in the literature. Spirituality in the workplace has become a common topic. Many management books reference principles from Eastern philosophies. Management development programs now include forms of self-development, as well. Dialogue groups enhance meaning for members. Interventions such as coaching and peer coaching seem to be on the rise. Consultants specialize in facilitating the rituals inherent in managing change. Consultants promise "learning relationships" with clients.

## *Another Perspective – Appreciative Inquiry (AI)*

AI is a fairly recent breakthrough in organizational and management development. Perhaps the best description of AI comes from its founder:

> *"Appreciative Inquiry is about the coevolutionary search for the best in people, their organizations, and the relevant world around them. In its broadest focus, it involves systematic discovery of what gives "life" to a living system when it is most alive, most effective, and most constructively capable in economic, ecological, and human terms. AI involves, in a central way, the art and practice of asking questions that strengthen a system's capacity to apprehend, anticipate, and heighten positive potential. It centrally involves the mobilization of inquiry through the crafting of the "unconditional positive question" often-involving hundreds or sometimes thousands of people. In AI the arduous task of intervention gives way to the speed of imagination and innovation; instead of negation, criticism, and spiraling diagnosis, there is discovery, dream, and design. AI seeks, fundamentally, to build a constructive union between a whole people and the massive entirety of what people talk about as past and present capacities: achievements, assets, unexplored potentials, innovations, strengths, elevated thoughts, opportunities, benchmarks, high point moments, lived values, traditions, strategic competencies, stories, expressions of wisdom, insights into the deeper corporate spirit or soul -- and visions of valued and possible futures. Taking all of these together as a gestalt, AI deliberately, in*

*everything it does, seeks to work from accounts of this "positive change core"—and it assumes that every living system has many untapped and rich and inspiring accounts of the positive. Link the energy of this core directly to any change agenda and changes never thought possible are suddenly and democratically mobilized."*

From Cooperrider, David and Whitney, Diana, A Positive Revolution for Change: Appreciative Inquiry (paper, 2000) http://appreciativeinquiry.case.edu/uploads/whatisai.pdf

See the AI resources listed at "Organizational Development and Change (including Appreciative Inquiry)" on page 504 in Appendix D. Those resources describe AI and its many approaches, and refer you to additional resources, as well.

Also see the AI Commons at http://appreciativeinquiry.case.edu/. Those resources provide comprehensive information about AI and, in turn, will reference other resources from which you can learn more about AI.

## Methods of Appreciative Inquiry Used in This Field Guide

This Field Guide uses several AI techniques, including:

1.   **Use of "presenting priority" rather than "presenting problem."**
     The latter phrase is commonly used in literature about methods of consulting and organizational development. The former phrase removes the term "problem," thereby inviting a more positive and strength-based image.

2.   **Ability for reader to substitute another term for "problem."**
     At several places in this Field Guide, you and your client are invited to use a term other than "problem."

3.   **Guidelines to generate recommendations based on your client's strengths.**
     During the phase, Discovery and Feedback, when generating recommendations, you are invited to produce recommendations that build on the strengths of your client.

4.   **Use of the stories technique for generating information.**
     The stories technique invites people to think of a situation in the past that reflects their best traits and then to use those traits to accomplish goals for the future.

     See "Stories (to Convey Positive, Individualized Learning)" on page 381 for a description of the stories technique and how to use it.

5.   **Nature of present and forward-looking questions used in coaching.**
     The Field Guide suggests questions for coaching that, primarily, are based on the present and future. The questions guide people away from analyzing past problems.

     See "How to Coach for Deep Problem-Solving and Learning" on page 68 for examples of useful coaching questions.

# Maintaining Professionalism

As a professional consultant (external or internal), it is imperative that you adopt principles to ensure ethical consulting, recognize the boundaries within which you should work in an organization, understand the legal liabilities and risks inherent in organizational consulting and attend to regular and ongoing professional development activities. Guidelines in this section will help you ensure that you operate truly as a professional in your consulting work. The guidelines are relevant to all phases of collaborative consulting.

## Principles for Effective Consulting

Consultants have different perspectives on effective consulting. The following guidelines might be useful as you reflect on your own principles for effective consulting.

1. **The "answer" to complex problems lies between you and your client.**
   The "answer" emerges during the project as you and your client work collaboratively to clarify current issues and address them, while learning at the same time.

2. **Encourage and recognize diverse values and perspectives.**
   An experienced organizational consultant remembers there are many perspectives on an issue in the organization. Those perspectives should be encouraged and explored because they often lead to more successful problem solving.

3. **When working with your client, start from where they are now.**
   Understand your client's perspective on their issues, including what they have tried, what has worked, what has not worked and what they think should be done now. It is better to go slower *with* your client than faster without them.

4. **There is no blame in consulting situations.**
   It is rare that anyone sets out to hurt someone else or an organization. An atmosphere of blame only serves to inhibit people in your client's organization from the trust, collaboration and commitment necessary for successful change.

5. **Come to the project with a basic consultation framework in mind.**
   Early in a project, the major purpose of the framework can be used as a common frame of reference when talking about the project goals, methods, evaluation and learning. Be willing to modify that framework as you and your client work together.

6. **Your value is in the flow of the process, not in the details of the project.**
   Your client will value you if both of you continue to work together in a process that is collaborative, well understood, communicated to all and focused on results.

7. **Success comes from who you are as from your expertise.**
   This is true, especially if your client perceives you to be authentic and respectful, and consulting with focus on results and learning. Similarly, one of the most powerful influences that can have with your clients is to model the behaviors that you want from them.

8. **Do what you say you are going to do.**
   In the midst of your client's confusion, you can help a great deal by remaining grounded and

centered, clear and consistent. Your consistency builds trust and commitment with clients, as well.

9. **Know yourself.**
You are an "instrument" of change with your client, so you should be willing to suspend your overall biases, assumptions and beliefs when working with people. Be honest about them when they arise during a project.

10. **Do not tell your clients to do something just because you said so.**
Always first explain the reasons for your advice and the benefits that might come to your client as a result. Then provide time for your client to respond to your advice. This is usually true even if you are a leader acting as an internal change agent.

11. **It is up to your client to use your advice or not.**
This is sometimes one of the hardest principles for new consultants to accept. It helps if you remember that people learn only what they are ready to learn.

12. **Do not take it personally.**
Often your client struggles with an issue, in part, because of their role in the issue. They may not want to change themselves and might resist your attempts to help them. In those instances, remember that those responses are their choices, not yours.

# Principles for Ethical Consulting

Simply put, ethics involves learning what is right or wrong, and then doing the right thing. Ethics includes the fundamental ground rules by which we live our lives. Values that guide how we ought to behave are considered moral values, for example, values such as respect, honesty, fairness and responsibility. Statements around how these values are applied are sometimes called moral or ethical principles.

Ethical consultants must have a set of principles, which defines ethical behavior and guides the consultants' actions toward those behaviors. This is true whether you are an external consultant or an internal leader wanting to lead staff members fairly and equally. Many times, those principles are documented as a code of ethics. Also, consultants must be able to recognize ethical dilemmas and have at least one tool to use to address the dilemma. Information in this subsection will help you to develop your principles for ethical consulting, recognize ethical dilemmas and resolve those dilemmas, as well.

## Codes of Ethics to Avoid Behaviors That You Perceive as Unethical

It is critical that you establish some major principles, or guideposts, to ensure that you consult in a manner that is fair and equitable and also that minimizes your liabilities as a consultant. Those principles are your "inner compass" in the midst of the confusion and complexity that are typical at various times in an organizational change effort. Many times, consultants start developing that compass by developing descriptions of their mission and vision for their consulting work and the way that they want to work.

See "How to Articulate Your Professional Mission and Values" on page 54 for guidelines to articulate your professional mission and values.

Consultants might refine description of their preferred values and behaviors by developing a code of ethics or conduct of conduct. Here are some important ethical guidelines for consulting during organizational change.

1. **Do no harm to your client.**

2. **Keep client information private unless the client or law requests otherwise.**

3. **Do not create dependence by you on your client, nor by your client on you.**

4. **Anticipate and avoid conflicts of interest (for example, representing two interests at once).**

5. **Do not act in the official capacity as an advocate for your client.**

6. **Do not go beyond your own expertise.**

7. **Do not skip the discovery phase of consulting.**

8. **Treat others the way you want them to treat you.**

One of the hallmarks of established professions are codes of ethics for those professions. Here are two relevant examples of codes of ethics that you might reference.

American Society for Training and Development at http://www.astd.org/ASTD/Membership/Local_Chapters/ethics.

Organization Development Institute at http://www.odinstitute.org/ethics.htm

## *Avoiding Behaviors That Clients Perceive as Unethical*

To avoid unethical behaviors, you also should develop strong self-awareness, including about your own biases and assumptions and about the limits of your own expertise. This self-understanding is critically important.

See "Understanding Yourself as an Instrument of Change" on page 43 for many guidelines to help you to develop deep awareness of your nature and skills in consulting.

When first establishing a relationship with your client's organization, you should make every effort to learn the culture, or personality, of their organization. The culture is reflected in a variety of values, some of them actually enacted and others that are preferred by members of the organization. Ethical behaviors should conform to the values of that culture, as well as your own professional values.

See "How to Work in Multicultural Environments" on page 58 for guidelines to learn the most important values in the culture of your client's organization.

## *Examples of a Consultant's Unethical Behaviors*

To further your understanding of ethics, it might help to consider examples of unethical behaviors. Ethics is often a highly subjective matter. Consequently, not everyone might agree that all of the following are examples of unethical behaviors.

1.  Because the consultant wants to have a good relationship with the client, the consultant quickly adopts the client's perspective on all issues and does not voice any disagreement with the client, thereby colluding with the client.

2.  Because the consultant offered guidance or advice that was well beyond their expertise, the client's organization implemented action plans that were destructive to the organization.

3.  Because the consultant did not conduct enough discovery (or "diagnosis") to further examine the client's reported issue, the client's organization implemented action plans that were incomplete or destructive to the organization.

4.  Because the consultant wanted the client to promptly do as the consultant advised, the consultant pushed their point of view well beyond what the evidence of the discovery process revealed in the client's organization.

5.  Because the client wanted the consultant to come to the same conclusion about the issue as the client, the client somehow did not tell "the whole story" to the consultant who, in turn, made the wrong recommendations based on inadequate information.

6.  Because the consultant wanted to further help the client's organization, the consultant did not terminate the current consulting project when the outcomes (that were specified in the project's work plan) are achieved.

7.  Because the consultant wanted to help the overall community, the consultant told funders information that the client believed was being held in confidence between the consultant and client.

8.  Because the consultant wanted to help the client's organization, the consultant arranged a meeting to report concerns about the Chief Executive Officer to the members of the Board, without telling the Chief Executive Officer of the consultant's attendance at the Board meeting.

9.  When the consultant learned about a particular new model or technique, for example, in program evaluation, he or she tried to convince the client of an issue with the client's program to create an opportunity to apply that new learning.

10. During the discovery phase of the consulting process when interviewing one of the entry-level staff members, the consultant tried to build trust with the member by sharing his or her confidential impressions of what he or she has concluded about the Chief Executive Officer so far.

### *Identifying and Resolving Ethical Dilemmas*

The nature of nonprofits and the manner in which they undertake organizational change are highly diverse. In addition, the role of the organizational consultant usually includes guiding people through change processes in which there is always the possibility of strong power differences among people, conflicting values and even unfair treatment. Unfortunately, too, there are times when you or your client act in a manner that, while expedient or self-protecting, results in unfair treatment of others.

In these situations, it is not uncommon that people can feel that something wrong or improper has occurred; they can even have widely varying opinions about what is right and wrong and what is proper and improper. Thus, there is always the strong possibility that ethical dilemmas can arise.

An ethical dilemma exists in a situation where there are strong, conflicting values and several viable alternatives to the situation, each of which seems reasonable and fair, yet could have significant effect on those involved. Ethical dilemmas are seldom as straightforward as "doing the right thing." Many times, the right thing to do is not nearly as recognizable and straightforward as people would hope. That is why the professional organizational consultant is sensitive to the potential of ethical dilemmas.

Your code of ethics is an important tool for recognizing and resolving ethical dilemmas. The code sensitizes you to the behaviors that you prefer. Your understanding of the culture of your client's organization is another major tool. It helps you to recognize the behaviors that your client prefers.

 See "Complete Guide to Ethics Management: An Ethics Toolkit for Managers" for several tools and procedures for addressing ethical dilemmas, at http://www.managementhelp.org/ethics/ethxgde.htm

## How to Maintain Proper Boundaries

There are certain types of organizational activities which you should avoid, depending on whether you are an external or internal consultant. The nature of the activities in which you become involved depends on what you and your client have agreed upon as your roles and responsibilities. As a professional consultant, you must monitor the types of activities in which you are – and are not – involved. That monitoring is especially important during the phases of Engagement and Agreement; Action Planning, Alignment and Integration; and Implementation and Change Management.

### *Scope of Contract*

If you are an external consultant, your work within your client's organization should be within the scope of the formal agreement that you have with your client. Do not work on activities that are outside of that scope without your client's permission – and probably not without a new or amended contract. For example, if your contract is to facilitate Board development, then do not also consult to developing a Fundraising Plan, even though you strongly believe that you can contribute a great deal to that Plan.

Your client has recruited you to work on certain matters within the organization. If you are involved in other matters, the client might become alarmed that you are a "loose cannon" shooting all over their organization. That situation could be frightening to them and cause the client to lose trust in you. You have a formal agreement to focus only on specific matters. If you stray from that agreement, your client could sue you for malpractice.

Even if your client greatly appreciated that you were helping out in other areas, you could be hurting the real project by causing "project creep." That occurs when your project seems to never end because the requirements for the project continue to somehow expand. Eventually, the project loses its focus and effectiveness. Despite your hard work, your client may no longer understand the project and where it fits into their organization.

Note that the above guidelines are applicable primarily to consultants whose practice involves a series of new clients. Some consultants work primarily with the same few clients and in a wide, informal scope of work within their organizations. In those situations, it still is advisable to form some type of agreement regarding the current scope of work for the consultant. The small amount of effort that it takes to formalize an agreement is well worth the protection that it affords the consultant and client in case there are any disagreements regarding the consultant's activities.

## Supervising Employees

Generally, supervision includes exercising formal authority to establish goals and priorities for employees who report directly to the supervisor, along with monitoring the timeliness and quality of progress toward the goals. The supervisor usually works according to personnel policies to reward or "punish" the employees' behaviors accordingly and also conducts a formal performance review. How supervision is carried out depends on the culture and policies of the organization.

As an external consultant, unless you have specifically contracted with your client to perform some or all of the duties of a supervisory role, you should not put yourself in the position of supervising employees. If, for example, your services involve guidance to the supervisor, you should guide and support the supervisor to, in turn, effectively supervise their own employees.

## Matters of Employment Laws

As an external consultant, unless you are an expert in employment laws and have been hired by your client to review and update personnel policies, you should avoid offering advice about matters of hiring, compensation and benefits, or record keeping. Similarly, you should not offer legal advice unless you are qualified to offer that type of advice and have been hired by your client to provide that advice. However, you should know of competent resources to which you can refer your clients, should you become concerned about a personnel or legal issue.

## Interaction with Staff

When you and your client first meet to clarify the desired outcomes and goals of the project (in a "contracting" meeting, in the case of an external consultant), you should also talk about what organizational resources need to be accessed by you and how. If you need to interact with certain staff members, both you and your client should be clear about the purpose of that interaction, and about which members will be involved and how. In addition, your client should notify each of those members and explain the purpose of the work with those members.

## Joining Client's Board of Directors

Occasionally, your client will be so impressed with your performance as an external consultant that your client asks you to join their Board of Directors. You should not join the Board before you and your client terminate your consulting contract, along with terminating any associated compensation to you. The reason for this is to avoid any apparent or active conflict-of-interest. Directors have a duty of loyalty to their nonprofit organization, which includes not engaging in Board-related activities that could personally benefit the director by providing money or other assets to that member. That duty ensures that the Board member's activities and deliberations are always focused primarily on benefiting the nonprofit organization – that the Board member does not have an apparent or actual conflict-of-interest in their role.

### Summary – Guide Your Client to Decide How to Decide

As an external consultant, you usually should not be making ongoing operating decisions about the governance, leadership and management of your client's organization, unless you have been hired to hold an interim position as a leader or manager in the organization. However, you should focus as much as possible on helping your client decide how to make those decisions. That is true because, often when people struggle in their organizations, they have gotten away from the fundamental systems and processes (plans, policies, roles and procedures) that are necessary to effectively make decisions and solve problems.

## How to Minimize Legal Liabilities and Risks

Information throughout this subsection applies primarily to external consultants. The extent of risk and liability in your work depends on the nature of your services. Consultants who work with clients to guide organizational change efforts probably carry little risk or legal liability. However, some clients might require that you carry professional liability insurance. The purpose of that insurance is to protect you against large financial losses if your client wins a lawsuit against you.

Although the risk of lawsuits might seem low, there are still some considerations that you should address. The following guidelines are offered to assist you in minimizing your risk and liabilities in your practice. The guidelines are not to be interpreted as legal advice.

### General Guidelines to Protect Yourself

1.  If you are providing services that are closely related to activities that are directly affected by various laws and regulations, you should obtain legal advice regarding your liability protection. Examples of those kinds of consulting services include developing personnel policies, advising on health care services or advising on compensation and benefits.

2.  If your place of business is in your home, you should consider getting general liability insurance. That insurance can protect you in case a client is injured in your home.

3.  Certain aspects of your consulting business can include some legal risk. Those aspects include, for example, contracts with clients and billing procedures.

4.  Certain practices constitute good preventive maintenance to minimize your risks and legal liabilities. Those practices include:

    a)  Get all agreements with clients in writing and confirmed with your signatures, including the project's contract. Follow that practice no matter how much you trust your client.

    b)  Engage in continuing professional development.

See "How to Continuously Improve Your Skills as a Nonprofit Consultant" on page 39 for many guidelines and ideas to improve your skills.

c)  Develop and adopt a code of ethics to guide your consulting services.

d)  Have a lawyer review your boilerplate, or standard contract.

e)  If a client insists on specifying your potential liabilities in contracts with you, limit those liabilities to the amount of the total project fees or do not do business with that client.

f)  Be able to explain your choices and advice to your client, and to others, if required.

## If You Encounter Questionable or Illegal Practices

The likelihood that you will encounter illegal practices during your consulting activities depends on:

1.  The nature of the activities of your client's organization and your consulting project.

2.  Law and regulations regarding those activities.

3.  Terms of your consulting contract.

The types of illegal practices that you might encounter might be in the areas of:

- Misappropriation of funds

- Fraud

- Theft

- Violation of employment laws, causing, for example, discrimination or harassment

- Breach of contract

If you encounter any of these questionable or illegal practices, consider the following courses of action:

1.  Describe the situation to your client.

2.  If they do not respond to the situation, consider describing the situation to a higher level in the client's organization.

3.  If they do not respond to the situation, you can either quit the project or report the situation to an appropriate legal authority.  If you choose to contact a legal authority, consider contacting your own attorney first.

## Protecting Your Intellectual Property

Intellectual property (IP) concerns copyrights, patents and trademarks (or service marks).  Simply put, copyrights are to protect ownership (authorship) of written words, for example, in books and pamphlets. Patents are to protect ownership of processes or technologies. Trademarks and service marks are to protect ownership of names, titles, slogans, images, etc. Copyrights and trademarks are usually the two aspects of IP to which organizational consultants should give attention during projects.

In a highly collaborative approach between you and your client, it is likely that both of you will be using materials that you developed before or during the project (the materials are your intellectual property). For example, you might distribute articles that you wrote about organizational change, forms and templates that you developed, or questionnaires and other assessment instruments that you designed. Early in the project, ideally within the contract, both of you should be clear about the rights of ownership and use of these materials during and after the project.

As an organizational consultant, you may want to use your materials with other clients and in various marketing activities in the future. You may also want to ensure that other consultants and clients are not able to claim ownership of your items, potentially resulting in lost revenue to you and even in lawsuits. Therefore, you should take steps to ensure that your ownership is protected.

To protect ownership of text that you have written and want to own in the future, you should use a copyright mark ("©") on those items that contain the text, for example, at the bottom of the page. To protect ownership of items associated with the identity or personality of your business, such as logos and slogans, put a trademark ("TM") or service mark ("SM").

In some projects, you might agree that you will own certain items produced during the project, for example, if you are generating a manual for them. In those situations of "work for hire," you and your client should specify the ownership of those items in a written agreement.

Consider including the following standard paragraph about IP in all of your written agreements with your clients. The paragraph may need to be modified depending on your arrangement for the project.

> Ownership of Intellectual Property. The consultant will retain all rights of intellectual property on materials developed by the consultant before, during and after the project.

## Conforming to Revenue Agency Requirements

An important consideration for you and your client is whether the particular government agency in the locale of your project would classify you as an independent contractor (an external consultant) to your client or as an employee of your client's organization. That classification can make a big difference in how your personal income is taxed. In the United States, the Internal Revenue Service (IRS) makes that distinction. In Canada, the Canada Customs and Revenue Agency (CCRA) makes that distinction. The following information should not be interpreted as legal advice. Rather, it is to help you ensure that you and your client develop an appropriate contractual relationship.

The concern of the IRS and CCRA is as follows. Some organizations hire people as "independent contractors" who should really be classified as "employees." In those situations, the taxing agencies might assert that the organizations should have withheld payroll and other taxes from the people. The taxing agencies can levy fines and other penalties on the organizations, as well. Consequently, you and your client must be careful when entering into a consulting relationship to ensure that the taxing agency does not deem your relationship to be an "employer-employee" relationship.

In the United States, the IRS has issued guidelines about how to discern if a relationship is really an employee relationship rather than an independent contractor relationship. The IRS guidelines are similar to the guidelines from the CCRA in Canada. Whether someone is deemed by the IRS or CCRA to be an employee or an independent contractor depends primarily on the extent of control that the organization has over the person. The less control in the relationship, the less likely the person will be deemed an employee.

Consider the following actions when attempting to specify your relationship with your client.

1.      Carefully specify your relationship with the person in a written contract.

2.      The terms of the relationship (specific services, fees, project start and stop dates, etc.) should be specified in the contract.

3.      Attempt to arrange fees to be based on results or tasks, rather than on time.

4.      In the contract, specify the relationship to be with an "independent contractor" who is responsible to pay his or her own taxes.

5.      The person doing the work should have all or considerable discretion in how services are carried out, including the process and scheduling. This criterion is not so clear in a highly collaborative relationship.

6.      The person doing the work should be responsible to obtain and pay for his or her own training to carry out the services.

7.      The person should not be required to carry out his or her services at the offices of the client.

8.      The person should have or be making obvious efforts to maintain business with other clients.

9.      The person should have his or her own place of business.

The more a person appears to act as a manager in the organization (for example, makes operating decisions, supervises people and allocates resources), the more likely that a government agency will deem the service provider an "employee" and not an independent contractor.

More information about the United State's Internal Revenue Service requirements is available at
http://www.irs.gov/businesses/small/article/0,,id=99921,00.html

Consider the following standard paragraph to include in all of your written agreements with your clients. The paragraph may need to be modified by you and your client, depending on your arrangements for the project.

<u>Independent Contractor.</u> Both the client and the consultant agree that the consultant will act as an independent contractor in the performance of its duties under this contract. Accordingly, the consultant shall be responsible for payment of all taxes, including Federal, Provincial and/or State taxes arising out of the consultant's activities in accordance with this contract, including by way of illustration but not limitation, Federal, Provincial and/or State income taxes, and any other taxes or business license fees as required.

# How to Continuously Improve Your Skills as a Nonprofit Consultant

If you want to consider yourself a professional, you should regularly engage in professional development. This is true whether you are an external or internal consultant. Considering the recent significant innovations in organizational and management development, it is important that you engage in ongoing professional development, as well. Also, it is critically important that you have a good understanding of nonprofits – you should not start consulting to them without this understanding. There are a variety of useful approaches for continuous professional development.

## *Engage in Continuous Learning and Development*

One of the most powerful forms of professional development is learning from your own consulting experiences. Many experienced consultants maintain a Learning Journal in which they regularly record their thoughts about what worked in a project, what did not work, what they learned from the project, and how they can use that learning in life and work. This form of development is quite powerful because it follows key principles of adult learning to learn from reflecting on one's own experiences.

 See "Cultivating and Guiding Learning" on page 213 for principles of learning and continuous learning, and designing systematic learning plans.

## *Know Your Community's Resources for Nonprofits*

Depending on the size of the community, there is often a wide range of resources for nonprofits in the community. As a consultant to nonprofits, you should know what resources exist and when to refer your nonprofit clients to those resources. Community resources often include, for example:

- Nonprofit service providers that provide technical and management services to nonprofits.

- Consulting firms that serve nonprofits in a wide variety of services, including technical and managerial.

- Educational and training centers that provide programs, courses, seminars or workshops about nonprofit topics and practices.

- Donors, such as foundations, corporations, government agencies and individuals, who support provision of services to nonprofits.

- Associations that provide opportunities for members to share feedback, materials and networking, along with regular conferences and discounts on purchases.

Appendix B includes listing of several national organizations. Contact those nearest you to identify resources for nonprofits in your community. Also, consult your local telephone directory.

## Use Internet Search Engines

Probably the largest source of assistance to you is the amazing amount of free resources on the Internet. Of course, there is no guarantee of the quality of the information that you will find there just like there is no guarantee of the quality of information that you will get from books or trainings. As with any adult in learning, you are often the "expert" at knowing what is useful for you to learn and when to learn it.

The Google search engine is one of the most powerful Internet search engines. Go to http://www.google.com or your favorite search engine.

## Find a Mentor

Many might argue that it is unethical for you to begin consulting on organizational and management development projects without having first worked with more experienced consultants or mentors. Without having a mentor, you might hurt the health of your client's organizations and even yourself. The problem is that, even after having read a great deal of literature about consulting and organizational development, you still might not realize what you need to know, but still do not know. The concept of "shadow consulting," or working closely with a more experienced consultant, is becoming much more common that even a decade ago.

See "Sources of Nonprofit Consultants and Mentors" on page 465 in Appendix B for sources of possible mentors.

A rather novel approach to mentoring is virtual mentoring. You might find a mentor willing to provide you guidance and support by using various means of telecommunications, for example, on-line forums or discussion groups.

See "Web Sites and On-Line Forums" on page 466 in Appendix B for major, on-line forums that might be useful for virtual mentoring.

## Engage in Networking

Networking with other consultants can be useful means for you to exchange useful information and materials about established and state-of-the-art tools and techniques. It is not uncommon that networking activities among organizational consultants also includes internal consultants – experts who are employees of organizations and responsible to consult to other departments in that organization. Thus, networking can be a useful means to advertise and promote your consulting business.

Professional organizations usually provide wonderful opportunities for networking and many of them have chapters in various states. Numerous organizations are listed in Appendix B.

Frequently, consultants organize small, local networking groups among themselves.

See "Sources of Nonprofit Consultants and Mentors" on page 465 in Appendix B, for organizations that can provide you, or refer you to, networking groups.

See "Web Sites and On-Line Forums" on page 466 in Appendix B for major, on-line forums in which you might conveniently network.

## *Obtain Ongoing Support*

Many professions use practitioners support groups, for example social workers, therapists and lawyers. The activities of organizational consulting can be quite frustrating at times, depending on your nature and the nature of your particular consulting project. Thus, a support group might be an extremely useful resource for you.

Note that consultants can gain support from a variety of types of resources. That might be an important consideration for you because, among some consultants, the notion of "support groups" might seem a little too "touchy feely." An irony here is that many times, from networking and problem solving groups, consultants report that one of the most useful outcomes is support.

Consultants might gain support from a variety of sources, for example, from mentors and peer groups. Forms of useful peer groups might include study groups, discussion groups, dialogue groups or peer coaching groups.

See "Sources of Nonprofit Consultants and Mentors" on page 465 in Appendix B for sources of organizations to join or get referrals from, and to join or form support groups.

## *Absorb Additional Readings*

Start your practice by reading literature about consulting. Much of that literature is about starting a consulting business, for example, conducting an inventory of consulting skills, developing marketing materials or setting up a home office. Sometimes that literature also includes very basic guidelines for identifying and solving problems in client's organizations.

See the annotated list of resources in "Consulting" on page 501 in Appendix D for books about consulting.

Next, read literature about the field of Organization Development (OD). OD focuses particularly on guidelines and materials to conduct effective organizational change. Thus, OD literature is critical to the consultant who seeks to work with nonprofits on projects that are significant in scope.

See the annotated list of resources in "Organizational Development and Change (including Appreciative Inquiry)" on page 504 in Appendix D for books about guiding change.

See the long list in "Recommended Readings – an Annotated List" on page 499 in Appendix D for numerous other useful publications about nonprofit functions, for example, nonprofit Boards of Directors, strategic planning, leadership and supervision, programs and evaluation.

There is a wide variety of national publications about nonprofits.

Two of the most prominent publications are the *Nonprofit Times* (http://www.nptimes.com/) and the *Chronicle of Philanthropy* (http://www.philanthropy.com/).

## Attend Training Sessions

There are an increasing amount of conferences, courses, seminars and workshops about consulting, organizational change and nonprofits.

See "Professional Organizations" on page 464 in Appendix B to identify or get referrals to organizations that provide training sessions.

## Volunteer Your Services

One of the most powerful approaches for you to learn about nonprofits might be for you to volunteer your services to nonprofits. For example, you might join a Board of Directors. Nonprofits that value their Boards often arrange for training and orientation sessions for Board members.

Your locale might have an organization that provides volunteers to nonprofits.

See "Professional Organizations" on page 464 in Appendix B and consider contacting one of the chapters of the professional organizations to investigate opportunities for volunteering.

3.       Notice what situations typically evoke those emotions in you.

4.       Notice the difference between your emotions and your outward responses to those emotions – what others would see you do and say. Ask yourself how you choose to feel about something and whether your behavior is aligned with that choice.

5.       Realize that it is OK to have strong emotional reactions. It is what you do with those emotions that can be a problem for you and others.

6.       Notice how long you retain those emotions. What changes them?

7.       Notice what makes you happy and plan for those situations on a regular basis.

8.       Notice how you make conclusions about other peoples' feelings. What are they doing or saying?

# Understand Your Natural Approaches to Problem-Solving and Decision-Making

Different people have quite different preferences and approaches for solving problems and making decisions. Those differences can often cause conflict between people unless they each understand their own particular preferences.

The following preferences represent probably the most common preferences. It is important for you to note that any preference is not necessarily better than others. Certain preferences might work better in certain situations. The important point for you to realize is the diverse ways that people – including you – address problems and decisions. Always consider that diversity in your consulting projects.

## *Rational Versus Organic Approach to Problem Solving*

### Rational

A person with this preference often prefers using a comprehensive and logical approach similar to the following procedure. For example, the rational approach, described below, is often used when addressing large, complex matters in strategic planning.

1.       Define the problem.

2.       Examine all potential causes for the problem.

3.       Identify all alternatives to resolve the problem.

4.       Carefully select an alternative.

5.       Develop an orderly implementation plan to implement that best alternative.

6.       Carefully monitor implementation of the plan.

7.       Verify if the problem has been resolved or not.

A major advantage of this approach is that it gives a strong sense of order in an otherwise chaotic situation and provides a common frame of reference from which people can communicate in the situation. A major disadvantage of this approach is that it can take a long time to finish. Some people might argue, too, that the world is much too chaotic for the rational approach to be useful.

## Organic

Many believe that it can be quite illusory to believe that an organizational consultant is there to identify and solve problems for the client. Some people assert that the dynamics of organizations and people are not nearly so mechanistic as to be improved by solving one problem after another. Often, the quality of an organization or life comes from how one handles being "on the road" itself, rather than the "arriving at the destination." The quality comes from the ongoing process of trying, rather than from having fixed a lot of problems. For many people it is an approach to organizational consulting. The following quote is often used when explaining the organic (or holistic) approach to problem solving.

> *"All the greatest and most important problems in life are fundamentally insoluble ... They can never be solved, but only outgrown. This "outgrowing" proves on further investigation to require a new level of consciousness. Some higher or wider interest appeared on the horizon and through this broadening of outlook, the insoluble lost its urgency. It was not solved logically in its own terms, but faded when confronted with a new and stronger life urge."*

From Jung, Carl, *Psychological Types (*Pantheon Books, 1923)

 See "Another Perspective – Organic, Holistic OD" on page 26 to learn about the holistic and organic approach to organizational development.

A major advantage of the organic approach is that it is highly adaptable to understanding and explaining the chaotic changes that occur in projects and everyday life. It also suits the nature of people who shun linear and mechanistic approaches to projects. The major disadvantage is that the approach often provides no clear frame of reference around which people can communicate, feel comfortable and measure progress toward solutions to problems.

## Intuitive Versus Sensing Approaches to Gathering Information

There are a variety of assessment instruments that are often referenced when helping people understand their own unique styles when solving problems and making decisions, for example, the Myers-Briggs Type Indicator® instrument. One of the dimensions of the Myers-Briggs is "Intuitive versus Sensing," which considers how a person gathers information. (Myers-Briggs is a registered trademark of Consulting Psychologists Press, Inc.),

## Intuitive

A highly intuitive person often gathers information instinctively. They thrive on ideas and possibilities. They might seem oblivious to what is going on around them, yet they often effectively solve problems and make decisions based on surprisingly valid information. Many times, they might not even know how they did it. Some experts on leadership and management assert that highly experienced people often have developed intuition that enables them to make quick, effective decisions. A major advantage of this approach is that it can save a great deal of time. A major challenge can be how to explain their choices to others.

### Sensing

These people thrive on facts and information. They are detail-oriented and accuracy is important to them. They are aware of their physical surroundings, of who is saying what. They solve problems and make decisions by considering the "data" around them. One of the major advantages of a sensing person is that their actions are often based on valid information. Thus, they are able to explain their reasoning and their actions to others. A major challenge is the time and care required for them to solve problems and make decisions.

## *Thinking Versus Feeling Approaches to Process Information*

Another major dimension of the Myers-Briggs Indicator® instrument is "Thinking versus Feelings," which considers how a person makes decisions about information.

### Thinking

A thinking person often uses a highly objective, sometimes rational approach to organizing, analyzing and making decisions about information. At their extreme, they might shun consideration of emotions. The thinking person probably prefers the rational approach to problem solving as described above in this subsection. The advantage of this approach is that it often generates valid problem solving and decision-making. A major challenge can be that it might require an extensive amount of time to come to action.

### Feeling

The feeling approach is used most often by individuals who are quite sensitive to their values in processing information. When people focus on their values, emotions often come into play. A major advantage of this approach is that it can help to ensure that people are happy and fulfilled in the situation – that their values have been considered during the process and are reflected in the outcome. A major challenge is that there are a variety of short-term factors that can influence a person's emotions other than the current major problem or decision, for example, their not having had enough sleep or having eaten right.

## Understand Your Preferred "Lens" Through Which You View Organizations

One of the most frequent reasons that organizational consultants argue about the best methods for organizational change is because consultants often have different perspectives, or lens, through which they view organizations. The impact of these differences is often underestimated. For example, you can have two different consultants interact with an organization and they might later provide different descriptions of the same organization. Therefore, it is critical that consultants understand their own perspective and be sensitive to the organizational perspectives of others.

One of the most useful resources to explain these perspectives is *Reframing Organizations* (Bolman and Deal, Jossey-Bass, 1991). The authors depict four quite different and major organizational perspectives among researchers, writers, educators, consultants and members of organizations.

## Table I:3 – Various "Lens" Through Which We View Organizations

| Lens | Examples of What is Noticed or Talked About from That Lens |
|---|---|
| Structural | Goals, objectives, roles, responsibilities, performance, policies and procedures, efficiency, hierarchy and coordination and control |
| Human Resource | Participation, feelings, fulfillment, communication, needs of people, relationships, motivation, enrichment and commitment |
| Political | Power, conflict, competition, authority, experts, coalitions, allocation of resources, bargaining and decision making |
| Symbolic | Rituals, culture, values, stories, different perspectives, language, expressions, myths, commitment and metaphors |

Note that these are horizontal lens regarding what different people notice across the activities in organizations. There are also many vertical lens through which we view intra-personal dynamics, for example, the many perspectives put forth in the increasing amount of books on personal development.

It is important for you to realize that no lens, or perspective, is better than the others. Experienced consultants have learned that the more perspectives that they can get from their clients about an issue in their organization, often the more accurate and useful are the plans to address that issue. Thus, the more lens through which you can view organizations, the more useful you will be to yourself and your clients.

# Understand Your Preferred Focus on Organizations

People naturally focus on different areas of the same organization during the same project. That difference can cause conflict and confusion, especially during the initial phases of the project. Therefore, it is important for you to recognize your own preferred scope during projects and, if possible, recognize the scope preferred by your clients. The following are probably some of the most common areas of focus viewed by people during projects.

## *Focus on "20/80" (Pragmatic Approach)*

This perspective tends to generate activities focused on quick, up-front, practical action plans that take 20% of your client's time and energy, but might address 80% of the problems in your client's organization. The disadvantage of the 20/80 approach is that ongoing, renewed action plans are sometimes necessary to generate long-term results.

## *Focus on Functions (Silo Approach)*

This perspective focuses primarily on the scope of the "presenting" priority – the priority that is first noticed and reported to you by your client. It might be a major problem in the organization that your client wants to solve, or it could be an exciting goal that your client wants you to help them to achieve. Note that the presenting priority often is a symptom of deeper, more entrenched problems. For example, many nonprofit leaders complain about ineffective fundraising, yet their real problem is ineffective strategic and program planning. A major advantage of this silo approach can be that it often gives quick comfort to your client who wants a "quick fix" and strongly believes where the problem lies in the organization. A major disadvantage is that, because organizations are complex and often rapidly changing, problems often require a larger focus than the particular function first reported as having the problem

## *Focus on Holistic, Systems Approach*

This perspective places strong focus on the overall system (for example, on the entire organization or program) and especially on the relationships among subsystems within the system (for example, on the coordination among processes, such as strategic planning, program planning and fundraising). This is an example of whole systems thinking. A major advantage of this approach is that it is more likely to effectively address complex challenges in organizations. A major challenge is in mastering systems thinking and use of systems tools.

# How to Inventory Your Skills as an Organizational Development Consultant

There can be a wide range of services and associated skills that are applicable to organizational change projects. Without a clear understanding of one's strong interests and skills as a consultant, you are more likely to lose motivation and succumb to burnout. Also, you are much more likely to hurt your client's organization and your own professional career. In addition, you will not know when and how to adapt your approach to consulting in various situations. You will not know when to ask for help or even when to leave a project, if necessary. One of the most important assets of any consultant is their reputation, their credibility. Credibility often comes from doing what you say you are going to do and doing it well, so credibility often comes from knowing what skills you are good at.

Therefore, it is critical for you to have a clear sense about what services you are excited about and interested in, and what services you dislike and often want little or nothing to do with. That sense can come from conducting an inventory of your skills and expertise. They can be organized into a variety of categories, but the following three might be most clear and meaningful to you:

1. **Technical**
   Includes mastery of content-specific information and practices, for example, with phases of consulting or with specific functions and processes in organizations.

2. **Interpersonal**
   Includes mastery of skills to understand and manage oneself and others and to maintain high-quality relationships with others.

3. **Process**
   Includes mastery of skills to work with others to effectively and efficiently develop and implement project plans.

Consider the following guidelines when attempting to identify what consulting services you want to provide and what skills you have to provide those services.

## *General Guidelines for a Self-Inventory*

1.  **Use the 20/80 rule.**
    Attempt to identify the 20% of interests and skills that generate 80% of the most fulfilling services that you could provide as a consultant.

2.  **Reference a list of competencies, if possible, regarding your general interest.**
    Many professions have established a list of competencies (knowledge, skills and attitudes and the ability to apply them for change) associated with high-performers in that field.

     See "Competencies for OD Consultants" on page 53 for more information.

3.  **Consider major types of consultants.**
    Many times, it is easier for us to relate broad roles rather specific service areas, such as Boards, marketing or finance.

     See "Major Types of Consultants to Nonprofits" on page 5 for descriptions of standard roles.

4.  **Get feedback from others.**
    Our opinions of what we like and dislike can often change, depending on our moods, or even if we have not been sleeping well lately. Thus, we often get a much more accurate and valid impression of our preferences if we ask family, friends or peers to give us their opinions about us.

5.  **Reference past experiences more than fantasies and daydreams.**
    Consider past experiences when identifying your preferences. Our history is often a more reliable indicator of our preferences than, for example, our fantasies or daydreams about the future.

6.  **Start with your feelings first.**
    What services are you passionate about? What gives you "goose bumps," or thrills? In contrast, what services do you dislike?

7.  **Next, consider your interests.**
    What have you been reading or talking about lately regarding services to organizations?

8.  **Then, consider trends in the particular service.**
    For example, you might prefer to provide services in the areas of face-to-face fundraising. However, a great deal of fundraising is now being done over the Internet. That might change your preference.

9.  **Assess your skills in your preferred area of service.**
    A powerful approach to assessing your skills is to work with a mentor in that area. For example, you might find an organization in which you could volunteer and work with a more experienced consultant to get an impression of your skill level.

See "Professional Organizations" on page 464 in Appendix B to contact any of the professional organizations where you might find, or get referrals to, opportunities to volunteer or find a mentor.

## *Competencies for OD Consultants*

One powerful approach for organizational change consultants to inventory their relevant skills is to review a list of recommended competencies. The focus of the field of Organization Development is on the values, theories and models, and tools and techniques to successfully accomplish organizational change. Therefore, it might be useful for you to examine a list of competencies for high-performing OD consultants.

 One of the more comprehensive studies of OD competencies was led by Roland Sullivan for the Organization Development Institute. That effort resulted in a free report, *The Knowledge and Skills Necessary for Competence in OD,* located on the Web at http://www.odinstitute.org/skills.htm. Note that some OD consultants might consider that list of skills as an ideal.

 Another useful self-assessment tool for consultants is from the Bayer Center for Nonprofit Management. The tool is located at http://www.pacepgh.com/assessmenttool.pdf

## *Knowledge Areas for Nonprofit Organizational Development Consultants*

In addition to the competencies suggested for consultants in the field of Organization Development, there are certain major nonprofit functions about which you should have knowledge. The degree of knowledge required depends on the nature of the particular services that you offer as a consultant. All organizational consultants should have at least basic, general knowledge about some of the major functions, including:

1.  **Differences between nonprofit and for-profit organizations**
    There are certain differences between the two types of organizations (although there are many more similarities than people realize). You should understand those differences, especially the role of volunteers, fundraising and priority on service (rather than generating a profit).

2.  **Board of Directors**
    Board members should be aware of, and sometimes approve and oversee, consulting projects that affect a significant portion of the organization. You should understand at least the roles and responsibilities of a governing Board, including how they compare to the roles and responsibilities of staff.

3.  **Strategic planning**
    Project plans for organization-wide projects are often most effective if integrated into an overall strategic planning process. You should have a fairly good working knowledge of the typical strategic planning process, including its major phases and activities.

4.    **Programs**

Nonprofits provide services to their clients, primarily in the form of programs. Consulting projects often are meant, ultimately, to improve programs. You should have at least a basic understanding of the design of a typical program, including the nature of staffing, and the types of outputs and outcomes from programs.

5.    **Staffing (Human Resources)**

It is likely that staff members will be highly involved in your projects. You should have at least a basic understanding of how staffing roles (including volunteer roles) are typically analyzed, how members are trained and organized, and how members are supervised.

6.    **Financial management**

Projects will likely incur substantial cost to your client's organization and various types of financial transactions. You should be aware that financial management typically includes budgeting, projecting, recording transactions, generating financial statements and analyzing those statements on a regular basis.

7.    **Fundraising or revenue generation (Sustainability)**

Fundraising is comprised of the activities used to generate revenue from donations by contributors, for example, individuals, foundations, corporations and/or government. Many nonprofits rely on fundraising to ensure sufficient funds to provide services. Charging fees for services, or a combination of fundraising and charging fees also can generate revenue.

8.    **Evaluation**

Evaluation of your projects might be more efficient in they are integrated with evaluation activities that are already underway. Nonprofits might conduct evaluations of staff members, programs, the Chief Executive Officer and the Board.

You might require some degree of knowledge in other major functions in nonprofits, including market research, advertising and promotions, facilities management and collaborations.

PART II, starting on page 111 , is all about nonprofit organizations, including differences between nonprofits and for-profits, and major functions in nonprofits.

To learn even more about nonprofits and each of the major functions in nonprofits, see Recommended Readings on page 499.

# How to Articulate Your Professional Mission and Values

Your professional mission and values serve as your "compass" in life and work. This is true whether you are an external or internal consultant. They guide how you make decisions and solve problems, especially during complex and challenging activities. For many of us, our mission and values are implicit – we have not taken the time to clarify them explicitly or to write them down. Without explicitly proclaiming the mission and values from which we want to operate as professional consultants, we are prone to getting ourselves into situations – and operating in those situations – in a manner that does not match our nature and needs. Your professional mission and values can be communicated to clients to help them to understand and trust you, which is critical in collaborative consulting. Therefore, it is important for professional consultants to consider articulating their own mission and value, ideally in mission statements and values statements.

## Developing Your Professional Mission Statement

Your professional mission statement describes at least the overall purpose of your consulting activities. There are various perspectives on mission statements. Some people believe the statements should describe an overall purpose. Some people believe the mission should also include a description of a vision, or future state. Some people believe the mission should also include a description of overall values. Mission statements can be just a few sentences long.

There are also various perspectives on how to develop a mission statement. The suggestions below are associated with one of the ways to develop your own professional mission statement to describe the purpose of your consulting activities.

The process of producing your own professional mission statement is as important as the mission statement itself. Therefore, it is important for you to carefully think about your own mission before you reference any mission statements produced by others.

When you write your professional mission statement, it should:

1.    Succinctly describe the purpose of your consulting activities.

2.    Succinctly describe the overall type(s) of clients you serve in your work.

3.    Mention the particular results (new knowledge, skills and/or conditions) that you work to help your clients achieve.

4.    Convey a strong public image.

5.    Mention any particular strengths and expertise that you have.

6.    Be clearly understandable by you and your clients.

## Developing Your Professional Values Statement

Your professional values statement describes the most important priorities in the nature of how you want to operate as a consultant. Some people might prefer to do a principles statement. Principles are descriptions of values in action and often begin with the phrase, "I will ..." or "I believe ..." Similar to the mission statement, the process of producing the values statement is as important as the values statement itself. The following guidelines will be helpful to you as you develop your own professional values statement.

1.    **When identifying values, think about behaviors produced by those values.**
      Many of us struggle to directly identify desired values. We can get bogged down in words that seem too general, idealized – even romanticized – to be useful. Often, it helps first to identify desired behaviors and then the values that produce those behaviors.

2.    **Consider any relevant laws and regulations that pertain to your consulting.**
      Identify behaviors or values that will help you operate in a manner so as to avoid breaking these laws and to follow the necessary regulations.

3.    **Consider suggested overall goals and assumptions for effective consultants.**
      Block (2000) suggests certain overall goals and working assumptions for any consultant.

See "Most Important Goals for Consultants" on page 7 and "Working Assumptions for Consultants" on page 7 to read Block's suggestions.

4.      **Consider suggested principles for effective consulting.**
Consider behaviors and values that are in accordance with the most important principles for consulting for you.

See "Principles for Effective Consulting" on page 29 for a listing of one suggested set of principles.

5.      **Consider your own lens, biases, style, response to feedback and conflict.**
You might identify behaviors and values that will help you to counter any potential misperceptions or obstacles that you might develop because of your own particular nature and needs.

6.      **Consider any current, major issues in your work.**
Identify the behaviors needed to resolve these issues. Identify which values would generate those preferred behaviors. There may be values included that some people would not deem as moral or ethical values, for example, team-building and promptness, but for many, these practical values may add more relevance and utility to a values statement.

7.      **Consider any ethical values that might be prized by your clients.**
For example, consider expectations of clients, suppliers, funders and members of the local community. Before you identify these "public relations" values, be careful that you do not select values that you really cannot adhere to in your work.

8.      **From the above steps, select the top five to ten values.**
You cannot be all things to all people, including to yourself. Even if you do include all the values on your statement, it is still important for you to carefully think about which values are most important to you.

9.      **Associate with each value, two example behaviors which reflect each value.**
Examples of behaviors for each value make the values much more explicit and understood to you and to others.

10.     **Update the statement at least once a year.**
The most important aspect of the statement is developing it, not the statement itself. Continued dialogue and reflection around your values cultivates awareness and sensitivity to act in accordance to your values. Therefore, revisit your statement at least once – preferably two or three times – a year.

See "Principles for Ethical Consulting" on page 30 for information about ethical consulting and for references to examples of codes of ethics, which are also a form of values statement.

## Summarize Your Learning About Yourself as a Change Agent

Answers to the following questions will help you practice explaining key terms and activities that you might need to explain to your clients. Answers might also help you to develop a clearer understanding of yourself as an instrument of change. The questions are about the information provided throughout PART I.

### Table I:4 – Exercise: Summarize Learning About Yourself

1. How do you define "consultant"? "Organizational development consultant"?

2. What kind of consultant are you now?

3. How do you define collaborative consulting?

4. What are the advantages of collaborative consulting?

5. What are the seven phases of organizational consulting in this Field Guide?

6. If you consider yourself to be an OD professional, how do you define "OD"?

7. What are your overall goals and working assumptions as a consultant?

8. Describe your biases (everyone has them) about leading and managing.

9. Do you prefer to see priorities as "problems" or "opportunities"?

10. Describe your consulting style. Consider your preferred use of humor, pace, questions versus comments, and content versus process.

11. How do you respond to conflict? To feedback about yourself?

12. What are your preferences for problem solving and decision-making? Consider rational versus organic, intuitive versus sensing, and thinking versus feeling.

13. What is your "lens" on organizations? Consider structural, human resource, political and symbolic.

14. What is your current, natural focus on organizations? Consider 20/80, functional and holistic/systems.

15. What are your current areas of expertise in consulting?

16. What are your professional mission and most important values for operating as a consultant?

# Building Trust, Commitment and Collaboration with Clients

The success of your consulting project rests as much on the quality of your collaborative relationship with your clients as on any other aspect of your consultancy. This is true whether you are an external or internal consultant. The more collaboratively that you can work with your client, the more likely that your client will gain the motivation, vision, political support and momentum necessary for successful change. The most important requirement for a collaborative consultancy is openness, honesty and trust between you and your client.

Guidelines in this section will help you to work with your client in an approach that is open and honest and is based on clear and supportive communication. The guidelines will help you and your client recognize and appreciate differences, and all the while, ensure clear and realistic expectations about each other and your overall project. The guidelines are relevant to all phases of the collaborative consulting cycle. Note that the various topics in this overall section are all highly integrated.

## How to Work in Multicultural Environments

Participants need to feel that they are being understood and respected throughout the project. They need to feel that their ideas and concerns are being heard. Those conditions create strong motivation and momentum for change.

It can be a major challenge to work in multicultural environments where your clients' organizations have values, beliefs and certain conventions that are distinctly different from yours. Consultants to nonprofits might experience that situation more frequently than consultants to large, for-profit organizations because nonprofits are usually formed to address certain needs in the community. Often, those needs exist among various culturally-specific communities.

Although multicultural consulting comes with its own unique challenges, it comes with many benefits, as well. There are few other such powerful experiences in which you can learn so much about people and organizations and also about yourself. The range of nonprofits is highly diverse and consultants who can work in multicultural environments often have a wider range of potential consulting projects than the consultant who is fearful or disinterested in those environments.

An organization's culture is driven by the values throughout that organization. Quite often, decisions in organizations are based on the strong values among its members. To help your client make meaningful decisions – and to understand decisions that they may have made already – it is extremely important that you have some understanding of the culture and values of your client's organization.

The following guidelines are intended to focus on the most practical suggestions for working with clients in multicultural environments.

### *Cultural Diversity Has a Huge Affect on Projects*

There are often major differences – realize that. For example, Western cultures tend to be highly rational and value things that are handy in meeting a current need. They value rugged individualism and competition. Some cultures might value patience, a sense of community and getting along with others, and still others might value direct authority and privacy.

Differences between cultures can lead to increased resistance during a project. You and your client might not understand each other because you have different values. Those differences can hamper the progress of your project, if not stop it altogether.

Some cultures may be overly deferential to the consultant. The nature of good consulting can be quite indirect. A good consultant will help clients to count on each other as much as on the consultant.

Some cultures are deeply guarded about private matters. Thus, techniques of supportive questioning, which might produce strong commitment and deep learning in some cultures, might not be appropriate in other cultures at all.

There are no universal laws to ensure conformity in each culture. Because of complexities in continually learning the cultures of your clients' organizations, it is critical for you to continually 1) be open to differences and 2) ask for help from your client.

## *Basic Guidelines to Culturally-Specific Consulting*

1.  **Be aware of your personal biases, style, preferences, lens and focus.**
    This is critically important for successful consulting in any type of culture. You make a major difference in your client's organization just by exposing the organization to your own nature and style of working.

     See "Understanding Yourself as an Instrument of Change" on page 43 and "Staying Grounded and Centered" on page 91 for guidelines to understand yourself and work in a manner that suits your nature and needs.

2.  **Realize that each part of an organization probably has a unique culture.**
    For example, the secretarial staff might interact with each other in a manner quite different from that of the program staff. In larger organizations, there are often several differences, for example, between senior management, program staff and support staff.

3.  **Promptly convey to your client that you want to be sensitive to their culture.**
    You should start in your first interaction with your client. State that you recognize that different people might approach the same project differently depending on their own personalities and the culture of the overall organization. Ask your client how you can understand the nature of their organization.

4.  **Consider getting a project mentor, or representative, from the organization.**
    Attempt to get someone from your client's organization to help you understand their culture and how to work in a manner compatible with the culture of the organization. This request is not a sign of weakness or lack of expertise, rather it is an authentic request that better serves you and your client.

## *Become Knowledgeable About Key Cultural Aspects*

Consider asking your client to help you understand how each of the following aspects might be unique in the culture of their organization. Key cultural aspects that might affect your consulting project include:

1. **Assertiveness**
   Are members of your client's organization comfortable being honest and direct with each other? If not, how can you still be as authentic as possible and help them to be as authentic as possible, as well?

2. **Body language**
   Are there any specific cues that you can notice to help you to sense how others are experiencing you?

3. **Communication styles and direction**
   Is communication fairly direct and specific or more indirect and general? Does information flow mostly "upward" to executives or is it widely disseminated?

4. **Conflict**
   Is conflict considered to be bad and avoided? Or is conflict accepted as normal and directly addressed when it appears?

5. **Eye contact**
   Are members of the organization comfortable with sustained eye contact during communication or not?

6. **Gestures**
   Are there any specific gestures that can cause members of the organization discomfort or confusion?

7. **Humor**
   Is use of humor in the organization rather widespread? Is there anything about the use of humor about which you should be aware?

8. **Information collection**
   Should you be aware of any potential problems or use any certain precautions when conducting interviews or using assessments?

9. **Physical space**
   For example, are members of your client's organization quite conscious of having a minimum amount of space around them when they work or speak with others?

10. **Power**
    Are members attuned to certain people of power when solving problems and making decisions? Is power based on authority and/or respect?

11. **Silence**
    Are members uncomfortable with silence during communication? Or is it a common aspect of communicating in their workplace?

12.     **Time**
        Is time a precious commodity that seems to underlie many activities, or can activities take as long as they need to take to be done effectively?

13.     **Wording**
        Are there certain words or phrasings that cause discomfort when people from different cultures interact?

## Hints for Talking with Others About Management Activities

It is not uncommon for people of any culture to experience confusion or engage in protracted arguments about activities only to realize later on that they have been in agreement all along – they had been using different definitions for the same terms.  Therefore, it is important to ensure that all of you are "speaking the same language" about activities.  The following three guidelines are most important when ensuring that you and your client continue to understand each other when talking about management activities.

### Recognize Difference Between Terms That Refer to Results Versus Activities to Produce Those Results

It is common for people from different cultures to become confused because different people are talking about results and others about the activities to produce the results.  For example, some people refer to the "plan" to be the document, and others refer to the "plan" to be the activity of developing the plan.  It is usually most clear to use the term "plan" to refer to the document itself, and use the term "planning" for the activities that produces the plan.

Here is another example.  Inexperienced consultants sometimes assert that, because the client does not have a tangible plan/document on the shelf and does not explicitly reference the document on a regular basis, the client does not have a plan.  That assertion can alienate the consultant from clients who believe that they have been doing planning all along (but probably implicitly) and also have a good plan – they just have not been calling their process "planning" and have not produced a written plan document.  Therefore, it is important for you to recognize if your clients have their own form of a certain activity and how that form is carried out in their organization.

### Be Able to Separate a Term from the Meaning of That Term

If your conversations with others about management seem to get stuck or mired in confusion, it often helps to separate terms from the intent of those terms.  For example:

- Rather than talking about "vision" or "goals," talk about "what" the nonprofit wants to accomplish overall.

- Rather than talking about "strategies," talk about "how" to accomplish "what" you want to accomplish overall.

- Rather than talking about "action plans," talk about "who is going to do what, and by when."

## Hints for Talking with Others About Leadership Activities

The topic of leadership has become so prominent and passionate with so many people that it sometimes causes great confusion.  Here are a few tips to help you and your client to "stay on the same page" when talking about leadership.

1.   **Be clear about whether you are talking about leadership roles or traits.**
     When people talk about leadership, they might be talking about traits of leaders, such as being charismatic, influential and ethical. However, when others talk about leadership, they might be talking about roles of leadership, such as the Board Chair or the Chief Executive Officer. Both discussions are about leadership, but both are about quite different aspects.

2.   **Be clear about the domain of leadership about which you are talking.**
     For example, when talking about leading yourself, you might be talking about leadership skills, such as being assertive or having good time and stress management skills. When talking about leading other individuals, you might be talking about skills, such as coaching, delegating or mentoring. When talking about leading groups, you might be talking about skills, such as facilitation or meeting management. When talking about leading organizations, you might be talking about skills, such as strategic planning or business planning. In each of these four cases, the term "leadership" refers to different sets of skills.

# How to Remain Authentic with Yourself and Others

Block (2000) asserts that authenticity is the building block upon which all other aspects of the consulting process are built. He suggests that authentic behavior is telling your client how you are experiencing your client, especially when you want to draw attention to a particular behavior of your client.

The concept of authenticity has received a significant amount of attention recently as people search for meaning and happiness, particularly in their work lives. Like many other popular concepts, different people have different views about authenticity and many people feel strongly about their own views. Some people assert that authenticity involves many features, for example, always being centered with themselves and others, living in a completely integrated fashion with their own values and principles, or always feeling complete meaning or sense of purpose in their lives. Consequently, they might assert that authenticity is a life-long pursuit. Other people have more short-term, specific and concise views, as will be explained immediately below.

## *Major Benefits of Authenticity*

Block (2000) asserts that authenticity is one of the critical aspects of successful consulting (along with successfully carrying out the phases of consulting). There are several reasons for the importance of authenticity.

1.   **Encourages clients to be open, honest and direct in the here-and-now.**
     The collaborative consultant wants the client to be as open and honest as possible. The consultant can encourage open and honest behavior in others by modeling that behavior themselves. This helps the consultant to fully understand the client and provide useful feedback that the client will hear, as well.

     Authenticity from your client also provides extremely valuable feedback to you. Frequently, you do not have sufficient opportunity to continually learn about yourself, particularly in settings with your clients. Clients who choose to be authentic around you are offering you a precious gift that can be used by you to cultivate a collaborative consulting relationship with them and others.

2.  **Builds client's trust and confidence in your relationship.**
    You can build a strong relationship with your client by showing them that you trust them enough to be able to handle the truth. In turn, they will do the same thing for you. Trust and confidence are critical ingredients for a successful working relationship between you and your client.

3.  **Deals with issues before the issues fester.**
    When people express themselves honestly in the here-and-now, they are much more likely to report issues as soon as they notice them. This ensures that issues are addressed when they occur, rather than festering until they show themselves as major forms of resistance to change during the project.

4.  **Considers important "data" about the client's situation.**
    Information that you gather from your other senses is important data about your client's situation. The more open and honest that you can be about your own perceptions, the more likely that the data from your senses will be accurate. Many times that data can be used to more accurately understand your client's situation.

5.  **Ensures organizational change efforts remain relevant, realistic and flexible.**
    Plans rarely are implemented as planned. Authentic behavior from your clients helps all parties involved to accurately perceive and talk about any changes in the project so, as a result, plans can be updated with those changes and thereby remain up-to-date. Perhaps Terry (1993) puts it best: "authenticity self-corrects."

## Key Guidelines to Authentic Behavior

Block and various schools of psychology, for example, Carl Rogers' self-directed therapy, describe the following core characteristics of authentic behavior. Considering their descriptions, authentic behavior is more attainable than many believe and it might help you to work easier rather than work harder in your projects for change.

1.  **Honest**
    Speak the truth.

2.  **Direct**
    Speak in terms that are clear, concise and focused.

3.  **About here-and-now**
    Speak about what is going on right now.

4.  **From you**
    Report your *own* experience of the here-and-now.

5.  **Non-judgmental of others**
    Speak about what you are experiencing around others, not of your judgments of others.

Unless you are authentic in a supportive manner, clients might feel like you are being aggressive. Aggressive behavior is perceived as demanding, forceful, arrogant and even hostile. That can cause discomfort, alienation, confusion and distrust between you and your clients. Experienced consultants have learned to employ authentic communication in a manner that is completely honest, yet remains supportive and respectful.

Note that authentic behavior does not always mean the consultant's speaking the truth about anything and everything all the time. Sometimes the consultant senses that the client is not yet ready to hear about the consultant's speculations, for example, about causes of issues or the client's role in those issues. Sometimes these speculations would simply overwhelm and confuse the client.

In every case, it is up to the consultant's judgment as to how much they "think out loud." However, usually there is more of a downside to not being authentic than the downside of sharing your thoughts and impressions with your clients.

## How to Really Listen to Your Clients

Listening is a critical skill for all adults to have. It is one of the most important skills for you to use as you learn about your clients, their organization and their problems. Also, it is one of the most important activities for you to use to establish a strong rapport with clients.

There have been numerous books written about effective listening skills. The following guidelines can help you accomplish effective listening in the vast majority of situations.

1.  **Be sure you can hear the speaker.**
    It is surprising how often people do not really listen to other people. It is just as surprising how often people do not realize that they cannot even hear other people. So always make this your first guideline in any situation for effective listening.

2.  **Overall, attempt to listen 75% of time – speak 25% of time.**
    This is one of the most powerful guidelines. Use of the guideline depends on your situation. For example, if you are making a presentation, you will speak more. Otherwise, ensure that your client speaks more than you do – and listen to them.

3.  **Adopt a culturally compatible physical posture to show you are interested.**
    This can be powerful means to show your client that you are interested in hearing them. For example, you might lean forward and maintain eye contact. Whatever physical gestures you make, be sure they are compatible to the culture of the speaker.

     See "How to Work in Multicultural Environments" on page 58 for guidelines to identify what is compatible to the culture of your client's organization.

4.  **Do not think about what to say while you are also trying to listen to the speaker.**
    Your brain goes four times faster than a speaker's voice. Thus, your brain can easily leave the speaker behind. Instead, trust that you will know how to respond to the speaker when the speaker is done.

5.  **Notice the client's speaking style.**
    Different people have different speaking styles. Do they speak loud or soft? Slow or fast? Are there disconnects between what they say versus what their body language conveys? Some people convey the central idea first and then support it with additional information. Other people provide information to lead the listener to the same conclusion as the speaker.

6.  **Listen for central ideas, not for all the facts**.
    Experienced consultants develop a sense for noticing the most important information conveyed by their client. They hear the main themes and ideas from their client. If you notice the major ideas, then often the facts "come along" with those ideas.

7.  **Let the speaker finish each major point that they want to make.**
    Do not interrupt – offer your response when the speaker is done. If you do have to interrupt, do so to ensure you are hearing your client. Interrupt tactfully. For example, put up your hand and say, "Might I interrupt to ask you to clarify something?"

8.  **Reflect back and ask if you are hearing their point accurately.**
    This is also one of the most powerful guidelines. Start by asking if you can reflect back, or summarize, to your client after they have spoken. Then progress to where you can ask your client to summarize back to you what you have just said to them.

9.  **Regularly share indications that you are listening to them.**
    Those indications can be, for example, nodding your head, saying "Yes" to short points that you agree with.

10. **Learn the art of supportive questioning.**
    Coaching involves the use of powerful questions to understand your client's perceptions, assumptions and conclusions. The coach must practice effective questioning skills to really understand the client.

     See "How to Coach for Deep Problem-Solving and Learning" on page 68 for guidelines to do powerful coaching by using supportive questioning.

11. **Ask others to provide you feedback about your communication skills.**
    Often, people do not know what they do not know about themselves. An example is the consultant who prizes themselves on their strong listening skills, yet regularly interrupts others when they are speaking. Another example is the consultant who speaks only in conclusions, but does not share how they came to those conclusions. Thus, others do not understand the consultant's rationale.

# How to Recognize and Understand Body Language

## *Interpreting Your Client's Body Language*

Resistance, confusion, distaste, passivity, etc., all show up in the body language of your client, regardless of what they are saying. Experienced consultants have learned often to trust what they see more than what they hear. Body language is always present. Too many speakers and listeners are unaware of body language.

The nature of a person's body language is highly dependent on the person's nature. For example, some people are intent on sitting or standing upright with their hands at their sides in a stance of attention and respect. Other people might slouch in their chair or extend their legs, in part, to convey that they feel comfortable around others in the room.

It is difficult to make overall conclusions about body language, especially because it is culturally dependent. However, people trust non-verbal communication more than they do verbal (spoken) communication, so learn to notice non-verbal communication, and be aware of your own.

In general, notice:

1.      **Style of voice, for example, loud, soft, frequent, irregular.**

2.      **Movement of the body, for example, gestures, face, eyes.**

3.      **Distance, space and time between speaker and listener.**

Specifically, notice:

1.      **Eye contact.**
        In the United States, this often conveys sincerity. In other cultures, though, it might convey aggressiveness or hostility.

2.      **Frequent movements of the body.**
        Frequent movements might convey nervousness, poor listening.

3.      **Openness of the body.**
        Arms crossed may mean defensiveness, which impedes communication.

## Interpreting Your Own Body Language

Your body language is often the true "compass" about your impression of the quality of a project. For you to remain authentic, you need to be in touch with your own non-verbal communication. Different people have different physical reactions in different situations. Consider the following.

1.      **Are you moving your arms and legs a lot?**
        If so, maybe you are afraid, frustrated or confused about something about your client or project.

2.      **Is your mouth dry?**
        Then maybe you are afraid of something.

3.      **Is your body position closed?**
        Are your legs and arms crossed? Perhaps you feel attacked somehow?

4.      **Is your brow furled?**
        Perhaps you are confused – or you are really interested in what your client has to say.

5.      **Are you looking away from the client a lot?**
        Then there is likely something about your client that is bothering you. Or, perhaps your style is to look away so you can think more clearly. If that is the case, realize that your client might be seeing you as having poor eye contact.

6.      **Is your heart racing?**
        Perhaps you are afraid of your client or the project, or you are excited about the project.

# How to Make Sure Your Client Really Hears You

Usually, your most frequent form of communication to your clients is spoken words. As with non-verbal communication, spoken communication is highly dependent on the particular culture in which you are working. For example, culture can affect how people speak about conflict, use humor, are honest and direct with each other, use silence, and use certain wording.

 See "How to Work in Multicultural Environments" on page 58 for guidelines about understanding the culture of your client's organization.

Consider the following general guidelines, which might be useful in a wide variety of cultures.

1. **Know the main point that you want to convey.**
   Sometimes, people begin speaking with the hope that if they talk long enough, they are bound to say what they want to say. Before you speak, take the time to think about the main points that you want to convey.

2. **Convey one point at a time.**
   That approach ensures that the listener is more likely to continue to understand you, rather than being overwhelmed with too many ideas delivered at too fast a rate. You might even find that you understand your own thoughts more completely.

3. **Speak too slowly rather than too quickly.**
   A good way to practice this guideline is to speak along with a news anchor when you are watching television. You will likely find that they speak much more slowly than you realize. They are professionals who have learned an effective rate of speaking.

4. **Vary your voice.**
   Always avoid monotone. A monotone voice might convey to the listener that you are bored or controlled. It is likely to lull you and/or the listener into a stupor. Varying your voice takes practice, but it is well worth the effort.

5. **State your conclusion before describing how you came to that conclusion.**
   Some speakers convey their recommendations or advice by conveying the necessary information to lead the listener to the same conclusions as the speaker's. Instead, it is often more reliable to first state your point and then explain it.

6. **People speak more frequently and completely when they are comfortable.**
   Therefore, get comfortable with the person to whom you are speaking. Skills in authentic expression can be useful in these situations. For example, if you are uncomfortable or confused, simply say so.

7. **Ask the listener to repeat the main points of what you just said to them.**
   This guideline ensures that the listener is indeed hearing what you wanted to convey. Be tactful when asking the listener to repeat what you said. For example, say "I want to be sure that I made sense to you just now, so I would appreciate if you could tell me what you heard me say."

8.  **Ask others to provide feedback about your spoken communication.**
    One of the most powerful ways to learn about yourself is to ask others for feedback.
    Therefore, ask others about how you might improve your speaking skills.

 See "How to Share Useful – and Respectful – Feedback" on page 45 for guidelines to get feedback, including about your spoken communications.

# How to Coach for Deep Problem-Solving and Learning

One of the major goals of a consultant is to help their clients learn to be more effective at solving problems and learning. One of the most powerful services that you can provide to your client is coaching your client to a) closely examine their own perceptions, assumptions and conclusions about their current problem or goal; b) take relevant and realistic actions; and c) learn by continuing to reflect on those actions and experiences.

You can use coaching at almost any time during your project when your client seems to be struggling to address an issue or achieve a goal. Coaching can be useful, for example, during the initial meeting when your client is reporting the current issue or goal for the project, or during regular meetings with your client when they are describing current challenges in implementing plans.

## What Is Coaching? How Is It Useful in Consulting?

There are a variety of views on coaching. In addition to the obvious example of coaching in sports, many supervisors consider coaching to be what others might consider to be delegating. Delegating is usually considered to be working with direct reports (employees who report directly to the supervisor) to establish goals or tasks, and then providing ongoing feedback, guidance and support to help the employee achieve the goals.

Another perspective on coaching is that of personal and professional coaching, which has fast become a major consulting service. Coaching provides conditions that are ideal for adult problem solving and learning. In the midst of continual change and development, people rarely struggle because they lack some key piece of information or some precise procedure from a course or a book. Rather, they often get stuck in how they think and feel about themselves or their situations in life and work. In addition, for people to learn, they often need ongoing support and guidance to take realistic risks and then learn from reflecting on their experiences. Coaching guides and supports that kind of problem solving and learning; thus, it is often quite powerful when used during a consulting project.

While there are also a variety of views about the nature, goals and techniques of personal and professional coaching, most coaches would probably agree that their approach to coaching is to work in a collaborative approach. This provides structure, guidance and support for their clients to:

1.  **Take a complete look at their current situation,**
    including their assumptions and perceptions about their work, themselves and others.

2.  **Set relevant and realistic goals for themselves,**
    based on their own nature and needs.

3.  **Take relevant and realistic actions toward reaching their goals,**
    ensuring that the actions are specific, measurable, achievable, relevant and timely.

4.    **Learn by continuing to reframe (or take apart) how they see their current situation,** and by reflecting on their actions along the way.

Note that coaching is not the same as therapeutic counseling.  The focus of your coaching is not on the analysis of an individual's personal history and character in order for them to overcome current, entrenched emotional or spiritual challenges in their lives.  Instead, the focus of your coaching is to guide and support members of the organization to achieve the goals and actions necessary to accomplish change in their organization.  While there is some general overlap between these two areas of focus, a consultant for organizational change should not attempt giving therapy unless they are trained therapists and unless that type of service is in the consulting contract.

Consultants to nonprofits know that one of the major challenges in achieving success is implementation and follow-through of action plans by members of the nonprofit.  Nonprofits often have very limited resources and attending to implementation in an ongoing focused fashion can be extremely difficult.  Another challenge in nonprofits is that the nature of small- to medium-sized nonprofits, and the people in them, tends to be highly diverse.  Consequently, methods to help nonprofits must be adaptable to diverse views and approaches.  Coaching is highly adaptable to the nature of the client being coached because it works from people, rather than at them.  It helps them to closely examine their own style, or the framework, of their thinking and problem solving.  In systems theory language, it helps them to examine their mental models.

 See "How to Analyze Mental Models – How People Think" on page 418 for more tools to solve problems by reframing them.

## *Guidelines for Designing a Coaching Session*

The nature of a coaching conversation can be distinctly different from a typical workplace conversation.  A typical conversation is usually a spontaneous exchange of information that almost seems to "ping pong" casually back and forth among the participants.  The focus of the conversation can move with whatever comments are offered by participants.  In contrast, coaching is usually a much more focused conversation in which the nature of exchange is based, in large part, on asking powerful questions of your client, while using effective listening and feedback skills, as you support your client in thoughtfully answering the questions.

Coaching is useful when it seems that an individual is struggling with a particular problem or is interested in how to achieve some goal, and wants help from another person.  In those situations, you need to intentionally prepare yourself and your client for a coaching session.  Consider the following guidelines.

1.    **Briefly describe the nature of coaching and its benefits to your client.**
      Mention that one of the most powerful ways to help someone solve a problem or clarify plans to achieve a goal is through use of a coaching session.  Explain how coaching helps the person reframe the problem, carefully think about action plans, and learn at the same time.  Explain the role of questions during coaching.

2.    **Ask the client if they would like you to coach them.**
      You should always get your client's permission to be coached.  Otherwise, your client may feel uncomfortable, manipulated and distrusting during questioning.

3.   **Consider any culturally specific conventions.**
     Depending on the conventions in the particular culture of your client's organization and on the personality of your client, your client might not appreciate getting questioned by you. In some cultures, questions might be perceived as disrespectful.

 See "How to Work in Multicultural Environments" on page 58 for guidelines to understand if questioning is acceptable in another's culture.

4.   **Focus on organizational issues, not just on the individual's issues.**
     Your role as a consultant is to facilitate organization-wide change, not only to facilitate change in one individual. Thus, you should maintain focus on the desired results of the project for organizational change in addition to the current challenges of the person whom you are coaching.

5.   **Use the guidelines for effective listening.**
     For example, be sure that you can hear your client, listen more than talk, and acknowledge your client's responses.

 See "How to Really Listen to Your Clients" on page 64 for guidelines to really listen to your clients when coaching them.

6.   **Respectfully and supportively offer probing questions.**
     Questions are the heart of the coaching session. The rest of this subsection provides numerous guidelines about traits of useful and not so useful questions, along with examples of powerful questions.

7.   **Limit advice during the questioning.**
     Sometimes, you might feel an urge to answer a question that your client seems to be struggling to answer. Your client might be struggling because they are searching for the best answer. That search can yield a great deal of learning for your client.

8.   **Limit general discussion during the questioning.**
     A general discussion can diffuse the focus on the questioning. Instead, keep focused on asking questions of your client. Each question might be based on answers to the previous question. There can be other times in the project for general discussion.

9.   **Avoid lecturing your client.**
     This guideline is relevant to probably any supportive and respectful communication with your client. Lecturing can be detected by regular use of phrases, such as "you should" or "you have to." Lecturing leaves your client feeling judged and angry.

10.  **Use questions to help your client develop action plans.**
     Often, it is useful to help your clients come to conclusions about their issues by helping them decide whether they even want to take action on those issues and what those actions should be. Often, actions "shake loose" solutions and generate learning.

11. **Use questions to help your client learn from the coaching session.**
   Your client can generate valuable insights from thinking about and responding to useful questions from you. It is important for you to help your client to identify and take ownership for that learning.

12. **Close the coaching session.**
   Always use some means for specifically ending the coaching session. For example, thank your client, ask your client what they have learned, mention the value of the coaching session to you, or physically move to a different location. Ask the client to summarize their learnings and ask them about next steps.

## Why Questions Are So Important in Coaching

The core "engine," or tool in personal and professional coaching, is you respectfully and supportively posing powerful questions to your client. There are several advantages to questioning.

1. **Helps your client to recognize their own perceptions and assumptions.**
   Usually, a coaching session starts with your client describing some issue or goal that is important to them. For example, if your current client is the Chief Executive Officer (CEO), the CEO might explain to you that he or she believes that there is a significant management problem. The CEO might add that he or she has tried hard to address the problem, but does not seem to be getting anywhere. The CEO might suggest that he or she needs to take a time management course.

2. **Helps your client to clarify their own assumptions.**
   As the CEO continues to think about the questions posed by you, he or she usually provides more information about the reasoning that led to those current conclusions about the issue. For example, the CEO might mention that other leaders seem to get more done, and feel much less frustrated.

3. **Helps your client to verify their own assumptions.**
   As you pose more questions, your client may begin to question how they see their issue and any conclusions about it. For example, the CEO might question himself or herself about whether others really get more done, whether the CEO is being realistic about the amount of tasks to get done in a day, and ultimately, whether the time management problem might be a symptom of another larger problem.

4. **Helps your client to modify their views on the issues.**
   Many times, finding the right problem is at least as important as finding the right answer. As the coaching session progresses, the CEO might seem to be talking about another problem or goal. For example, the CEO might mention that he or she wishes for more guidance from the Board of Directors about setting priorities and providing more resources for the CEO, but he or she is reluctant to ask for help for fear of appearing incompetent.

5. **Helps your client to arrive at realistic conclusions about what to do.**
   Many times, leaders in nonprofit organizations are faced with so many challenges and options for meeting those challenges that they do not know what to do. Other times, leaders of nonprofits are so inspired and driven that they struggle to be realistic. Coaching helps people to move on to action-oriented conclusions that are relevant and realistic.

6. **Helps you and your client to develop powerful skills in inquiry and reflection.**
In our example, over several coaching sessions, the CEO often begins to develop his or her own skills in asking useful questions to others and themselves. Conversations become more focused, especially on useful actions and learning. The CEO is learning to solve his or her own problems and identify learning, too.

7. **Helps you to help your client without knowing extensive background on issues.**
One of the major advantages of using questions during coaching is that often you can help your client without ever having to know a great deal of history about the particular issue or goal faced by your client. Actually, the more that you know about how your client got stuck on a particular issue, the more that you can sometimes get as stuck as your client during coaching. Many times, clients struggle because of strong misperceptions. The more that you closely examine the background and thinking about those misperceptions, the more that you might adopt those misperceptions yourself. You can avoid that trap by resorting to asking questions during coaching sessions.

## Traits of Destructive Questions

Before suggesting guidelines to conduct supportive questioning, it is important for you to know what types of questions to avoid. Consider these guidelines.

1. **Avoid asking questions that can be answered simply with "yes" or "no."**
You and your client gain little understanding or direction from such pointed questions that have such short answers. Instead, consider questions that start with "What," "How," "When," and "Where."

2. **Avoid leading questions.**
Leading questions are questions that are asked to lead your client to a certain pre-determined conclusion or insight. Those questions can be perceived by your client as being manipulative and dishonest. Leading questions often can be answered with "yes" or "no," for example, "You did what I suggested, right?"

3. **Avoid frequently asking questions that begin with "Why."**
Those types of questions can leave your client feeling defensive, as if they are to be accountable to you to justify their actions. That feeling of defensiveness can damage feelings of trust and openness between you and your client.

## Traits of Useful Questions

Consider these guidelines.

1. **Where possible, use open-ended questions.**
Open-ended questions are those that are not answered with "yes" or "no." They generate thinking and reflection on the part of your client. They also ensure that your client keeps focused in the questioning session.

2. **Focus questions on the here-and-now.**
The goal of coaching is to help your client go forward by reframing their problem, identifying realistic actions to take, and learning from those actions.

3.     **Ask questions to clarify what your client is saying.**
Clarifying questions help you and your client understand the key point or "bottom line" of what he is saying.  This can enable them to move on to the right question.

4.     **Ask questions about the client's perspectives, assumptions, actions, etc**.
Adults can learn a great deal by closely examining their own thinking.  Often, they struggle because of inaccurate perceptions or assumptions.  Therefore, ask questions about their thinking, assumptions and beliefs about current priorities.  Do not ask lots of questions about other people – you cannot coach people who are not with you.

5.     **Ask your client for help.**
It can be powerful when you show enough trust and confidence in the relationship with your client that you can ask them for help with helping them.  For example, you might ask your client, "What question should I ask you?" or "What additional questions should I be asking now?"

## *Examples of Powerful Questions for Coaching*

It is common that a coaching session with clients goes through a certain life cycle.  Initially, your client will report some major problem, goal, challenge or priority.  Your questions can be useful at that time to help your client report their problem, and then closely examine and clarify that problem.  Next, you can help your client identify useful actions to take to effectively resolve their problem.  Lastly, you can help your client learn from the coaching session itself.  Consider the following questions when coaching your client and notice the grouping of the questions into the various life cycles of a useful coaching session.

## Table I:5 – Useful Questions to Ask When Coaching Others

**1. To Help Clients Report Their Issue:**

- What do you want to work on today?

- What is wrong? What is missing?

- What would be exciting to achieve?

- What would you like from me today?

- How would you like to get it?

**2. To Help Clients Clarify Their Issue:**

- What is important?

- How is this issue important?

- What do you think the real problem is?

- What is your role in this issue?

- Where do you feel stuck?

- Is what you are doing getting what you want?

- What is the intent of what you are saying?

- Where are those strong feelings coming from?

- What would you like me to ask?

**3. To Help Clients Move to Action:**

- Have you experienced anything like this before? What did you do? How did it work out?

- What do you hope for?

- What is preventing you from...?

- What would you be willing to give up for that?

- If you could change one thing, what would it be?

- Imagine a point in the future where your issue is resolved. How did you get there?

- What can you do before the next meeting?

- Who will do that action? By when? What will it look like when done? How will you know it is done?

**4. To Help Clients Deepen Their Learning:**

- Have you said everything that you want to say?

- How did this coaching session go for you?

- What is the learning in this for you?

# How to Share Useful – and Respectful – Feedback

Feedback is information about performance and is information that people can act on. Frequently, you share feedback with individuals and groups in your client's organization. Usually, feedback is what your client wants you to provide. The feedback might be about your client's actions and ideas, or the results of assessments in your client's organization. Feedback is extremely useful during evaluations of the project and in generating learning from activities in the project.

Feedback can be powerful means of identifying and solving problems. However, the feedback must be shared in a manner that is understandable to your client and is perceived by them as being provided in a highly respectful manner. Sharing feedback involves guidelines from several other subsections in this overall section, especially the skills in authenticity, effective listening and verbal communication. Consider the following guidelines, as well.

1.  **Be clear about what you want to say.**
    You might have already sensed what feedback you want to convey to your client. However, you should think about what points you want to convey and how you want to convey those points.

2.   **Be concise and specific.**
     People often lose specificity when they speak because they say far too much, rather than not enough.  Or, they speak about general themes and patterns.  When giving feedback, give details about what you see or hear.

3.   **Avoid generalizations.**
     Avoid use of the words "all," "never," and "always."  Those words can seem extreme, lack credibility and place arbitrary limits on behavior.  Be more precise about quantity or proportion, if you address terms of quantities, at all.

4.   **Be descriptive rather than evaluative.**
     Report what you are seeing, hearing or feeling.  Attempt to avoid evaluative words, such as "good" or "bad."  It may be helpful to quickly share your particular feeling, if appropriate, but do not dwell on it or become emotional.

5.   **Own the feedback.**
     The information should be about your own perception of information, not about their perceptions, assumptions and motives.  Use 'I' statements as much as possible to indicate that your impressions are your own.

6.   **Be careful about giving advice.**
     When giving feedback, it is often best to do one thing at a time – share your feedback, get their response to your feedback, and then, when they are more ready to consider additional information, share your advice with them.

Note that if you are sharing feedback in a meeting with members of your client's organization, for example, about results of an assessment, you should follow a carefully designed agenda for the meeting.

See "You and Your Client Share Feedback with Others" on page 307 for guidelines about designing a feedback meeting.

# How to See Your Client's Point of View – Your Skills in Empathy

## *What Is Empathy?  Why Is It So Important?*

Empathy is the ability to accurately put yourself "in someone else's shoes" – to understand their situation, perceptions and feelings from their point of view – and to be able to communicate that understanding back to the other person.  Empathy is a critical skill for you to have as an organizational consultant.  It contributes toward accurate understanding of your clients, their perceptions and concerns.  It also enhances your communication skills because you can sense what your client wants to know and if they are getting it from you or not.  Ideally, your client can learn skills in empathy from you, thereby helping them to become more effective leaders, managers and supervisors.

Note that empathy is sometimes confused with sympathy.  Sympathy involves actually being affected by the other person's perceptions, opinions and feelings.  For example, if the client is frustrated and sad, the sympathetic consultant would experience the same emotions, resulting in the consultant many times struggling with the same issues as the client. Thus, sympathy can actually get in the way of effective consulting.

## *Guidelines to Develop Empathy*

1.  **Experience the major differences among people.**
    One of the best examples of strong skills in empathy is people who have traveled or worked in multicultural environments. They have learned that the way they see and experience things is often different from others. People with little or no skills in empathy might have an intellectual awareness of these differences. However, until they actually experience these differences, their skills in empathy will probably remain quite limited.

2.  **Learn to identify your own feelings – develop some emotional intelligence.**
    Many of us are so "processed" and "sophisticated" about feelings that we cannot readily identify them in ourselves, much less in others. For example, we might perceive thoughts to be the same as feelings. So when someone asks you how you feel about a project, you might respond, "I think we have a lot to do." Or, we might not distinguish between seemingly related emotions, for example, between frustration and irritability or between happiness and excitement.

    See "What is Your Emotional Intelligence?" on page 46 for basic guidelines about emotional intelligence.

3.  **Regularly ask clients for their perspectives and/or feelings regarding a situation.**
    Silently compare their responses to what you might have thought they would be. This approach not only helps you to sharpen your own empathic skills, but also helps you to learn more about your client.

# How to Keep It Real – Managing for Realistic Expectations

Many times, personnel in nonprofits – and consultants – are passionate and sometimes idealistic about what they want to accomplish. While those traits can be useful when working to make a major difference in communities and the world, they often pose major obstacles when trying to accomplish significant change in an organization. Also, it is not uncommon that when people have been struggling with a major issue, they urgently search for quick fixes to address those issues. That search can cause a great deal of despair and cynicism. Consequently, one of the most important requirements for a successful consulting project is for you and your client to share the same relevant and realistic expectations during the project. Consider the following approaches to ensuring that outcome with your client.

1.  **Use authentic behavior to verify whether plans are relevant and realistic.**
    It is important for you and your client to speak up if you have any confusion and concerns whatsoever about suggestions, recommendations, plans or actions. For example, are they relevant to addressing the overall issue and are they realistic to accomplish?

2.  **Regularly ask your client for their perceptions of how the project is doing.**
    It is important that both you and your client frequently discuss the quality and progress of the project. One of the outcomes from those discussions is verification of your mutual expectations of the project, especially as they may shift over time.

3.  **Avoid quick fixes.**
    The typical nonprofit is short on time, money and people. There can be tremendous pressure on consultants to get a lot done and do it quickly. Change takes time. You are far better off to take your time and do it right, rather than have your client be disappointed in you because results of your work did not last.

4.  **Acknowledge both the ups and the downs that occur in your projects.**
    Experienced consultants sometimes count on optimism and good wishes to motivate people for change. That approach may work for the short-term, but rarely does so for the long-term. Trust and respect your client enough to tell them the whole story.

5.  **Use written action plans, specifying who is doing what and by when.**
    At the end of each one-on-one and group meeting, always review who is going to do what and by when. Soon after each meeting, you and your client should document the plans and share them with others involved in the effort.

6.  **Conduct coaching sessions around your client's current issues and goals.**
    Coaching sessions can be useful for relevant and realistic action planning, to specify who is going to do what and by when, and especially, whether those plans are realistic. The sessions also collect key learning about plans and actions.

 See "How to Coach for Deep Problem-Solving and Learning" on page 68 for guidelines to coach your clients, including coaching them to be realistic.

# How to Help Your Client Appreciate Accomplishments

## *Why Is the Ability to Appreciate Accomplishments So Important?*

Particularly with personnel in small- to medium-size nonprofits, it is rare that there is not a large amount of work to do. In addition, their mission is usually about meeting some large, unmet need in the community. It is rare, too, that the nonprofit somehow completely meets that need. For many personnel in nonprofits, it can seem like nothing ever gets done.

Because time is such a precious commodity in these nonprofits, it is common that their people cannot provide sustained effort to a consulting project. Many times, the project gets put on "hold" for a few weeks as people attend to other sudden demands for their time, for example, developing a major grant proposal for funds that they suddenly found out about, the Chief Executive Officer's leaving for vacation, preparing for their annual meeting, or finishing a large program evaluation. For you and your client, it can seem that the project has stalled out completely.

Sometimes we create long lists of tasks to get done, and yet do we finish all of those tasks on our lists? When we do finish tasks, there are always many more to replace those on the list that were finished. Our nature is to focus on what needs to get done, do it and then forget about it.

For many of us, it can seem like we are stuck in a merry-go-round that never goes anywhere and we cannot seem to get off. By ignoring our accomplishments, we are ignoring vast portions of our lives and our work – our perspective can become skewed and incomplete. That perspective can be a major obstacle to the success of any consulting project.

## *How Can You Maintain Appreciation for Appreciation?*

As a consultant, you can make a big difference in your effectiveness and that of your client's accomplishments if both of you have the ability to recognize and appreciate your accomplishments regularly. Consider the following guidelines.

1.  **Convey the importance of appreciation when you start working with clients.**
    Mention how important it is to maintain an accurate perspective on the project as the project progresses – that accomplishments should be recognized as well as the tasks yet to be done.

2.  **Ask clients for ideas about how to regularly recognize completion of tasks.**
    Different cultures have different practices. Some might prefer a simple "Thank you," while others might have a ritual of some sort. Therefore, it is important early in a project to get ideas from your clients.

3.  **When planning with clients, build in acknowledgement of completion in plans.**
    Planning always results in a list of things to do. Too often, the design of the plans does not include means to recognize accomplishments. Planning is one of the best opportunities to regularly build in means to recognize accomplishments.

4.  **Design project tasks so it is clear whether they were finished or not.**
    This is often one of the biggest challenges in developing a sense of appreciation. Ideally, goals, objectives and other tasks are designed to be SMART, an acronym for specific, measurable, achievable, relevant and timely.

5.  **Regularly acknowledge the completion of the tasks or progress on tasks.**
    Always seek to find opportunities to appreciate the work of your clients. That practice can be a powerful means to model behaviors that they learn from in their lives and work.

# Dealing with Resistance from Individuals

## What is Resistance?  What Causes It?

An important skill for you to have as an organizational consultant is to effectively recognize and address resistance from clients.  This is true whether you are an external or internal consultant.  Resistance in a consulting project is when your client (a person or a group in the organization) reacts against recommendations from you or against changes in the organization that seem threatening to them.  Resistance is quite common in consulting projects that focus on changing a significant part or process in the organization.  After all, the way your client's organization has been operating in the past is because one or more people felt strongly that their organization should be operating that way (even though the way they were operating may have caused problems or needs to be changed).  Thus, any perceived change in their organization can be threatening.

The resistance can be direct or indirect.  Direct resistance is your client's authentic (direct, honest and open) expression about the perceived threat and why they are not going to follow the recommendations or support the change.  Indirect resistance is when your client does not authentically admit their concern and, instead, does not cooperate with you.  Usually, resistance is indirect and, therefore, can be difficult for you and your client to effectively address.

If you do not see resistance, look again.  Resistance is useful because it tells you that your client perceives that something must change soon or is already changing.  If there is no resistance at any time during your project, it is likely that the project is not really addressing the root cause of issues in your client's organization.

## How to Recognize Another Individual's Resistance

Block (2000) provides elegant advice about how to deal with resistance.  The first step is to recognize the resistance.  Resistance, in consulting projects, can be occurring when:

- Your client does not return your calls.

- Your client continues to question the same piece of advice, even after you have repeated your answer several times.

- Your client tells you that they will have to think about your advice, then takes a few weeks to think about it, and still does not come to a conclusion.

- Your client postpones meetings with you.

- Your client suddenly calls you on the phone to say, "Everything's fine now.  You do not need to come back.  We'll send you your check.  Goodbye."

If their resistance is direct – if they are talking directly to you about their deep concerns (which may, in fact, not be resistance at all, but valid concerns) – the project is probably doing fine because your client is being authentic with you.

# How to Respond to Another Individual's Resistance

Despite the complexities, challenges and frustrations about resistance in consulting projects, you need not make the situation any more difficult than it already is. Actually, one of the best ways to deal with resistance is to be authentic about it. Consider the following guidelines when experiencing resistance from another person.

See "How to Address Resistance in Groups" on page 390 for guidelines to deal with resistance when working with groups, rather than individuals.

1. **Recognize it.**
   Usually, you first experience resistance by feeling confused and/or frustrated about your client's recent behavior. It is important then to identify the form of resistance that you are encountering. What is your client doing that you did not expect or not doing that you did expect? What do you see with your eyes and hear with your ears?

2. **Report it to your client.**
   Be authentic. Describe what you expected and did not get, or what you did not expect and did get instead. Do not embellish your description. It should be as simple and direct as possible within the conventions of your client's culture.

3. **Let them respond.**
   Resistance does not always occur for logical reasons. Usually, it occurs because of a strong reaction or emotion to some perceived threat. So your client may need to vent their emotions for a while. Let them vent, even if that venting is at you.

See "How to Manage Interpersonal Conflicts" on page 84 for guidelines about how to address situations where others are angry at you.

4. **Do not take it personally.**
   Remember that your client is reacting to a perceived threat in the consulting project, not from any particular personal feature about you, the consultant. If you take it personally, you are likely to feel defensive, inadequate or angry, and you can lose your perspective and effectiveness as a consultant.

5. **Ask what they want to do about the situation.**
   If you direct your client to do something, your client will likely resist that direction from you, as well. So at this point, your client should take the responsibility to decide what to do next. If their suggested course of action seems inappropriate or ineffective to you, give them an authentic response.

Consider the following examples of authentic and inauthentic responses from a consultant when experiencing various forms of resistance from clients.

## Table I:6 – Examples of Inauthentic and Authentic Responses

| Client Action | Inauthentic Response from Consultant | Authentic Response from Consultant |
|---|---|---|
| Client arrives 20 minutes late for 10 a.m. meeting and does not mention being late. | (Feels irritated. Makes no comment) | "I thought our meeting started at 10 a.m.?" |
| Client seems irritable with consultant. | (Feels alarmed. Makes no comment) | "You seem irritated to me. Are you?" |
| Client suggests that no one tell the Board about the project. | (Is concerned.) "Well, OK. If you say so." | "The project seems important enough to tell the Board. It is more likely to be implemented with their support. I am concerned that they are not involved." |
| Client rambles on. | (Is confused and bored. Feigns interest.) | "I am struggling to get your point. Can you summarize what you would like me to understand?" |
| Client is suspicious when hearing about collaborative consulting. | (Is embarrassed, concerned, irritated. Changes subject.) | "You seem concerned about collaborative consulting. Let's explore your concerns." |
| Client talks at length about their personal problems. | (Is flattered.) Says, "Let's continue talking." | "Should we set aside some time to talk more about your problem or attend to the project? How can I be most helpful to you?" |
| Consultant struggles to organize himself at start of meeting. | (Is embarrassed. Looks away from the group.) | "I need a minute to organize my things. I apologize. Give me a minute, please." |
| Group members do not seem interested in presentation. | (Is irritated, concerned. Continues presentation anyway.) | "Some of you seem distracted. I'm wondering if there is a better way for me to make my point?" |

# How to Manage Your Own Resistance

Not only your clients express resistance during projects. You probably express resistance – especially indirect resistance – to certain situations yourself. As a professional, it is important for you to recognize your own forms of resistance during projects and to know how to manage that resistance, as well. Consider the following typical forms of resistance from consultants.

## *Common Forms of Resistance from Consultants*

See if you recognize any of the following forms of resistance in yourself.

1.  **Being overly optimistic in your estimates to your client.**
    Promising far too much in the project to impress your clients, avoid conflicts and motivate others.

2.  **Avoiding the Discovery and Feedback phase.**
    Generating recommendations right away in a project to show your expertise and generate quick results.

3.  **Avoiding having to ask for help.**
    Working only on issues and recommendations that make use of your particular expertise, rather than admit that you need help.

4.  **Avoiding contact with your clients.**
    Postponing phone calls and meetings with your client, fearing that you might experience negative feedback or conflict.

5.  **Trying to motivate others to change merely by preaching at them.**
    Resorting only to exhorting people to change, to avoid the hard work of researching issues and generating recommendations to change systems.

6.  **Not verifying that your client did what they said they would do.**
    Assuming that your clients are completing tasks on time, rather than investigating the situation and confronting clients, if necessary.

7.  **Assuming that actions were done because they were in the plan.**
    Putting all of your work into producing the plan document to avoid the hard work of guiding and monitoring change.

8.  **Avoiding your client's resistance.**
    Ignoring obvious signs of resistance from your client to avoid conflict and being assertive with your client.

9.  **Not being authentic with your client.**
    Purposely using vague and complex terms with your client when discussing difficult situations to avoid conflict and being assertive.

10. **Postponing your project activities.**
    Continuing to reschedule meetings with your client to avoid doing work that you do not like, experiencing negative feedback or conflict.

## *How You Can Manage Your Own Resistance*

### Manage Yourself

1.  **Tell at least one other person about how you express indirect resistance.**
    Just by telling one other person, you admit that you need help and you acknowledge that you want to be more direct.

2. **Develop your emotional intelligence (EI).**
Learn to recognize and name the uncomfortable feelings that your methods of indirect resistance are working hard to avoid. Some consultants use a shadow consultant while they are developing their emotional intelligence. Others use a shadow consultant as a sounding board, on an ongoing basis.

 See "What is Your Emotional Intelligence?" on page 46 for basic guidelines about emotional intelligence.

3. **Recognize how you typically deal with feedback and conflict.**
Understand your typical reactions to the extent that you can describe them to others, including how you feel and what you do in situations of feedback and conflict.

4. **Practice direct resistance.**
Direct resistance includes directly expressing your feelings of fear and concern so you and others can address those feelings.

## Manage Your Professional Skills

1. **Know your skills and competencies.**
List the professional skills about which you feel confident. Consider your knowledge, skills and abilities and also how you are able to apply them for change.

 See "How to Inventory Your Consulting Skills" on page 51 for guidelines to help you identify your professional skills and competencies.

2. **Pursue only those consulting contracts that involve your strong skills.**
You will soon find that you are much more comfortable in projects in which you have complete confidence in yourself.

3. **Develop a network of other consultants with other skills.**
When you find yourself in project situations that are beyond your skills, you can comfortably ask other consultants to help you.

4. **Say "no" when you are not comfortable with your workload.**
You are far better to do a good job in several projects than to sometimes struggle and be uncomfortable in many more projects.

5. **Say "no" when you are not comfortable with the project.**
Learn to trust your intuition. If your gut tells you not to take on a project, delve deeply to find out why not. If you gut feeling does not change, do not do the project.

## Manage Your Role in Your Project

1. **Specify your role in each project proposal and contract.**
Specify what you will and will not do in projects. Do not be reluctant to refer your client to that specification, if necessary.

2. **Do your homework – be prepared.**
   This is perhaps the best piece of advice. There is no substitute for having a good grasp on what needs to be done by both you and your client to accomplish successful change.

3. **View the project as a long conversation, a relationship.**
   Experienced consultants have learned that, despite the ups and downs during their projects, clients will value the consultants if they remain open, honest and respectful.

4. **Do not dwell on the details.**
   With significant organizational change, your credibility is in the process, not in the details.

# How to Manage Interpersonal Conflicts

Interpersonal conflict can occur, especially when you are addressing resistance from your client. It can occur at other times in the project, too, for example, if there is not a match between your style and someone else's in your client's organization. In those situations, you may need your interpersonal skills, particularly in effective listening, verbal communication and empathy. The following basic guidelines will also be useful in addressing the conflict.

1. **As a consultant, know what you do not like about yourself.**
   We often do not like in others what we do not want to see in ourselves.

   a) Write down 5 traits that really bug you when see them in others.

   b) Be aware that these traits are your "hot buttons."

2. **Manage yourself.**
   If you and/or the other person are getting heated up, manage yourself to stay calm by:

   a) Speaking to the person as if the other person is not heated up – this can be very powerful!

   b) Avoid use of the word "you" – this avoids blaming.

   c) Nod your head to assure them you heard them.

   d) Maintain eye contact with them.

3. **Move the discussion to a private area, if possible.**

4. **Give the other person time to vent.**
   Do not interrupt them or judge what they are saying.

5. **Verify that you are accurately hearing each other.**
   When they are done speaking:

   a) Ask the other person to let you rephrase (uninterrupted) what you are hearing from them to ensure you are hearing them.

   b) To understand them more, ask open-ended questions (avoid "why" questions – those questions often make people feel defensive).

6.  **Repeat the above step, this time for them to verify that they are hearing you.**
    When you present your position:

    a)  Use "I," not "you."

    b)  Talk in terms of the present as much as possible.

    c)  Mention your feelings.

7.  **Acknowledge where you disagree and where you agree.  Seek common ground.**

8.  **Work the issue, not the person.**
    When they are convinced that you understand them:

    a)  Ask "What can we do to fix this problem?" They will likely begin to again.

    b)  Then ask the same question.  Focus on actions you both can do.

9.  **If possible, identify at least one action that can be done by one or both of you.**

    a)  Ask the other person if they will support the action.

    b)  If they will not, ask for a "cooling off period."

10. **Thank the person for working with you.**

11. **If the situation remains a conflict, then:**

    a)  Consider whether to agree to disagree.

    b)  Consider seeking a third party to mediate.

Note that the above guidelines are rather basic, but still applicable in many situations.  Interpersonal conflicts can be complex, ranging from people who just do not like each other because "of personal chemistry" to people struggling in the middle of complex, entrenched organizational dynamics.

 For more information and guidelines about addressing interpersonal conflict, see the topic "Addressing Interpersonal Conflict" in the Free Management Library at
http://www.managementhelp.org/intrpsnl/conflict.htm

# Administrative Skills for Consultants

There are a variety of administrative skills required by organizational consultants. The focus of this Field Guide is on organizational change with nonprofits, and not on all aspects of consulting, such as setting up or marketing your consulting business. This overall section is about administrative skills specific to ensuring a well designed, coordinated and communicated project for organizational change. The guidelines apply whether you are an external or internal consultant.

## How to Design Systematic – and Flexible – Project Plans

Systematic means that the general flow of activities in the project plan includes: 1) establishing clear goals to be achieved during the project, 2) regular activities to ensure that the goals are being achieved and, 3) making adjustments to achieve those goals, if necessary. Systematic project planning skills are important, especially when working on a fairly large and complex project.

Project planning can lend a strong sense of order and understanding between you and your client. It also provides a common frame of reference from which you and your client can effectively communicate on a regular basis, and can also ensure that plans are relevant, realistic and flexible. Therefore, it is critical for you to have good project planning skills, especially during the second and fourth phases of a project.

First, understand the terms that are common to project plans. Then follow the guidelines to work collaboratively with your client to develop a project plan suitable to you both. Consider the following terms and guidelines.

Note that project planning is usually conducted in Phase 2: Engagement and Agreement and in Phase 3: Discovery and Feedback.

### *Most Common Terms in Project Planning*

Project planning typically uses the following key terms, which are typically addressed in this order.

1.  **Project plan (work plan)**
    Overall, the project plan is a documented description of how the project will be conducted. The plan often includes description of the desired results (goals or outcomes) from the project, the methods to be used to produce those results, any tangible deliverables to be produced, schedule, budget and specification of your role as a consultant and their role as client. Usually, you develop a proposed project plan that you provide to your client in a project proposal. The particular name, content and format of the plan depend on the preferences of you and your client.

2.  **Goals and/or outcomes (project results)**
    Project plans usually specify certain results, such as problems to be solved or other accomplishments to be achieved. In a consulting project, results are often specified in terms of goals and/or outcomes. Frequently, groups of goals are associated with certain, overall outcomes – all of those goals must be achieved to achieve that overall outcome.

    Some people might prefer the term "objectives" instead of goals. Some consultants, particularly those who help to design nonprofit programs, might specify that outcomes are only in regard to changes in clients who participate in the programs.

In any case, goals, objectives and outcomes should be described as specifically as possible in project plans, ideally with numbers and/or percentages.

3. **Methods**

These are the approaches, activities and processes that, when integrated, result in achievement of the results. There is a wide range of consulting methods (or "interventions") that might be used, for example, training, facilitating meetings or coaching leaders.

4. **Deliverables (and/or Indicators)**

These are tangible results, or outputs, that will be produced during, or at the end of, a project, for example, written reports, facilitated meeting or various types of plans. Often, the deliverables are used as measures, or indicators, to suggest the extent of progress toward achieving the desired results of the project.

5. **Resources**

Resources include the people, materials, technologies, money, etc., required to use the methods. The costs of these resources are often depicted in the form of a project budget. Consulting projects often specify what resources are needed in a project and who is to provide them.

6. **Schedule**

The plan usually specifies when your project is to start and end, and often includes dates for specific deliverables to be provided to, or by, your client. Other considerations of time might include frequency of certain activities during the project, dependencies among certain activities due to timing, and critical path considerations (critical path is the certain sequence of activities that must occur in order for the project to be successful).

7. **Budgets**

The project budget specifies how much money is needed to pay you, and to obtain and support any resources needed during the project, such as money for supplies and travel.

8. **Roles and responsibilities**

The plan might include description of the roles and responsibilities of you and your client, for example, about communication between both parties, provision of resources, or coordination and administration of project activities. (Note that you and your client may choose to further specify the roles and responsibilities in a written and signed contract.)

See "Sample Proposal for Organizational Development Services" on page 470 for a sample project plan.

## *Designing Systematic Project Plans*

Each project plan is highly unique to each project, including how you prefer to work in your projects. However, you can design powerful project plans by working in conjunction with your client. It is likely that you will provide the first version of your project plan to your client. Make it clear that the plan is a draft, or working plan, that can be changed based on feedback from your client. Then you should work collaboratively to modify the project plan to suit your mutual nature and needs.

See "Collaborative Planning for Relevant, Realistic and Flexible Plans" on page 316 for guidelines to conduct collaborative planning.

# How to Take Useful Notes During Projects

This might seem like a trivial matter to address in a guidebook about consulting. It is not. Especially when working with nonprofits that have very limited resources, it is important to always be clear about who said what and who is going to doing what. Nonprofit personnel are often extremely busy, which often means that details get forgotten. Also, you can get a lot of credibility with your client just by doing a good job keeping notes and tracking details. The following guidelines will be useful in all phases of the collaborative consulting cycle.

## *Regarding Conversations*

Take notes during, or right after, every exchange with your client. Document:

1.    The date of the exchange.

2.    If it was a phone call or meeting.

3.    Who was involved in the exchange.

4.    Highlights, for example, who is going to do what and by when.

5.    Keep a copy in your file for your client.

Put the notes in your client's file that you keep for yourself.

## *Regarding the Time You Worked on the Project*

Those notes can be precious information when assessing your time and contributions to a project, especially when billing your client. Each day that you work on the project, document:

1.    Date that you worked on the project.

2.    Highlights of what you worked on.

3.    Time of the day that you started.

4.    Time of the day that you finished.

Put the notes in your client's file that you keep for yourself.

## *Taking Notes During Group Meetings*

Consultants might struggle to be effective at facilitating a meeting and taking notes from a meeting at the same time. Therefore, it is often useful to arrange with your client to provide a meeting recorder – someone who can document and distribute information from the meeting. Suggest that the recorder collect information about:

1.  Purpose of the meeting.

2.  Date of the meeting.

3.  Time the meeting started.

4.  Who attended.

5.  Who did not attend and was excused (before the meeting, they informed someone from the meeting that they could not attend the meeting and why).

6.  Who did not attend and was not excused (they did not inform anyone that they would be gone).

7.  Topics addressed during the meeting.

8.  Major decisions made during the meeting.

9.  Specific actions from the meeting, including who will do what by when.

10. Attach, or reference, any materials provided before or during the meeting.

 See "Meeting Design, Management and Interventions" on page 375 for guidelines to design and facilitate meetings.

# How to Write Meaningful Project Reports

Project reports should be distributed regularly to ensure that you and your client always have the same perceptions about the project, including what has been done, what is yet to be done, and whether there are any current issues that need attention. The plans can also be used by you to verify "for the record" that your client has approved the quality of your work so far. Lastly, the reports ensure a well-organized, complete record of the history and progress of the project.

Consider having your client provide you reports of the status of their work on the project, as well. That practice can be a convenient means for you to sense if your client is still committed and participating in the project. A report from your client to you could follow the same guidelines as those that you use to send reports to your client as provided below.

The scope, content and frequency of the reports can be clarified between you and your client in your initial meetings in the project.

## Send Your Report to At Least Two People

This is a safe practice to follow in case, for example, one of the two people leaves the organization, or the quality of the relationship between you and one of the two people deteriorates. In an organization-wide project, try to have your reports go at least to the Chief Executive Officer and the Chair of the Board of Directors.

## *What to Include in a Basic Report*

In reports, specify:

1.     Highlights of what was done since the last report.

2.     Highlights of what will be done over some specific period of time in the future.

3.     Any issues that must be addressed soon, by when in the project, and who you recommend to address them.

4.     A deadline by which the readers of the report are to get back to you if they have any concerns or questions about the contents of your report.  That deadline can come in handy later on if your client has a problem with the way that you are handling a project.  If that occurs, you can always remind your client that you reported the information to them before and that if they had a problem with your plans then they should have gotten back to you by the deadline specified in the report.

Put the report in your client's file that you keep for yourself.

# Staying Grounded and Centered

Your instincts – your "gut" feeling – help guide you to solve problems and make decisions as a consultant. Therefore, it is important for you to stay in touch with yourself – to be centered – during your consulting. This is true whether you are an external or internal consultant. The guidelines in the following subsections will help you stay in touch with who you are. The guidelines are useful in all phases of the collaborative consulting cycle, but especially in the phases of Action Planning, Alignment and Integration, and Implementation and Change Management.

## Frustrations of Consulting for Organizational Change

There can be a variety of sources of frustration during a project, particularly when working with small- to medium-sized nonprofit organizations. The frustrations are not from the nature of people in the nonprofits; rather they can be from working with organizations that often have limited resources and, meanwhile, are attempting to address major, unmet needs in their communities.

But there are other sources of frustration. One is from addressing the resistance that can arise during a project. For example, clients might not return phone calls, reschedule meetings, arrive late or leave early from meetings, or not attend to required actions by certain deadlines.

The extent to which you are frustrated by these situations depends, in large part, on your nature. If you are a rather detail-oriented person who likes to see tasks get done on time, you might need to manage your frustrations when faced with various forms of resistance. If you like to make decisions in an orderly and logical fashion, you might also need to manage your frustrations when, as typical happens, plans keep changing. Particularly with nonprofits, surprises can keep occurring during a project, for example, an executive might leave the organization, funds from potential donors might not arrive, or other urgent issues might suddenly arise.

See "Challenges and Rewards of Capacity Building with Nonprofits" on page 196 for descriptions of many of the potential sources of frustration.

## How to Motivate Yourself During Long Journeys for Change

Consultants are like everyone else. They must manage for balance in their lives and their work. Therefore, consultants must give attention to managing their own personal motivation – and it can be managed.

1. **Clarify your purpose in consulting and how you want to do consulting.**
   That purpose and those values might seem so intuitive to you that they are difficult to articulate. However, during times of stress, confusion or burnout, it can be powerful to stand back and reflect on why you chose to consult with nonprofits and how you want to do that consulting.

   See "How to Articulate Your Professional Mission and Values" on page 54 for guidelines to think about why and how you want to do consulting.

2. **Even if you do not like goals, set some professional goals, however small.**
Without goals, you may not know if you are really accomplishing anything. Working hard is not necessarily an end in itself. Set some small goals. It will be good practice for you if you have not done that before. Besides, if you do not like goals, you are in for a major challenge in consulting with nonprofits because consulting is about achieving goals.

3. **Celebrate accomplishments.**
Many hard-working people seem to believe that celebrating accomplishments is a form of complacency, that the job should be celebration in itself. Those beliefs can hold true maybe for the first couple years of a consultant's job. Then the grind gets old. It is critical for consultants to recognize that they are accomplishing something – it is usually not enough to be continually "working for the cause." Take time out to recognize what did get done and celebrate the accomplishments.

4. **Ask for help.**
It can be quite difficult for a consultant to ask for help. However, consultants can gain an incredible amount of help from peers as mentors, fellow members of a support group, or members of a networking group. Consider getting a personal and professional coach. The coach can use a variety of techniques to help you clarify current goals, how you want to pursue those goals, and how you can learn at the same time.

5. **Get some direct contact with clients of nonprofits you have served.**
Few things are as motivational as hearing from a client about how they have benefited from the programs and services of a nonprofit that you have helped.

6. **Follow simple guidelines of time and stress management.**
Those guidelines are included later on in this Field Guide. With a few simple steps, you can make a major difference in managing your stress, often by first addressing how you spend your time.

 See "How to Manage Your Time and Stress – Avoiding Burnout" on page 93 for guidelines to manage your time and stress.

7. **Watch your diet. Get enough sleep.**
Do not resort to lots of caffeine and sugar to give you a boost. Research shows that the boost is usually followed by a major let down in energy. It is better to take a short walk, get some protein and do some stretches. Also, it is interesting how bleak the world looks to people who do not eat right or get enough sleep. A little bit of good food and more sleep can make the world seem a lot better.

8. **Get some variety in your work.**
Do not get lost in the "circle of paperwork." The only way that you will probably get some variety in your work is to schedule it. Schedule time to do something simple from which you can get a sense of satisfaction. Clean out the storage closet. Wash the dishes.

9. **Get some professional development.**
Go to a course. Join a professional networking organization. Read professional journals that relate to your services. Join a Speakers Bureau to share your knowledge.

See "How to Continuously Improve Your Skills as a Nonprofit Consultant" on page 39 for guidelines to continue your professional development.

10. **Write status reports for yourself and your client.**
Status reports can be weekly and document what you have accomplished with your client, including any highlights, trends and issues that currently exist, and what you plan to do next. One of the most important outcomes from this activity is actually standing back and thinking about your work, and noticing that you are actually getting a lot done.

See "How to Write Meaningful Project Reports" on page 89 for guidelines about writing status reports.

11. **Know when to leave certain consulting projects.**
Occasionally, it may be that you and your client have to part because you simply are no longer motivated in your work. Any separation from the project should be done in a highly ethical fashion and according to the terms of any signed contract.

See "Knowing When to Leave Project" on page 111 for guidelines about what to think about if you leave a project.

# How to Manage Your Time and Stress – Avoiding Burnout

The two topics of time management and stress management are often addressed together because they are so closely interrelated.

## *Myths About Stress and Time Management*

1. **All stress is bad.**
No, some stress is good and some is bad. Good stress can include excitement or thrills. The goal is to recognize your personal signs of bad stress and deal with them.

2. **Planning my time just takes more time.**
Planning helps you work smarter, rather than harder. The attitude that stopping to plan is a problem is itself a symptom of stress and time management problems.

3. **I get more done in more time when I use caffeine, sugar, alcohol or nicotine.**
Wrong! Research shows that the body always has to "come down." When it does, you will not be effective in your work, which offsets whatever gain you achieved from the boost from stimulants.

4. **A time problem means there is not enough time to do what I need to do.**
No, a time management problem is not using your time to your fullest advantage to get done what you want done. You need to know what you really want to do.

5. **The busier I am, the better I am using my time.**
You may only be doing what seems urgent, and not what is important. Doing what is important often addresses the many matters that seem to be urgent.

6.    **I feel very hurried and busy, so I must have a time management problem.**
Not necessarily. You should verify that you have a time management problem. This requires knowing what you really want to get done and if it is getting done or not.

7.    **I feel OK, so I must not be stressed.**
In reality, many adults do not even know when they are really stressed out until their bodies tell them so. They miss the early warning signs from their body.

## Major Causes of Stress

1.    **Not knowing what you want or if you are getting it – poor planning.**
If you ask adults where they are needed, they can give you many answers. If you ask them what they want, they often struggle to answer.

2.    **The *feeling* that there is too much to do.**
One can have this feeling even if there is hardly anything to do at all. Knowing what you want to do often helps address the vague feelings that there is too much to do.

3.    **Not enjoying your work.**
This can be caused by lots of things, for example, not knowing what you want or not eating well.

4.    **Conflicting demands in your work.**
Unless you have some sense of your priorities, it is likely that you will feel conflicting demands in your work.

5.    **Having insufficient resources to do your work.**
As a consultant, one of your most important resources is usually your time. You will benefit a great deal from finding your own style of time management.

6.    **Not feeling appreciated.**
This can be a major problem for organizational consultants. You can ask clients to tell you how you are doing. You have to accept and remember their compliments.

## Biggest Time Wasters

1.    **Interruptions**
There will always be interruptions. The interruptions are not the problem. The problem is how they are handled.

2.    **Hopelessness**
People "give in," "numb out" and "march through the day." This is probably the worst time and stress management problem. Other guidelines in this section can help you to avoid this time waster.

3.    **Poor delegation skills**
This involves not asking for help and/or sharing work with others. You can ask your client for help, consider working with colleagues, or cut back your workload.

## Common Symptoms of Poor Stress and Time Management

1.  **Irritability**
    Your family, friends, peers and clients usually notice this before you do. If your clients have noticed your symptoms, you will have to find a better means to manage your time and stress.

2.  **Fatigue**
    How many adults even notice this? We often work with a vague sense of tiredness. Your body sends the first message of problems, so learn to sense your own fatigue.

3.  **Difficulty concentrating**
    You can often get through the day without even concentrating. Thus, this symptom often goes unnoticed.

4.  **Forgetfulness**
    If you cannot remember what you did all day, what you ate today or whom you talked to, you need to address your time and stress problem as soon as possible.

5.  **Loss of sleep**
    This affects everything else! Recognize what you can do to have a full night's sleep, for example, cut back on coffee or do not work late.

6.  **Physical disorders**
    Common symptoms are headaches, rashes, tics or cramps. At worst, withdrawal and depression.

## Wise Principles of Good Stress and Time Management

1.  **Learn your signs for being overstressed or having a time management problem.**
    Ask your friends about you. Perhaps they can tell you what they see when you are overstressed. Their feedback is often more accurate than your own perceptions.

2.  **Most people *feel* that they are stressed and/or have a time problem.**
    Verify that you really have a problem. What do you see, hear or feel that leads you to conclude that you have a time or stress problem?

3.  **Do not have the illusion that doing more will make you happier.**
    Is it quantity of time that you want or the quality? If not quantity or quality, then what?

4.  **Stress and time problems usually require more than one technique to fix.**
    You do not need a lot of techniques, but usually more than one. Pick a few that are realistic and practical, get started, notice your successes, and give yourself credit.

5.  **One of the major benefits of time planning is feeling that you are in control.**
    It might even help at this point to think about what you mean by "control." Does it mean that you control everything in your life or only what is most important in the long run?

6.  **Focus on results, not on "busyness."**
    This guideline is the main point about performance – a person can seem very busy, but that does not mean they are actually accomplishing what is most important.

7.  **It is the trying that counts – at least as much as doing the perfect technique.**
    As people get older and wiser, they let go of frustrations around not achieving enough quantity of things. Instead, they focus on the quality of the process.

## Simple Techniques to Manage Stress

There are a lot of things people can do to cut down on stress. Most people probably even know what they could do. It is not the lack of knowing what to do to cut down stress – it is doing what you know you have to do. The following techniques are geared to help you do what you know you have to do.

1.  **Talk to someone.**
    You do not have to fix the problem. Similar to addressing resistance and conflicts, it often makes a big difference just to recognize and name the issue.

2.  **Notice if any of the muscles in your body are tense.**
    Just noticing that will often relax the muscle. Pay attention to your neck, shoulders, arms and legs. Tightness? Soreness?

3.  **Ask your client if you are doing OK.**
    This simple question can make a lot of difference. Also, it further helps to build trust and openness between you and your client.

4.  **Ask for help.**
    Ask peers. Hire some help. Get a mentor. Get a coach. Join a support or networking group.

 See "How to Know When to Ask for Help" on page 108 for guidelines to know when to ask for help.

5.  **If you take on a technique to manage stress, tell someone else.**
    They can help you be accountable to them and yourself. Otherwise, your attempts to use techniques can get lost in the other time and stress problem that you have.

6.  **Cut down on caffeine and sweets.**
    It is difficult to cut down on something without replacing it with something else instead. Do isometric exercises. Chew sugarless gum.

7.  **Use basic techniques of planning, problem-solving and decision-making.**
    Concise guidelines are in this Field Guide. It might help to focus on the 20/80 rule. Remember, it is often the trying that counts.

8.  **Monitor the number of hours that you work in a week.**
    Tell your family, friends and peers how many hours that you are working per week now and how many hours that you intend to work.

9.  **Write status reports.**
    Reports can be drudgery to finish, but they are usually helpful to remind you of what you have gotten done. You should be writing reports to clients, anyway.

10.     **"Wash the dishes."**
        Do something simple that you can feel good about. Following that guideline, as with others, starts with gumption: making that initial effort to move yourself.

## *Simple Techniques to Manage Time*

The goal of time management should not be to find more time. The goal is set a reasonable amount of time to spend on these roles and then use that time wisely.

1.      **Start with the simple techniques of stress management above.**
        Many times, techniques of stress management are useful in managing time, as well.

2.      **Practice.**
        Practice asking yourself throughout the day: "Is this what I want or need to be doing right now?" If yes, keep doing it. If not, get help from family and friends.

3.      **Analyze your time.**
        Logging your time for a week in 15-minute intervals is not that hard and does not take up that much time. Do it for a week and review your results. This is both realistic and an objective way to analyze your time.

4.      **Do a "to do" list for your day at the end of the previous day.**
        Mark items as "A" and "B" in priority. Set aside two hours right away each day to do the important "A" items and then do the "B" items in the afternoon. Let your voicemail or someone else take your calls during your "A" time.

5.      **At the end of your day, spend five minutes cleaning up your space.**
        Use this time, too, to organize your space, including your desktop. That will give you a clean and fresh start for the next day.

6.      **Learn the difference between "Where am I needed?" and "What do I want?"**
        The former question is about your client's time. The latter question is about yours.

7.      **Learn the difference between "Do I need to do this now?" and "Do I need to do it at all?"**
        Finding the answer might require some careful reflection about what has been important in the past and what is important to you now.

8.      **Use a "Do Not Disturb" sign!**
        During the prime part of the day, when you are attending to your important items (your "A" list), hang this sign on the doorknob outside your door.

9.      **Sort your mail into categories: "read now," "handle now," "trash," and "read later."**
        You will quickly get a knack for sorting through mail. You will also notice that much of what you think you need to read was not really all that important anyway.

10.     **Read your mail at the same time each day.**
        That way, you will likely get to your mail on a regular basis and will not become distracted into any certain piece of mail that ends up taking too much of your time.

11. **Have a place for everything and put everything in its place.**
That way, you will know where to find it when you need it. Perhaps the most important outcome is that you have a *feeling* of being in control.

12. **Schedule 10 minutes to do nothing.**
That time can be used to just sit and clear your mind. You will end up thinking more clearly, resulting in more time in your day. The best outcome of this practice is that it reminds you that you are not a slave to a clock – and that if you take 10 minutes out of your day, your business will not fall apart.

## Summary Principles to Stay Sane During Change

Each person finds his or her own way to "survive." The following summary guidelines will help you to keep your perspective and health. Some of the guidelines are adapted from above.

1. **Monitor your work hours.**
The first visible, undeniable sign that things are out of hand is that you are working far too many hours. Note how many hours you are working per week. Set a limit and stick to that limit. Ask your family, friends and peers for help.

2. **Recognize your own signs of stress.**
Different people show their stress in different ways. Some people have "blow ups." Some people get forgetful. Some people lose concentration. For many people, while they excel at their jobs, their home life falls apart. Know your signs of stress. Tell someone else what those signs are. Ask them to check in with you every two weeks to see how you are doing. Every two weeks, write down how you are doing – if only for a minute. Stick in it a file marked "%*#)%&!!#$."

3. **Have at least one person in your life with which you are completely honest.**
Even if you communicate primarily via e-mail, develop at least one person with whom you can be completely honest. That person can be a wonderful resource both to help keep you true to yourself and provide ongoing support.

4. **Distinguish between what is important and what is urgent.**
One of the major lessons that experienced consultants have learned is to respond to what is important, rather than what is urgent. It can seem like your day is responding to one crisis after another. As you gain experience, you quit responding to crises. You get an answering machine or someone else to answer the phone. You develop a filing system to keep track of your paperwork. You learn basic skills in conflict management. Most important, you recognize that consulting is a process – you never really "finish" your to-do list – your list is there to help you keep track of details. Over time, you learn to relax.

5. **Recognize accomplishments.**
Our society promotes problem solvers. We solve one problem and quickly move on to the next. The culture of many organizations rewards problem solvers. Once a problem is solved, we quickly move on to the next one to solve. Pretty soon we feel empty. We feel as if we are not making a difference. So in all your plans, include time to acknowledge accomplishments.

# Special Topics in Nonprofit Consulting

There are certain situations that can occur in an organizational consulting project, depending on the nature of your client's situation and priorities and on whether you are an external or internal consultant. Each situation might occur in a completely different fashion. If you find yourself in any of these situations, the following guidelines will be useful to you. The situations include:

1.      How to define project "success"

2.      How to work with nonprofit service providers during projects

3.      How to collaborate with consulting teams ("tag teams")

4.      How to work for a committee

5.      How to work when contracting to provide recommendations only

6.      How to know when to ask for help

7.      How to know when to leave a project

## How to Define Project "Success"

Your client's perception of project "success" is the basis from which your client concludes, for example, whether the project of high quality, that money paid to you was well spent, that you did a good job as a consultant, and whether you might be hired again (if you are an external consultant). Early in the project, it is important for you and your client to discuss how to determine the success of the project. Letts, Ryan and Grossman (1998) suggest that the three overall outcomes of capacity building with nonprofits include: 1) helping the nonprofit to do what it already does, but better; 2) improving its ability to grow; and 3) improving its ability to change.

Unfortunately, determining whether a project was successful or not is not nearly as easy as it might seem because there are numerous perspectives on what is project "success." Therefore, it is important to consider all of these perspectives, especially about a complex – and usually changing – project. Consider the following possible definitions of what might be considered as "success" in your consulting project, and work with your client to select one or more.

1.      **Desired outcomes and results listed in the project agreement are achieved.**
         Both you and your client should somehow specify the overall results that the project is to achieve. Ideally, the results are described in terms such that you both could readily discern if the results were achieved or not. This outcome is often a measure as to whether the project was successful or not.

2.      **The client's problem is solved.**
         More times than people realize, the originally specified project results have little to do with actually solving the most important problem in your client's organization. That occurs because, as you and your client work together to examine and address their overall problem, you both realize that there is a more important problem to address. At that time, it is wise to change your project plans if both of you agree. Discuss the new results that you prefer and how you will know whether or not they are achieved.

Still, later on, your client might believe that any agreed-to results that were achieved from the project were not as important as addressing any current, unsolved problems, so your client might still conclude that the project was not as successful as it should have been. Or, your client might believe that any achieved results were actually more useful than addressing the original problem that you discussed, so your client might still conclude that the project was highly successful.

3.  **The project is finished on time and within budget.**
    Often, your nonprofit client has limited resources in terms of money and time. Therefore, any project that did not require more time and money than expected might be considered successful. That might be true, especially if your client has the philosophy that there are always problems to be solved in any organization and that the project was done as best as could be done.

4.  **You and your client sustain a high-quality, working relationship.**
    As explained throughout this Field Guide, the quality of your relationship with your client is often directly associated with what the client perceives to be the quality of the project. In a highly collaborative approach to consulting, you want your relationship with your client to be as open, honest and trusting as possible. The nature of the relationship supports your client's strong, ongoing commitment and participation in the project itself, which, in turn, helps to ensure that the project effectively addresses problems in their organization.

5.  **Your client learns to address similar problems by themselves in the future.**
    This outcome should be one of the major goals for any consultant. However, the exact nature of the problem may never arise in the client's organization again, so it is often difficult to assess if the client has learned to solve that problem. Also, few consultants are willing to scope a project to the time required to assess whether a client really can solve the same type of problem in the future.

6.  **Your client says that they would hire you again (if you are an external consultant).**
    One of the most powerful outcomes is that you both are willing to work with each other again. One of the ethical considerations for any consultant is to avoid creating a dependency of the client on the consultant – where the client cannot capably participate in the organization without the ongoing services of the consultant. However, it is not uncommon that the client strongly believes that the quality of the relationship with the consultant is as important as the consultant's expertise. The client might choose to use that consultant wherever and whenever they can in the future.

7.  **You get paid in full.**
    This perspective might sound rather trite to include in this Field Guide. However, you might feel good about the quality and progress of a project only to conclude, later on, if you have not been paid as promised, that the project was not successful.

# How to Work with Nonprofit Service Providers During Projects

As an external consultant, there are a variety of situations in which another nonprofit service provider (a provider other than yourself) might be associated with your project. These situations seem increasingly common and might include:

- A management and technical service provider (for-profit or nonprofit) that hired you to provide services to a particular nonprofit organization.

- A foundation that hired you to provide services to a grantee.

- A foundation that provided funds to the grantee and the grantee hired you to provide services.

In any of those situations, the other provider might be considered one of your clients, as well as certain people in the nonprofit organization that is the direct recipient of your services. If you are working with a nonprofit service provider during a project, the provider might have various preferences about how you do your consulting. If so, the provider and nonprofit should inform you of those preferences. The following guidelines will help you think about your role and the role of a provider during your projects.

## What Is a Nonprofit Service Provider?

There is a diversity of nonprofit service providers. For example, providers might focus on certain types of services, certain types of nonprofits or certain geographic areas. Examples include:

- Associations

- For-profit consulting firms

- Foundations

- Nonprofit consulting firms (management support organizations)

- Training centers

## How Do Providers Usually Operate?

Depending on the situation, the provider might perform a variety of activities, including some or all of the following:

1. Interview the nonprofit organization to understand its "presenting" priority.

2. Enter into a contract with the nonprofit regarding project results, services, fees, etc.

3. Work with the nonprofit to ensure the most suitability between the nonprofit and a potential consultant.

4. Arrange the first meeting between the nonprofit leaders and you.

5. Demand that the nonprofit and/or you make certain changes in the nonprofit's organization.

6. Contact certain nonprofit personnel on a regular basis about the quality of the project.

7. Contact you to get impressions of the project.

8. At the end of the project, conduct some form of evaluation about the project.

## *Guidelines for a Successful Relationship During the Project*

If you are working for, or will be working with, a nonprofit service provider during a project for major organizational change, the following guidelines will be useful to you. Your activities during the project depend to a great extent on the situation in which the provider is involved, how the provider prefers to operate, and how the recipient of your services prefers to be involved.

1.  Make sure there are written contracts for the project. Depending on the situation, there might be a contract between you and the provider, you and the nonprofit, and/or between all three parties. The contract should specify the roles, rights and requirements of each of the parties, and what kinds of information should be shared with whom and when.

2.  Encourage that all three parties see and sign the contracts to ensure key personnel are aware of all roles, rights and requirements. Otherwise, one or more parties are left to speculate – and sometimes be suspicious and resentful – about the role of the other parties.

 See "Proposals, Contracts and Letters of Agreement" on page 251 for considerations when developing a contract.

3.  If the provider initiated the contract with the recipient of services, ask to see the provider's proposal and/or contract with the recipient. Review the roles, rights and requirements of all parties in that contract.

4.  If the provider brought you to the project to address certain issues, fully understand the provider's "diagnosis," or conclusions and recommendations, about the presenting priority in the nonprofit's organization and how those conclusions were made.

5.  Negotiate to make changes to contracts and diagnoses, if necessary.

6.  If you have not yet been selected for the project, seek to understand the provider's and recipient's requirements for selecting a consultant. Ensure that those requirements meet your nature and needs as a professional.

7.  Before the first meeting with the provider and the nonprofit, understand who will attend, your role in the meeting, and how much time you will have to talk during the meeting. Also understand any limitations on what you can say, as suggested by the terms in any contracts.

8.  Arrange to see the results of any project evaluations conducted by the provider and/or nonprofit during and after the project.

9.  Arrange to obtain letters of recommendation from the provider and/or nonprofit after the project.

10. During the project, always provide written status reports to relevant parties per the terms of any contracts.

# How to Collaborate with Consulting Teams ("Tag Teams")

The following guidelines are about working with groups of consultants on a particular project, both external and internal to the organization. The guidelines apply to external consultants.

The guidelines are not about forming and working with a group of internal consultants within an ongoing business that attends to ongoing projects.

## *Benefits of Consulting and/or Project Teams*

It can be a major advantage to collaborate with a team of consultants or members of your client's organization during a project, especially during a large, complex project. Benefits include:

- Occasionally, a client or nonprofit service provider will specify that they want a team of consultants on the project because the project requires substantial expertise and resources.

- The team can provide a wide variety of expertise and perspectives during the project, often resulting in a more accurate understanding and resolution of problems in the client's organization.

- If the team is designed well, members often provide useful ongoing support and feedback amongst each other, as well.

- If a consultant suddenly is not able to work on the project, other consultants can step in to cover for the missing consultant.

- As a result, consultants enjoy a more successful project and develop a network of trusted peers.

A team on a project might include:

- An organizational change consultant to guide development of the collaborative relationship and overall project plan.

- Board trainers who ensure the Board of Directors is sufficiently developed to oversee the organizational change project.

- A strategic planning facilitator to guide development of an overall strategic planning framework in which the organizational change plan can be integrated.

- Program specialists to guide development of program plans, including outcomes, groups of clients to serve, methods to achieve outcomes and the designs of evaluations.

- Marketing consultants to provide expertise, for example, in market research, public relations, branding, and advertising and promotions planning.

- Fundraisers to guide development of fundraising plans.

- Trainers to convey "expert" content at various times to various members of the client's organization.

## *Guidelines to Form and Operate Consulting and/or Project Teams*

Similarly to other successful teams, a project team needs to be built carefully. It requires certain systems and structures to operate effectively. A team is essentially an organization. Consequently, the ideal approach to building and operating teams is to do all of the things necessary to develop, lead, manage and operate an organization. Usually, that extent of care and resource is not available for teams. However, the following guidelines will ensure that your team has the necessary systems and structures in place to start operating together and to learn and adjust as necessary to operate as an effective team.

 PART V will be useful to you when forming the team of consultants and managing for productive meetings.

1.     **Leadership roles.**
The leadership of the group is responsible to set the direction and guide others to follow that direction, including providing means to identify and solve any problems in the group, and making decisions in the group. Other guidelines in this topic apply to the leadership role. There should always be one lead consultant who is ultimately responsible for the function of the team, including clarification of roles, communication with the client, and intercommunication among group members.

Note that different "sub-leaders" might be needed at different times. For example, the strategic planning facilitator might lead the participation of the team of consultants during the strategic planning activities. Afterwards, the program consultant might lead the marketing and fundraising consultants during program development. Note that getting a Field Guide for each of the team members could be useful to address the following guidelines.

2.     **A suitable match among the natures and needs of the team members.**
Just as a strong self-awareness of consultants helps them work effectively with clients, that self-awareness helps them work effectively with other consultants. Therefore, each consultant should understand their own personal biases, style, lens on organizations, and preferences for solving problems and making decisions. Information from PART I of this guide can be helpful to members of the team to develop their own self-awareness.

3.     **Common values and language about the way they work.**
Consultants to the same type of client organizations can have different ways of working. For example, it is not uncommon that facilitative (process) consultants have a different way of working than expert consultants. The direction and energy for the facilitative consultant often comes from the client. The direction and energy for the expert consultant often comes from the consultant. The organizational consultant might talk about terms, such as change, systems and performance. The expert consultant might talk about goals, objectives, training methods and procedures. Therefore, it is important early in formation of your team to discuss the potential differences in how consultants might work even when in the same team.

4.     **A clear understanding of the team's overall purpose and each individual's role.**
Each consultant or member of the team should know where he or she fits into the overall project plan. Members of the team should review the overall project plan to understand their role. They should understand when and where they come into the project. The lead

consultant should ensure that the client is always of aware of which consultant will be working with them and how.

5.  **Mechanisms to effectively communicate with each other.**
    Each consultant or member of the team will need to be aware of the progress of the overall project, including current status regarding deliverables and scheduling. Each member will need to coordinate the hand-off to the next member. The lead consultant will ensure that hand-off is carried out successfully. All members should share the same mechanisms for communication, for example, have regular status meetings or share an e-mail list.

6.  **Means to thoroughly identify and resolve problems in the team.**
    The types of problems that can occur in a team are usually about:

    a)  Unclear expectations among members regarding roles and timing to work with the client.

    b)  When the client struggles to work with numerous members.

    c)  When one or more members need to leave the team.

    The other guidelines in this topic are all useful in addressing these most common types of problems in teams in projects.

# How to Work for a Committee

Occasionally, a project is configured so you are accountable to a group during the project, such as a Board committee. This is true whether you are an external or internal consultant. You might be asked to regularly report to the committee. The committee members, as a whole, might make project decisions about the project.

There are certain challenges in that situation. For example, members might have different perceptions of problems in the organization and what needs to be done to address them. Committees might struggle to come to agreement in a timely fashion. Sometimes, members of the committee are members of the Board of Directors. Board members are almost always volunteers to the nonprofit organization and have full lives outside of their work with the nonprofit. Board members usually do not give ongoing, complete attention to the project. Therefore, they may spend their time on the committee in trying to remember what they talked about when they last met. All of those challenges can be a major obstacle to the success of any consulting project.

As to how you might work to address those challenges, you need to be tactful, always being respectful and supportive. The following guidelines might be useful when you are reporting to a committee.

1.  **As much as possible, interact with members as an entire committee.**
    At various times during the project, you might find yourself interacting differently with various members of the committee. For example, you might be spending much more time with certain members or you might be sending reports to some members and not others. As much as possible, attempt to avoid those situations. If those situations do occur with certain members, ask those members how all other members will learn about the results of your interactions with them. Encourage members to ensure all other members are always up-to-date about the project.

2. **Gently help committee members to competently operate amongst themselves.**
   For example, even though you may have not been hired to help the committee to operate effectively, you still might offer them any materials with guidelines that might seem useful. Offer the materials in that spirit – that you are just trying to be helpful. You should offer the materials right away in the project, not later on after you might have experienced problems with the committee. After providing them the materials, do not push the matter any further. Leave it up to the members as to whether they use the materials or not.

   See "Guidelines to Form and Operate Consulting Teams and/or Project Teams" on page 104 for guidelines that might be useful to committee members.

   PART V, starting on page 369, also includes many guidelines that might be useful to committee members at various times during the project.

3. **Ensure that the committee has reviewed the consulting project plan.**
   The plan usually specifies the results to be achieved during the project, the methods to achieve those results, and the schedule to carry out the methods. As to finding out whether all members of the committee have seen and actually approved the plan or not, you should be tactful. For example, you probably should not demand that all members sign the project plan. However, in a meeting or on a written communication to members, you can pose the question as to whether all members have seen the project plan or not.

4. **Ask the committee to establish consistent communication with you.**
   For example, strongly encourage that you have ongoing, face-to-face meetings with the entire committee. Suggest that you send all members regular written project reports. Follow practices of effective project reports, including description of highlights of past actions, plans for upcoming activities, and especially, the request for any member to get back to you by a certain date if they disagree or have concerns about anything on the report.

5. **Encourage committee members to participate in various phases of the project.**
   Without direct involvement in project activities, members can get so detached that they lose motivation and interest in the project altogether. As a result, they lose their usefulness to the project. This can be true, especially for volunteer Board members who do not spend a great deal of time on the project. One of the most powerful ways to re-energize and refocus members of the committee is to involve them in project activities, such as developing action plans or coaching leaders in the organization.

# How to Work When Contracting to Provide Recommendations Only

Occasionally, clients might specify that the major result of your project is to write a report. This is true whether you are an external or internal consultant. There are several situations in which that might be useful for your client, for example, your client wants to:

- Find out what the problem is before they commit resources to solving the problem.

- Ensure they are satisfied with the nature and quality of your work before they contract with you to actually implement recommendations from the report.

- Provide a report to a funder.

This situation can be a challenge for the consultant who prefers to work in a highly collaborative fashion, and greatly values what can be accomplished and learned from taking action. Also, many experienced consultants have learned that far too many reports just end up on shelves. Therefore, it is important in this situation to ensure that the report is useful to your client.

Consider the following guidelines.

1. **Clarify the client's desired outcomes from using the report.**
   Ask your client to describe what people would be able to do as a result of reading the information in the report. Be clear that you are not focusing on what people would do as a result of implementing recommendations from the report, rather only from reading the report.

2. **Clarify who the specific audiences of the report will be.**
   Different audiences might value different information from the report. For example, Board members might want an Executive Summary with highlights. Staff members might want more detailed information about how problems were identified. If your client plans to use an outside consultant to resolve problems described in the report, the report will likely need sufficient information to describe the dynamics of the problem.

3. **Early in the project, address matters of implementation of recommendations.**
   Mention that, many times, recommendations from reports are not implemented. Ask your client for ideas on how they can ensure the recommendations are implemented. By asking them, you are reminding them of the difference between reading a report and actually implementing recommendations from the report. Hopefully, you are also cultivating their interest and participation in carefully designing the report.

4. **Focus on relevance, utility and practicality.**
   Reports that focus on scientific accuracy, validity and reliability can generate extensive amounts of data that generate solid conclusions. However, far too often, the reports end up sitting on a shelf because the authors did not consider the usefulness of the report and how its recommendations might actually be applied.

5. **Remind your client, developing the report is as important as the report itself.**
   This guideline is similar to developing other plans, for example, strategic plans or business plans. The report's development process is where the learning is generated.

6. **Use the collaborative approach to consulting to also develop the report.**
   If you develop the report yourself, the contents of the report are not likely to be nearly as useful as when you include the various perspectives and learning from other members of the organization.

7. **Involve the right people in developing the report.**
   Similar to guidelines for developing effective plans, the people who will be involved in implementing the recommendations from the report should be involved in developing the report. That approach ensures the report includes all key perspectives to the problem and the

solution, and also cultivates ownership and commitment to implement any recommendations later on.

8.     **Include an Implementation Section.**
       If possible, include a section in the report that specifies what roles should do what, in what order and by when. Consider including guidelines for monitoring implementation of the plan, as well.

9.     **Ensure your client reviews ongoing drafts of the report as it is written.**
       That practice ensures that the report starts out in the right direction before you put a lot of effort into it. It also reminds busy clients that the report is another project to which they need to provide attention.

# How to Know When to Ask for Help

Because an organizational project often focuses on changing a significant portion or all of an organization, it is common that the project includes changing various systems and functions about which you are not an expert. One of the major ethical principles of good consulting is to ensure that you do not expand your role in a project beyond that of your own skills and expertise. Therefore, it is critical for an organizational consultant to know when to ask for help. This is true whether you are an external or internal consultant. Consider the following guidelines when faced with this type of situation.

1.     **Have you ever done the activity before?**
       If not, what makes you think you can do it now, to the extent that your client might pay you for it?

2.     **Do you want to gain that expertise that you do not have now?**
       Then consider "coat tailing" an expert – to ask to work alongside an expert in the project. Or, ask someone to "shadow" you, providing a sounding board and expert help as you work through the project.

3.     **Consider the same reasons that people hire consultants in the first place.**
       Those may be the reasons that you and your client bring in new expertise.

See "Reasons Nonprofits Work with Consultants" on page 4 to review numerous reasons that consultants are hired.

4.     **Have a list of resources available to provide a range of specific expertise.**
       For example, fundraising, Board training, grant writing, computer installation, and maintenance or evaluation design.

5.     **If you bring in extra help, consider forming a consulting team.**
       There are several advantages to forming a team of consultants.

See "How to Collaborate with Consulting Teams ("Tag Teams")" on page 103 for the advantages of consulting teams and how to form them.

Realize that you could end up hurting your client and their organization – and your credibility, a precious asset for a consultant – if you stretch yourself to consult in an area of expertise in which you are not an expert.

# How to Know When to Leave a Project

## *Why Would You Leave a Project Before It Is Over?*

There are many reasons why you might consider leaving a project, especially if you are an external consultant. For example, major changes in your clients' organization might make it extremely difficult for you to finish the project, such as your client no longer having sufficient funds to pay you. Or, you might have become quite ill.

However, it is rare that reasons for leaving a project are that straightforward. Instead, reasons are usually less clear, for example, you might be faced with leaving because:

- You have encountered sustained resistance from various members of your client's organization, regardless of your various attempts to address that resistance and, as a result, there is decreased likelihood of project success.

- The quality of your relationship with your client has greatly deteriorated, for example, you experience ongoing conflicts and little trust, even though the project seems to be progressing in terms of addressing problems in the organization.

- You encounter unethical practices or other activities that are directly in conflict with your values.

## *Considerations If You Choose to Leave*

We often learn the most from our mistakes, from our major challenges in life and work. Therefore, be careful about concluding that you should leave the project. Consider the following questions.

1. **If you are working with another service provider, have you involved them?**
   For example, if you are working for a nonprofit service provider, than you should immediately notify the provider of your concerns. The provider may be the party ultimately and legally responsible for performing according to the terms of the contract, so they must be told as soon as possible about any issues. The provider may be able to help you with some ideas to improve the situation.

2. **Have you really tried hard to address your issues with your client?**
   What have you done to manage your stress management lately? For example, have you had an authentic discussion with your client about your concerns? What resources have you tapped? Have you asked any peers for feedback and support to address your issues with your client? What else might you still do?

3. **What is in your contract with your client?**
   Contracts often specify the terms of project termination, for example, "Either party can terminate this contract with at least 30 days written notice to the other party." Are there other clauses that pertain, for example, clauses about penalties or reimbursement for damages.

4.  **What will be the impact on your client's organization?**
    Realize that the effects might be dramatic. For example, members of the organization might conclude that their problem is so hopeless that you chose to leave the organization. What would be the effects of that conclusion? What project activities are underway in the organization and what might be the impact on those activities? Have you discussed this situation with peers to ensure that you are aware of any hurt or damage that might be caused by your leaving?

5.  **What are the alternatives for your client?**
    Can your client bring in another consultant? How would that transition from you to the new consultant occur? What if your client does nothing? Are there actions that you can recommend that your client can undertake in the short-term? Long-term?

6.  **What if the client fights hard to make you stay?**
    It is surprising how often we can assume that others have the same perceptions and feelings as we do about an event, especially when our perceptions are clear and feelings are strong. Unless you have had an authentic discussion with your client, you should be aware that your client could have any kind of reaction to your intention to leave, even if you believe that your client really wants you to go. How will your client respond to your intentions to leave and how do you know?

7.  **How might this affect your reputation?**
    One of the most important assets of any consultant is his or her reputation. It is surprising how small the community of nonprofits and consultants really is. Particularly, if your client has strong negative feelings about you and your leaving, word could spread quickly, causing substantial damage to your reputation and credibility as a consultant.

8.  **What can you learn from this situation?**
    How did you get yourself in this situation in the first place? What could you have done differently? What might you do differently in the future? Is there any learning that you can share with your client? If so, be careful to offer it as feedback from you, not as judgments about them.

If you have thoroughly addressed the above-listed questions and still decide to leave the project, then if you are working for a provider, termination should be according to their preferences. If you are not working for a provider, promptly comply with the terms of your contract, for example, submit a written letter of termination to your client. Be sure to copy at least two people in your client's organization. Do not go into extended analysis of the cause of your leaving. Instead, mention "for personal reasons" or "because I can no longer be useful in helping the client."

# PART II:

# OVERVIEW OF

# NONPROFIT

# ORGANIZATIONS

# AND SYSTEMS

# What Is a Nonprofit?

To successfully consult to nonprofit organizations, it is critically important for you to fully understand the workings in the organization, including all of the major activities and how they all fit together. This is true whether you are an external or internal consultant. A successful consulting process for a large corporation likely will not work for most nonprofit organizations, which tend to be much smaller in size. Far too often, new consultants set out to conduct a comprehensive, in-depth and detailed consulting process for a nonprofit, only to realize that members of the nonprofit have soon lost all interest in – and have even come to resent – the consulting process entirely because it does not suit the nature and needs of their organization. Information in this part of the Field Guide will give you a good foundation on which to apply principles of systems thinking, performance management and organizational change to accomplish successful nonprofit consulting.

## Nonprofit Compared to For-Profit Corporations

Perhaps the best way to explain the nature and role of a nonprofit organization is to contrast it to a for-profit organization, a form with which most of us are quite familiar. The following table depicts major differences between both types of organizations.

### Table II:1 – Nonprofit Compared to For-Profit Corporations

| For-Profit Corporations | Nonprofit Corporations |
| --- | --- |
| Owned by stockholders | Owned by the public |
| Generates profit for the owners | Serves the public |
| Success is making sizeable profit | Success is meeting the needs of the public |
| Board members are paid | Board members are volunteers |
| Employees can make a very sizeable income | Staff should make a reasonable, not excessive, income |
| Money earned over and above that needed to pay expenses is kept as profit and distributed to owners | Money earned over and above that needed to pay expenses is retained as surplus, and should be spent soon on meeting the public need |
| The Chief Executive Officer is often on the Board of Directors, and may even be the President of the Board | Conventional wisdom suggests that the Chief Executive Officer not be on the Board |
| Usually not exempt from paying federal, state/provincial and local taxes | Can often be exempt from paying federal taxes, and some state/provincial and local taxes |

While there are these distinct differences, the nature of a large nonprofit is more like a large for-profit than a small nonprofit organization. Similarly, a small nonprofit is more like a small for-profit business than a large nonprofit organization. This similarity is most evident in the kind of organizational issues that arise and how they are resolved.

# Primary Forms of Nonprofit Organizations

It is important for you to recognize that the term "nonprofit" can mean a variety of types of nonprofit organizations. Knowing those types and why they are formed will enrich your understanding of your client's organization, and help ensure your credibility when communicating about nonprofits with your clients.

## *Informal Nonprofits (Unincorporated)*

If the purpose of the organization's effort is to address an occasional, and often not extremely critical, need in the community, perhaps the need can be filled by an informal nonprofit, rather than by a formal nonprofit organization. In an informal nonprofit, people gather often for a short time, for example, to clean up their neighborhood.

## *Formal Nonprofit Corporations (Chartered, Incorporated)*

If the organization is intended to meet a current, ongoing need in the community, the organization often incorporates as a separate legal entity. In the United States of America (USA), a corporation is formed by filing various papers with the state, usually obtained from the state's Secretary of State's office. In Canada, a nonprofit corporation can be formed either at the provincial or federal levels, or under a variety of regulations, for example, a provincial Societies Act or Companies Act, or the federal Canada Corporations Act. In Canada, it is necessary to be incorporated to become a charity.

Depending on the country in which the nonprofit is formed, benefits of incorporation might be that the nonprofit corporation can:

- Own property and have its own bank account.

- Enter into contracts.

- Continue operations as a legal entity after the founders are gone.

- Be eligible to conduct tax-exempt activities (see below).

- Be eligible for tax-deductible donations (see below).

- Conduct operations for which Board members are not personally liable (in most cases).

## *Tax-exempt Nonprofits*

If a nonprofit organization wants to be exempt from paying various taxes, they file with the appropriate government agency to gain tax-exempt status. For example, in the USA, they file with the Internal Revenue Service (the nonprofit almost always needs to first gain corporate status). To qualify for tax-exempt status in the USA, the nonprofit must serve a need that is religious, educational, charitable, scientific or literary in nature. If the IRS grants tax-exempt status to the nonprofit, it will send the nonprofit a determination letter. Rules for tax-exempt status are in the USA Tax Code in section 501(c). Thus, tax-exempt nonprofits are often referred to as 501(c) nonprofits. In Canada, tax-exempt status can be granted even at the provincial level. Note that all nonprofits still must pay employment (or payroll) taxes.

## *Charitable Nonprofits*

Depending on the nature of the mission of the nonprofit corporation, it might also be granted tax-deductible (or charitable) status, for example, from the IRS in the USA or the Canada Customs and Revenue Agency in Canada. Being tax-exempt is not the same as being tax-deductible. Tax-deductible or charitable means that people can reduce their federal and/or state/provincial tax liabilities based on their contributions to the nonprofit organization. Tax-deductible status is granted usually to nonprofits that serve needs in regard to the arts, charitable, civic affairs, education, the environment, health and social services, literary, scientific and religious matters.

In the USA, the IRS does not grant tax-deductible, or 501(c)(3), status to all nonprofits. For example, the IRS does not grant tax-deductible status to social welfare nonprofits, 501(c)(4)'s, that exist primarily to lobby, or to associations, 501(c)(6)'s, that exist primarily to support networking and development of their members. They are tax-exempt, but not tax-deductible.

# Three Major Levels within Nonprofit Corporations

There are a variety of designs of nonprofit corporations. Because the organization is incorporated, it requires a Board of Directors. Board members choose to have Board committees or not. Board members choose to have staff or not. The nonprofit might have one program or many.

## *Governance and Boards*

The governance aspect of a nonprofit is responsible to provide overall strategic direction, guidance and controls. Often the term "governance" refers to Board matters. However, many people are coming to consider governance as a function carried out by the Board and top management. Effective governance depends to a great extent on the working relationship between Board and top management.

## *Central Administration*

Central administration includes the staff and facilities that are common to running all programs. This usually includes at least the Chief Executive Officer and office personnel, such as finance staff or executive assistants. Nonprofits usually strive to keep costs of central administration low in proportion to the cost of running programs. Small nonprofits might not have separate administrative staff, or any paid staff at all.

## *Programs*

Typically, nonprofits work from their overall mission, or purpose, to identify a few basic service goals, which must be reached to accomplish their mission. Resources are organized into programs to reach each goal. It often helps to think of programs in terms of inputs, process, outputs and outcomes. Inputs are the various resources needed to run the program, such as money, facilities, clients and program staff. The process is how the program is carried out, for example, clients are counseled, children are cared for, art is created, and association members are supported. The outputs are the units of service, for example, number of clients counseled, children cared for, artistic pieces produced, or members in the association. Program outcomes are the impacts on the clients from participating in the nonprofit's services, for example, increased mental health, safe and secure development, richer artistic appreciation and perspectives in life, and increased effectiveness among members.

# Key Roles in Nonprofit Corporations

## Clients

Everything in a nonprofit is ultimately directed to serving clients. Clients are the "consumers" or "customers" of the nonprofit. Services can be in the form of tangible or intangible products, and are often provided in the form of nonprofit programs.

## Board Members

The Board is comprised of individuals from the community served by the organization and, ideally, represents the needs of that community. Law and theory dictate that the Board is in charge and directly accountable for the overall direction and policies of the organization. Powers are given to the Board by the Articles of Incorporation or other governing documents, for example, Articles of Association or its Constitution. The Board can configure itself and the nonprofit in whatever structure it prefers to meet the organization's mission, and usually does so via specifications in the By-Laws. Members of nonprofit Boards are generally motivated by a desire to serve the community and the personal satisfaction of volunteering. Usually, nonprofit Board members do not receive direct monetary compensation for serving on the Board. Board members only have authority when they sit in Board meetings, not as individuals.

## Board Chair

The Board Chair's role is central to coordinating the work of the Board, Chief Executive Officer and Board committees. The Chair's role may have power to appoint Chairs and members of Board committees, depending on what is specified about this role in the By-Laws. The true power of the Board Chair is usually through persuasion and general leadership ability.

## Committees or Task Forces

The Board might choose to carry out its operations using a variety of Board committees or task forces. If so, examples of common committees are the Executive Committee, Finance Committee, Fundraising Committee, Marketing Committee, Programs Committee and Personnel Committee. The types of committees formed by the Board depend on the current overall strategic goals and priorities of the nonprofit, as well as the commonplace skills of organizational management. The Board should appoint members to each committee. Members of the committees include at least one Board member, and may also benefit from staff or volunteer members.

## Chief Executive Officer

The Board might choose to retain a Chief Executive Officer role in the nonprofit organization. If so, the Board typically chooses to have this role be ultimately responsible to carry out the wishes of the Board. The Chief Executive Officer is directly accountable for the work of the staff and supports the work of the Board committees. The Chief Executive Officer is a staff role. This role might not be compensated in a small nonprofit.

## Staff

Staff other than the Chief Executive Officer usually report to the Chief Executive Officer and may support the work of Board committees at the request of the CEO. As mentioned above, the role of Chief Executive Officer is a staff role. Staff, in this context, might refer to program directors /

managers, accountants, executive or administrative assistants, or people who provide direct services to clients. Small nonprofits might not have any paid staff.

## Volunteers

Volunteers are unpaid personnel who assist staff, can serve on Board committees, and generally work under the direction of the Chief Executive Officer or other supervisor. In many nonprofits, the volunteers are every bit as valuable, or more valuable, to the organization as the paid staff.

# Roles and Responsibilities of the Nonprofit Board of Directors

The following description is to orient you to the roles of a nonprofit Board of Directors so that you can recognize the importance of the Board members role in the organization and in your consulting projects. Also, you can realize how the Board plays a key role in the success of your projects.

## Responsible to the Public

A for-profit corporation is owned by its stockholders. The Board of Directors is responsible to those stockholders. A more progressive perspective is that the Board is responsible to the stakeholders – to everyone who is interested in and/or can be affected by the corporation.

A nonprofit corporation is owned by the public. The Board of Directors is responsible to the stakeholders, particularly the communities that the nonprofit serves.

## Establish Overall Plans and Policies, Staff Implements Them

Boards are responsible to establish top-level plans and policies that define the purpose and direction for a nonprofit. The Chief Executive Officer (if the Board chooses to have a CEO in the organization) is responsible to manage the nonprofit's resources in an effective and efficient manner according to the plans and policies of the nonprofit. How this all occurs in a nonprofit depends on the structure and culture of the organization.

## Power Vested in All Board Members, Not Individual Members

Individual Board members do not have formal authority. Formal authority and approval of the nonprofit's major plans and policies must be made by the Board as a body of its members. Boards, in turn, have policies and procedures (for example, By-Laws or policies for staffing) that determine how the Board acts as a body to approve those plans and procedures.

## General Responsibilities

Ingram (2002) itemizes the following 10 responsibilities of nonprofit Boards.

1.    Determine the organization's mission and purpose.

2.    Select the Chief Executive Officer.

3.    Support the Chief Executive Officer and review his or her performance.

4.    Ensure effective organizational planning.

5.    Ensure adequate resources.

6.    Manage resources effectively. (This is often done by appointing a Chief Executive Officer to manage the organization.)

7.    Determine and monitor the organization's programs and services.

8.    Enhance the organization's public image.

9.    Serve as a court of appeal.

10.   Assess its own performance.

To learn more about nonprofit Boards of Directors, see the list of recommended resources on page 499.

# Roles and Responsibilities of the Chief Executive Officer

It is likely that, as an organizational consultant, you will work directly with the Chief Executive Officer (or Executive Director). The Chief Executive is the major "player" in the nonprofit, the person who often knows the most about the nonprofit is services and clientele. It is common that the first Chief Executive of the nonprofit is also the founder of the nonprofit. The Chief Executive plays a major role in first organizing the Board and helping members to do their job as Board members. The following paragraphs provide a general overview of the major responsibilities of the role of Chief Executive Officer.

## Board Administration and Support

Theory and law assert that the Board oversees and governs the nonprofit organization. Many experts note that it is often the Chief Executive Officer (CEO) who actually facilitates the Board to perform those roles. The CEO often knows much more about the nonprofit organization than do the members of the Board. Consequently, the CEO must continually update Board members about the nonprofit organization, often by providing written reports to Board members that are reviewed during Board meetings. An effective Board hires the CEO and regularly evaluates the CEO's performance. The CEO often helps with Board development and administration, often through a Board Governance Committee.

## Program, Product and Service Delivery

The CEO is an expert about the nonprofit and its programs, knowing who the clientele are, what their needs are, and how those needs should be met. The CEO oversees design of programs to ensure they continually meet the needs of clients in a highly effective fashion. Programs must be advertised and promoted to community stakeholders, particularly to clients and funders. The CEO works with the Board in this regard, often in a Programs Committee, to ensure Board members are up-to-date about programs and their effectiveness.

## Financial, Tax, Risk and Facilities Management

The CEO works with the Board Treasurer to develop the yearly budget. The budget should be derived from results of the Board's yearly strategic planning. Once the budget is established, the CEO must operate the nonprofit in accordance with the Strategic Plan, the budget, and in a manner consistent with various laws and regulations, as well as the policies of the Board. This includes paying all relevant taxes. It also includes managing the facilities of the organization in an efficient and safe fashion. The CEO works with the Board in this regard, often in a Finance Committee.

## Human Resource Management

The CEO leads the effort to design organizational roles and assign responsibilities among staff. These roles and responsibilities should be derived directly from results of yearly strategic planning. The CEO oversees staffing, training and supervision of personnel. These activities must closely conform to up-to-date personnel policies and procedures that are reviewed on a regular basis by an employment law expert and approved by the Board. The CEO works with the Board in this regard, often in a Personnel Committee.

## Community and Public Relations

The CEO often takes the lead in ensuring that the community continues to have a strong positive image about the nonprofit and its services. It is often most productive if the CEO works from a comprehensive Marketing Plan developed in conjunction with a Board Marketing Committee and approved by the Board in general.

## Fundraising

One of the primary responsibilities of a nonprofit Board of Directors is assure adequate funding and to help with fundraising. Unfortunately, many Board members do not assume this full responsibility. In any event, the CEO usually leads the fundraising efforts, clarifying the amounts of money needed to reach strategic goals, where to go to appeal for those monies, how to make those appeals, and making the appeals themselves. It is often most successful if the CEO works from a comprehensive Fundraising Plan developed in conjunction with a Board Fundraising Committee and approved by the full Board.

To learn more about the role of the nonprofit Chief Executive Officer and other staff, see the list of recommended resources on page 503.

A good way to depict the role of the Chief Executive Officer is by providing a job description. Take a minute or two to review the job description on the following page.

## Table II:2 – Example Job Description of Chief Executive Officer

**Title:**　　　　　　　　　　Chief Executive Officer (Executive Director)

**Responsible to:**　　　　　Board of Directors

**Major Functions:**

1. Implement the strategic goals and objectives of the organization.

2. With the Chair, to enable the Board to fulfill its governance function.

3. Give direction and leadership toward the achievement of the organization's philosophy, mission, strategy, and its annual goals and objectives.

**Major Responsibilities and Accountabilities:**

1. Board Administration and Support – Supports operations and administration of the Board by advising and informing Board members, interfacing between Board and staff, and supporting Board's evaluation of Chief Executive Officer.

2. Program, Product and Service Delivery – Oversees design, marketing, promotion, delivery, and quality of programs, products and services.

3. Financial, Tax, Risk and Facilities Management – Recommends yearly budget for Board approval and prudently manages organization's resources within those budget guidelines according to current laws and regulations.

4. Human Resource Management – Effectively manages the human resources of the organization according to authorized personnel policies and procedures that fully conform to current laws and regulations.

5. Community and Public Relations – Assures the organization and its mission, programs and services are consistently presented in strong, positive image to relevant stakeholders.

6. Fundraising – Oversees fundraising planning and implementation, including identifying resource requirements, researching funding sources, establishing strategies to approach funders, submitting proposals, and administrating fundraising records and documentation.

(This job description might be used by a policy governing Board, one of the major types of structures of Boards.)

*Date of Board Approval of Job Description:* _____ *Board Chair:* _____

# Board and Staff Coordination – How They Fit Together

During projects, you often will interact with members of staff. Depending on the nature of the project, you might interact with members of the Board, as well. It will help you to have a basic understanding of the major roles in the organization and how they relate to each other. The following graphic depicts the relationships in a nonprofit where Board members have chosen to have committees and a Chief Executive Officer (Executive Director) role.

*(Adapted from and used with permission of Greater Twin Cities United Way)*

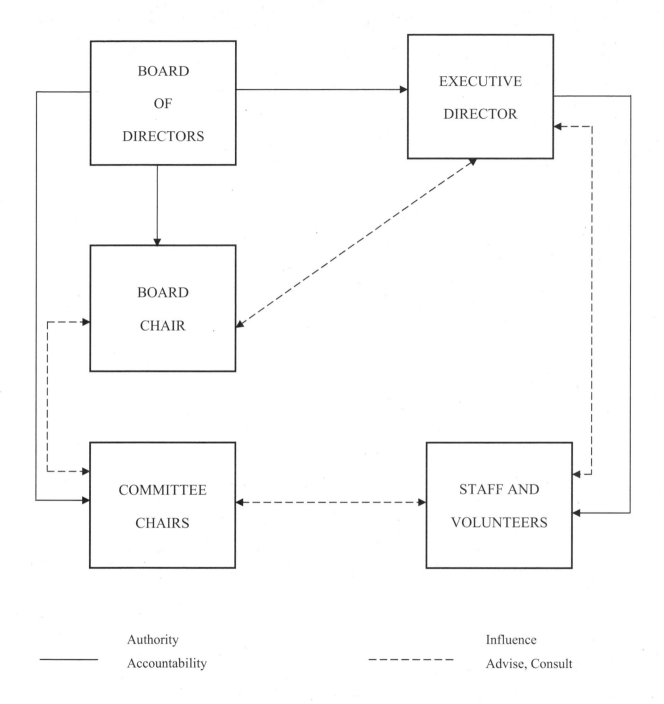

| | |
|---|---|
| Authority | Influence |
| ——— Accountability | - - - - - - - Advise, Consult |

# Board and Staff Roles – Who Often Does What

## Table II:3 – Common Roles Between Board and Staff

| Organizational Planning | Responsibilities |
|---|---|
| Initiate and direct the process of long-range planning | Board |
| Provide input to mission and long-range goals | Joint |
| Approve mission and long-range goals | Board |
| Formulate annual objectives from long-range goals | Staff |
| Approve annual objectives | Board |
| Implement operational plan | Staff |
| Follow-up to ensure implementation of all plans | Board |

| Board of Directors | |
|---|---|
| Select new Board members | Board |
| Orient, train and organize members into committees or task forces | Board |
| Plan agenda for Board meetings | Joint |
| Ensure Board operations are highly effective | Board |

| Programs | |
|---|---|
| Assess stakeholder needs (of clients', funders', community's, etc.) | Joint |
| Identify program outcomes and goals | Staff |
| Approve program outcomes and goals / monitor, receive reports | Board |
| Ensure evaluation of products, services and programs | Board |
| Maintain program records, prepare program reports | Staff |

| Financial management | |
|---|---|
| Prepare preliminary annual budget based on long-range plans | Staff |
| Approve annual budget | Board |
| Approve expenditures outside authorized budget above certain amount | Board |
| Ensure annual audit of financial accounts | Board |
| Ensure that expenditures are within budget during the year | Joint |

| Fundraising | |
|---|---|
| Establish fundraising goals (amounts / goals to be raised) | Board |
| Organize fundraising campaigns | Joint |
| Lead the solicitation of contributions during fundraising campaigns | Board |
| Manage grants (tracking grant budgets, reporting progress, etc.) | Staff |

| Personnel Activities (staff and volunteers) | |
|---|---|
| Employ and supervise Chief Executive | Board |
| Decide to add general staff and / or volunteers | Joint |
| Select / train general staff and / or volunteers | Staff |
| Direct work of the general staff and /or volunteers | CEO |

| Public / Community Relations Activities | |
|---|---|
| Present / describe organization to community | Joint |
| Write descriptions of organization (newsletters, web, etc.) | Staff |
| Provide linkage with other organizations | Joint |

## Mission and Vision – Compass for Where Change Goes

All systems have a purpose, or mission, in their life. They also have certain methods, or strategies, to work toward that mission. For example, think of people who have complained that they do not feel meaning in their lives. Often, it is because they are not in touch with their purpose or mission. Usually, when people discover their mission in life, they feel much more fulfilled. They may even develop a clear vision for themselves, that is, clear depiction of what they want to be by a certain time in the future or what kind of world they want to live in.

Some people prefer to set goals along the way while working toward their vision, for example, goals to finish college, have a family or establish a career. They often set about to find ways, or strategies, to achieve their goals, for example, enroll in college, start dating or get career counseling. They may set timelines for achieving their vision and their goals. After they have set timelines, they think about what resources they will need, for example, money, house or training.

Other systems are similar, especially organizations. To be effective, leaders need to be clear about the mission, or purpose, of their organization, program or team. Leaders will also need to establish a clear vision and goals along the way while working toward the mission. And, leaders will need some useful strategies to achieve the vision and associated goals.

## Values – Compass for How Change Occurs

While the mission is the compass for the direction of change, the values are the compass for the nature of how change is carried out. Attention to organizational values has increased substantially because people are recognizing and benefiting from the tremendous diversity of values, perspectives and opinions among nonprofit stakeholders. In addition, experts in organizational change are recognizing the critical role of values during change.

Like people, organizations have actual, enacted values and also preferred, espoused values. All organizations have overall actual values in how they operate. The actual values reflect the current culture of the organization. Those values are either explicit (acknowledged and written down) or implicit (often not recognized and acknowledged). Actual values can be detected with your senses – with what you see, hear and feel about what is currently happening in the organization. Preferred values are the overall priorities in how the organization wants to operate. Often, the preferred values are articulated in the form of a values statement during the strategic planning process. Just like people, organizations' preferred values are often quite different from their actual values.

During change, both types of values are important. As the consultant working to help change the organization, you will be faced with behaviors and opinions that reflect the actual values of the organization. During change, you and your clients often will talk about how the organization should operate – its preferred values.

Successful organizational change usually involves working to change the culture of your client's organization. Rarely can you, as a consultant, change the culture of your client's organization. Your clients have to do that, but it can take years. Change in culture often results from recognizing both the actual and the preferred values of the organization. It comes from ongoing communication about what currently exists versus how the organization wants to exist (its vision). It comes from continuing to take action to achieve that vision – and from learning at the same time. Probably the most powerful form of help that you can provide is by facilitating a highly collaborative approach with your clients to examine and understand the current state of your client's organization, articulate where the organization wants to be, and then guide the organization to get there.

# Critical Role of Strategic Planning in Nonprofits

The success of your consulting project is based largely on how well the project is aligned with the strategic mission, goals and strategies of the organization. Thus, as an organizational development consultant, it is important that you understand the role of strategic planning in nonprofits and are aware of your client's Strategic Plan.

The strategic planning process affects every aspect of your client's organization. Most organizations conduct strategic planning. Some take a highly formal and explicit approach, while others take a less formal and implicit approach. Unless you are consulting to facilitate strategic planning for your client, you probably do not need to understand a great deal about how their plans are formed, but you should understand the overall process and its key terms to talk about the Strategic Plan with your client.

Nonprofit organizations establish mission, goals and strategies during the strategic planning process. Many organizations also develop vision statements and values statements. To be effective, the strategic planning process must include action plans that specify who will do what and by when to implement the Strategic Plan. The process must also include timelines for completion of goals and a list of resources needed to implement the strategies. The list of resources often includes a budget, or list of what funding is needed and how it will be spent.

Perhaps one of the easiest ways to explain strategic planning is by using a simple analogy. The following table depicts a comparison between strategic planning for an organization and vacation planning for a family.

For more information about nonprofit strategic planning, see the list of recommended resources on page 506.

## Table II:4 – Analogy of Strategic Planning to a Family Vacation

| | |
|---|---|
| Strategic planning is like: | Arranging a trip we will take |
| Mission is like: | The reasons we are traveling, for example, relax, gain renewal, strengthen the family, educational experiences, etc. |
| Values are like: | Our priorities in how we carry out our trip, for example, have a good time, listen, talk, quiet places, opportunities to meet new people, etc. |
| Vision is like: | Where we want to end up and what we will be doing at our ultimate destination |
| External analysis is like: | Checking the weather, road conditions, etc. |
| Internal analysis is like: | Checking our available vacation time, condition of our car, who can drive, etc. |
| Goals are like: | Major stops along the way |
| Strategies are like: | Major routes we will take to the major stops |
| Action planning is like: | Identifying who will drive each route, check the map, make reservations, etc. |
| Budgeting is like: | Identifying how much money we will need to spend and tracking our expenses along the way. |
| Implementing and adjusting plans is like: | Getting in the car and starting our vacation, then noticing that some roads are under construction and changing routes, etc. |
| Evaluation is like: | Hearing from family members about whether they enjoyed the vacation and what they learned. |

# Unique Challenges of Typical Nonprofits

Information that clearly conveys the differences between the typical nonprofit and, for example, large for-profit organizations will be especially useful to you in your work with nonprofits.

The nature of a typical new nonprofit tends to be a rather tight-knit group of people, each very dedicated to the mission of the organization.  They will chip in to help wherever and whenever they can.  Often, they are like a small family.  This tends to change as the organization goes through its life cycles.

(Adapted with permission from Sandra Larson, previous Executive Director of The Management Assistance Program for Nonprofits, St. Paul.)

1.      **There is a unique balance of power between Board and Chief Executive Officer.**
         At the heart of any successful nonprofit is an effective Chief Executive Officer and Board of Directors, assuming the organization is big enough to warrant having a Chief Executive. These leaders must work as a team with vision, skill and sufficient resources to accomplish the organization's mission.  While leadership is shared, critical management skills must rest with the Chief Executive Officer.  However, the Board must be sufficiently skilled in

management to assess the work of this Chief Executive Officer and assist in strategic decision making.

2.  **Consulting and problem solving are value-laden.**
    Values are the driving force in a nonprofit. The bottom line is the realization of a social mission, not profit. This poses complex problems for the leadership team. How are programs agreed upon, progress monitored and success measured? How are priorities set and consensus reached? How are staff members rewarded and what control systems are applicable? Skilled consultants may be needed from time to time to assist the team in answering these qualitative, value-laden questions and focusing on appropriate management systems.

3.  **Nonprofit personnel are often highly diverse.**
    Diversity is reflected not only by different races and ethnic groups, but also by different values and perspectives. This strong diversity is a major benefit to the nonprofit because input from a wide variety of perspectives usually ensures complete consideration of situations and new ideas. However, nonprofit personnel must ensure they cultivate, and remain open to, the various values and perspectives.

4.  **Problems are especially complex for the nonprofit.**
    The majority of nonprofits have small staffs and small budgets, for example, less than $500,000. This compounds the leadership and management problems they face, especially given the magnitude of community needs with which they deal. Those new to nonprofits may believe that, because nonprofits tend to be much smaller in size than large for-profit corporations, issues in nonprofits should be simple in nature. On the contrary, the vast majority of organizations (regardless of size) experience similar issues, for example, challenges in planning, organizing, motivating and guiding. However, when these issues are focused in a small organization, the nature of the organization becomes dynamic and complex.

5.  **Sufficient resources to pay leadership may be lacking.**
    With lack of sufficient money, attracting and retaining paid management also can be problematic. Hard work with little career development opportunity encourages turnover of Chief Executives and staff. This can stall the organization's work. Expertise brought in to advise the management may be lost once that leadership leaves.

6.  **Lack of managerial training is problematic for the nonprofit.**
    Many nonprofit managers have been promoted primarily out of non-management disciplines and do not have the managerial skills that are needed to run a nonprofit organization. Training and consultation can do much to help these new leaders gain the skills they seek and help them up the myriad of learning curves.

7.  **Chief Executives wear too many hats.**
    A nonprofit Chief Executive has to be a current expert in planning, marketing, information management, telecommunications, property management, personnel, finance, system design, fundraising and program evaluation. Obviously this is not possible, regardless of the size of the organization. A larger organization may be able to hire some internal experts, but this is certainly not the case for the smaller organization. Furthermore, the technology of management progresses too rapidly today for the non-specialist to keep abreast of new thinking and expertise, whatever the size. Outside expertise, therefore, is often a must for both the large and small organization.

8.   **The nonprofit is too small to justify or pay for expensive outside advice.**
     Most nonprofits, even larger ones, hesitate to spend money on administrative "overhead" such as consultants or other outside experts because this is seen as diverting valuable dollars from direct service. Of course, many nonprofits have no choice. They do not have enough money to even consider hiring consultants at for-profit rates. Low-cost, volunteer-based assistance is often an appropriate solution.

9.   **One-shot assistance often is not enough**.
     While most consultant organizations want to teach managers "how to fish" rather than give them a "fish," "fishing" (management skills) is not something that can be learned in one consultation. Especially in more technical arenas such as computerization, learning comes while grappling with an issue or management problem over a period of time. Building internal management capacity takes more time than a one-shot consultation. Repeat help, therefore, is not a sign of failure but of growth – a new need to know has surfaced.

10.  **Networks are lacking.**
     Many people outside the nonprofit sector observe, "Why don't those Chief Executives get together more, share more ideas, undertake cooperative ventures?" There are many reasons. First of all, running a successful organization (delivering the quality service that fulfills the organization's mission) is not enough. Most nonprofit Chief Executive Officers run a second business – raising money to support the first. Both are complex and time-consuming activities, especially when the Chief Executive Officer wears all the management hats and often some program hats as well. Second, developing networks or researching joint ventures is time-consuming, expensive and risky. Third, the nature of most funding specifies how funds are to be spent, and can make collaboration with other agencies virtually impossible.

11.  **Nonprofits usually have little time and money.**
     Many funders are hesitant to fund what might not succeed. While nonprofits may be more entrepreneurial than funders, they also have little capital to risk. Collaborative planning will be enhanced by computerization and telecommunications, but these investments also are difficult to fund. In some ways, affordable consultants can substitute for expensive, up-front research and development costs, at least at the feasibility level. In many cases, consultants can carry an organization through the needed planning to actually develop a new system of collaboration, merger or automation.

12.  **Nonprofits need low-cost management and technical assistance.**
     Nonprofits are valuable community assets that must be effectively managed. The need to provide affordable, accessible management and technical assistance to nonprofit organizations is clear for all the reasons stated above, including the complexity of the task, the lack of Board and internal expertise, the lack of time and money, changing needs, the learning curve, and finally, the importance of the results to the community. What is well done is based on what is well run.

13.  **The typical nature of planning in nonprofits is on current issues.**
     Many nonprofits do not have a lot of time, money or resources for sophisticated, comprehensive strategic planning. The focus is usually on identifying the major issues facing the nonprofit and quickly addressing them. Typical major challenges for the consultant are basic training of personnel about planning concepts and processes, helping the nonprofit to focus and sustain its limited resources on planning, ensuring strategies are really strategic rather than operational/efficiency measures, and helping design small and focused planning meetings that produce realistic plans that are implemented.

# Diversity of Nonprofits

You can further your understanding of nonprofits by realizing their tremendous diversity, including the types of needs that they work to meet in the community, configurations of Boards and staff, types and configurations of programs, and the approaches used to build those diverse programs. This is true whether you are an external or internal consultant.

## Culture (Personality) of Organizations

As you read in the subsection, "How to Work in Multicultural Environments," in PART I, the nature of how consulting is carried out in an organization depends to a great extent on the culture of the organization – culture tends to influence what people perceive, how they make assumptions, what they believe, and how they act in their organization.

Organizational change is largely a matter of cultural change. Consequently, it is important for you to get a good sense about the culture of your client's organization. However, as an organizational consultant, you can rarely change your client's culture – usually only your client can do that. Changing culture often takes six months to several years. Therefore, changing culture may require more time than can practically be included in a consulting contract

Differences in culture can be observed in a wide variety of aspects, for example:

- Where power lies in the organization.

- How decisions are made.

- The nature of language, including wording, emphasis and use of silences.

- What people brag about.

- How facilities are arranged.

- What people wear.

- How people interact.

- Peoples' perceptions of, and value placed on, time.

- People's perceptions of personal space.

- Sense of urgency to address tasks.

One way to get a clearer understanding of the concept of organizational culture is to consider several disparate types of cultures. There are probably as many types of organizational cultures as there are personalities in human beings. Researcher Jeffrey Sonnenfeld, in *Matching Leadership Style to Diverse Strategic Cultures,* identifies the following four major types of cultures. Although their names include terms not often associated with nonprofits, the types of cultures are common across the range of nonprofit organizations.

1. **Academy culture**

   Employees are highly skilled and stay in the organization, while working their way up the ranks. The organization provides a stable environment in which employees can develop and exercise their skills. Examples include medium- to large-sized nonprofit services in education, arts, environmental protection and social services.

2. **Baseball team culture**

   Employees are "free agents" who have highly prized skills. They are in high demand and can rather easily get jobs elsewhere. This type of culture exists in fast-paced, high-risk organizations, such as technology and health care.

3. **Club culture**

   The most important requirement for employees in this culture is to fit into the group. Usually, employees start at the bottom and stay with the organization. The organization promotes from within and highly values seniority. Examples are the military, religious and civic organizations.

4. **Fortress culture**

   Employees do not know if they will be laid off or not. These organizations often undergo massive reorganization. There are many opportunities for those with timely, specialized skills. In today's environment of tight funding for nonprofits, almost any type of nonprofit, especially small- to medium-size, might be an example here.

Quite often, a nonprofit leader has a good sense of the culture of their organization. They just have not made that sense conscious to the extent that they can fully learn from, and lead within, the culture. Unless they make conscious their awareness of the culture, they struggle to really understand the culture and explain it to others.

Different people in the same organization can have different perceptions of the culture of the organization. This is especially true for the different perceptions between the top and bottom levels of the organization. For example, the Chief Executive Officer may view the organization as being highly focused, well organized and even rather formal. On the other hand, the receptionist might view the organization as being confused, disorganized and sometimes even rude.

Note that there may not be close alignment between what the organization says it values (for example, creativity, innovation and team-building) and what you are actually seeing (for example, conformity and risk-avoidance). This disparity is rather common in organizations.

Culture is a concept about which many books have been written and it typically is discussed in the abstract. However, when you operationalize the concept to a more practical level, such as that needed when guiding change, you often end up using the same types of tools and techniques as described in this Field Guide. This Field Guide is about the process to guide successful organizational change – that type of change always involves successful organizational cultural change.

 If you want to learn a more about organizational culture, see Edgar H. Schein's book, *Organizational Culture,* 3rd Edition, Jossey-Bass, 2004. This is a classic book on the subject.

# Life Cycles of Organizations and Programs

Organizations go through different life-cycles just like people do. For example, people go through infancy, child-hood and early-teenage phases that are characterized by lots of rapid growth. People in these phases often do whatever it takes just to stay alive, such as eating, seeking shelter and sleeping. These people make impulsive, highly reactive decisions based on whatever is going on around them at the moment.

Start-up organizations are like this, too. Often, founders of the organization and its members have to do whatever is necessary just to stay in business. Leaders make highly reactive, seat-of-the-pants decisions. They fear taking the time to slow down and do planning.

In our comparison of organizations to people, we note that, as people continue to mature, they begin to understand more about the world and themselves. Over time, they develop a certain kind of wisdom that sees them through many of the challenges in life and work. They learn to plan and to use a certain amount of discipline to carry through on those plans. They learn to manage themselves.

To survive well into the future, organizations must be able to do this, as well. Experienced leaders have learned to recognize the particular life cycle that an organization or program is going through. These leaders understand the types of problems faced by the organization or program during the life cycle. That understanding gives them a sense of perspective and helps them to decide how to respond to decisions and problems in the workplace.

## *Three Perspectives on Life Cycles*

Perhaps it is most useful if you can get a variety of perspectives on life cycles. The following useful table is summarized from Daft (1992), which, in turn, is based on information from Quinn and Cameron (1983). Remember that the following information is about life cycles of systems, and is appropriate to organizations, programs and even your consulting projects.

## Table II:5 – One Perspective on Life Cycles

| Aspects | Birth | Youth | Midlife | Maturity |
|---|---|---|---|---|
| **Size** | Small | Medium | Large | Very large |
| **Bureaucratic** | Non-bureaucratic | Pre-bureaucratic | Bureaucratic | Very bureaucratic |
| **Division of labor** | Overlapping tasks | Some departments | Many departments | Extensive, with small jobs and many descriptions |
| **Centralization** | One-person rule | Two leaders rule | Two department heads | Top-management heavy |
| **Formalization** | No written rules | Few rules | Policy and procedures manuals | Extensive |
| **Administrative intensity** | Secretary, no professional staff | Increasing clerical and maintenance | Increasing professional and staff support | Large– multiple departments |
| **Internal systems** | Nonexistent | Crude budget and information system | Control systems in place: budget, performance, reports, etc. | Extensive – planning, financial and personnel added |
| **Lateral teams for coordination** | None | Top leaders only | Some use of task forces | Frequent at lower levels |

## Another Perspective

Simon (2001) provides another perspective on life cycles of nonprofit organizations.  In summary, the author identifies the following stages.

- Stage One: Imagine and Inspire ("Can the dream be realized?")

- Stage Two: Found and Frame ("How are we going to pull this off?")

- Stage Three: Ground and Grow ("How can we build this to be viable?")

- Stage Four: Produce and Sustain ("How can the momentum be sustained?")

- Stage Five: Review and Renew ("What do we need to redesign?")

Simon also provides numerous considerations and suggestions for discerning life cycles, and guiding organizations to the next cycle.  The book also includes a comprehensive, yet practical life-stage assessment tool.

### Table II:6 – Another Perspective on Life Cycles

This author often views life cycles in the following phases (rather than stages). As with any life cycles, they are highly integrated and not always sequential in order. The phases include infancy, growth and maturity. Decline, stagnation or growth can occur between the infancy, growth and maturity phases. This simple approach to life cycles is straightforward to describe to clients and easy for clients to apply on their own.

| Infancy Phase | Growth Phase | Maturity Phase |
|---|---|---|
| ▪ Clarify mission, vision and values | ▪ Focus on effectiveness of services | ▪ Sustain momentum |
| ▪ Firm up the leadership systems, including Board and CEO role | ▪ Focus on efficiencies through policies and procedures | ▪ Focus on innovation |
| ▪ Clarify clients and stakeholders | ▪ Expand services, especially current services to new clients | ▪ Cultivate renewal |
| ▪ Clarify desired outcomes from services | ▪ Accomplish fundraising streams for increased sustainability | ▪ Focus on succession planning and risk management |
| ▪ Clarify methods to deliver services | ▪ Document successful operations | ▪ Diversify resources, including funding |
| ▪ Build image in community | ▪ Attend to longer-range planning | ▪ Share learning with other people and organizations |
| ▪ Build infrastructure and lay groundwork for future sustainability | ▪ Implement and polish plans | ▪ Expand services, especially new services to new clients |
| | ▪ Expand evaluations and accountabilities, and capture learnings | ▪ Seek to successfully duplicate model elsewhere |
| | ▪ Systematize major functions, including systematic plans | ▪ Attend to even longer-range planning |
| | | ▪ Manage change and transformation |

# Types of Community Needs Met by Nonprofits

The types of needs served by nonprofits are so wide-ranging as to be impractical to identify completely. However, the following major categories of needs are rather common.

- Arts
- Civic affairs
- Economic development
- Education
- Environment

- Health
- Literary
- Religion
- Scientific
- Social services (or human services)

# Diversity of Board Structures

It is important to realize the various structures in which Board members choose to organize themselves. Otherwise, you might encounter a nonprofit Board that is not organized in a structure with which you are familiar. As a result, you might get confused and even make strong recommendations that do not suit the particular design of the Board. Board members might conclude that you are inexperienced with Boards and, thus, you can lose a great deal of credibility.

Members of a Board of Directors usually choose to organize themselves and operate a certain way. Hopefully, they make that choice in an intentional way, as a result of careful planning. Whatever structure the members end up using often has great influence over how members work together to govern the organization and how staff might interact with them. Therefore, it is important to have some basic understanding of the various structures from which Board members might choose to operate. Some are quite informal and loosely structured, and others are formal and highly structured. There is no one "perfect" Board design for all types of nonprofits.

## *Working Governing Board (Administrative Governing Board)*

In a "working" Board, Board members attend to the top-level strategic matters of the organization, and at the same time attend to the day-to-day matters of the organization. This structure often arises when the organization is just getting started, cannot afford staff or prefers to operate completely on a volunteer basis. The nature of this Board structure is usually rather flexible and informal. Board members and staff (if the nonprofit has staff) work together to do whatever they can. Ideally, Board members remember that they are responsible for the governance of the organization and develop the organization's plans (although too often not strategic in nature) and policies. They might conduct Board operations in the form of Board committees. Many times, there is no Chief Executive Officer role in the organization. In that case, Board members need to be aware of which "hat" they are currently wearing, be it Board member of volunteer staff member.

## *Policy Governing Board*

A "policy" Board is often viewed as more "mature," having passed through the "working" Board stage. For example, on a policy Board, paid and/or volunteer staff members have been recruited and organized. Thus, Board members attend primarily to strategic matters, while staff members attend to day-to-day matters. The definitive characteristic of a policy Board is the presence of a variety of Board committees and a Chief Executive Officer who reports to the Board.

## *Policy Governance® Board*

The structure of the Policy Governance® Board is designed to ensure that Board members always operate in a fashion that maintains strong, strategic focus for the organization. Members of this Board structure focus on policies that determine the "ends" for the organization to achieve and leave the "means" up to the staff to decide. Board members set limits within which the Chief Executive Officer operates, for example, financially or strategically. This structure is characterized by few, if any, distinct officer roles or Board committees. ("Policy Governance" is a registered trademark of Carver Governance Design, Inc.)

## Collective Board

The "collective" Board is the epitome of a "team" effort. Board members and staff share equal responsibility in deciding strategic matters and carrying them out, as well. This type of Board is often popular among cultures that highly value equality and power sharing for the good of the community.

## Other Board Structures

There are other structures too. Church Boards tend to be organized and operate according to the regulations of its particular church law. School Boards are often highly structured Boards that resemble policy Boards, but not always. Other local community Boards, for example, Chambers of Commerce, can have their own way of operating as well.

Member-driven Boards, such as those in associations, vest authority in the members of the association to staff the Board and approve major policies from the Board. In those situations, members usually provide their preferences and approvals during the association's annual meeting.

In any Board structure, it is important for Board members to realize that the law sees them as maintaining a legal responsibility and public trust to ensure that the nonprofit operates according to its mission – a mission to meet a community need in accordance with applicable laws and regulations.

# Organization Chart of Typical Start-Up Nonprofit

It is common that a start-up nonprofit organization has one major program carried out by a hands-on group of volunteers, some of whom act as the Board of Directors and others who act as staff. Both groups might be involved in providing services to clients. A new nonprofit often does not include the role of Chief Executive Officer.

Note that there is no certain standard that suggests whether a nonprofit is categorized as small, medium or large in size. However, conventionally, small nonprofits usually have no paid staff or only one or two programs.

Also note that the charts on this and the following pages are functional in design. Functional design of organizations is based on a top-down hierarchy of positions. Certainly, there are other designs of nonprofit organizations that do not follow this design. For example, self-organizing organizations might have different forms at various times, depending on the strategic priorities and culture of the organization.

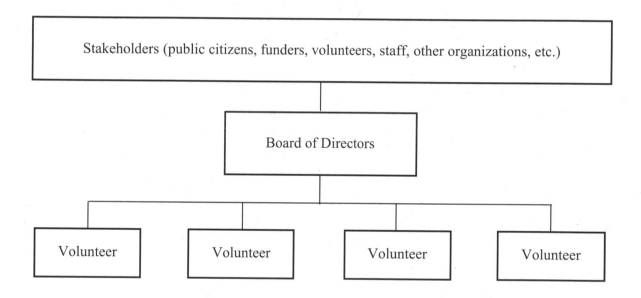

## Organization Chart of Typical Small Nonprofit with CEO

A nonprofit might have a part-time or full-time Chief Executive Officer (CEO) in a paid or volunteer position. If the nonprofit has staff in addition to the CEO, the CEO supervises the other staff members, who also might be part-time or full-time, and occupy paid or volunteer positions. The CEO reports to a Board of Directors comprised of volunteers, and the Board members supervise the CEO.

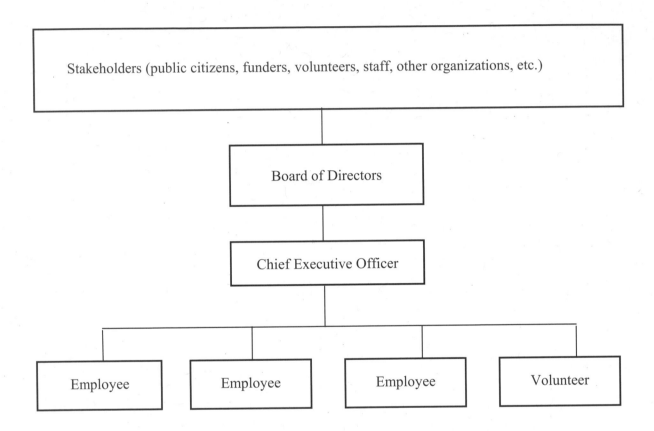

## Organization Chart of Typical Medium-to-Large Sized Nonprofit

An organization like this usually has a paid Chief Executive Officer, often on a full-time basis, and who supervises various staff members, again who might be paid on a full-time or part-time basis. Staff might also include volunteers. The Chief Executive Officer reports to a Board of Directors comprised of volunteers, and the Board supervises the CEO. This nonprofit often has more than one program, is managed by employees, and is staffed by employees or volunteers.

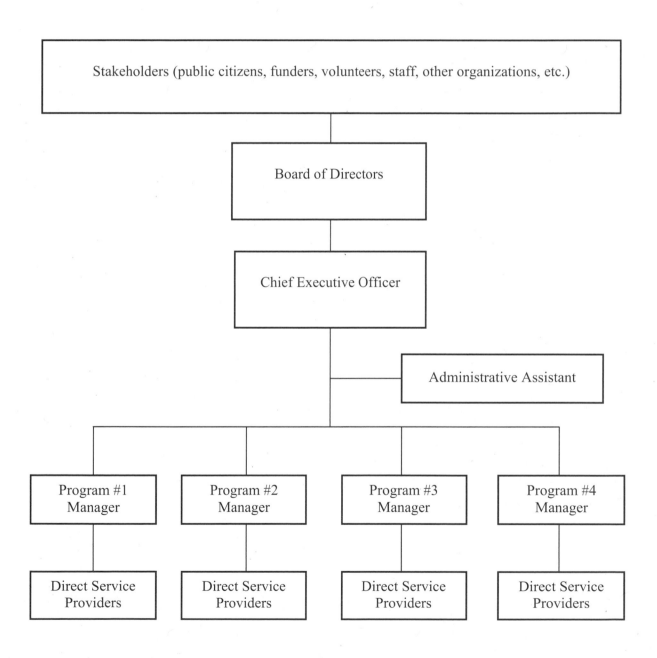

# Nonprofit Programs, Configurations and Types

As an organizational consultant, it is important for you to have some sense about what a nonprofit program really is.

## Discerning Programs from Activities

### Activities

Activities are a set of events that, although they are or seem beneficial to the community, are so loosely or informally conducted that it is difficult to readily ascertain if the events are truly needed by the community and/or are making any substantive difference in the community.

There are many types of activities that can be useful to a community, even someone standing on a corner and handing out food to whomever happens to walk by. On first impression, that event might seem beneficial to the community. However, without knowing whether the food is safe, whether those walking by really need the food or not, or whether handing out the food on the corner is the best means to provide the food, it is difficult to ascertain whether the event deserves the ongoing investment of resources from the community.

### Programs

A nonprofit program is an integrated set of services conducted to meet specific, verified community need(s) by achieving certain specific outcomes among specific group(s) of clients in that community. Services include ongoing systematic evaluations, as much as possible, to ensure that the specific outcomes are indeed being achieved and that the community's resources are best invested in that particular program.

The community need and the services to meet that need are verified by more than anecdotal evidence – by using credible, valid means of research to collect information and make conclusions. Information is collected from primary sources (those persons in need, community leaders, etc.) and, as much as possible, from secondary sources (census data, other established program models, etc.).

The research and conclusions together suggest a concise, systematic "theory of action" or "chain of events" that, in turn, suggests and explains why the new program will work – or how the established program works as it does. The theory of action may require program personnel to specifically define and/or set parameters around certain key terms, for example, "leadership" or "youth."

In essence, a well-designed program is similar to a well-designed research project from which a community can benefit and a great deal can be learned. Common examples of nonprofit programs are food-shelf programs, transportation programs, training programs, health services programs and arts programs.

Nonprofits often define their programs during strategic planning. Programs become major methods, or strategies, to reach strategic goals. For example, a nonprofit might have a mission to "Enhance the quality of life for young adults by promoting literacy." Major strategies, or programs, to work toward that mission might be a High School Equivalency Training Program and a Transportation Program to get the young adults to the Training Program.

The typical nonprofit organizational structure is built around programs. Two other major aspects of the nonprofit structure are its governance (the Board and, for some, the Chief Executive Officer) and its central administration. The Board oversees the entire nonprofit organization. The central administration exists to use the nonprofit's common resources primarily to ensure each program is developed and operated effectively.

## *Program Configurations*

Programs have two major types of configurations, including:

1.      Free-standing program, where the program's services are delivered completely within the context of the program.

2.      Multi-program effort, where two or more programs are tightly integrated to provide a common set of services to meet one, major unmet need in the community.

The organizations that provide programs can be:

1.      Free-standing, where a program, or multi-program effort, is provided completely within the context of one organization.

2.      Multi-organization (or collaborative) effort, where a program, or integration of programs, is provided by two or more organizations that work closely together to meet a major, unmet need in the community.

 To learn more about nonprofit programs, see the recommended list of resources on page 506.

# Various Approaches to Building Programs

There are at least five different common approaches to developing a new nonprofit program. Each of the approaches is described in the rest of this topic. Some approaches seem to start out slow and soon stop altogether. Other approaches start out fast and then end in a flurry of confusion. Still, other approaches start out carefully and go on to make a huge difference for their clients. The approach you use depends on various factors.

Note that sometimes the approach to development of a new nonprofit organization is essentially the same as the approach to development of its new program, particularly if the organization is new or only has one program. In that case, it might be difficult to detect any difference between the approaches to developing the overall organization and its new program. Whether it is a new organization or a new program, the development process depends on several factors.

1.      **The nature and complexity of the organization's programs and services**
        For example, the process to develop a program that provides mental health services would probably be more complex than the process to develop a program that provides a food shelf to low-income families.

2.      **The resources and stability of the overall organization**
        For example, if the organization has been in operation for several years and its current programs have been using the same processes and procedures over those years, the organization probably has more accurate and reliable processes from which to design new or

139

related programs. On the other hand, if the organization is relatively new, it likely has limited expertise and resources from which to design programs.

3. **The extent of program development expertise in the organization**
   It is not surprising to find that many nonprofit leaders have little, if any, formal training in developing programs. There have been few comprehensive resources in this regard. Many nonprofits have resorted simply to doing whatever seems reasonable for the day, while collecting as many resources as possible and hoping that they will be useful.

Following are descriptions of five common approaches to developing nonprofit programs. The nature of the approaches can overlap somewhat.

## *"Build It and They Will Come" Approach*

This approach is common to new nonprofit organizations, especially if their founder is rather inexperienced in program development, in conducting marketing analysis, and/or has a strong passion – even an obsession – about meeting a perceived need in the community. In these situations, the founder believes that there is an unmet need in the community. He bases his belief almost entirely on his own perception, even though there is sometimes no verified evidence of a strong unmet need. In this approach, the founder:

1. On his own, designs a method (often a roughly designed program) to meet the need that they perceive in the community.

2. Applies for funding to a donation source (individuals, corporations, foundations or the government) and is turned down due to lack of evidence that the perceived unmet need really exists.

3. Advertises the program to the community, usually through word-of-mouth, flyers, brochures and direct mailings.

4. Experiences a great deal of frustration that most of the people having the perceived unmet need do not flock to the program.

5. Substantially increases the advertising throughout the community.

6. Continues to experience frustration that most of the people having the unmet need do not flock to the program.

7. Either abandons the effort or, if the unmet need really does exist, persists and accomplishes the seat-of-the-pants approach to program development. The program, however, often suffers from Founder's Syndrome, where the nonprofit is operated according to the personality of someone in the organization (usually the founder), rather than according to the mission of the organization.

## *Seat-of-the-Pants Approach*

This approach is common to many new nonprofit organizations, especially if their founders are rather inexperienced in organizational development and management. In these situations, the nonprofit organization and its primary program are so highly integrated that it is difficult to discern what resources go directly into providing services to clients versus those resources needed to run the entire organization. The seat-of-the-pants program development process usually parallels the development of the organization itself, and might best be described to include the following steps:

1.      A person realizes a major, unmet need in the community. The person starts doing whatever they can to meet the need, mostly through their own efforts.

2.      The person realizes that they cannot do it all, and/or others start to chip in and help the person. Over time, all the people involved start to agree on who is going to do what to be more efficient. At this point in the program, all the participants are often still volunteers.

3.      Over time, some or all of the people realize that they need more help, including money, to continue to meet the community need. To get funding, they usually start to form a nonprofit corporation by filing Articles of Incorporation, usually with the Secretary of State's office in their state. Filing for incorporation requires that the nonprofit have a Board of Directors. They are soon granted the status of nonprofit corporation. Next, they often seek tax-exempt status from the Internal Revenue Service so they do not have to pay federal taxes. So they apply for tax-exempt status and may eventually get tax-deductible/charitable status, too.

4.      They continue to work to meet the major need in the community, while they continue to organize themselves, usually by having a volunteer Chief Executive Officer and other volunteers.

5.      As mentioned earlier in this guide, organizations go through life cycles. Nonprofit organizations and/or programs rarely get through the first life cycle until they have established the necessary processes and structures to sustain continued growth. Hopefully, the nonprofit realizes that they need yet more planning and organization of resources to meet the community need in a more effective and efficient fashion. If they do not achieve this realization, they can succumb to Founder's Syndrome.

6.      At this point, whether the nonprofit achieves more organization of its resources or not, it has developed a program geared to meet the unmet need of the community. The program development approach was somewhat seat-of-the-pants in nature – people scraped the program together by doing whatever they had to and whenever they had to do it. The program just kind of came together.

While this seat-of-the-pants approach often works when first developing a nonprofit organization, it certainly is not the best way to go forward or to add other programs.

## Incremental Planning Approach

People can probably develop a new program without having to resort to the high-risk, seat-of-the-pants approach or to a more comprehensive, in-depth process if:

1.      They know their client needs well (they should be careful about assuming that they do!),

2.      They plan to meet those needs by using program methods with which they are familiar, and

3.      The cost and risk of starting the new program are quite low.

If the above conditions are true, they can develop their new program with a straightforward plan that specifies:

1.    Outcomes and/or goals for the new program to achieve.

2.    Program methods or activities to accomplish those goals.

3.    Any minor changes that must be made to current programs in order to implement the new program methods.

4.    Who is responsible to implement the program methods and make the minor changes.

5.    Timelines for achievement of the goals.

6.    Budget that lists the funds necessary to obtain the resources required to achieve the goals.

## Business Planning Approach

There are a variety of views, formats and content regarding business plans. Usually, a business plan includes careful analyses of:

1.    A major unmet need in the community.

2.    Program method(s) to meet the need.

3.    How the community and nonprofit can engage in a productive, ongoing relationship where the nonprofit program continues to meet the community need and the community, in turn, returns sufficient value to the nonprofit.

4.    How the program methods can be implemented and managed.

5.    What the costs are to build and implement the program methods.

Usually, the business plan includes contents that are organized into several other subordinate (or smaller) plans, including a marketing plan, management plan and financial plan.

You might have recognized that a business plan is essentially the same as a well-written fundraising proposal; thus, it might be said that the more you use a business-planning approach in your program development, the more probable it is that you will get funds from donors.

Particularly in the for-profit world, bankers and other investors often require a business plan because the plan includes a careful look at all aspects of a project. Business planning is often conducted when:

- Expanding a current organization, product or service.

- Starting a new organization, product or service.

- Buying an organization, product or service.

- Working to improve the management of a current organization, product or service.

People should do a business plan for a nonprofit program if any of the following conditions exist:

1.    The nature of the program is new to the organization.

2.      They will need funding to develop and operate the program.

3.      They are not familiar with the program's clients and their needs.

4.      They are not completely sure how to meet their needs.

## *Business Development Approach*

> *"Nonprofits have to recognize that they are businesses, not just causes. There is a way to combine the very best of the not-for-profit, philanthropic world with the very best of the for-profit, enterprising world. This hybrid is the wave of the future for both profit and nonprofit companies."*

> From *Genius at Work*, an interview with Bill Strickland, CEO of Manchester Craftsmen's Guide and the Bidwell Training Center

A new trend in nonprofit program planning is focus on nonprofit business development, which might take program planning to an even higher level of quality than that done in business planning. Note that nonprofit business development includes the business planning process so, technically, it is not a completely different alternative to business planning. However, business development usually includes more upfront, rigorous examination for numerous opportunities to provide products and services among a variety of stakeholders to generate revenue and still work toward the mission of the organization. Business development often helps groups of clients identify new needs that they did not even realize, whereas processes that start right away with business planning are based on one currently known, particular need among clients without rigorous analysis for many other opportunities. Business development is quite market-driven, whereas business planning can be quite program-driven. Andy Horsnell, co-founder of Authenticity Consulting, LLC, describes the main phases in the business development process, including:

1.      Clarifying the current, overall situation of the nonprofit and its external environment, particularly to ensure a solid base from which to develop current or new programs.

2.      Inventorying the assets and capabilities of the nonprofit, particularly those that can contribute toward developing current or new programs.

3.      Brainstorming, screening and selecting a short list of opportunities in which to sell products or services, particularly those that might be used to deliver more of current programs to current clients, new programs to current clients, current programs to new clients, and new programs to new clients.

4.      Researching the short list for feasibility and selecting the most appropriate opportunities, including careful consideration to likely sales and profitability, business models, payers and competitors, processes and materials required to develop each idea, and the influence of laws and regulations.

5.      Strategizing and planning to implement the selected opportunities, including developing a business plan.

6.      Implementing the plan and adjusting it to reality.

## *Program Building Approaches Compared to Good Program Management*

You should realize that the business planning and business development approaches are usually much more comprehensive and in-depth than the "build it and they will come" and seat-of-the-pants approaches to program development. The business planning and business development approaches form the foundation for good program management because the approaches are likely to ensure:

- More accurate understanding of community needs.

- Higher quality of service by focusing on what you do best.

- More effective and efficient operations in your organization.

- Increased financial resources, notably through increased mission-related earned income.

- Better use of financial resources.

- More freedom and choices of resources to meet community needs.

- Improved coordination between Board and staff.

- Better relationships with clients and other external stakeholders.

- Enhanced credibility with clients and funders.

So, rather than thinking of business planning or business development as processes to develop programs, you might benefit best from thinking of the business planning and business development processes as activities required for good program management.

# Context-Sensitive Features – What Makes Each Nonprofit Unique

All organizations are systems and all systems have similar features. Yet, there are aspects of these features that can make systems act differently, at different times. It is critical for you to recognize these differences when you are working with your clients to identify organizational issues and how to address them.

The following list includes some major considerations for you to address when attempting to identify the unique aspects of your client's organization. It includes brief descriptions of some of the most important considerations. (Guidelines to address those considerations are integrated throughout PART IV.)

1.  **Culture of the organization**
    You would work differently with your client's organization, depending on the organization's culture. An organization's culture is similar to its overall "personality." For example, some nonprofit organizations operate in a highly "business-like" fashion with extensive formality of rules and regulations. Other organizations pride themselves on operating in a highly informal, relaxed fashion.

2.  **Life cycle of the organization**
    The particular life cycle of a nonprofit can make a big difference in how consulting should be carried out because organizations often operate differently during different life cycle stages. For example, the nature of their planning, policies and procedures can change substantially between stages.

    > See "Life Cycles of Organizations and Programs" on page 130 for more information about life cycles of organizations and how to identify them.

3.  **Size of the organization**
    The larger the organization, the sometimes more complex the nature of its issues and the more complex the actions needed to address those issues. Consultants usually consider the size in terms of the number of programs and personnel (employees and volunteers) because those features are most often associated with specific organizational issues. Sometimes people consider the size of the budget. However, that can be misleading because a small organization might have a large "pass through" grant about which another organization actually does the work to meet the requirements of that grant.

4.  **Source of the top-level leadership**
    For example, if the source of leadership in a nonprofit is the Board (the nonprofit is Board-driven), then you will need to carefully consider the role of the Board in your project. Although theory and law assert that Boards are to govern corporations (whether nonprofit or for-profit), experienced consultants have learned that, in many cases, the senior staff members actually facilitate the Board members to do their jobs. In staff-driven nonprofits, you will need to carefully consider the role of the Chief Executive Officer in your project.

5.  **Style of the leadership used by your current client**
    You learned in PART I that you might have different clients at different times in the same project. In this paragraph, consider your client to be the person with whom you are currently working most closely to set direction and follow that direction in the project. As much as possible, you should accommodate to your client's style of leadership. There is a variety of leadership styles to consider, ranging from highly involved to detached, and from highly directive to highly participative.

6.  **Structure and strategies of the organization**
    In this context, strategies refer to the overall approaches used by the organization to effectively meet the needs of its external environment, especially the needs of its clients and stakeholders. Those approaches include how the organization identifies the environment's needs and then uses its resources (for example, programs, people and facilities) to meet those needs. The structures are the result of the organization's overall strategies (the principle that "form follows function"). Structures include organizational design, policies, plans, procedures and roles. There are numerous types of nonprofits and although they might be similar in terms of other context-sensitive features, they are different from other types of nonprofits. For example, arts organizations have their own similar nature, as do community development corporations, libraries, grassroots, associations and churches.

7.  **Rate of change in the external environment**
    Certain types of nonprofit services are in the midst of tremendous change. Often, the faster the rate of change in the external environment, the more that your projects will need to focus on helping your clients recognize and guide change in their organizations, as well.

145

# Understanding Nonprofits as Open Systems

Before you can change a system, you need to understand it. Fortunately, there have been recent, major breakthroughs in helping people to closely examine and understand systems, including the systems in and around organizations. As a result, we have come to view organizations from a new perspective – a systems perspective.

The systems perspective may, at times, seem quite basic. Yet, decades of organizational and management development activities have not worked from a systems perspective. Only recently, with tremendous changes facing organizations and how they operate, have we come to embrace this new way of looking at organizations and their various parts and processes. As a result, the systems perspective has brought about a significant change (or paradigm shift) in the way that people understand and resolve problems in organizations.

Another level of understanding can be gained by working from an open systems perspective, which considers: 1) the subsystems in the organization, 2) the system of the overall organization, and 3) the various influences and interactions between the organization and its environment.

The following two subsections might seem somewhat theoretical in nature. Yet, from reading and fully understanding them, you will learn how to see – and work with – the "big picture" of nonprofit organizations and how they interact with their environments.

## What Is a System?

Simply put, a system is an organized collection of parts that are highly integrated to accomplish an overall goal. The system has various inputs, which go through certain processes to produce certain outputs, which together, accomplish the overall desired goal for the system.

Note that a system is usually made up of many smaller systems, or subsystems. For example, a nonprofit organization is made up of programs, groups and people. If one part of the system is changed, the nature of the overall system is changed, as well.

Systems range from simple to complex. There are numerous types of systems. For example, there are biological systems (for example, the heart), mechanical systems (for example, a thermostat), human/mechanical systems (for example, riding a bicycle), ecological systems (for example, predator/prey) and social systems (for example, groups, supply and demand and also friendship).

Complex systems, such as social systems, are comprised of numerous subsystems, as well. These subsystems are arranged in hierarchies, and integrated to accomplish the overall goal of the overall system. Each subsystem has its own boundaries of sorts, and includes various inputs, processes, outputs and outcomes geared to accomplish an overall goal for the subsystem. Complex systems usually interact with their environments and are, thus, open systems.

A high-functioning system continually exchanges feedback among its various parts to ensure that they remain closely aligned and focused on achieving the goal of the system. If any of the parts or activities in the system seems weakened or misaligned, the system makes necessary adjustments to more effectively achieve its goals. Consequently, a system is systematic.

A pile of sand is not a system. If you remove a sand particle, you have still got a pile of sand. However, a functioning car is a system. Remove the carburetor and you have no longer got a working car.

 See "Systems Thinking, Chaos Theory and Tools" on page 507 in Appendix D for recommended readings to understand more about chaos theory.

## Inputs

Inputs are items that are used by the various processes in the system to achieve the overall goal of the system. General types of inputs include, for example, people, money, equipment, facilities, supplies, people's ideas and people's time. Types of inputs to a nonprofit program that provides training to clients might include trained teachers, clients, training materials, classrooms, funding, and paper and pencils. Inputs can also be major forces that influence the organization and its programs. For example, various laws and regulations influence how the program is operated. Inputs are often identified with the cost to obtain and use them. Simply put, a program's budget is a listing of the program's inputs and the costs (expenses) to obtain and use them, along with any monies expected to be earned or raised (revenues).

## Processes (Methods to Produce Results)

Processes, or activities, are series of activities conducted by the organization or program that manipulate the various inputs to achieve the overall desired goal of the organization or program. For example, the major processes used by a nonprofit program that provides training to clients might include recruitment of clients, pre-testing, training, post-testing and certification. Processes can range from the simplicity of putting a piece of paper on a desk to the complexity of manufacturing a space shuttle. Nonprofit leaders are usually concerned primarily with the most important recurring processes in the organization, for example, its plans, programs, policies and procedures.

Some nonprofit experts, especially fundraisers, often refer to the processes as the program "activities," "methods" or "throughputs."

## Outputs (Tangible Results)

Outputs are the tangible results produced by the organization or any of its various programs. Outputs are often described by using numbers, for example, the number of clients who finished a certain program. Outputs are often mistaken to indicate the success of an organization or one of its programs. For example, nonprofit leaders might mistakenly assume that because a program served a large number of clients, the program must have been quite successful. That is not a valid assumption. The success of a nonprofit organization or program is determined, not by the range and number of clients trained (the program's outputs), but by how the clients benefited that training (the program's outcomes, described later on below).

## Goals (Desired Results)

Goals are the ultimate results that the system wants to accomplish. All systems are goal-directed. For example, plants, animals and people strive to stay alive and to replicate themselves. Nonprofit organizations and programs must have clear goals, as well. It is important for leaders to establish goals and thoroughly communicate them throughout the organization.

The overall goals of the nonprofit organization are usually described in terms of its mission, or purpose. In addition, many nonprofits often associate a vision, or clear depiction, of what the nonprofit or its clients will look like when working successfully at some point in the future. The mission, vision and strategic goals are usually determined during strategic planning. Thus, strategic planning is an important responsibility of the role of nonprofit leader.

Note that an organization can have goals in a variety of dimensions, for example, goals regarding activities of the organization, activities of clients or impacts on clients (these impacts are often referred to as program outcomes – see below).

## Feedback

Feedback is continuously exchanged among the various parts of a nonprofit organization and its programs and, ideally, with the environment external to the organization, as well. Feedback comes from a variety of sources, for example, from external stakeholders (clients, community leaders, funders), Board members, the Chief Executive Officer and other staff. Feedback can also come from evaluations of the organization, programs and personnel. This ongoing feedback, or communication, is absolutely critical to the success of the organization and its programs. A nonprofit has to continually include ongoing feedback within the organization and with its environment.

## Assessment and Evaluation

Assessment means to make some measurement from the feedback. Evaluation means collecting information, or feedback, in an orderly manner and making judgments to make important decisions. An effective nonprofit is continually collecting and assessing feedback to evaluate effectiveness in the organization. Often, assessment and evaluation are focused on various outputs, or measures, from the system. Evaluation in nonprofits can be focused on the entire organization or any of its subsystems, including programs, groups, processes or employees. Evaluation can be with regard to the quality of ongoing activities in the organization (formative evaluation) or the activities final results (summative evaluation).

## Learning

Learning is enhanced knowledge, skills and attitudes that are gained to remain or become more effective in achieving desired results. Learning occurs within people and, ideally, within groups, processes and the organization itself. Learning often is the result of the assessment and evaluation of feedback in and around the organization. People in and around nonprofits often speak of "capacity building," the activities to strengthen the effectiveness of organizations to work toward their various missions. Learning is critical because it ensures that the organization is continually improving its understanding of itself and its environment.

# What Is an Open System?

An open system is a system that regularly exchanges feedback with its external environment. Open systems are systems, of course, so inputs, processes, outputs, goals, assessment and evaluation, and learning are all important. Aspects that are critically important to open systems include the boundaries, external environment and equifinality.

Healthy open systems continuously exchange feedback with their environments, analyze that feedback, adjust internal systems as needed to achieve the system's goals, and then transmit necessary information back out to the environment.

See "Overview of the Open System of a Nonprofit Organization" on page 150 for a depiction of the open system of a nonprofit organization.

## Boundaries

All systems have boundaries, although the boundaries can be difficult to identify because systems can be very dynamic.  Open systems have porous boundaries through which useful feedback can readily be exchanged and understood.

Closed systems, unlike open systems, have hard boundaries through which little information is exchanged.  Organizations that have closed boundaries often are unhealthy.  Examples include bureaucracies, monopolies and stagnating systems.

## External Environment

The external environment includes a wide variety of needs and influences that can affect the nonprofit, but which the nonprofit cannot directly control.  Influences can be political, economic, ecological, societal and technological in nature.  For example, there is a wide range of community needs that affect how the nonprofit chooses and designs its programs to meet those needs.

A highly effective nonprofit is regularly exchanging feedback with its external environment – it is an open system.  Healthy nonprofits regularly try to understand their environments through use of environmental scanning, market research and program evaluations.  These nonprofits often try to influence their external environment, as well, for example, through use of public relations, advertising and promotions, lobbying and advocacy, and educating community leaders about those needs.

## Outcomes (Results Among Program Participants)

Program outcomes are critically important to the success of nonprofit.  Outcomes are in regard to the changes that participants accomplish as a result of participating in a certain program.  Outcomes are usually specified in terms of changed:

1.      Knowledge (usually short-term outcomes).

2.      Behaviors, notably those that comprise useful skills (often intermediate outcomes).

3.      Attitudes, values and conditions, such as increased security, stability or pride (usually long-term outcomes).

Some examples of outcomes from a program are when clients accomplish the ability to read, live alone or drive a car.  Notice the difference between program outcomes (measures of changes in clients) and outputs (measure of activities in programs).

### *Equifinality (More Than One Way to Accomplish the Same Result)*

Equifinality means that the same or similar results can be achieved by using a variety of different processes. For example, management can achieve the same results by using different inputs or by using different processes with the same inputs. Equifinality suggests that there is no one right way to accomplish important results in an organization.

In contrast, closed systems have one right way to do things. For example, in heavily bureaucratic organizations, a person must finish the necessary procedures regardless of how useful an intended result will be for the organization – the focus is on doing things right, rather than doing the right things.

The concept of equifinality explains why there is no one right way to lead or manage organizations. It explains why there is no one right way to guide organizational change. You should keep this in mind when adopting various solutions-based best practices, diagnostic models and assessment tools.

## Overview of the Open System of a Nonprofit Organization

The graphic on the following page depicts the overall open system of a nonprofit organization. In the following depiction, remember that the general flow of activities in the system is in a large loop or cycle. Each phase exchanges feedback (for evaluation and learning) with other phases and, as a result, some phases are changed and/or repeated in the overall cycle. Remember that the following graphic is a model of the workings of a system. Do not confuse the graphic to be the actual system of a nonprofit organization.

# Table II:7 – Overview of the Open System of a Nonprofit Organization

| Goals | Goals | Goals | Goals |
|---|---|---|---|

**Inputs**

Standard materials and concepts used by a nonprofit, for example:

- People
- Ideas
- Time
- Money
- Facilities
- Technologies
- Clients
- Location
- Collaborators
- Etc.

**Processes**

Subsystems to process the inputs and generate outputs and outcomes, for example, activities of:

- Individuals
- Teams
- Projects
- Programs
- Processes (cross-functional)
- Functions

**Outputs**

Tangible results from the organization or program, for example, the amount of:

- Trained clients
- Courses
- Books
- Reports
- Revenue
- Fixed cars
- Patients
- Etc.

**Outcomes**

Impacts on clients (in the external environment) from participating in program, such as:

- Employed clients
- Literate clients
- Independent clients
- Healthy clients
- Adopted clients
- Mobile clients
- Etc.

**Feedback Between All Parts and External Environment for Evaluation, Learning and Adaptation**

Feedback in from the environment is especially from standard inputs, environmental scanning, market research and program evaluations. Feedback out to the environment is especially from outputs, public relations, advertising and promotions, and outcomes.

151

# Benefits of Open Systems View of Nonprofits

Today, consultants and clients are learning to more clearly recognize the various parts and processes of the nonprofit organization, and, in particular, their inter-relationships and alignment, for example, the coordination between the Board and the Chief Executive Officer, or integration between the Strategic Plan and other plans. Understanding of inter-relationships and alignment is not only about parts and processes within the system, but also to the system and its environment – an "open systems" approach.

Consultants and clients now focus much more attention on the feedback among the various major parts and processes in the nonprofit and between the nonprofit and its environment. Consultants examine problems, not just by focusing on what appears to be separate parts, but on the larger patterns of interactions within the parts. They focus on structures that provoke behaviors that determine events – rather than reacting to events as was done in the past. They maintain perspective on performance by focusing on the outcomes that the nonprofit wants to achieve, particularly in its external environment.

The following paragraphs itemize some of the major benefits when looking at your clients' nonprofit organizations from an open systems perspective.

## More Effective Problem Solving

Without clear understanding of the "big picture" of a nonprofit organization, consultants and nonprofit leaders tend to focus only on the behaviors and events associated with problems in the workplace, rather than on the systems and structures that caused the problems to occur in the first place. To effectively solve problems in any type of organization, it is critical to be able to identify the real causes of the problems and how to address those causes. A systems view provides clear understanding of the "big picture."

## More Effective Leadership

The most important responsibilities of a leader are to set direction and to influence others to follow that direction. It is difficult to establish direction for an organization and to keep that organization on its course if you do not understand how the organization works in the first place. Without a clear understanding of the overall nature and needs of an organization, the leader can get lost in the day-to-day activities, never really giving attention to the more important activities, such as planning the organization's overall direction and organizing their resources. As a result, the leader "cannot see the forest for the trees." The leader ends up working harder, rather than smarter. A systems view helps the leader to really understand the overall structures and dynamics of the nonprofit and what must be done to guide the nonprofit towards it strategic vision and goals.

## More Effective Communication

One of the most important ingredients for the success of any system is ongoing feedback, or communication, among all the parts of the organization. Some of the first symptoms that an organization or consulting project is in trouble are sporadic and insufficient communication. In these situations, people often struggle to see beyond their own roles in the organization or project. Consequently, people are much less effective than they could be otherwise. Without a clear understanding of the parts of an organization or project and how they relate to each other, it is difficult to know what to communicate and to whom.

## More Effective Planning

The planning process is basically working one's way backwards through the system of an organization or project. It includes identifying desired results (goals and outcomes), what outputs (tangible results) will indicate that those results have been achieved, what processes will produce those outputs, and what inputs are required to conduct those processes in the system. A systems view often makes the planning process much more clear and orderly to planners.

## More Effective Design of Projects and Programs

An advantage for project and program designers who have a systems view is that they have stronger knowledge of the primary parts of their project or program and how they should be aligned to more effectively reach desired goals. A systems view also promotes focus on achieving overall results, so the day-to-day details of the project or program do not become the most important activities for people to address – so people do not become focused in matters that are urgent, rather than important.

## More Effective Organizational Results

The most successful projects and organizations often use a variety of methods to achieve results. In projects, methods can include, for example, coaching, facilitating, training or provision of resources. In organizations, methods can include strategic planning, program development, management and leadership development, team building, supervisory development, organizational and employee performance management, and principles of organizational change. Any consultant or leader would be hard-pressed to employ these various methods in an effective fashion without a good understanding of the overall systems of their project or organization. Consequently, having a systems view is critical to accomplishing successful results.

## Avoid Founder's Syndrome

Founder's Syndrome occurs when an organization operates primarily according to the personality of one of the members of the organization (usually the founder), rather than according to the mission (purpose) of the organization. When first starting their organizations, founders often have to do whatever it takes to get the organizations off the ground, including making seat-of-the-pants decisions to deal with frequent crises that suddenly arise in the workplace. As a result, founders often struggle to see the larger picture and are unable to suitably plan to make more proactive decisions. Consequently, the organization gets stalled in a highly reactive mode characterized by lack of funds and having to deal with one major crisis after another. The best "cure" for this syndrome is developing broader understanding of the structures and processes of an organization, with an appreciation for the importance of planning.

# Overview of the Open System of a Nonprofit Program

## Logic Models – Depictions of Systems

The previous subsection described how you can understand and portray the overall open system of any organization, including a nonprofit. The format of that portrayal is called a logic model. A logic model can be a powerful tool to understand and analyze your client's organization or any of its programs. The benefits of doing a logic model about a program are essentially the same as the benefits of having a systems view of an organization.

The level of detail in a logic model is usually sufficient that you can grasp the major inputs that go into the system, what processes occur to those inputs, the various outputs produced by the system, and the overall benefits (or outcomes) that occur for the clients or customers who have participated in the system.

A logic model depicts only the major, recurring processes in the system, rather than the one-time processes. For example, it does not include the initial activities to build the program, such as "construct the building" and "register with appropriate government authorities." The logic model depicts primarily the processes required to manipulate the various inputs to produce the desired outputs and outcomes, for example, "hold training sessions for clients," or "conduct certification assessments of clients."

The size of the logic model is usually such that readers can easily study the model without extensive reference and cross-comparisons among many pages. Ideally, the logic model is one or two pages long.

The graphic on the following page depicts the logic model of a sample nonprofit program. As noted previously, the graphic is a model – or simulated depiction – of the workings of a program. Do not confuse the graphic to be the actual system of a nonprofit program.

Logic models are extremely important tools for consultants to nonprofit organizations to understand and utilize, especially for identifying program outcomes. One of the best resources available is *Measuring Program Outcomes: A Practical Approach* available from the United Way of America (1996).

# Table II:8 – Example of a Logic Model for a Nonprofit Program

The following example is intended to portray the scope and level of detail in a program's logic model. The model depicts a fictional program called the Self-Directed Learning Center (SDLC). The mission, or purpose, of the program is to enhance the quality of life for low-income adults by providing free, on-line training materials and programs and by helping them help each other to learn. Feedback from the environment is from inputs, environmental scanning, market research and program evaluations. Feedback to the environment is principally from public relations, advertising and promotions, outputs and outcomes.

| Inputs | Processes | Outputs | Short-Term Outcomes | Intermediate Outcomes | Long-Term Outcomes |
|---|---|---|---|---|---|
| • Collaborators<br>• Computers<br>• Free articles and other publications on the Web<br>• Funders<br>• Self-directed learners<br>• Supplies<br>• Volunteers<br>• Web | • Provide peer-assistance models in which learners support each other<br>• Provide free, on-line training program: Basics of Self-Directed Learning<br>• Provide free, on-line training program: Basic Life Skills<br>• Provide free, on-line training program: Passing Your GED Exam | • 30 groups that used peer models<br>• 100 finished training programs<br>• 900 learners who finished Basics of Self-Directed Learning<br>• 900 learners who finished Basic Life Skills<br>• 900 learners who finished Passing Your GED Exam | • High-school diploma for graduates<br>• Increased likelihood and interest for learners to attend advanced schooling | • Full-time employment for learners in jobs that require high-school education<br>• Independent living for learners from using salary to rent housing<br>• Strong basic life skills for learners | • Improved attitude toward self and society for graduates<br>• Improved family life for families of graduates<br>• Increased reliability and improved judgment of learners |

155

# Management Systems and Why You Should Understand Them

## *What Is a Management System?*

A systems perspective notices the recurring patterns and themes in a system, including its inputs, processes and outputs. It will help you a great deal when addressing issues in nonprofits, if you can develop a systems perspective on the particular management activities in those nonprofits. That view helps to ensure that you fully examine and understand all of the important aspects of activities around the issues. (Your examination will be during the phase, Discovery and Feedback, of the collaborative consulting phase.) A systems view helps you to more readily understand what might be the causes and effects of the issues. It helps you recognize how each issue might be affecting other areas of the organization, as well. Finally, it helps you generate useful recommendations to address each issue.

Each sub-system in the overall organization has its own management system. For example, there is a management system for each of the following: Board operations, CEO activities, program operations, marketing, financial management, fundraising and evaluations. Each management system has a systematic design, although members of the nonprofit may do the activities in the system in an implicit and unsystematic manner. The activities in the system do not occur together in a step-by-step, linear fashion, but are closely integrated and cyclical in nature. Ideally, the activities in the system are aligned with each other and with the external environment.

The exact activities and how they are conducted depend on the particular nonprofit organization, including whether the activities are being designed for the first time or have been in operation for a while. For example, it is common, especially for new and/or small nonprofits, to conduct activities on a rather reactive, as-needed basis, rather than on a proactive, plan-based basis.

The best management systems operate as open systems – they carefully consider inputs to their system and then adjust their management activities accordingly to produce high-quality outputs for the rest of the organization. A logic model can be used to depict a management system. After the following paragraphs, there are several examples of management systems for common types of management activities in nonprofits. There is also depiction of the overall management system for a nonprofit organization.

### Inputs

The type of inputs to each management system depends on the purpose and focus of the system. Generally, inputs are in terms of people, best practices, plans, policies, money, equipment, facilities, supplies, people's ideas and people's time. For example, inputs to the Board operations include the Strategic Plan, results of past evaluations of Board operations, annual calendar for the Board and availability of volunteers to join the Board.

### Process

The process includes four major phases: planning, developing, operating and evaluating.

#### Planning

Planning activities answer the questions: What do we want to accomplish? How do we accomplish it? What resources do we need? Examples of planning activities could include updating Board policies and procedures to set direction and make decisions, the Board Organization Chart and Board Committee work plans.

### Developing

Development activities include obtaining resources and enhancing them to be useful for achieving the desired results. Examples could include forming a Board Governance Committee to guide development of the Board, and recruiting, training and organizing new Board members.

### Operating

Operating activities include using the resources to implement the plans, such as Board members attend meetings, make decisions, guide strategic planning, supervise the CEO and participate in fundraising.

### Evaluating

Evaluation activities determine if the desired results are being achieved by the management system, such as Board members conduct an annual self-evaluation to determine the quality of activities regarding its planning, development and operations.

## Outputs

The type of outputs from each management system depends on the purpose and focus of the system. Generally, outputs are in terms of products and services for internal and external customers. For example, outputs from Board operations might include directions to the CEO, public speeches, program reviews, financial reviews, donations, minutes from Board meetings, Board decisions, Board Development Plan, and updated Board policies and procedures.

## *Overall Management System for Nonprofit Organization*

The following table depicts the overall management system for an entire nonprofit organization.

## Table II:9 – Overview of the Management System of a Nonprofit Organization

| Inputs: people, money, equipment, facilities, supplies, people's ideas, people's time, etc. | | |
|---|---|---|
| **System Loop** | **Major Functions** | **Comments** |
| **Planning** ⇕ | Strategic planning for organization (mission? vision? values? goals?) | ▪ All activities are integrated with each other. |
| | Planning for programs (similar to business planning) (clients? outcomes? services? marketing? costs?) | |
| | Resource planning (people? fundraising/revenue? technologies? other?) | ▪ Driving force behind all activities is leadership among Board and staff. |
| **Developing** ⇕ | Revenue / fundraising development (for major activities) | |
| | Board, staff and volunteer development (recruiting, training, organizing) | |
| | Development of other resources (facilities, supplies, policies, procedures, etc.) | ▪ Leadership sets direction, guides resources toward the direction, and makes adjustments to keep resources on track. |
| **Operating** ⇕ | Supervision and teamwork | |
| | Program operations | |
| | Advertising and promotions | |
| | Facilities management | |
| | Financial management | ▪ Strategic goals set direction for organization and suggest performance goals for Board and staff. |
| | Administration | |
| **Evaluating** | Board | |
| | Individuals | |
| | Programs | |
| | Processes | |
| | Organization | |
| Outputs: community needs met by nonprofit, trained Board and staff members. | | |

The following descriptions are of each of the major functions listed in the previous table, Overview of the Management System of a Nonprofit Organization. The descriptions are organized according to the four major phases of a management system.

## Planning

1.  **Strategic planning**
    Members of the Board and staff conduct strategic planning to determine the overall purpose (mission) and direction (vision and goals) for the nonprofit, as well as the methods (values, strategies and programs) for the nonprofit to work toward the purpose and direction. The strategic planning process provides input to all other major functions in the organization, especially program planning and resource planning. Thus, if strategic planning is not done well, the entire organization can be adversely effected.

2.  **Planning for programs**
    Programs are designed or refined as means to implement the service-oriented strategies from the Strategic Plan. During program planning, the marketing research (or "inbound marketing") activities are conducted to identify, for example, specific community needs for the nonprofit to meet, what outcomes are needed to meet those needs, what specific groups of clients to serve, and how to serve them to achieve those outcomes. Program planning provides input to many other functions, such as resource planning (regarding staff, funds, people), financial management, advertising and promotions, and also fundraising. Many problems commonly associated with fundraising and promotions are really the result of poor program planning.

3.  **Resource planning**
    Planners identify what resources are needed to implement the strategic and program plans. Usually, resources include people, funding, facilities, equipment, supplies, and even certain polices and procedures. Budgets usually are developed that include listings of resources that are needed, along with the estimated costs to obtain and support the use of those resources. Resource planning directly affects the quality of all operating activities because, without adequately identifying what resources are needed, major functions in the organization struggle to be effective.

## Developing

4.  **Revenue / fundraising development**
    Planning for programs specifies how much money the programs might earn (expected revenues), how much money they might cost (expected expenses) and if there are any deficits (expenses exceeding revenue) for the programs. The deficits often are addressed by fundraising. The planning for fundraising is often carried out by developing and implementing a Fundraising Plan, which specifies the overall amounts of money that must be raised, where it might be raised, how it will be raised, by who and when. If the planning for fundraising is not done systematically and comprehensively, nonprofits miss opportunities for funding and, instead, focus their fundraising activities on a few methods, for example, continued fundraising events.

5.  **Board, staff and volunteer development (leadership and management)**
    Members of the Board and staff are developed by first identifying what expertise is needed to achieve the goals in the strategic and program plans. Development activities continue by obtaining, training and organizing members to better achieve the strategic and program goals. Note that many nonprofits recruit and develop personnel as an activity somewhat

apart from their strategic and program planning activities. That approach may result in the nonprofit being run more by personalities than by plans. The results of successful development of the Board and senior staff greatly influence the success of the nonprofit because Board and staff provide the leadership that drives the entire system with its phases of planning, developing, operating and evaluating. However, strategic planning and program planning must occur before development of the Board and staff to provide direction for how they should be successfully developed.

6. **Development of other resources**

There usually is a variety of types of resources (other than money and people) that needed to be obtained and developed, for example, facilities, equipment, policies and procedures. Perhaps most important among these resources are policies and procedures. They form the "glue" that aligns and integrates the resources of money and people. If those policies and procedures are not integrated and up-to-date, they can cause inefficiencies in the operating activities. As a result, members of the organization experience increasing inefficiencies and conflicts. Successful leaders have learned to focus on developing a firm foundation of plans and policies from which their organizations can more reliably grow.

## Operating

7. **Supervision and teamwork**

A supervisor is someone who oversees the progress and productivity of people who report directly to the supervisor. Thus, a Board supervises the Chief Executive Officer, and a CEO supervises, for example, the Program Director. Teamwork is about how people work together to coordinate goals, roles, leadership and communication. The activities of supervision and teamwork are critical to the success of a nonprofit because those activities ensure that goals are established in accordance with strategic and program goals, progress toward the goals is monitored, and adjustments are made among individuals to more effectively achieve the goals. Many times, recurring problems in other types of operating activities are really symptoms of poor teamwork.

8. **Program operations**

This includes the ongoing activities that provide services directly to the clients. The nature of these activities depends on the types of needs met by the program. For example, health services often require highly trained program staff and technologies. Food shelves require large facilities to store groceries. The success of programs depends a great deal on the effectiveness of strategic and program planning and of teamwork in the organization.

9. **Advertising and promotions**

These "outbound" marketing activities are geared to inform stakeholders (clients, funders, community leaders) about new and current programs, and also to keep those programs in the minds of stakeholders. Many times, problems in advertising and promotions are the result of poor program planning, such as unclear identification of what specific groups of clients should be served, the needs of each group, and how the programs meet each need.

10. **Facilities management**

This includes identifying what major facilities will be needed, such as buildings, equipment and computer systems. The need for major facilities is identified during resource planning. Thus, problems caused by lack of facilities often are a result of poor resource planning. Problems caused by ineffective use of facilities often are a result of poor staff development.

11.  **Financial management**

Activities of financial management include documenting financial transactions (bookkeeping), generating and analyzing financial statements, and making adjustments to budgets based on the various analyses. This is usually done to Board-approved fiscal policies and procedures. Many times, people report problems with finances when they really mean problems with inadequate funding. Those problems are often caused by ineffective program planning, resource development and/or fundraising activities. Problems that are truly about financial management often can be addressed by training personnel about bookkeeping, and about generating and analyzing financial statements.

12.  **Administrative activities**

This includes the extensive range of detailed activities that must be coordinated and conducted on a daily basis to ensure the efficient operations of the nonprofit. Many people think of these activities as clerical, or "paperwork." Problems with administrative tasks often are the result of poor resource planning and staff development, or lack of appreciation for policies and procedures.

## Evaluating

13.  **Board self-evaluation**

Members of the Board of Directors should regularly evaluate the quality of their activities on a regular basis. Activities might include staffing the Board with new members, developing the members into well-trained and resourced members, discussing and debating topics to make wise decisions, and supervising the CEO. Probably the biggest problem with Board self-evaluation is that it does not occur frequently enough. As a result, Board members have no clear impression of how they are performing as members of a governing Board. Poor Board operations, when undetected, can adversely affect the entire organization.

14.  **Staff and volunteer (individual) performance evaluation**

Most of us are familiar with employee performance appraisals, which evaluate the quality of an individual's performance in their position in the organization. Ideally, those appraisals reference the individual's written job description and performance goals to assess the quality of the individual's progress toward achieving the desired results described in those documents. Continued problems in individual performance often are the results of poor strategic planning, program planning and staff development. If overall planning is not done effectively, individuals can experience continued frustration, stress and low morale, resulting in their poor overall performance. Experienced leaders have learned that continued problems in performance are not always the result of a poor work ethic – the recurring problems may be the result of larger, more systemic problems in the organizations.

15.  **Program evaluation**

Program evaluations have become much more common, particularly because donors demand them to ensure that their investments are making a difference in their communities. Program evaluations are typically focused on the quality of the program's process, goals or outcomes. An ineffective program evaluation process often is the result of poor program planning – programs should be designed so they can be evaluated. It can also be the result of improper training about evaluation. Sometimes, leaders do not realize that they have the responsibility to verify to the public that the nonprofit is indeed making a positive impact in the community. When program evaluations are not performed well, or at all, there is little feedback to the strategic and program planning activities. When strategic and program planning are done poorly, the entire organization is adversely effected.

16.    **Evaluation of cross-functional processes**
       Cross-functional processes are those that span several systems, such as programs, functions and projects. Common examples of major processes include information technology systems and quality management of services. Because these cross-functional processes span so many areas of the organization, problems in these processes can be the result of any type of ineffective planning, development and operating activities.

17.    **Organizational evaluation**
       Ongoing evaluation of the entire organization is a major responsibility of all leaders in the organization. Leaders sometimes do not recognize the ongoing activities of management to actually include organizational evaluations – but they do. The activities of organizational evaluation occur every day. However, those evaluations usually are not done systematically. As a result, useful evaluation information is not provided to the strategic and program planning processes. Consequently, both processes can be ineffective because they do not focus on improving the quality of operations in the workplace.

## *Examples of Management Systems for Specific Functions*

The following tables depict various examples of common management systems. Knowledge of the systems will come in handy later on when working with your client to analyze issues in their organization and what can be done to address those issues.

Each of the tables depicts highlights of the activities in that particular management system – not all possible activities in that system. Examples include management systems for:

- Board operations

- Strategic planning

- Management development

- Staffing (hires and volunteers)

- Financial management

- Advertising and promotion

- Fundraising

- Program evaluations

## Table II:10 – Examples of Management Systems for Specific Functions

| Management System for Board of Directors | | | | | |
|---|---|---|---|---|---|
| Inputs | Processes | | | | Outputs |
| | Planning | Developing | Operating | Evaluating | |
| • Past evaluation results of Board<br>• Annual calendar<br>• Mission, vision, values, goals<br>• Community leaders<br>• Experts<br>• Staff<br>• Best practices on Boards | • Board policies and procedures<br>• Job descriptions<br>• Board organization chart<br>• Board Committee work plans | • Form Board Develop. Committee<br>• Recruit members<br>• Provide Board Manual<br>• Train members about Boards<br>• Orient members about nonprofits<br>• Organize members into committees | • Attend meetings<br>• Research, discussions, debates<br>• Motions, decisions<br>• Strategic planning<br>• Supervise CEO<br>• Public relations<br>• Review programs<br>• Review financials<br>• Fundraise | • Meeting evaluations<br>• Quality of attendance, participation, teamwork, strategic decisions?<br>• Board self-evaluation annually<br>• Board Develop. Plan to address results of evaluations | • Board minutes with decisions<br>• Directions to CEO<br>• Public speeches<br>• Program reviews<br>• Financial reviews<br>• Donations<br>• Board Develop. Plan<br>• Updated Board policies and procedures |

| Management System for Strategic Planning | | | | | |
|---|---|---|---|---|---|
| Inputs | Processes | | | | Outputs |
| | Planning | Developing | Operating | Evaluating | |
| • Past evaluation results of nonprofit<br>• Past Strategic Plan<br>• Board, staff members<br>• Community leaders<br>• Researchers<br>• Program experts<br>• Best practices on planning | • Clarify purposes of planning<br>• Decide time span of Strategic Plan<br>• Select planning model<br>• Select participants<br>• Identify needed outside help<br>• Identify needed materials | • Form Planning Committee<br>• Hire, orient facilitator<br>• Announce planning process<br>• Train on strategic planning<br>• Orient experts on nonprofit<br>• Design research plans<br>• Schedule sessions | • Develop/ review mission, vision, values<br>• External analysis<br>• Internal analysis<br>• Establish strategic goals<br>• Develop action plans<br>• Develop Operating Plan<br>• Develop Budget | • Provide clear mission, goals, actions, budget?<br>• Satisfaction checks during planning<br>• Plan being implemented?<br>• Implementation on schedule? | • Strategic Plan<br>• SWOT information<br>• New/updated mission, vision, values, goals<br>• Action plans<br>• Operating Plan<br>• Budget<br>• Performance goals for Board and staff |

**Table II:10 – Examples of Management Systems for Specific Functions (Cont.)**

| Inputs | Processes | | | | Outputs |
|---|---|---|---|---|---|
| | Planning | Developing | Operating | Evaluating | |
| <div align="center">**Management System for Management Development**</div> | | | | | |
| ▪ Mission, values, goals<br>▪ Strategic Plan<br>▪ Action plans<br>▪ Operating Plan<br>▪ Program plans<br>▪ Personnel policies<br>▪ Current managers<br>▪ New managers<br>▪ Best practices on leadership, management | ▪ Assessment of current leadership and management capacities<br>▪ Identify training goals (needed capacities)<br>▪ Update personnel policies on compensation, hiring, delegating, firing, etc. | ▪ Form Board Personnel Committee<br>▪ Design training methods<br>▪ Develop training materials (or select courses)<br>▪ Develop evaluation plans<br>▪ Integrate training goals in performance plans | ▪ Organize leaders and managers into trainings<br>▪ Conduct in-house trainings<br>▪ Attend outside trainings<br>▪ Conduct on-the-job trainings<br>▪ Apply new learning to the workplace | ▪ Evaluate during training activities<br>▪ Quality of planning, organizing, leading, controlling?<br>▪ Delegating?<br>▪ Managing conflicts?<br>▪ Managing meetings?<br>▪ Redo assessment at end of trainings | ▪ Initial assessment results<br>▪ Training plans<br>▪ Applied learning from participants<br>▪ Updated personnel policies<br>▪ Final assessment results |

| Inputs | Processes | | | | Outputs |
|---|---|---|---|---|---|
| | Planning | Developing | Operating | Evaluating | |
| <div align="center">**Management System for Staffing (Paid and Volunteer)**</div> | | | | | |
| ▪ Mission, values, goals<br>▪ Strategic Plan<br>▪ Action plans<br>▪ Operating Plan<br>▪ Program plans<br>▪ Personnel policies<br>▪ People<br>▪ Best practices on leadership, management | ▪ Update personnel policies and procedures<br>▪ Update job descriptions<br>▪ Update staff organization chart<br>▪ Select recruitment methods and tools | ▪ Form Board Personnel Committee<br>▪ Recruit, hire members<br>▪ Provide Personnel Manual<br>▪ Develop training methods<br>▪ Orient, train, organize members<br>▪ Develop equipment, supplies, etc. | ▪ Establish goals for staff<br>▪ Share feedback<br>▪ Administer the offices<br>▪ Operate programs<br>▪ Marketing<br>▪ Financial management<br>▪ Fundraising<br>▪ Evaluations | ▪ Goals achieved by staff, volunteers?<br>▪ Low conflicts, turnover?<br>▪ High morale?<br>▪ Do annual performance reviews<br>▪ Reward positive performance<br>▪ Implement performance improvement plans | ▪ Status reports<br>▪ Meeting minutes<br>▪ Program reviews<br>▪ Financial reviews<br>▪ Updated personnel policies<br>▪ Update job descriptions, charts, etc.<br>▪ Performance reviews |

**Table II:10 – Examples of Management Systems for Specific Functions (Cont.)**

| | Management System for Financial Management | | | | |
|---|---|---|---|---|---|
| Inputs | Processes | | | | Outputs |
| | Planning | Developing | Operating | Evaluating | |
| • Laws and regulations<br>• Fiscal policies and procedures<br>• Strategic Plan<br>• Action plans<br>• Operating Plan<br>• Program plans<br>• Last year's budget<br>• Best practices on financial management | • Update fiscal policies and procedures<br>• Review plans to identify needed resources<br>• Identify costs to obtain and support resources<br>• Identify fundraising target<br>• Develop Budget | • Form Board Finance Committee<br>• Train Board on how to analyze finances<br>• Obtain software to manage financial information<br>• Obtain expertise to do bookkeeping, statements | • Enter bookkeeping transactions<br>• Generate financial statements<br>• Analyze statements<br>• Support annual audit<br>• Implement recommendations from audit | • Transactions tracked fully?<br>• Financial statements reviewed?<br>• Shortage of funds?<br>• Bills paid on time?<br>• Cash crises?<br>• Issues addressed from audit? | • Updated fiscal policies and procedures<br>• Budget<br>• Fundraising target<br>• Financial statements<br>• Audit findings<br>• Invoices, receipts, checks, etc. |

| | Management System for Advertising and Promotions | | | | |
|---|---|---|---|---|---|
| Inputs | Processes | | | | Outputs |
| | Planning | Developing | Operating | Evaluating | |
| • Mission, vision, values, goals<br>• Strategic Plan<br>• Program's market research and methods<br>• Staff<br>• Experts<br>• Best practices on advertising and promotions | • Specify each program's benefits<br>• Clarify each program's target groups<br>• For each group, associate program benefits with target's needs<br>• Specify preferred public image for nonprofit | • Form Board Marketing Committee<br>• Develop methods to advertise each program to its target groups (brochures, flyers, etc.)<br>• Develop methods to convey public image (logo, slogans, etc.) | • Use methods to convey each program's benefits to its target groups<br>• Use methods to cultivate public image with important stake-holders | • Implementation of advertising plan on schedule?<br>• Implementation of PR plan on schedule<br>• Increase in contacts to programs?<br>• Increase in clients for programs?<br>• Increased relationships with stake-holders? | • Advertising and Promotions Plan<br>• Flyers, brochures, testimonials, presentations, etc.<br>• Logo, slogans, web site, newsletters, etc. |

**Table II:10 – Examples of Management Systems for Specific Functions (Cont.)**

| Inputs | Processes | | | | Outputs |
|---|---|---|---|---|---|
| | **Management System for Fundraising** | | | | |
| | Planning | Developing | Operating | Evaluating | |
| ▪ Mission, vision, values, goals<br>▪ Budget<br>▪ Donors<br>▪ Board, staff members<br>▪ Program goals and outcomes<br>▪ Advertising and Promotions Plan<br>▪ Best practices on fundraising | ▪ Establish fundraising target<br>▪ Design research plans on prospective donors<br>▪ Select donors to approach<br>▪ Decide who approach, when and how<br>▪ Develop Fundraising Plan | ▪ Develop Fundraising Committee<br>▪ Train Board and staff on fundraising<br>▪ Conduct research<br>▪ Write grant proposals about needs, vision and methods, evaluation, budgets<br>▪ Develop solicitation kits | ▪ Approach each donor<br>▪ Send grant proposals<br>▪ Coordinate site visits<br>▪ Manage database of solicitations<br>▪ Acknowledge received grants<br>▪ Manage grant spending<br>▪ Reports to funders | ▪ On schedule to approach each donor?<br>▪ Percentage donors giving funds?<br>▪ Fundraising Committee functioning?<br>▪ Board involved?<br>▪ Fundraising target reached?<br>▪ Reports to funders on time? | ▪ Fundraising Plan<br>▪ Proposals<br>▪ Meetings with funders<br>▪ Donations from individuals, foundations, corporations and/or government<br>▪ Database of potential and active donors |

| Inputs | Processes | | | | Outputs |
|---|---|---|---|---|---|
| | **Management System for Program Evaluations** | | | | |
| | Planning | Developing | Operating | Evaluating | |
| ▪ Program process<br>▪ Program goals<br>▪ Program outcomes<br>▪ Board and staff<br>▪ Best practices for evaluations | ▪ Identify which program aspects to evaluate (process, goals, outcomes, etc.)<br>▪ What information is needed?<br>▪ How get information, who and when? | ▪ Form Board Programs Committee<br>▪ Develop information collection methods<br>▪ Develop Program Evaluation Plan<br>▪ Train staff to use methods | ▪ Collect information<br>▪ Analyze information<br>▪ Identify strengths, weaknesses, issues, progress to outcomes, etc.<br>▪ Generate recommendations to address findings | ▪ Programs implemented on schedule?<br>▪ Adjust Plans?<br>▪ Adjustments to make to programs right away? | ▪ Information collection methods<br>▪ Collected information<br>▪ Evaluation reports<br>▪ Recommendations to programs |

## *Role of Leadership in Management Systems*

The term "leadership" has become so popular lately that many different people have many different interpretations of the term – and people often have strong passions about their own particular interpretations.  In this context, the term "leadership" is intended to mean setting direction and influencing people to follow that direction.  Thus, a person can lead themselves, other individuals, other groups or an entire organization.

See "Major Roles During Change and Capacity Building" on page 6 for information about the key roles during change.

Executive leadership roles in a nonprofit are filled primarily by the Board of Directors, a Chief Executive Officer (if the Board chooses to hire a CEO) and by middle-management roles, for example, Program Directors.  It is the role of the Board of Directors to ensure that the nonprofit establishes a clear purpose (mission), clear direction (vision and strategic goals) and how that direction can be followed (values, strategies, plans and policies).  Some Boards hire a Chief Executive Officer (CEO) to carry out the Board's strategic policies.  In those cases, the CEO plays a major role in ensuring that the development and operating activities are carried out in an effective and efficient fashion.  Although theory and law assert that the Board is responsible to govern the organization, the Board and CEO often work together as partners to establish the nonprofit's overall direction and how it can be followed.

# Typical Types of Systematic Plans in Nonprofits

Many plans include contents that correspond in nature to the four phases of a systematic management system: overall planning, developing, operating and evaluating. Note that each nonprofit tends to customize the plans according to the nature and needs of their nonprofit.

### Advertising and Promotion (Per program)

- Target group(s) served by the program?
- Program's benefits to each target?
- How to convey benefits to each target?
- Who conveys benefits and when?
- How to convey the benefits?
- What resources do they need?
- Costs to get and use those resources?

### Board Development Plan

- Results of Board assessment?
- Areas that need improvement?
- Action plans to address each area?
- Who conducts each action and when?
- Schedule for re-assessment?
- What resources do they need?
- Costs to get and use those resources?

### Evaluation Plan (per program)

- Audience for evaluation results?
- Decisions that evaluation helps to make?
- What information is needed?
- How to get that information and when?
- Who gets that information?
- How to analyze and report information?

### Fundraising Plan (per organization)

- What deficit(s) exist?
- Desired percentage mix of donors?
  - From individuals, corporations?
  - From foundations, government?
- Which specific donors to approach?
- How will donors be approached?
- Who will approach each donor?
- How will grants be administered?
- Resources needed to implement plan?
- Costs to obtain and use resources?

### Grant Proposal (basic proposal)

- What specific community need exists?
- Vision, goals, outcomes to meet need?
- Program(s) and methods to meet need?
- How will programs be evaluated?

### Program Plan (or Business Plan)

- Description of program/service?
- Marketing plans:
  - What specific market need(s) exist?
  - What outcomes and benefits needed?
  - What target markets served?
  - What products/services provided?
  - Potential competitors and collaborators?
  - How to provide ("package") services?
  - Pricing structure(s)
- Management and staffing plan:
  - What expertise (people) is needed?
  - How is expertise organized?
  - Who leads the expertise?
- Financial:
  - Estimated revenues?
  - Estimated expenses (to operate)?
  - Estimated break-even?

### Public Relations (per organization)

- Desired public image for organization?
- Convey image to which stakeholders?
- Convey what message to each stakeholder?
- Who conveys it and when?
- How to convey it?
- What resources do they need?
- Costs to obtain and use resources?

### Strategic Plan

- Mission, vision, values
- Critical issues
- Core strategies
- Goals and strategies
- Action plans
- Budgets

# PART III:

# NONPROFIT

# PERFORMANCE,

# CHANGE AND LEARNING

# Nonprofit Performance Management

From having read PART II, you know about the major parts and processes in the system of a nonprofit.  You know about how they are all supposed to work together.  Now you are ready to learn about how nonprofit leaders make sure that those pieces are always operating together as effectively as possible.  The guidelines throughout this section apply whether you are an external or internal consultant.

An understanding of nonprofit performance management is critical to have if you are to be a successful consultant for organizational change in nonprofits.  That understanding helps you and your clients to recognize:

1.      Where organizational change – including your project – fits into the overall workings of a nonprofit organization.  This helps you avoid doing change for the sake of change, which should always be avoided.

2.      Where the roles of major management models, such as strategic management and Total Quality Management, fit into the workings of a nonprofit organization.  Those models and others can be powerful means to support performance in nonprofits.

3.      Where common concepts, such as "best practices" and "organizational effectiveness," fit into the overall workings of a nonprofit.  Those phrases are often talked about without full understanding of their role in performance.

Without a good understanding of performance management, consultants sometimes lose sight of the "big picture" – of what is really important in their client's organization.  As a result, they forsake the overall effectiveness of the organization for the achievement of the specific goals of their particular project.  Without an understanding of organizational performance management, your projects for organizational change will likely lack a clear sense of order and might even damage your client's efforts to serve their own clients.

Later on in this section, you will read about the many benefits from having a performance management perspective while completing the various phases of the collaborative consulting cycle.

## What Is Nonprofit Performance?
## Why Is It So Important Now?

Nonprofit organizations are faced with major challenges.  Changing demographics and current political policies have resulted in many more needs in many more communities – communities that are often highly diverse.  Increased public scrutiny has resulted in increased demand for accountability to show how nonprofit monies are spent.  Increasing competition from for-profit businesses has meant that nonprofits must be much more careful about their choice of strategies to successfully compete with the for-profits.  This overall situation has put much more focus on nonprofits having to prove that they are indeed meeting needs in the community – the nonprofits have to prove that they are performing.

Performance means effectively and efficiently meeting goals – it means doing what you say you are going to do and doing it well.  Nonprofit performance means accomplishing organizational and program goals, including strategic goals and program outcomes.  Employee performance means accomplishing the duties and responsibilities in the employee's job description and, if applicable, annual performance goals. Project performance means accomplishing the goals for the project, including consulting projects. The most important result for nonprofits is to meet needs in communities. Therefore, strong performance in nonprofits means that the nonprofits are indeed meeting specific needs in the communities.

Note that people, groups, projects, programs and organizations can all seem extremely busy, but that does not mean that they are performing. In poorly performing organizations, "busyness" is often mistaken for strong performance – people who appear to be busy are often deemed to be very useful employees. That is a misperception. If they are not directly contributing toward achieving the goals of the organization, they are participating in "busyness," not performance.

# Overview of the Performance Management Process

Performance management is what successful leaders and managers attempt to do all the time – they just are not used to referring to those activities as "performance management." Also, they may do those activities in an implicit and unsystematic manner, so the activities are not nearly as effective as they could be. Basically, performance management is a systematic approach to:

1.    Clarify the overall goals of a system and its various subsystems, for example, strategic goals for the nonprofit and the goals for its various programs.

2.    Ensure that the subsystems continue to be aligned in an optimum arrangement to effectively achieve the overall goals. For example, ensure that all goals of all programs are aligned and integrated with each other and, in turn, aligned with strategic goals.

3.    Take ongoing measurements of various indicators to see if the overall goals are being achieved or not. This includes, for example, ongoing assessments and evaluations of program goals to ensure they are being achieved.

4.    Reinforce, or reward, behaviors that are useful to achieving the goals. For example, if progress is clearly being made toward achieving a certain program's goals, program staff should be rewarded for their performance.

5.    Make adjustments, where necessary, to more effectively achieve the goals. If program goals are not being achieved, a project for organizational change might be initiated to improve the program.

Similar to any organizational change effort, the performance management system is always best implemented according to the particular nature and needs of the organization.

## *Domains of Performance Management in Nonprofits*

In this Field Guide, a performance domain is referred to as any system or subsystem from which results are expected, including:

1.    Position (for example, the Chief Executive Officer)

2.    Teams (collection of people to accomplish a specific purpose)

3.    Projects (one-time efforts, such as automating the billing process or moving to a new building)

4.    Processes (cross-functional processes, such as information technology or quality management)

5.    Functions (for example, Board operations, strategic planning or marketing)

6.    Programs (for example, day care program or food shelf program)

7.    The organization in its entirety

Planners of a performance management system might choose other systems than those listed above to be their performance domains. For example, they might choose systems that they refer to as "behavioral" or "operational." This Field Guide chose the above-listed domains because they are most recognizable and discussed in nonprofit organizations.

When working to improve performance of the overall organization, it is usually wise to focus not only on the performance of each particular domain but also on the quality of the inter-connections between the domains.

## Phases of the Performance Management Process

Systematic performance management often includes several ongoing, major activities, that are organized into the following three overall phases. The steps in each phase are generally followed in sequence. Remember that the phases may apply to any system in an organization, or to the entire organization itself.

### Phase One: Performance Planning

The activities of performance planning are conducted during any type of planning or goal establishment. Steps in performance planning include:

1.    Identification and prioritization of desired results, including outcomes in the external environment and other goals regarding the external and internal environments.

2.    Establishing means to measure progress, for example, indicators toward achieving those results.

3.    Sometimes setting organization-wide standards for assessing how well results were achieved, for example, "exceeds expectations."

4.    Establishing means to monitor measures to assess the quality of performance toward achieving results.

### Phase Two: Performance Assessment

Performance assessments are conducted when monitoring progress toward achievement of results, such as strategic goals or program goals. Many times, those assessments are done informally by sharing commentary or status reports.

1.    Tracking and measuring the indicators to identify progress toward results.

2.    Exchanging ongoing feedback about the extent of achievement of results.

3.     Reinforcing activities that achieve results.

Note that the third phase of the collaborative consulting cycle, Discovery and Feedback, is also a type of performance assessment.

### Phase Three: Performance Improvement Planning

The activities of performance improvement planning are done so frequently and informally that we often do not recognize those activities as means to improve performance. They are part of the day-to-day problem solving.

1.     If performance is not acceptable, identifying what can be done to improve performance, for example, adjusting goals and measures, or providing more resources (time, expertise, money, training, etc.).

2.     Developing and implementing action plans to improve performance.

3.     Repeating phases two and three until performance is acceptable.

Note that the fourth and fifth phases of the collaborative consulting cycle, Action Planning, Alignment and Integration and also Implementation and Change Management, are types of performance improvement planning.

The flow chart on the next page shows the relationship between these three phases in a typical performance management process.

# Benefits of Performance Management Perspective

There are numerous benefits as you use the performance management perspective to address the presenting priority in your client's organization. Your client will benefit from the perspective long after your project has been completed.

## *Cultivates System-Wide, Long-Term View of the Organization*

It is easy for anyone, when dealing with the many issues in the day-to-day operations of a nonprofit, to lose sight of what is really important. An effective performance management process follows a systems approach to examining the organization and its various parts, all the while keeping strong focus on desired overall results for the organization. The systems view helps people to always see the "big picture." A performance management perspective helps you to know what is most important now in that big picture.

## *Focuses on Results, Not Just Behaviors and Activities*

A common misconception among members of an organization is that behaviors and activities are the same as results. An example is the employee who manually reviews completion of every form and procedure, rather than supporting automation of the review. The supervisor may conclude the employee is committed to the organization and works hard, thus, deserving a high performance rating. However, an employee may appear extremely busy, but not be suitably contributing at all toward achieving the goals of the organization.

## The Performance Management Process

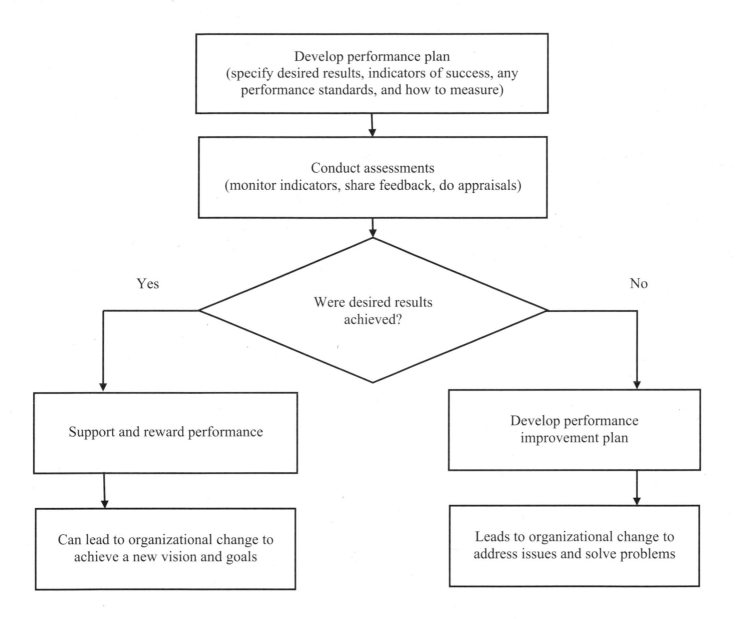

### *Develops a Culture of Accountability and Credibility*

Best practices and the implementation of plans for change alone do not make for successful change. Performance has to become part of your client's culture. As your client focuses on matters of achieving results and monitoring measures toward results, you will notice that the values of accountability and credibility become more of a part of their culture. Your client can readily speak to you and other stakeholders in terms of achieving results and focusing on performance. Stakeholders often feel that your client's nonprofit is highly accountable and credible in its dealings. As a result, your client's organization often has more influence, for example, when seeking funds from various donors.

### *Aligns All Goals with the Overall Goals of the Organization*

Performance management includes clarifying overall organizational goals, then identifying other smaller goals that are needed to achieve the overall goals, and then developing indicators (measures) of progress toward achieving all of the goals. This "chain" of measurements is continually examined to ensure alignment of all of the parts and processes of the nonprofit to achieve the overall goals of the organization.

### *Produces Meaningful Measurements for Many Applications*

These measurements have a wide variety of useful applications. They are useful in benchmarking, in setting standards for comparison with best practices in other organizations. They provide consistent basis for comparison during internal change efforts. They indicate results during improvement efforts, such as employee training, management development or quality management. They help ensure equitable and fair treatment to employees based on performance.

### *Makes Sure Everyone "Is on the Same Page"*

A performance management process provides a common language for everyone in the organization or project for organizational change. People refer to terms, such as results, indicators, assessments, performance planning and performance improvement. All the while, everyone is focused on achieving the most important, overall goals in the organization.

# Examples of Performance Management Systems in Nonprofits

It might help you in your understanding of performance management systems if you review some rather common systems in nonprofits. The table on the following page provides an overview of performance management systems.

## Table III:1 – Examples of Performance Management Systems in Nonprofits

| Function | Identify Desired Results | Performance to Achieve Desired Results | Evaluate Performance Toward Results | Reward and/or Improve Performance |
|---|---|---|---|---|
| Board | 1) Strategic Plan and 2) evaluation of Board both specify goals and expertise needed by Board | Recruit Board members and train Board members, supervise Chief Executive Officer, represent organization to community, oversee planning, ensure adequate resources, and ensure effective performance | Conduct Board evaluation toward achieving desired results | Celebrate accomplishment and/or conduct Board development as needed |
| Strategic Planning | 1) Stakeholder analysis and 2) organizational analysis both identify needs to be met by overall implementation of Plan | Clarify mission, vision and values statements, establish goals and strategies toward statements, develop action plans to implement strategies, implement action plans | Evaluate progress of implementation of plan toward meeting overall stakeholders' needs | Reward positive performance and/or adjust organizational operations to improve performance as needed |
| Program Planning | 1) Market research identifies specific client needs to be met by program and 2) program evaluation specifies adjustments to program | Clarify program vision and desired outcomes for clients, develop program methods to achieve outcomes, deliver services to clients | Conduct program evaluation toward meeting client needs | Celebrate accomplishments and/or adjust program operations to improve performance as needed |
| Human Resource Management | 1) Strategic Plan and 2) evaluation of staff both specify goals staff must meet | Supervise staff (establish goals for each member, provide feedback and coaching) | Conduct employee performance evaluations | Reward performance and/or implement employee performance improvement as needed |
| Fundraising | Strategic plan estimates deficits (amount expenses exceed revenues) which become fundraising goals | Establish fundraising goals, identify sources of funding, develop action plans and assignments to approach funders | Evaluate progress of fundraising | Celebrate accomplishments and/or adjust fundraising operations as needed to achieve fundraising goals |
| Financial management | Fiscal policies and procedures specify financial practices | Conduct accounting and bookkeeping to track and monitor transactions, analyze financial statements | Evaluate financial activities | Reward performance and/or adjust financial operations as needed |

# Models of Organizational Performance Management in Nonprofits

Now that you have an understanding of the performance management system, it will be useful for you to understand some of the most common performance models used by nonprofits to manage organizational performance. Often, people have heard of many of the following models – they just have not thought of them as organized approaches to organizational performance management. Any or all of the models listed in the following paragraphs will improve organizational performance depending on whether they are implemented systematically.

Note that there are many other practices that can make a significant contribution to the effectiveness of an organization. However, the practices are usually not ongoing and systematic in nature and, thus, are not established models for organizational performance management. Examples of these practices include strategic planning, business development, business planning, program planning, nonprofit capacity building and benchmarking.

The following models are listed in alphabetical order.

## Balanced Scorecard

This method focuses on developing four overall indicators, or measurements, to assess progress toward achieving organizational results. The indicators address customer perspective, internal business processes, learning and growth, and financials. Although the method can require extensive use of resources, the Balanced Scorecard is beginning to receive strong attention among many nonprofit leaders.

## Continuous Improvement

This method focuses on improving customer satisfaction – a primary outcome from achieving the most appropriate organizational results – through continuous and incremental improvements to internal processes, and/or by removing unnecessary activities and variations. It is highly likely that many nonprofits already pursue some course of continuous improvement without recognizing the method as such. Proponents of continuous improvement point out that the benefit of the method is that it forms a comprehensive, detailed approach to process improvement – not a reactive, hit-or-miss approach. Continuous improvement is often perceived as a quality management initiative.

## ISO 9000 Quality Management Series

ISO 9000 is an internationally recognized standard of quality and includes guidelines to accomplish the ISO 9000 standard. Organizations can be audited to earn ISO 9000 certification. The ISO 9000 has been enhanced by numerous other ISO-related standards. There have been several additions to the ISO 9000 family of models, producing various new names with numbers in the 9000 series, for example, ISO 9001 and ISO 9002. The ISO quality management initiative is not used widely among nonprofits at this time.

## Knowledge Management

This method (or movement) focuses on collection and management of critical knowledge in an organization to increase its capacity for achieving results. Knowledge management often includes extensive use of computer technology. In and of itself, this is not an overall comprehensive process assured to improve performance. Its effectiveness toward reaching overall results for the organization depends on how well the enhanced, critical knowledge is applied in the organization. At this time, knowledge management is receiving spotted attention among nonprofit service providers.

## *Learning Organization*

This method (or movement) focuses on enhancing organization systems and people to increase the organization's capacity for performance. It includes extensive use of principles of systems theory. In and of itself, this is not an overall comprehensive process assured to improve performance. Its effectiveness toward reaching overall results for the organization depends on how well the enhanced ability to learn applies to the organization.

## *Management by Objectives (MBO)*

This method aims to identify and closely align organizational goals and subordinate objectives throughout the organization. Ideally, employees get strong input to identify their own goals and objectives. It includes extensive, ongoing tracking and feedback in the processes to reach objectives. Similar to continuous improvement, many nonprofit leaders already implement some version of MBO, but probably not to the extent that experts in MBO would recognize as MBO in the various nonprofits.

## *Strategic Management*

Strategic management is one of the more common models for organizational performance management in nonprofits – many people just do not recognize their organizational activities as a means of strategic management. Basically, strategic management is the systematic, ongoing development and implementation of strategic planning. Strategic planning is well known in nonprofits for determining a nonprofit's mission, vision, values, goals, strategies, objectives, timelines and budgets.

See "Strategic Management (for "Diagnosing" Organizations)" on page 422 for guidelines to use strategic management as a diagnostic model.

## *Total Quality Management (TQM)*

TQM involves carefully implementing a set of comprehensive and specific management practices throughout the organization to ensure the organization consistently meets or exceeds customer requirements. The process involves strong focus on process measurement and on controls to ensure continuous improvement. TQM is considered to be a quality management initiative. At the time of this writing, TQM has not become a major model for performance management in nonprofits.

# Maximum Performance – Different Things to Different People

Despite the recent attention to achieving maximum performance, there is no standard interpretation of what that means or what it takes to get it. Still, you should be aware of the various views and be able to choose your own. Information in this subsection will orient you to what people are suggesting that it takes for nonprofits to achieve maximum performance.

## *Exploring Nonprofit Organizational Effectiveness*

The phrase, "organizational effectiveness," is commonly referred to when discussing nonprofits that have achieved maximum performance. Perhaps one of the best overviews of the concept of organizational effectiveness is provided by Herman and Renz (2002). The authors identify nine fundamental propositions about organizational effectiveness.

1. **Nonprofit organizational effectiveness is always a matter of comparison.**
   When determining the effectiveness of an organization, to what are you comparing the organization to conclude whether it is effective or not? For example, are you comparing to a certain set of best practices or to another highly respected nonprofit?

2. **Nonprofit organizational effectiveness is multi-dimensional.**
   Nonprofit organizational effectiveness cannot be measured by one indicator. For example, a budget surplus or a strong program outcome does not guarantee that the nonprofit has achieved overall maximum organizational effectiveness.

3. **Boards make a difference in organizational effectiveness, but how is not clear.**
   There is a correlation between effective Boards and effective nonprofit organizations. However, it is not clear that one necessarily causes the other.

4. **Nonprofit organizational effectiveness is a social construction.**
   The concept of organizational effectiveness is "in the eye of the beholder." One person might have a completely different interpretation than another person.

5. **More effective nonprofits are more likely to use correct management practices.** The authors are careful to point out that the reverse is not necessarily true – that nonprofits that use correct management practices will be judged as being effective. (The correct practices were identified during focus groups in various studies.)

6. **Claims about "best practices" warrant critical evaluation.**
   The authors explain that the results of their study do not agree with the wide assertion that certain practices, for example, automatically produce the best Boards.

7. **Measures of responsiveness may offer solutions to differing judgments.**
   This proposition reframes the concept of effectiveness for a nonprofit to be about how well that nonprofit is doing in responding to whatever is currently important.

8. **It can be important to distinguish different types of nonprofit organizations.**
   This is true to make progress in understanding the practices, tactics and strategies that may lead to nonprofit organizational effectiveness.

9. **Network effectiveness is as important to study as organizational effectiveness.**
   This proposition recognizes that the effectiveness of a nonprofit might depend to a great extent on the effectiveness of the wide network of nonprofits in which the particular nonprofit operates.

## Suggested Capacities for Organizational Effectiveness

Letts, Ryan and Grossman (1998) suggest four key capacities for organizational effectiveness.

1. **Adaptive capacity**
   is the ability of a nonprofit to maintain focus on the external environment of the organization, particularly on "performing" (meeting the needs of clients), while continually adjusting and aligning itself to respond to those needs and influences. Adaptive capacity is cultivated through attention to assessments, collaborating and networking, assessments, and planning.

2. **Leadership capacity**
   is the ability to set direction for the organization and its resources and also guide activities to follow that direction. Leadership capacity is cultivated through attention to visioning, establishing goals, directing, motivating, making decisions and solving problems.

3. **Management capacity**
   is the ability to ensure effective and efficient use of the resources in the organization. Management capacity is accomplished through careful development and coordination of resources, including people (their time and expertise), money and facilities.

4. **Technical capacity**
   is the ability to design and operate programs to effectively and efficiently deliver services to clients. The nature of that technical capacity depends on the particular type of service provided by the nonprofit.

The authors assert that most nonprofits attend to developing managerial and technical capacities, yet their strongest need is to develop their adaptive and leadership capabilities.

In addition, many experts in nonprofits identify a fifth key capacity.

5. **Generative capacity**
   is the ability of the nonprofit to positively change its external environment. This capacity is exercised by engaging in activities to inform, educate and persuade policy makers, community leaders and other stakeholders.

## Suggested Aspects for Performance

Blumenthal (2003) suggests improved performance might result from improvements in one or more of the following four aspects:

1. **Organizational stability**
   is in regard to whether program services are consistently delivered and the organization survives.

2. **Financial stability**
   is based especially on short-term survival, for example, the nonprofit has the ability to pay its bills. Financial stability is often ignored as an area of importance during capacity building.

3.     **Program quality**
       is based on indicators of impact, including adequate research about effective programs and
       an outcomes management system. This aspect also is often ignored.

4.     **Organizational growth**
       is based on attracting resources and providing more services. Blumenthal adds that growth
       alone is not an indicator of performance.

## *Putting Best Practices into Perspective*

While working to improve the effectiveness of nonprofits, consultants often refer to various
performance standards as conveyed in "best practices" and "standards of excellence." The
performance standards correspond to the levels of quality in certain nonprofits that are widely
viewed by others as being high performing nonprofits. Those views usually reflect conventional
wisdom, but not necessarily findings from research. Consultants often use the standards to assess the
quality of practices in their client's nonprofit and then what must be done to improve that quality.

Although the practices and standards can be somewhat useful in getting some quick perspective on
the quality of a particular function, you need to be careful about how you choose them and about
how you draw conclusions from any comparisons. The best use of best practices for an organization
depends on a variety of factors, including the culture of the organization, nature of the programs that
the nonprofit provides, expectations of major stakeholders, and effects of change in the environments
of the nonprofit. The open systems concept of equifinality suggests there is no one right way, or best
practice, for leading, managing or guiding organizations and change.

If you are working in a highly collaborative approach with your clients, you are much more likely to
work toward best practices in a manner that aligns those best practices with the nature and needs of
your client's organization.

 See "How to Select from Among Public Data Collection Tools" on page
412 for examples of various organizational assessment tools, some of
which include best practices information.

# Organizational Change and Capacity Building

### *Understanding the Nature of Change and Capacity Building*

Organizations – nonprofit, for-profit and government – change all the time, even after they have been carefully designed to achieve certain results. That is why your client needs to continually measure their progress toward achieving results. When measurements indicate that your client's nonprofit is getting "off course," then it is important to initiate an organizational change effort. Change might be initiated, not just to get back on course, but also to set a completely new course for the nonprofit.

Many people argue that organizations are changing like never before. Some of those changes are intended and others occur as sudden surprises. Usually, organizational change is provoked by some major, outside driving force, for example, substantial cuts in funding, major new markets/clients, or the need for dramatic increase in productivity/services. Experts on organizational change assert that most change efforts are provoked by some sort of crisis.

As stated elsewhere in this Field Guide, any consultant who provides services in capacity building should have an understanding of the nature and principles of systems, performance management and organizational change. This is true whether you are an external or internal consultant. Otherwise, you are likely to address a current, major problem in one particular part or process in your client's organization, only to find that your solution has created another, major problem in another part of their organization.

The subject of organizational change has reached evangelical proportions. There is an explosion of literature about the subject and an accompanying explosion in the amount of consultants who offer services in this general area. When people struggle to accomplish successful organizational change – whether in for-profit, nonprofit or government organizations – it is often because they do not understand the nature of planned change. Information in this overall section will help you to understand the nature of organizational change, including types of change, barriers to change, major phases in guiding change and various models for guiding change.

Note that the purpose of capacity building activities is to accomplish some form of organizational change. Therefore, the phrases "capacity building" and "organizational change" are often used together in this section interchangeably.

> Guidelines throughout PART IV and PART VII will show you and your client how to conduct successful consulting and organizational change, using principles of systems thinking and successful change.

## Major Types of Organizational Change

Typically, the phrase "organizational change" is about a significant change in the organization, such as reorganization or adding a new program. This is in contrast to smaller changes, such as adopting a new computer procedure. Organizational change can seem like such a vague phenomena that it is helpful if you can think of change in terms of various dimensions as described below.

## Organization-wide Versus Subsystem Change

Examples of organization-wide change might be a major restructuring, collaboration or "right-sizing." Usually, organizations must undertake organization-wide change to evolve to a different level in their life cycle, for example, going from a highly reactive, entrepreneurial organization to one that has a more stable and planned development. Experts assert that successful organizational change requires a change in culture – cultural change is another example of organization-wide change.

Examples of a change in a subsystem might include addition or removal of a program, reorganization of a certain department, or implementation of a new process to deliver services in a program.

## Transformational Versus Incremental Change

An example of transformational (or radical, fundamental) change might be changing an organization's structure and culture from the traditional top-down, hierarchical structure to a large amount of self-directing teams. Another example might be Business Process Re-engineering, which tries to take apart (at least on paper, at first) the major parts and processes of the organization and then put them back together in a more optimal fashion. Transformational change is sometimes referred to as quantum change.

Examples of incremental change might include continuous improvement as a quality management process or implementation of new computer system to increase efficiencies. Many times, organizations experience incremental change and its leaders do not recognize the change as such.

## Remedial Versus Developmental Change

Change can be intended to remedy current situations, for example, to improve the poor performance of a program or the entire organization, reduce burnout in the workplace, help the organization to become much more proactive and less reactive, or address large budget deficits. Remedial projects often seem more focused and urgent because they are addressing a current, major problem. It is often easier to determine the success of these projects because the problem is solved or not.

Change can also be developmental – to make a successful situation even more successful, for example, expand the amount of clients served, or duplicate successful programs. Developmental projects can seem more general and vague than remedial, depending on how specific goals are and how important it is for members of the organization to achieve those goals.

Some people might have different perceptions of what is a remedial change versus a developmental change. They might see that if developmental changes are not made soon, there will be need for remedial changes. Also, organizations may recognize current remedial issues and then establish a developmental vision to address the issues. In those situations, projects are still remedial because they were conducted primarily to address current issues.

## Unplanned Versus Planned Change

Unplanned change usually occurs because of a major, sudden surprise to the organization, which causes its members to respond in a highly reactive and disorganized fashion. Unplanned change might occur when the Chief Executive Officer suddenly leaves the organization, significant public relations problems occur, poor program performance quickly results in loss of clients, or other disruptive situations arise.

Planned change occurs when leaders in the organization recognize the need for a major change and proactively organize a plan to accomplish the change. Planned change occurs with successful implementation of a Strategic Plan, plan for reorganization, or other implementation of a change of this magnitude.

Note that planned change, even though based on a proactive and well-done plan, often does not occur in a highly organized fashion. Instead, planned change tends to occur in more of a chaotic and disruptive fashion than expected by participants.

# Why Change and Capacity Building Can Be Difficult to Accomplish

Change can be difficult for you and your client to accomplish for a variety of reasons.

- **People are afraid of the unknown.**
  They communicate their fear through direct means, such as complaining about the plans for change. Or, they communicate their fear indirectly, for example, by not attending meetings to plan the change.

- **People think things are just fine.**
  This might occur if the executives in the nonprofit have not adequately communicated the need for the change.

- **Many people are inherently cynical about change.**
  This cynicism often occurs if earlier attempts at change were unsuccessful, and not explained to employees.

- **Many doubt there are effective means to accomplish successful change.**
  They may have read publications in which writers assert that most organizational change efforts fail.

- **There may be conflicting goals in the organizational change effort.**
  A conflicting goal might be, for example, to significantly increase resources to accomplish change, yet substantially cut costs to remain viable. That conflict can occur, especially if staff were not involved in plans for the change.

- **Change often goes against values held dear by members in the organization.**
  The change may go against how members believe things should be done. For example, they might disagree that nonprofits should pursue "making a profit" when implementing plans for an earned-income venture.

- **The original reason for the change, changes.**
  This situation is not uncommon, particularly in nonprofits with clients whose needs are rapidly changing or in nonprofits with rapidly changing environments.

- **People get burnout during the change effort.**
  Organizational change usually takes longer to achieve than most people expect. Some experts assert that successful change can take from several months to several years.

- **Leaders of the change end up leaving the organization.**
  Especially in smaller nonprofits or nonprofits with very limited resources, leaders might not believe they are receiving sufficient value for what they are investing in the nonprofit. They might conclude that it is better to just leave. Or, the change may not be going as expected, and the leaders are asked to leave.

- **Participants do not understand the nature of planned change.**
  Frequently, participants expect the change to be according to a well-designed, well-organized effort that has few surprises. When surprises do occur, they lose faith in the change effort and seek to abandon it.

- **The relationship between the consultant and the client "sours."**
  The relationship can deteriorate, especially if your client does not want to change or if the project struggles because of one or more of the above-listed barriers to change.

You can overcome many of the barriers if you work with your client in a highly collaborative fashion. Overall guidelines for successful collaborative consulting are provided throughout this Field Guide. Also, overall guidelines for successful organizational change are provided throughout this section.

# Requirements for Successful Organizational Change

Cummings and Worley (1995) describe a comprehensive, five-phase, general process for managing change, including: 1) motivating change, 2) creating vision, 3) developing political support, 4) managing the transition and 5) sustaining momentum. That process seems suitable for organizing and describing general guidelines about managing change.

Whatever model you choose to use when guiding organizational change, that model should include the priorities and areas of emphasis described in the following five phases of change. The collaborative consulting model described in PART IV integrates highlights from all of the five phases.

## Motivating Change

This phase includes creating a readiness for change in your client organization and developing approaches to overcome resistance to change. General guidelines for managing this phase include enlightening members of the organization about the need for change, expressing the current status of the organization and where it needs to be in the future, and developing realistic approaches about how change might be accomplished. Next, organization leaders need to recognize that people in the organization are likely to resist making major changes for a variety of reasons, including fear of the unknown, inadequacy to deal with the change and whether the change will result in an adverse effect on their jobs. People need to feel that their concerns are being heard. Leaders must widely communicate the need for the change and how the change can be accomplished successfully. Leaders must listen to the employees – people need to feel that the approach to change will include their strong input and ongoing involvement.

## Creating Vision

Leaders in the organization must articulate a clear vision that describes what the change effort is striving to accomplish. Ideally, people in the organization have strong input to the creation of the vision and how it can be achieved. The vision should clearly depict how the achievement of the vision will improve the organization. It is critically important that people believe that the vision is relevant and realistic. Research indicates that cynicism is increasing in organizations in regard to change efforts. People do not want to hear the need for the latest "silver bullet" that will completely turn the organization around and make things better for everyone all the time. They want to feel respected enough by leaders to be involved and to work toward a vision that is realistic, yet promising in the long run.

Often the vision is described in terms of overall outcomes (or changes) to be achieved by all or parts of the organization, including associated goals and objectives to achieve the outcomes. Sometimes, an overall purpose, or mission, is associated with the effort to achieve the vision, as well.

## Developing Political Support

This phase of change management is often overlooked, yet it is the phase that often stops successful change from occurring. Politics in organizations is about power. Power is important among members of the organization when striving for the resources and influence necessary to successfully carry out their jobs. Power is also important when striving to maintain jobs and job security. Power usually comes from credibility, whether from strong expertise or integrity. Power also comes from the authority of one's position in the organization.

Some people have a strong negative reaction when talking about power because power often is associated with negative applications, for example, manipulation, abuse or harassment. However, power, like conflict, exists in all human interactions and is not always bad. It is how power and conflict are used and managed that determine how power and conflict should be perceived.

Matters of power and politics are critically important to recognize and manage during organizational change activities. Change often means shifts in power across management levels, functions, programs and groups. To be successful, the change effort must recruit the support of all key power players, for example, senior management, subject matter experts and others who are recognized as having strong expertise and integrity.

A strong mechanism for ensuring alignment of power with the change effort is to develop a network of power-players who interact and count on each other to support and guide the change effort. Means to manage power can include ensuring that all power-players are involved in recognizing the need for change, developing the vision and methods to achieve the vision, and organization-wide communication about the status of change. Any recommendations or concerns expressed by those in power must be promptly recognized and worked through.

## Managing Transition

This phase occurs when the organization works to make the actual transition from the current state to the future state. In consultations, this phase usually is called implementation of the action plans. The plans can include a wide variety of "interventions," or activities designed to make a change in the organization, for example, creating and/or modifying major structures and processes in the organization. These changes might require ongoing coaching, training and enforcement of new policies and procedures. In addition, means of effective change management must continue, including strong, clear, ongoing communication about the need for the change, status of the change, and solicitation of organization members' continuing input to the change effort.

Ideally, the various actions are integrated into one overall Change Management Plan that includes specific objectives, or milestones, that must be accomplished by various deadlines, along with responsibilities for achieving each objective. Rarely are these plans implemented exactly as planned. Thus, as important as developing the plan, is making the many ongoing adjustments to the plan with key members of the organization, while keeping other members up-to-date about the changes and the reasons for them.

## Sustaining Momentum

Often, the most difficult phase in managing change is this phase when leaders work to sustain the momentum of the implementation and adjustment of plans. Change efforts can encounter a wide variety of obstacles, for example, strong resistance from members of the organization, sudden departure of a key leader in the organization, or a dramatic cut in funding. Strong, visible, ongoing support from top leadership is critically important to show overall credibility and accountabilities in the change effort. Those participating in the change effort often require ongoing support, often in the form of provision of resources, along with training and coaching. The role of support cannot be minimized – despite its importance during organizational change, the role of support is often forgotten. At this point in a consulting project, it may be wise for you to ensure you have ongoing support (often from other consultants) that can provide you ongoing objectivity, affirmation, provision of resources and other forms of support. Employee performance management systems play a critical role in this phase of organizational change, including in setting goals, sharing feedback about accomplishment of goals, rewarding behaviors that successfully achieve goals and accomplish change, and addressing performance issues.

# Various Organizational Change Models

The purposes of an organizational change model are to 1) provide guidance to leaders of the change effort and 2) give a common perspective and frame of reference for participants when communicating about their change effort. The following paragraphs provide a general overview of some of the more prominent change models. The purpose of the overviews is to increase your general knowledge about approaches to change and help you grasp the diversity of approaches. The overviews are not intended to provide you detailed guidelines about implementing any of the models.

Note that there are many other change models, many of them formed by modifying the well-known models, such as Lewin's action research. Also note that, because there is no standard definition for a change model, some readers might consider some or all of the following as ways to effect change, rather than as change models.

## Unfreeze, Move, Refreeze

Lewin's (1951) model is probably the most well known. Its simple, but powerful, premise is that to change a system, you first have to "unfreeze," or loosen up those structures and influences that currently hold the system together. Without attention to these structures, actions to accomplish desired changes will not likely be successful because those actions will encounter strong resistance from members of the organization. Structures can be loosened in a variety of ways, for example, by enlightening members of the organization about the gap between where they are now and where they could be. The next general phase is moving the change along, primarily by cultivating new knowledge, skills and perspectives among members. The final phase is developing and implementing new structures, such as new plans, policies and procedures, which freeze, or hold, the current state of change in place.

## Action Research

Lewin's action research process is based on an overall cycle of researching a situation to establish actions to take, taking those actions, and then learning from the actions. The cycle has been embellished to include more specific steps in the general sequence: 1) clarifying the current problem in the system, 2) involving a specialist or consultant, 3) gathering data and diagnosing the situation, 4) providing feedback to people in the system, 5) incorporating members' feedback to further clarify the problem and its causes, 6) establishing action plans to address the problem, 7) taking actions, and 8) gathering data to assess the effects on the problem.

There have been various, recent modifications to the action research model. Modifications include more involvement of members of the organization in the process, less focus on "diagnosis" (as done in a medicinal model) and more focus on joint discovery, more focus on strengths and opportunities and less on weaknesses and problems, and more focus on learning.

The action research model forms the basis of the collaborative consulting cycle described throughout PART IV.

## Business Process Reengineering (BPR)

This method aims to increase organizational performance by radically re-designing the organization's structures and processes, by starting over from the ground up. BPR can be demanding on nonprofit staff, who are often already overloaded with other work. There are many proponents – and increasingly, it seems – opponents of BPR. Still, the process might be one of few that really forces nonprofit leaders to take a complete, fresh look at systems in their organization and how to re-develop those systems anew.

## Future Search Conference

Future Search Conference is an example of a recent category of change models, called large-group interventions. An overall goal of large-group interventions is to quickly engage all key stakeholders to align the organization with its external environment and, thus, more effectively achieve the organization's goals. The interventions involve a large group of participants, often lasting from one to three days. Involvement of all key stakeholders is an example of a "whole systems" approach to change. Large-group change is an example of transformational, organization-wide change.

Wesibord (1987) developed the future search approach, which involves 30-100 people who work together, usually over three days, to find a preferred future and to develop action steps to accomplish that future. The consultant works with a small planning group to design the event. All key internal and external stakeholders are encouraged to attend. Participants examine the past, present and future of the organization from the perspective of the participants themselves, the organization and its industry. Participants discover their shared values and assumptions to clarify a preferred future or vision. The vision emerges from various scenarios, built from considering what has worked and what has not worked in the past, but especially what has worked. Short-term and long-term action plans are established. Emphasis is on building to the desired future, rather than on solving problems.

## McKinsey 7S Model

The model was developed by Watermann and Peters (1982) and depicts 7 dimensions of organizations that must be considered when accomplishing organizational change. Imagine a circle of six circles with one circle in the middle. The middle circle is labeled "shared values." Shared values represent the overall priorities in how the organization chooses to operate. The six outer circles include "strategy," "structure," "systems," "skills," "staff" and "style."

Strategy is the overall direction of the organization and how it is going to follow that direction. Structure is the organization of the company, defining its roles and lines of authority. Systems include the processes and procedures that guide day-to-day activities in the organization. These three are the hard S's.

Skills are the capabilities of the organization. Staff includes the organization's people and how their expertise is utilized. Style is how the organization is led. These three are the soft S's.

The point of the model is that an effective organization has to accomplish a fit between all 7 S's, and to realize that a change in any one of the seven dimensions will effect a change in all others.

# Major Roles During Change and Capacity Building

The process of organizational change can include a variety of key roles. These roles can be filled by various individuals or groups at various times during the change process. Sometimes, individuals or groups can fill more than one role.

## Change Initiator

It is conventional wisdom among organizational development consultants that successful change is often provoked by a deep "hurt" or crisis in the organization, for example, dramatic cut in funding, loss of a key leader in the organization, warnings from a major funder, or even actions of a key competitor. It is not uncommon then that someone inside the organization reacts to that deep hurt and suggests the need for a major change effort. Often the person who initiates the change is not the person who becomes the primary change agent.

## Change Agent

The change agent is the person responsible for organizing and coordinating the overall change effort. The change agent role can be filled by different people at different times during the project. For example, an outside consultant might be the first change agent. After the project plan has been developed and begins implementation, the change agent might be an implementation team comprised of people from the organization. If the change effort stalls out, the change agent might be a top leader in the organization who intercedes to ensure the change process continues in a timely fashion.

## Champion for Change

Change efforts often require a person or group who continues to build and sustain strong enthusiasm about the change. This includes reminding everyone of why the change is occurring in the first place, the many benefits that have come and will come from the change process. The champion might be the same person as the change agent at various times in the project.

## Sponsor of Change

Usually, there is a one key internal person or department that is officially the "sponsor," or official role responsible for coordinating the change process. In large organizations, that sponsor often is a department, such as Human Resources, Strategic Planning or Information Technology. In smaller organizations, the sponsor might be a team of senior leaders working to ensure that the change effort stays on schedule and is sustained by ongoing provision of resources and training.

### *Leadership, Supervision and Delegation*

In this Field Guide, leadership is defined as setting direction and influencing people to follow that direction. A person can lead themselves, other individuals, other groups or an entire organization. Supervision is guiding the development and productivity of people in the organization. Effective supervisors are able to achieve goals by guiding the work of other people – by delegating.

See "Client's Delegation to Maintain Motivation and Momentum" on page 354 for guidelines to productive delegation.

Note that supervisors exist throughout a nonprofit organization, depending on the particular structure of the Board and staff. For example, the Board of Directors supervises the Chief Executive Officer (CEO), the CEO supervises program directors or executive assistants, and program directors supervise other program staff.

The topic of leadership has become one of the most prominent topics in all of management literature today. It is almost impossible to find a general management book that does not include frequent mention of the topic of leadership. There are a variety of reasons for this, one of the most important being that successful organizational change requires strong, ongoing and visible leadership in support of that change. Leaders must model the type of behaviors that they want to see in their organization. Other reasons include:

- Leaders who work with others in the organization to clarify those desired results define the vision and goals, or desired results, for change.

- Leaders in the organization must "walk their talk" – they must behave according to the same values and behaviors that are to be accomplished by the change effort.

- Leaders must ensure the ongoing accountabilities, resources and support to ensure that actions are taken to accomplish the overall change effort.

There simply is no substitute for the role that leadership and supervision play in accomplishing successful organizational change. Thus, it is extremely important that leaders and supervisors in the organization have a strong understanding of basic principles of successful change in organizations.

See "Organizational Change and Capacity Building" on page 183 about principles, roles and activities for conducting successful change.

## How to Make Sure the Board of Directors Participates in the Project for Change

Especially in projects for change in small- to medium-sized nonprofits, the Board can be the leverage point – the point in the project that can make the biggest difference – for success in your project for change. In these situations, your client seems reluctant to involve their Board, at all, in your project, you should seriously consider whether your client is really ready for a project to accomplish significant change in their organization.

To ensure that the Board of Directors in your client's organization provides strong contribution to your project, consider the guidelines in this subsection.

See "Roles and Responsibilities of the Nonprofit Board of Directors" on page 117 to learn more about a nonprofit Board of Directors.

## Benefits of Board Involvement in the Project

1. **The Board ensures the project is fully resourced and shows political support.**
   Board members have full authority for allocation of resources for the nonprofit. Consequently, Board members can ensure that the project has all necessary resources, including people, money and time. Their allocation shows strong political support for change, which can sustain ongoing motivation and momentum for change.

2. **The Board ensures that project plans are developed and implemented.**
   The Board supervises the Chief Executive Officer, having full authority over the CEO. Although staff members (including the CEO) usually develop and implement many of the action plans in the project for change, the Board can ensure that those plans are fully developed and completely implemented.

3. **Board members provide a wide range of useful expertise.**
   Board members often have a wide range of useful skills for governing the organization, such as planning, leadership, management, supervision and problem solving. They may also have technical knowledge of the organization or the industry. . Those skills can be useful during a project for change.

4. **The Board provides time and energy to help implement plans for change.**
   Staff members often are already overloaded. Giving them yet more work to do (during your project) can completely overload them such that they collapse altogether, which could significantly damage the organization. Although the Board is responsible to govern the organization by establishing broad plans and policies, Board members still can help with implementation of various plans by helping to develop and oversee development of plans. Plans might be to address issues in strategic planning, programs, marketing, staffing, financial management or fundraising.

5. **The Board provides objective assessment on project issues and results.**
   Board members usually are not involved a great deal in the day-to-day activities of a project. Consequently, they often retain an objective perspective on the activities and results of the project. Their perspective can be useful when addressing issues in the project and evaluating results of the project.

6. **Involvement of Board members is a powerful means to Board development.**
   One of the best ways to get good Board members is to give them something to do. One of the best ways to get rid of Board members is to give them something to do. Your project can be useful means to give Board members something to do – and, thus, develop the Board.

## *Ensuring the Board Is Highly Involved in the Project*

1.  **The Board should be involved in first meeting with you, the consultant.**
    In projects that are intended to accomplish significant change in a nonprofit, members of the Board certainly should be aware of – and have approved – the project. The Board Chair should participate in the first meeting with you during Phase 2: Engagement and Agreement.

2.  **Both the Board Chair and the Chief Executive Officer should sign the contract.**
    The Board Chair should sign the contract along with the Chief Executive Officer. That approach helps to ensure that the Board is indeed aware of, and supports, the project.

3.  **Educate Board members about successful organizational change.**
    Members of the Board are almost always volunteers to the nonprofit organization. Thus, they usually already have full-time jobs and are quite busy. Still, you should briefly educate them about what it takes to accomplish successful organizational change. You might provide them a short article, or brief presentation.

    See "Requirements for Successful Organizational Change" on page 186 for information about successful change that you can share with a Board.

4.  **Involve at least one Board member in the Project Team.**
    In projects for change, you should try to form a Project Team comprised of key personnel from your client's organization. Ensure that at least one Board member, ideally the Board Chair, is included on the Team.

    See "Establish the Project Team" on page 260 for guidelines to form a Project Team.

5.  **Ensure that all members of the Board get feedback from the discovery phase.**
    Near the end of Phase 3: Discovery and Feedback, you and your client will present the findings and recommendations from your analysis of the organization. Those results are important information for all Board members to know about. Ensure that you provide that information to all Board members, whether in a meeting and/or a written report.

6.  **Board members should be highly involved in activities that affect the Board.**
    Board members should participate in various aspects of the project, depending on its scope. For example, if the project includes Board development and development of the CEO position, Board members should be highly involved in setting and achieving project goals.

7.  **Include Board development in the project if many issues exist in the organization.**
    If your activities during the Discovery and Feedback phase identify many issues in your client's organization, it is likely that the client's Board of Directors has major problems, as well. Otherwise, the Board would have been effectively governing and the many organizational issues would not have existed. Also, one of the most powerful approaches to addressing problems among staff and programs is to build up the Board to help you to address those problems. Therefore, during the Phase 4: Action Planning, Alignment and Integration, include action plans to develop the Board.

> For detailed guidelines to develop a Board of Directors, see the
> recommended list of resources on page 499.

8.  **If there are CEO and/or staffing issues, form a Board Personnel Committee.**
    A Board Personnel Committee is responsible to ensure that staffing (including the CEO) is
    carefully planned and fully utilized. That includes providing ongoing coaching to the CEO
    to ensure that his or her role is competently filled. A Board Personnel Committee can be of
    tremendous value to your project, especially after you have gone, to coach the CEO through
    the struggles of making major changes.

9.  **All Board members should be copied on project reports.**
    All Board members have a responsibility to govern the organization. All Board members
    should always be able to access any information inside the nonprofit organization.
    Consequently, they should be copied on reports about the status of your project.

10. **The Board should formally approve the Change Management Plan.**
    During Phase 4: Action Planning, Alignment and Integration, you and your client will
    develop various action plans to address the presenting priority and any other issues in your
    client's organization. Those plans will be in an overall Change Management Plan. Formal
    approval of the Plan by the Board can help to ensure that Board members have seen and will
    support the Plan.

11. **The Board Executive Committee should "police" implementation of action plans.**
    Ensure that the Board Executive Committee regularly reviews the implementation status of
    the Change Management Plan.

12. **Board members should be highly involved in reviewing evaluation results.**
    Finally, the Board should ensure that the project actually addresses the presenting priority
    and any other issues found in the organization. They should regularly review results of
    evaluations of project activities as those activities occur. Also, they should review results of
    evaluations of the quality of final results from the project.

# Common Capacity Building Activities and How Clients Choose Them

## Types of Capacity Building Activities

There are many approaches to providing capacity building services, including:

- Providing access to repositories of information and resources (for example, databases, libraries and web sites)

- Publications

- Trainings (public, customized or on-line)

- Consultation (for example, coaching, facilitating, expert advice and conducting research)

- Coordinating alliances

The following table lists many of the types of common capacity building activities. The following list is by no means complete. However, it does include many of the types of capacity building in nonprofits. Near the end of the phase, Discover and Feedback, when you are generating recommendations to your client, you might be making recommendations that include some or all of the following activities.

## Table III:2 – Common Types of Capacity Building Activities

| | |
|---|---|
| ▪ Assessments | ▪ Management development |
| ▪ Board development | ▪ Marketing (research, promotions) |
| ▪ Business planning | ▪ Meeting management |
| ▪ Business development | ▪ Mergers |
| ▪ Collaboration planning | ▪ Networking opportunities |
| ▪ Conflict resolution | ▪ Organizational development |
| ▪ Convening | ▪ Peer learning |
| ▪ Earned-income development | ▪ Program design |
| ▪ Evaluation | ▪ Project management |
| ▪ Facilities planning | ▪ Quality management |
| ▪ Financial management | ▪ Referrals |
| ▪ Funding | ▪ Research |
| ▪ Fundraising | ▪ Risk management |
| ▪ Information technology | ▪ Staffing (selection, development) |
| ▪ Leadership development | ▪ Strategic planning |
| ▪ Legal | ▪ Team building |

## How Clients Choose Types of Capacity Building Activities

Clients often describe projects in terms of the types of capacity building activities in the project, rather than of the overall nature of the project. For example, they might refer to the project as "fundraising" or "strategic planning," rather than "resource development" or "setting the long-term direction for the organization. Clients often hire consultants based on how closely the consultant's services match what the client believes the activities should be. For example, they might seek a fundraiser or a strategic planner. Consequently, consultants often list their services in terms of common capacity building activities.

However, there usually is more to how clients select a type of capacity building then merely by matching terms. Many times, clients do not even realize how they chose a particular capacity building service or consultant. Connolly and York (2003) suggest that the type of capacity building activities undertaken by a particular nonprofit depends on certain factors, including:

1.  **Organizational resources**
    Including time, skills, expertise, money, facilities and equipment

2.    **Organizational readiness**
      Especially if the nonprofit has the ability to discern real underlying causes of issues

3.    **Organizational life cycle**
      For example, new nonprofits need help to create, while others focus on efficiency

4.    **Access to capacity builders and associated resources and tools**
      For example, to trainings, consultants or peer networks

# Challenges and Rewards of Capacity Building with Nonprofits

## Unique Challenges in Consulting with Typical Nonprofits

Due to the unique nature of the typical nonprofit, there can be several major challenges in consulting with them. Many nonprofits do not have the funds sufficient for professional development. The members of the organization start nonprofits out of a passion for meeting a particular need in the community. Other members are promoted often on the basis of their particular expertise in providing certain kinds of services, not on their expertise in general leadership and management. Consequently, members often have little or no knowledge about standard management practices in organizations.

Similar to for-profits, nonprofits are in the midst of tremendous change. The personalities of members of nonprofits are often highly diverse as are the cultures of the nonprofits themselves. Many nonprofits are small in size, for example, having staff size of 20 or less and budget size of under $500,000. There is increasing pressure on nonprofits to be more accountable with funds they receive from donors, including from the public.

Consequently, there can be numerous challenges for you when working with the typical nonprofit during an organizational change project, such as:

- Decisions take more time than usual because more people often have to be involved, so activities, such as planning, may take longer than expected.

- Decisions are often based on values, rather than practicality and expedience, so a variety of decision-making techniques might be needed.

- Issues are every bit as complex as in large organizations – sometimes in small organizations, the dynamics of issues evolve at an even faster rate.

- Expertise conveyed to certain personnel, for example, during trainings, may be lost once those personnel leave, so re-training may be required.

- Personnel sometimes have little formal training in management practices, so training may be required in areas, such as planning, organizing, leading and coordinating resources.

- The Chief Executive has to wear many "hats," so it is often hard to get the person in that role to retain focus on one thing at a time.

- People often are reluctant to spend money on resources other than dedicated to providing direct services to clients, so it might be difficult to procure and support additional resources in a project.

- Planning and projects are usually focused on current, major issues facing the organization and quickly addressing them now.

 See "Unique Challenges of Typical Nonprofits" on page 125 for more complete description of the above-listed challenges.

## *Rewards of Consulting with Nonprofits*

Although the challenges when working with nonprofits might be many, the rewards can be at least as numerous, including

- Opportunities to provide meaningful assistance to organizations.

- Learning about diverse people and problems in organizations and communities.

- Learning about what works and what does not to solve those problems.

- Ongoing revenue streams (there is sometimes a major myth that nonprofits have no money at all and, therefore, cannot afford to pay consultants).

- Opportunity to learn about many aspects of organizational and management development, particularly by volunteering to assist in those areas.

- Feeling the deep appreciation from people who greatly need your services.

- Tremendous satisfaction from making a major difference in communities.

- Opportunity for personal and professional growth.

# Evaluation of Performance and Change

## Evaluation and Assessment

The terms "evaluation" and "assessment" are often used interchangeably. Webster's *Dictionary* defines each term by using the other. Certainly not all people perceive the terms to have the same meaning. For example, some people might interpret an assessment to be gathering information to take a measurement of something, for example, the extent to which some process or program achieves "best practices." In contrast, a common interpretation of evaluation is gathering information and then making judgments about that information to make a major decision. Based on that particular interpretation, evaluations might include use of various assessments.

Despite the similarity in meaning between the two terms, the terms are often mentioned differently in different applications. For example, phrases such as "program evaluation," performance evaluation" and "Board self-evaluation" are common. However, the phrase "organizational assessment" is far more common than "organizational evaluation." For many people, the term "assessment" seems less intimidating than the term "evaluation" because the term "evaluation" implies judgment of them.

This Field Guide uses both terms interchangeably, but also attempts to use each term in its most conventional application. However, you might choose to use whichever term seems most comfortable for you and your client. This is true whether you are an external or internal consultant.

## Value of General Knowledge About Evaluation and Assessments

As an organizational change consultant, you should have a good understanding about how to systematically design and implement evaluations or assessments in a variety of applications. Information in this section will help you to achieve that level of understanding.

There are many philosophies about evaluation and many kinds of evaluation, as well. It can seem almost overwhelming to get clear perspective on evaluation. Therefore, it often helps to understand the general knowledge about evaluation, including its major categories, common types and common levels. That general knowledge is described in this overall section, as well. You would benefit most from reading about this general knowledge before developing an evaluation or assessment design, or plan, for your project.

 Certain portions of the information in this section were excerpted or adapted from the publication, *Field Guide to Nonprofit Program Design, Marketing and Evaluation* (McNamara, 2003).

# Evaluation and Assessment – Means to Performance and Learning

Evaluation plays a critical role in ensuring strong performance in your client's nonprofit organization – and it plays a strong role in ensuring that your consulting project remains high quality. There are certain major myths about evaluation that can cause people to doubt the relevance of evaluations and, in some cases, be intimidated by the thought of doing evaluations at all. However, many times, people are already conducting evaluations and are not even aware of it because their evaluation activities are conducted implicitly (not written down and discussed with others). For example, the overall practices in successful leadership and management involve continually collecting feedback about various situations and then making judgments. Thus, evaluation is often a part of everyday life in organizations. However, to benefit the most from evaluations it is useful to develop and implement evaluation designs in an explicit and systematic fashion.

Many times, the activities of evaluation and assessment are, themselves, major methods to accomplish change in organizations. The activities can mobilize members of the organization to realize that they have unattended priorities that must be addressed soon in their organizations. Results of the activities can lend strong focus to the strategies and operations of the organization, as well.

One of the most profound learnings for experienced consultants is to always include some form of evaluation or assessment in their projects. Many times, they strongly believed that they knew the "truth" about their clients' problems and issues in organizations. Later on, after gathering more information, they realize that their initial impressions were not at all accurate. Many consultants would assert that it is unethical not to conduct some form of evaluation or assessment early on in projects.

# Benefits of Evaluation and Assessment

Sometimes people have a negative reaction to the term "evaluation." That is an unfortunate reaction because there are many benefits from evaluation. As we will discuss, the process of evaluation is similar to how adults learn, so there can be tremendous learning generated during evaluations. It might be useful for you to reference the following benefits when explaining to your client how evaluation is important to your consulting project with them.

Benefits of evaluation include that it:

1.    Enhances learning for participants as they continue to collect feedback, and make interpretations and judgments about how to support or improve their performance.

2.    Improves performance as participants continue to make adjustments to what they are doing on the basis of learning from their evaluations.

3.    Improves accountabilities and credibility among nonprofits and stakeholders at a time when nonprofits are competing hard for resources from communities and donors.

4.    Supports participation of people because the evaluation process, especially when conducted in a collaborative fashion, considers their feedback, opinions and conclusions.

5.    Cultivates realistic expectations as participants continually reference real-world results and compare them to their initial expectations in processes and projects.

6.    Facilitates meaningful communication among participants in the project – perhaps the most important benefit from the evaluation process.

# Myths About Evaluation and Assessment

One of the major reasons that people sometimes struggle to appreciate and support evaluations is because they entertain various myths about the process. The following paragraphs address those myths and might be useful to you as you work with your clients to help them appreciate and support evaluation activities in your consulting projects.

## Myth #1 – Evaluation Generates Boring, Useless Data

This was a problem with evaluations in the past, when evaluation designs were chosen largely on the basis of achieving complete scientific accuracy, reliability and validity. This approach often generated extensive data from which carefully chosen conclusions were drawn. Usually, generalizations and recommendations were avoided as much as possible. However, as a result, evaluation reports sometimes reiterated the obvious and left people disappointed and skeptical about the value of evaluation in general. More recently, especially because of Patton (1986), evaluation has focused on relevance, utility and practicality at least as much as on scientific accuracy, reliability and validity.

## Myth #2 – Evaluation Is a Complex Process That Requires Experts

Many people believe they must completely understand terms such as validity and reliability before they can conduct an effective evaluation on a project or program. On the contrary, they do not have to completely understand those terms. They do, however, have to consider what decisions they need to make and then how they will get and use that information to make those decisions.

## Myth #3 – Evaluation Is About Proving Success or Failure

This myth assumes that projects and programs can be implemented perfectly the first time and will operate themselves perfectly well into the future – all without ever having to make any adjustments to themselves. This does not happen in real life. Project and program success is based largely on remaining open to continuing feedback and then adjusting the project or program accordingly. Evaluations provide this continuing feedback.

# Major Dimensions and Categories of Evaluation

There are so many different applications for – and ways to conduct – evaluations that it can seem quite difficult to keep a clear perspective, much less to design an effective evaluation plan. One of the easiest ways to get a clear perspective is to first identify which dimension or category of evaluation you are undertaking.

## Two Major Dimensions of Evaluation

### Self-Directed Versus Other-Directed Evaluation

Self-directed evaluations occur when the evaluation of a set of activities, for example, a project, is designed and conducted by the people who also designed and implemented the project, as well. In that case, the people who designed the project and are implementing it are also collecting information about the project to make conclusions about its quality. A common example of a self-directed evaluation is use of self-assessments, such as self-assessment of learning styles or personality preferences.

In the above example, other-directed evaluation occurs when an "outside" evaluator evaluates the project. The outside evaluator designs the plan to conduct the evaluation, collects information about the quality of operations of the project, analyzes the information and then reports on the results of the analysis.

### Informal Versus Formal Evaluation

Informal evaluation activities are not organized into any consistent, methodical design.  For example, occasional questions about the quality of a project might be interpreted as informal evaluation.  Note that many experts on evaluation would probably argue that informal evaluation is not evaluation at all, but rather is just a random collection of information.  Those people who believe that there is such a thing as informal evaluations would probably argue that informal evaluations occur frequently and are a regular part of the activities to lead and manage organizations.

Formal evaluation activities are organized into a systematic framework, which lends a consistent form (thus "formal") to collecting, analyzing and reporting information.

## *Two Major Categories of Evaluation*

### Formative Evaluations

Formative evaluations are conducted as a process (in a project or program) while the process is being formed or implemented (thus, the use of the term "formative").  The primary purpose of formative evaluations is to continue to improve the quality of that process.  Thus, a formative evaluation of a consulting project might be conducted to ensure that your project is 1) operating according to the expectations of you and your client, and 2) heading toward achieving the results that both of you desire.

There are various types of formative evaluations, for example, implementation evaluation and process evaluation.  It is likely that your project will include at least a process evaluation.  Note that many of the organizational performance management models and quality management initiatives are centered largely around continuous formative evaluations, for example, strategic management, Balanced Scorecard, Total Quality Management (TQM) and continuous improvement.

 See "Common Types of Evaluation and Evaluation Questions" below for more information about implementation and process evaluations.

### Summative Evaluations

Summative evaluations are conducted after completion of a process to make conclusions about overall results and effectiveness.  For example, project results are often specified in terms of desired goals to be achieved by the project.  Occasionally, certain groups of desired goals are listed together in project plans under the same overall desired outcome.  It is likely that your project will include at least a results-based evaluation that judges the quality of the project's achievement of the goals and/or outcomes.

# Common Types of Evaluation and Evaluation Questions

There are many types of evaluation, for example, accreditation, cost-benefit analysis, descriptive, goals-based, goal-free, needs assessments, results, outcomes, performance, personnel, process, implementation, product, quality assurance and program.  Probably the most common types of evaluation used in consulting projects include implementation, process and results evaluation.  Each of these is described below.

Evaluations can be wide-ranging and generate tremendous amounts of information. Therefore, it is important to sustain strong focus during evaluation activities, especially when gathering, analyzing and reporting information. Focus in evaluations comes from the nature of the questions that must be answered, for example, "What are the strengths and weaknesses of the process?" or "What can be done to improve the process?" In addition to information about the most common types of evaluations in projects, the following paragraphs also suggest useful evaluation questions for each type of evaluation.

## Implementation Evaluation

The purpose of an implementation evaluation of a project is to discern whether the project is being implemented as specified in the project work plan. Patton (2002) suggests that, if an organization has limited resources with which to conduct an evaluation, there are occasions in which an implementation evaluation would be of greatest value. It is not uncommon to set out to implement a particular project design only to find out later that project staff has modified the process, sometimes substantially. It is often of no use to conduct a process or results evaluation if you do not know what process your project is really using to achieve those results in the first place. Therefore, seriously consider conducting an implementation evaluation.

An implementation evaluation gathers as much descriptive information as possible about as many aspects of the project's process as possible. This is particularly useful during the development phase of a project.

### Some Evaluation Questions to Consider When Doing an Implementation Evaluation

The following list of questions is by no means a standard and required set of evaluation questions that must be addressed whenever conducting an implementation evaluation. Rather, this list provides examples of evaluation questions to help you get a clearer sense about the purpose of an implementation evaluation and the nature of evaluation questions that might be useful when designing an implementation evaluation.

- How much is your client involved in developing and implementing the project? Is it to the extent desired by you and your client?

- What project activities are being conducted to achieve the desired results of the project? Are the results what were specified in the project plan?

- What resources, such as people, facilities and money, are being used to conduct the project? Are they what were specified in the project plan?

- What has been the timing of completion of the project's major activities so far? Is that what was specified in the project plan?

- What are the deliverables that have been produced by the project and when? Are they what were specified in the project plan?

- How does the implemented project differ from the planned project, so far? Are those differences important enough to change the implemented project or project plan?

- So far, what can be learned from current evaluation activities to improve future evaluations and project activities?

## *Process Evaluation*

Process evaluations are geared to understand how a process produces the results that it does. The focus is on "how" the process works, not so much on "what" activities are in the process (the latter is the focus of an implementation evaluation). Process evaluations focus on the dynamics of the processes and how they influence each other to produce results. These evaluations are useful in a consulting project, especially if your client reports many complaints or if there appear to be significant inefficiencies in project activities. Process evaluations are also useful for accurately portraying to outside parties how the process truly operates, which would be useful, for example, when considering replication of the process elsewhere.

### Some Evaluation Questions to Consider When Doing a Process Evaluation

1. What do you and your client consider to be the major strengths and weaknesses of the process?

2. What do you and your client like or dislike about the process?

3. What do other members of your client's organization consider to be the strengths and weaknesses of the process?

4. What do the members like or dislike about the process?

5. What can you, your client and other members recommend to improve the process?

6. What can you, your client and other members do to improve the process?

7. What is the best process to use now to achieve the desired results?

## *Results-Based Evaluation (Goals-Based and/or Outcomes-Based)*

Projects are established to meet one or more specific, desired results. Results are often specified in terms of goals and/or outcomes in the original project plans. Results-based evaluations evaluate the extent to which projects are meeting desired goals and/or outcomes.

Note that the process to design an outcomes-based program evaluation is often different than the process used to design an outcomes-based project evaluation.

### Do Not Focus Evaluation Only on Attainment of Desired Results

Results evaluations are useful to ascertain whether the project is achieving desired results or not. However, singular focus on attainment of results can substantially limit the learning from the evaluation. In addition to assessing the extent of progress toward achieving results, results-based evaluation can also be enlightening about:

- How the desired results were established.

- How the project worked toward the desired results.

- Whether the current desired results are realistic or not.

- How the desired results can be changed if necessary.

- Whether any new desired results should be added.

- How the project can be modified to pursue the new desired results.

 For detailed guidelines and forms to conduct an outcomes-based program evaluation, see the list of recommended resources on page 505.

By focusing results evaluations only on achievement of initially determined results, you can even impose arbitrary limits on the project itself. It is common that project plans are modified as the plans are implemented. As a result, desired results from the project often are changed, as well. Thus, results evaluations can be limiting if focused only on initially determined desired results.

### Some Evaluation Questions to Consider When Doing a Results Evaluation

1. Have the goals and outcomes been achieved? If not, what else needs to be achieved?

2. Have all of the issues in the organization been addressed? If not, which issues still need attention? What should be done?

3. Has the vision for change been achieved? If not, what else needs to be accomplished to achieve the vision? How should that be done?

4. Have the action plans been implemented? If not, which action plans are yet to be accomplished?

5. Have the performance indicators for success been achieved? If not, which ones still need attention?

6. Do leaders in the organization agree that the project has been successful? If not, which leaders disagree? What else needs to be done?

# Major Levels of Evaluation

It is common practice among evaluators, particularly in training and development activities, to consider various levels of evaluation that are commonly referred to as the Kirkpatrick (1994) levels. It will be helpful for you to keep these levels in mind when designing and conducting evaluations in your projects. These levels give you some indication as to the usefulness of evaluations in achieving long-lasting change in your client's organization. The significance of the levels tends to increase with each level. The complexity in conducting the evaluations tends to increase with each level, as well. Also, achieving higher levels of evaluation often requires that lower levels were conducted successfully, as well. Here is an overview of the various levels.

## *Level One – Reactions (What Was Your Experience?)*

This is probably the most commonly used level of evaluation. We are most used to experiencing it at the end of training sessions when the trainer hands out an evaluation form for us to complete. Some people call the forms "reactionnaires" or "happy forms" because the forms evaluate our reactions and feelings about the training. This level of evaluation is the least reliable in terms of making valid conclusions about the effectiveness of development activities, especially regarding progress toward organizational effectiveness.

Despite this level being the least reliable, the level is useful in getting quick impressions of the likelihood of participants' continued participation in development activities, such as projects for organizational change. You can assume that your client will not accomplish significant types of learning and change if they do not have positive reactions to your services. Thus, level-one evaluations can be useful in that regard.

## Level Two – Learning (Any New Knowledge, Skills, Attitudes?)

Evaluation at this level is about the extent of learning achieved by participants. Learning is interpreted by trainers and educators to be enhanced knowledge, skills and/or attitudes. Evaluations regarding knowledge often include measurements of a participant's knowledge before and after an experience. Evaluations regarding skills often include observation of the participant when conducting an activity, sometimes before and after, but usually after, an experience. Evaluations about participants' attitudes is often more complex and can involve collecting information from them about their perspectives and opinions before, during and after an experience.

Note that there is often a direct association between the major aspects of outcomes (a popular type of nonprofit program evaluation) and learning. Short-term outcomes often are associated with changes in program participants' level of knowledge. Intermediate outcomes are associated with changes in skills. Long-term outcomes are associated with changes in attitudes, conditions and perspectives.

## Level Three – Transfer (How Is Learning Being Used?)

Evaluations at this level are about participant's ability to apply their new learning towards successfully completing certain tasks. This level is often called the "transfer level" because it is associated with evaluating whether new learning has been successfully transferred from the service provider (for example, the trainer, consultant or coach) to the learner. The best forms of learning are those that can be used "to get something done." This level is often the most important type of evaluation because it can be used to make conclusions about whether learning was really useful or not. Also, this level of evaluation can still be somewhat practical to conduct (as compared to level four evaluation). Thus, this level is often the most meaningful to conduct during projects.

## Level Four – Results (What Is the "Bottom Line?")

In accordance with principles of performance management, results at this level mean that the participant can apply new skills in the organization such that the organization can more successfully achieve its overall results. This is the level at which most organizational change consultants hope to show positive conclusions from evaluations. This is the level that seems to reveal the overall effectiveness of the consultation.

However, it is also the level at which it is extremely difficult to conduct relevant evaluations. There are a variety of reasons for this predicament. For an effective evaluation, evaluators usually must work with participants after the consulting project has been completed to determine the short-term and long-term effects of the consultation. Usually, the project is not designed to provide that kind of long-term involvement. Also, it can be quite difficult to identify any "theory of action" or "chain of events" that could convince people that organizational effectiveness was a direct result of staff participation in a project. Also, by the time a project is finished – and especially if the project seems to have been successful – clients usually have lost motivation to take part in further evaluation.

Despite the challenges in designing a highly relevant and credible evaluation at level four, there are several advantages to making the attempt. The focus on performance and learning that can come from a level-four evaluation often makes it well worth the effort. If you think about it, the overall process of performance management is itself an attempt at level-four evaluation. The process includes carefully collecting information to decide if the organization is achieving its overall desired results.

# Various New Perspectives on Evaluation

In the past, evaluations often were conducted in a highly scientific manner with strong emphasis on accuracy, validity and reliability. Those comprehensive evaluations treated the focus of the evaluation almost like a "black box" to be objectively examined from "the outside looking in." Far too often, that type of scientific evaluation produced reports that were impenetrable to the average reader. They were difficult to readily apply in the day-to-day activities of leading and managing organizations.

That major problem has spawned a variety of new perspectives on evaluation. Some experts assert that evaluation has, in itself, become a new form of capacity building. The following paragraphs explain some of the more prominent new perspectives. Each tends to suggest that the more your client is involved – collaborates – in all of your evaluation activities, the more likely that your evaluation will be useful.

## Qualitative Evaluation

Qualitative information from an evaluation is about the thoughts, feelings and perceptions from participants. In contrast, quantitative information is about specific indications, such as those produced by numbers, ratings, rankings, yes's, and no's.

In the past, evaluations were based, in large part, on quantitative information. Evaluators and other researchers have come to realize the primary limitation of using only quantitative information – it usually does not accurately reflect the totality of the participants' beliefs and perceptions about their own experiences. It is those beliefs and perceptions from which participants choose to make decisions and take actions in their projects and organizations. Thus, quantitative information can be quite limiting when used solely as the basis for understanding your clients and how they make decisions during a project.

Patton (2002) explains how qualitative information is used much more now than in the past in various forms of research, such as evaluations. Researchers have produced more ways to collect and analyze qualitative information, including ways to identify various patterns, themes and conclusions that emerge from the information.

## Utilization-Focused Evaluation

Patton (1986) asserts several premises about utilization-focused evaluation. First, the driving force for an evaluation should be concern for utilization, or applicability and usefulness. Second, the priority on utilization should be paramount throughout the design and implementation of evaluation plans. Third, evaluations should be user-oriented, specifically to the people who will use the results of the evaluation. Fourth, the users of the evaluation should be actively involved in decisions about the evaluation. Fifth, there will be various interests from various stakeholders about an evaluation. Those interests must be considered, along with the limitations by which evaluators can suit all those interests.

Utilization-focused evaluation places strong emphasis not only on producing useful evaluation results, but also on recognizing the limitations of the evaluator and participants in conducting evaluations. Limitations are in the form of limited time, energy and knowledge. The advantage of utilization-focused evaluation is the strong likelihood that results will be useful to you and your clients. A drawback can be lack of credibility from external stakeholders (for example, funders) who seek more comprehensive, scientific rigor in methodologies and findings.

## Holistic Evaluation

Holistic evaluations produce conclusions about the quality of some phenomena in its entirety, rather than about its specific parts. Depending on the availability of resources and time to produce conclusions from evaluations, holistic evaluations are likely to include a variety of means to collect a variety of types of information about many aspects of the phenomena. Then the various pieces of information are integrated into conclusions about the overall quality of the phenomena. Project evaluations conducted from a holistic perspective are careful to focus on as many aspects of the project as possible, and not just on whether certain project goals were achieved or not. That overall, holistic perspective greatly enhances your understanding of the project and your client's organization. The major advantage of holistic evaluation is that the evaluator often gains a more focused, and sometimes complete and accurate, understanding of some phenomena. The disadvantage is that, in seeking to focus on the system as a whole, important nuances about the system can go unnoticed.

## Participatory Evaluation

Participatory evaluation has become a major approach to evaluation, particularly in efforts that involve diverse values and perspectives. The approach can be used to transform organizations and communities, particularly when the focus is on change and learning. Whyte (1991) explains that participants in the evaluation engage in the actual planning and implementation of the evaluation process itself. There is not an external evaluator doing an evaluation *on* people, rather it is the people who are doing an evaluation *amongst* themselves. Major advantages of participatory evaluation are that the approach can be a powerful means for participants to build community among themselves, develop strong skills in continuous learning (skills in reflection and inquiry), and improve how they live and work. A major challenge for consultants is maintaining strong participation from nonprofit leaders who likely are already overworked and fighting various day-to-day crises in their nonprofits.

## Developmental Evaluation

In developmental evaluation, there are no pre-established goals and outcomes to be used as the basis for evaluation, rather the evaluation emerges over time. Patton (1994) first suggested developmental evaluation as a means to ensure that evaluations remain relevant, particularly in projects and programs that are likely to have unexpected changes. Few projects occur exactly as specified in project plans. Instead, plans are changed as you and your client learn more about the various problems or goals to be addressed by the project. The developmental approach helps you and your client to be aware of what is actually occurring during a project, remain open to any necessary changes during a project, and learn from those changes.

# Barriers to Evaluation and Assessment and How to Overcome Them

## *Barriers*

Before giving attention to guidelines about evaluating organizational change projects, you should be aware of some common barriers to evaluation. The barriers can crop up in any kind of project and with any kind of organization, but occur chiefly with small- to medium-sized nonprofit organizations. Barriers can occur as a result of:

- A new, major issue that suddenly became more important than the original issue that the project was supposed to address.

- Resistance from participants because they have negative feelings, and sometimes major myths, about evaluation.

- Resistance from participants because it goes against their values, for example, they feel they are judging people.

- People who are cynical about the real value of evaluation.

- Lack of expertise to design a relevant, credible and practical evaluation.

- People who succumb to burnout during the project.

- People believe that things are already just fine and do not understand the need for an evaluation.

## *Helping Clients Overcome Barriers*

As a consultant, you can address these barriers. Consider the following guidelines.

1.  Explain what evaluation is. Help clients realize that they are probably already doing evaluation, but just not calling it that.

2.  Explain the major myths about evaluation. Ask them if they have any of those myths. Debunk the myths.

3.  Explain that evaluation focuses on relevance and utility and practicality, not just on complete accuracy, validity and reliability.

4.  Explain that evaluation is often associated with a great deal of learning.

5.  Ensure that your evaluation design suits the nature and needs of your client's organization.

# Guidelines for Successful Evaluation and Assessment

The following guidelines are useful in any type of evaluation or assessment that you design for your projects.

1.  **Ensure the evaluation design matches the nature and needs of your client.**
    One of the best ways to ensure a close match is to involve your client as much as possible in the design and implementation of the evaluation plan. That highly collaborative and participatory approach enjoys all the benefits of collaboration (the benefits explained throughout this Field Guide), especially the benefits of strong relevance of the evaluation plan and the participation of your client in implementing that plan.

2.  **Discuss evaluation with your client in the early phases of the project.**
    Evaluation occurs throughout a project. The best forms of evaluation include the commitment and participation of your client. Therefore, it is best if you involve your client, as soon as possible, in the design and implementation of evaluation plans. Also, the sooner that you discuss evaluation in the project, the sooner that you can begin collecting useful information for the evaluation. In the early discussions, mention the benefits of evaluation.

     See "Benefits of Evaluation and Assessment" on page 199 for a description of the benefits of evaluation.

3.  **Focus on relevance, utility and practicality as much as on "scientific" priorities.**
    Scientific priorities are in regard to accuracy, validity and reliability. Far too many highly "scientific" evaluation reports sit collecting dust on shelves because the reports have little utility and practicality and, thus, little relevance to the readers of the reports. Therefore, it is far better to err on the side of less scientific value and more on usefulness of the report by focusing on relevance, utility and practicality.

4.  **Integrate project evaluation with other ongoing evaluations in the organization.**
    Many organizations conduct various forms of evaluation as part of their ongoing management activities, for example, as part of ongoing employee performance management, program evaluations and strategic planning. Integrating your project evaluations with these other activities in the organization helps your client to leverage their evaluation activities and, thus, save time and energy.

5.  **First, reference the results (goals and/or outcomes) specified in the project plan.**
    Your client will be interested in whether your project is achieving the results needed to solve a specific problem or achieve a specific goal. Therefore, the design of your evaluation plans should first be focused on whether the project is achieving those results or not. That usually means including a results evaluation.

6.  **Focus on short-term, intermediate and long-term results, if possible.**
    Successful change in organizations can take from several months to several years to accomplish. It is important that you and your client be as realistic as possible when determining what results should occur and by when. By focusing evaluation on near-term results, you can verify quick successes that provide motivation and credibility for the project. By focusing evaluation on more long-term results, you can establish more realistic and meaningful results and then verify that those results are actually achieved.

7.   **Include some form of process evaluation, too.**
     Projects rarely are implemented exactly as planned. Instead, various adjustments, or continuous improvements, must be made as participants learn more about the problems or goals to be addressed by the project. Process evaluation is essential for strong, continuous improvements to your project.

8.   **Include a mix of methods to collect information.**
     For example, review relevant documentation such as strategic plans, policies, procedures and reports. Then administer practical questionnaires to quickly collect information anonymously if appropriate. Follow up your questionnaires with various interviews. Interviews might be closed (by asking specific questions that evoke specific answers) or open-ended (asking general questions that can evoke a wide range of responses) and with individuals or groups.

9.   **Place high priority on capturing learning during evaluations.**
     Learning involves gaining new knowledge, skills or perspectives – learning is not merely finding new things to do. The best forms of learning from evaluation are those that are focused on solving the problems or achieving the goals that are the primary focus of your project with your client.

 See "Cultivating and Guiding Learning" on page 213 for more explanation about the learning process and how the process can be systematically included in consulting projects.

10.  **Be careful about using only pre- and post-project assessments in evaluation.**
     Occasionally, you and your clients might want to conduct an evaluation of a project specifically by comparing the situation that existed before the project with the situation after the project has been completed. This is commonly referred to as a pre- and post-test approach to evaluation. Although this approach can be useful, it should not be the only approach used in evaluation. A great deal of learning can be gleaned by using process evaluations during a project, as well. In addition, the pre- and post-project assessment might show little or no difference, and yet your client might have gained a great deal during the project because of the learning gained from project activities.

11.  **Share learning from evaluations as soon as you have them**.
     There is a tendency to put off acting on the results, or conclusions, from evaluations until the project has been finished. That approach treats the project like a "black box" that should not be tampered with until the project is over. That approach also minimizes the tremendous value that evaluations have for making continuous improvement. By promptly sharing results with your clients, you can make ongoing adjustments to the project to ensure that the project remains high quality. You also help to ensure strong buy in among your clients.

12.  **Produce written evaluation reports**.
     One of the best ways to ensure that all participants clearly understand the results of evaluations is to produce a written evaluation report. At a minimum, the report should document the purpose of the report, how data was collected and analyzed, findings and conclusions, and recommendations.

# How to Design Successful Evaluation and Assessment Plans

The more focused you are about the purpose of your evaluation, the more effective and efficient you can be in the design and implementation of evaluation plans, and the more useful your evaluation results will be. That kind of focus comes from using a formal approach to evaluation, which requires using a formal approach to designing your plans for evaluation, as well. Consider the following key questions when designing any kind of evaluations or assessments.

1.  **Who are the primary audiences?**
    For example, is the information for Board members, management, staff, funders or clients? Each of these audiences might need to make specific decisions about the project. Also, they might require that project evaluation information be organized and presented in a certain manner to really be useful to them.

2.  **What are the primary purposes?**
    For example, the purpose of the evaluation might be to answer certain management questions, such as: How do we address problems and improve the project? How do we discern if the project is achieving its goals, or clarify and verify what benefits the organization is realizing by participating in the project?

3.  **What questions must be answered?**
    If the decision that you need to make is about improving the project, you might have a range of evaluation questions to answer, such as: What are the strengths and weaknesses of the approach in the project? Is the project achieving its goals and if not, why not?

4.  **What types of information are needed?**
    For example, if you want to know if you need to improve the project or not, then you might need information on staff and client complaints, costs of the project, or the changes that clients report from having participated in the project.

5.  **From what sources should the information be collected?**
    For example, should it be collected from individual employees, individual clients, groups of clients, groups of employees or also from program documentation?

6.  **What are the best methods to collect the information?**
    Can you get the information from reviewing documentation, using questionnaires, conducting interviews? Are there assessment instruments that you can use? Should you use an instrument that has already been developed or should you develop your own? Is it best to use a mix of these methods?

7.  **What context-sensitive considerations must be made?**
    Each organization has unique features, such as its culture, nature of leadership, rate of change in its environment, nature of programs and services, and size. How do these features influence how you will gather your information?

8.  **What is the best timing for getting the information?**
    Do you need to provide a report by a certain date? Are there problems that need to be addressed right away? How often can you get access to the sources of the information that you need? How long will it take to collect information?

9.    **Who should collect the information?**
Ideally, someone from outside the project does the information collection, analysis and reporting. That approach helps to ensure that the evaluation is carried out in a highly objective and low-bias manner. However, it is often unrealistic for small- to medium-sized nonprofits to afford an outside evaluator. Consequently, it is important to select personnel who can conduct the evaluation in a manner as objective as possible. Equally as important is to ensure that the project operations are designed so they automatically generate much of the information that will be useful in evaluating the project.

10.    **How will you analyze the information?**
How the information is analyzed depends much on the focus of the evaluation questions and on the nature of the information, for example, whether the information will contain lots of numbers or comments.

11.    **How will you make interpretations and conclusions?**
You will need some frame of reference from which to make judgments about the information, for example, performance indicators, best practices, theories or standards of performance.

 See "Maximum Performance – Different Things to Different People" on page 179 for more information about best practices.

12.    **How will you report the information?**
How the evaluation results are reported depends on the nature of the audience and the decisions that must be made about the project. For example, you might provide an extensive written report or a presentation to a group of people.

13.    **Should you test your evaluation and assessment plans?**
Depending on the complexity of your plans, you might benefit from field testing them by using data-collection tools with a certain group of people to discern if the tools are understandable to them.

14.    **What ethical considerations must be made?**
For example, do you want to report any information unique to any of the participants? If so, you will need to get their expressed consent. In any case, you will need to tell any of your potential participants of your evaluation plans.

# Cultivating and Guiding Learning

Despite many of us having participated in years of formal education and schooling, we still have vague, confused perceptions about learning. Yet learning plays a critical role in how we perform in life and work. This overall section of the Field Guide will help you to understand learning, including its role in change and performance, key components of learning, various myths about learning, state-of-the-art concepts in learning, and how to integrate learning plans into your projects with your clients. Information throughout this section applies whether you are an external or internal consultant.

## Learning, Change and Performance

Educators and trainers typically view learning as enhancing one's knowledge, skills and attitudes – they often use the acronym "KSA" to refer to these three concepts. The essence of learning is change – you cannot successfully change something without first learning about it and you cannot successfully learn something without it changing you.

People learn a great deal in life and work. Ultimately, learning is enhancing one's capacity to perform. The most important learning in organizations is learning tied to performance of individuals, groups, processes or the entire organization itself.

As a professional consultant, one of your most important goals is to ensure that, as a result of your guidance, your clients are more able to solve their own problems and achieve their own goals. You and your clients cannot achieve that overall goal without focusing on learning during your projects.

Many of us naturally accomplish learning without really thinking about it. We learn from activities, such as discussions, reflection and analyses. However, the best type of learning is learning made conscious so we can communicate about it – and build on it – with others. Therefore, it is important to integrate opportunities for learning into your projects and to take advantage of those opportunities to more effectively solve problems and achieve goals.

## Key Components of Learning

You can get a clearer perspective on the concept of learning by getting clear on various components and on several related terms. The following paragraphs provide definitions of key terms related to learning.

### Information

At its most basic form, a piece of information about something is a "unit of awareness" about that thing. Information alone is not learning. Some people think that this awareness occurs only in the brain and, therefore, usually comes from some form of thought. Other people also accept information as a form of realization from other forms of inquiry, for example, intuition.

### Knowledge

Knowledge is gleaned by getting some sense of the value and organization of the information. Typically, information evolves to knowledge by the learner's mulling it around in their heads, talking about it with others, being tested on it, or somehow using the information. Knowledge is the most basic form of learning.

## Skills

Skills are a higher form of learning than knowledge. Skills are developed by applying knowledge in an effective and efficient manner to accomplish tasks and goals in life and work. People notice skills in others, usually by observing their behavior. The value of knowledge is often judged by what you can do with that knowledge.

## Attitudes, Perspectives

The most powerful form of learning is when people develop new ways of perceiving things. People take actions based on their beliefs and their beliefs are often based on their perceptions. Changes in perception are often considered to be the highest form of learning. Later on in this section, we will explore more about this when we discuss single-, double- and triple-loop learning.

## Training

This term is often interpreted as the activity when an expert and learner work together to effectively transfer information from the expert to the learner to enhance the learner's knowledge, skills and attitudes so the learner can better perform a current task or job. Compare this to the terms education and development, described below.

## Education

Education is accomplishing a new understanding of the world and your role in it, so your life and work are substantially enhanced, as well. In a sense, education is becoming socialized, or immersed in a culture, to better understand society and how you can effectively function in that society.

## Development

This term is often viewed as a broad, ongoing, multi-faceted set of activities to bring someone or an organization up to another threshold of performance. Development includes a wide variety of methods, for example, orienting about a role, training in a wide variety of areas, ongoing training on the job, coaching, mentoring and self-development. Some view development as a life-long goal.

# Myths About Learning

Despite having participated in years of schooling, we entertain certain myths about learning – myths that can greatly inhibit our learning in life and work. The following advice is geared to help learners avoid those myths.

## Myth #1 – Information Is Knowledge

Too often, when we want to learn something, we take a course, gain lots of new information and then consider ourselves as having learned the information. Yet how much of the material from those courses did we actually apply? New information is not necessarily the same as learning unless you also apply that information and think about what you learned from applying it. Paulo Freire, who is possibly responsible for educating more human beings than anyone in history, asserts that "without practice, there is no knowledge."

## Myth #2 – Entertainment Is Enlightenment

Go to your personal library and look at the hundreds or maybe thousands of books there. How many of them did you buy because you were thrilled by the title of the book, but after having purchased it, you did not read the book at all? Now think about trainings that you attended where the trainer was highly inspirational and entertaining, but you did not use any of the information from the trainings at all. Sometimes, new learning comes from uncomfortable situations, when we have to push ourselves to actually apply the new information.

## Myth #3 – Rational Analysis Is the Only Way to Learn

Assignments over the years sometimes ask us to analyze the content of some expert source of material and then write a paper. Yet, Eastern philosophies that have existed thousands of years remind us of the role of intuition, and of the role of reflection on our experiences and on our practices. We can learn both from our hearts and souls and from our heads. Experienced leaders and consultants have learned to trust their intuition at least as much as their skills in rational analysis.

## Myth #4 – Learning and Actions Are the Same Thing

Ask action-driven people what they have learned lately and it is likely that they will tell you the latest actions that they added to their "to do" lists. Remind them that learning is new knowledge, skills or attitudes, not actions, and they might just stare at you – they are not used to thinking about learning at all. Certainly, learning can come from action and useful learning should produce action, but learning and actions are not the same things.

# Barriers to Learning During Projects

There are a variety of barriers that can affect learning during projects. The following paragraphs describe those barriers. One of the most powerful approaches to overcome the barriers is to integrate opportunities for continuous learning in your projects – an upcoming subsection explains the concept of continuous learning. Another approach is to work collaboratively with your client to design systematic learning plans into your project – another upcoming subsection explains how to design systematic learning plans.

1. **Myths about learning**
   As mentioned above in this subsection, "Myths About Learning," people often have major myths about learning, assuming that it is the same as gaining new information (rather than knowledge), is the same as being entertained, is the same as taking action, and is produced only from highly rational thought processes. Those myths can be strong barriers to real learning in life and work.

2. **Uncomfortable, previous experiences with learning**
   Misdirected educators can convey the impression that learning results only from working hard to memorize information conveyed by some expert source and then to pass rigorous tests to prove that we learned the information. Many of us end up believing that schooling is an uncomfortable experience where we are treated more like sheep than people. We end up feeling that learning is something to be avoided altogether.

3. **Dependence on others for learning**
   Years of schooling can convince us that learning comes only from experts and not from ourselves, which can be a barrier to learning. Management literature frequently includes

mention of various "gurus," or larger-than-life experts. Often, the credibility of new theories and practices is measured by whether the information came from a guru. Many of us discount our own judgment in lieu of depending on the latest pronouncements from gurus.

4. **Mismatched learning styles**
People prefer to learn in a variety of ways. Some people learn primarily by seeing or visualizing information, others through hearing and others through experience. Some learn by analyzing information and others by acting on it. Experienced trainers have learned to integrate a variety of learning styles into their training methods. A mismatch between learning styles can be a strong barrier to learning, for example, if participants in a project prefer to learn by doing, but the consultant prefers to train by delivering extended lectures.

5. **Learning seen as a luxury**
Occasionally, clients with limited time and energy view learning as if it is an activity in which they cannot afford to indulge. When consultants ask their clients to reflect on their own experiences to learn from those experiences, clients may be reluctant to do so. This can cause a major barrier to learning during a project.

# Different Kinds of Learning (Loops of Learning)

Key breakthroughs in helping people understand the dynamics of learning are the concepts of single-loop, double-loop and triple-loop learning. These concepts help you to realize and appreciate the kinds of learning that you and your client can glean during a project. The concepts are largely from the works of Argyris and Schon (1974).

## *Single-Loop Learning (Following the Rules)*

The conventional example used to explain this concept is the thermostat. It operates in one mode. When it detects that the room is too cold, it turns on the furnace. When it detects that the room is too hot, it turns off the furnace. In other words, the system includes one automatic and limited type of reaction – little or no learning occurs and little or no insight is needed. Experts assert that most organizations operate according to single-loop learning – members establish rigid strategies, policies and procedures and then spend their time detecting and correcting deviations from the "rules."

You might exhibit this kind of learning when you notice that your client has not produced a certain deliverable on time during a project, so you get angry at your client and demand that your client produce the deliverable – without ever really exploring why your client did not produce the deliverable in the first place.

## *Double-Loop Learning (Changing the Rules)*

In double-loop learning, members of the organization are able to reflect on whether the "rules" themselves should be changed, not only on whether deviations have occurred and how to correct them. This kind of learning involves more "thinking outside the box," creativity and critical thinking. This learning often helps participants understand why a particular solution works better than others to solve a problem or achieve a goal. Experts assert that double-loop learning is critical to the success of an organization, especially during times of rapid change.

To continue the above example of your client not producing a deliverable, double-loop learning occurs when you engage your client in discussion about their reasons for the absence of the deliverable, and whether your expectations were realistic or not. Results of the discussion might be, for example, that project timelines are changed or that communications between consultant and client are improved.

### Triple-Loop Learning (Learning About Learning)

Triple-loop learning involves "learning how to learn" by reflecting on how we learn in the first place. In this situation, participants would reflect on how they think about the "rules," not only on whether the rules should be changed. This form of learning helps us to understand a great deal more about ourselves and others regarding beliefs and perceptions. Triple-loop learning might be explained as double-loop learning about double-loop learning.

To continue the above example, triple-loop learning occurs when, after having engaged in discussion with your client, both of you discuss the dynamics of your conversation, including how it was conducted, what learning was produced from the conversation, and how that learning was produced.

## Continuous Learning

### Ability to Learn to Learn

The concept of continuous learning has received a significant amount of attention during the past decade because it holds tremendous promise in enhancing the performance of individuals and organizations. It follows that consulting projects also can benefit from integrating concepts of continuous learning into various phases of the consulting project.

Simply put, continuous learning is the ability to learn to learn. Learning need not be a linear event where a learner goes to a formal learning program, gains areas of knowledge and skills about a process, and then the learning ceases. If the learner can view life (including work) as a "learning program," then the learner can continue to learn from almost everything in life. As a result, the learner continues to expand his or her capacity for living and working.

### Skills in Reflection and Inquiry

Continuous learning is not achieved by continuously attending training sessions, courses, workshops and seminars. Rather, continuous learning, or learning how to learn, is developed primarily from skills in reflection and inquiry. Skills in reflection are the ability to examine one's own experiences and to learn how to deal with new experiences as a result. Skills in inquiry are the ability to ask powerful questions that cultivate learning. These two skills are the essence of continuous learning. This learning is often in the form of "Aha!"s, or flashes of insight.

## Key Principles of Adult Learning

During a consulting project, you and your client can often learn a great deal. However, the most important learning seldom comes from the same traditional means used in all of your years of schooling. Rather than learning from gaining a great deal of new knowledge that you memorize and repeat on tests, you and your client usually learn according to the following principles of adult learning.

### Growth Requires Willingness to Experience, to Develop

Learning often involves new skills, developing new behaviors. After many years of classroom education, it is easy for us to take a course where all we must do is attend each meeting, take notes and pass tests – and call this learning. A person can finish a Masters in Business Administration (MBA), but unless they are willing to actually *apply* new information, they will most likely end up with an office full of un-referenced textbooks and a head full of data, but little knowledge and wisdom. For the learning process to succeed, the individual must be willing to take risks, be open to new ideas, be able to share doubts and fears about new information and situations, apply the new information to current and real-world challenges, and then learn, especially by asking themselves and others powerful questions about their experience.

### Growth Involves the Entire Learner

If learning is to be more than collecting new information, then we must involve ourselves completely in our learning experiences. Unfortunately, too many development programs still operate from the assumption that the learner can somehow separate personal development from professional development. So we end up getting a great deal of help with information about finance and sales, but little help with stress and time management. Then when we enter the hectic world of management, we struggle to keep perspective and we are plagued with self-doubts. True learning involves looking at every aspect of our lives, not just at what is in our heads.

### Growth Requires Ongoing Feedback

Many of us do not know what we need to learn – we do not know what we do not know. Therefore, feedback from others is critical to understanding ourselves and our jobs. Feedback is useful in more ways than telling us what we do not know. Feedback also deepens and enriches what we do know. Research indicates that adults learn new information and methods best when they a) actually *apply* the information and methods, and b) exchange feedback around those experiences. However, we are often reluctant to seek advice and impressions from others, particularly fellow workers. We are sometimes reluctant to share feedback with others, as well. The courage to overcome our reluctance and fear is often the first step toward achieving true meaning in our lives and our jobs.

### Trust Your Instincts to Learn

Learning does not come only from other people telling you what you need to know and how you need to learn it! The highly motivated, self-directed learner can make a "classroom of life." Everything becomes an experience from which to learn. A person can design their own learning experiences. They can think about what they want to learn, how they might learn it and how they will know if they learned it.

## Forms of Peer Learning for Your Projects

### What Is Peer Learning?

Peer learning has become a major form of providing and enhancing capacity building activities. De Vita (2001) suggests that peer learning is one of the eight requirements for an effective capacity building activity. The Environmental Support Center and Innovation Network, Inc. (2002) assert that peer learning is one of the nine principles for effective capacity building.

The concept of peer learning is popular in personal, professional and organizational development today. It is highly valued by business leaders and managers, whether for-profit or nonprofit. It is written about by educators, researchers, writers and consultants. It is used by consulting services, training centers, associations, businesses and citizens.

While the phrase "peer learning" is used a great deal, it can mean many different things to many different people. Perhaps the best definition is simply that "peer learning" means peers who are learning from each other. All of the people in a peer learning activity are equally dedicated to helping others to learn. In that sense, they all are "peers" to each other, regardless of their status in life or work.

## Why Is Peer Learning So Popular Today?

There are numerous advantages to peer learning activities, depending on the particular design of the activity.

1.   **It is ideal for adult learning.**
     Senge (Doubleday, 1990), points out that adults learn best when they are 1) working on current, real-life challenges and 2) exchanging feedback with others in similar situations. Various forms of peer learning, especially when applied to real-life challenges, such as those in consulting projects, provide ideal conditions for adult learning.

2.   **It can expand, deepen and enrich traditional forms of training.**
     Peer learning activities can be used to make traditional forms of training and development much more powerful, for example, courses, workshops, seminars or consultations during a project. Rather than one-shot sessions in which experts talk *at* learners, peer learning activities encourage peers to share feedback, materials and support each other's learning.

3.   **Peers can manage their own learning and development.**
     Peers can manage their own learning by setting learning goals, methods and means to evaluation. Thus, forms of peer learning can set the foundation for successful self-directed and continuous learning in life and work.

4.   **Peer learning can be very cost-effective.**
     Peers do most of the work in peer learning activities. Expensive consultants and materials often are not needed. Thus, the learning can be quite cost-effective, especially when designed to complement other traditional forms of services. This can be valuable to organizations with limited resources, such as nonprofit organizations.

5.   **Programs accommodate the busy schedules of peers.**
     One of the most frequent complaints among adult learners is that they cannot find the time to attend professional development sessions. In peer learning activities, peers can schedule and locate their own learning sessions, which makes the sessions accommodating to their busy schedules.

6.   **Peer learning builds teams.**
     Working and learning together results in a common understanding of team roles. Learning how team members learn and what team members' priorities are leads to opportunities to support and assist each other. Ultimately, it builds positive regard among team members.

A downside of peer learning can occur when there is little useful experience or expertise among the peers from which they can learn. Still, peers can help each other by sharing ongoing feedback, support and accountabilities to take actions to get things done – and learn from reflection on those actions.

## *Various Forms of Peer Learning*

You will recognize the various forms of peer learning listed below. They are common to many of us – so common that the power of these forms of learning has been taken for granted.

The following peer-based models are popular forms of group (two or more people) activities in which learning can occur intentionally or unintentionally.

### Table III:3 – Common Types of Peer-Learning Models

| Model | Common Uses | Role of Learning |
|---|---|---|
| Action learning groups | Small groups of people organized to work on real-world priorities | Intentional |
| Committees | Groups of people organized toward a common purpose or goal | Unintentional |
| Debates | Convince people of one point of view over another | Unintentional |
| Dialogues | Deepen understanding, and especially meaning, around a topic or question | Intentional |
| Discussion | Share comments and opinions to make a decision or enhance understanding | Often unintentional |
| Self-help groups | Groups of people organized to personally benefit each member | Intentional |
| Study groups | Groups of people organized to learn a common topic or skill | Intentional |
| Teams | Groups of people organized toward a common purpose or goal | Unintentional |

There are a variety of other forms of peer groupings that are less common in training and development, for example, clearing committees, communities of practice, elder circles, peer mentoring and peer review groups.

Any of these can be powerful forms of learning during consulting projects, particularly if they are integrated with frequent opportunities for reflection and inquiry to identify new learning. Many of these forms can be integrated into project activities.

### *Power of Peer Coaching Groups (Action Learning)*

Action Learning has quickly gained wide attention as a powerful means to ensure actions in the workplace and learning at the same time. Action Learning includes ongoing meetings of peers to address real-world issues or goals and learn at the same time. Between meetings, peers take action on their issues or goals and learn from reflection on those actions.

One format of the Action Learning process is peer coaching groups in which each peer is coached by others during the meeting. Peers use the same process as the personal and professional coaching process.

See "Coaching for Deep Problem-Solving and Learning" on page 68 for guidelines to do coaching. Group members can use these guidelines, too.

## Integrating Learning into Your Projects

One of the most successful ways to reliably cultivate and capture learning during your projects is to integrate a systematic Learning Plan into your project. The plan need not be extremely detailed and in great depth to be useful. However, as with any other type of plans in your project, the Learning Plan should be developed in a highly collaborative fashion with your client.

See "Develop a Learning Plan to Capture Learning During the Project" on page 334 for guidelines to develop a Learning Plan.

# PART IV:

# COLLABORATIVE

# CONSULTING CYCLE

# Description

## *Prerequisite Readings and Knowledge*

Guidelines throughout PART IV will guide you and your client through the various phases of the collaborative consulting cycle. Depending on your current knowledge and expertise about consulting and nonprofits, you might benefit from first reading other sections in the Field Guide. Proceeding through PART IV without having read other necessary sections in the Field Guide would be like trying to cook a meal by reading through the recipe even though you do not have the necessary food ingredients.

| Consulting Cycle: |
|---|
| Client's Start-Up |
| Engagement |
| Discovery |
| Action Planning |
| Implementation |
| Adoption |
| Termination |

See "How to Use the Field Guide" on page xix to understand how to best use this Field Guide, including what sections to read and in what order.

Also, before proceeding through the phases, be sure that you have read the general description of the collaborative consulting cycle, including its history and the factors that influence how you proceed through the phases.

See "Overview of the Phases of the Collaborative Consulting Cycle" on page 22 for a general overview of the cycle.

## *Use of the Term "Problem" Throughout PART IV*

There are many occasions in which a project is conducted, not to solve some major current problem, but to achieve a more forward-looking overall goal. To solve the problem, a project usually establishes various "goals" to be achieved during the project. On those occasions, use of the term "problem" might not be appropriate and use of the term "goals" might be confusing.

Because many organizational change projects are undertaken to solve a major problem or meet a major need, and because there can be confusion with multiple uses of the term "goal" in a project, the term "problem" is used throughout this PART IV to refer to the problem, need, opportunity or overall goal to be addressed by the project.

## *Overview of Collaborative Consulting Cycle*

The following table depicts the cycles and the types of activities that occur in each phase in the cycle. In a highly collaborative approach to consulting, both you and your client would undertake the activities in each phase, except in the Client Start-Up phase.

### Table IV:1 – Overview of Collaborative Consulting Cycle

| Phases | Activities |
| --- | --- |
| 1. Client's Start-Up | Client realizes the presenting priority and need for a consultant |
| 2. Engagement and Agreement | Client and consultant meet, discuss presenting priority and form an agreement about how to work together |
| 3. Discovery and Feedback | Identify information needed to analyze presenting priority |
| | Identify best sources and methods to collect information |
| | Collect information |
| | Organize and analyze information |
| | From the information, identify critical issues and recommendations for the project to address |
| 4. Action Planning, Alignment and Integration | Identify actions to address issues |
| | Develop vision and actions into overall action plans |
| | Ensure actions are aligned and integrated together |
| | Develop plans for evaluation, learning and communications |
| | Develop Change Management Plan |
| 5. Implementation and Change Management | Implement and monitor Change Management Plan, including sustaining motivation, momentum and learning |
| 6. Adoption and Evaluation | Evaluate results of implementing the Plan to ensure desired change has occurred throughout system |
| 7. Project Termination | End the project |

# Phase 1:  Client's Start-Up

Other books on consulting and organizational development might combine the activities described in this phase with activities in the next phase. However, combining these phases often ignores important activities for change that occur even before you and your client agree to work on a project together.  That is why this phase is called the Client's Start-up.

| Consulting Cycle: |
| --- |
| Client's Start-Up |
| Engagement |
| Discovery |
| Action Planning |
| Implementation |
| Adoption |
| Termination |

## What Consultants Learn from This Phase

It is important for you to understand the types of activities that occurred in this phase.  That understanding helps you to:

1. Start from where your client is now – this is an extremely important principle when working with clients to accomplish major change in their organizations.

2. Be aware of initial key stakeholders concerned with your client's change effort, especially those involved in detecting the need for the project.

3. More effectively talk with your client about early activities during the change effort and relate better to your client's reality.

4. Gain some perspective on how long the need for the project existed and what your client has done so far to address that need.

5. Be aware of the results of your client's efforts, including what they sought to accomplish, what worked, what did not and what learning was generated.

6. Be aware of other potential or related issues and goals regarding your client's organization.

7. Understand your client's efforts so far to gain assistance to help them address the need in their organization.

8. Understand the reasons your client decided to seek a consultant and their criteria for selecting the consultant.

9. Think of useful questions to ask during your first meetings with your client when you are trying to discover more about the history of the need for the project.

10. Understand more about the overall culture of your client's organization, particularly how its members make decisions and solve problems.

11. See the project as part of an overall change effort, rather than only as a consulting project defined by a contract between you and your client.

You can gain understanding about your client's start-up activities by collecting information, especially during the upcoming phases, Engagement and Agreement and also Discovery and Feedback.

# Recognizing the Need for Change

## What Were the Early Indicators of the Need for Change?

### Remedial Change?

The need for change can arise when people notice the symptoms of current issues in your client's organization (remedial change). For example, these indicators for change might be about any of the major internal functions, such as Board operations, strategic planning, programs, staffing, marketing, finances, fundraising or evaluations. Usually, complaints are about various aspects of these functions, for example, high turnover or interpersonal conflicts among Board members and also among staff members, lack of participation among Board members, persistent shortages of cash, complaints from clients about programs and services, or complaints about the performance or nature of certain Board or staff members.

### Developmental Change?

The need for change can also arise when your client has the desire to achieve some vision for the future or to install some new major system or practice (developmental change). Those changes might not necessarily be associated with addressing current issues. For example, your client might have recently finished a strategic planning process, which produced a long-term vision for the organization to achieve. Or, your client might have completed an organizational assessment that pointed out the need for attention to certain practices within the organization and that set some standard of "best practices" for the organization to achieve. Or, your client might have decided that they want to adopt a new performance management system, such as the Balanced Scorecard.

See "Major Types of Organizational Change" on page 183 for more information about remedial versus developmental change.

## Who First Asserted the Need for Change?

### External Stakeholders?

Your client's change effort could have been suggested initially by external stakeholders, such as community leaders, funders, volunteers or clients. Major change efforts in nonprofits often are initiated by external stakeholders, particularly with remedial projects.

Initial and ongoing involvement of external stakeholders can be useful during projects, to:

1.  **Provide broad, initial perspective on the need for change.**
    Quite often, employees of the organization are so close to the issues in the organization that they cannot see any solutions to those issues. In contrast, external stakeholders are removed enough to maintain broad perspective on the change effort.

2.  **Help to define "success" for the project.**
    One of the most important criteria for a nonprofit to be deemed successful is for the nonprofit to meet the needs of the community. External stakeholders in the community often can help to clarify those needs and whether they are being met.

3.    **Support your client's efforts to gain resources for the project plans.**
External stakeholders, such as community leaders or members of foundations, can contribute time, money and energy to help a nonprofit meet a current need in the organization.

4.    **Be a "policing" influence to ensure the nonprofit takes necessary actions.**
There can be tremendous resistance from members of the organization toward taking the necessary actions to accomplish successful change. Members often are more inclined to take actions when they are accountable to external stakeholders.

5.    **Provide more objective assessment of the ongoing success of a project.**
Because external stakeholders often have a broad perspective on the need for change and clear perception of the terms of success for the project, they may be a reliable means to assess whether the project has achieved success.

It might be important for you and your client to build on the insights and strengths of these external stakeholders when developing and implementing your project plans.

## Internal Stakeholders?

Your client's change effort could have been suggested initially by internal stakeholders, such as members of the Board of Directors or staff. Often, the internal stakeholders are the first to sense that some kind of issue exists within the organization and that the issue needs to be addressed soon. However, the internal stakeholders may be so close to the issue that they cannot get a clear perspective on causes and solutions. Or, those stakeholders might feel inhibited from taking action because they fear they might lose their jobs. These challenges for internal stakeholders might contribute to the reasons that your client decided to work with a consultant.

The benefits of involving internal stakeholders are similar to those of external stakeholders, as listed above. However, the involvement of internal stakeholders is often even more important because change efforts are more successful if they have the ongoing commitment and participation of internal stakeholders.

Similar to the benefits of working with external stakeholders who were first involved in the change effort, it is important to build on the insights and strengths of these internal stakeholders when developing and implementing your project plans.

## *When Was the Need for Change First Noticed?*

1.    **Did the need suddenly arise or result from a planned or scheduled activity?**
There often is strong urgency to attend to sudden problems, and consultants enjoy strong motivation from clients in those situations. However, resources can be difficult to mobilize when there is short notice. In contrast, scheduled activities often include sufficient planning to ensure adequate motivation and resources.

2.    **How long ago did the need first arise?**
Was the need around for many years or many months before anyone attended to it? If so, then why did the need persist before getting sufficient attention? Why is your client initiating a change effort now? Is your client any more interested or involved in meeting the need now? How do you know?

3.  **Has the need been recurring – did it go away and then return?**
    It is common for members of an organization to recognize a major problem that needed to be solved or a goal to be achieved, but then not be able to take actions right away. What caused the need in your client's organization to go away in the past? What caused it to return? You should ensure that the need is met permanently, if possible.

# Preliminary Efforts to Accomplish Change

1.  **What did your client decide to try?**
    Did they try to solve a problem by using consulting? Gain new knowledge by using training? Guide a group of people by using facilitation? Get ongoing individual help by using coaching? Install a new system, process or program? Or a mix of these?

2.  **What did your client want to accomplish?**
    Did they want to solve a problem? Achieve a new goal or vision? Did your client have some impression of what success would be for their efforts? Was that impression vague or clearly defined? How did they define success?

3.  **How did your client decide what to try?**
    For example, did your client take a systematic approach or resort to a highly reactive, "knee-jerk" approach? (Be careful here. Your client might be highly intuitive, rather than merely being reactive.) Was there priority on involving all key stakeholders in a highly participative approach or did one person make the decision?

4.  **Was the focus on performance?**
    What did your client do to ensure that current or new services were effectively or more effectively provided to clients during the change effort? Did they establish specific goals for their efforts? How did they use those goals during the effort?

5.  **What resources did your client contribute to the effort?**
    What people, time, money, facilities, etc., were contributed to the effort? How were those resources organized and managed and by whom? Who made the decisions? Were the resources adequate for the effort?

6.  **How did your client manage the change effort?**
    Did your client understand the nature of planned change? How did leaders in the organization motivate others in the effort? By involving them in the planning? By preaching at them? By threats? Did the effort seem to have the commitment and participation of others in the organization?

7.  **What were the results of your client's efforts? Did they focus on learning?**
    What worked? What did not work? What obstacles did they encounter? What strengths did they realize? What learning was gained from the effort? Think of learning in terms of new knowledge, skills or perspectives.

# Decision to Get Help

1. **What sources of assistance were selected?**
   Did your client consider assistance from funders, management support organizations, associations, others? Was the emphasis primarily on internal or external sources of help? Did your client seek volunteer and/or hired help?

2. **How did your client select those sources of assistance?**
   Did they consider their degree of access to certain trainers, consultants, coaches, researchers, etc.? Did your client consider their own resources in terms of time, skills, expertise, money, etc., to match that source of assistance? Did they consider their readiness for change?

3. **Why did your client choose to use a consultant?**
   For example, did your client not have the necessary internal expertise to meet their need? Did external stakeholders require a consultant? Did the project need the credibility provided by a consultant? Other reasons?

 See "Reasons Nonprofits Work with Consultants" on page 4 to review the various reasons that nonprofits hire consultants.

# Approach to Selecting a Consultant

The following guidelines apply when the client decided to recruit an external consultant.

1. **How did your client establish criteria for selecting a consultant?**
   Who established the criteria? Did they develop a Request for Proposal form and are they seeking proposals from various consultants? Are they working with a management support organization (MSO) that is providing a consultant?

 See "How to Work with Nonprofit Service Providers During Projects" on page 100 to understand the roles that various MSO's undertake.

2. **Where are they looking for consultants?**
   Did they get referrals from other nonprofits? Use the Yellow Pages? Seek professionals from local corporations, professional associations or universities? Other sources?

3. **How will they select a consultant?**
   Is your client using a Search committee to review proposals from consultants? If so, from where did the committee membership come? What is the deadline for selecting a consultant?

## Table IV:2 – Example of a Client's Start-Up Phase

In the Transitioning Nonprofit (TN), leaders in the organization decided to seek a consultant after its major funder, the We Have Had It Foundation, informed TN's Executive Director, Ed, that it would not renew its funding unless TN got some professional help soon. The following information explains how TN made its decision.

Program officers in the Foundation had explained to Ed that they were concerned about TN's latest grant request because, despite TN's having recently received increased funding from the Foundation, TN continued to experience shortages of cash, including submission of emergency requests in each of the past two years to the Foundation. Program officers also expressed concern that they had requested a Strategic Plan and program outcomes evaluation from TN several times over the past two years, yet TN had not yet provided a Strategic Plan or evaluation results. In addition, the Foundation expressed concern that there seemed to be increasing turnover on TN's Board and staff, and that Board members did not seem to be involved in TN's fundraising efforts or strategic planning.

The current situation was highly unusual. In the past, it had seemed much easier for TN to get money. TN's programs had grown at a rapid rate and so had grants from donors. Members of the Board and staff had been excited to have anything to do with TN and Ed.

During the past year or so, Ed had responded to recurring cash shortages by calling emergency meetings of the Board, demanding that Board members help Ed raise funds quickly. (Otherwise, the Board met every three months on a regular basis, usually with no clear agenda – Board members usually "rubber stamped" whatever Ed suggested in the meeting.) In response to each cash shortage, Ed would submit numerous grant requests to a wide variety of donors. He would implore his Board members to make phone calls to those donors. Lately, those donors were turning down TN's grant requests.

Also during the past year, there had been increasing turnover on the Board and staff. At first, Ed felt that those people who had quit were disloyal and had abandoned TN. He admitted that he had been glad to see them go because they had complained a lot about the same problems happening over and over again. Even now, Ed noticed that certain people on the staff seemed to complain a lot. He talked to the Board about firing those people. The Board members cautioned Ed against that because they were worried that it would be hard to replace those people. Things just seemed to be getting worse. Board members really were not sure what to do – neither was Ed.

At first, Ed resented the Foundation's ultimatum and felt that the Foundation was discriminating against TN. Ed told Board members that he felt the Foundation's position was unfair. After some discussion, Ed and the Board members agreed that if they did not get any funding from the Foundation, TN would not be able to continue providing services to its clients. As a result of the Foundation's ultimatum, they reluctantly decided that they would seek some outside help, but only if the Foundation would help to pay for that outside help. The Foundation later agreed to fund half of the costs of a consulting project, with the stipulation that TN fund the other half.

During the next month, Ed asked some other nonprofits for references of good consultants, especially good fundraisers. He got names of several consultants, including an organizational development consultant, and called each of them for an interview.

# Phase 2: Engagement and Agreement

This phase is usually where the relationship between you and your client starts. This is true whether you are an external or internal consultant. Experts assert that this phase is one of the most – if not the most – important phases in the consulting process. Activities during this stage form the foundation for successful organizational change. The quality of how this phase is carried out usually is a strong indicator of how the project will go.

| Consulting Cycle: |
| :---: |
| Client's Start-Up |
| Engagement |
| Discovery |
| Action Planning |
| Implementation |
| Adoption |
| Termination |

This section includes a variety of questions that will be helpful for your client to answer. Your client might not have immediate and clear answers to those questions. However, even your posing of the questions will help your client begin thinking more comprehensively and systematically about the project – and the questions will help to increase your credibility with your client, as well.

It might take several meetings to finish this phase. In addition, you might not address the following subsections in the order in which they are included below. Instead, your conversations with your client might wander a bit. Your job will be to ensure that you have addressed all of the subsections by the time that you formalize an agreement with your client.

Occasionally this phase needs to be repeated, for example, if a new problem arises in your client's organization and, therefore, a new project design and plan is needed. On other occasions, you and your client might decide to contract for various phases of an overall project. For example, you might contract to finish an assessment and then contract to guide your client through implementing the recommendations from the assessment.

Note that the information in this section refers to "your client," even though, in the early activities of this phase, your potential client and you might not have formalized an agreement to work together on the project yet.

## Purpose and Goals

The overall purpose of this first phase in consulting is to see if there is a fit between the natures of you and your client, how you both can benefit from that fit in a consulting project, and then to decide the specific next steps to begin the project.

Goals of this phase include the following and in the following general sequence:

1.      Exchange introductions, including information about how each of you prefers to work in a project, and about your values and style.

2.      Clarify who the official client is. Also identify who direct and indirect clients might be.

3.      Get a description of your client's need for a project (the presenting priority).

4.      Scope the project, identifying the major problem to be solved and/or its preliminary goals, when the project should start and stop, and what and whom you can access in the project.

5.  Understand how the project can be coordinated and administered, including how project decisions can be made and how communication can occur.

6.  Get some sense of your client's and your own readiness to undertake the project.

7.  Decide whether both of you want to work together now on a project or if any additional activities are needed, such as another meeting, follow-up proposal or reference check.

8.  Gain agreement on the overall approach to the project, including a collaborative approach to further discovery, feedback, action planning, implementation and evaluation.

9.  Arrange a formal agreement, for example, a letter of agreement or contract, and decide what terms might be included in any of those documents.

10. Obtain information for you to understand more about your client's organization.

11. Identify next steps, such as if there should be any more meetings between you and representatives from the client's organization or if a preliminary assessment should be done.

# Arrange the First Meeting with Your Potential Client

## *Guidelines for the First Conversation to Arrange the First Meeting*

At some point in the project, you will have your first face-to-face meeting with your client, usually scheduled during an initial telephone call. The call may be initiated by your client or by an intermediary (such as a management support organization) for your client. The following guidelines will help ensure that your first meeting is highly productive. They will be useful during the initial telephone call with your client.

See "Meeting Design, Management and Interventions" on page 375 to prepare for this meeting with your client.

1.  **Find out if your client has issued a Request for Proposal (RFP).**
    An RFP usually specifies your client's desired outcomes and other terms and conditions for the project. An RFP, if available, is important to review before the first meeting. (An RFP is used usually when the client is seeking an external consultant.)

2.  **Mention your goals for this meeting.**
    For example, your goals could be to accomplish introductions, hear about your client's problem or need for change, understand more about the organization, decide whether to proceed or not and then specify next steps. Ask what goals the client has for the meeting.

3.  **Attempt to have key stakeholders in the meeting.**
    Attempt to have your client include at least the Chief Executive Officer and Board Chair. These two stakeholders are often critical to the success of the project – the sooner that they are involved, the better. Their participation develops the strong political support that is critical for successful organizational change. If the Board Chair will not be at the meeting, ask your client why not.

4.     **Ask who else needs to be there.**
Strongly encourage that the meeting is attended by whoever makes decisions about the project or will be greatly influenced by the outcomes of project. The sooner that you establish contact with these other stakeholders, the more likely that your project will have the commitment and support of all of the important stakeholders.

5.     **Clearly understand how much time you will have for the meeting.**
Ask for at least an hour for the meeting. If your client wants the meeting to be half an hour or shorter, then use your skills in authenticity to express your concern.

6.     **Ask your client about any culturally specific considerations for the meeting.**
For example, you might ask what you should wear. This question can lead to a request for your client to be as frank or honest as possible about what conventions work best with the particular culture of your client's organization.

7.     **Ask if you can take notes during the upcoming meeting.**
Some clients are reluctant to have consultants take notes during meetings with them, especially when the clients have not met the consultants before and are not sure that they will hire those consultants. It will be useful now to explain your ethical principles pertaining to confidentiality.

8.     **Ask for materials to help you to learn more about your client's organization.** You can learn a great deal about your client's organization by reviewing certain documentation, for example, the latest Strategic Plan, Annual Report, marketing materials and website. (This preliminary activity should not be confused with the more formal and comprehensive assessments conducted during the upcoming Discovery and Feedback phase of the consulting process.)

> See "How to Review Documentation" on page 397 for guidelines about reviewing documentation to learn about your client's style.

## *Preparation for the First Meeting*

There are a few administrative activities that will prepare you for your upcoming face-to-face meeting.

1.     **Closely review the materials provided by your client.**
For example, analyze the RFP, Strategic Plan, annual report, financials, marketing information and the client's website.

2.     **Customize a resume for your client's project.**
Many consultants have an extensive resume, which they customize to apply for certain types of projects.

3.     **Start a file on your client.**
Experienced consultants have learned to retain and carefully organize all information about their client and the project.

See "Administrative Skills for Consultants" on page 86 includes guidelines to polish your administrative skills.

# Understand the Client's Perception of the Need for Change

## *Focus on Understanding the Client Now, Not on "Selling" Yourself*

New consultants often come into this phase with a strong desire to "sell" themselves to their client – to convince the client that they should be hired. That "sales" mentality often results in them doing most of the talking, rather than listening to the client.

That approach is usually a major mistake. Clients often hire consultants based on how well the client believes that the consultant actually listened and understood the situation. There are several opportunities in this phase for you to tell your client about yourself and do so in a meaningful and focused fashion. The guidelines throughout this phase will ensure that you are focused on listening and understanding your client.

## *Use Your Interpersonal Skills to Hear the Presenting Priority*

If you are an external consultant, the first meeting with your client is sometimes an ambiguous and somewhat confusing experience because you and your client are talking about an important need in the client's organization, yet you hardly know each other. If you are an internal consultant, you might have already established a rapport with your client. In either case, you will need to use your interpersonal skills to build trust, commitment and collaboration. The more effective your skills are in these areas, the more likely that you and your client will have a firm foundation from which to share complete and accurate information, thereby resulting in a more successful project.

See "Building Trust, Commitment and Collaboration with Clients" on page 58 for extensive guidelines to polish your interpersonal skills.

In these meetings, it is critically important to effectively use your skills in developing high-quality, interpersonal relationships. For example, carefully listen to the client's choice of words. You might use those same, or similar, words in your spoken and written communication during your meetings in this phase and throughout your relationship.

In one or more face-to-face meetings, your client will explain their perceptions of the problem or goal that needs to be addressed by the project (the presenting priority). Remember that their explanation often centers on symptoms, rather than on the root cause of the problem.

During the meeting, you might ask your client to describe their organization to you, and you might describe what you know about their organization, based on what you learned from reviewing the materials that they provided.

## Focus on Hearing About – Not Solving – the Presenting Priority for Now

Listen to your client's perception of their need for organizational change. It is important not to start giving advice about how to solve their problem now. Even if you are convinced that you know how to solve their problem, you still have not conducted sufficient assessment to be sure you clearly understand the situation. (Those activities will be conducted in the phase, Discovery and Feedback.) Besides, if you start solving the problem now, your client is likely to jump at the chance for some quick fixes to their situation – often those quick fixes are wrong and usually they do not involve your services.

Therefore, if your client asks for an opinion on how to solve the problem, let them know that you heard them, for example, you might summarize what you heard them answer in response to your questions. You might let them know what the causes of the problem *might* be, but always add that you need to get more information to understand more. Also, it is important for you not to "take sides" or blame anyone in disagreements or conflicts described by your client.

## Ask Useful Questions to Clarify the Presenting Priority

You might ask the following questions to learn more about your client's problem or goal. Be sure that you let your client know that you are hearing their responses.

 See "Phase 1: Client's Start-Up" on page 227 to review the kinds of activities that your client might have undertaken before meeting with you.

For now, you should ask:

1. What did your client see or hear that brought them to their conclusions about the priority?

2. What has been the effect of the priority on the rest of the organization (the system), for example, on Board operations, Chief Executive Officer role, operations of staff, program operations and marketing activities?

3. When did they first notice the priority? Who reported it?

4. What has your client done so far to address the priority? What did they want to accomplish? How did they choose those activities? Who was involved?

5. What happened as a result of their efforts to address their priority? What worked? What did not work? What did they learn?

6. Why do they want to address the priority now?

7. What will happen if nothing is done about the priority?

8. How did they conclude that they needed a consultant now?

9. What might be their role in causing the problem?

You might mention now that, at this point in a project, problems often seem hopeless, but that they are not. Add that you will work with your client to find out what is causing the problem and what you both can do to solve it.

# Clarify Desired Outcomes, Timing and Resources

It is possible that the specific scope of the project will change during the project, as a result of Phase 3: Discovery and Feedback. However, it is important for you and your client to have a common impression now of the current scope of the project. Answers to the following questions and use of the following guidelines will help you to achieve that common understanding. Note that, if your client has issued a Request for Proposal (RFP), then answers to the following questions might already be in that RFP.

1. **What will be an overall successful project?**
   For example, will it be solving the problem, not spending more than is budgeted for the project, achieving some goal, or installing a new program or system? Will it please certain external stakeholders?

2. **What are the specific results that your client would like to achieve?**
   Try to get specifics about what your client wants to see as a result of a successful project. What would people be doing? How would clients be served better? How would internal operations be better? What new learning would be accomplished (new knowledge, skills and perspectives)?

3. **When should the project start and stop?**
   The start date of a project is usually the date that a formal agreement is established, for example, that a contract or letter of agreement is signed by you and your client. The stop date sometimes changes during the project as you and your client work together to further clarify desired outcomes from the project and how those outcomes will be recognized.

4. **Does your client have any preferences about what methods are used?**
   Occasionally, clients have strong preferences about the methods that are to be in a consulting project. For example, clients might prefer that the project include Board training, strategic planning or fundraising. It is surprising how often clients have this strong initial preference, yet, after further assessment indicates that quite different methods are needed, clients are open to changing their preferences.

5. **What resources does your client have to support the project?**
   Your client might have already allocated certain people, funds and plans for the upcoming project. This question helps you and your client to begin discussions about the often-difficult activity of freeing up people from their busy day-to-day activities in the organization to instead take part in a consulting project.

6. **Who, specifically, does your client expect to be involved in the project?**
   One of the most precious resources for nonprofits is the time of its members. Successful projects for major organizational change almost always require the ongoing commitment and participation of certain roles, including the Board Chair and Chief Executive Officer. Now is the time to ensure that these important roles are, or soon will be, involved in the project.

# Decide How the Project Could Be Coordinated and Administered

Projects that are intended to accomplish major change in organizations can last from several weeks to several months or longer. It is important that you and your client maintain regular communication about project status, expectations and results. It is also important to be clear about what major roles exist in the project, including who will make major decisions and who will be your formal contact in your client's organization. Answers to the following questions will help you and your client to set a firm foundation for effective coordination and administration early on in your project. If you are an internal consultant, you might play some of the following roles yourself.

1. **Who can make decisions about the project?**

   This question is useful for identifying who the current client is. It is extremely important for you to always know who the current client is – it might not be the same person all the time in the same project.

    See "Who Is the Client? How to Know Who Your Current Client Is" on page 14 for guidelines to understand who your current client is.

2. **Who can make decisions if your client is not available?**

   This is an important question because if your client is not available, you will need someone else to work with. The answer to this question will tell you what to do if, for example, your client decides to leave the organization.

3. **Who will be officially responsible – be the sponsor – for the project?**

   Sometimes, projects have a role or person officially responsible to manage the project, including coordinating communication, helping to get decisions made, and ensuring that the project has sufficient resources. The sponsor can be helpful in coordinating the project with you.

    See "Major Roles During Change and Capacity Building" on page 6 for information about key roles, such as the sponsor, in organizational change.

4. **Who is the champion for the project?**

   Sometimes, projects have a "champion" who has taken it upon himself or herself to ensure that participants keep up momentum and participation in the project so it is successful. The champion can be helpful as you work together to sustain momentum during the change effort. That role might be played by different people at different times. Try to detect who is most enthusiastic and supportive of the project now.

5. **Who should receive your written status reports?**

   Explain that you will be providing written status reports during the project. Ensure that your reports go to at least two people in your client's organization, ideally to the Chief Executive Officer and Board Chair. If your project will be affecting a significant portion of the organization, including the Board, encourage the Board Chair to share reports with all Board members. Your reports should also go to whomever will be making decisions about your project and, preferably, to those who will be affected by your project.

6.   **With whom and how often should you meet?**
     Establish regular face-to-face meetings with decision makers. This is critical to the success of your project. It helps to sustain the political support necessary for successful organizational change. Attempt to get agreement for meetings at least once a month if not every two weeks during your project. Ideally, the key decision makers will be in that meeting, as will the project sponsor.

7.   **Who else will help administer the project?**
     Although the role of administrators might not seem as important as those of executives in your client's organization, it is the administrators who can ensure that attention is given to the many important details, such as scheduling meetings, distributing meeting minutes and other reports, and coordinating communication.

# Help Your Client Start Thinking About Project Evaluation

The more involved your client is in the project's evaluation activities, the more useful the results of those activities will be, and the more likely that the project will be high quality. However, members of nonprofit organizations often have limited resources, especially in terms of time and energy, so you cannot assume that your client will take part in evaluation merely because you want them to. To get adequate involvement from your client, they have to understand the benefits of evaluation and how they might take part in it. Thus, it is useful at this point to begin discussions about evaluation.

Your goals in this discussion are to:

1.   Ensure your client has a basic understanding of evaluation.

2.   Gain the level of participation required from the client to conduct effective evaluations during the project.

3.   Get even more specific about what the client wants to see regarding quality of the consulting project's process and results.

See "Evaluation of Performance and Change" on page 198 for descriptions of evaluation and how to describe it to others.

## *Help Your Client Realize the Involvement Needed from Them*

Some clients have a negative reaction to the term "evaluation." In that case, it is useful to explain that evaluation is collecting information to make effective decisions during and at the end of the project. Add that evaluation does not have to involve extensive resources and that the focus of evaluation is on being highly practical and realistic.

Clarify that evaluation can be focused on the quality of the project's activities (formative evaluation) and the quality of the project's results (summative evaluation). Mention that you can work with your client to design evaluation activities that are highly relevant, realistic and flexible.

Mention that there will likely be various "outputs" during the project, such as project reports, meetings and trainings, that can provide useful means of evaluation. Clarify that information about various outputs probably would need to be collected by members of your client's organization. Ask your client for their reaction to your comments about outputs, suggestions about project evaluation, and the level of involvement that might be needed from them.

Note that the extent of your client's willingness to participate in planning and conducting the evaluation is often an indicator of how much they see themselves responsible for the overall quality of the consulting project.

## Help Your Client Further Clarify "Success"

Often, at this point in the project, your client does not have a clear impression of how they would assess the project's quality or results as being "successful." Mention that one of the biggest mistakes when planning how to evaluate a project is to have clients make evaluations based only on their feelings, beliefs and perceptions. Suggest that clients avoid this mistake by specifying what *behaviors* they would like to see from themselves and others during and after the project to conclude that the project was successful.

This is an important discussion. It helps your client to think more about what "success" is in the project and, as important, how success can be measured.

See "How to Define Project 'Success' " on page 99 for options to determine project success.

Ask your client if they have any preliminary suggestions about what to evaluate regarding the project. Hear from them first. Then you might suggest some aspects of the project to evaluate, including the overall quality of the:

1.      Consultant's services during the project.

2.      Client's participation during the project.

3.      Achievement of project goals.

4.      Learnings from the project.

## Establish Evaluation Questions Regarding the Quality of Project Activities

You learned in PART III that evaluations are best designed to answer certain evaluation questions. At this point, you are talking with your client about how you will, later on, evaluate the quality of the project's ongoing activities (a formative evaluation). You are not ready to consider evaluation of the project's final results (a summative evaluation) because you have not finished the project yet. The following evaluation questions should be mentioned to your client now.

1.      What do you consider to be the major strengths and weaknesses of the project?

2.      What do you like or dislike about the project?

3.      What do other members of your client's organization consider to be the strengths and weaknesses of the project?

4.        What do the members like or dislike about the project?

5.        What can you, your client and other members recommend to improve the project?

6.        What can you, your client and other members actually do to improve the project?

7.        What is the best process for the project to use now to achieve the desired results from the project?

You might wait to finish a formal, documented evaluation plan with those questions until you have signed a contract with your client. Typically, you will develop the evaluation plan during Phase 4: Action Planning, Alignment and Integration.

See "Guidelines for Successful Evaluation and Assessment" on page 209 and "How to Design Successful Evaluation and Assessment Plans" on page 211 to develop evaluations plans.

# You and Your Client Learn About Each Other

Use of the guidelines throughout this subsection depends on whether you are an external or internal consultant. As an internal consultant, you probably already have some rapport with your client. Still, you should work to cultivate a relationship where you and your client understand how each of you prefers to work.

Many consulting projects fail, not because the project's goals were not achieved, but because you and your client failed to establish a strong working relationship. In failed projects, both parties too often focus primarily on achieving the project's goals, the technical aspects of delivering various capacity building services, and written status reports. They did not attend to cultivating and sustaining a high-quality relationship between the consultant and client. That type of relationship creates the motivation, political support and momentum critical for successful organizational change.

If your client feels comfortable around you, feels that you respect them and understands your overall approach to the consulting project, you will have earned a significant amount of trust, commitment and participation from your client. Those benefits can start by your making an effort to establish a high-quality relationship now.

## *Explain Your Style and Goals as a Consultant*

Mention to your client that you would like to take a few minutes to explain how you prefer to work. This activity can help you to establish strong credibility with your client and further ensure that you have an effective working relationship. In your explanation, consider the following guidelines. You might even create a brief document about yourself that you provide to your client. That way, after you have described yourself to your client, you can leave the document with them to review later on, if needed.

The guidelines throughout PART I will be particularly useful to you now as you explain the role of consultants, collaborative consulting, your ethics, your preferred boundaries in consulting, your nature and preferred approach to consulting. Guidelines for building trust, commitment and collaboration will also be useful to you now.

1. **Mention your primary goals as a consultant.**
   For example, mention your goals that your clients learn to solve problems for themselves, you both work in a highly collaborative fashion, and your working relationship be as important as the steps in the consulting process.

2. **Mention the major assumptions by which you work.**
   For example, mention that projects are more successful if based on accurate information and feedback from members of your client's organization, members believe they have input to plans and decisions, and members are committed to participating in the project.

3. **Mention the principles and ethics that are important to you.**
   Here is where it is especially useful to provide a document to your client, rather than recite each principle. Mention examples of information that you keep confidential, for example, problems in the organization and information about personnel. Mention that you do not divulge any information without your client's explicit permission.

4. **Highlight your expertise and resources that might be useful in the project.**
   You might mention any previous training, work experience or types of projects that convey your credibility to work the project with your client. Now is a good time to begin talking about learning and its importance in the project – share what you have learned in the past and how you learned it.

5. **Describe the overall consulting process that you use.**
   For example, mention any major phases and what tends to occur in each. (You might use the phases in this PART IV or develop your own.) Be prepared to explain why you prefer to include additional assessments in your consulting activities.

6. **Clarify that you prefer to work in a highly collaborative fashion.**
   Clarify that there is a "50/50" responsibility for the work in the project. (During this discussion, your client might voice some preference that you would do all of the work. Be prepared to explain the advantages of collaborative consulting to them and be prepared to "flex" the 50/50 balance in one direction or the other.)

7. **Mention any boundaries that you hold in your consulting work.**
   For example, you might refuse to assume roles where you are supervising people in your client's organization, or providing legal advice. You certainly are not acting as an official member of the Board of Directors.

8. **Mention that you prefer to build in learning plans in your projects.**
   Explain that the plans help to ensure that your client learns how to solve problems that remain solved, can enhance their leadership and management skills, and can more effectively manage change in the future.

9. **Your client might ask about your fees.**
   By now you likely have, or soon will have, your own approach to setting your fees. You might share your fees with your client at this time. (This Field Guide is not focused on guidelines to establish your consulting business or on setting your fees.)

See the list of resources in "Consulting" on in Appendix D for more information on setting fees.

## *Starting Learning About Your Client's Style and Organizational Culture*

At this point, your client might be a little confused as to why you are seeking the following types of information from them. Stress that it is important for you to understand how your client wants to work with you. One of the most powerful ways to discern the style of your client is to ask them. You can learn a lot by asking your client the following questions.

1. **How would you describe your leadership and management style?**
   How do you set direction? How do you ensure that that direction is being followed? What if it is not being followed? Who do you admire as leaders? What is it about them that you admire? What should be your role in this project?

2. **How do you like to make decisions and solve problems?**
   Do you like to carefully lay out a variety of options or make more of an intuitive decision? Do you like to involve others a lot or depend primarily on your own judgment? If it depends, what does it depend on?

3. **What kind of people do you get along with best, talkative or quiet?**
   For example, people who are more outgoing and share their thoughts out loud? Or, people who think a lot on their own and then share their conclusions?

4. **Do you prefer having a lot of fun in your work or "getting down to business"?**
   Your client might report that they want you to focus on the business of the project – on achieving results. However, you might find, after further discussion, that they highly value sharing information about their family and friends, as well.

5. **Do you prefer to get information in spoken or written form?**
   The answer indicates if you should share project information primarily in written reports or in spoken contact. Spoken communications might be either in person or by phone. Written reports might be shared through email or faxes in addition to postal mail. Ask what their preferred methods are. Even if your client prefers written, encourage them to meet with you, as well. You can learn a great deal and enhance communications in a face-to-face, rather than written format.

6. **Do you prefer reference to "problems" or "opportunities"?**
   Explain how some people believe that problems exist primarily because people see certain situations as problems, rather than as opportunities. Ask your client if they have any preference as to how you refer to situations in your project. (If they prefer the term "opportunities", then you can replace the term "problems" with "opportunities" when using information from this Field Guide.)

7. **What do you know about change management? What would you like to know?**
   How have they managed change in the past? What did they learn? There seems to be an explosion of literature about change management lately. It is not unlikely that your client has encountered some of it. Offer to share information with them.

 See "Requirements for Successful Organizational Change" on page 186 as a purchaser of this Field Guide, you are authorized to provide your client a copy that three-page subsection.

8.  **Do you view organizations as structures and processes or relationships of people?**
    Mention that different people can see the same organization quite differently, depending on their "lens" on organizations. Add that, as a consultant, you can communicate more successfully with your client if you talk in the same terms they do. (Often, you can detect their view by listening to the words that they use, for example, "plans and policies" versus "Tom, Jack and Sally.")

9.  **Are there any cultural considerations that should be made?**
    Usually, if your client views the culture of their organization as being highly unique and as having clear values for how people should interact, your client already has strong preferences about how you should work within their organization.

     See "How to Work in Multicultural Environments" on page 58 to review how to learn about the culture of your client's organization.

10. **What else would you like to discuss regarding a working relationship?**
    You want to understand as much as possible about what your client desires in an effective working relationship. In case there is anything else that you should know, but have not asked so far, now is the time to ask this "bottom line" question.

# Assess Client Readiness for the Project

One of the most important goals in this phase of the consulting cycle is to assess if your client is really ready for a major change effort in their organization. If you are an internal consultant, you might play some of the following roles yourself. This assessment is critical to sustaining motivation and momentum for change during the project. Information in this section will guide you to the most important considerations when making this assessment.

## *Explain the Criteria for Successful Organizational Change to the Client*

Rothwell, Sullivan and McLean (1995) assert the following conditions for an organizational change effort to be successful.

1.  At least one top decision-maker believes in the need for change and other leaders do not oppose that need.

2.  The reason for change is caused by conditions within the work environment – the conditions are under the control of people in the organization.

3.  The organization leaders are willing to commit to a long-term effort to make the change.

4.  Leaders are open to other perspectives about causes and solutions to problems, including their own roles in the problems.

5.  There is sufficient trust in the organization such that people can work together to conduct the project for change.

6.  Leaders are willing to commit the resources to support the change effort.

## Ask Key Questions to Discern the Client's Readiness for Change

You can learn a great deal about the readiness of your client's organization by asking the following questions. Some of the questions are related with others – still, it helps to ask the questions separately.

Introduce this topic to your client by mentioning that is it is important to carefully consider what must be done to get ready for the project. Do not introduce the questions as some sort of assessment that your client will pass or fail. Usually, your client will appreciate your asking the following questions. If they do not, you already have one clear indication that they probably are not ready for making a major change effort.

 See "Checklist to Assess Client's Readiness for Change" on page 468 in Appendix C for a form that might be useful for you to use now.

1.  **Have they allocated any funds for the project?**
    At this point, they might ask you for preliminary estimates of the cost for your services. It is OK for you to say that you would owe them a careful answer before you respond, as long as you tell them when you will have an estimate. You can tactfully ask if they have any funds available for the project now or do they intend to seek funds from a funder. Be wary of undertaking a project in which there are no funds now and no clear idea of how to obtain those funds soon.

2.  **What obstacles might they see for this project?**
    For example, might they struggle to get funds or to free up time to participate in the project? If they see no obstacles at all, delve deeper. The remaining questions in this subsection will be especially useful to you now.

3.  **Are there any major events coming up that might affect the project?**
    Major events might include an annual meeting, a major fundraising drive, change in senior leadership, or a move to a new facility. Ask your client how any events might impact the project. Be wary of undertaking a project in which the project "somehow will have to fit in" with other activities in the organization.

4.  **Is the client open to other perspectives from you regarding the problem?**
    Other perspectives might be about causes of the problem or solutions to the problem. Often, your client will respond that they are completely open to hearing perspectives other than their own. It is useful now to ask what other people should be involved soon and why. Be wary of undertaking projects where your client seems irritable about this question and/or insists their conclusions are final.

5.  **What might be their role in the problem?**
    Hopefully, your client offers several ways in which they might be involved in causing the problem – or at least have not been effective in solving it in the past. Be wary of undertaking projects where your client seems irritable about this question and/or offers little or no information about how they might be somehow involved in the cause of the problem.

6.  **Did the client use a consultant before and, if so, how did the project work out?**
    If they did use a consultant before and that project was not successful, you can learn a lot now about how your client might successfully or unsuccessfully work with you. Be wary of

undertaking projects where your client used many consultants before to solve the same problem and/or seems to blame previous consultants for the outcomes of unsuccessful projects.

7.  **Are any important people missing from your meetings?  If so, how will they be involved?**
    For example, is the Board Chair missing?  Other senior people?  Why are they not in attendance?  How will they become apprised of and involved in the project?  Be wary of undertaking projects where important people seem to struggle to find the time to attend important meetings in a project – the first meeting.

8.  **Can you be assured access to the people needed by the project?**
    Mention that you will likely conduct some assessments near the beginning of the project to get clarity on problems and identify solutions for the project.  Add that it is useful if members of the Board and senior staff participate in those assessments.  Clarify that the assessments might involve brief questionnaires and then maybe a follow-up interview of up to an hour with certain people.  Ask if you can gain access to do those assessments.  Be wary of undertaking projects where your client does not seem to cooperate in finding even small amounts of time from senior people in the organization.

9.  **Are there any certain people or specific activities that are off limits?**
    Depending on the focus of your project, it might be reasonable for your client to insist that certain people not be involved, for example, people who are new to the organization.  However, do not be afraid to respectfully challenge your client if they insist that certain resources are off limits.  Be wary if your client insists that certain Board members or senior staff be off limits.  Hiding information can make them distrustful of the project, thereby decreasing the chances of success.

10. **Are there any people who might be uncomfortable with this project?**
    If any members of the Board or senior staff will be uncomfortable with the project, ask your client how that discomfort should be addressed.  Avoiding communication with those people could undermine the project later on.  Be wary of undertaking a project in which certain senior people are to be avoided at all times.

11. **How can they be sure that they have the time and energy to participate?**
    Now is a good time to really focus on this question with your client.  One of the most important resources for nonprofits is the time and energy of their members.  It can be difficult to free up that time to attend to activities other than providing direct services to clients.  Be wary of undertaking projects in which your client does not appear committed to making the time and energy for a project.

12. **Are there any other warning signs for you?**
    Sometimes, especially if you are a highly intuitive person, you might sense that something is wrong for you about the project.  For example, someone in the room is not saying anything or there are uneasy glances among people.  Even if you do not know why you feel uneasy, recognize that you do.  Be wary of undertaking a project that you did not feel good about in the first place.

# Decide If You and Your Client Should Work Together

## *Decide Now If the Project Is Really Appropriate for You*

Now is the time to for you to decide if the project is really appropriate for you. If you are an internal consultant, you might not have much influence as to whether you accept the project or not. Otherwise, as an external consultant, you need to consider the following questions. Depending on how you make decisions (rationally or intuitively) you might need to take time alone to think or you might prefer to talk with your client. In your decision, consider your client's answers to the above questions to assess readiness for change and your answers to the following questions.

1.  **Do your capabilities match those needed for the project?**
    The primary expertise of an organizational development consultant is guiding change in a significant portion of the organization or throughout the entire organization itself. To do that, you do not have to be an expert in every specialty in organizations. Your skills in organizational change (and the guidelines and materials in this Field Guide) will help you identify what specialties are needed and the order in which they should applied. So do not exclude yourself from the project just because you do not have expertise in all required specialties – you can recommend that your client bring in that other expert help.

    However, if your client insists that they want expertise only in a certain area – an area in which you are not an expert – and they are not committed to a project for significant organizational change, you should consider backing out from the project. You might recommend someone else to help your client.

    See "How to Know When to Ask for Help" on page 108 to further explore when you should ask for help or quit a project.

2.  **Does your schedule match that needed for the project?**
    One of the worst decisions that you can make is to accept the project with the intent of somehow integrating it into your already busy schedule. You will end up resenting the project, getting burnout, and not being useful to your client or yourself. If you don't have the time required for the project, you can suggest different timing or decline the project.

3.  **Does your nature match that of the leaders in the organization?**
    Even if you do have the capabilities and time for a project such as this, there are times when the "chemistry" is not right – the nature of your client is not enough of a match for your own. For example, perhaps your client is very "down to business," whereas you prefer use of more humor and interaction with others.

4.  **If you have decided that the project is not for you, tell your client now.**
    Now is the time to let your client know if you have decided that the project is not right for you. Do not waste any more of your client's time. Perhaps your client will engage you in conversation about your thoughts and decision – you might end up changing your mind. In any case, your client will respect you for being authentic with them.

5.  **You might need more time to make your decision.**
    It is OK not to make your decision now. Perhaps the upcoming discussion about your client's readiness (included immediately below) will help you to further consider your own decision about the project. However, you will need to decide before you are asked to sign a

formal agreement, such as a contract or letter of agreement (these agreements are discussed further on in this section).

## *Decide If the Client Is Ready for the Project*

1.   **Discuss your client's readiness for the project.**
     The discussion can be enlightening for your client regarding their true ability to successfully engage in a project for change.  The discussion will also lend tremendous credibility to you as a consultant for your client.

2.   **Start the discussion by reviewing criteria for successful organizational change.**

> See "Explain the Criteria for Successful Organizational Change to the Client" on page 245.

3.   **Pose any remaining questions you have about your client's readiness.**
     You might pose only those questions about which you are still concerned.

> See "Ask Key Questions to Discern the Client's Readiness for Change" on page 246.

4.   **You and your client share conclusions about the client's readiness.**
     Try to end this discussion with a conclusion from your client about their readiness for a project – do not leave the question undecided.

5.   **If your client is not ready, you might help them decide how to get ready.**
     How they get ready depends on why they are not ready.  Perhaps they need to reduce the scope or postpone the project.  Perhaps they need to attend to more basic matters of leadership, such as Board and/or leadership development or time and stress management.

## *If You and Your Client Are Committed, Decide How Each Wants to Proceed*

Even if you and your client are ready for a project, that does not mean that your client has selected you as their consultant for the project.  Therefore, you should consider asking your client the following questions.

1.   **How do you feel about the meeting so far?**
     This question helps you and your client to take a few minutes to reflect and learn from what you have done so far, including how you have worked together.  The question also helps your client to affirm the results of the meeting.

2.   **How would you like to proceed?**
     At this point, your client might have a course of action in mind, for example, to:

a)   Hire you.
     In this case, congratulations!  You should formalize an agreement now by signing a contract with your client.  You also should strongly consider developing a detailed project work plan that you propose, along with that contract.

b)  Not hire you.
There are a variety of reasons why a client might not hire you.  (See below.)

c)  Meet with you again soon.
If so, get clear on the reasons for the next meeting, who will attend and when.  Ask if you can provide a detailed proposal before the next meeting.  Perhaps that will make your meeting more focused and productive.

d)  Get a proposal from you.
If so, ask if they have any specifications for the content of the proposal.  If they do not, the following subsection will guide you to develop a thorough proposal.

## *If the Client Decides Not to Hire You*

Perhaps your client had one or more of the following reasons.  Do not be afraid to ask them for their reasons.  Your response to their reasons depends on whether they have already hired another consultant.

1.  **They just wanted to "pick your brain" for ideas to do themselves.**
Occasionally, clients already have ideas about what they need to do.  They are not sure if they want a consultant or not, but find that it is useful to talk to a consultant to refine their own ideas about what to do.  Consequently, after getting the ideas, they decide not to hire a consultant.

2.  **They just do not like you.**
Perhaps the "chemistry" is not there, for example, your personality is not a match for your client's.  They probably will not admit this, but if they could, you might learn something important about your personality and how to make yourself more appealing to others.

3.  **They have already selected another consultant.**
Perhaps the job was "wired" – they were required to get bids or proposals from a certain number of consultants, and they had already selected another consultant.  However, they might not admit this to you lest you get irked at their wasting your time.

4.  **They are not certain about doing a project at all.**
Sometimes, major problems exist in organizations because they struggle to make decisions.  If you can, help them talk about how they make decisions – that discussion might be a tremendous gift to them.

5.  **They have concerns and fears about your approach.**
In this situation, try to help them get specific about their discomfort.  Are they uncomfortable about the level of their involvement, your consulting process – what?  Perhaps you can address their discomfort by further clarifying certain information or doing a better job of hearing them.

6.  **Your approach takes too much in resources.**
In this situation, try to find out what resources they are concerned about and how they decided your approach took too much in resources.  Perhaps they misunderstood your approach or you can make negotiations about those resources or be flexible about your role and theirs.

7.      **They want someone less expensive.**
        Many experts on consulting assert that clients rarely decide not to hire you because of your fees – instead, if your client really wants to hire you, they will work hard to negotiate fees with you. Still, if you are not hired because of your fees, you might renegotiate them with your client or reconsider how you set your fees.

# Proposals, Contracts and Letters of Agreement

## General Guidelines for Designing and Processing These Documents

Guidelines throughout this subsection apply primarily to external consultants. However, internal consultants should also establish some type of agreement to ensure that they are in clear agreement with their clients. Internal consultants might resort to verbal agreements or letters of agreements, while external consultants might resort to written contracts and letters of agreements.

Always use some form of written agreement with your client, especially for major organizational change efforts. If you have followed the guidelines in this Engagement and Agreement phase, formalizing your agreement in a written document should be straightforward.

Agreements can be specified in a variety of ways. For example, before your client decides to work with you, they might request a proposal from you about how you might work with them if you are hired. A proposal can go a long way towards reaching an agreement with your client because it can guide you and your client to carefully discuss the major aspects of a project before a contract form or letter of agreement is signed. A contract specifies the agreement between you and your client regarding the project and becomes legally binding after you and your client have signed the contract. Letters of agreement are used for less complex projects in which the project requirements and consulting activities are rather routine and well understood. Letters of agreement become legally binding when you and your client clearly indicate your mutual approval of the agreement. The contents of any of these three documents depend on the degree of formality expected by you and/or your client and on the complexity of your project.

When designing a formal agreement, consider these guidelines.

1.      **Ask your client if they have a preference about these documents**.
        Newer organizations usually do not have such preferences and resort to recommendations from you, the consultant. However, you can save yourself a lot of work and editing if you know your client's preferences beforehand.

2.      **Be sure to indicate the document is open to discussion and negotiation.**
        Many consultants have lost out on projects because clients interpreted the documents to be unchangeable. Proposals should be just that – proposed approaches to working with your client on a project.

3.      **When does your client want the document? To whom should it be submitted?**
        Make sure that the document promptly gets to whoever will be making decisions based on the document. If your client has a legal department, expect delays in finalizing a contract form.

4.      **Mark each page of the document as "draft" and number and date all pages.**
        This practice helps to ensure that any copies of the document that existed before a final agreement do not mistakenly become the official documents for the project. It also helps

you and your client manage any changes made to the documents until finished. When numbering pages, use a format, such as "Page 1 of 8."

5.  **Get documents signed before you incur expenses or provide services.**
    Unless you have an agreement signed by you and your client, you might not have a strong legal basis to recoup any expenses you incur or payment for services you provide. For example, you might not be reimbursed for airline tickets or preliminary assessments that occur early in a project.

6.  **Obtain signatures of both the Chief Executive Officer and Board Chair.**
    In small- to medium-sized nonprofits, this practice is useful to ensure that the top leaders in the organization are aware of, and in full support of, your project. The practice reduces the chance that there will be major surprises as project activities begin to involve Board members. Those members may need to provide information and resources and also approve major decisions during the project.

## Core Elements of a Proposal

The following elements are often found in proposals. As mentioned above, the final content of your proposal should be determined from discussions with your client. For example, you both might choose to include elements in your proposals that are typically included in contracts (listed in the next topic). You might choose to use different terms in the following phrases, as well.

1.  Title page
2.  Background information
3.  Project goals and/or outcomes
4.  Project work plan
5.  Deliverables

6.  Approach to evaluation
7.  Project schedule
8.  Roles and responsibilities
9.  Fees and payment terms
10. Resume and references from past clients

See "How to Design Systematic – and Flexible – Project Plans" on page 86 for guidelines about designing systematic project plans to include in your proposals.

See "Sample Proposal for Organizational Development Services" on page 470 for a sample of a project proposal.

## Core Elements of a Consulting Contract

The following elements are often found in consulting contracts. Similar to proposals, the final content of your contract should be determined from discussions with your client.

1.  Title page

2.  General description of both parties (you and your client), including name and contact information

3.  Brief and general description of the nature of the services

4.  Official contacts (name and positions) for each party

5.  Start and stop dates for the project

6.  Goals and/or outcomes from the project (might refer to an attached proposal)

7.  Tangible deliverables from the project (might refer to an attached proposal)

8.  Approach to evaluation (might refer to an attached proposal)

9.  Roles and responsibilities (might refer to an attached proposal)

10. Where the work will be done

11. Ownership of materials brought to, or produced during, the project

12. Billable fees, expenses and materials

13. How the contract can be terminated

14. Terms of confidentiality

15. Specification that you are an "independent contractor"

16. Space for both parties to include their signatures and for date of the contract signing

If the scope and costs of your project are relatively small, for example, under $5,000, the proposal itself might be signed as representing a formal contract.

See "Sample Basic Contract Form for Consulting Services" on page 478 for a sample of a basic contract.

## Additional Elements Sometimes Included in Consulting Contracts

The following elements are sometimes included in consulting contracts, especially when the contracts are used by large, well-established organizations.

1.  How decisions are made between consultant and client

2.  How communication occurs between consultant and client

3.  How the document can be changed

4.  A "kill fee" which specifies what your client or you pays if either of you suddenly terminates the contract

5.  Number of hours required from each party to finish the project

6.  Indication of compliance with applicable laws and regulations

7.  Insurance requirements

8.  Warranties of service

9.  Avoidance of solicitation to employees

10. Remedies/arbitration if major disagreements occurs

11. The project proposal as an attachment, especially with complex projects

## Core Elements of Letter of Agreement

A Letter of Agreement is usually a one- or two-page document that is less formal and complete than a contract. Typical elements of a Letter of Agreement include:

1.  Brief description of the nature of the services and project.

2.  Contact information for both parties.

3.  Billable fees and expenses.

4.  Specification that you are an "independent contractor."

5.  Space for both parties to sign the Letter of Agreement.

## Table IV:3 – Example of Engagement and Agreement Conversation

The Transitioning Nonprofit (TN) had scheduled interviews with various consultants as a result of an ultimatum from the We Have Had It Foundation. The ultimatum was that TN gets outside help or the Foundation no longer would fund TN.

One of the consultants that TN phoned was an organizational development consultant, OD Bob. In that phone call, Executive Director, Ed, explained that TN needed a consultant for a variety of services, including fundraising, strategic planning and outcomes evaluation. Ed added that fundraising was the most important need. OD Bob agreed to attend an interview and mentioned that he would send information about himself to TN beforehand. OD Bob's information was about his experience and credentials, his mission and values as a consultant, his priority on a collaborative approach and his focus on systems and learning in organizations. He also asked that materials about TN be sent to him before the interview.

Ed, Bob and members of the Board's Search Committee attended the interview. Ed began the interview by welcoming OD Bob to TN. Ed explained that TN had some current challenges that needed a consultant. He said that mostly TN needed cash right now, so fundraising would be the most important. He added that a local Foundation, the We Have Had It Foundation, funded a large portion of TN's budget. He explained that the Foundation also wanted TN to produce a Strategic Plan and an outcomes evaluation for each of its programs. He mentioned that people in TN were already very busy serving clients, so they didn't have a lot of time for a consulting project. He asked OD Bob if he could raise the cash and then write the Plan and the evaluations. The members of the Search Committee were noticeably quiet so far.

OD Bob responded by commending TN on its past performance. He clarified that, by performance, he meant TN's effectively achieving outcomes with its clients. Then he summarized back what he had heard Ed say during the past few minutes. He said that he recognized that TN had a variety of challenges, and that he believed he could help TN. He said he had some quick information and questions to share with the participants, but first he wanted to quickly review how he worked as a consultant. Then OD Bob quickly reviewed his mission, values, and collaborative and systems approach.

Next, OD Bob posed some questions. How had TN concluded that it had problems? How had the problems affected the rest of the organization, such as the Board, staff, programs, finances, fundraising or evaluations? What had TN done in the past to resolve the problems and what were the results? What had TN learned? How had TN managed change in the organization?

Ed did all the talking. He explained that TN had a lot of clients to serve and that that required a lot of money. Ed had been very successful in fundraising in the past, but now donors seemed to be getting pickier. He explained that the Foundation had turned down Ed's latest grant request, wanting strategic planning, outcomes and more Board involvement.

Ed added that it seemed like TN now had one problem after another now, including lack of cash, Board and staff members leaving, and people bickering in the workplace all the time. Ed asserted that he had a very good Board, though, adding that, "The members are always there when I need them."

### Table IV:3 – Engagement and Agreement Conversation (Cont)

OD Bob again summarized what he had heard Ed say. Then OD Bob asked if he could share another perspective on TN's problems. He suggested that problems, such as cash shortages and conflicts, were recurring because efforts to resolve the problems so far weren't really getting at the root cause of those problems – instead, people were dealing with the symptoms.

OD Bob went on to explain, "There is a cycle of activities that happens in organizations. The cycle starts with overall planning, then developing resources, and then doing the day-to-day operations. The learning from those operations feeds back into the overall planning. All parts of the cycle are interrelated. If any part of that cycle, or system, is not well attended to, other parts of the system have problems, too. For example, recurring problems with developing resources, such as fundraising, often are symptoms of poor overall planning. It's no one's fault really – people are so close to the day-to-day activities that they lose perspective on the overall situation. To fully address those recurring problems, we need to ensure that the overall cycle of activities is aligned and completely focused on achieving outcomes with clients – focused on performance."

OD Bob headed off participants' concerns by adding, "Many times, people are concerned about that systems approach because they worry that it takes too much time. However, as they develop as leaders, they realize that a systems approach isn't working harder, rather it's working smarter – and in the long run, they're actually saving more time because they are dealing with fewer crises." OD Bob finished by saying, "TN has been so successful that it has outgrown its way of doing things – now TN needs to firm up its internal foundation so it can support even more of the rapid growth that you had before. You all get a lot of credit."

Ed seemed quiet for a while, as did the Board members on the Search Committee. Then Ed turned to the Board members and asked, "What do you think?" After a few seconds, the Board Chair responded, "Ed, I think OD Bob is on to something. It seems like we're always having crises where we're short of cash. Each time, you work yourself to exhaustion getting TN more money, but then we're soon out of money again. It seems that if we work to get more money again right now, we'll just have the same problems in the near future. We've got to do something different, Ed. However, I'm not sure I understand everything here, though, Bob."

Ed added, "I'm not completely clear either, Bob. I'm still not completely sure that we shouldn't just focus on fundraising to raise more money right now. Why not?"

OD Bob replied, "Respected donors probably won't give you much money, especially on an ongoing basis, unless they see your Strategic Plan. They want the Plan because they want to know that the nonprofit knows where it wants to go. They want to know how their investment fits into the nonprofit's overall plans. But to create a really good Strategic Plan, the Board should be involved – planning is a major part of the Board's responsibility. That sometimes requires briefly reminding the Board about its roles and responsibilities. So there are other things to attend to before fundraising."

Ed said, "OK, supposed we hired you. I'm still not sure what you would do."

## Table IV:3 – Engagement and Agreement Conversation (Cont)

OD Bob said, "I highly recommend that we collaborate to do a quick, highly focused assessment of all of the most important activities in your organization.  The results of that assessment can be used for us to develop some specific action plans.  Then we'll collaborate to implement those action plans until we've addressed all of the issues from the assessment.  I'll coach and guide you through all phases of our project.  The project will produce the Strategic Plan, outcomes evaluations and more Board involvement that the Foundation wants."

Ed said, "I'm not sure that I want my people doing an assessment.  They're very busy."

OD Bob replied, "We want to always be realistic and flexible with your extremely busy staff.  So that assessment might need only an hour or so from each of your senior staff and Board members for now.  We'll collaborate to design the assessment together.  There are numerous benefits to that assessment.  It will point to the root causes of problems in TN.  It will energize Board and staff members and get them focused on the project.  It will provide information that we can give to the We Have Had It Foundation to show them that we are spending their investment wisely.  We'll keep the assessment practical and useful."

OD Bob added, "During the project, I'd like to regularly meet with you and a few other people who are the decision-makers in the project.  I call them the Project Team.  I would collaborate with that Team to guide the development and implementation of the various action plans from the project.  The Team would ensure that the project remains extremely practical and useful to TN.  I would provide regular written reports to the Project Team, too.  Again, I'd provide ongoing coaching with a focus on managing change and capturing learning."

The Board Chair asked OD Bob, "Do you really think we're ready for a project like this?"

OD Bob thought for a few seconds, then replied, "Any organizational change project needs certain things for success.  It needs clear action plans.  Top management has to consistently show support for plans.  We need to intentionally manage the change process.  The more stakeholders are involved, the more successful the project will be.  We need to remain open and honest with each other.  We need to keep an open mind about what we all decide and what we're learning.  We need to focus on performance – high-quality services to your clients.  We need to carefully manage the change in TN.  Do you think TN is ready?"

For the next few minutes, the participants talked about whether TN was really ready for a major project.  Ed asked OD Bob how much time the project would take from the Board and staff.  OD Bob suggested that he provide a detailed proposal, and all agreed.  The next week, OD Bob sent a detailed proposal, along with materials about organizational change.  Two weeks later, TN selected OD Bob.  A week later, they signed a contract.

# Phase 3: Discovery and Feedback

## *This Phase Is Critical to the Success of Your Project!*

| Consulting Cycle: |
| :---: |
| Client's Start-Up |
| Engagement |
| Discovery |
| Action Planning |
| Implementation |
| Adoption |
| Termination |

Whether you are an external or internal consultant, you and your client will work together to understand more about the presenting priority and how you can effectively address it. It might be a major problem in the organization or an exciting goal to achieve. You will collect information about the priority, analyze it to identify findings and conclusions, and then make recommendations from that information. Sometimes the data-collection effort is very quick, for example, facilitating a large planning meeting. Other times, the effort is more extensive, for example, evaluating an entire organization and developing a complete plan for change.

Too many consultants minimize the importance of – or altogether skip – this critical phase. Do not! It is unethical to initiate a project for organizational change without fully understanding the presenting priority and the quality of operations in your client's organization. Rushing to conclusions and actions without this full understanding can be harmful to your client's organization because your project can end up dealing with symptoms, rather than the root causes of issues. When working for significant change in organizations, you should always start from where your client is – do not impose major change on them simply based on what you want them to accomplish no matter what. That approach usually backfires on both you and your client.

See "Evaluation of Performance and Change" on page 198 for general knowledge about evaluation and assessments, if you have not yet read that information.

## *The Most Important Result Is Client's Mobilization for Change*

Your activities for discovery do not have to be all-inclusive. The activity of working with you to understand more about their organization can itself cause major change in their organization. For example, the activity helps your client become more enlightened about the organization and excited about making necessary changes. It helps members see that their opinions and concerns are being heard – that perception is critical to sustaining the type of motivation and momentum required for successful change. Perhaps the most important result from discovery is mobilizing your client for change.

Note that the Discovery and Feedback phase accomplishes certain activities in the overall performance management process – conducting assessments and then deciding if results meet performance standards.

See "Overview of the Performance Management Process" on page 172 for information about the overall performance management process.

## *Importance of Research Planning*

The nature of the overall activity in this phase is to conduct an assessment or evaluation to further understand the presenting priority described to you by your client during the Engagement and Agreement phase. Assessments play a major role in consulting projects, especially in projects that are designed to accomplish significant change in organizations. Probably the most common application for the following guidelines is when you and your client are conducting assessment activities as part of this Discovery and Feedback phase of the collaborative consulting cycle. Another application for the guidelines is when you have been hired as an external consultant primarily to conduct a comprehensive assessment and then provide a detailed written report with recommendations to your client, without being involved in the implementation.

Assessments are forms of research. Therefore, the process used to develop a well-designed assessment plan is the same process used to develop a well-designed research plan. You and your client should develop a comprehensive, systematic research plan before actually conducting the research. To develop a complete research plan, both of you should follow each of the guidelines in each of the following subsections and do so in the order in which they are included. Throughout this section, the term "research" can be used interchangeably with the terms "evaluation" and "assessment." As with any of the guidelines in this Field Guide, the more collaboratively you work *with* your client, the more likely the following guidelines will contribute to the success of the project.

Note that the guidelines in this section can be useful in a variety of major applications, including:

- Discovery activities in a project for organizational change (guidelines throughout this section are provided in that context of a major change effort).

- External and internal assessment activities as part of an overall strategic planning process.

 See the listing of resources in "Strategic Planning" on page 506 in Appendix D for more sources of learning about strategic planning.

- Conducting an evaluation and reporting results.

 See the listing of resources in "Program Evaluation" on page 505 in Appendix D for more sources of learning about program evaluation.

# Purpose and Goals

The primary purpose of the discovery phase is to fully understand the presenting priority, by identifying all areas of the organization that need attention and what kinds of attention each area needs. By collaborating heavily with your client during this phase, you orient your client to accepting feedback about issues in their organization and how those issues can be addressed.

Rothwell, Sullivan and McLean (1995) mention the following benefits of an assessment:

1. Identifies the causes of problems in the organization.

2. Provides the basis for sharing feedback between you and your client.

3.  Provides background information for upcoming action planning.

4.  Provides a basis for tracking and evaluating the project activities.

The most important outcome of this phase, though, is energizing and engaging your client around the project. The activities of the discovery phase alone often are powerful means to improve the organization.

The goals of this phase are for you and your client to collaboratively:

1.  Decide what information is needed, starting with the presenting priority.

2.  Decide how that information can be collected and by whom, in a realistic and practical fashion.

3.  Gather that information, usually by conducting an assessment of some kind.

4.  Understand the information. Often, this is not nearly as difficult as it might seem.

5.  Identify key issues that are revealed from the collected information.

6.  Share mutual impressions of what the information indicates. The mutual impressions are critical to the next phase, Action Planning, Integration and Alignment.

# Establish the Project Team

At this point, it will be useful to form a project team. The team members can be an invaluable asset to you. They will act as a liaison between the project and the rest of your client's organization.

## *"Job Description" for the Project Team*

The "job description" for the team might be to work with you to:

1.  **Customize plans and activities during upcoming phases in the consulting cycle.**
    Team members could give you feedback to ensure that project activities suit the nature and needs of your client's organization. Team members often know more about the organization's culture and how to work within that culture.

2.  **Review various drafted results from the consulting process.**
    For example, team members can help develop and review plans for data collection, collect and analyze that data, generate preliminary recommendations and conduct presentations.

3.  **Monitor progress of the project.**
    Team members should know the project plans and be aware of the implementation status. Members can help, for example, by modifying plans and/or activities to get back on schedule or by changing schedules.

4.  **Sustain momentum throughout the planning process.**
    Team members can show enthusiasm and support for the project. Other members of your client's organization can be inspired if they see team members really believing in the project.

5. **Answer various questions from you during the project.**
   There will be times when you do not understand various terms and practices within the client organization. Team members can explain what is happening, any effects on the project, and suggest how the project might be modified.

## *Who Should Be on the Project Team?*

The team should include five to eight highly committed individuals. That size often seems to provide the most appropriate range of energy, participation and decision-making ability. Membership on the team depends on the desired project outcomes and the scope of activities. If the nonprofit's staff is 10 people or less, you might include the entire staff on the team. It often helps if the team is comprised of a cross-section of the staff, representatives from the executives, program leadership, direct service providers and clerical activities. A cross-functional team can help to ensure that all levels of the organization have a chance to provide input to the development and implementation of the action plans for change, increasing the ownership and participation. Also, a cross-functional team can bring a rich diversity of ideas often useful in generating diverse perspectives and opinions during the project.

You should seek to include the people who can make decisions about the project, can ensure that the project is fully resourced to achieve its desired results and are affected by the project. Ideally, the Team can include members from outside the organization, such as funders and community leaders. The following guidelines will be helpful.

1. **The Chief Executive Officer (CEO) should be on the team.**
   The CEO provides ongoing visible legitimacy, along with the ability to make decisions and provide historical information about the nonprofit. If there is a likelihood that the CEO will not be on the team, members of the Board and the CEO should have clear and credible reasons for excluding the CEO.

2. **Include the person responsible to ensure the project is finished.**
   Usually that person is the CEO. If someone else has primary responsibility, find out who that person is as soon as possible – that person is critical to the success of your project.

3. **Encourage the Board Chair to be on the team.**
   Especially if your project involves significant change in your client's organization, the Board should consistently be aware of, and approve of, project activities. One of the best ways to ensure that kind of awareness is to include a key member of the Board on the team.

4. **Include a "champion."**
   The champion helps to maintain enthusiasm during the project. Different people might fill the role of champion at different times, but you should always know who the current champion is.

5. **Include someone to help administer the project.**
   For example, this person would ensure that materials and facilities are provided for meetings and that meeting results are well documented. This person can also take notes during meetings and distribute them to key personnel.

6. **Consider having the leader of each major program on the team.**
   It is extremely important that the project retains or enhances the performance of your client's

services to its own clients during the project. One of the best ways to ensure that quality of performance is to involve program leaders in the team.

7.  **Consider including members from outside the organization.**
    Examples of external members include funders, community leaders or clients. These members can provide extremely valuable insight as to how planned changes will be perceived and can affect external stakeholders. Inclusion of funders on the team can provide significant credibility for the client to the funders, as well.

See "How to Build Highly Effective Teams" on page 372 for guidelines to build and organize effective teams, including your Project Team.

## Train Team Members About the Nature of Organizational Change

Despite the popularity of the term "change" today, it is surprising how little people really know about the principles and activities required for successful change in organizations. Even highly experienced leaders and managers often do not realize what brought about successful change in their organizations – they often conclude that things just seemed to work out well somehow.

Team members can be much more valuable to your project if they have at least some basic understanding of the nature of planned change in organizations. Often, they can quickly gain that understanding by reading and discussing basic principles of successful change, key roles during change and the numerous ways in which successful change is brought about in organizations.

See "Requirements for Successful Organizational Change" on page 186 for information to give team members an overview of guiding change.

# Select a Specific Organizational Diagnostic Model Now

It is not enough merely to brainstorm a lot of ideas for change and then discuss each with your client. The Discovery and Feedback phases involve collecting data about the presenting priority in your project, reporting findings and conclusions, and then forming some ideas about how to address the results of the data collection. That requires you to make certain judgments about the data that you collect. Fortunately, there are a variety of approaches to help you form your judgments before you are faced with what might be an extensive range of data. The field of Organization Development refers to those approaches as organizational diagnostic models.

(Historically, literature in the field of Organization Development has included reference to "diagnosing" systems. This term is criticized today because it suggests that an organization is a static system that can be analyzed by an external expert who then tags the organization as having some certain "disease." However, the term still does describe the nature of activity that occurs when trying to understand issues in an organization and what to do to address those issues. Also, the phrase "diagnostic model" is still in use. Therefore, this topic in the Field Guide retains use of the term "diagnostic.")

See the list of resources at "Organizational Development and Change" on page 504 for resources to learn about Organization Development.

## *What Is a Diagnostic Model?*

There are differing opinions about diagnostic models. Some people suggest that these models should come without bias or suggested solutions, and should be used to accomplish an objective, unfolding understanding of organizations. Others believe that models should suggest:

1.      What types of practices should be occurring in the organization.

2.      The order in which those practices should be occurring.

3.      Standards of performance for various domains, such as individual positions, teams, projects, processes, functions, programs and the organization.

Thus, a diagnostic model can be useful in an organizational change effort to:

1.      Analyze results of data collection.

2.      Identify issues that should be addressed by the organizational change effort.

3.      Suggest what actions should be taken to address the issues.

4.      Evaluate the success of the organizational change effort.

There are numerous organizational diagnostic models available, depending on one's beliefs on what the roles of the models should be. Some of the best examples of models that suggest solutions are those of organizational performance management. Common examples include strategic management, Balanced Scorecard, Total Quality Management and Management By Objectives.

See "Models of Organizational Performance Management in Nonprofits" on page 178 for brief descriptions of models of organizational performance.

A prominent organizational diagnostic model is the open systems model. The model is effective at depicting the major activities in an organization and how they interact with each other and their external environment.

See "Overview of the Open System of a Nonprofit Organization" on page 150 for depiction of the open systems model of a nonprofit organization.

Examples of other diagnostic models are types of "best practices" and "standards of excellence," as well as benchmarks (or standards of performance) for certain types of industries.

See "Maximum Performance – Different Things to Different People" on page 179 for more information about best practices.

Still more examples include Weisbord's 6-box model, McKinsey 7S model and Nadler-Tushman Congruence Model.

### Models and Tools Are Methods to Collect and Organize Data – They Are Not Solutions

Tools, such as questionnaires and assessments, are means to collect data about your client's organization. Be careful, especially when using diagnostic and organizational assessment tools, to not adopt the tools and their associated questions as depicting how the "perfect" nonprofit organization should operate. Answers to the questions in the various tools should be informed by your understanding and views of how organizations operate.

Certainly, there are experts who would not use a specific, documented assessment tool when entering a client's organization. They might believe that such a tool would prematurely impose certain "solutions" on the client's organization – solutions that do not address the most important issues, at all. Instead, they would intuitively ask a series of diagnostic questions, continually informed by the most recent learning about the client's organization. This is an option for you, as well as the use of explicit tools. However, your tuition should be developed from years of experience, which might include careful use and learning from application of various data collection tools.

### Strategic Management Is a Straightforward Model

You should come to your organizational-change projects with at least one model or framework in mind for how to guide change. The strategic management performance model is surprisingly easy to use as a diagnostic model. Many people are aware of the activities of strategic management – they just do not know them by that name. Basically, strategic management is the systematic implementation of a Strategic Plan. Strategic planning is a common activity in nonprofit organizations.

Strategic management becomes a straightforward diagnostic tool. This Field Guide includes a depiction of that system. You are strongly encouraged to gain a good understanding of that system – it can be extremely useful to you as a consultant for organizational change.

 See "Strategic Management (for "Diagnosing" Organizations)" on page 422 to understand how strategic management can be used as a diagnostic tool.

That organizational diagnostic tool is a powerful means to help you:

1.      During the rest of this Discovery and Feedback phase, to localize the root causes of issues in the organization (for example, the presenting priority).

2.      During the upcoming Action Planning, Alignment and Integration phase, to identify what actions to take and in what order to take them.

## Focus the Research (Data Collection)

Ideally, the research conducted by you and your client would be useful to everyone in your client's organization. However, without a clear and specific focus, the research can quickly become a demanding and wide-ranging set of activities that can produce a tremendous amount of seemingly disconnected information – information that can end up being useful to no one. Therefore, it is extremely important to get as much focus as possible before you and your client start the research.

There is no specific formula that can be applied in every project to promptly compute the specific focus of the research. That focus comes from you and your client carefully thinking about the presenting priority and how that priority integrates with the rest of the organization. It comes from identifying questions that the research should answer.

The following guidelines will help you and your client significantly focus the research. Do not feel overwhelmed while proceeding through the guidelines. There are several extensive examples to which you can refer. Also, remember that, as long as you effectively intervene somewhere in a system, you are likely to affect other parts of the system, as well – hopefully, you will affect those parts in a positive way. While proceeding throughout this section, you will finish a comprehensive worksheet that results in a customized research plan.

## What Is the Performance Domain of the Presenting Priority (Boards, Programs, Teams)?

When selecting what data you will need, start by focusing on the presenting priority. You probably learned a lot about the presenting priority during the Engagement and Agreement phase. When your client first invited you to the project, they described some current major need that they had, for example, to solve a major problem in the organization or to help them achieve some exciting vision or goal.

Think about the priority. What performance domain is it in? Is the priority primarily about:

1.     An individual position, team, project, cross-functional process, function, program or the entire organization?

2.     Is the priority in more than one domain?

See "Nonprofit Performance Management" on page 171 for information about performance management, including about domains.

### Include Board Operations, Strategic Planning and Program Planning

The functions of Board operations, strategic planning and program planning affect all other aspects of the nonprofit organization. If any or all of those functions are not planned and implemented well, other activities will suffer, including staffing, marketing, finances, fundraising and evaluations. You want to be sure that your project identifies any major issues in those three critical functions. Therefore, focus on those three functions in the research planning.

See "Management Systems and Why You Should Understand Them" on page 156 for description of the importance of the three functions.

### Fill in the "Planning the Research" Worksheet

If you and your client are planning the research now, then in the worksheet, "Planning the Research," in Appendix C, fill in the section, "Domain(s) of presenting priority."

265

## *Is the Presenting Priority a Remedial or Developmental Effort?*

A remedial effort is made to solve a current problem in the workplace. For example, the priority might be Founder's Syndrome – where the organization is struggling because it has been operating more according to the personality of someone in the organization than to the mission of the organization. Research during discovery about remedial priorities usually covers how the issue was caused and what can be done to resolve it.

In contrast, the organization might be undertaking those same activities to get ready to effectively achieve a new vision. Research about developmental priorities usually addresses the new vision and what must be done to achieve it.

That distinction between past and future activities is not always clear or meaningful. For example, to achieve a new vision, you should ensure that your client's organization already has a firm, current foundation from which to work. To gain that assurance, assess the quality of current operations. This close relationship between the current and future events in an organization is one of the primary reasons that organizational development consultants focus a great deal of their research on current activities, regardless of the nature of the presenting priority.

## *Presenting Priority and Its Fit in the Organization*

### Value of Using Research Questions

The research gains much more focus by associating specific questions that must be addressed during the research. Reasons for the use of questions include:

1. **Research questions can provoke reflection and learning.**
   One of your major goals as a consultant is to help your clients to learn. Your clients can learn a great deal during the Discovery and Feedback phase of a project. Questions are powerful means for adults to learn by reflecting on their experiences and identifying learning from those experiences.

2. **Research questions can form the basis for questionnaires, interviews, assessments, etc.**
   Many times, the overall research questions can become specific questions that you and your client can use in data collection efforts, whether in questionnaires or interviews with Board members and members of staff.

3. **Research questions can form the basis of your coaching with leaders.**
   Coaching often is best conducted by posing powerful questions to help your client clarify what they want to accomplish, what they can do specifically to accomplish it, what they have done so far and what they have learned so far. Research questions can become powerful questions to pose when coaching your clients.

 See "How to Coach for Deep Problem-Solving and Learning" on page 68 for guidelines to powerful coaching questions.

Although research questions might seem wide-ranging, do not be concerned. There are a variety of tools that might be used to quickly collect answers to the questions. Finally, even if you do not get answers to all of the questions, your posing the questions and your client's attempts to answer them are powerful means to change the organization.

### First, Include Standard Questions About Current Issues and Recommendations

The following questions are standard during any discovery activity.

1.  What do you think are the most important issues to address in your organization?

2.  What do you recommend should be done to address those issues?

3.  How are your suggestions realistic?

4.  In what order should your suggestions be followed?

### Next, Include Questions About the Management System of Presenting Priority

Do not jump merely to posing the questions: What is broke? How do we fix it? Indeed, those are useful questions. However, far too often, that limited set of questions results in fixing only one part of the system. As a result, the problem recurs and can cause more problems throughout the rest of the system. That approach cultivates only single-loop learning. By posing more systematic questions that are focused on performance, you can cultivate double- and triple-loop learning.

 See "Different Kinds of Learning (Loops of Learning)" on page 216 to understand the types of learning.

In a project for organizational change, essential and necessary research questions are about the systematic management activities associated with the performance of the presenting priority. When identifying those activities, it will help you and your client to take a systems approach. At this point, you might develop a logic model of the management system for the presenting priority.

 See "Management Systems and Why You Should Understand Them" on page 156 to understand management systems.

 See "Logic Model (to Depict Systems and Identify Relationships)" on page 423 for guidelines to develop a logic model.

The research could be designed to answer the following questions:

1.  What is the quality of the inputs, or resources, to the domain?

2.  What is the quality of the overall planning regarding that domain?

3.  What is the quality of the resource development for that domain?

4.  What is the quality of the operating activities for that domain?

5.  What is the quality of the evaluation and learning activities for that domain?

6.      What is the quality of the actual results produced by the domain?

7.      What is the quality of the governance, leadership and supervision around the domain?

## Next, Include Questions About Any Systems Directly Integrated with the Presenting Priority

1.      **Use chaining of logic models to depict integrated systems.**
A logic model is straightforward means to depict a system, describing the system's inputs, processes, outputs and outcomes. A powerful technique for understanding how various systems are directly integrated with each other is by chaining together each of the logic models that depicts each of the systems. The chaining technique depicts how the outputs of one system become the inputs of another.

> See "Chaining Logic Models (for Aligning and Integrating Systems)" on page 424 for guidelines about how to identify which systems are directly aligned with each other and how to depict those with logic models.

2.      **Include questions about management systems for directly integrated systems.**
Consider the above-listed seven questions for each management system directly integrated with the presenting domain. This might seem insurmountable, at first. However, you soon come to realize that the systems in a nonprofit are so closely integrated that information about one system usually is relevant to other systems, as well. Even if you do not comprehensively gather answers to all questions, merely by posing them to your client, you cultivate a great deal of learning.

## Finally, Include Questions About Domains that Interact with the External Environment

Remember how a healthy nonprofit is an open system? Certain functions in the nonprofit regularly exchange feedback with the external environment of the nonprofit. It is important that you assess the quality of those functions (or domains).

1.      **Consider each function that gathers feedback from the environment.**
Feedback from the environment often comes from environmental scanning (during strategic planning), market research (during program planning) and program evaluations.

2.      **Consider each function that provides feedback to the environment.**
Feedback to the environment occurs through advertising and promotions, and from strong outcomes with participants of the nonprofit's programs (program operations). Feedback also can be provided through lobbying and advocacy, and educating community leaders about needs in the community.

## Fill in the "Planning the Research" Worksheet

> For each research question that you and your client selected, make a copy of the worksheet that contains the header, "Research Question and Data Collection," in the document, "Planning the Research," in Appendix C. Then document each question on a copy.

# What Data Do You and Your Client Need to Collect and How?

This subsection helps to continue focusing the research by identifying the types of data that both of you will need to answer the research questions. At the end of this topic, there is a handy table that depicts seven of the most common areas of presenting priorities and the kinds of data that would be helpful to collect for each priority.

## *What Data Is Needed to Answer Each Research Question?*

Now think about each of the research questions about the presenting priority. The following table suggests what types of data might be useful for some standard, systematic research questions about your presenting priority. Remember that your presenting priority is usually about some domain (individual position, team, project, cross-functional process, function, program or the entire organization). A cross-functional process spans multiple domains, for example, information technology or quality improvement processes.

## Table IV:4 – Useful Information to Answer Research Questions

You will recognize that the following questions are about the quality of activities in the management system of the presenting priority.

| Research Question About Presenting Priority | Types of Data That Might Be Useful |
|---|---|
| Inputs to domain? | ▪ What specific, tangible items are needed by the domain?<br>▪ What expertise is needed?<br>▪ What technology is needed?<br>▪ What other resources are needed (people, funding, materials, etc.)? |
| Quality of overall planning? | ▪ Were the right people involved in the planning?<br>▪ What overall desired results did the planning establish?<br>▪ How were the results identified?<br>▪ What goals were identified to achieve the overall results?<br>▪ How were those goals identified? |
| Quality of resource development? | ▪ What resources were identified as being required to achieve goals?<br>▪ How were those resources identified?<br>▪ What was done to get the resources?<br>▪ Were all resources obtained?<br>▪ How were people sure that the resources were sufficient? |
| Quality of operating activities? | ▪ Were plans implemented and resources used effectively – did they achieve the desired results?<br>▪ Were plans implemented and resources used efficiently – were activities cost-effective?<br>▪ What issues occurred during implementation?<br>▪ How were those issues addressed? |
| Quality of activities of evaluation and learning? | ▪ How did people conclude if the desired results were achieved or not?<br>▪ How did people conclude if the operating activities were effective and efficient?<br>▪ How did people report the results of their evaluations? |
| Quality of actual results from the domain? | ▪ What are the criteria for evaluating the actual results?<br>▪ Does each desired result meet those criteria?<br>▪ If not, what should be done to improve operating activities? |
| Quality of governance, leadership and supervisory activities? | ▪ How were overall purpose and direction established?<br>▪ How were plans communicated?<br>▪ How was the implementation of plans monitored?<br>▪ How were decisions made?<br>▪ How were problems solved? |

## *Possible Types of Organizational Data for Research*

Guidelines throughout this Discovery and Feedback phase will help you and your client to narrow the selection of the types of data that will be most useful to understanding your client's presenting priority and how to successfully address it. The following table depicts a wide variety of types of data that might be useful in a project for organizational change. Guidelines throughout this subsection will help you and your client to select which types of data will be useful to the research.

### Table IV:5 – Possible Types of Data to Collect

| Dimension | Examples of Types of Data |
|---|---|
| Time | Past, present and future |
| External stakeholders | Clients, funders, community leaders, political leaders and experts in program services |
| External trends | Political, economic, societal, technological and environmental |
| Management activities | Planning, organizing, leading and controlling |
| People in the organization | Employees, volunteers and Board members |
| Performance domains | Individual position, team, project, cross-functional process, program, function (see below) or organization |
| Functions | Board operations, strategic planning, program operations, teamwork, marketing, financial, fundraising and evaluations |
| Services | Program services, outcomes, collaborators, competitors, target markets, unique value proposition, best practices and benchmarks |
| Context-sensitive (unique) considerations | Age, size, structure, positions, strategies and policies, source of leadership, style of leadership, culture, life cycle and rate of change in environment |

## *Get a Quick Snapshot of the Quality of All the Major Activities*

Note that it is extremely useful to target the research on the quality of as many aspects of your client's organization as possible. For example, if you have been recruited to help with fundraising, then you still should conduct a quick assessment to discern if your client's Board is operating successfully, if a Strategic Plan has been developed and is being implemented, and if programs have plans that are being implemented. An organization-wide assessment can be conducted rather quickly – and it might be much easier to do than you think.

Near the end of this section, in the subsection about methods of collecting data, the Field Guide suggests a specific organizational assessment tool that can be used to quickly gather data about many aspects of the organization.

See "Consider Using the Nonprofit Management Indicators Tool" on page 277 for suggestion of one organizational assessment tool.

## *Common Presenting Priorities and Data to Collect*

The table on the following pages depicts six common presenting priorities: Board operations, strategic planning, teamwork, financial management, fundraising, and advertising and promotions. Next to each priority, the table associates the specific types of data that are typically needed to address that priority.

Notice that, in many cases, the suggested data is in accordance with answering the previously suggested research questions about the quality of management activities and the leadership, governance and supervision of the presenting priority.

Remember that, at this point, you and your client are identifying the types of data that will need to be collected during the research. You and your client are not yet identifying the sources of that data or the methods to use to collect that data. Guidelines for those upcoming activities are included later on in this section.

### Fill in the "Planning the Research" Worksheet

If you and your client are planning the research now, then in the worksheet, "Planning the Research," in Appendix C, fill in the section, "Data to collect."

## Table IV:6 – Common Presenting Priorities and Data to Collect

**Board operations**

Collect data about how Board members and leaders on the staff:

- Ensure members understand and can perform their roles as members of a governing Board.
- Clarify the roles between the Board and CEO.
- Decide what new expertise is needed on Board.
- Ensure that members attend and participate fully in Board meetings.
- Set direction, make decisions and solve problems among themselves.
- Ensure that the organization has a clear purpose, vision and strategic priorities, and also how members ensure that those are being followed effectively and efficiently.
- Ensure that the CEO is performing his or her role competently.
- Ensure that they are conducting their operations in a high-quality manner each year.
- Understand how the quality of Board operations affects the work of other positions and functions in the organization.
- Believe that issues exist? How do they affect the organization? What should be done?

**Strategic planning**

Collect data about how Board members and leaders on the staff:

- Ensure that the planning process suits the nature and needs of the organization, and considers continuous feedback about the quality of all major systems in the organization.
- Clarify the overall purpose, vision and values of the organization.
- Ensure that strategic goals and objectives are established for the organization.
- Ensure that all members of the organization and its external stakeholders are aware of the organization's purpose, vision, values and goals.
- Ensure that the organization's resources are focused and aligned toward the purpose, vision and goals of the organization.
- Ensure that each Board member, Board committee and staff position clearly knows how they contribute towards the purpose, vision and goals of the organization.
- Ensure that progress is being made in an effective and efficient fashion toward the purpose, vision and goals of the organization.
- Understand how strategic planning affects all other systems in the organization.
- Believe that issues exist? How do they affect the organization? What should be done?

**Teamwork**

Collect data about how leaders on the staff:

- Identify what expertise is needed in the organization.
- Specify roles and responsibilities for each position.
- Set direction, make decisions and solve problems with staff members.
- Evaluate performance, or achievement of goals, in the workplace.
- Organize positions in the organization, including into overall teams.
- Organize teams, clarifying the purpose of team, results to be achieved by team, resources to the team, and how team members will communicate.
- Ensure that staff members are aware of each others' roles and value to the organization.
- Understand how the quality of their work affects all other systems in the organization, especially the work of other positions and services to clients.
- Believe that issues exist? How do they affect the organization? What should be done?

**Table IV:6 – Common Presenting Priorities and Data to Collect (Cont.)**

### Financial management

Collect data about how Board members and leaders on the staff:

- Know what the organization, including its central administration and programs, costs to operate.
- Know how much money can be generated from the organization's services.
- Know how much money is needed to be raised from fundraising and/or fees from services.
- Are sure of how, and where, all of its monies are being spent.
- Are sure that its monies are being spent wisely, ethically and legally.
- Are sure that money is available to pay current bills or any sudden expenses that arise.
- Are sure that financial management activities are being conducted in a highly efficient and cost-effective fashion.
- Understand how the quality of financial management affects all other systems in the organization, especially tracking and control of adequate resources for all activities.
- Believe that issues exist? How do they affect the organization? What should be done?

### Fundraising

Collect data about how Board members and leaders on the staff:

- Know how much money needs to be raised from fundraising and/or fees from services.
- Are sure their programs indeed provide unique features and benefits to the community.
- Are sure that the organization can present a highly credible case to a potential donor to donate funds to the organization.
- Know who the most likely donors to the organization are.
- Are sure of how each donor should be approached.
- Decide who will approach each donor.
- Are sure that donations will be tracked and reported.
- Understand how the quality of fundraising planning and implementation affects all other major systems in the organization, especially provision of adequate resources for all activities.
- Believe that issues exist? How do they affect the organization? What should be done?

### Advertising and promotions for each program

Collect data about how Board members and leaders on the staff:

- Are sure that there really is a need for their programs in the community.
- Are sure that their programs indeed provide unique features and benefits to the community.
- Know of each specific group of clients served by each program.
- Are sure that each program is indeed benefiting specific groups of clients in the community.
- Are sure that each group understands the features and benefits most appealing to them.
- Know that the overall public image is effectively conveyed (this data is in regard to effective public relations for the entire organization, rather than one specific program).
- Understand how the quality of advertising and promotions for each program affects all systems in the organization, especially the success and provision of adequate resources for each program.
- Believe that issues exist? How do they affect the organization? What should be done?

## *Best Sources for This Data*

The next topic, "Best Methods to Collect Data," includes a table that depicts typical sources of data for six common priorities for consulting projects. For now, review the following guidelines in this topic to understand more fully how to select the best sources for data in the research.

### General Types of Sources

There is a wide variety of sources for you and your client to collect the data that you need during the research. Possible sources of data include:

- Board members

- Clients

- Community leaders

- Documentation within the organization

- Experts on program services

- Funders

- Researchers and educators on trends

- Results of other research, for example, census data

- Staff members

- Volunteers

- Websites

### Who to Consider When Selecting People as Sources

The presenting priority of your project might be about helping your client to address certain problems that started at some time in the past or to achieve more forward-looking goals. Regarding projects to address problems, you might not know the root causes of the problems now, but you probably know the symptoms of the problems as reported by your client. In that situation, consider getting information from:

1.  People who are closest to the symptoms of the problem.

2.  People who are most affected by the symptoms of the problem.

3.  People who are most interested in the project, for example, the people who hired you if you are an external consultant.

4.  People who make decisions about the project, such as Board members and the Chief Executive Officer.

With projects to achieve a vision or specific goals, consider getting information from:

1.      People who established the goals.

2.      People who provide the authorization and resources to achieve the goals.

3.      People who are responsible to achieve the goals.

### Fill in the "Planning the Research" Worksheet

If you and your client are planning the research now, then in the worksheet, "Planning the Research," in Appendix C, fill in the section, "Source(s) of data."

## *Best Methods to Collect Data*

The overall goal in selecting data collection method(s) is to get the most useful information to answer the research questions and do so in the most cost-effective and realistic fashion.

### Overview of Common Data Collection Methods

There are a variety of methods to collect data during research. Many of the methods are quite common, for example, reviewing documentation, using questionnaires and conducting interviews. Other methods might include using various assessment tools that are available, such as tools to assess the quality of Board operations, strategic planning and programs. You might even choose to design your own methods to collect information.

See "Major Methods of Data Collection" on page 397 for an overview of major methods to collect information, including various assessment tools.

### Guidelines to Selecting Methods

Consider the following questions:

1.      How accurate will the information be from using those methods?

2.      Will the data collection methods get all of the needed information?

3.      What additional data collection methods should and could be used if additional information is needed?

4.      Will the information be credible to those who will use the results of the research?

5.      How do you naturally collect information, for example, by using your intuition (your internal "detector") or by sensing (focusing on external data)?

See "Understand Your Natural Approaches to Problem-Solving and Decision-Making" on page 47 identify how you prefer to gather data.

6.  Do you have the expertise and time for the selected methods? For example, you might have little or no expertise in conducting systematic surveys. In that situation, you should seek additional help. If there are limited resources available to you and your client during the research, especially in terms of time and access to people in your client's organization, you and your client should consider methods that are highly focused and practical, for example, questionnaires and short, follow-up interviews.

7.  Does your client have the resources for applying the methods, considering their time, energy and expertise for completing assessments for all areas of the organization?

8.  Will the nature of the particular source of information (for example, members of Board and staff) conform to the data collection methods, for example, will they fill out questionnaires carefully, engage in interviews or focus groups, and let you examine their documentation?

See "Address Context-Sensitive Considerations" on page 282 for more guidelines to ensure that the methods of data collection suit the nature of the participants in the research.

## For a Whole Systems Approach, Consider Using the Nonprofit Management Indicators Tool

One of the most useful organizational assessment tools is the Checklist of Nonprofit Management Indicators developed by the Greater Twin Cities United Way. (The tool is not from the United Way of America.) The tool helps members of the organization conduct a quick, comprehensive assessment of all major, internal aspects of their nonprofit organization. By using the assessment, each person indicates whether or not he or she thinks a particular aspect of the nonprofit needs attention. Each person's responses can be compared to "best practices" information in the assessment. The results of the assessment give a fairly good impression of how the nonprofit is doing overall when compared to best practices for nonprofits. As with any tool, the user should be careful not to apply it as a pre-established set of solutions that an organization must apply "as is" without customizing the tool to the organization.

See "Organizational Assessment Tool with Best Practices" on page 480 in Appendix C.

Although the Indicators assessment is quite comprehensive, it can be completed by almost anyone in about thirty minutes. To use the assessment:

1.  Consider having each Board member finish the assessment. If that is not practical, have each Board officer and/or the Chairs of Board committees finish the assessment.

2.  Request that the Chief Executive Officer finish the assessment.

3.  Consider having each staff member finish the assessment if the total size of staff is less than five to eight members. If the total size of staff is more than that, consider having staff leaders finish the assessment (for example, program managers and supervisors of staff).

4.  The completed assessments are sent to you for analysis. Analysis would include: a) compiling the responses by totaling the number of responses for each question; and b)

generating a report that highlights which areas of the nonprofit need the most attention, from comparing responses to best practices.

5.      If it is not practical to have the staff and Board members finish the assessment, then each planner might finish the assessment and then analyze their own results. Afterwards, in the entire group, planners can share their results, including conclusions about how the nonprofit might be doing when compared to best practices in nonprofits.

## Integration of Methods

Ideally, you and your client will use a combination of data collection methods (this is called triangulating the research). For example, you both might do the following.

1.      Start with a review of documentation to understand as much as possible about the organization and presenting priority. Once you have obtained that documentation, your review often can be done without extensive involvement of other people in the organization. The learning from that review often provides you credibility later on when doing other forms of data collection with participants, such as conducting interviews and focus groups.

2.      Next consider administering questionnaires to quickly gather a lot of information about people's knowledge, perceptions, feelings and opinions.

3.      Then consider conducting interviews that include questions that were honed during your review of documentation and analysis of the results from the questionnaires.

See "Major Methods of Data Collection" on page 397 for guidelines for using each method.

## Example of Sources and Methods of Data Collection

The table on the following pages depicts typical sources and methods of data collection for six common presenting priorities: Board operations, strategic planning, teamwork, financial management, fundraising, advertising and promotions. Remember that, at this point, you are identifying the methods to collect the data that you need from certain sources. You are not yet collecting and analyzing that data.

## Table IV:7 – Common Sources and Methods of Data Collection

**Board operations:**

- Review Board Bylaws, job descriptions, committee descriptions, description of Board versus staff roles, etc., to understand Board's stated preferences for how it organizes itself, and operates and interfaces with staff.
- Review Board's annual calendar of activities – are they on schedule?
- Review the Board's written procedures for identifying, orienting, training and organizing new Board members to understand how the Board states that it prefers to staff itself with fully developed new members.
- Review Board meeting agendas and meeting minutes to ascertain rate of attendance, participation of members, nature of decisions, follow-through on decisions, etc.
- Administer questionnaire to members and CEO to understand each member's perceptions of the Board's quality of teamwork, decision-making, problem solving, implementation of procedures and plans, quality of participation of all Board members, etc.
- Observe actual Board meetings to see how Board meetings are facilitated, including adherence to the agenda, how topics are addressed, how decisions are made, etc. Do the activities match what documentation and interviews revealed?
- Interview CEO about how the Board sets direction for the organization and CEO, and how it monitors implementation of plans. Is there evidence of clear documentation about plans and status of plans?
- Review results of the Board's self-evaluation. Were the results effectively addressed – or are there plans to address results?
- Review the Board's written evaluation of the CEO. Was it comprehensive and focused on implementing strategic goals?
- Do members believe issues exist? How do issues affect the organization? What should be done?

**Strategic planning:**

- Review the most current Board-approved Strategic Plan document. At a minimum, does it describe the mission and strategic goals? If action plans (specifying who will do what by when) are not in the Plan, where are they? Did the Plan produce an annual budget?
- Interview Board members and senior staff about how the Plan was developed, how implementation feedback was collected about implementation, how the Plan was communicated and to whom.
- Did the planning process carefully consider external trends and needs, with input from external stakeholders?
- Did the planning process carefully consider the quality of internal operations?
- If a Strategic Plan is not available, interview Board and staff members to understand how they are sure they have the same mission and goals and that everyone is working toward them. Understand how they made the decision not to develop a Strategic Plan document.
- Administer a questionnaire that asks all Board and staff members about their awareness of the mission and strategic goals.
- Review program plans, including each program's outcomes and target groups of clients, to understand their accordance with the Strategic Plan.
- Review the operating (annual) budget. How is it in accordance with the Strategic Plan?
- Are there problems with strategic planning? How do they affect the organization? What should be done?

## Table IV:7 – Common Sources and Methods of Data Collection (Cont.)

**Teamwork:**

- Review Personnel Policies to understand how staff members are supposed to be hired, assigned performance goals, rewarded and compensated for performance, and how performance issues are addressed.

- Review the Organization Chart to understand the roles in the organization and how those roles are integrated.

- Review job descriptions. Do they have specific up-to-date responsibilities in accordance with the latest Strategic Plan?

- Review written status reports about what each role does. Do the activities on the reports match the nature of work on the job descriptions?

- Interview senior staff to understand what program teams and other teams exist, and the charter for each (charter specifies purpose and specific objectives of each team).

- Administer a questionnaire about organizational climate, including respect, morale and coordination of staff.

- Observe staff meetings. Are they facilitated to an agenda? Are actions and issues recognized and addressed? Meeting minutes issued?

- Interview executives to understand how tasks are assigned, decisions are made, conflict is managed and communication occurs among individual staff members. Are activities in accordance with Personnel Policies?

- Examine the rate of employee turnover, etc.

- Do people believe that issues exist? How do issues affect the rest of the organization? What should be done?

**Financial management:**

- Review the current annual operating budget. Does it reflect priorities from the most recent Strategic Plan?

- Review current and past year's financial statements, including Statement of Financial Activities (income statement) and Statement of Financial Position (balance sheet). Is there a budget-versus-actual and/or cash flow report? Are they complete? How often were they issued? Who reviews them?

- Review the fiscal policies and procedures. Do they ensure accurate and legal collection, control and disbursement of funds?

- Review the latest financial audit from an outside auditor. Are all accounting standards followed? Are the auditor's recommendations followed?

- Interview Board members. What do they know about reviewing financial information? How are they sure the information is accurate?

- Interview the Board Treasurer. How are finances tracked and analyzed?

- Interview the bookkeeper. How are transactions entered and statements generated? To whom do they go? What do others do with them?

- Interview program staff. How were program pricing policies established?

- Interview the CEO or Board Treasurer. How do they know there are sufficient funds to pay current bills?

- Do people perceive that there are issues in financial management? How do issues affect the rest of the organization? What should be done?

**Table IV:7 – Common Sources and Methods of Data collection (Cont.)**

**Fundraising:**

- Review the Fundraising Plan. Does it specify a fundraising target, sources of donations, how to approach each, who will approach each and by when? How will grants be administered?
- If a Plan does not exist, are key members of the Board and staff aware of all of the information that should be in a Plan?
- Is the fundraising target derived from projected deficits as depicted in the last annual operating budget that, in turn, resulted from the Strategic Plan?
- Interview Board members. Are members participating in fundraising? Were they trained for effective fundraising?
- Review several grant applications. Do they specify the need for the funds, and vision, goals, methods, budget and approach to evaluation for funds for the program?
- How are grants managed? Are donations recognized and reports submitted to donors for their grants?
- Do people believe there are issues with fundraising? How do issues affect organization? What should be done?

**Advertising and promotion:**

- Review the Strategic Plan and/or program plans. What evidence exists that there are indeed unmet needs for programs to meet?
- Review program plans. What specific groups of clients are served by each program? What are the unique features and benefits of each program?
- Review results of program evaluations. Are program results being achieved? What are the strengths of the program?
- Review the Advertising and Promotions Plan. How are the features and benefits conveyed to each group of clients?
- Interview the CEO. Who is responsible for advertising and promotion? Are those activities effective?
- Interview several major clients. What do they think of the nonprofit? How could advertising and promotion be more effective?
- Do people believe there are issues with advertising and promotion? How do those issues affect rest of organization? What should be done?

## Fill in the "Planning the Research" Worksheet

If you and your client are planning the research now, then in the worksheet, "Planning the Research," in Appendix C, fill in the section, "Data collection method(s)."

## *Best Timing to Collect Data*

When determining the start and stop dates for data collection, consider:

- Timing of access to sources of information in your client's organization.

- Timing required to utilize various data collection methods, either by you or others in the organization.

- Context-sensitive considerations, for example, how long it might take for participants to understand and utilize various data collection tools (see the next subsection).

Similar to the other major considerations in designing the research plan, the timing to collect data also depends on the needs of those who will use the research. For example, typical deadlines for people to use the research might be related to:

- Identifying the causes and solutions to problems and, thereby, increasing current organizational performance as soon as possible.

- Identifying what is needed to achieve a new vision as soon as possible.

- Making changes to the current project work plan to address problems during the project.

- Providing a report to the Board by a certain date.

- Providing a report to a funder by a certain date.

- Generating advertising and promotions materials by a certain date.

If you have been collaborating with your client to develop the research plans, the plans are likely to already meet any scheduling requirements of your clients.

### Fill in the "Planning the Research" Worksheet

 If you and your client are planning the research now, then in the worksheet, "Planning the Research," in Appendix C, fill in the section, "Timing of data collection."

## Address Context-Sensitive Considerations

Context-sensitive considerations in regard to the unique features of your client's organization are extremely important to consider when conducting research within your client's organization. Depending on the culture and language, source and style of leadership, and nature of products and services in your client's organization, the activities of collecting information can range from being perceived as highly threatening to a true gift. Thus, you need to carefully consider each of the unique features of your client's organization. This is good practice for whole systems thinking.

 See "Context-Sensitive Considerations (What Makes Organizations Unique)" above to understand each of the considerations.

The most important skills in conducting context-sensitive research are "people" skills – those skills about building trust, commitment and collaboration.

 See "Building Trust, Commitment and Collaboration with Clients" on page 58 for many guidelines to develop your people skills.

## *Culture and Language of the Client's Organization*

If the culture is business-like, you and your client will want to conduct the research in a formal and orderly style. If the culture is informal, you both might act in a rather informal fashion to be in accordance with how people are in the workplace – unless it will benefit your client's organization to be more formal. If the culture seems rather secretive, you should carefully design how you collect information and you might also need to settle with less information than you had expected. You might even decide to collect data anonymously or privately with certain people. In any case, you and your client will need to be sure that members of the organization understand the words and language used during data collection. Consider how members of your client's organization might feel about "evaluating" others, for example. Ask your client to help you understand any cultural requirements.

See "How to Work in Multicultural Environments" on page 58 for guidelines for recognizing and working in a certain type of culture.

## *Life Cycle of the Client's Organization*

If your client's organization is in its early life stages, it is likely that members of the organization are extremely busy – even highly reactive – when dealing with the numerous day-to-day crises in the organization. Thus, members might struggle to find the time to participate in research activities, so the research design should be highly focused and include highly practical methods to collect information. Also, members might need to be convinced why they should spend their precious time engaged in research activities with you. Obviously, if the organization is in its later stages of development, members might have more time for the research. If the later stage is one of decline, there might even be some cynicism you will have to deal with when conducting the research.

See "Life Cycles of Organizations and Programs" on page 130 to review information about life cycles.

## *Size of the Client's Organization*

The larger the organization, the more levels of management you and your client might want to involve in the research, including gaining their approval and later on reporting results to them. Also, the larger the organization, the more likely that the culture will be rather formal with established policies and procedures that you will need to consider. In contrast, the culture of smaller, new organizations is likely to be less formal with less emphasis on policies and procedures.

## *Source and Style of the Client's Top-Level Leadership*

If your client's organization is Board-driven (most of the overall directives come from the Board), members of the Board might want to be aware of the strategic intent of the research, if there are any external stakeholders involved, and how research results will be used. In a staff-driven organization, those same concerns might exist, but might be addressed via communication with the Chief Executive Officer.

The effects of styles of leadership on the research are similar to the effects of culture. If a style is autocratic – based on control and formal authority – be sure that the research goes through proper channels. You and your client might need to conduct the research in a business-like style, as well.

### Fill in the "Planning the Research" Worksheet

If you and your client are planning the research now, then in the worksheet, "Planning the Research," on page 494 in Appendix C, fill in the section, "Context-sensitive considerations."

## Who Should Conduct the Data Collection?

You might not always be the best person to conduct the research during the Discovery and Feedback phase. Guidelines in this topic will help you and your client to select the best persons to conduct that research.

### Selecting the Right Researcher

In addition to being available when needed, the researcher should have expertise in:

- Understanding the various context-sensitive considerations in your client's organization, such as its culture, size and styles of leadership.

- Using the various data collection methods.

- Analyzing qualitative and quantitative information.

- Communication skills to collect data and report results of the research.

The extent of expertise desired or required depends on the:

- Complexity of the context-sensitive considerations.

- Complexity of the data collection tools.

- Complexity of the types of data generated from the research.

- Focus of the project.

### Should Your Client Conduct Interviews with Members of Their Organization?

Data collection from members of the organization is one of the rare occasions where a highly collaborative approach between you and your client may not be the best approach. This is true especially during interviews and focus groups to collect data from within your client's organization. Members sometimes feel inhibited or intimidated from sharing information about issues in the organization if other members are requesting that information in a direct, personal exchange. Therefore, you might arrange to conduct those interviews and focus groups yourself or have someone other than a member of the organization help you with those data collection methods. However, your client can help collect data by using other less personal means of data collection, for example, reviewing documentation and administering questionnaires.

### Fill in the "Planning the Research" Worksheet

If you and your client are planning the research now, then in the worksheet, "Planning the Research," on page 494 in Appendix C, fill in the section, "Who will conduct research."

## Field-Test Research Plans

You and your client might want to field-test the research plans to ensure that the data collection tools are understandable for everyone to use and that the tools will generate the kinds of data that you need. Also, you both will want to ensure that the use of the tools is compatible with any context-sensitive requirements, such as cultural preferences for data collection and the styles of leadership used in interactions among members.

If you and your client developed the research plans in a highly collaborative approach, it is likely that your client has already worked to ensure that the data collection tools will be useful in their organization.

Whether the plans are field-tested or not depends on the complexity of the:

- Context-sensitive considerations.

- Data collection tools.

- Types of data generated from the research.

- Focus of the project.

However, one of the most important considerations is the amount of time and other resources that would be required to field-test the research plans. Therefore, field-testing is less likely to occur with clients that have very limited amounts of time and resources.

### Fill in the "Planning the Research" Worksheet

If you and your client are planning the research now, then in the worksheet, "Planning the Research," on page 494 in Appendix C, fill in the section, "Field-testing research plans."

# Collect Meaningful Data

## Announce the Project to Members of the Organization

To ensure a highly successful project, it is critical that the project gains and maintains the commitment and ownership of participants. That accomplishment sustains motivation and momentum for the organizational change effort. Probably the most critical point in which to start cultivating that buy-in is when first announcing the project to others in the organization. The announcement must be done carefully to help participants quickly realize and accept the need for the project – so that they do not react to the project as just another fad or "silver bullet" intended to save the day. Here are some suggestions to consider:

1.  **CEO and Board member(s) announce the project to staff.**
    The project should be announced by the Chief Executive Officer or by a Board member to the staff, especially to those who will participate in the project. They should explain the purpose and benefits of the project to the organization. Special care should be given to ensuring sufficient time for reactions, questions and suggestions.

2.   **Accompany the announcement with an official memo.**
     The memo should reiterate reasons for the project, benefits of the project, project goals, management's full support of the project, as well as the project's start and stop dates.

3.   **Mention organizational change activities over the last few years.**
     Mention any successes or failures in the past, and what is being done to avoid those failures this time around. This type of information when presented in an authentic manner often helps to minimize cynicism about the project.

4.   **Mention the list of participants in the Project Team if there is one.**
     It helps for participants to realize that the project was designed and is being implemented by a team of fellow members from the organization.

5.   **Provide the name of one contact person.**
     This is useful in case anyone has any private concerns, questions or suggestions about the upcoming project.

## Prepare Participants Before Data Collection

You and your client should carefully prepare others who will be providing data during the research. You should not start simply by asking those people for certain types of data. Consider the following guidelines:

1.   **Leaders introduce the researcher to others in the organization.**
     One of the most powerful ways to do this introduction is in a group, for example, in a staff meeting. The introduction should include the researcher's description of the upcoming data collection effort and provide the opportunity for others to ask questions.

2.   **Tell each participant what is expected of him or her.**
     Explain how the data will be collected, and when and how the participant can participate. Mention if any pre-work would be useful for them to undertake, and any topics or activities that they should think about before participating in the data collection.

3.   **Contact each participant before conducting the interviews.**
     Interviews can be a rather personal form of data collection. It helps a great deal if the researcher calls each participant before the actual interview to introduce themselves, verify the timing of the upcoming interview and see if the participant has any questions.

4.   **Be prepared to clarify any terms of confidentiality of the data.**
     Some participants might ask the researcher to consider certain data from them as private – "off the record." The researcher should be clear and frank about any client or funder requirements for confidentiality. The researcher can offer to attempt to protect the privacy of the participant – to not include identifiable information about the participant in reports about results of the data collection. However, the researcher should be careful about making strong promises because if illegal activities are discovered during data collection, the researcher might not be able to guarantee that degree of privacy if subpoenaed by a court of law.

5.   **Tell participants whom they can call if they have questions.**
     Occasionally, participants have certain questions or comments about their role in the data collection. For example, they might ask about terms of confidentiality or they might want to

further clarify something they said during an interview. Provide them with the name of someone they can contact.

6.    **Review organizational documentation before contacting anyone.**
Documentation review is a major form of data collection. The researcher can learn a great deal about the organization from reviewing various forms of documentation, such as the Strategic Plan, marketing information and organization charts. That understanding provides the researcher strong credibility during the upcoming data collection activities because participants soon realize that the researcher already knows a great deal about the organization.

## Finish the "Planning the Research" Worksheet

 If you and your client are planning the research now, then in the worksheet, "Planning the Research," on page 494 in Appendix C, fill in the section, "How you will prepare participants."

# *Prepare Researcher(s) for Data Collection Activities*

This data collection activity is probably the first time that you and/or other researchers interact with many participants in the project. Data collection activities can be powerful means to start mobilizing members of the organization to accomplish major organizational change. The activities can help members realize the need for change and excite them to participate in accomplishing that change.

You also have a wonderful opportunity now to help members develop the types of behaviors needed to effectively address the presenting priority. For example, if the presenting priority is about improving planning or teamwork, members might need to learn how to be more systematic in their planning and more cooperative with others. You can model those types of systematic and cooperative behaviors yourself now during the data collection effort.

The guidelines in these sections in PART I will be especially useful to you now as you directly interact with others during data collection:

- Maintaining Professionalism

- Understanding Yourself as an Instrument of Change

- Building Trust, Commitment and Collaboration with Clients

- Administrative Skills for Consultants

The guidelines for data collection in PART VI will also be useful. In that section, each major tool for data collection is explained, along with guidelines for applying that tool.

In addition, if you will be collecting data during group meetings, the guidelines in PART V will be useful to you now.

Lastly, you and any other researchers should become familiar with the research plan.

## *Implement the Research Plan*

By now, you will have collaborated with your client to carefully develop a research plan by using the previous guidelines in this section and completing the worksheet, "Planning the Research." The research plan will have specified:

- Domain(s) of the presenting priority (individual position, team, project, cross-functional process, function, program or organization)

- Research questions

- Data to collect, sources of data and data collection methods for each research question

- Timing of data collection

- Context-sensitive considerations

- Who will conduct the research

- Field-testing research plans

- How you will prepare participants

Data collection is now a matter of collaboratively implementing the research plan.

## *If You Encounter Questionable or Illegal Practices*

Occasionally, data collection activities uncover organizational activities that seem immoral, for example, a violation of your professional standards and those in society, significant lies in the workplace or intentionally withholding very useful information from others. You might even encounter activities that are illegal, such as misappropriation of funds, fraud, theft or violation of employment laws.

See "Principles for Ethical Consulting" on page 30 and "How to Minimize Legal Liabilities and Risks" on page 35 for guidelines to address questionable or illegal situations.

# If Discovery and Feedback Stall, Cycle Back

Clients often are highly motivated to take part in the activities that identify issues and recommendations, so this phase rarely stalls during those activities. If it stalls, it might be because:

- Your client was not really ready for change.

- Your client does not fully understand the reason for discovery in their organization.

- The data collection effort is too large and complex for your client to undertake with you.

- Another major priority arose in the organization, which became more important than the presenting priority.

The following guidelines are standard, brief reminders of what to do whenever a particular phase of the consulting process seems to have stalled.

See "How to Do Collaborative Consulting with Busy Clients" on page 16 for a more complete description of each of the following actions.

1. **Be authentic.**

2. **Remind your client of the importance of the project.**

3. **Recognize the other priorities of your client.**

4. **Realize your client's lack of participation may be a form of project resistance.**

5. **Remind your client: choices about the project are choices about the nonprofit.**

6. **Continue to recognize accomplishments in the project so far.**

7. **Use small-group instead of large-group activities where possible.**

8. **Use coaching to identify obstacles and how to remove them.**

9. **Resort to the "Sanity Solution."**

10. **Decide if you should cycle back to Phase 2: Engagement and Agreement phase.**

# Identify Issues and Recommendations from the Data

## Organize the Data Collected by You and Your Client

### Prepare for Organizing the Data

Before you and your client begin organizing data and coming to conclusions about what you both found, be sure that both of you are fully prepared. Consider the following guidelines:

1. **Be sure that your client, including the Project Team, is highly involved.**
   One of the best outcomes from identifying issues is the learning gained by your client from noticing those issues and what might have caused them. Also, the more collaboratively that you work together, the more likely that you will identify the most important issues and how to address them later on.

2. **Determine any need for experts or program specialists.**
   If the results of data collection are in areas in which you and your client do not have expertise, get that expertise now. For example, you might need a specialist in a particular area, such as health care, information technology or market research.

3. **Identify any diagnostic models that you and your client will use to identify issues.**
   You and your client probably identified model(s) early in the Discovery and Feedback phase, such as strategic management, best practices, benchmarks and industry norms. If not, think now about how you both will make judgments regarding the data. How will both of

you conclude if the quality of performance of some major activity does not meet a certain performance standard?

 See "Maximum Performance – Different Things to Different People" on page 179 for more information about performance standards.

## Organize the Data

The following guidelines refer to quantitative and qualitative information. Quantitative data is data other than commentary, such as ratings, rankings, yes's and no's. Qualitative data includes commentary (not numeric ratings and rankings), usually about peoples' beliefs, perceptions and feelings.

Make copies of data and store the master copy away in a safe place. Use the copy for making modifications, such as edits, cutting and pasting.

1. Regarding quantitative data, add up the number of ratings, rankings, yes's or no's for each question from your questionnaire or interview guide.

2. For questions where a number is chosen by the respondents, consider computing a mean, or average, for each question. This is often more meaningful than indicating, for example, how many respondents ranked 1, 2 or 3.

3. Regarding quantitative data, you still might embellish your information on averages by conveying the range of answers, for example, 20 people ranked "1", 30 ranked "2" and 20 people ranked "3".

4. Regarding qualitative information, read through all the commentary at least twice. Mark any comments that were "off the record" or confidential.

5. Then organize quantitative and qualitative data into similar categories, for example:

   a) Per research question

   b) Per domain (for example, of the presenting priority, domains that share inputs and outputs with the presenting priority, and domains of overall planning)

   c) Strengths and weaknesses

   d) Frequency of complaints and compliments

   e) Categories suggested by the diagnostic model

6. Label each category of information.

Keep all data for several years after organizing it in case it is needed for future reference. Be sure to secure the information to protect it from access by people who are not involved in the project.

## *Identify Critical Issues*

If the research covered many aspects of your client's organization, it might seem like there are many issues to address – it might even seem overwhelming.  However, because the organization is a system with many integrated parts, you can often make a huge difference in the quality of operations by focusing on just a few parts.  You and your client will work together to prioritize those issues to address the most important ones.  Usually, there is a great deal of learning that can be gained.

Near the end of this topic is a table that depicts many of the most common types of issues discovered in nonprofit organizations.

### You and Your Client Consider Effects of Yourselves as Instruments of Change

The first major consideration for you and your client, even before identifying issues, is to realize any effects that each of your personal natures might have on interpretation of the data.  Discuss the following considerations with your client now so that both of you can recognize each of your natures and how it might influence the data analysis.  Consider:

- The "lens" through which either of you views organizations, for example, structural, human resources, political or symbolic.

- Your biases about leadership and nonprofits.  For example, should they be "more businesslike"?  Should they emulate a certain style of leadership?

- Your personal preferences for how you collect and interpret information.  For example, do either of you shy away from lots of data and prefer to make intuitive judgments?

- Your strengths and weaknesses as a consultant or leader.  Do not stray into analyzing any areas in which you do not have expertise.

> See "Understanding Yourself as an Instrument of Change" on page 43 for many guidelines about understanding your lens, biases, styles and preferences.

However, do not be timid about including your professional advice and opinions when identifying issues and recommendations – that is what your client is paying you for.

### Consider These Domains When Identifying the Issues

As you get ready to identify issues, consider your analysis to be of the following domains and in the following order.  After reviewing the following three paragraphs, go on to the next paragraphs that guide you to actually identify issues in each of the domains.

1.   **Focus on the quality of the management system of the presenting priority.**
     For example, if your client recruited you to improve fundraising, start there.  That approach ensures that you address your client's initial concerns and helps to retain your client's interest and motivation in the project.

2.   **Then focus on domains that share inputs and outputs with the presenting priority.**
     For example, if the presenting priority is fundraising, focus on domains that interact with fundraising, for example, program planning and strategic planning.  Those domains share

clarification of program costs, groups of clients to be served by each program, and the desired outcomes for each group of clients served.

See "Management Systems and Why You Should Understand Them" on page 156 for ideas of what domains might share inputs and outputs with certain other domains.

3.      **Analyze the quality of the overall planning activities.**
The overall planning activities are strategic planning, program planning and resource planning. Issues in any of those activities will adversely affect the quality of activities in many other activities, as well. Thus, always be sure that the overall planning activities are included in your research somehow, if only for a quick assessment of those activities.

## Identify the Issues in Each Domain

Now is when you and your client must use your collective judgment to identify issues by comparing data to relevant standards of performance. You might benefit now from reviewing guidelines about working with groups (within your client's organization) as you organize information and make decisions based on that data.

Guidelines through PART V are about group skills to manage meetings, organize information, make decisions and facilitate groups.

Consider the following guidelines to identify issues:

1.      **Compare the quality of management in the domains to certain performance standards.**
The standards should be agreed upon between you and your client.

a)   Standards from your performance model

b)   Industry standards

c)   Frequency of appearance

d)   Other best practices or standards of excellence

2.      **For each comparison, describe findings as differences from standards.**
You might use wording such as: less than, greater than, equal to, similar to, different from, occurring or not occurring.

The table on the following page depicts many of the types of issues discovered in nonprofits. The issues are organized into various domains.

## Table IV:8 – Common Types of Issues in Nonprofit Organizations

**Board operations**

- Low attendance at meetings
- Low participation in meetings
- High turnover of Board members
- No, or poor, decision making
- Rubber-stamping recommendations from the Chief Executive Officer
- Conflict among Board members
- Micromanagement of the nonprofit's day-to-day activities

**Strategic planning**

- Lack of clear focus for building programs and making major decisions
- Frequent suggestions from Board and/or staff for new programs
- Continual shortage of funds across the organization
- Low attendance and participation from Board and/or staff members
- Poor program results
- Conflict among Board and staff members about priorities, roles and responsibilities

**Program planning**

- Lack of clear goals and outcomes with programs
- Shortage of resources for programs
- Little or no results from programs
- Frequent complaints from program staff members
- Conflict and turnover among program staff members

**Management development**

- Poor planning, organizing, leading and administration of resources
- Lack of direction and guidance to staff members
- Conflict among staff members
- High employee turnover
- Poor communication between staff and Board members
- Incomplete implementation and evaluation of programs
- Board is not involved at all, or far too much, in planning and leadership

**Staff development**

- Frequent turnover
- Frequent complaints and conflict
- Poor performance
- Compliance ("going through motions") on the job
- (See symptoms of problems with program planning as listed above in this table)

**Table IV: 8 – Common Types of Issues in Nonprofit Organizations (Cont.)**

**Teamwork**
- Conflict between team members
- Inefficiencies in activities
- High turnover of members
- Confusion about decision making and problem solving
- Poor performance among members
- Ineffective meetings
- Low morale

**Financial management**
- Shortage of resources for programs
- Lack of understanding of costs of various resources
- Bills continually not paid on time
- Problems reported by annual financial audits
- Numerous requests for funds
- Frequent refusals from donors to fund programs
- Financial goals for fundraising are not clear

**Advertising and promotions**
- Little or no available feedback from program participants
- Strong testimonials and results from program participants, yet little growth in programs
- Confusion among clients about program benefits and activities
- Lack of program resources

**Fundraising**
- Poor program evaluations
- Shortage of resources for programs
- Little or no results from programs
- Frequent complaints from program staff members
- Numerous requests for funds to develop new programs
- Frequent refusals from donors to fund programs

**Program evaluations**
- Confusion among staff members about the program
- Inability to successfully describe program to others
- Poor program results
- Frequent complaints and conflicts among staff members
- Ineffective advertising and promotions
- Ineffective fundraising for programs

## *Generate Relevant and Realistic Recommendations*

### You and Your Client Probably Know More Now Than You Think You Do

Now you and your client are ready to identify what should be done to address the issues that were discovered in the research. As you both identified various issues, you both probably sensed recommendations to address them, as well. As a consultant with expertise in certain areas, you might sometimes take the lead in generating recommendations about certain issues. That is fine. However, remember that the best solutions to complex problems result from collaboration between you and your client.

The recommendations do not need to address all of the issues. Because your client's organization is a system with many integrated parts, you and your client often can make a significant difference even if the recommendations affect only a few of those parts. Then, as those parts become healthier, they positively affect the rest of the organization. Besides, there are some standard recommendations that can be used to address a wide range of issues – just like there are some standard healthy habits that can address a wide range of health issues (habits, such as get sleep, eat well and exercise).

Solutions recommended by you and your client do not have to be perfect solutions. Many times, your most useful service to the members of your client's organization is to help them to see their issues "in a different light" – to reframe how they see those issues and then help them to come up with additional recommendations.

See "How to Analyze Mental Models – How People Think" on page 418 for tools to help people solve problems by reframing them.

### Preparation for Generating Recommendations

The same considerations that you used to prepare for identifying issues can be used now to prepare for generating recommendations. Those considerations included to be sure that your Project Team and other key stakeholders were involved in this activity, involve any experts who might be needed because of the nature of the issues, and have a diagnostic model and other performance standards to reference.

Near the end of this topic is a table that depicts many of the most common types of actions (or recommendations) to address issues commonly discovered in nonprofit organizations.

### Level of Detail to Plan For in Recommendations from You and Your Client

You and your client might consider this phase of the consulting process to be focused primarily on identifying recommendations about *what* your clients will do, while the next phase of the consulting process (Action Planning, Alignment and Integration) is focused on *how* your clients will implement those recommendations. The recommendations of you and your client in this phase will probably be less detailed than in discussions during the next phase. In this phase, identify recommendations to address most, or all, of the issues.

Descriptions of recommendations might include only the nature of the actions to take with the recommendations, and not include specification of who should take those actions, when and how. However, make recommendations more detailed if your client has little time in which to implement recommendations or has little expertise with which to refine recommendations. If there are many issues and recommendations, you might divide the recommendations into two categories: broad goals and more detailed recommendations associated with each goal.

## Describe the Recommendations in Understandable and Specific Terms

Whatever level of detail you and your client decide to include in the recommendations, describe each in terms that are clearly understandable and specific – specific to the extent that it would be obvious whether someone had followed the recommendations or not. For example, the recommendation, "Try to build up the Board," is not specific. In contrast, "Conduct Board training, coach the Board Chair and conduct a self-evaluation of the Board," are all specific recommendations.

Later on, your client will decide which of the recommendations to follow and will identify specific actions to take to follow each recommendation. The descriptions of those actions should be specific, measurable, achievable, relevant and timely.

## Consider These Domains When Preparing to Generate Recommendations

Similar to when you identified issues before, start your analysis for recommendations with the presenting priority, then domains that share input and outputs with the presenting priority, and then domains of the overall planning activities.

## General Considerations Before Generating Recommendations

1. **If many issues exist, then a grand, forward-looking vision might not be helpful.**
   A rather common mistake that consultants make in organizational change efforts is to work with clients first to establish a grand, inspirational vision that must be achieved during the change effort. While that type of vision can be motivational to many, it might be useless – or even hurtful – if the organization currently faces many issues that must be addressed before the grand vision should even be considered.

    See "Develop a Vision for Change Now?" on page 320 for more guidelines about developing a vision for change, including a grand or strategic vision.

2. **Focus recommendations on structures and processes, not just on personalities.**
   Another common mistake is to encourage change only by evoking people to work harder or to somehow change their nature. That approach inspires some, but the change soon dissipates. An important systems principle is relevant here: structures determine behaviors, which determine events. Do not focus on changing behaviors without also changing structures, such as plans, policies and job descriptions.

3. **Focus recommendations at least one level "above" where the issue occurs.**
   For example, if the operational activities of fundraising are not effective, do not focus only on doing those activities even harder. Focus on the overall planning activities, including strategic planning and program planning.

## Now You and Your Client Generate Recommendations for Each Domain

Block (2000) recommends that recommendations be:

- Something about which your client has control to change.

- Clearly important to the organization.

- Focused on items which the organization has a commitment to work on.

In addition, some or all of the following approaches might be useful as you and your client generate recommendations to address the issues that were discovered during the research. Note that there will be additional considerations that you and your client will need to address in the upcoming phase, Action Planning, Alignment and Integration.

1.   **Associate judgments about issues with their level of performance.**
     You and your client might use words, such as applicable, not applicable, meets requirements, does not meet requirements, is urgent, is important, do first and do later.

2.   **Consider what has and has not worked.**
     Think about what your client has told you about what they already tried. Think back about what they said to you during the Engagement and Agreement phase. Recommendations should build on what worked and avoid what did not.

3.   **Build in some quick successes.**
     Build in activities that are easily accomplishable and for which resources are readily available, such as convening a Project Team or developing a project schedule. Quick successes help to mobilize and organize people in the early phases of the project.

4.   **Include recommendations to develop or update the leadership (Board and executives).**
     The "leverage point" in the system of an organization – the place where the least amount of effort often makes for the most long-term difference – is ensuring that the leadership provides effective planning and oversight of the organization. So, even if the performance of Board members and the executives was already of high quality, they will need to understand the result of the change effort and how they should further develop their performance to achieve those results.

5.   **Ensure that recommendations would not hurt services to clients.**
     When identifying recommendations, always ask, "Might this hurt the quality of our services to our clients?" That level of performance must be protected at all times.

 See "Finish the Action Plans – Alignment, Integration and Reality Check" on page 328 for guidelines to analyze effects of recommendations.

6.   **Consider use of various tools to analyze systems.**

     a)  You might use a force-field analysis to identify the driving forces that are "pushing against" and "pushing for" change in a system – resulting in the system being stuck. That information can tell you and your client what forces to support and which to minimize in the recommendations.

b) You might use a polarity tool to resolve two seemingly conflicting choices and to clarify how to avoid overdoing any of recommendations.

c) You might use a logic model to clearly depict a system and the relationships between the parts of that system.

d) You might use rational problem solving methods to identify all options to solve a problem, compare them to each other and then carefully select the best option.

e) You might use the upside/downside tool to carefully examine if an option might have any unexpected consequences.

See "Analyzing Systems" on page 417 for a variety of tools to analyze systems and the guidelines to use each of them.

7.  **Consider principles for successful organizational change and capacity building.**
    There are a variety of principles that can be useful to you at this point. Include relevant principles in recommendations generated by you and your client.

    See "Changing Systems" on page 438 for a description of the key principles for successful change.

8.  **Consider the many types of capacity building.**
    There are many types of capacity building listed in this Field Guide. They might give you ideas for recommendations.

    See "Common Capacity Building Activities and How Clients Choose Them" on page 194 for a listing of many types of capacity building.

9.  **Build on strengths in the organization.**
    For example, if the organization has a strong financial position, include recommendations that involve purchasing additional resources to implement other recommendations. If there are plenty of volunteers, incorporate the role of volunteers in recommendations. A powerful approach to identifying strengths is to refer to stories about past successes in the organization. This is a technique often used in Appreciative Inquiry.

    See "Stories (to Convey Positive, Individualized Learning)" on page 381 for guidelines to use the stories technique.

10. **Decide now if additional help will be needed.**
    For example, if recommendations include developing the Board, but you do not have expertise in that area, you might need to bring in a Board specialist. Similarly, you might need a strategic planning facilitator, financial management expert or fundraiser.

11.     **It might not be useful to put a lot of detail into recommendations now.**
For now, you and your client might suggest what overall actions need to be taken.  However, you both should probably wait to suggest what specific objectives need to be accomplished and when in order to conduct the overall actions.

Recommendations might end up being changed during the upcoming feedback meeting.  In addition, participants in the meeting can be overwhelmed by lots of detail in recommendations.  Sometimes you can lull them into passivity with an impressive presentation – that passivity could come back to haunt the project later on during the implementation phase.

The table on the following page depicts the most common recommendations to address issues discovered in nonprofits.  This table suggests formation of a variety of Board Committees.  Depending on the size and commitment level of the Board members, it might not be realistic to create all these committees.  Each Board should determine the committee or organizational structure that will support them in their work for the organization.

Note that various different cultures might use different terms than those in the following recommendations.

 See "How to Work in Multicultural Environments" on page 58 for hints about using certain terms with other people.

## Table IV:9 – Common Recommendations and Order of Implementation

### Board operations

Form a Board Governance Committee to oversee the following actions: (Coach the Board Chair to work with the entire Board to do the actions.)

- Conduct at least a one-hour Board training session each year about roles and responsibilities of a governing Board of Directors and Chief Executive Officer.
- Conduct at least a one-hour Board orientation each year about the Board's unique practices.
- Ensure annual strategic planning to identify the nonprofit's mission, goals, strategies, objectives, specific responsibilities to achieve each, timelines, etc.
- Ensure Board staffing procedures are based on obtaining expertise needed to achieve the most up-to-date strategic goals.
- Ensure each Board member has something specific to do, such as membership on a Board Committee.
- Ensure each Committee has a work plan that specifies the objectives and timelines for the Committee to achieve during the year. Each Committee regularly reports the status of implementation of its work plan in each Board meeting.
- Establish a Board Executive Committee to be comprised of Committee Chairs and to "police" that work plans are being implemented on a timely basis by each Committee.
- Establish a Board Personnel Committee to supervise the Chief Executive Officer in effectively working with the revamped Board and staff.
- Ensure the Chief Executive Officer has annual performance goals and is evaluated against those goals.
- Conduct a Board self-evaluation each year and ensure that results are addressed.
- Enact a Board attendance policy to sustain strong attendance.

### Strategic planning

Form a Board Planning Committee to oversee the following actions:

- Ensure involvement of, and/or input from, staff, clients and other stakeholders in the strategic planning process.
- Ensure effective Board development, especially regarding their responsibility to ensure effective strategic planning and implementation. The Board Governance Committee should oversee the activities listed in the previous section of this table.
- Develop a "plan for plan" that ensures that upcoming strategic planning is relevant, realistic and flexible to suit the needs and nature of the organization.
- Conduct strategic planning to clarify the organization's mission, strategic goals, objectives and action plans (that specify who will do what and by when).
- In the planning, consider learning and evaluation results from day-to-day operations.
- Ensure that strategic priorities (goals, objectives, etc.) are associated with a relevant Board Committee that monitors achievement of those goals and objectives. For example, ensure the Board Programs Committee oversees program goals, the Board Personnel Committee oversees staffing planning and development, etc.
- Update each Committee's work plan and each staff position's job description and performance goals to reflect the latest strategic goals.
- Communicate the Strategic Plan to all key stakeholders.
- Ensure the Strategic Plan is approved by the Board and its implementation is monitored by the Executive Committee.

**Table IV:9 – Common Recommendations and Order of Implementation (Cont.)**

### Program planning

Form a Board Programs or Marketing Committee to oversee the following actions:

- Conduct market research to clearly identify:
  1) Unmet community needs to meet with programs.
  2) Which groups of clients will be served by which programs.
  3) What outcomes to achieve with each group of clients.
  4) Methods to effectively meet the needs of each group.
  5) Potential collaborators and competitors.
  6) What resources are needed to provide the services.
  7) The cost of those resources.
  8) How the program should recover the costs.
- In the research, consider learning and evaluation results from day-to-day operations.
- Ensure program staff is resourced (clear roles, time, energy and expertise) to carry out their roles in the program.
- (Nonprofits rarely ask for help with "program planning," rather they ask for help with program advertising, even though program planning may be where they really need help.)

### Management development

Form a Board Personnel Committee to oversee the following actions:

- Train staff in the standard roles of Board and Chief Executive Officer.
- Establish up-to-date policies and procedures regarding creating staff positions, recruitment and selection of staff, how performance goals are established, how delegation is conducted, how performance issues are addressed, and a compensation system commensurate with performance. Incorporate policies and procedures into a Personnel Policies Manual reviewed by an expert on employment laws and approved by the Board.
- Develop skills in leadership and management by providing training in at least the following skills:
  1) Time and stress management.
  2) Planning process, including setting direction (vision and goals), methods (strategies) to achieve goals and resource planning to implement strategies.
  3) Communication, written and spoken, for example, presentations and meeting management.
  4) Basic skills in supervision, such as setting goals, delegating, giving feedback and evaluating performance.
  5) Conflict management.

### Staff development

Form a Board Personnel Committee to oversee the following action plans:

- Conduct strategic and program planning for clear focus, roles and alignment of roles.
- Ensure staff members receive specific performance goals.
- Assess staff members' needs for training, resources and supervision to achieve goals.
- Ensure effective supervision, including mutually established goals, delegation, feedback, performance reviews and rewards.
- Obtain strong staff input about issues and how they can be addressed – ensure a participatory approach to leadership and management.
- Establish and train staff in up-to-date personnel policies that conform to recent employment laws and regulations.

## Table IV:9 – Common Recommendations and Order of Implementation (Cont.)

### Teamwork

Form a Board Personnel Committee to oversee the following actions:

- Ensure up-to-date job descriptions and performance goals for each staff member.
- Develop charters and work plans for teams, including:
  1) Purpose of the team.
  2) Results to be achieved by the team and by when.
  3) Resources available to the team.
  4) How decisions will be made.
  5) Roles on the team.
  6) How the communications will occur inside and outside the team.
- Develop the staff and management appropriately.

### Financial management

Form a Board Finance Committee to oversee the following actions:

- Conduct strategic planning, identifying resources needed to achieve strategic goals and the financial resources required to obtain and support ongoing usage of those resources.
- Conduct program planning, identifying costs to develop programs and the expected revenue and expenses for each program.
- Train Board members in how to review financial information.
- Train staff about financial management, including how to document each financial transaction, generate financial statements, analyze those statements and report important information from the analysis.
- Establish, revise and ensure ongoing implementation of fiscal policies and procedures to ensure effective and legal financial management and cash controls.

### Advertising and promotions

Form a Board Marketing or Promotions Committee to oversee the following actions:

- Develop and implement an Advertising and Promotions Plan for each program and the organization overall that clearly identifies:
  1) Specific groups of clients served by the program.
  2) Unique benefits of the program to each group.
  3) What messages to convey to each group.
  4) How each message will be conveyed.
  5) Who will convey the message.
  6) When.
- Monitor status of implementation of the Advertising and Promotions Plan.
- A Marketing Committee might also be responsible for marketing analysis, for example, for clarifying what community needs should be met by each program, what specific groups of clients should be served, and what competitors and collaborators exist for each program.

## Table IV:9 – Common Recommendations and Order of Implementation (Cont.)

### Fundraising

Form a Board Fundraising Committee to oversee implementation of the following actions:

- Conduct strategic planning to identify what programs are needed and how those programs should be integrated into the organization. A Board Planning Committee might oversee this strategic planning.
- Conduct program planning to clearly identify which community needs should be met, what outcomes to achieve, what methods to achieve outcomes and cost of resources to develop programs.
- Orient fundraisers (internal or external) about program clientele and program results.
- Develop and implement a Fundraising Plan specifying what monies need to be raised, what funding mix is desired (among individuals, corporations, foundations and government), what donors to approach, how to approach them, when to approach them, who will approach them and how funds will be administered.
- For revenue development, conduct market research to identify fees-for-services opportunities, then conduct feasibility studies on each of the most likely opportunities, and then business planning for each of the best opportunities.

### Program evaluations

Form a Board Program Evaluation or Programs Committee to oversee the following actions:

- Conduct program planning to clarify program process, goals and/or outcomes.
- Train program staff about evaluation, including its benefits and how to identify:
  1) Types of evaluation.
  2) What type to use.
  3) What information is needed for each type.
  4) How to get that information.
  5) How to analyze and interpret it.
  6) How to report it.
- Conduct a program process evaluation to determine the effectiveness and the ineffectiveness of the program process.
- Conduct a program goals evaluation to determine achievement of goals.
- Conduct a program outcomes evaluation to determine what benefits were realized by participants.
- Determine how to package and share evaluation findings with marketing, fundraising and future planning activities.

## Always Prioritize the Recommendations from You and Your Client

It is important that members of your client's organization clearly understand the recommendations generated by you and your client. If you have more than five to seven overall recommendations, you should carefully organize the recommendations so that they are easy to comprehend. Your client can use one or more of the following categories to prioritize and organize the recommendations.

1. **Short-term versus long-term recommendations**
   Consider short-term to be recommendations that can be followed in the next 1-3 months. The scope of these terms is up to you and your client to decide.

2.     **Per domain**
       Organize the recommendations by domain: by individual or position, team, project, process, program, function or the entire organization.

3.     **Essential versus desired**
       Essential recommendations are those that, if not followed, certainly will block the organization from successfully dealing with its most important issues. You also might refer to the essential recommendations as "critical success factors."

4.     **Broad goals and narrow recommendations (goals versus objectives)**
       You might organize each of the recommendations under five to seven more broad goals, each with specific objectives to achieve that goal. For example, for a goal of Board development, have objectives, such as Board training, coach the Board Chair and update Board policies.

## Document the Findings and Recommendations from You and Your Client

You and your client should report the results of the research, including findings and recommendations, in a written document. The level and scope of the content of the written report depends on:

- **The target audience for the written report.**
  For example, Board members might want a report that includes the highlights of findings, accompanied by a face-to-face presentation. The Chief Executive Officer might want a more comprehensive report that focuses on the presenting priority and what can be done to address it.

- **Whether you were recruited to provide recommendations only.**
  This situation often requires a more complete and formal written report. Information in the report should be sufficient such that the report can be fully understood by others without explanation from you.

- **Whether recommendations are part of the Discovery and Feedback phase.**
  If so, the report might require primarily "talking points" for you to reference during a face-to-face meeting with your client.

At a minimum, a written report should include:

1.     An executive summary.

2.     Description of the organization, the project and role of the research.

3.     Explanation of the research purpose and questions, data collection methods and analysis procedures.

4.     Listing of findings and conclusions.

5.     Any relevant attachments, for example, inclusion of data collection methods, such as questionnaires and interview guides.

6.      Pages marked as "proprietary" and "draft" until finished.

If the research discovered gross misbehavior or extremely poor performance of the Chief Executive Officer, you might label the report "To Board Members Only."

## Comments to Reduce Your Client's Resistance to Findings

The report might include information that members of your client's organization will interpret as negative criticism. In that situation, you and your client might include the information in the following table early on in the written report in order to minimize resistance to accepting the information.

## Table IV:10 – Sample Text to Include in Reports to Reduce Resistance

*There is no blame.*
*No person ever sets out to damage an organization. Everyone is doing the best that they can with what they know at that time in an organization. It is extremely rare that major, ongoing struggles are addressed merely by replacing certain people. Struggling organizations have broken systems, not broken people. Thus, attention should be toward improving those systems.*

*Be open to new perspectives about current issues.*
*In a struggling organization, each leader usually has very strong opinions about what caused the issues and what will resolve them. Consequently, it can be a major struggle for readers to objectively read the contents of an assessment report when those contents do not closely match the reader's opinions. One of the first challenges in improving an organization is for its leaders to be open to new perspectives and ideas about issues.*

*Read the report several times.*
*It is common for readers to have strong reactions to information in a comprehensive assessment report. Those reactions can inhibit the reader from accurately understanding other information in the report. Therefore, after reading the report for the first time, set it down for a few hours and then re-read it. Underline key phrases. Discuss your reaction with other readers.*

*Evaluate the report based on overall information, not on incidental details.*
*The report includes an extensive amount of information. A few minor details might not be completely accurate, some details might be missing, etc. Those details can be corrected. Therefore, focus especially on the overall issues described in the report and on the recommendations to address those issues.*

*Evaluate the report's recommendations based on the accuracy of major recommendations.*
*Some people evaluate recommendations based on their novelty and complexity. That approach is based on the myth that major issues are resolved by using new, complex techniques. Instead, issues are usually resolved by helping people to reframe how they see those issues and then by coming to agreement on how to resolve the issues.*

*You cannot judge the quality of an organization merely by counting its issues.*
*Healthy organizations have learned to evolve through life cycles. For those organizations, their transitions were characterized by an increase in the amount and complexity of issues. It is not how many issues an organization has, but how the organization addresses those issues that makes the biggest difference in achieving long-term health for the organization.*

## Example of Overall Recommendations

The information in the following table depicts one example of overall recommendations. In the research report, you and your client should include more detailed recommendations in accordance with each of the overall recommendations provided in the example. Recommendations should be based entirely on the results of the research and not on the following example. Note that the example includes only a description of the overall recommendations and not the issues that generated those recommendations.

## Table IV:11 – Example of Overall Recommendations

The following overall recommendations address the specific areas that our research indicated need attention. They are in the general order in which they should be followed. Our research report includes detailed recommendations for each of the following recommendations.

Implementation of the plans will result in more Board-driven, participative and proactive leadership with focus on achieving systematic and strategic results. Effective, overall organizational development could take six months to a year to achieve.

1.  First, Board development should occur according to a specific Board Development Plan reviewed and approved by the Board. The Plan should include specific goals, timelines and responsibilities. This ensures strong Board leadership structures to ensure that plans are developed and implemented in a timely manner.

2.  Next, based on the Board's enhanced leadership structure, a Strategic Plan should be developed with focus primarily on developing internal systems and with short-term specific goals and timelines. Each of these overall recommendations should be associated with a strategic goal in the Strategic Plan.

3.  Next, a Program Plan should be developed for each major program/service, specifying goals and outcomes for the program, methods to achieve goals and outcomes, resources needed for the program, and performance indicators to be evaluated regularly.

4.  Next, Personnel Policies should be updated and approved. Policies should address staff and volunteer management, and include systematic procedures for how performance goals are established, staff and volunteers are developed, performance is monitored and evaluated, performance issues are addressed, and performance is associated with equitable and fair compensation.

5.  Next, a Fundraising Plan should be developed that specifies what monies need to be raised for what programs, donors/sources for those monies, who will approach the donors, how and when they will approach the donors, and who will manage grant information and requirements.

6.  Each of the strategic goals in the Strategic Plan should be integrated into a specific work plan for each Board Committee. Implementation of the Strategic Plan should be monitored by the Board's Executive Committee, which should be comprised of Chairs of each of the Committees.

# You and Your Client Share Feedback with Others

Now that you and your client have identified various issues and overall recommendations to address those issues, both of you are now ready to share that information with the rest of the members of the organization in a feedback meeting. The manner in which you share that feedback can greatly influence the effectiveness of your project in accomplishing successful organizational change. A successful feedback experience can establish strong motivation, vision, political support and momentum for change.

If your Project Team included all members of your client's organization, the feedback activities are not needed because all members are already aware of the issues and recommendations. However, that is true only if *all* members of the organization, including the full Board of Directors, were on the Team. Otherwise, you will need a meeting to share important feedback with others who were not directly involved in the discovery activities.

If you have been working in a highly collaborative fashion with your client, now is the time that that collaboration will really pay off. There will be few surprises when hearing the results of the discovery activities. The results will be much more useful. There will be much less resistance to the recommendations.

It is important that you and the Project Team work as partners to present the results of the research to the rest of the organization. That partnership brings a great deal of credibility and comfort to other organization members.

There is often an overlap in the nature of activities between identifying what actions to take (during discussions in the feedback meeting) and the action planning activities of the next phase, Action Planning, Alignment and Integration. During the feedback meeting, your client is deciding *what* actions to take. In the next phase, your client decides *how* to take those actions.

## *Preparation*

Before you work with your client to design the agenda (in the next topic) for the feedback meeting, there are certain considerations that need attention now.

1. **Your client may prefer that the written report go to certain people before meeting.**
   That is your client's prerogative. Encourage those people who received the report to still attend the meeting. Ensure that the report is marked "draft" until any feedback from the meeting has been incorporated into the report.

2. **Be sure that your client understands the purpose of the upcoming meeting.**
   Explain that the meeting is intended to share results of the research, that there will be no blame put on anyone, that your goal is to ensure that participants understand the research results, and that in the meeting they will begin to identify actions to address the issues.

3. **How will group decisions be made in the meeting?**
   You will want participants to make – and support – prompt decisions during the meetings. Before the meeting begins, be sure that you and your client have decided how participants in the meeting will make decisions about recommendations. For example, with they use a consensus method? Vote?

4. **What will participants in the meeting want to know about the research?**
   You and your client may know what you want those decision makers to learn from attending the meeting, but that is entirely different than knowing what they want to learn. Often, they feel apprehensive about the results of the research. They want to know if they are to blame somehow. They want to know how much time your project will take from their current duties. The best way to find out what participants want from the meeting is to ask them. To pose that question, you might share your proposed agenda with them and then ask them if anything is missing from the agenda.

5. **With what style should the information be presented during the meeting?**
   Ask your client to advise you on how decision makers like to get information. For example, they might prefer a presentation followed by a discussion. Or they might prefer handouts that highlight certain information, along with attachments having more detailed information.

## Design the Feedback Meeting

The particular design of the meeting is up to you and your client. There are various aspects of the meeting to carefully consider, including what goals to achieve during the meeting, what topics need to be covered, how much time to allocate to each topic, who should attend the meeting, what parts of the meeting you will lead and what parts your client will lead, how long the meeting will be, and who will document major decisions and actions from the meeting.

In addition, it will be helpful now to consider what obstacles or challenges might arise during the meeting and how those might be addressed. For example, you might encounter strong resistance from certain people within the organization.

PART V includes many guidelines for achieving successful meetings, such as the design of agendas, establishing ground rules, time management, evaluating meetings and dealing with various forms of resistance from groups.

### Desired Outcomes from the Meeting

1. Key members of the organization agree on the issues facing their organization and, ideally, on most of the actions to address those issues.

2. Members feel ownership and commitment to take those actions soon.

3. Members understand that the actions will be further refined in the next phase, Action Planning, Alignment and Integration.

### Selecting Participants for the Meeting

1. **The most important decision makers should participate in the meeting.**
   Without their participation, it is often extremely difficult to gain their strong, ongoing support for your project. Their participation is critical to sustaining the political support necessary for successful organizational change. They may not pose an obstacle for your project – however, that is not the same as proactively supporting your project.

2. **If all Board members will not be in attendance, find out why.**
   If the scope of your project means major change to the nonprofit's programs, staffing and/or resources, then all members of the Board of Directors should be at the meeting. Sometimes, your client might be hesitant to agree to this. If that is the case, arrange for you to attend a portion of an upcoming Board meeting during which you can share the major findings and conclusions from the research.

3. **For those who will be missing, how will information be communicated to them?**
   Get this question answered before you conduct the feedback meeting. Otherwise, there may be a long delay in getting the necessary information out to those who did not attend the meeting.

## Agenda and Allocation of Timing

Block (2000) is a good source of information about how to carefully design and conduct feedback meetings. He makes the following two points well.

1. **A common mistake is to allocate far too much time to discussion about issues.**
   People assume that the more the participants know about the issues, including the dynamics of causes and effects, the more they will be able to address those issues later on. That assumption is not valid because issues rarely have simple, rational causes that can be fully understood. Delving into the issues usually results in participants feeling deep despair and anxiety. Besides, most members of the organization usually are already aware of the issues that exist – members usually want to move forward to address those issues as soon as possible, rather than delve into the past.

2. **Allocate most of the meeting to agreement on actions to take – to get the decisions.**
   It is critical that by the time participants leave the meeting, they have formally agreed on what actions they will take to address the various issues. If participants suggest that they decide on actions after the meeting, promptly and strongly encourage them to make their decisions during the meeting. Otherwise, you will have lost a precious opportunity to get their clear commitment for participation during the rest of the project.

## Table IV:12 – Suggested Topics and Timing for Feedback Meeting

| Topic | Length of Time (minutes) |
|---|---|
| Welcome and brief introductions | 10 |
| Review the agenda, goals of the meeting and its ground rules | 3 |
| Describe the project, including your role and the role of the research | 2 |
| Describe the focus of the research and its research methods | 3 |
| Explain that issues are from broken systems, not from broken people | 2 |
| Describe the overall issues discovered from the research | 20 |
| Describe the overall recommendations from you and your client | 30 |
| Decide on which recommendations to follow | 30 |
| Identify any actions to address the issues and also any learnings so far | 10 |
| Evaluate the feedback meeting | 10 |
| **Total Time** | **120** |

## *Skills Needed to Facilitate the Feedback Meeting*

Different groups of people might participate very differently in the meeting. Therefore, it is important to be aware of the major values and traditional behaviors in your client's organization. Skills in communication are critical during this meeting. You must carefully listen to each participant, to both their words and body language. You will need to ensure that the terms and phrases that you refer to in the upcoming meeting will be understood by participants. For example, they might have different interpretations for "strategic planning" or "leadership". This meeting is all about sharing feedback with others. Therefore, you should brush up on your skills in communications.

See "Building Trust, Commitment and Collaboration with Clients" on page 58 for guidelines to brush up on various skills in communications.

The feedback meeting can be somewhat uncomfortable for some participants. They might feel apprehensive, scared and confused. After all, they might be hearing about issues that they do not want to hear about. They might believe that they are somehow to blame for those issues. The success of your meeting depends on how well you recognize those feelings among participants and help them deal with those feelings in a constructive manner. Your skills in empathy will come in handy.

See "How to See Your Client's Point of View – Your Skills in Empathy" on page 75 to polish your skills in empathy.

Many times, issues in your client's organization exist because of previous actions taken by participants who now are in the feedback meeting. During the meeting, participants hear recommendations that can directly conflict with what participants believe they should do to address their issues. Conflicts during the meeting can be within various participants or with others, such as with you and other facilitators in the meeting.

See "Understand Your Natural Responses to Feedback and Conflict" on page 45 to clarify how you respond to conflict and how to manage conflict.

If you have worked in a highly collaborative manner with your client, your client will help you to lead the meeting. Still, in the middle of discussing issues and what can be done to address those issues, clients sometimes can quickly become quite confused. In those situations, you might need to take a clear, assertive role in facilitating the meetings. This is one of the few times that you might need to take a strong role other than a highly collaborative role. Therefore, before you conduct the feedback meeting, you might need to polish some of your skills in working with groups.

PART V, starting on page 369, has guidelines about preparation for any group activity, such as getting ready to facilitate, making group decisions, enhancing group participation and managing resistance during meetings.

## *Conduct the Feedback Meeting*

At this point, you and your client are ready to decide who will lead the discussion of each of the topics on the agenda for the feedback meeting. For each topic, consider the following guidelines:

1. **Welcome and brief introductions (10 minutes).**
   Usually, all the participants know each other, but you do not know them. So brief introductions are a chance for you to get settled and others to get acquainted with you. Do not spend more than 10 minutes on this activity.

2. **Review the agenda and goals of meeting (3 minutes).**
   Give a crisp, concise overview of the agenda. Ask if participants have any questions so far. Just quickly hear the nature of each question and then indicate where on the agenda their question will be addressed later on in the meeting.

3. **Describe the project, including your role and role of research (2 minutes).**
   Give a concise overview of the project, including the presenting priority, goals and outcomes. Mention the phases of the consulting process and where the discovery phase fits in the process.

4. **Describe the focus of the research and research methods (3 minutes).**
   Briefly mention any research questions, what information was needed to address the presenting priority, how that information was collected and from whom. Now is a good time to thank those in the room who provided the information. Mention how your client was involved in designing and conducting the research.

5. **Explain that issues are from broken systems, not broken people (2 minutes).**
   This is an important point to establish early in the meeting. It helps participants focus on plans, not on personalities, during the meeting. It helps them to alleviate their anxieties and hear what you are saying when you talk about their issues.

 See "Comments to Reduce Your Client's Resistance to Findings" on page 305 for comments to include in your report to address any resistance from others while reading the report.

6. **Describe the issues discovered from the research (20 minutes).**
   Describe the most important five to seven issues. Explain how you and your client derived them, for example, by using certain standards of performance or best practices. Do not mention recommendations yet – make sure that participants focus first on the issues.

   Confine your explanation to systems that are not working, what broken systems tended to affect other systems, and challenges of certain life cycle stages. Do not go into extensive analysis. Do not bury the participants in details about the issues.

   Mention the domains of the issues (for example, the Board, strategic planning and teamwork) and how they are connected with each other. Focus discussions on understanding your descriptions of the issues, not on the causes of the issues or what they can do about them yet. Once they understand the issues, then promptly move on to the next topic.

7. **Describe the recommendations (30 minutes).**
   You and your client explain the most important five to seven recommendations. Explain

how you derived them, for example, reference to standards of performance or best practices. Talk in terms of systems and performance, not of specific people. Describe how you and your client grouped the recommendations (short-term versus long-term, essential versus desired, etc.).

Mention that you considered what worked before and what did not in your client's organization. Explain how the recommendations will not hurt the current quality of service to clients. Mention that the recommendations build on the strengths of the organization and give examples of some of those strengths.

Be willing to change the recommendations if participants make a strong case for those changes. However, remember that the recommendations are the result of careful research.

8. **Decide on recommendations and actions (30 minutes).**
Block (2000) reminds consultants that their entire focus at this stage should be on getting participants to decide what actions they will take to address the issues. The decision is theirs to make, not yours. Be factual, not judgmental. If the discussion seems to get away from decisions on actions, bring the participants back to making decisions again.

Do not push participants too hard to accept the recommendations. After all, the recommendations might be wrong. However, if they decide not to follow a certain recommendation, then promptly ask them to decide now what they do want to do about the particular issue associated with that recommendation.

Remind them that the actions they select will be further refined and verified during the next phase, Action Planning, Alignment and Integration. Assure them that, if the actions that they selected later on prove to be highly ineffective or unrealistic, the actions can be changed in the next phase.

See "How to Manage Group Conflict and Come to Decisions" on page 391 for guidelines to manage group conflict.

9. **Identify actions and learning (10 minutes).**
Have someone recite the decisions that were made during the meeting, along with the actions that need to be done and by whom. That technique helps participants feel that their meeting was constructive. It ensures that each person knows what is expected of him or her as a result of the meeting.

Then ask the participants, "What have you learned from this meeting? Have you gained new knowledge or insights?" The group may be quiet for several seconds. Remain quiet yourself. Give participants time to think. After they have shared, then share any learning that you have gained.

10. **Evaluate the meeting (10 minutes).**
A powerful technique is to have each participant evaluate the meeting out loud to the rest of the participants.

See "Evaluating the Overall Meeting" on page 377 for a powerful technique to evaluate meetings.

## *After the Meeting*

1.  **Ensure that an official list of approved actions is documented.**
    The actions that participants select should be described in a document, such as the meeting minutes or Board meeting minutes. That official listing can be useful later on when focusing your efforts to develop action plans for each recommendation.

2.  **Distribute meeting minutes.**
    Ensure that the minutes, or documentation of major decisions and actions from the meeting, are distributed soon after the meeting.

3.  **Communicate the results of the meeting to other decision makers.**
    Work with your client to identify how the results of the meeting will be explained to those decision makers who did not attend the meeting.

4.  **Distribute the assessment report.**
    Update the assessment report with the results of the feedback meeting. Remove the word "draft" from the document now. Distribute the report to the key decision makers identified by your client.

5.  **Discuss a contract for the remainder of the project?**
    If your contract with your client was to do the assessment only, you might contract soon to guide the implementation of recommendations, as well.

    Frequently, nonprofits get a grant to conduct a needs assessment and, later on, get another grant to implement the recommendations that result from the assessment. That might be the case with your client.

6.  **Schedule action-planning sessions.**
    Begin scheduling the upcoming planning sessions for the next phase, Action Planning, Alignment and Integration.

7.  **Discuss any contract revisions needed because of changes in the project's focus?**
    If the scope and depth of the project changed from its original specification in your contract, you should seriously consider doing a new contract with your client or amending your current contract. The more accurate the focus of your contract, the easier it is to evaluate the project and to avoid project "creep." Project creep is when the requirements of your project keep changing, resulting in an ongoing project that never seems to end. Project creep can result in a perceived failure because of the gap between what was contracted, what was done and what was expected.

# Phase 4: Action Planning, Alignment and Integration

| Consulting Cycle: |
|---|
| Client's Start-Up |
| Engagement |
| Discovery |
| **Action Planning** |
| Implementation |
| Adoption |
| Termination |

In the previous phase, Discovery and Feedback, you and your client conducted research, discovered various issues that needed attention, generated recommendations to address those issues, and shared your information with others in a feedback meeting. Part of that meeting included discussions – and, hopefully, decisions – about the specific actions that your client should take to address the issues.

This phase is focused on further clarifying those actions, along with developing them into various action plans, including plans for evaluation, communication, motivation and learning. The various plans are integrated into an overall Change Management Plan. Thus, the early activities in this phase overlap and are a continuation with the activities near the end of the Discovery and Feedback phase. This is true whether you are an external or internal consultant.

Action plans and the Change Management Plan together provide a clear vision for change. They provide the "roadmap" for managing the transition from the present state to the desired future state. Development of the various action plans is often an enlightening experience for your client. They begin to realize a more systematic approach to their planning and day-to-day activities.

The nature of action planning tends to occur throughout a project for organizational change. Note that this action-planning phase accomplishes the critical step of developing a performance improvement plan in the overall performance management process.

See "Nonprofit Performance Management" on page 171 for information about the overall performance management process.

Much of the following information about action planning is adapted from the publication, *Field Guide to Nonprofit Strategic Planning and Facilitation* (McNamara, 2003).

## Purpose and Goals

The primary purpose of this phase is to ensure that each issue in the organization will be addressed in an approach that is relevant, realistic and flexible for the organization.

The goals of this phase for you and your client include to:

1. Develop complete action plans for each action that was selected during the Discovery and Feedback phase. Plans include objectives, responsibilities, timelines and how the achievement of objectives will be monitored.

2. Align and integrate the action plans with each other to ensure complete effectiveness and efficiency of all action plans throughout the system of the organization.

3.      Ensure action plans are relevant, realistic and flexible so they remain credible and retain the commitment and participation of all members of the organization.

4.      Combine action plans into an overall Change Management Plan that includes associated plans for communicating the Plan, evaluating results of the Plan and recognizing accomplishments.

5.      Integrate and communicate the contents of the Change Management Plan throughout the organization, and integrate contents into all major plans and policies in the organization, as well.

# Collaborative Planning for Relevant, Realistic and Flexible Plans

In this phase of the collaborative consulting cycle, you and your clients work together to develop several types of plans, for example:

- Action plans to address various issues in the organization.

- An Evaluation Plan for the quality of the project's process and its final results.

- A Learning Plan to ensure that the project generates useful learning.

- A Recognition and Motivation Plan to ensure each participant makes strong contributions to the project.

- A Communications Plan to ensure all major stakeholders are aware of the change effort and how they participate in it.

- An overall Change Management Plan.

Before you and your client focus on developing these plans, it is important that you fully understand how to collaborate for highly effective planning. That type of planning ensures the motivation, vision, political support and momentum that are critical for successful change. The following guidelines will be useful, especially during this phase of the collaborative consulting cycle.

## *General Guidelines for the Planning Process*

A common failure in planning is that the plan is never really implemented. Instead, all the focus tends to be on writing a plan document. Too often, the plan sits collecting dust on a shelf.

Guidelines about successful planning could probably encompass a book of several hundred pages. The following general guidelines will help to ensure that the planning process is carried out and implemented – or that deviations from the intended plan are recognized and managed accordingly.

1.      **Involve the right people in the planning process.**
        When planning, get input from everyone who will be responsible to carry out parts of the plan, along with representatives from groups who will be affected by the plan. Of course, people should be involved if they will be responsible to review and authorize the plan.

2.  **Convey that the recurring planning process is as important as the plan document.**
    Far too often, primary emphasis is placed on the plan document.  This is extremely unfortunate because the real treasure of planning is the planning process itself.  During planning, planners learn a great deal from ongoing analysis, reflection, discussion, debates and dialogue around issues and goals in the system.

3.  **Ensure the nature of the process is compatible with the nature of planners.**
    For example, the linear nature of the traditional top down planning process, such as that typically used in strategic planning, may feel rigid for some planners.  If so, consider other less linear ways to conduct planning.

4.  **Ensure plans are systematic.**
    Systematic plans include activities to identify:

    a)  Overall goals to accomplish.

    b)  How those goals will be accomplished.

    c)  How to evaluate if the goals are being accomplished or not.

    d)  How to modify activities to more effectively achieve goals, if necessary.

5.  **Build in successes early in the planning process.**
    For example, build in activities that seem straightforward and for which resources are readily available, such as convening a project team or developing a project schedule.  Quick successes help to quickly mobilize and organize people in the early phases of the project.

6.  **Organize the plan into phases.**
    For example, Phase I of the project might be focused on generating a report and Phase II focused on implementing the report.  That approach helps to make the planning and implementation of the overall plan more comprehensible and easy to manage.

7.  **Consider the key aspects of any major plan.**
    Key aspects include the following:  (Note that, depending on the nature and needs of the planners, your client might choose to use different terms for these aspects.)

    - Outcomes

    - Goals

    - Methods

    - Objectives

    - Deliverables

    - Resources

    - Schedule

    - Budgets

    - Roles and Responsibilities

See "Designing Systematic – and Flexible – Project Plans" on page 86 for a description of each of the above key terms in planning.

8.  **As much as possible, specify goals and/or objectives to be "SMART".**
    SMART is an acronym for:

    a)  Specific
        For example, it is difficult to know what someone should be doing if they are to pursue the goal to "Think about writing a paper." It is easier to understand "Write a paper."

    b)  Measurable
        It is difficult to know what the scope of "Writing a paper" really is. It is easier to appreciate that effort if the goal is "Write a 30-page paper."

    c)  Achievable
        It should be realistic to be able to achieve the goal in a preferred time frame. A person should not expect to write a 1,000-page paper overnight.

    d)  Relevant
        The goal should be closely related to the overall purpose of the plan. A person should not be assigned a goal of cleaning the facilities if their major role is to write a 30-page research paper over the next week.

    e)  Time-bound
        It may mean more to others if I commit to a realistic goal to "Write a 30-page paper in one week." However, it will mean more to others (particularly if they are planning to help me or guide me to reach the goal) if I specify that I will write one page a day for 30 days, rather than allowing the possibility that I will write all 30 pages on the last day of the 30-day period.

9.  **Integrate methods to achieve goals with other current activities.**
    If the plan describes methods to achieve an overall goal, consider how those methods can be integrated with ongoing activities in the organization. For example, if the plan is about developing the Board or improving a program, include those new activities in the nonprofit with current strategic planning or program evaluation activities.

10. **Build in accountabilities for results and implementation monitoring.**
    Plans should specify who is responsible for achieving each result, including goals and objectives. Dates should be set for completion of each result, as well. Responsible parties should regularly review the status of the implementation of the plan. Be sure to have someone of authority "sign off" on the plan. Ideally, those who are responsible for executing the plan should also sign off on the plan. Include responsibilities for completion of, for example, the plan, relevant policies, procedures, job descriptions and performance review processes.

11. **Build in occasions to identify and capture learning.**
    One of the best outcomes from consulting projects is learning. Learning is most powerful when made conscious. With extremely busy clients, the occasions for making learning more conscious are rare. It helps to build in brief, highly focused discussions to uncover learning gleaned from developing and implementing plans.

> See "Cultivating and Guiding Learning" on page 213 for
> general information about recognizing and capturing learning.

12. **Describe how the plan can be changed.**
Few plans are ever implemented exactly as intended. Therefore, it is important to specify how plans can be changed. Consider including the following procedure in each plan document.

    a) Notice the need for the change, why it is needed and what it should be.

    b) Notify leaders of the proposed change before making the change.

    c) Get approval for the change.

    d) Make the change and revise the dates of the document.

    e) Notify key stakeholders of the change, describing the reason for it, how each stakeholder is affected, and whom to contact if they have questions.

13. **Note deviations from the plan and re-plan accordingly.**
It is OK to deviate from the plan. The plan is not a set of rules. It is an overall guideline. As important as following the plan is noticing deviations and adjusting the plan accordingly.

14. **Evaluate the planning process and the plan.**
During the planning process, regularly collect feedback from participants. Do they agree with the planning process? If not, what do they not like and how could it be done better? In large, ongoing planning processes (such as strategic planning, business planning and project planning), it is critical to collect this kind of feedback regularly.

    Finally, take 10 minutes to write down how the planning process could have been done better. File it away and read it the next time you conduct a planning process.

15. **Write down the planning information and communicate it widely.**
Project planners often forget that others do not know what the project planners know. Even if people do communicate their intentions and plans orally, chances are great that others will not entirely hear or understand what the planners want done. Also, as plans change, it is extremely difficult to remember who is supposed to be doing what, according to which version of the plan. Also, key stakeholders may request copies of various plans. Therefore, it is critical to write plans down and communicate them widely.

16. **Celebrate the production of the plan document.**
It is easy for planners to become tired and even cynical about the planning process. One of the reasons for this problem is that, far too often, emphasis is placed only on achieving the results. Once the desired results are achieved, new goals are promptly established. The process can seem like having to solve one problem after another, with no real end in sight. Yet when one really thinks about it, it is a major accomplishment to carefully analyze a situation, involve others in a plan to do something about it, work together to carry out the plan and actually see some results. So acknowledge this – celebrate your accomplishments.

# Develop a Vision for Change Now?

## *Developing Visions for Change Can Be Powerful – But Be Careful*

Some people prefer to focus their overall organizational change efforts on a broad, compelling vision. Many times, that vision for change becomes the same as, or replaces, the overall organizational vision that was developed during strategic planning. The vision for change can be a powerful means to sustain the type of motivation and momentum critical for successful change. The activities of developing that vision can be exciting, as well.

However, be careful. Expending too much energy on first developing an exciting vision sometimes leaves planners too tired to attend to the important task of developing and refining action plans. Therefore, you and your client might choose not to include a vision for change in the project. If you do decide to include a vision for change, you can carefully develop that vision now, or you might wait until after you have developed all of your action plans and then develop your vision based on the expected outcomes from having implemented those action plans later on.

See "Develop Action Plans" on page 323 if you decide to do action plans now, rather than develop a vision for change.

## *Many Approaches to Developing a Vision for Change*

The more people that you can involve in the visioning process, the more likely that you will cultivate strong motivation and momentum for change. There are a wide variety of approaches to developing a vision, depending on:

- How well members of the organization understand their clients and their clients' needs

- Effectiveness of discussions and decision-making among members of the Board and staff

- Value of inclusiveness and consensus in decision making among members of the Board and staff

- Time available to develop the vision

The guidelines in this subsection for developing a vision are designed to promptly produce a vision in a practical fashion. Certainly, some experts and planners would disagree with the guidelines, not because they might not produce an acceptable vision, but because they might not be according to the strong preferences and values they have about the extent of participation when developing a vision. As with any of the guidelines in this guidebook, planners have the prerogative to vary from the guidelines and design their own approaches.

### What Is a Vision for Change?

A vision for change provides a vivid description of the organization and its clients at some point in the future. The purpose of the vision is to provide direction and motivation for members of the organization, in addition to that provided by the mission statement. Another benefit of a vision is that it can be used to help identify goals and actions by working backwards from a point in the future.

## Use a Grand Vision or a Strategic Vision?

A grand vision is a broad description of an ideal condition for the organization and its clients. It can be useful for inspiring and motivating others. For example:

> Children of the world enjoy the love and support of loving, dedicated parents.

Certain cultures might prefer a grand vision because it is more compatible with their values. For example, various nations of Native American Indians refer to "working for the 7th generation." They prefer to work toward a long view into the future. Another application of a long-range vision might be when using the Appreciative Inquiry (AI) process.

See "Another Perspective – Appreciative Inquiry (AI)" on page 27 for more information about AI.

A strategic vision describes the organization and its clients after certain goals and actions have been accomplished. For example:

> 10% of the children ages 1-7 in south-central Minneapolis are enrolled in a suitable school system as a result of participating in our programs.

Decide what type of vision you want to generate. Some planners might prefer to establish a vision by imagining from the present to the future, and others by imagining from the future to the present. In general, nonprofits with limited resources that are facing a variety of issues might be better to work from the present to the future, particularly if developing a vision for change. That approach can be easier for planners to conceptualize and it often results in a more realistic, and therefore meaningful, vision for change.

## Establish Criteria for the Written Description of the Vision for Change

Planners should carefully prepare for generating their vision. Establish up-to-date criteria for evaluating the description of the vision. The criteria might be established first by having one or more planners recommend a set of criteria and next by getting reactions from members of the Board and key staff to finish the criteria. Consider the following as criteria for the new vision and perhaps rank your criteria in terms of importance when evaluating the description of your vision:

1.    Clearly understandable by people internal and external to the organization.

2.    Depicts the desired future state of the organization and its clients at some point in the future.

3.    Inspirational to members of the organization and key stakeholders.

4.    Depicts the environment in which the nonprofit operates and how its clients benefit from its services.

5.    Depicts the strengths of, and opportunities for, the organization.

## Generate a New Vision

There is no one standard approach to generating a vision. The following approach can be practical and adaptable for a wide variety of types of organizations. The approach recognizes that, no matter how tightly focused are the members of the Board and key staff when discussing information about the vision, it almost always helps if they have a draft of a vision to look at during their discussions.

When generating the vision, consider the following suggestions:

1.  Identify why you are doing a vision. What is its purpose? How will it be used?

2.  Nonprofits exist primarily to serve clients, not to develop and operate organizations. Therefore, first develop a vision around future conditions for your client, rather than conditions in the organization.

3.  Use a group of people from your client's organization to develop the vision. If your client values a highly participative process, you and your client will need to plan enough time for that extent of involvement from all members of the organization. Remember, the more people involved in the visioning, usually the more useful is the vision. Regardless of the process used, it still will require careful design and facilitation of group activities to develop the vision.

     See "Forming Groups and Teams" on page 371 and "Meeting Design, Management and Interventions" on page 375 for many guidelines to form and facilitate teams, and address many of the challenges that can occur.

4.  There are a wide range of techniques that can be used to generate ideas and wording for a vision. Whatever techniques are used, they should conform to the culture of your client's organization and how people prefer to work together. Collaborate with your client to select and apply those techniques.

     See "How to Collect and Organize Useful Information in Groups" on page 380 for a variety of techniques.

5.  From the larger group's ideas and wording, use a smaller group of two to three people to draft at least one version of the vision. They should mark their version as "draft". The group should not attempt to develop the "perfect" vision. Rather, they should develop a draft that at least seems to meet the pre-established evaluation criteria. Then the group of writers should present the draft, along with criteria to evaluate the draft, to the members of the Board of Directors and staff for their review and feedback about the draft.

6.  Changes should be made to the vision until it is acceptable to the members. Changes might be made by repeating steps three through five in this procedure. Then the vision should be widely communicated and referenced by all members of the organization.

# Develop Action Plans

## *Typical Contents of an Action Plan*

A complete action plan specifies:

1.  What must be accomplished (what many people call "objectives") to achieve each overall action or goal.

2.  Who is responsible for achieving each objective.

3.  The timing to start and finish each objective.

4.  What resources might be required.

5.  How the action plan will be monitored.

You and your client may have already gotten to that level of detail in descriptions of the actions to address issues. More than likely, though, you described the nature of the action, but did not specify various objectives and responsibilities to carry out the actions.

Action plans can be done in a wide variety of formats. The following table depicts a rather common format for an action plan. The sample action plans in the following table are to develop a Board of Directors, based on the results of a recent project. Note that Board development is a common result from a project because the Board needs to be enhanced and organized to guide implementation of the project's results. Your client might choose to use other than the Board Committees recommended in the following table.

## Table IV:13 – Example of Action Plans

| Goal 1:  Install new Board systems suggested in Change Management Plan | Start | Stop | Responsibility |
|---|---|---|---|
| 1.  Develop Committee work plans (objectives and time lines) for each Board Committee | | | Board Governance Committee |
| 2.  Board approves Board Development Plan | | | Board |
| 3.  Board approves new annual Board calendar | | | Board |
| **Goal 2.  Ensure Board is fully resourced to govern.** | | | |
| 1.  Review and update Board staffing policies to recruit and select new Board members with expertise to achieve the organization's goals | | | Board Governance Committee |
| 2.  Select new Board members | | | Board Governance Committee |
| 3.  Ensure all Board members receive Board orientation about our nonprofit's practices | | | Board Governance Committee |
| 4.  Ensure all Board members receive Board training about roles of a governing Board | | | Board Governance Committee |
| **Goal 3.  Ensure full participation and dedication of all Board members.** | | | |
| 1.  Ensure all Board members are on at least one Committee | | | Board Governance Committee |
| 2.  Approve and enact Board attendance policy | | | Board |
| 3.  Approve conflict-of-interest policy | | | Board |
| **Goal 4.  Ensure all Board meetings are highly focused and strategic.** | | | |
| 1.  Propose a procedure for making Board decisions, such as consensus, then voting if necessary | | | Board Governance Committee |
| 2.  Ensure meeting materials are provided at least one week before full Board meetings | | | Board Governance Committee |
| 3.  Adopt a meeting evaluation procedure | | | Board |
| **Goal 5.  Ensure Board leadership rigorously coordinates Board activities.** | | | |
| 1.  Reorganize Executive Committee to include Chairs of Committees | | | Board Governance Committee |
| 2.  Provide ongoing guidance and support to ensure an effective Board Chair position | | | Board Governance Committee |
| 3.  Analyze goals and timetables in work plan of each Committee | | | Executive Committee |
| 4.  Ensure each Committee operates according to work plans in their charters | | | Executive Committee |
| **Goal 6.  Ensure continuous improvement of the Board.** | | | |
| 1.  Conduct Board self-evaluation once a year | | | Board |
| 2.  Develop updated Board Development Plan based on self-evaluation results | | | Board Governance Committee |
| 3.  Conduct Board retreat focused on improving results | | | Board |

## Guidelines to Collaboratively Develop Action Plans

The following guidelines will be useful to you and your client as you collaborate to develop your action plans.

1. **The format of action plans is up to the leaders of the organization.**
   Some nonprofit leaders prefer highly specific and organized action plans, while others prefer less formal action plans. More formal plans include the content in the previous example, plus specification of what resources are need to achieve the objective and performance targets that specify how much of the objective needs to be achieved and by when.

2. **Staff members should be highly involved in action planning.**
   Identification of specific objectives and the timing to achieve them usually requires strong knowledge of the day-to-day activities in the organization. Staff members usually have that information more than Board members. However, Board members should work with staff to develop those action plans.

3. **Start with the simplest activities when developing action plans.**
   For example, if the overall change management activities include developing the Board, start developing action plans around the straightforward activities of scheduling a consultant to train Board members. That simple approach helps planners to more quickly learn how to develop action plans in a manner that suits the nature and needs of their organization.

4. **Organize the action plans into relevant categories.**
   The categories might correspond directly to the categories of recommendations (from the Discovery and Feedback phase). For example, categories might include short-term versus long-term, order of implementation of the action plans, per domain (a program, project, Boards, information technology, an individual position, etc.), essential versus desired, most important five to seven actions, or broad goals versus specific actions to achieve each goal.

## Identifying Objectives in Action Plans

1. **Pose these two questions about each overall action:**

   a) What needs to be done (to accomplish the overall action)?

   b) How will that be done?

   Often, several repetitions of these two questions generate a number of objectives about a specific strategy.

2. **Work forwards or backwards from the overall action.**
   Some staff might find it easier to identify objectives by working backwards from an image of achievement of the goal or the strategic issue. Other staff might find it easier to work forward from the present.

3. **Number and complexity of objectives varies.**
   The number of objectives in an action plan depends on the range, depth and complexity of the overall actions and on the degree of specificity preferred by your client.

4. **Use group decision-making methods if working with a group.**
   If the activities required to accomplish an objective might involve a group of five or more people, use group-based decision-making methods.

   See "Organizing Information and Making Decisions" on page 380 for guidelines to facilitate group-based decisions.

## Assigning Responsibility for Objectives

1. **Think in terms of roles in the organization, not specific people.**
   That approach helps you to be more systematic in how you view the organization – you focus on plans and positions, rather than personalities. Sometimes, the objective might be achieved by a group of people. In that case, the objective still should be assigned to the one position that has specific responsibility to ensure that the group achieves the objective.

2. **Do not forget about current workloads among Board and staff members.**
   A common mistake made by planners when developing their action plans is to forget about the current workload already assigned to positions in the organization. This mistake usually results in action plans that do not get implemented because people are already busy doing their current jobs in the workplace and, therefore, cannot find the time to do any new tasks or objectives.

3. **Be careful how your client delegates objectives to each position.**
   The manner in which a supervisor assigns an objective to a person is extremely important to the success of the objective. Skills in delegation are critical.

   See "Client's Delegation to Maintain Motivation and Momentum" on page 354 for guidelines for effective delegation.

## Identifying Timelines in Action Plans

1. **Timing is often the feature of action planning that planners resent the most.** Setting a particular time period puts pressure on the person responsible to accomplish the objective (otherwise, the person could wait forever!). Ironically, one of the advantages of associating timing with an objective is that it helps planners ensure that accomplishing the objective is realistic in the first place.

2. **Associating timing with objectives is an important management skill.**
   One of the biggest challenges for new supervisors is attempting to determine the time required for subordinates to accomplish tasks. Action planning can be a wonderful experience for management development.

3. **When identifying timing, consider scope, activities and sequence of activities.**
   Consider the scope of the activities that must be conducted to accomplish the objectives, and the likely sequence of the activities. Those considerations often give planners a good sense of how long it might take to achieve an objective, and when the activity should start and stop.

4. **The specificity of timing depends on scope of the objective.**
   For example, if it might take someone six months to accomplish a particular task, timing information might be described in terms of months.  Smaller objectives might be associated with terms of weeks.  Usually, the larger the organization and extent of strategies, the more likely that action plans should specify start and stop dates for accomplishments of objectives.

5. **Some planners simplify the action plan by identifying only a deadline.**
   While this certainly makes action planning easier, it also runs the risk of not being useful for planners and leaders when attempting to closely analyze the relevance and reality of the action plans.

6. **Work backwards or forwards.**
   When identifying the timing, planners often work backwards from a particular deadline, or they can work forwards from a reasonable start date.  The more issues that the organization is facing, the more useful it might be for planners to work from the present to the future.

7. **Include the person who will be responsible for achieving the objective.**
   That person often has the most useful knowledge as to when the objective can be started and finished, based on that person's current skills, resources and workload.

## Identifying Resources for Action Plans

Resources are usually specified in terms of people, time, materials, equipment, facilities and money.  Sometimes, planners simplify their action plans by including estimates of:

1. Number of people needed to accomplish the objective.

2. Amount of money that might be needed to support the resources required to achieve the objective.  Usually, though, planners make mention of the money needed primarily to obtain and support any materials, equipment or facilities.  They might not mention budgeting information about compensation for the people working to accomplish the objective, unless the scope of the objective is quite large and/or an independent contractor (consultant) is included in the activity.

Careful planning and specification of resources can provide strong verification and justification when raising funds to implement parts of the entire Strategic Plan.

## Identifying Who Will Monitor the Action Plan

This includes specifying the position that will regularly monitor the status of the implementation of the action plan, along with the date of the last monitoring activity.  Usually the responsibility for monitoring goes to the supervisor of the person responsible to accomplish the objective.

Note that the Board of Directors is responsible to supervise the Chief Executive Officer (CEO) and, thus, would be responsible to monitor accomplishment of any objectives assigned to the CEO.

See "Use These Tools to Track Status of Implementation" on page 358 for extensive guidelines and tools to monitor the implementation of plans.

# Finish the Action Plans – Alignment, Integration and Reality Check

A mistake frequently made by inexperienced consultants is to not align and integrate action plans with each other. Blumenthal (2003, p. 19) writes, "Many studies show that the consistency, or fit, between components is more important than the choice of any particular component." Guidelines in this subsection help you ensure that your action plans are optimally aligned and integrated for maximum effect in your client's organization.

## *Ensure Action Plans Are Complete and Integrated with Each Other*

Once all of the various action plans have been drafted, then planners should carefully examine them to ensure that they are complete for each action and organized efficiently for the entire organization. Next, planners should align and integrate action plans with each other. The following guidelines will help you.

### Ensure Each Action Plan Is Complete

For each action plan, one at a time, consider: Are there any objectives obviously missing from the plan? If someone suggests one, put it in the plan. Consider using a brainstorming technique to generate more ideas for objectives.

See "Brainstorming (to Generate Creative Ideas)" on page 380 for guidelines for using the brainstorming technique.

### Ensure the Objectives in the Action Plans Are All Integrated with Each Other

Next, consider if the implementation of any of the action plans might cause problems, or help with, implementation of other action plans. Consider these questions:

1. Is there any duplication of objectives across different action plans?

2. Should any of the objectives across separate action plans be combined into one action plan?

3. Do any of the objectives conflict with each other – accomplishment of one objective would make it almost impossible to accomplish an objective in another action plan?

4. If one or more of the objectives is accomplished, might it contribute to accomplishing one or more objectives in another action plan?

5. Should any of the objectives be divided into one or more other objectives?

6. Finally, what is the potential or real impact that achievement of a particular objective will have on other parts of the organization?

## Ensure All of the Action Plans Are Aligned with Each Other

Now it is often handy to consider the order in which the action plans affect each other. Certain action plans provide outputs that are used by other systems in the organization. For example:

- Action plans for Board development might influence action plans for strategic and program planning, because the success of those two types of planning depends on how well the Board is developed.

- Action plans for strategic and program planning might influence resource development (obtaining and developing resources) for staff and funding.

- Action plans for strategic and program planning might influence action plans for advertising and promotions and for fundraising.

To align your action plans, consider using the technique of chaining logic models.

 See "Chaining Logic Models (for Aligning and Integrating Systems)" on page 424 for guidelines to identify which systems are directly aligned with each other and how to depict those with logic models.

## *Conduct Reality and Compatibility Checks of All Action Plans*

Once the action plans have been well integrated, then planners should carefully examine each of them to ensure that they are realistic. Plans should be realistic if they are to sustain the type of motivation and momentum necessary for successful change. Consider the following for all of the action plans together:

1. **Are there enough people in the organization to attend to all of the objectives?**
   For example, the action plans might specify that eight people are needed to work toward accomplishing objectives in March through June. However, the nonprofit only has five people in the organization at that time and only 20% of their time can be allocated to working on the action plans.

2. **Is there enough money to support implementation of the action plans?**
   For example, if the action plans specify budgets that total $25,000 to support activities to work toward objectives from March through June, can the nonprofit provide that much money for that period?

3. **Are there enough resources to support the implementation of the action plans?**
   Are there enough materials, equipment and facilities? For example, across all of the action plans, if two conference rooms need to be available at the same time in March, can the nonprofit provide those facilities then?

4. **Are the action plans acceptable to the organization's culture?**
   For example, the culture of some organizations is not conducive to detailed specification of actions, or objectives. If that is the case with your client's organization, work with your client to accomplish a description of what is expected of others and by when. Rather than referring to "action plans" or "objectives," refer to the intent of those terms.

5. **Will implementation of the action plans have any adverse effect on services?**
   It is critically important that the organizational change effort does not hurt current or future services to clients – those services are the most important type of performance that the organization must give. Program staff should be highly involved in answering this question.

6. **Will the implementation of the action plans be sustainable?**
   Actions plans produce sustainable change by being integrated throughout the structures of the organization and by enjoying the strong, ongoing support of Board and executives in the organization.

7. **Might there be any unexpected side effects or risks with the action plans?**
   Invite planners to play "devil's advocate" – to imagine the worst that can happen and then to identify strategies to prevent that worst situation from happening. While that exercise can be frustrating, it often provokes useful insights and helps planners avoid "group think" – the situation where everyone goes along with the group for the sake of going along with the group.

8. **Are there any other "red flags"?**
   Even if planners just feel like the action plans together are a lot for the organization to do, planners should talk about their impressions and, for example, try identify what they are seeing or reading that leads them to be concerned.

# Identify Performance Indicators of Success

It is good practice to identify certain measures, or performance indicators, that will suggest whether you have successfully addressed the issues that were identified during the Discovery and Feedback phase. Now is a good time to identify those measures before you begin implementing the various action plans. Those measures will be used during upcoming phases to evaluate the progress of the change effort.

Performance measures are an essential part of the overall performance management process. The primary purpose of the consulting cycle in an organization is to systematically conduct certain aspects of that performance management process.

See "Nonprofit Performance Management" on page 171 to understand the performance management process and the role of the consulting cycle.

Note that if you had tried to identify those measures earlier in the consulting cycle, you probably would have realized back then that you did not have enough clarity to identify overall measures. Now, after having carefully developed various action plans, you usually have much more clarity about what needs to be done.

To identify the performance measures, consider the following guidelines:

1. **Consider "success" as defined during the Engagement and Agreement phase.**
   Occasionally, clients are quite specific about what they consider to be success for the project. Many times, though, those specifications are changed a great deal during the Discovery and Feedback phase. If those original specifications still seem accurate, they might contribute to defining measures of success now.

See "How to Define Project "Success" on page 99 to consider various options for defining "success."

2. **Consider each of the overall goals or actions recommended during Feedback.**
If those goals were described in specific terms, they might be helpful to use as overall measures of success. Many times, though, the recommended goals are changed when developing specific action plans to achieve the overall goals. If those goals still seem accurate, they might contribute to defining measures of success now.

3. **If you and your client included a vision for change, reference the vision.**
The vision for change described what your client's organization would look like after its issues had been addressed. Therefore, the vision can be useful when identifying overall measures of success.

4. **Consider the overall results that will occur from implementing action plans.**
If you and your client identified a wide range of numerous action plans, it could be a major challenge to identify measures of success by referencing those plans. Still, it is useful to do the best that you can for now. Occasionally, the measures need to be changed. That is fine, as long as the measures are changed systematically.

See "Systematically Adjust Plans When Really Needed" on page 359 for guidelines about systematically changing plans.

Information in the following table depicts an example of measures of success. The information is an example only. You and your client should select your measures based on the findings and plans of your project.

## Table IV:14 – Example of Performance Indicators For Success

**Board operations:**

Indicators:

> The Board of Directors has approved and implemented a Board Development Plan, resulting in specific work plans for each Board Committee. The Board has recruited, trained and organized new members to fully staff each Committee. Each work plan is associated with a strategic goal in the current Strategic Plan. Each work plan includes objectives, responsibilities, timelines and methods to monitor implementation. The Executive Committee assures that work plans are implemented on schedule.

Outcomes:

> Board-driven, focused, participative and proactive governance.

**Strategic planning:**

Indicators:

> The Board of Directors has approved a three-year Strategic Plan. The Plan includes specific strategic goals and action plans. Each action plan has specific objectives, responsibilities, timelines and methods to monitor implementation. The Plan includes an annual operating budget. The CEO assures that action plans are implemented on schedule.

Outcomes:

> Clearly communicated vision, how to achieve the vision and verified progress toward that vision.

**Program evaluation:**

Indicators:

> Each program has a documented Program Evaluation Plan that specifies general outcomes, outcomes targets, outcomes indicators, needed data, methods to collect the data, and who will collect the data and by when. The Program Director assures that each program evaluation is completed by the beginning of the third fiscal quarter. The CEO and Chair of the Board Programs Committee ensure Evaluation Plans are implemented.

Outcomes:

> Each program has specific goals and measured progress toward achieving each of those goals.

**Fundraising planning:**

Indicators:

> A Fundraising Plan was developed and approved by the Board of Directors. The Plan specifies what monies need to be raised and for what programs, donors/sources for those monies, who will approach the donors, how and when they will approach the donors, and who will manage grant information and requirements. The Plan includes specific responsibilities, timelines and methods to monitor implementation. The CEO and Chair of the Board Fundraising Committee assures that the Plan is implemented on schedule.

Outcomes:

> Most effective and focused fundraising activities that generate all needed funds from funders.

# Develop an Evaluation Plan to Evaluate the Quality of Final Results

Now that you and your client have established the overall actions (or goals) and associated action plans to achieve during the organizational change project, you are ready to decide how you will evaluate whether or not your desired results are being achieved. You are not deciding now whether the project has achieved its desired results – you are planning for how you will make the decision later on, probably during the Adoption and Evaluation phase. The best way to be ready to conduct an effective evaluation later on is to develop a systematic Evaluation Plan that all people know about and understand. The best way to ensure that level of understanding is to include the Evaluation Plan in the Change Management Plan.

 See "Evaluation of Performance and Change" on page 198 to read about the myths, benefits, types and levels of evaluation, barriers and how to overcome them, and guidelines to develop evaluation plans.

## *Evaluation Questions to Consider*

You learned in PART III that evaluations are best designed to answer certain evaluation questions. The following evaluation questions might be useful when evaluating the progress toward achieving the final results from the project.

### Questions Regarding the Achievement of Desired Results

1.      Have the goals and outcomes (listed in the contract for the project) been achieved? If not, what else needs to be achieved?

2.      Have all of the issues in the organization been addressed? If not, which issues still need attention? What should be done?

3.      Has the vision for change been achieved? If not, what else needs to be accomplished to achieve the vision? How should that be done?

4.      Have the action plans been implemented? If not, which action plans are yet to be accomplished?

5.      Have the performance indicators for success been achieved? If not, which ones still need attention?

6.      Do leaders in the organization agree that the project has been successful? If not, which leaders disagree? What else needs to be done?

### Questions Regarding the Learning from the Project

You and your client might develop a Learning Plan that you include in the overall Change Management Plan.

1.      What new learning have you gained from the project? Think in terms of enhanced knowledge, skills and abilities.

2.      How did you gain that new learning?

3.      What did you learn about how you learn?

4.      How might you take that learning forward in your life and work?

# Develop a Learning Plan to Capture Learning During the Project

One of your primary goals as a consultant is to help your client learn how to solve problems for themselves in the future. You can ensure that you meet this goal – and learn a great deal yourself – by working with your client to integrate a systematic Learning Plan into your project. That Plan will be integrated into the overall Change Management Plan

 See "Cultivating and Guiding Learning" on page 213 to read about the key components of learning, myths, barriers to learning, different kinds of learning, continuous learning, key principles of learning, forms of peer learning, and how to reliably integrate learning into your projects.

## *Developing Your Learning Plan*

Consider the following guidelines to develop your Learning Plan.

1.      **Identify five to seven goals for learning.**
        Think of the most useful type of knowledge, skills and perspectives to have to accomplish successful change. For example, useful goals might be to learn:

        a) How to discover the "real" causes of issues, rather than the symptoms.

        b) The value of working collaboratively with others.

        c) How to build trust, commitment and participation.

        d) How to design systematic plans.

        e) The nature of organizational change.

        f) General guidelines for accomplishing successful change.

2.      **For each goal, describe how you will evaluate whether learning was achieved.**
        For example, you will see some type of activity from learners, such as completion of certain tasks, provision of certain advice, or answers to certain questions.

3.      **For each goal, specify methods to achieve that learning.**
        Consider methods, such as trainings, readings, discussions, reflection, peer discussions, peer coaching and study groups.

4.      **During the project, integrate the various methods to achieve learning.**
        Phase 5: Implementation and Change Management, provides a wide range of diverse activities into which you could integrate methods for learning.

5.       **For each method, identify what outputs, or tangible results, might be produced.**
The outputs provide the basis from which you can evaluate whether the goals were achieved. For each output, use your evaluation method as specified in item 2 above.

6.       **For each major learning, discuss these questions with your client.**

a) How did you accomplish that learning?

b) How can you take the learning forward in your work?

## *Benefiting from Your Learning Plan*

1.       **For new learning, answer "How will this be useful in life and work?"**
Learning for the sake of it can be fun and entertaining, but without putting it into practice, the learning can be quickly forgotten. A primary goal of learning is to get things done, so ensure that learning objectives are associated with useful activities.

2.       **Integrate learning methods that include double-loop and triple-loop learning.**
Those types of learning can come from highly focused discussions among you, your clients and peers in their organizations. They can also come from using the coaching technique because the technique centers on the use of inquiry and reflection (continuous learning). Other opportunities for learning include:

a)    Finishing each meeting by reflecting on what was learned during the meeting.

b)    Mentioning new learning in written reports.

c)    Asking for new learning during interviews, questionnaires, evaluations and coaching.

3.       **Do not worry about whether or not your Learning Plan is perfect.**
The key is to get started. Start simple, but start. Do the best that you can for now. There is no perfect plan. You are doing the plan according to the nature and needs of your client. Also, it is not important to stick to the plan for the sake of the plan. Deviations from the plan are to be expected. However, it is important that deviations are recognized and explained.

4.       **Remember that learning is a process.**
Just like the organizational change process itself, the learning process takes time. Usually, people first learn new knowledge, then they use that knowledge to develop skills and then from applying those skills, they develop new perspectives – all of this is learning.

# Develop a Recognition and Motivation Plan

It is important to systematically look for achievement of goals and objectives during implementation of the Change Management Plan. Those accomplishments should be recognized and rewarded. That approach builds tremendous credibility to the change effort. It shows that top leaders in the organization are in complete support of the change effort. It helps further to build trust, commitment and collaboration among members of the organization. Ultimately, it sustains the motivation and momentum that are required for successful change.

A Recognition and Motivation Plan need not be extensive and detailed – it can be a set of practices that you use with each employee. Those practices can be your Plan – and can be integrated into the overall Change Management Plan. The practices should match the culture of the organization. They should be developed with others in the organization. People need to feel a sense of ownership and commitment in development of the practices. Consider the following guidelines.

 The following guidelines are adapted from the publication, *Field Guide to Leadership and Supervision for Nonprofit Staff* (McNamara, 2002).

## Steps Your Client Can Take to Help Staff Members Motivate Themselves

It is critical that members of your client's organization feel highly motivated to implement the Change Management Plan. However, simply put, you or your client cannot motivate someone else. Your client can only provide the optimum environment in which others can motivate themselves. The following specific steps can help your client to provide that kind of environment. You might share the list with your client.

1. **Make a list of three to five things that help each staff member to motivate themselves.**
   It is important to understand what motivates, or rewards, each of the staff members. Different people are motivated by different influences. For example, some people prefer money, promotions, time away from the office or relationships.

    See "Table IV:15 – Checklist of Categories of Typical Motivators" on page 339 and have your client and their staff members finish the checklist.

2. **Ensure each staff member's motivations are considered in the plan for change.**
   For example, staff members might be rewarded with more family time or more recognition, if that is important to them. Your client should identify the various ways in which staff members are motivated and ensure suitable reward systems are in the plan for change.

3. **Use one-on-one meetings with each staff member to build relationships.**
   In the workplace, many staff members are motivated more by care and concern for them than by attention to their work. Your client should consider getting to know their staff members and members' families, hobbies, favorite foods, etc. This can sound manipulative – and it will be if not done sincerely. However, even if your client sincerely wants to get to know each of the staff members, it may not happen unless your client intentionally sets aside time to be with each of them.

4. **Cultivate strong skills in delegation.**
   Delegation includes conveying responsibility and authority to specific staff members so they can carry out certain tasks. Delegation also allows members to take a stronger role in identifying the tasks and how they can be achieved. Delegation usually results in more fulfillment and motivation in their jobs, as well.

See "Client's Delegation to Maintain Motivation and Momentum" on page 354 for guidelines to successful delegation.

5. **Implement at least the basic principles of performance management.**
Good performance management includes identifying goals, measures to indicate if the goals are being met or not, ongoing attention and feedback about measures toward the goals, and corrective actions to redirect activities back toward achieving the goals when necessary. Good performance management techniques usually provide strong motivation for staff members because they clearly understand what is expected of them, feel that they are being treated fairly and feel rewarded when they have done a good job.

6. **Clearly convey how staff members' results contribute to organizational results.**
Members often feel strong fulfillment from realizing that they are actually making a difference. This realization often requires clear communication about organizational goals, progress toward those goals and celebration when the goals are met.

7. **Reward desired behaviors from staff when your client *sees* the behaviors.**
A critical lesson for new managers and supervisors is to learn to focus on behaviors, not on personalities. One of the best ways to ensure focus on behaviors is to use the eyes more than the feelings. A supervisor can get in a great deal of trouble (legally, morally and interpersonally) for focusing only on how he or she *feels* about a staff member rather than on what the supervisor is actually *seeing* with their eyeballs.

8. **Or, reward the desired behaviors soon after your client sees them.**
This helps to reinforce the notion that your client highly prefers the behaviors that they are currently seeing. Often, the shorter the time between a staff member's action and the reward for the action, the clearer it is to the member that their supervisor highly prefers that action.

9. **Be balanced – be realistic – do not overdo rewards.**
Do not overdo recognition and rewards. Staff members need to believe that their supervisor is being sincere and honest with them. Members who perceive constant rewarding, whether through constant compliments or other forms of recognition, will soon lose their appreciation for those rewards. Members will likely question the sincerity of the supervisor, as well.

10. **Celebrate achievements.**
This critical step is often forgotten. Celebration of achievements is not a direct means of motivating staff members; rather, it cultivates an environment where members can more readily feel a sense of accomplishment, and thus, fulfillment in their jobs. New managers and supervisors are often focused on getting "a lot done." This usually means identifying and solving problems. Experienced managers come to understand that acknowledging and celebrating a solution to a problem can be every bit as important as the solution itself. Without ongoing acknowledgement of success, staff members become frustrated, skeptical and even cynical about efforts in the organization.

11. **Let staff members hear from their clients (whether internal or external).**
Let members hear clients proclaim the strong benefits from the members' services. For example, if the member is working to keep internal computer systems running for other staff members (internal clients) in the organization, have those clients express their gratitude to the member. If a member is providing a product or service to external clients, bring in a client to express their appreciation to the member.

When considering recognition and motivation, do not forget the means to motivate you, the consultant.

 See "How to Motivate Yourself During Long Journeys for Change" on page 91 for guidelines for motivating yourself as a consultant.

## Primary Responsibility for the Implementation of the Recognition and Motivation Plan

The Plan should specify who has primary responsibility for ensuring implementation of the Plan. Usually, the Chief Executive Officer has the primary responsibility to ensure implementation of this Plan. However, the CEO might delegate that responsibility to someone else. In any case, the practices should be documented in the Personnel Policies and become part of the standard training for supervisors.

## Table IV:15 – Checklist of Categories of Typical Motivators

To help you identify what motivates (or rewards) you, consider the following categories of typical motivators. Rank the categories, starting with "1" as the highest. You might have several categories that rank a "1". Do not worry about getting your ranking to be "perfect." The point is to go through the process of thinking about what motivates you. Consider discussing the results with your supervisor, peers, subordinates, family and friends.

\_\_ Career Development / Success

\_\_ Comfort / Relaxation

\_\_ Health / Balance

\_\_ Influence / Leadership

\_\_ Learning / Knowledge / Discovery

\_\_ Materials / Possessions

\_\_ Recognition / Praise

\_\_ Security / Money / Home

\_\_ Social Affiliation / Popularity / Acceptance

\_\_ Status / Prestige / Stand Out / Reputation

\_\_ Task Accomplishment / Problem Solving / Achievement

\_\_ Teaching / Guiding Others

\_\_ Vitality / Energy

\_\_ Others? _____

Are there other comments you could make that would help you (and maybe others) to more clearly understand what motivates you? Take a moment to consider this question and write down your answers.

# Develop a Communications Plan

One of the most powerful means to ensure the success of organizational change is through ongoing, systematic communication to all stakeholders about the status of the change activities. Communication reduces people's resistance to change. It maintains their focus on the vision and actions for change. It shows them that the top leaders continue to support the change effort. Ultimately, it helps to maintain the motivation, vision, political support and momentum to accomplish successful change.

Unless your client has a large organization, you need not have an extensive and detailed Communications Plan. Extensive plans often identify what messages need to be conveyed to which specific groups of stakeholders, along with how, who and when. To develop a practical, systematic Communications Plan, consider the following guidelines. (Note that your Communications Plan will be integrated into the overall Change Management Plan.)

1.  **Decide what to communicate.**
    Your communication should include at least the following types of information:

    a) Need for change

    b) Vision and actions for change and how they were chosen

    c) Expected results of achieving the vision

    d) Responsibilities for achievement of vision and actions and when

    e) Status of vision and actions

    f) Major accomplishments

    g) Ups and downs of the effort (admit mistakes, too)

2.  **Identify opportunities for communication.**
    There are numerous opportunities in the workplace to continue to communicate about the project for change. Consider:

    a) Board meetings

    b) One-on-one meetings

    c) Program reviews

    d) Staff meetings

    e) Spoken commentary

3.  **Select tools for communication.**
    Your client probably uses many of the following items in the day-to-day activities in their workplace. It takes little effort to include information about the project for change.

    a) Action plans

b)  E-mail messages

c)  Board Work plans

d)  Chief Executive Officer report to the Board of Directors

e)  Memos

f)  Newsletter about the change effort

g)  Planned-Versus-Actual budget reports

h)  Status reports

i)  To-do lists

4.  **Identify who should receive which communication, using which tools.**
    For example:

a)  Board members

b)  Managers

c)  Staff

d)  Consultant

e)  Funder

f)  Others

5.  **The most important communication tool is the behavior of leaders.**
    Leaders need to "walk their talk."  They should act the way that they want others to act in the workplace.  For example, if leaders want more effective teamwork in the organization, their own behavior should reflect effective participation in teams.

# Develop an Overall Change Management Plan

It helps a great deal to assemble the many plans and actions for change into one overall Plan.  That approach ensures that the many activities for change are highly integrated, resulting in more efficient activities, as well.  It also makes it easier to communicate the change effort to others because ongoing communications are from one document.  Also, it makes it much easier to have one person have overall responsibility for the change effort because that person has one consolidated set of actions for which he or she is responsible.  Finally, one of the biggest advantages might be that the Plan can be provided to a funder to get further funding for resources to implement the Plan.  Guidelines in this subsection will help you to develop your Plan.

## *Organize Phases of Activities into Overall Plan*

The Plan often is more manageable if actions are organized into various phases. You might organize phases based on:

1.      The quickest actions first, then the more long-term actions next.

2.      Overall planning activities first, including strategic planning, program planning and resource planning.

3.      Per domain (individual position, team, project, cross-functional process, function, program or organization).

4.      Essential actions done first, then desired actions later on.

5.      The most important five to seven actions done first, then other actions later on.

## *Develop a Grand Timeline for Implementation*

The following table depicts one example of a grand timeline. You might refer to the timeline as an example of a format that you could use. The content of your timeline should be based on the content of your Change Management Plan.

## Table IV:16 – Example of Grand Timeline Template

In the Timeline, the left-hand column includes "Categories of Action Plans." Each category has various action plans and each action plan is associated with a row under that category. Note that each action plan has its own objectives, along with the responsibilities, start dates and stop dates. The contents of each action plan are not in the following timeline.

| Categories of Action Plans | J | F | M | A | M | J | J | A | S | O | N | D |
|---|---|---|---|---|---|---|---|---|---|---|---|---|
| **Board Development:** | | | | | | | | | | | | |
| Include new practices and roles in operations | | | | | | | | | | | | |
| All members oriented and trained | | | | | | | | | | | | |
| Meeting evaluation procedure enacted | | | | | | | | | | | | |
| Conduct Board self-evaluation | | | | | | | | | | | | |
| Address evaluation results in retreat | | | | | | | | | | | | |
| **Program Development:** | | | | | | | | | | | | |
| Develop program framework for each program | | | | | | | | | | | | |
| Develop Business Plan for Program A | | | | | | | | | | | | |
| Decide disposition of Program B | | | | | | | | | | | | |
| Identify partnerships for Program C | | | | | | | | | | | | |
| Identify opportunities to replicate Program D | | | | | | | | | | | | |
| **Marketing:** | | | | | | | | | | | | |
| Develop & implement Public Relations Plan | | | | | | | | | | | | |
| Develop & implement Newsletter Plan | | | | | | | | | | | | |
| Develop & implement Website Management Plan | | | | | | | | | | | | |
| **Resource Development:** | | | | | | | | | | | | |
| Develop & implement Fundraising Plan | | | | | | | | | | | | |
| Develop & implement Facilities Plan | | | | | | | | | | | | |
| Develop & implement Staffing Plan | | | | | | | | | | | | |
| **Finances:** | | | | | | | | | | | | |
| Expand Finance Committee | | | | | | | | | | | | |
| Update fiscal policies and procedures | | | | | | | | | | | | |
| Develop program-based operating budget | | | | | | | | | | | | |
| Identify fundraising targets | | | | | | | | | | | | |

## *Establish Accountabilities in the Change Management Plan*

There should be one person directly responsible for the implementation of the Plan. Note that the Board ultimately is responsible for all activities in the organization. However, the person directly responsible for the Plan should be someone who has the authority and prompt access to the resources to implement the Plan. Various individuals are responsible for each action plan and its objectives. If each action plan has been well designed, it includes specification of who is responsible for the action plan and for each of its objectives. Consider the following examples.

1.  **If the Plan includes change to the Board, the Board Chair is responsible.**
    In theory, Board members have responsibility for the plan. However, responsibility assigned to many often is assigned to no one. Therefore, the responsibility should lie with the Board Chair to ensure that successful change occurs. Note that if a Board Governance Committee exists, it might be the members' responsibility to implement that Plan – but the Board Chair should ensure that the Plan is implemented.

    An effective approach to ensuring implementation of plans is to assign the Board's Executive Committee to oversee implementation of those plans. For example, the Executive Committee might review status of the various action plans in the overall Change Management Plan.

2.  **If the Plan includes a change to the entire organization, the CEO is responsible.**
    The CEO has the most authority and direct access to the resources necessary to make changes to the entire organization, although other people certainly will be involved in making those changes. Hopefully, the CEO has good skills in delegation so those other people are effectively involved.

3.  **If the Plan includes change to a program, the Program Director is often responsible.**
    Reasons for this are the same as reasons for the CEO to be responsible for organization-wide change.

 See "Use These Tools to Track Status of Implementation" on page 358 for numerous tools to track status of implementation.

## *Develop a Budget*

You might need a variety of resources to be able to implement your Plan. For example, your client might need to pay for more of your time, for an expert to conduct trainings or provide materials, or for a program specialist to work on various programs. Your client might be planning to get a grant to pay for implementation of the Plan. Consider the following guidelines to develop a budget to implement your Plan.

### Step One – Select a Time Period for the Budget

Your time period may correspond to the grand timeline that you developed earlier. Or the time period might correspond to the particular grant cycle of one of your client's favorite funders.

## Step Two – Identify Expenses

1.      Estimate personnel costs, including:

   a)  Costs for salaried personnel, including salaries and fringe benefits (plan 40% of salaries as fringe)

   b)  Costs for hourly personnel (plan 30% of salaries for fringe)

   c)  Costs for any temporary employees

   d)  Costs for contracted help, for example, accountants, lawyers and fundraisers

   e)  Costs associated with making those personnel productive, for example, training, membership dues and travel

   f)  Other(s)?

2.      Estimate costs regarding facilities. Consider:

   a)  Furniture, such as desks, file drawers and tables

   b)  Other(s)?

3.      Estimate other costs. Consider:

   a)  Tools

   b)  Inventory

   c)  Marketing materials

   d)  Documentation, for example, texts and manuals

   e)  Office equipment, such as computers, copiers, faxes and telephones

   f)  Other(s)?

## Step Three – Obtain Review and Approval of the Budget

The Chief Executive Officer should review and approve the budget for the project. If the scope of the Plan includes change for a significant part of the organization, the Board should review and approve the budget.

## *Contents of a Typical Change Management Plan*

The most important consideration when designing the format of the Plan is "What audiences will get the Plan?" Various audiences might get different versions of the Plan, depending on the use that the audience will have for the Plan. Consider the following major sections:

1.      **Title page**
        Include the name of the nonprofit, indication that it is a Change Management Plan, the scope of the Plan (organization and/or programs), time span of the Plan and indication if it is

official (for example, has been approved by the Board – if it is not official, include the word "draft").  Include the date that the Plan was drafted or approved.

2.    **Cover letter**
The Chief Executive Officer (and Board Chair, if possible) should include a cover letter, noting his or her complete support of the Plan and intentions to ensure the Plan is implemented and evaluated on a regular basis.

3.    **Executive summary**
This is one of the most important parts of the Plan.  The Executive Summary usually should be no more than 1-2 pages in length.  It should at least include:

a)    The purpose of the Plan, including how the Plan will be used and any overall results expected from implementing the Plan

b)    When implementation of the Plan will be started and finished

c)    Most important issues, goals and actions that were identified during the project

d)    How implementation of the plan will be monitored

4.    **Description of domain(s) of the project**
For example, the domain might be a team, project, cross-functional process, function, program or organization.  Note that if the Change Management Plan is focused primarily on one individual, that is commonly referred to as a Performance Improvement Plan.

5.    **Key issues and the vision and/or goals to address the issues**
Along with the Executive Summary, this information is one of the most important parts of the Plan.

6.    **Action plans**
Some planners might prefer to include those in a separate document and refer to them from the Plan document.

7.    **How implementation of the Plan will be monitored**
Here is where you specify where responsibility for monitoring lies.

8.    **Budget for implementation of the Plan**
 Include the budget that you developed earlier.

9.    **Reference to related plans or documents**
There might be reference to other related plans and documents, for example, program plans, marketing analysis or program evaluation plans.

10.    **Appendices**
The appendices are often reserved for information used to derive the body of the Plan, for example, data from the Discovery and Feedback phase.

### *Celebrate Completion of the Change Management Plan*

At this point, participants have achieved some major accomplishments during the project.  It is likely that they have:

- Identified the most important issues facing their organization.

- Established meaningful goals and actions to achieve the issues.

- Identified specific objectives to do the actions.

- Developed a variety of associated plans, for example, for evaluation, learning, recognition and communication.

- Learned a great deal along the way.

Work with your client to find a suitable way to recognize these accomplishments with all participants in the project.

# If Action Planning Stalls, Cycle Back

Action planning can stall for a variety of reasons including:

- Your client does not understand the value of action planning.

- Your client does not understand how to design an action plan.

- Your client is reluctant to assign actions to people in the organization.

- Your client is overwhelmed by the various plans in this phase.

The following guidelines are standard, brief reminders of what to do whenever a particular phase of the consulting process seems to have stalled.

 See "How to Do Collaborative Consulting with Busy Clients" on page 16 for a more complete description of each of the following actions.

1.  **Be authentic.**

2.  **Remind your client of the importance of the project.**

3.  **Recognize the other priorities of your client.**

4.  **Realize your client's lack of participation may be a form of project resistance.**

5.  **Remind your client: choices about the project are choices about the nonprofit.**

6.  **Continue to recognize accomplishments in the project so far.**

7.  **Use small-group instead of large-group activities where possible.**

8.      **Use coaching to identify obstacles and how to remove them.**

9.      **Resort to the "Sanity Solution."**

10.     **Decide if you should cycle back to Phase 2: Engagement and Agreement phase.**
        You and your client may need to carefully re-establish priorities in the project.

# Phase 5: Implementation and Change Management

At this point in the project, you and your client have worked together to identify the major issues facing the organization and identified what actions should be taken to address those issues. You both developed the actions into action plans, each of which specified various objectives to be accomplished, along with who will be accomplishing them and when. Then you both integrated the action plans, along with plans for evaluation, learning and communication, into an overall Change Management Plan. In this phase, you and your client will work together to implement that Plan. This is true whether you are an external or internal consultant.

| Consulting Cycle: |
| --- |
| Client's Start-Up |
| Engagement |
| Discovery |
| Action Planning |
| Implementation |
| Adoption |
| Termination |

The challenges of nonprofits can make your job now even more difficult. Nonprofits, especially small- to medium-sized ones, have major challenges to overcome when trying to accomplish successful change in their organizations. They face shortages of funds, time and energy. Decisions can take longer than in for-profit organizations because decisions are often based on values, rather than on "the bottom line." Nonprofits often cannot afford the types of training and development afforded by for-profits.

Although you want to work in a highly collaborative manner with your client, it is your client who must implement that Plan in the workplace. Your role is to guide and support your client along the way. Now is when you must muster all of your skills as a consultant because you will be working to get a lot done, but will be working through others to do it. You might struggle just to know what is happening regarding the implementation of plans. You might need to confront your clients about why more progress is not being made. Other times, you will congratulate them on their accomplishments.

Guidelines in this section will help to effectively implement the Change Management Plan. You might need to modify the Plan at times and that will be fine as long as you make those changes systematically.

## Purpose and Goals

The purpose of this phase is to successfully address the issues in your client's organization by implementing the Change Management Plan, along with continued actions to sustain motivation and momentum during the implementation.

Goals of this phase include:

1.      Integrate the Change Management Plan and its various subordinate plans throughout the systems in your client's organization.

2.      Ensure continued motivation and momentum to implement the Change Management Plan.

3.      Keep monitoring the status of implementation using the measures of success identified during the action planning.

4.      Continue to show support from top leaders in the organization.

5.      Regularly communicate status to everyone in the organization.

# Integrate the Change Management Plan Throughout the Organization

One of the most important approaches that can be used to ensure the implementation of the Change Management Plan is to work in a highly collaborative fashion with your client. Certainly, there are other means. While exhorting others to change can be a powerful means for inspiration and motivation, that type of persuasion seldom is long lasting. One of the most effective overall approaches to ensuring that organizational change is successfully accomplished is to integrate the action plans throughout the structures (plans, roles, policies and procedures) in the organization.

The integration of action plans into other systems in the organization sends a clear message that the change effort has the strong political support of leaders in the organization. That type of support and involvement from leaders further helps to maintain the type of motivation and momentum critical to successful organizational change.

## *Authorization of the Change Management Plan Document*

The authorization of the document by the members of the Board indicates that they officially are in support of the implementation of the Plan and will work to ensure that the Plan is implemented. In fact, the Board is responsible to be sure that these types of significant plans are effectively implemented. That is one of the most important responsibilities of the Board.

## *Allocation of Resources*

One of the most visible gestures to ensure implementation of the Plan is to allocate the resources necessary to implement the Plan. Often, that official allocation comes in the form of the Board's approval of a budget to be used to obtain and support the use of resources to implement the Plan.

## *Board Work Plans*

Work plans might be accomplished by the Board, in total or by various Committees on the Board. Work plans should be updated soon after completion of the Change Management Plan. The following table represents one format and content of an overall, top-level work plan.

| Year 2005 Actions | Jan | Feb | Mar | Apr | May | Jun |
|---|---|---|---|---|---|---|
| **Strategy 3.1: Develop Strategic Plan** | | | | | | |
| 3.1.1. Recruit consultant help | --- | | | | | |
| 3.1.2 Plan for a plan | | --- | | | | |
| 3.1.3 Strategic planning | | | --- | --- | | |
| 3.1.4 Board review of plan | | | | --- | | |
| 3.1.5 Obtain Board approval of plan | | | | | --- | |

## Policies and Procedures

Policies and procedures should be developed, or updated, to guide activities toward implementing action plans produced from the project. For example, action plans might indicate that the Board needs to be developed, staff needs to be hired and financial management needs to be improved.

Policies are broad guidelines that can be referenced by members of the Board or staff to make decisions. The most prominent examples are Board policies, personnel policies and fiscal policies. Board policies address how Board members want to interact with each other when governing the nonprofit organization. Personnel policies address how staff are recruited, hired, supervised, guided, rewarded and fired. The policies also help to ensure that management practices conform to important employment laws and regulations. Fiscal policies address how the organization should manage its financial information and processes.

Procedures are step-by-step directions about how to accomplish a policy. Examples are how to use a computer system, ensure that facilities are locked and safe, and use the kitchen facilities.

## Job Descriptions

A job description is a written description of the responsibilities of a certain position, or job, in the organization. Management should have a job description for each job in the organization. The description should specify the general responsibilities of the position along with some of the specific duties to be conducted by the person in that role, the title for the position, and any special skills, training or credentials required. The responsibilities should be updated to include expectations associated with that role and associated action plans.

## Performance Goals

In addition to a job description, certain roles in the organization, particularly management roles, often have an associated list of specific accomplishments that they are to accomplish by a certain time in the organization. Probably the best example of performance goals is the list of goals that a Board of Directors might establish for the Chief Executive Officer in an organization.

# Reminders – Critical Ingredients to Maintain Successful Change

Here are some quick reminders of what to do to maintain successful change, especially during the implementation phase. You have probably already been doing many of them so far in your project.

See "Requirements for Successful Organizational Change" on page 186 for a more complete description of each of the following items.

## Maintain Motivation

1.    Test for readiness before people undertake new activities.

2.    Deal with resistance as it arises, whether from individuals or groups.

3.      Keep people enlightened about need for change, describing the issues that the organization faces and what will happen if nothing is done.

4.      Stay realistic – there is already too much cynicism in our organizations today.

5.      Keep giving people opportunities to provide input to the project.

## *Focus on Vision and Action Plans*

1.      Keep the vision and action plans in front of people at all times.

2.      Be sure that people continue to have input to the vision and plans, and modify them, if needed, in order for them to remain relevant and realistic.

3.      Remind people of how the vision and plans will successfully address the issues in the organization.

4.      Keep managing people's expectations by ensuring vision and plans are realistic and by sharing the successes and failures of project activities.

## *Ensure Political Support*

1.      Be sure that top leaders authorize sufficient resources to support and sustain project activities.

2.      Be sure that people see that leaders are actively involved in the project activities.

3.      Be sure that top leaders' suggestions and concerns are addressed in a timely manner.

## *Manage Transition*

1.      Engage in ongoing coaching, facilitation and training where needed, to ensure people are fully resourced and guided to implement plans.

2.      Ensure plans and actions are focused on changing systems.

3.      Ensure that implementation of the Change Management Plan is monitored on a regular basis.

## *Sustain Momentum*

1.      Ensure clear and specific accountabilities to achieve plans and actions.

2.      Ensure that top leaders are aware of those accountabilities. Reward strong performance and address poor performance.

3.      Ensure supervisors delegate.

# Consultant's Coaching to Maintain Motivation and Momentum

As the consultant, you should maintain focus on the following topics about implementation of the Change Management Plan. This is true whether you are an external or internal consultant.

1.   **Monitor status of implementation of the Change Management Plan.**
The Communications Plan portion of the Change Management Plan should have specified how communication of status would be provided to you. As soon as you notice that you are not receiving communication or implementation has stalled, be authentic and speak up.

2.   **Consider coaching to address problems during implementation.**
Coaching is a powerful practice to ensure ongoing trust, commitment and collaboration during implementation. Those three conditions are vital to the successful implementation of the Change Management Plan. Coaching also can be used to solve problems and cultivate learning because it helps people to fully understand their current challenges and customize action plans to address those challenges.

> See "How to Coach for Deep Problem-Solving and Learning" on page 68 for guidelines and techniques of coaching.

3.   **Be sure to keep project activities realistic.**
Far too many projects are based entirely on grand expectations for change without any realistic action plans to support them. Unrealistic expectations can quickly spawn cynicism about your project. Be sure to continually manage for realistic expectations. Your client will greatly appreciate your efforts to be realistic with them.

> See "How to Keep It Real – Managing for Realistic Expectations" on page 76 for guidelines to keep projects realistic.

4.   **Keep discussing the process evaluation questions.**
During Phase 2: Engagement and Agreement, you and your client discussed certain evaluation questions that should be addressed during the project. Those questions will lend strong focus and momentum to the project as long as you and your client continually discuss the questions and any answers to them so far.

> See "Process Evaluation" on page 203 to view a list of suggested questions for process evaluations.

5.   **If the status of implementation gets completely stuck, be authentic.**
Implementation can get stuck for a variety of reasons. Your client might realize that the organization lacks the resources necessary to implement the Change Management Plan. There might be tremendous resistance from various members of the organization. Another major priority might arise and replace the original focus of the project.

See "If Implementation Stalls, Cycle Back" on page 360 for guidelines about how to respond when implementation gets stuck.

6.   **Recognize accomplishments as they occur for your client.**
This is one of the most powerful practices for sustaining motivation and momentum. Your client and other members of the organization are usually focused on the day-to-day details of running the organization. They are focused on what is not getting done and what issues are not yet addressed by the project. You can provide precious benefit from reminding them of the successes of their efforts so far.

See "How to Help Your Client Appreciate Accomplishments" on page 77 for guidelines to recognize and appreciate accomplishments.

# Client's Delegation to Maintain Motivation and Momentum

One of the most powerful approaches to ensure implementation of plans is your client's ongoing delegation to their staff members. Therefore, this subsection is in this Field Guide, even though the guidelines are for your client to follow.

Delegation is when supervisors give responsibility and authority to subordinates to finish a task by a certain date, and then work collaboratively with staff members to identify how the task can be accomplished. (Remember that supervisors exist throughout the organization. For example, the Board supervises the Chief Executive Officer and the CEO supervises direct reports.)

Effective delegation develops people who are ultimately more fulfilled and productive. Supervisors become more fulfilled and productive themselves as they learn to count on their staff members and are freed up to attend to more strategic issues. Effective delegation sustains the type of motivation, vision, political support and momentum that are critical for successful change.

Delegation is often difficult for new leaders, particularly if they have had to scramble to start the organization themselves. Many leaders and managers want to remain comfortable, making the same decisions they have always made. They believe they can do a better job themselves. They do not want to risk losing any of their power and stature during delegation (ironically, they do lose these if they do not learn to delegate effectively). Often, they do not want to risk giving authority to subordinates in case they fail and impair the organization.

However, there are basic approaches to delegation that, with practice, become the backbone of effective supervision and development. Horton (1992, pp. 58-61) suggests general steps to accomplish delegation. The following guidelines build on those steps. You might share the guidelines with your client.

1.   **Client should specify preliminary desired results to themselves.**
It will be difficult for your client to delegate to others in their organization if they cannot convey at least some basic description of the results that are to be achieved. Usually, the more clear and specific the description, the more clearly that staff members understand the results. Therefore, your client should first think about the results that are to be achieved and how to describe those results to others. Note that the specification of results usually becomes even more complete during delegation to others.

2. **Client should delegate tasks ultimately to one lead person, to one subordinate.**
   If the tasks are to be achieved by a group, there still should be one lead person who ultimately is responsible for the work of the group. This approach makes it easier for the supervisor to monitor status. It also gives the lead person a strong sense of responsibility and greatly increases their motivation.

3. **Client should select the best subordinate to lead the project.**
   To make the best selection, consider the expertise and timing most likely to be required to achieve the desired results. Then select the staff member with the most expertise and available timing. If timing for the project is not extremely urgent, then also consider the developmental needs of staff members. Perhaps there is time in the project for various other staff members to participate to further develop their skills.

4. **As much as possible, your client should collaborate with the lead person.**
   The extent of collaboration depends on the supervisor's style of leadership and expertise of the lead person. The more expertise he or she has, the more collaboration there may be between the supervisor and lead person. As much as possible, the supervisor should let the person choose how to achieve the desired results.

5. **Client should have the lead person summarize their impressions of the project.**
   Your client should explain to the lead person that this summary is not a measure of his or her competence to understand the client, but rather is to ensure that both share the same clear impression of the project.

6. **Client gets ongoing non-intrusive feedback about progress on the project.**
   The client should continue to get regular reports from the lead person. Written reports often are the most clear and credible. Reports might describe what the lead person did last week, plans to do next week, and any potential issues. Regular meetings with the person should include this ongoing feedback, as well.

7. **If the client is not satisfied, they should not take the project back from the lead person.**
   The client should continue to work with the lead person to ensure that they perceive the project as being their responsibility. The client should look for the cause of their dissatisfaction. For example, is it lack of communication, training, resources or commitment? The client should promptly share their concerns with the lead person.

8. **Client should evaluate and reward performance of staff members**.
   Evaluate the progress that was made toward achieving the desired results more than the methods that staff members used to achieve those results. Address insufficient performance by developing performance improvement plans. Reward successes, especially by using whatever means each member prefers for motivating themselves, for example, awards, merit increases or time off from work.

# Important Reminders for Consultants During Implementation

## *Professional Management*

1. **Recognize which roles you should play and when.**
   As a consultant, at various times you might choose the role of facilitator, coach, expert or trainer. By choosing the right role at the right time, your efforts are more targeted and effective. In addition, your client better understands you and the reasons for your actions.

   See "How to Know What Consultant Role to Play and When" on page 19 for guidelines to discern what role to play.

2. **Keep track of who your current client is.**
   Remember that there are different types of clients, such as direct and indirect and also situational and project clients. Knowing who your current client is and working effectively with them results in greater leverage for your efforts and more impact during the project.

   See "Who is the Client? How to Know Who Your Current Client Is" on page 14 for guidelines to recognize your current client.

3. **Recognize when you need to deal with resistance and how.**
   Different people might show resistance in different ways during the project. Also, remember that resistance can be direct or indirect. Indirect resistance is often the most difficult to recognize and address. When you respond effectively to resistance, you help your client to progress in the project and learn at the same time.

   See "Dealing with Resistance from Individuals" on page 80 for guidelines to deal with resistance from your client.

4. **Maintain your professionalism.**
   This includes maintaining your principles of consulting and ethics, and appropriate boundaries during consultation. Prolonged efforts for change can involve a variety of challenges and ongoing frustrations. In those situations, it can be tempting to compromise your values for the sake of getting things done more quickly or of minimizing stress. The results of such compromises come back to haunt you.

   See "Maintaining Professionalism" on page 464 for guidelines to maintain your professionalism.

5. **Recognize when you might need help.**
   Sometimes, there is the illusion that asking for help indicates that you are somehow inadequate in your role as consultant. However, significant change in an organization often requires a wide variety of skills. Your job is to recognize the types of skills needed and then help your client to obtain and utilize those skills.

356

See "How to Know When to Ask for Help" on page 108 for guidelines to know when you need help.

6.  **Recognize when you need to quit the project even if it is not yet completed.**
    There can be the illusion that quitting a project means failure for you, your client and the project. However, quitting the project sometimes can be the best thing for you and your client. That action might signal to the client that a different approach has to be taken for change to occur in their organization. It might signal to you that you need to be more careful about which projects you undertake and how.

See "How to Know When to Leave a Project" on page 111 for guidelines to know when to quit a project.

## Self-Management

1.  **Be sure that you remain grounded and centered.**
    Do not lose yourself during the sometimes long journey of change. You need to remain mindful of what best suits you in how you work, especially your values and ethics. You must effectively manage your time and your stress. Each person manages differently. Know what works best for you.

See "Staying Grounded and Centered" on page 91 for guidelines to remain grounded and centered.

2.  **Keep getting support and objective feedback from others.**
    This is true, especially during a large project for change. Social workers, therapists and members of other helping professions often use various forms of support for themselves. Recruit and appreciate that form of help for yourself.

See the list of resources in "Professional Organizations" on page 464 for sources, or referrals to sources, of support.

3.  **Remain open to feedback about your performance.**
    The more that you are willing to hear feedback about yourself, the more likely that you will grow both as a person and a consultant. In addition, your openness provides a powerful model for your client to be open to learning, as well. We all have certain natural responses to feedback. Know what your responses are and how to manage them for maximum learning.

See "Understand Your Natural Responses to Feedback and Conflict" on page 45 to clarify how you receive feedback.

# Use These Tools to Track the Status of Implementation

The following tools can help you and your client to carefully monitor the status of implementation of the Change Management Plan. Without knowing that status, it is extremely difficult to manage the transition of the organization. Some of the tools might have been included in your Communications Plan.

## *Spoken Word*

This is probably the most frequent form of getting information about the status of an activity in the workplace. Although it is the most frequent, it is usually the least reliable because information is usually incomplete or about a small aspect of an overall activity needed to implement an action from the Change Management Plan. Spoken commentary should be used primarily to clarify information from other written tools of communicating status. However, supervisors should remain highly accessible to their direct reports to continue to exchange commentary as much as possible.

## *"To-do" Lists*

To-do lists are probably the most frequent means by which people manage what they need to do in the workplace. The list usually includes a brief mention, or listing, of the tasks to attend to, and the status toward completion of the tasks. Supervisors sometimes request to-do lists from each of their subordinates.

## *Status Reports*

Status reports are written descriptions of an individual's work activities. The reports are usually provided on a regular basis, perhaps weekly or biweekly. They should be dated and describe:

1.      What activities were done over the past time period

2.      Any current actions or issues that must be addressed by management

3.      Plans for activities on the next time period

Some supervisors might prefer written status reports, rather than to-do lists. Status reports are usually more complete. The time to prepare these is about 15 minutes if done weekly.

## *Staff Meetings*

Staff meetings are regular meetings among members of the staff to exchange information about activities in the organization, often including status of what each member is doing and will be doing. Staff meetings should be held with supervisors and their direct reports at least once a month. Ideally, they are held with all members of the organization at least once a month or quarterly if in larger organizations.

## *Action Plans*

Action plans are a handy means to report the status of progress toward specific objectives from the Strategic Plan. Action plans should be updated and provided to senior managers at least once a month or to members of the Board of Directors at least quarterly.

### Chief Executive Officer Report

These written reports usually come from the Chief Executive Officer to members of the Board, and are provided at each Board meeting. The reports briefly describe the highlights from activities since the last Board meeting and highlights of any future activities that are expected before the next Board meeting.

### "Planned Versus Actual" Budget Reports

These reports can be extremely useful, particularly to members of the Board and management team. The reports can give a quick picture of the status of financial activities. The reports usually include specification of:

1.    All categories of expenses

2.    The amount of money planned for each month in that account category

3.    The amount of money actually spent for each month in the account category

The reports should be reviewed once a month by senior management and members of the Board of Directors.

### Program Reviews

Reviews are regular examinations of the activities to assess how well they are being conducted. Reviewers examine whether activities are following the original plan. Usually, there are key indicators about the status of activities, such as:

- What major problems exist and what is needed to address them?

- What are the actual costs compared to the planned costs?

- Are any actions needed to avoid financial problems?

- What are you learning from the program implementation so far?

- What would you do differently about the program if you could do anything?

- What limitations are holding you back from what you would ideally do if you could?

- How are you acknowledging and celebrating the accomplishments?

Program reviews usually occur on an irregular basis. Reviewers look for major milestones or deliverables that are specified on a project plan.

## Systematically Adjust Plans When Really Needed

Plans are rarely implemented as designed. That is not a problem – it is acceptable to adjust plans. The plan is only a guideline – not a strict roadmap, which must be followed exactly as specified when first written. Plans must be flexible.

Reluctance to change plans under any circumstances results in loss of credibility to the plans. The vision for change soon becomes unimportant. Eventually, members of the organization lose their motivation to take part in the change effort. Soon, momentum for the effort is lost altogether.

There are valid reasons and invalid reasons for changing plans. Valid reasons are usually about:

- Changes in the organization's external environment, for example, decreased need for the nonprofit's services.

- Changes in the availability of resources necessary to implement the plans, for example, funding for the project is not obtained.

- Changes in priorities in the organization, for example, a sudden, major crisis occurs that needs immediate attention.

Invalid reasons are usually about ineffective leadership, for example:

- There was little attention to monitoring the status of implementation of plans, so people let other priorities become more important – they focused on urgent, rather than important, matters.

- There was little attention to effective coaching and delegation so people lost motivation and momentum to implement plans.

- There was little visibility of top leadership supporting the plans, so people assumed the plans were some kind of passing fad.

Changes to plans should be done systematically. Consider these guidelines.

1. Recognize the need for a deviation from the plan.

2. Understand the reason for the deviation.

3. Decide what the change should be.

4. Communicate the need for the change to the plan and what the change should be (before making the change to the plan).

5. Obtain approval to make the change.

6. Make the change to the plan.

7. Update the version of the plan, for example, changing the date on each of the pages and adding commentary that explained the change.

8. Track the status of the plan.

# If Implementation Stalls, Cycle Back

This phase is more likely to get stalled than any other. This phase can get stalled for a variety of reasons, including:

- Another priority became more important to your client during implementation.

- A key person in the project left the organization.

- Your client's organization lacked sufficient resources to implement change.

- Your client lacks sufficient leadership to ensure that plans are implemented.

- Your client thought that merely having written plans would make a big difference.

- Your client thought that you would do the work.

- You encountered continued resistance from your client – or from yourself.

The following guidelines are standard, brief reminders of what to do whenever a particular phase of the consulting process seems to have stalled.

See "How to Do Collaborative Consulting with Busy Clients" on page 16 for a more complete description of each of the following actions.

1.   **Be authentic.**

2.   **Remind your client of the importance of the project.**

3.   **Recognize the other priorities of your client.**

4.   **Realize your client's lack of participation may be a form of project resistance.**

5.   **Remind your client: choices about the project are choices about the nonprofit.**

6.   **Continue to recognize accomplishments in the project so far.**

7.   **Use small-group instead of large-group activities where possible.**

8.   **Use coaching to identify obstacles and how to remove them.**

9.   **Resort to the "Sanity Solution."**

10.  **Decide if you should cycle back to Phase 2: Engagement and Agreement phase.**
     You and your client may need to carefully re-establish priorities in the project.

# Phase 6: Adoption and Evaluation

By now, you and your client have made a consistent and focused attempt to implement the Change Management Plan, along with associated plans for evaluation, learning, recognition and communications.

| Consulting Cycle: |
|---|
| Client's Start-Up |
| Engagement |
| Discovery |
| Action Planning |
| Implementation |
| Adoption |
| Termination |

## Purpose and Goals

This purpose of this phase is to ensure that your client's organization has integrated new approaches and practices identified from the project into the organization. This is the phase of the consulting process that really pays off if action plans have been focused on changing structures, plans, policies and roles.

Goals of this phase include to:

1.  Decide if the issues (that were identified during Discovery and Feedback) have been successfully addressed.

2.  Decide if the vision for change has been achieved (if your client decided to develop a vision for change during the project).

3.  Decide if the action plans have been implemented.

4.  Decide whether it is necessary to cycle back in the consulting cycle or proceed to the next phase, Project Termination.

Note that it might seem to your client that the issues have been successfully addressed even though the vision and action plans were not implemented. In that case, be extremely careful that your client is not really showing signs of resistance by rushing to say that things are "fixed" even though they are not. Guidelines in this section will help you to avoid that situation with your client.

## Common Barriers to Implementation

When assessing the extent of your client's adoption of the desired changes in their organization, it is useful to consider the reasons that implementation might not have occurred. Hopefully, none of these situations occurs during your projects.

1.  **The overall situation changes.**
    In nonprofits, a project might successfully identify a major issue and actions to address that issue, only to discover that a new, major issue has suddenly become much more important.

2.  **Key people succumb to burnout.**
    The stress of the change effort was such that some people lost their ability to sustain momentum and focus on their work. Consequently, they are no longer effective in the project – or their jobs.

3.  **Key people leave the organization.**
    Small nonprofits, especially, tend to have a high employee turnover rate – employees come

and go rather quickly. It can be a disaster to a project if your client suddenly leaves the organization.

4. **The relationship between the consultant and client degenerates.**
If you and your client have not worked at sustaining an effective working relationship, it can fall apart completely during the rigors of implementation.

5. **Key people in the organization just refuse to implement action plans.**
Experienced consultants have learned that it is not up to the consultants as to whether a client follows the consultant's advice or not. If key people in the organization consistently refuse to implement action plans, the project can come to a complete stop. When this occurs, it is time to cycle back.

# Indicators That Your Client Has Adopted New Systems

Now is the time for you and your client to decide whether your client's organization has adopted the necessary new systems (the systems required to address issues in their organization). It helps to look for certain indicators when making that decision. Note that your client might decide that not all of the following indicators need to be present for the project to have been successful. Consider:

1. Overall performance indicators of success.

> See "Identify Performance Indicators of Success" on page 330 for examples of indicators.

2. Whether all of the issues have been addressed.

3. Whether the vision for change has been achieved.

4. Whether the action plans have been implemented.

5. Whether leaders in the organization agree that the project has been successful.

# Evaluation of Project Results

Now you and your client are ready to conduct a systematic evaluation as to whether or not the indicators of success have really been achieved. If your client has been implementing the Evaluation Plan that was developed during the Action Planning, Alignment and Integration phase, then your evaluation activities now might merely be a matter of reviewing the findings from having implemented that Plan. Otherwise, you and your client will need to conduct an evaluation by developing and systematically implementing the Evaluation Plan.

> See "Develop an Evaluation Plan to Evaluate the Quality of Final Results" on page 333 to develop the Evaluation Plan now, if needed.

# If the Desired Results Are Still Not Achieved, Cycle Back

If, after having conducted the evaluation of progress toward achieving desired results, the results have not been achieved, then consider the following guidelines. These guidelines are standard, brief reminders of what to do whenever a particular phase of the consulting process seems to have stalled.

 See "How to Do Collaborative Consulting with Busy Clients" on page 16 for a more complete description of each of the following actions.

1.  **Be authentic.**

2.  **Remind your client of the importance of the project.**

3.  **Recognize the other priorities of your client.**

4.  **Realize your client's lack of participation may be a form of project resistance.**

5.  **Remind your client: choices about the project are choices about the nonprofit.**

6.  **Continue to recognize accomplishments in the project so far.**

7.  **Use small-group instead of large-group activities where possible.**

8.  **Use coaching to identify obstacles and how to remove them.**

9.  **Resort to the "Sanity Solution."**

10. **Decide if you should cycle back to Phase 2: Engagement and Agreement phase.**
    You and your client may need to carefully re-establish priorities in the project.

# Final Evaluation of the Project as a Whole

## *Include Questionnaires and Discussions*

Your evaluations so far have been on the quality of the project's activities (the formative evaluation) and achievement of the desired results from the project. There are other aspects of the project that you should evaluate now. Like many other types of evaluation, this one can produce significant learning for you and your client.

One of the most powerful approaches to this evaluation includes the use of at least two methods of data collection, usually a questionnaire and a highly focused discussion with your client. It is important for you to decide which of the two methods to use first.

Use questionnaires before discussions. That approach will give you quick feedback from which you might design your upcoming discussions. However, that feedback on the questionnaires tends to be less thoughtful than feedback provided during a discussion. In addition, your client might provide positive responses to the questions because they know that they will be meeting with you soon. An advantage of the questionnaire is that you will have documented evidence of your client's impressions of the quality of the project.

Use of the discussion method first often provokes more thoughtful responses. Those responses often are somewhat biased because people tend to provide more positive feedback about others when those people are in the same room as the respondent. However, the follow-up questionnaire will be completed more thoughtfully because your client had a chance to be more thoughtful about the project during the discussion method.

 See "How to Design and Administer Questionnaires" on page 403 for guidelines to design and administer questionnaires.

Unfortunately, at this point in projects – especially if they have been successful – clients usually want to move on to other priorities and struggle to find the motivation to take part in yet another evaluation. If this situation occurs to you, do not be put off. Persist in having this evaluation. The value of this project evaluation is so significant that, once you and your client have done the evaluation, they will greatly appreciate your having been persistent. This evaluation usually generates tremendous learning and appreciation for both you and your client.

Be sure that at least the following questions are asked during the discussion. Always let your client answer the questions first. Then your answer follows theirs.

 See "Discussion (to Permit Free-Floating Exchange of Information)" on page 382 for guidelines to use the discussion process.

1.  **What were the four to five most important results from the project?**
    Let your client decide what "results" mean.

2.  **What were the top four to five learnings for you from the project?**
    Remind your client that learning is new knowledge, skills and attitudes.

     It might be useful for you and your client to reference the Learning Plan that you developed as part of your Change Management Plan.

3.  **What were the strengths? Of the project? Client? Consultant?**
    What activities were most useful in producing results?

4.  **What were areas for improvement? Of the project? Client? Consultant?**
    If your client cannot identify any, keep asking and remain silent.

5.  **Were there any unexpected outcomes from the project?**
    Again, if your client cannot think of any, ask again and remain silent.

# Phase 7: Project Termination

| Consulting Cycle: |
| --- |
| Client's Start-Up |
| Engagement |
| Discovery |
| Action Planning |
| Implementation |
| Adoption |
| Termination |

## Purpose and Goals

This purpose of this phase of the consulting process is to recognize the termination of the original project plan and decide the future of the relationship between you and your client. If you are an internal consultant, that role might already be clear.

The goals of this phase are for you and your client to:

1. Ensure that there is a specific termination to your consulting project.

2. Identify the next steps for both of you.

3. Formalize the end of the project.

## Typical Reasons Projects Are Terminated

- Desired results of the project have been achieved.
- The end date of the contract is reached.
- Your client runs out of resources for the project.
- Your client leaves the organization.
- Your client's organization experiences a dramatic change of some kind.
- You or your client somehow violates one or more terms of the contract.
- Your client is not able to utilize the outcomes from the consultation work.

## Avoid Dependency and "Project Creep"

### Avoiding Dependency

Certainly, you helped your client a great deal when working to integrate those new systems into their organization. It is not uncommon that clients continue to ask consultants for assistance even after the goals of the project have been achieved. However, it is important at this point, that you continue to "wean" your client away from continued dependence on you. It is unethical for you to contribute towards that ongoing dependency. Indeed, one of the most important goals for consultants is to teach clients how to solve their problems for themselves.

For adoption to occur successfully, your client must have learned how to adopt various new systems into their workplace. Ideally, your client has learned how to use those new systems at least once now without your direct guidance and support.

To achieve that goal, sooner or later, you must begin separating yourself as a consultant from each project. It is during this phase that you and your client should begin the process of separating the consulting relationship – the relationship in which your client relies on you for guidance and materials to address problems or achieve goals in their workplace.

### Avoiding Project Creep

It is also important to avoid "project creep." That happens when your client keeps adding requirements to the project, even though the original requirements, as specified in the contract, have already been met. Nonprofits have major needs and they can use all the help they can get. Your client might inadvertently cause project creep without realizing it.

As a consultant, keep focused on the desired results for the project and whether or not they have been achieved. The most reliable and consistent description of those results usually is in the contract that you and your client agreed to during the Engagement phase.

If you are asked to do something outside the bounds of the contract, mention your concern to your client. You and your client may need to renegotiate the contract to add the tasks or extend deadlines, or you may want to develop a new contract for a new project.

## Identify Next Steps

Now that you and your client have agreed that the project's desired results have been achieved, there are several options available to both of you. Keep in mind that the relationship between you and your client has great value. Here are your options:

1.      Separate and never see each other again (if you are an external consultant).

2.      Establish another contract regarding a different issue.

3.      Remain as an advisor – be careful of unethically maintaining your client's dependency on you.

Certainly, there are other options, for example, to extend the contract or recycle certain phases. However, if the desired results of your current project indeed have been achieved, it would be unethical for you to pursue those other options.

## Formalize Termination of Project

### Letter of Project Termination

The following guidelines apply to external consultants.

By now, you have met with your client to evaluate the project. That activity included identifying any weaknesses, strengths and learnings regarding the project, you and your client. Now you should formally terminate the project with a letter to your client. This practice is too often forgotten, yet it is meaningful to ensure that you and your client clearly recognize that the project has indeed been terminated. Consider the following information to include in the letter.

1. Include the following sentence: "If you do not agree that the conditions of our contract have been fulfilled completely, please respond in writing to me within two weeks of receiving this letter." That useful phrase might protect you at some time in the future if your client ever decides that your project was not successful, after all.

2. You might reiterate any strengths and learnings from the project.

3. Request permission to use any of their complimentary comments as testimonials in your advertising literature about your services.

4. Congratulate them on their new developments and learning.

5. Add any final invoices.

## *Organize Your Administrative Information*

Clients often come back to you, especially if they considered the projects to be highly successful. In those situations, it often is useful to be able to quickly remember the details of those past projects.

Each project file is often two to four inches thick, at least. Now, at the end of a project, is the best time to organize your file. Usually, at this point, you want to just put the file away and move on to other activities. Do not! Instead, go through the file one more time, if only for 15 minutes, to weed out unnecessary documents and ensure that remaining documents have dates on them and are in the right order. Make any notes that will help you to quickly remember highlights from the project. Copy any documents that could be useful in other projects.

# PART V:

# TOOLBOX –

# GROUP SKILLS

# Forming Groups and Teams

Teams frequently conduct the process of organizational change. For example, you might encourage your client to form a project team to oversee development, implementation and evaluation of the project plan. Teams might be used to design and implement various assessments to attempt to identify root causes of organizational problems. Teams might be used to identify the most suitable action plans to address those problems. Certain teams might be used to implement certain action plans.

Therefore, a critical skill for you is to be able to work with your client to build various types of teams, communicate with them, work with them to help them decide what they want to do and how they want to do it, and to solve problems and make decisions. Guidelines in this section will help you to develop and use the necessary skills with teams and groups. This is true whether you are an external or internal consultant.

Group dynamics, like culture, is a concept about which many books have been written and it typically is discussed in the abstract. Similar to the concept of culture, when you operationalize group dynamics to apply in a project for change, you often end up using the same types of tools and techniques as described in this section of the Field Guide.

 To learn a great deal about group dynamics in organizational change, see Edgar H. Schein's book, *Process Consultation: Its Role in Organizational Development,* Addison Wesley, 1988. This is a classic work on the subject.

## What Determines Whether a Gathering is a "Group"?

This might seem like a silly question, but it is not. Gatherings of less than 10-12 people are considered by organizational development consultants to be a small group. Information in this section is about forming and facilitating small groups of 10-12 people or less.

Groups that are larger than that range tend to have another level of complexity not apparent in small groups. For example, larger groups are similar to entire organizations. They have their own culture, distinct subsystems (or cliques), diversity of leadership styles and levels of communication. While certain structures are useful in small groups, they are absolutely necessary in larger groups. Larger groups should have a clearly established purpose, and documented plans and policies for making decisions, such as means to decide ongoing leadership, decision making, problem solving and communication.

## How to Prepare to Facilitate

It is always important for you to be personally prepared for facilitation. This is true whether you are an external or internal consultant. In most cases, you are by yourself as the facilitator, while your group members look to you to guide them through a successful group activity. Depending on the goals of your group and the nature of its members, the experience of facilitation can range from fun and fulfilling to challenging and lonely. The following guidelines will help you to personally prepare for facilitation in any situation.

1. **Always know the goals, structures and membership of the group.**
   An important systems principle is that structures determine behaviors, which determine events. The behaviors and events in your group will be determined, in large part, by the plans, roles, policies and procedures in your group.

    See "How to Build Highly Effective Teams" on page 372 for guidelines to carefully design the goals, structures and membership of your meeting.

2. **Know what "centers" you – what calms you down before a meeting.**
   Different people "get centered" by different means. For example, do you meditate, take a walk, or memorize an opening to the meeting? Think about successful meetings that you have facilitated in the past. What worked to keep you centered?

3. **Remember how you successfully deal with feedback and conflict.**
   Remember your typical reactions to feedback and conflict and how you have learned to successfully manage those reactions.

    See "Understand Your Natural Responses to Feedback and Conflict" on page 45 for guidelines about how you respond to feedback and conflict.

4. **Use your emotional intelligence (EI).**
   Remember how you recognize and name uncomfortable feelings and how you have learned to successfully manage those emotions.

    See "What is Your Emotional Intelligence?" on page 46 for guidelines to develop emotional intelligence.

5. **Have an opening – something to say when you start the group meeting.**
   Always know what you are going to say for the first minute of the meeting. Your sense of purpose and direction will be contagious to group members. For example, memorize a certain opening to the meeting or tell a joke.

    See the list of recommended resources about facilitation on page 502.

# How to Build Highly Effective Teams

Teams, or small groups of people who work together on an ongoing basis to accomplish some common goal, are most effective when carefully designed. Too often, teams are formed merely by gathering some people together and then hoping that those people somehow find a way to work together. One of the best ways for you to build a successful team is to develop a clear charter when the team is first formed. In addition to the charter, you will need to attend to some other activities that are listed throughout this section – those activities come later on. For now, consider the following guidelines when chartering teams during your project.

1.  **Set clear goals for the results to be produced by the team.**
    The goals should be designed to be "SMART." This is an acronym for specific, measurable, achievable, relevant and time-bound. As much as possible, include input from other members of the organization when designing and wording these goals. Goals might be, for example, "to produce a project report that includes a project plan, schedule and budget to develop and test a complete employee performance management system within the next month." Write these goals down for eventual communication to and discussion with all team members.

2.  **Set clear goals for the effectiveness of the team process.**
    The goals should also be designed to be "SMART." Goals might be, for example, "to attain 90% participation of all members during the first 6 weeks of weekly attendance," and "achieve 90% satisfaction ratings among members or share facilitation of the group." Write these goals down for eventual communication to and discussion with all team members.

3.  **Determine time frames for commencing and terminating the team, if applicable.**
    Write these times down for eventual communication to and discussion with all team members.

4.  **Determine the membership of the group.**
    Consider the extent of expertise needed to achieve the goals, including areas of knowledge and skills. Include at least one person who has skills in facilitation and meeting management. Attempt to include sufficient diversity of values and perspectives to ensure robust ideas and discussion. A critical consideration is availability – members should have the time to attend every meeting and perform required tasks between meetings.

5.  **Determine the structure of the group.**
    Structure includes the number of people in the group, how often and when they will meet, who will be the leader of the group, other roles for other members, how members will communicate with each other and procedures for making decisions and solving problems.

6.  **Determine the process of the group.**
    Depending on the nature of the results to be produced by the group, the process might be focused on, for example, open discussion, action planning, problem solving and decision-making, or generating recommendations.

7.  **Identify any needs for training and materials.**
    For example, members might benefit from a training that provides a brief overview of the typical stages of team development and includes packets of materials about the team's goals, structure and process to make decisions.

8.  **Identify the costs to provide necessary resources for the team.**
    Consider costs, such as paying employees to attend the meeting, trainers, consultants, room rental and office supplies.

9.  **Contact each team member.**
    Before the first meeting, invite each potential team member to be a part of the team. First, send them a memo, and then meet with each person individually. Communicate the goals of the project, why the person was selected, the benefit of the goals to the organization, the time frame for the team effort, and who will lead the team (at least initially). Invite the team member to the first meeting.

10. **Plan the first meeting.**
In the first meeting, review the goals of the team, why each member was selected, the benefit of the goals to the organization, the time frame for the team effort, who will lead the team (at least, initially), when the team might meet and where, and any changes that have occurred since the individual meetings. Have this information written down to hand out to each member. At the end of the meeting, ask each person to make a public commitment to the team effort.

11. **Early on, plan team building activities to support trust and strong working relationships among members.**
Team building activities can include, for example, a retreat in which members introduce themselves, exercises in which members help each other solve a short problem or meet a specific and achievable goal, or an extended period in which members can voice their concerns and frustrations about their team assignments.

12. **Support team meetings and processes.**
At this point, it is critical that supervisors remain available to provide support and resources as needed. The supervisor should regularly monitor team members' progress on achieving their goals. Provide ongoing encouragement and visibility to members. One of the most important forms of support a supervisor can provide is coordination with other supervisors to ensure that team members are freed up enough to attend meetings.

# Meeting Design, Management and Interventions

## How to Design Highly Effective Meetings (Agendas)

Meeting management tends to be a set of skills often overlooked by facilitators and planners.  That can be a major mistake because, in projects to accomplish major change in organizations, your credibility is in the flow of the process, not in the details of the project.  Therefore, it is important that the process of your meetings be well designed.  This is true whether you are an external or internal consultant.

The following guidelines ensure that general purpose meetings are highly focused and results-oriented around certain topics.  (Note that the unique design for the agenda of the feedback meeting in the Phase 3: Discovery and Feedback should follow guidelines as presented in that section.)

1.  Design the agenda together with the organization's leadership – do not design it yourself.  Ensure an effective meeting by first reflecting on the goals for the meeting and then the activities to meet those goals.

2.  Think about how you label an event so people come in with that mindset.  It may pay to have a short dialogue around the label to develop a common mindset among attendees, particularly if they include representatives from various cultures.

3.  Include introductions or some type of "check in" early on so all members get involved early in the meeting.

4.  Be sure to dedicate time to reviewing the status of actions assigned in previous meetings.

5.  Allow time for brief evaluations, or "satisfaction checks," among the members.

6.  Next to each major topic, include the type of action needed, the type of output expected, and time estimates for addressing the topic.

7.  Review the agenda at the beginning of each meeting, giving participants a chance to understand all proposed major topics, change them and accept them.

8.  Ask participants if they will commit to the agenda.

9.  Keep the agenda posted at all times.

10.  Ensure a meeting recorder (or documenter) who documents major activities during the meeting and actions to be conducted after the meeting.  This person should issue meeting minutes shortly after the meeting (although meeting minutes may seem the most perfunctory duty from a meeting, the minutes can end up being the most useful part of the meeting by helping people remember all of the actions to be completed).

11.  In general, do not over-design the meeting.  Be willing to adapt the meeting agenda if members are making constructive progress toward the overall goals.

# How to Manage for Effective Meetings

## *Facilitator's Preparation for Meetings*

Remember that your behavior sets the tone for the meeting. You should become as comfortable as possible before each meeting.

 See "How to Prepare to Facilitate" on page 371 for guidelines to personally prepare for facilitation.

## *Opening Meetings*

1.     Start on time. This respects those who showed up on time and reminds any late-comers that the meeting and its scheduling are serious.

2.     Ask if anyone is missing who should be present. If there is anyone who should be there and is not, visit the reason for the absence and address how to get him or her involved.

3.     Ask if introductions would be useful. Even though members of the group might all be from the same organization, some members still might not know each other.

4.     Model the kind of energy and participation needed by the facilitator and meeting participants.

5.     Clarify your roles for that meeting, for example, note when you will be doing any training, facilitating or recording.

## *Establishing Ground Rules for Meetings*

The ground rules establish the overall "personality" of the meeting, so they are important to establish early on when working with a group.

The purpose of this technique is to suggest certain desired behaviors among participants during their meetings. Ground rules can be identified before the group meeting and then proposed to the group for their review, modification and/or approval. Or, the ground rules can be developed by members of the group in a group meeting. Common ground rules are:

1.     Meetings start and stop on time.

2.     Focus on priorities, not on personalities.

3.     Everyone participates.

4.     All opinions are honored.

5.     No interruptions.

6.     No sidebars (or conversations not involving the main group).

7.      Celebrate accomplishments.

## Time Management

One of the most difficult facilitation tasks is time management.  In a highly energized meeting, time seems to run out before tasks are finished.  Therefore, the biggest challenge is keeping the process moving.

1.      Consider asking the group for a volunteer to help monitor and remind the group about the time.

2.      If the planned time on the agenda is getting out of hand, present it to the group and ask for their input as to a resolution.

3.      Adjourn a meeting when scheduled – rarely deter from this guideline.  It is far better to adjourn a meeting even if members feel work is incomplete than to drag a meeting on and on with the illusion that everyone should leave the meeting with a strong sense of closure.  Adjourning a meeting on time ensures that all members feel their time is respected and they can continue to count on sound meeting management.

## Evaluations During Meetings

Evaluation of the quality of a meeting is a critical, but often overlooked, requirement for effective meetings.  Avoiding evaluations in an effort to "get more work done" in meetings is a good example of working harder, rather than smarter.  Far too many meetings end up with members going out of the room, remarking to each other that the meeting was not useful.  Get this impression *during* the meeting so you can do something about it.

Perhaps the most critical element of any successful meeting is each member's complete and responsible participation.  Regular evaluations can attain that level of participation.

If the meeting is a long one, for example, more than 1.5 hours, then every hour or so, conduct a five-minute "satisfaction check."  Have each member visit their "internal weather vane" and report their evaluation so each person is involved (have the senior management provide their evaluation last).  Round-Robin is a useful technique to collect evaluation from each person.

See "Round-Robin (to Ensure That All Ideas Are Heard from Everyone)" on page 381 for a procedure to use the Round-Robin tool.

## Evaluating Meetings

Leave 10 minutes near the end to evaluate the quality of the meeting.  Do not skip this portion of the meeting.  All the meeting participants can quickly learn a great deal about what is working and what is not.  Here is a powerful technique for evaluating a meeting.

Have each member privately write down a rating of the overall quality of the meeting, with 1 representing "very poor" and 5 "very good."  Then, one at a time, out loud, each member:

1.      Shows other members the rating that they wrote down.

2.    Very briefly explains why they gave that rating.

3.    Says what *they personally* could have done in that meeting to have earned a rating of 5 for the meeting.

Have the senior management provide their evaluation last.

This is not a chance for members to moan and groan about others – this is an opportunity for each member to take responsibility for the overall success of the meeting.

## *Capturing Learning*

1.    Ask to hear from a few participants regarding what they have learned during the meeting.

2.    Remind them that learning is enhanced knowledge, skills and perceptions.

3.    Share your own learning, as well.

## *Closing Meetings*

1.    Review actions and assignments from the meeting.  Ensure that someone will be distributing minutes (or documentation of the actions and assignments) from the meeting.

2.    Establish the time and location for the next meeting, if necessary.  Ask group members if they can make it or not (to get their commitment).

3.    Ask who should be at the next meeting and ensure that someone is assigned to invite them.

4.    Ask for agenda items for the next meeting.

# How to Know When to Intervene

The purpose of this technique is to bring the group members back to focus and/or behaviors that are most effective for the group process if:

- The ground rules are being broken.

- The group seems stalled or stuck.

- There is prolonged conflict among members.

- Some members are not participating.

The nature of the intervention depends on the nature of the problem in the group.

1.    If the group seems stuck, it is appropriate to point this out to the entire group.

 See "How to Get Groups Unstuck" on page 392 for ideas about how to address the situation when the group seems stuck.

2.	If there is prolonged conflict between certain members, it may be more appropriate to invite the members out of the group and to conduct an intervention among those members.

> See "How to Manage Group Conflict and Come to Decisions" on page 391 for ideas to address group conflict.

3.	If a ground rule is being broken, it may be appropriate to point this out to the entire group.

There are a wide variety of intervention techniques, for example, summarizing, confronting, making suggestions, asking questions, providing other perspectives, asking for clarity, reminding the group about their ground rules, and structuring activities.

Whenever intervening in a group, try to give the group an opportunity to take responsibility for recognizing the situation and deciding what to do about it.  If an intervention is to the entire group:

1.	Briefly describe what you are seeing or hearing (in the here and now) that leads you to conclude that there is a problem.  Do not just report what you feel or sense – try to be more specific.

2.	Ask the group what they want to do.

3.	Be silent while group members react and discuss the situation.

4.	Focus the discussion on the problem at hand.

5.	Ask them for a decision.

# Organizing Information and Making Decisions

## How to Collect and Organize Useful Information in Groups

The tools in this subsection should be used with sensitivity and consideration of the nature of the participants in the group. This is true whether you are an external or internal consultant.

 See "Building Trust, Commitment and Collaboration with Clients" on page 58 for guidelines to help you work with sensitivity and consideration.

The following tools are listed in this subsection:

1. Brainstorming (to Generate Creative Ideas)

2. Round-Robin (to Ensure All Ideas Are Heard from Everyone)

3. Stories (to Convey Positive, Individualized Learning)

4. Discussion (to Permit Free-Floating Exchange of Information)

5. Parking Lot (to Defer Disposition of Information)

### *Brainstorming (to Generate Creative Ideas)*

The purpose of the brainstorming technique is to generate a broad range of new and creative ideas, for example, in a group to identify:

- Opportunities, threats, strengths and weaknesses (SWOT)

- Strategic issues

- Strategic goals

- Strategies

- Objectives

To generate the list of ideas, brainstorming uses the following steps.

1. Specify the topic to be brainstormed to the planning group (if possible, do this step as pre-work before the next meeting).

2. Ask for a free-for-all generation of ideas from among members of the group.

3. Stress that there is no bad idea. All ideas are accepted, in brainstorming.

4. List all the ideas on a flipchart, holding back any reactions and/or discussion from any members of the group until all ideas are collected. (Members might ask a quick question about an idea, but only to understand its meaning, not to make a decision about the idea.)

After all ideas have been generated:

5.      Combine the ideas into common categories. This can be done by using the discussion, voting (ranking or rating) and/or consensus techniques.

6.      Select the most preferred categories and/or ideas. This can be done by using the discussion, voting (ranking or rating) and/or consensus techniques.

## Round-Robin (to Ensure That All Ideas Are Heard from Everyone)

The purpose of the Round-Robin technique is to ensure collection of all ideas from all members of the group. Use of the technique might be a little intimidating to people who are uncomfortable speaking in groups. Therefore, if someone seems to be uncomfortable when asked for ideas, do not push them hard for ideas – you might even let them pass or skip some turns.

1.      The facilitator clarifies the topic or goal to be addressed by the group, for example, to generate ideas to resolve a specific issue in the organization.

2.      Members get quiet time before the group meeting, or early in the group meeting, to identify ideas on their own.

3.      In the meeting, the facilitator collects a list of ideas by getting one idea from one person at a time, going around the table, until each member has shared all of the ideas from their list.

4.      Members do not analyze or discuss any of the ideas until all ideas have been collected. Members can ask a question during the Round-Robin, only to get clarification on a suggested idea.

5.      The facilitator and members avoid duplication of ideas on the list.

After all ideas have been generated:

6.      Combine the ideas into common categories. This can be done by using the discussion, voting (ranking or rating) and/or consensus techniques.

7.      Select the most preferred categories and/or ideas. This can be done by using the discussion, voting (ranking or rating) and/or consensus techniques.

## Stories (to Convey Positive, Individualized Learning)

The purpose of the stories technique is to focus individuals and groups of stakeholders on positive and holistic considerations about:

- Vision

- Values

- Action plans

This technique borrows from the field of appreciative inquiry.

The facilitator explains that the focus of this technique is on the positive by building on the strengths and opportunities of the organization and its stakeholders. The facilitator clarifies the goal of the technique, for example, to establish vision, values and/or action plans.

1.      Each member quietly reflects on their best experience with the organization and its clients.

2.      In pairs, members interview each other (each interview is 10 minutes long) about their best experience, including:

   a)  What made it the best experience? What were they doing? Who was involved?

   b)  What do they value about the organization and its clients now?

   c)  What would they like to be a core value in the organization?

   d)  Three wishes for the organization and its clients.

3.      The interviewer documents the top five to eight major themes in what the other person talked about, for example, "helping other people," "feeling of fulfillment" or "working in a team." The interviewer mentions the themes to the other person to get their agreement, disagreement or modifications to the themes.

4.      Use the Round-Robin technique in the group to collect all of the themes. Also, use the brainstorming technique to expand the list of themes if the group prefers.

5.      Use the voting technique (rating) to select the top five to eight themes to include in the vision and/or reflect in the values.

6.      Use the Round-Robin technique for each person to identify their action plans to enact the vision and/or values.

## *Discussion (to Permit Free-Floating Exchange of Information)*

The purpose of the discussion technique is to ensure interaction among group members to identify, clarify, analyze and/or select an item, for example, about:

   ▪  Issues

   ▪  Recommendations

   ▪  Objectives

   ▪  Responsibilities

   ▪  Timelines

The process of the discussion technique includes the following steps.

1.      Specify the discussion topic and the goal to the planning group (if possible, do this step as pre-work before the next meeting). The goal is usually to identify, clarify, analyze and/or select an item.

2.      It is often best if the topic is described in the form of a "yes/no" question or a choice from among alternatives, for example, "Should we approve ___?" or "Should we hire ____?".

3.      Specify when the discussion is to start and stop.

4.      Allow for open, unassigned exchange of information, for example, questions, suggestions or general comments until it is time to stop the discussion. Give the group a two-minute warning when time is almost up.

5.      Facilitate to focus the discussion around the topic.

6.      Attempt to capture key points on a flipchart.

Optional:

7.      Attempt to summarize the discussion by identifying conclusions or decisions from the discussion.

8.      The group can make selections from the results using voting (ranking or rating) and/or consensus techniques.

## *Parking Lot Technique (to Defer Disposition of Information)*

The purpose of the parking-lot technique is to postpone addressing, or even ignore, a certain topic or issue that can be dealt with later because the group is dealing with more important issues for now.

1.      One or more members of the group mentions that a matter before the group is not directly related to the established topic or goal that the group wants to address.

2.      The facilitator or a group member suggests that the matter go on the "parking lot."

3.      If group members agree with the suggestion, the matter is listed on a "parking lot" – for example, a flipchart sheet posted off to the side in the meeting room.

Before the end of the meeting, members agree how the "parking lot" matters will be addressed later on, if at all.

## How to Help Groups Make Meaningful Decisions

Similar to the use of the tools in the previous subsection, use of the tools in this subsection should be used with sensitivity and consideration of the nature of the participants in the groups. This is true whether you are an external or internal consultant.

See "Building Trust, Commitment and Collaboration with Clients" on page 58 for many guidelines to help you work with sensitivity and consideration.

The following tools are listed in this subsection:

1.      Voting (to Make Selection from Among Alternatives)

2.      Consensus Process (to Ensure Collaborative Decision Making)

3.      Reference-to-Authority (to Make Prompt Decisions Based on Formal Authority)

4.      Nominal Group Technique (for Thorough Decision Making)

## *Voting (to Make a Selection from Among Alternatives)*

The purpose of the voting technique is to make a selection from various alternatives, for example:

- Select the most important or desired item from a list of items (by ranking)

- Select a range of the most important or desired items from a list of items (by rating)

There are a variety of approaches to the voting technique.

### Show of Hands

The most common approach to the technique is simply to ask for a show of hands about each item on a list, one at a time, and the item that gets the most votes in a show of hands is the item selected from the list.

### Ranking

Ranking is assigning one distinct value to each item to select the single, most important item from a list. For example, a ranked list would have one item ranked as 1, another as 2, another as 3, etc.

### Rating

Rating is associating a value with each item in order to identify ranges of items from a list. Several items can have the same value associated with them. For example, a rated list might have several items rated as high, medium or low or as 1, 2 or 3.

### Dot-Voting

A common approach to using the technique is as follows.

1.      Each member gets a certain number of dots (votes) that he or she can use to vote for items on a list. The number of dots that they get is usually equal to the number of choices that are to be made from a list. For example, if three items are to be selected, each member gets three dots.

2.      Each member walks up to the overall list of items and places their dots next to the items that the member recommends be selected from the list.

3.      After all members have cast their votes, the items that received the most votes get selected from the list.

The dot-voting technique has variations. Different colored dots can represent more than one vote, or even a negative vote. Sometimes, each participant is given one vote of each weight and required to apply each vote to a different item. In other cases, a member is allowed to cast multiple votes for one item.

# Consensus Process (to Ensure Collaborative Decision Making)

The purpose of this particular consensus technique is to make a group decision in a highly participative, egalitarian fashion, and get a result that everyone can "live with." You might:

- Select the most important or desired item from a list of items (by ranking)

- Select a range of the most important or desired items from a list of items (by rating)

Often, there is confusion around the term "consensus." Consensus means that every member of the group can live with the group's final decision. It does not mean that every member completely agrees with the decision. Consensus is often the means by which highly participative groups members reach their decisions, especially if they favor a highly egalitarian approach to decision making.

There are several approaches to the technique of reaching consensus. One quick approach to consensus is to just ask for a quick conclusion from the group by 1) suggesting a specific answer to the decision that must be made by the group and 2) asking if everyone in the group can live with that suggestion. Although that approach might save a lot of time, it certainly does not support the kind of strategic discussion and thinking so important in strategic planning. Therefore, planners might consider the following, more thoughtful approach to reaching consensus.

## Before the Meeting

Members receive information that:

1.    Clarifies the decision to be made. It is often best if the decision is written in the form of a "yes/no" question or a choice from among alternatives, for example, "Should we approve ___?" or "Should we hire ____?".

2.    Is sufficient for each member to come to some conclusion on their own.

## Ground Rules During Consensus Activities

The facilitator explains ground rules to other members of the group, for example:

1.    Members do not interrupt each other.

2.    Members can disagree with each other.

3.    Members do not engage in side discussions.

4.    Silence is considered agreement with the decision to be made.

5.    When a decision is reached by consensus, all members act as a united front to support the decision.

## Consensus Process

The facilitator guides the procedure.

1.    The facilitator specifies a deadline by which to reach consensus in the meeting.

2.    In a roundtable fashion, each member:

   a) Gets equal time to voice their preferences and their reasons regarding the question.

   b) Focuses their perspectives on what is *doable*.

   c) Does not mention other members' names.

   The most senior leader or manager in the group voices his or her opinion last.

3.    At the end of each person's time slot, all members take a quiet minute to:

   a) Collect their own thoughts in response to the last speaker's preferences.

   b) Decide what they would be willing to compromise or have in common with the last speaker.

4.    At the deadline:

   a) The facilitator poses what seems to be the most common perspective voiced by members

   b) Asks all members if they can support that perspective.

5.    If no consensus is reached, members might choose one of following options:

   a) Have a discussion, based on what was learned from the consensus activity so far. Then repeat steps two through four to see if a consensus has been achieved.

   b) Consider further research until a specified future time. Decide what additional information is needed and maybe appoint a committee to do research. The committee researches and provides recommendations, preferably in writing to each member of the group before the next meeting. At the next meeting, members hear the committee's recommendations and initiate the consensus process again.

   c) Consider using a vote to decide (via rating or ranking). Some people would assert that voting is not consensus, but it sure is handy if the consensus process has not reached a conclusion by an absolute deadline.

   See "Voting Technique" on page 384 for a description of the rating and ranking approaches to voting.

## *Reference-to-Authority (to Make Prompt Decisions Based on Formal Authority)*

The formal structures of an organization are really just strategies to help the organization achieve its overall goals – "form follows function." The structures are usually referenced by members of the organization when making important decisions about matters in the organization. The following structures are often the most important in a nonprofit and they are often considered in the following order.

1.  **Decisions of the Board of Directors**
    In the United States, nonprofit corporations are owned by the public.  However, the public counts on a small group of people to ensure that the nonprofit is operated to meet the needs of the community.  The small group of people who are legally responsible for the nonprofit is the governing Board of Directors.  Thus, important decisions about the nonprofit must include strong involvement from Board members.

2.  **Formal design of the organization**
    The design of the nonprofit greatly influences how decisions are made.  For example, if the Board decides whether to include a Chief Executive Officer position in the organization, the Chief Executive Officer can often make certain decisions because of the authority vested in the position by the Board.

3.  **Board-approved personnel policies**
    These policies should be updated regularly, preferably by experts on labor laws to ensure that the nonprofit and its employees operate in a lawful and ethical fashion.  The policies should be referenced when making decisions regarding how employees should be supervised and compensated.

4.  **Board-approved Strategic Plan**
    The plan establishes the nonprofit's mission (or purpose), what the nonprofit wants to accomplish in the future and by when and how.  Thus, the Strategic Plan is one of the most important overall directives in a nonprofit.  When facing decisions that might affect the nonprofit's overall mission, vision, goals and strategies, the decision makers should reference the current Strategic Plan.

5.  **Various subordinate, approved plans**
    Often, the Strategic Plan generates a variety of other plans that guide decisions about their respective areas of focus.  For example, decision makers should consult the Marketing Plan when making decisions about the nonprofit's markets or programs.

## Nominal Group Technique (for Thorough Decision Making)

The purpose of the nominal group technique is to collect a wide range of ideas from among members of the group, organize the ideas into categories, and make a decision about which idea, or range of ideas, is most desired.  For example, it is often used to identify, collect, organize and select:

- Issues

- Recommendations

- Objectives

- Responsibilities

- Timelines

The nominal group technique (NGT) can be a powerful and versatile technique in the strategic planning process.  There are many versions of the nominal group technique (NGT), which, in any form, is a combination of various other techniques, including all of the techniques listed in the previous table.  This guidebook suggests various different approaches to the NGT, customized to the different steps in the planning process. Each time, a specific procedure for the NGT is provided at that point in the guidebook, for ease of use, rather than describing all of the variations here.

The technique usually includes various phases, including:

1.  The facilitator clarifies the topic or goal to be addressed by the group, for example, to select the most important items from a list.

2.  Ideas are collected from members of the group.

    a) The Round-Robin technique is often used to compile an initial list of ideas.

    b) Brainstorming is used to expand the initial list of ideas.

3.  The overall list is organized and analyzed.

    a) The discussion technique is often used.

    b) The list is analyzed for overlaps, duplications, conflicts and interdependences.

4.  Ideas are selected from the overall list, using any of the following techniques.

    ■ The discussion technique can be applied, depending on the nature of the members of the group.

    ■ The consensus technique can be applied if the group highly values strong participation and egalitarian approaches to decision making.

    ■ The voting technique can be used to make a final selection.

    ■ A straw vote or an indication of priorities can be made and then discussed or reviewed in terms of relationship to major issues.

# Common Challenges in Facilitating Groups

(Thanks to The Management Assistance Program for Nonprofits in St. Paul, Minnesota, for permission to include much of the information in this section.)

## How to Get All Group Members to Participate

One of the overall goals of this guidebook is to help ensure that the strategic planning process includes the strong participation of members of the Board and staff. Much of what supports the active participation of group members lies in how the meeting is designed and managed. This is true whether you are an external or internal consultant.

### *Meeting Preparation and Opening*

1. Meet offsite. This minimizes interruptions and members' preoccupation with their day-to-day activities.

2. At the beginning of each meeting, get them involved early. For example, include introductions or do a brief "check in" from each member.

3. Have people share information about themselves. This is usually easier to talk about and initially they may be more motivated to talk about themselves than planning.

4. Have each member state what he or she wants from the meeting. Ask each member of the group to help others achieve their goals for the meeting. Post a sheet of each person's wants. Review this list at the end of the meeting.

5. If a member is absent from a meeting, the Chief Executive Officer should acknowledge who is missing and find out why.

6. Review ground rules, including the ground rule that "everyone participates."

### *During the Meeting*

The group of planners should include members of the organization who are most vested in the planning process and implementation of the plan. Consider some or all of the following:

1. Use an "inner circle, outer circle" approach where the inner circle is comprised of planners and the outer circle includes experts who provide critical information and/or review this information at various times, as invited by members of the inner circle.

2. Use break-out groups, or small groups, to increase attention and participation among members. Be sure to provide specific directions about what the groups are to accomplish and by when. Be sure to have a spokesperson for the small group.

3. If the facilitator feels the group is in a lull, he or she should say so, and then ask the group if they agree and what they can do to get out of the lull.

4. Allow time for individual thinking and taking notes.

5.      Build in physical movement periodically throughout the meeting.

6.      Bring in some jokes or cartoons and share them at different times. Be careful not to offend members who might misinterpret the humor as being insensitive.

7.      Post the mission, vision and/or values statements on the walls where the meeting is held to remind people of why they are there.

8.      Do a Round-Robin about the current topic, asking each person what he or she thinks about the current activity or topic.

9.      Specifically address the quiet people, for example, mention, "We haven't heard from you yet." However, do not push hard on people who seem reluctant to speak.

10.     For some groups, it might help to have each person bring an object and share it with the group as an initial icebreaker. This can increase personal involvement, trust and confidentiality.

11.     Ask lots of questions for the group to answer.

12.     Use a variety of aids to ensure all learning styles are considered, such as spoken, visual and kinesthetic. This is important to keep members with varying styles equally engaged.

13.     Share facilitation roles. Let someone else facilitate as you take the time to record, organize and prepare information.

### During the Meeting Closure

1.      Recognize and document results at the end of each meeting. This shows progress, promotes satisfaction and cultivates fulfillment among members of the group.

2.      Within a week after the end of the meeting, have the meeting recorder (documenter) issue meeting minutes, including major actions and assignments from the meeting.

## How to Address Resistance in Groups

Dealing with resistance is one of the most important aspects of the facilitator's role. This is true whether you are an external or internal consultant. Some forms of resistance from your client may include, for example: getting items sent to you far too late for adequate preparation in an upcoming meeting, negativism, canceled or rescheduled meetings, coming late, not doing pre-work, silence, intellectualizing, extended analysis or passive compliance. Resistance must be recognized and effectively addressed to sustain the motivation and momentum necessary for successful organizational change.

Realize that the resistance is the members' reactions to the process, not to you. Do not take it personally. Also, remember that resistance is seldom managed with sound logic and arguments.

Consider the following general process:

1.      Acknowledge the resistance, name what behaviors you believe indicate the resistance.

2.      Use language that is simple, specific and brief.

3.      Explain that resistance is often an indirect expression of some strong emotion and typically happens in a group.

4.      Ask the group members for their reaction, and listen while you remain quiet.

Also, consider some or all of the following specific suggestions.

1.      Use a Round-Robin technique to get all views out in the open.

2.      Be sensitive to ethnic/cultural differences.  These differences are likely to become apparent only after the members who are resisting begin to communicate.  Ask group members if the resistance might be based on cultural differences such as language, group norms or styles.

3.      Remind members of the difference between an "either/or" and "both/and" perspective.  Do they feel they are in a win-lose situation?

4.      Focus on what the group agrees on, for instance by posting the mission, vision and/or values statements to remind people of why they are there.

5.      If resistance persists, consider off-line conversations with the resisting planners.

## How to Manage Group Conflict and Come to Decisions

If the facilitator detects prolonged conflict within the group, consider the following guidelines.  Sometimes, the conflict is consistently between certain members.  In that case, you might consider off-line conversations (or conversations outside the planning group) with the conflicting members.  Otherwise, consider the following general process:

1.      Acknowledge to the group that they seem to be stuck in conflict.

2.      Name or describe what behaviors you are seeing that indicate that the group seems to be in conflict.

3.      Explain that conflict is a natural occurrence, especially in healthy groups, and is not to be avoided, but should be managed.

4.      Ask the group for any reactions about the current situation, and listen while you remain quiet.

These comments often help members of the group to get to the needs and assumptions behind disagreements.

Also, consider some or all of the following specific suggestions.

1.      Explore whether differences really exist, or if the problem is poor communication techniques such as cross-talking.

2.      Organize ideas, for example, use movable sticky notes – this is often the best way to quickly record, present and reorganize ideas.

3.      Propose a majority vote if the discussion or consensus techniques are not useful.

4.      Focus on what the group agrees on, for instance by posting the mission, vision and/or values statements to remind people of why they are there.

5.      Have members restate their position. If it will take longer than three minutes, allow opportunities for others to confirm or question for understanding (not disagreement).

6.      Shift to prioritizing alternatives, rather than excluding all alternatives but one.

7.      If two or three people strongly disagree, try a role reversal – if person A and B disagree, have A assume B's point of view and try to defend it, and then B assume A's point of view and try to defend it.

8.      Draw structures such as process flowcharts or wheels to fill in and portray different viewpoints.

9.      Use the Nominal Group Technique to record and discuss ideas on a flipchart.

10.     Propose an "agree to disagree" disposition.

11.     If disagreement or lack of consensus persists around an issue, have a committee breakout to select options and then report back to the larger group.

12.     With the group's permission, bring in a neutral outside speaker. Have the speaker talk about the issue dividing the group.

13.     Tell stories of successes and failures in strategic planning, including how planners got past their differences and reached agreement.

14.     Ask the group, "If this disagreement continues, where will we be?"

15.     Have one or two of the organization's clients come in and remind the group of how important their work really is.

# How to Get Groups Unstuck

Sometimes, even if there is a lot of participation from members and no prolonged conflict, a group might not seem to be making any progress on particular planning activities. They may simply be stuck. Block (2000) suggests that you know you are stuck if you find that you are explaining something for the third time. The first two times should be good faith efforts to address a situation. The third time suggests that things are stuck.

Consider the same general process as when a group seems in prolonged conflict.

1.      Acknowledge to the group that the group seems to be stuck.

2.      Name or describe what behaviors you are seeing that indicate that the group seems to be stuck.

3.     Ask the group for any reactions about the current situation, and listen while you remain quiet.

Also, consider some or all of the following specific suggestions.

1.     Take a five-minute break to let members do whatever they want.

2.     Resort to some movement and stretching.

3.     Ask for five examples of "out of the box" thinking.

4.     Resort to thinking and talking about activities in which resources do not matter.

5.     Play games that stimulate creative thinking.

6.     Use metaphors, such as stories, myths or archetypal images. For example, ask each person to take five minutes to draw or write a metaphor that describes their opinions and position in the meeting.

7.     Have a five-minute period of silence, with no suggested tasks to do in this time.

8.     Take five to 10 minutes and in groups of two, each person shares with the other what they are confused or irritated about. The other person in the pair helps the speaker to articulate his or her views to the larger group. Then, reverse the roles, so each person has the opportunity to express themselves.

9.     Have each or some of the planners tell a story and include some humor.

10.    Use visualization techniques, for example, visualize reading an article about the organization's success some years into the future. What does the article say about how the success came about?

11.    Play reflective or energizing music (depending on the situation).

12.    Restructure the group to smaller groups or move members around in the large group.

13.    Have a period of asking question after question after question (without answering necessarily). Repetition of questions, "why?" in particular, can help to move planners into deeper levels of reflection and analysis, especially if they do not have to carefully respond to each question.

14.    Establish a "parking lot" for outstanding or unresolved issues, and then move on to something else. Later, go back to the stuck issue.

15.    Turn the problem around by reframing the topic and/or issue. Usually, questions help this reframing happen.

16.    Ask key questions, for example, "How can we make it happen? How can we avoid it happening?"

17.    Remember different learning styles. For example, the group may get more clarity by using visual aids.

18. Focus on what the group agrees on, for instance by posting the mission, vision and/or values statements to remind people of why they are there.

19. Ask the group, "If we continue to be stuck, where will we be?"

20. Have one or two of the organization's clients come in and remind the group of how important their work really is.

# PART VI: TOOLBOX –

# PRACTICAL DATA

# COLLECTION

# METHODS

# Major Methods of Data Collection

This section provides descriptions of each of the most common methods (tools) for collecting information during a research effort.  Each description includes guidelines about how to customize and use that particular tool.  Near the end of the section, guidelines suggest how to select from the free tools available on the Internet.  A listing of free organizational assessment tools is included.

The selection and use of any of the methods in this section should be from an overall systematic research plan that addresses certain questions.  This is true whether you are an external or internal consultant.

See "Guidelines for Successful Evaluation and Assessment" on page 209 and "How to Design Successful Evaluation and Assessment Plans" on page 211 for guidelines to design research plans for evaluations and assessments.

## Overview of Major Methods of Data Collection

The table on the following page depicts common methods of data collection, including the primary purpose, advantages and challenges in using the method.  The table will be useful to you, especially during Phase 3: Discovery and Feedback, when deciding what methods to use to collect the data.

See "Best Methods to Collect Data" on page 276 for guidelines about how to select methods to collect data.

## How to Review Documentation

The review of documentation is often the first place that consultants start when trying to learn more about clients' organizations.  There is usually a large amount of documentation that your client can promptly provide.  The documentation often covers a wide range of information about your client's organization, and you can review the documentation without requiring time from your busy client.

Of course, what you look for and what you conclude depend on the purposes and the questions to be addressed by the research.  It helps not only to look at the content of the documentation, but its style.  Table VI:2 lists some of the more common types of documentation reviewed by consultants and what they often look for in that documentation.

### *Reviewing the Content of Documentation*

Some standard questions when reviewing documentation include:

- Currency – how up-to-date is the documentation?

- Scope – does the documentation include typical contents of that particular type of document?

- Depth – how in-depth is the content of the document?

- Authorship – who has developed the various documents?

## Table VI:1 – Overview of Major Methods of Data Collection

| Method | Overall Purpose | Advantages | Challenges |
|---|---|---|---|
| Documentation review | To quickly learn about a process (project, program, etc.) without interrupting it; can include marketing materials, program evaluations, policies, procedures or meeting minutes | -get comprehensive and historical information<br>-does not interrupt programs, etc.<br>-information already exists<br>-few biases about information | - often takes much time<br>- information may be incomplete or out of date<br>- need to be quite clear about what looking for<br>- is not a flexible means to get data<br>- data restricted to what already exists |
| Observation of people and activities. | To gather accurate information about how a process actually occurs | - view operations of a process as they are actually occurring<br>- can adapt to events as they occur | - can be difficult to interpret behaviors<br>- can be complex to categorize observations<br>- can influence behavior of those being observed<br>- can be expensive<br>- can be influenced by observer bias |
| Questionnaires, surveys, checklists | To quickly and/or easily get lots of information from people in a non-threatening way | - anonymity<br>- inexpensive to administer<br>- easy to compare and analyze<br>- administer to many people<br>- can get lots of data<br>- sample tools often already exist | - might not get careful feedback<br>- wording can bias client's responses<br>- are impersonal<br>- in surveys, may need sampling expert<br>- does not get the full story |
| Interviews | To fully understand someone's impressions or experiences, or learn more about their answers to questionnaires | - get full range and depth of information<br>- develops relationship with client<br>- can be flexible with client | - can take much time<br>- can be hard to analyze and compare<br>- can be costly<br>- interviewer can bias client's responses |
| Focus groups | To explore a topic in depth through group discussion | - quickly and reliably get common impressions<br>- can be an efficient way to get range and depth of information in a short time<br>- convey key information about programs | - can be hard to analyze responses<br>- need a good facilitator<br>- can be difficult to schedule six to eight people<br>- individuals might influence others' opinions |
| Case studies | To fully understand or depict peoples' experiences; conduct examination through cross comparison of cases | - fully depict peoples' experiences<br>- powerful means to portray process to others | - usually quite time consuming<br>- represents depth of information, rather than breadth |

## Table VI:2 – Types of Documentation and What to Look For

| Item | Typical Contents | Notice for now (in addition to currency, scope, depth and authorship) |
|---|---|---|
| Strategic Plan | Mission, vision, values, external and internal analyses, goals, strategies, objectives, action plans, budget | • What terms did they use?<br>• How did they do planning?<br>• Do goals and actions result from analyses?<br>• How much of their Plan has been implemented? |
| Board organization chart | Board positions, committees and reporting relationships | • What positions and committees exist?<br>• Do the types of committees support current priorities in the organization? |
| Board policies and procedures | Bylaws, staffing, making decisions, attendance and conflict-of-interest | • Are the guidelines suitable for recruiting, selecting, orienting, training, organizing?<br>• Are members following those procedures? |
| Board meeting minutes | Frequency of meetings, attendance, topics and decisions | • What are the rates of attendance and participation?<br>• Are discussion topics strategic?<br>• Are members using their procedures? |
| Staff organization chart | Positions and titles, reporting relationships, and names of staff | • What is the number of staff?<br>• Who reports to whom?<br>• What programs do they have? |
| Financial information | Budgets, Statement of Financial Activities, Statement of Financial Position, cash flows and audit reports | • What reports do they use?<br>• What is the frequency of reports?<br>• What are the expenses?<br>• What are the sources of income?<br>• What are the sources of donations?<br>• Do they have sufficient cash now? |
| Annual report | History of organization, major accomplishments, future plans | • Are there any highlights from their history?<br>• What major accomplishments occurred over the past years?<br>• What are the major priorities for next year?<br>• What programs do they have? |
| Advertising literature | Program features and benefits | • Are there clear descriptions of who is served?<br>• Are there clear descriptions of program benefits?<br>• Do the benefits match the needs of clients? |
| Public relations materials | Identity and image of organization | • What is the overall image of the organization?<br>• What strengths do they convey? |
| Program evaluations | Program outcomes, strengths and weaknesses | • What do they evaluate? Processes? Goals? Outcomes? Other?<br>• Do evaluations seem to be effective? |

## *Reviewing the Style of the Documentation*

From the materials, get a sense of the culture of the organization.

1.  If there is a full range of these types of documents, you can probably assume that the organization highly values careful documentation when making important decisions, and will likely prefer the same during their projects for change.

2.  If these documents appear to be comprehensive and include a great deal of graphs, figures and numbers, you can probably assume the organization highly values careful research, analysis and conclusions, and will prefer the same during projects for change.

3.  Do they show strong considerations and documentation about, for example, sound fiscal management, expanding services, effectiveness of services and efficiency of services? They will probably show the same traits during projects for change.

# How to Conduct Observations

Observation can be one of the most useful forms of data collection. Observers use their five major senses (sight, hearing, touch, taste and smell) to collect information about environments, activities and interactions (spoken or otherwise). Observers can identify the information and interpret it using diagnostic models, and according to their own nature and needs. They can also adapt their observation as the program processes change. In some cases, they can actually experience the activities. However, observers can also influence the behavior of the research subjects, which can unduly influence the research results. Observation can also be quite costly because it takes up so much of the observer's time, both during the observations and later on when organizing, analyzing and interpreting the information.

Note that, to be good at observation during research, you need training and practice to notice and accurately record what you need to notice. As with any other research methods, you need to notice information that addresses the research questions. The following information includes the 20% of guidelines that generates 80% of useful observations. The remaining 20% of useful observations comes during the rest of the project.

## *Preparation*

1.  **Have clear and established research questions to guide the research.**
    Research questions are the questions that you are trying to answer by conducting the research. Usually, the clearer the research questions, the more focus you will have during the research. Remember that everything that occurs in the research environment (in which you will be observing) is data. You want to collect the data most relevant to the research questions.

2.  **Clarify whether you will be an "outside" observer or an observer-participant.**
    It might be easier for you to retain objectivity if you are an outside observer. You are not taking part in the activities under observation. However, as an observer-participant, where you participate in the activities along with the research subjects, you can also experience the program first-hand. In that case, it will be more of a challenge for you to focus on objectivity during data collection.

3.  **It is ideal to have more than one observer**.
    Then data collection includes more than one perspective and one set of tools. However, it is usually rare that an organization can afford two observers.

4.  **Use tools to help you record what you are noticing from your five senses.**
    This can speed up the data collection and also remind you of what to notice. For example, use a checklist of possible behaviors that you might see and when you see that behavior during your observations, note them on the checklist. You could also use audio and/or video recorders.

5.  **Test audio and/or video recorders.**
    Before you use this equipment in your research environment, test them to be sure that they function properly.

6.  **Think about categories of information that you will collect.**
    For example, if the research question is "How can we improve the program?", you will want to collect information about, for example, program activities and processes, what people complain about and ideas to improve the program. Some broad general categories that you might consider are about the research subjects' environment, how they come into the environment, what resources they use, what activities they undertake alone, what activities they undertake with each other, how the subjects leave the environment and actual results for subjects.

7.  **Practice use of data collection tools**.
    Before you actually go into the research environment, make sure you are familiar with them.

8.  **Be rested.**
    It can be tiring to conduct observations. You need energy to concentrate.

9.  **Do not plan for extended observation activities.**
    For example, you might limit observations to an hour followed by a rest period.

10. **Always get written permission from research subjects.**
    They deserve to know that they are taking part in a research effort and how you plan to use the information you collect from them.

11. **Fully disclose your research to participants.**
    Include the purpose of the research and the activities that you will be doing. Acquaint yourself to the research participants and them to you, as well. Explain what you will do with the research results and, especially, how the research will benefit the participants. Provide time for them to ask you questions.

12. **Allocate "clean up" time immediately after the observation.**
    You will use this time to collect your notes and write down information that you remembered, but did not record during the observations. Allocate the same amount of time for clean up that you used for your observations. For example, if you observed for an hour, then allocate an hour for clean up.

## *Conducting Observations*

1.    **Be sure that you are located in a place where you can see and hear what you want to observe.**

2.    **Set up data collection tools.**

3.    **Remember that you are the "eyes and ears" for the research effort.**
     You will want to be as thorough as possible in noticing important information and recording it thoroughly.

4.    **Remind the research subjects of why you are in the room.**
     Hopefully, you have talked to them beforehand and had each of them sign an information release form.

5.    **Begin collecting information.**
     Use all five senses. Do not rely on your memory. Write it down or capture it on the data collection tool, such as a recorder.

6.    **Take note of anything that will help you organize information captured by tools.**
     For example, write down notes about when the recorders were started or stopped.

7.    **Describe the environment.**
     Include, for example, the physical space and any major tools and equipment.

8.    **Describe the people.**
     Include their roles, relationships to each other and how they intend to interact with each other.

9.    **Describe the activities.**
     Include what people do alone and with each other.

10.    **Note what happened and what did not happen.**

11.    **Include quotations to mark any statements made by research subjects.**

## Reviewing Documentation to Learn More About the Culture in Your Client's Organization

A great deal can be learned by observing behaviors during conversations and meetings. You might ask to spend some time in the organization so you can get to know it better. This kind of observation should be done only after someone in the organization has introduced you to others, along with explaining why you are consulting to the organization. If you get an opportunity to observe people, notice their overall style. Remember that they will likely participate in a consultation in the same way.

When observing people in the organization, notice:

1.    Is there a high degree of participation among members?

2.    Are ideas encouraged and clarified?

3.  Is there closure about ideas, for example, are people taking notes to ensure completion of tasks?

4.  Do individuals support each other's comments? For example, are they highly team-oriented ("Let's work together"), individualistic ("It's your problem"), task-oriented ("Get things done!"), process-oriented ("Let's do it the right way") or crisis-oriented ("We've got to do something now!")?

## *Immediately After the Observations*

Overall, ensure that data is organized and coherent such that someone else could use it to get a clear impression of what the research subjects did.

1.  **Clean up your notes.**
    For example, clarify any miscellaneous notations, ensure pages are numbered and fill out any notes that do not make sense.

2.  **Note any special circumstances**.
    For example, note if you felt tired so your observations might not have been complete or accurate.

3.  **Describe any personal reflections on the experience.**
    For example, describe whether the subjects were active or seemed inhibited by your being there. Consistently ask yourself, "What did I see or hear that led me to the results of my reflections?"

# How to Design and Administer Questionnaires

## *Preparation*

Before you start to design your questions, clearly articulate what problem or need is to be addressed. Review why you are doing the evaluation and what you hope to accomplish by it. This provides focus on what information you need and, ultimately, on what questions should be in the questionnaire.

The following guidelines are relevant, whether you are conducting research by using questionnaires on hardcopy paper or via the Internet.

## *Directions to Respondents*

1.  **Include a brief explanation of the purpose of the questionnaire**.

2.  **Include a clear explanation of how to finish the questionnaire**.

3.  **Include directions about where to send or turn in the completed questionnaire**.

4.  **Note conditions of confidentiality.**
    Indicate who will have access to the information for evaluation purposes and whether you plan to restrict other access to responses. (Note that you should not guarantee confidentiality about their answers. If a court sued you to see answers, you would not likely be able to stop

access to this information. However, you can assure that you will make every reasonable attempt to protect access to the answers.)

## Content of Questions

1.  **Ask about what you need to know**.
    Get information about the goals or ultimate questions you want to address.

2.  **Ask questions that the respondent should be able to answer.**
    Make sure that the respondents can reasonably be expected to know the answers.

3.  **Ask questions that the respondents want to answer.**
    If the questions are too private or silly, the respondents may lose interest in the questionnaire or lose faith in the process.

## Wording of Questions

1.  **Will the respondent understand the wording?**
    For example, are you using any slang, culturally-specific or technical words?

2.  **Are any words so strong that they might lead a respondent to a certain answer?**
    Attempt to avoid use of strong adjectives in the questions, such as "highly effective government" or "prompt and reliable."

3.  **Ensure you are asking one question at a time.**
    Try to avoid the use of the word "and" in your questions.

4.  **Avoid using "not" in your questions if you are asking yes/no questions.**
    Use of "not" can lead to double negatives and cause confusion.

5.  **If you use multiple-choice questions, be sure your choices are mutually exclusive and encompass the total range of answers.**
    Respondents should not be confused about whether two or more alternatives appear to mean the same thing. Respondents also should not have a clearly preferred answer not listed among the choices of an answer to the question.

## Order of Questions

1.  **Be careful not to include so many questions that potential respondents are dissuaded from responding**.

2.  **Engage respondents early in the questionnaire to increase their motivation to finish it.**
    Start with fact-based questions and then go on to opinion-based questions. For example, ask people for demographic information about themselves and then go to questions about their opinions and perspectives. This gets respondents engaged in the questionnaire and relaxed, before encountering more challenging and reflective questions about their opinions. (Consider whether they can finish the questionnaire anonymously; if so, indicate this on the form where you ask for their name.)

3.  **Attempt to get respondents' commentary in addition to their ratings**.
    For example, if the questionnaire asks respondents to choose an answer by circling an

answer or provide a rating, ask them to provide commentary that explains their choices. Provide sufficient space and time for them to write the commentary.

4. **Include a question to get respondents' impressions of the questionnaire itself**.
Ask them if the questionnaire was straightforward to finish ("yes" or "no"), and if not, to provide suggestions about how to improve the questionnaire.

5. **Pilot your questionnaire on a small group of clients or fellow staff**.
Ask them if the form and questions seemed straightforward. Carefully review the answers on the questionnaires. Does the information answer the evaluation questions or provide what you want to know about the program or its specific services? What else would you like to know?

6. **Finish the questionnaire.**
Finish the questionnaire according to the results of the pilot. Put a date on the form so you can keep track of all future versions.

# How to Design and Conduct Interviews

Interviews are particularly useful for getting the story behind a participant's experiences. The interviewer can pursue in-depth information around a topic. Interviews may be useful as follow-up with certain respondents to questionnaires, to further investigate their responses.

Before you design your interviews, clearly articulate to yourself what problem or need is to be addressed by doing the interviews. This helps you keep a clear focus on the intent of each question.

Much of the information herein was adapted from Patton (1990).

## *Preparation*

1. **Choose a setting with little distraction.**
Avoid extraordinarily bright lights or noisy environments. Ensure the interviewee is comfortable (you might ask them if they are). Often, they may feel more comfortable at their own place of work or home. Keep in mind that it may be more difficult to control interruptions there.

2. **Explain the purpose of the interview.**

3. **Address terms of confidentiality.**
Note any terms of confidentiality. (Be careful here. Rarely can you absolutely promise complete confidentiality. Courts may get access to information, in certain circumstances.) Explain who will have access to their answers and how their answers will be analyzed. If their comments are to be used as quotes, get their written permission to do so.

4. **Explain the format of the interview.**
Explain the type of interview you are conducting and its nature. If you want the interviewee to ask questions, specify whether they should ask questions now, as they arise or wait until the end of the interview.

5. **Indicate how long the interview usually takes.**

6.     **Tell them how to get in touch with you later if they want to.**

7.     **Ask them if they have any questions before you get started with the interview.**

8.     **Do not count on your memory to recall their answers.**
Ask for permission to record the interview or bring along someone to take notes.

## *Types of Interviews*

1.     **Informal, conversational interview**
No predetermined questions are asked in order for the interviewer to remain as open and adaptable as possible to the interviewee's nature and priorities. During the interview, the interviewer "goes with the flow."

2.     **Interview guide approach**
The interview guide approach is intended to ensure that the same general areas of information are collected from each interviewee. This provides more focus than the conversational approach, but still allows a degree of freedom and adaptability in getting information from the interviewee.

3.     **Standardized, open-ended interview**
The same open-ended questions are asked to all interviewees (an open-ended question is where respondents are free to choose how to answer the question – they do not select "yes" or "no" or provide a numeric rating.). This approach facilitates faster interviews that can be more easily analyzed and compared.

4.     **Closed, fixed-response interview**
All interviewees are asked the same questions and asked to choose answers from among the same set of alternatives. This format is useful for those who are not practiced in interviewing. This approach facilitates the fastest interviews that can also be easily analyzed, but sometimes restricts the range of information from the respondent.

## *Types of Topics in Questions*

Patton notes six kinds of questions. A person can ask questions about:

1.     **Behaviors**
Regarding what a person has done or is doing.

2.     **Opinions/values**
Regarding what a person thinks about a topic.

3.     **Feelings**
Regarding what a person feels about something. Note that respondents sometimes respond with "I think ..." so be careful to note that you are looking for feelings.

4.     **Knowledge**
Regarding what a person knows about a topic.

5.     **Sensory information**
Regarding what a person has seen, touched, heard, tasted or smelled.

6.     **Background/demographics**
       Standard background questions, such as age or education.

Note that the above questions can be asked in terms of past, present or future.

## Sequence of Questions

1.     **Get the respondents involved in the interview as soon as possible.**

2.     **First ask for some facts.**
       With this approach, respondents can more easily engage in the interview while warming up to more personal matters.

3.     **Intersperse fact-based questions throughout the interview.**
       This approach avoids a long list of fact-based questions, which tends to disengage respondents.

4.     **Ask questions about the present before questions about the past or future.**
       It is usually easier for them to talk about the present and then work into the past or future.

5.     **The last questions should allow respondents to provide any other information.**
       This period can be enlightening when respondents realize they have other information to share that you have not yet asked about.

## Wording of Questions

1.     **Wording should be open-ended.**
       Respondents should be able to choose their own terms when answering questions.

2.     **Questions should be as neutral as possible.**
       Avoid wording that might influence answers, for example, evocative or judgmental words.

3.     **Questions should be asked one at a time.**

4.     **Questions should be worded clearly.**
       This includes knowing any terms particular to the program or the respondents' culture.

5.     **Be careful about asking "why" questions.**
       This type of question infers a cause-effect relationship that may not truly exist. These questions may also cause respondents to feel defensive, that they have to justify their response, which may inhibit their response to this and future questions.

## Conducting Interviews

1.     **Occasionally verify that the tape recorder (if used) is working.**

2.     **Ask one question at a time.**

3.     **Attempt to remain as neutral as possible.**
       Do not show strong emotional reactions to their responses. Patton suggests acting as if "you have heard it all before."

4.      **Encourage responses with intermittent nods of the head or occasional uh-huh's.**

5.      **Be careful about your appearance when note taking.**
   If you jump to take a note, it may appear as if you are surprised or pleased about an answer, which may influence answers to future questions.

6.      **Provide transition between major topics.**
   For example, "we have been talking about (some topic) and now I would like to move on to (another topic)."

7.      **Do not lose control of the interview.**
   This can occur when respondents stray to another topic, take so long to answer a question that times begins to run out, or even begin asking questions of the interviewer.

## *Immediately After Interviews*

1.      **Verify that the tape recorder, if used, worked throughout the interview**.

2.      **Make any notes on your written notes.**
   For example, to clarify any miscellaneous notations, ensure pages are numbered, or fill out any notes that do not make senses.

3.      **Write down any observations made during the interview.**
   For example, where did the interview occur and when? Was the respondent particularly nervous at any time? Were there any surprises during the interview? Did the tape recorder break?

# How to Conduct Focus Groups

## *Benefits of Focus Groups*

Focus groups are interviews, but of six to 10 people in a group. A person can get a great deal of information during a focus group session. Focus groups are a powerful means to understand peoples' perceptions and beliefs about issues, ideas and strategies. For example, during a consulting project, you might use a focus group to understand what the members of your client's organization believe about:

- What issues exist in the workplace.

- Causes of those issues.

- Goals to achieve in the organization.

- What should be done to address the issues or goals.

Focus groups can also be a powerful approach to help members of your client's organization feel strong participation and ownership in the project. Group members feel honored and respected by you and the top leaders in the organization because members' opinions are being listened to and respected.

## *Useful Tools and Techniques*

1. **Meeting design, management and interventions**
   The focus group requires careful attention to ensure its success. There should be clear goals for the meeting. Attendance should be selected carefully. The agenda should reflect the goals of the meeting, along with the timing to solicit the group's feedback to various questions during the meeting.

    See "Meeting Design, Management and Interventions" on page 375 for guidelines to clarify the meeting's goals and agenda.

2. **Selecting and posing useful questions**
   You should come to the focus group with five to six key questions that you will pose to them. The questions should be chosen carefully such that their answers will inform you and your client about how your project can proceed successfully. Questions should be posed in proper sequence, and clearly and concisely to ensure accurate answers from group members.

    See "How to Design and Administer Questionnaires" on page 403 for guidelines for designing questionnaires, including their use with focus groups.

3. **Conducting interviews**
   A focus group is basically a group interview, so skills in interview techniques will be useful to you. Group members will need to understand if the focus group is informal or formal in nature. You will need to guide the group to maintain focus on answering the questions. Concurrently, you will need to capture the main points of group members' answers.

    See "How to Design and Conduct Interviews" on page 405 for guidelines for conducting interviews, including in focus groups.

## *Preparing for a Session*

While a focus group can be a powerful means to learn from the members of your client's organization, it also can be a challenge to help the participants in the group to be as authentic as possible in the group session. Participants might feel inhibited from speaking the truth if they believe that their supervisors will somehow judge or evaluate the participants on what they say. Participants might feel inhibited from talking about various issues or the causes of those issues if they believe that others in the room are to blame for those issues.

Although there may be certain inhibitions in the focus group, the group still can be quite useful. Consider the following guidelines to make your focus group as useful as possible to your project and members of your client's organization.

1. **Work with your client to assess whether focus groups are compatible to the culture.**
   For example, in some cultures, it is disrespectful to pose questions to other people. In those situations, a focus group might actually be hurtful to members of the organization. In some cultures, there is strong deference to authority – even a strong fear of authority. In those

situations, participants in a focus group would be strongly inhibited from disagreeing with authority in the group.

 See "How to Work in Multicultural Environments" on page 58 for guidelines to help you identify whether questioning would work in the culture of your client's organization.

2. **Communicate the goals of the focus group and how it benefits participants.**
First, explain how the consulting project will benefit the organization. Then explain how the focus group will contribute to the project. Will it help to clarify issues or provide means to address issues?

3. **The focus group needs visible support from top management.**
Top management should announce the focus group to the intended participants, along with why management supports the group and how management will participate. Encourage openness among participants.

4. **If top management participates, have them show authentic behavior early on.**
The facilitator of the focus group might pose the first question to the Chief Executive Officer or other member of management, as an opportunity for that person to show significant candor or openness to other members.

The remainder of the guidelines in this subsection about focus groups will be useful to you, as well.

## Designing the Session

1. **Identify the major objective of the session.**
Is it, for example, to clarify issues, suggest goals or clarify strategies?

2. **Carefully develop five to six questions.**

   - The meeting should last one to two hours. In this time, you can usually ask at most five to six questions.

   - Focus groups are basically multiple interviews – use interview techniques. Many of the same guidelines for conducting focus groups are appropriate to conducting interviews.

3. **Plan your session.**

   - **Scheduling**
   Sessions are usually one to two hours long. Schedule sessions at a time when there are no other important or urgent activities that might interrupt the session.

   - **Setting and refreshments**
   Hold sessions in a conference room or other setting with adequate airflow and lighting. Configure chairs so all participants can see each other. Provide refreshments, even boxed lunches if the session is held over lunch.

   - **Ground rules**
   It is critical that all group members participate as much as possible. It is also important to move along while generating useful information. Because the session is often a one-

time occurrence, it is useful to have a few, short ground rules that sustain participation, yet help the group stay focused. Consider the following three ground rules: a) all opinions are honored, b) keep focused and c) maintain momentum.

- **Agenda**
  Consider the following agenda: welcome, review of agenda, review goals of the session, review ground rules, introductions, questions and answers, wrap up.

- **Membership**
  Focus groups are usually conducted with six to 10 members who have some similar nature, for example, similar age group, status in a program or interest in a project.

- **Plan to record the session**
  The facilitator should tell participants that notes will be taken to provide accurate feedback to the client. Then the facilitator should ask participants whether he or she can take notes. Ideally, someone other than the facilitator is available to take notes, leaving the facilitator to engage with participants.

4. **Work with an executive or top leader to invite participants to the session.**
   Send them a follow-up invitation with a proposed agenda, session time and list of questions the group will discuss. Plan to provide a copy of the final report from the session to participants and let them know that they will get the report.

5. **About three days before the session, call each participant to remind him or her.**
   This is a good opportunity to ask if the participant has any questions or concerns.

## *Facilitating the Session*

If you are the facilitator, the following guidelines will be helpful to you.

1. **Your goal is collecting useful information to meet the overall goal of session.**

2. **Introduce yourself and the co-facilitator, if there is one.**

3. **Explain the means you will use to record the session.**

4. **Carry out the agenda.**

5. **Carefully ask each question before that question is addressed by the group.**

6. **After each question is answered, carefully reflect back the group's answer.**

7. **Ensure even participation.**

8. **Adjourn the session – inform participants of results from the session.**

## *Immediately After the Session*

1. **Clean up your notes.**
   For example, clarify any scratching, ensure pages are numbered, and fill out any notes that do not make sense.

2.  **Write down any observations made during the session.**
    For example, where did the session occur and when? What was the nature of participation in the group? Were there any surprises during the session? Did the tape recorder break?

# How to Select from Among Public Data Collection Tools

## *Considerations When Selecting*

There is an increasing amount of freely available tools that you can use to collect data during a project. Several tools are mentioned at the end of this subsection. However, before you begin reviewing those tools, be sure that you are aware of the major types of tools, the advantages and disadvantages of using each, and general guidelines for applying each type of tool.

 See "Overview of Major Methods of Data Collection" on page 397 to be aware of the major types of tools and impacts of using each of them.

In addition to the considerations mentioned in the above-referenced subsection, there are several additional considerations that must be addressed when selecting a publicly available tool.

1.  **Focus**
    Does the tool focus on Boards, strategic planning, programs, Chief Executive Officer, staff, marketing, finances, fundraising or evaluations?

2.  **Purpose of the tool**
    For example, to detect strengths and weaknesses, or to compare to certain "best practices?"

     See "Maximum Performance – Different Things to Different People" on page 179 for information about best practices.

3.  **Values and assumptions**
    For example, does the tool assume a specific Board structure or top-down leadership?

4.  **Languages**
    English? Other(s)?

5.  **Audiences for the tool**
    To whom will the tool be applied?

6.  **Administrator of the tool**
    Who will guide the application of the tool? An outside person? Self-assessment? Will the data collection be participatory?

7.  **User guide**
    Are there adequate descriptions of procedures for how to use the tool and analyze the results?

8.  **Duration and frequency**
    How long will it take to use the tool? Is the tool to be applied at certain times? More than once?

9.      **Cost**
        What are any costs to obtain the tool? Use the tool?

10.     **Availability**
        How soon can the tool be made available?

11.     **Technical support for the tool**
        If you have questions or need guidance, can anyone help you?

12.     **Modification**
        You might need permission if you seek to modify the tool.

## *Available, Free Organizational Assessment Tools*

There are many freely available tools (especially on the Internet) that are appropriate for use in a nonprofit organization. The following list includes free, on-line tools, each of which assesses numerous aspects of a nonprofit organization. However, before selecting an already designed tool, be sure that you have addressed the considerations listed immediately above. Keep in mind that these types of tools include some inherent bias. To the author's knowledge, none of these tools has been tested for reliability or validity.

### United Way Management Indicators (includes best practices)

This is a well designed, comprehensive, behaviors-based tool that also includes a suggested "best-practices" standard, as well. This tool is in Appendix C.

### McKinsey Capacity Assessment Grid

This is a comprehensive grid that suggests seven elements of organizational effectiveness, each with descriptions of four possible levels of performance for each element. Go to http://www.emcf.org/publications/emcf-reading-room/tools-and-guides/assessing-your-organizational-capacity/

### Minnesota Council of Nonprofits "Principles and Practices"

This is a widely recognized, comprehensive, principles-based assessment tool that suggests principles for effectiveness in many of the major functions in nonprofits. Go to http://www.mncn.org/info_principles.htm

### Maryland Association of Nonprofit Organizations "Standards of Excellence"

This is a widely recognized, principles-based assessment tool that suggests principles for effectiveness in many of the major functions in nonprofits. Go to http://www.marylandnonprofits.org/html/standards/04_02.asp

## Understanding Organizational Success: Self-Assessment Tool for Nonprofit Organizations

This is a comprehensive, well-designed tool that nonprofits can use to assess their organizations. Directions to apply and analyze the tool are included. Go to http://smifoundation.org/NPAssessmentTool.pdf

## Self-Assessment Tool for United Way Agencies

This is a medium-sized, straightforward assessment tool regarding major functions in nonprofits. Go to http://www.uwac.org/uwac/repositories/Download/oat_uw.pdf

# PART VII:  TOOLBOX –

# ANALYZING AND

# CHANGING SYSTEMS

# Analyzing Systems

Guidelines in this section will help you to carefully examine and understand the dynamics of the various systems in your client's organization, including the overall system of their organization and any major problems that exist within that organization. This is true whether you are an external or internal consultant.

See "Changing Systems" on page 434 for guidelines to help you change those systems.

## What is Systems Thinking?

One of the major breakthroughs in understanding the complex world of organizations is the field of systems theory. The field studies systems from the perspective of the whole system, its various subsystems and the recurring patterns in the relationships between the subsystems. Systems theory has greatly influenced how we understand and change organizations.

The application of this theory is called systems analysis. One of the major tools of systems analysis is systems thinking. Basically, systems thinking is a way of helping a person to view systems from a broad perspective that includes seeing overall structures, patterns and cycles in systems, rather than seeing only specific events in the system. This broad view can help you to quickly identify the real causes of issues in organizations and know just where to work to address them. Systems thinking has produced a variety of principles and tools for analyzing and changing systems.

See "Benefits of Open Systems View of Nonprofits" on page 152 to understand the many benefits of having a systems view.

By focusing on the entire system, consultants can attempt to identify solutions that address as many problems as possible in the system. The positive effect of those solutions leverages improvement throughout the system. Thus, they are called "leverage points" in the system. This priority on the entire system and its leverage points is called whole systems thinking.

Remember information about the open systems model? That model puts priority on recognizing the interaction between a system and its external environment. The model, in conjunction with whole systems thinking, is a powerful means to analyzing and changing systems.

Systems theory has evolved to another level called chaos theory. In this context, chaos does not mean total confusion. Chaos refers to the dynamics of a system that apparently has no, or little, order, but in which there really is an underlying order. In these systems, small changes can cause complex changes in the overall system. (In technical terms, chaos theory applies to complex non-linear dynamics systems.) Chaos theory has introduced new perspectives and tools to study complex systems, such as biological, human, groups, weather, population growth and the solar system.

See the resources in "Systems Thinking, Chaos Theory and Tools" on page 507 in Appendix D to learn more about systems thinking, chaos and tools.

Note that systems theory and systems thinking are not the same as being systematic. In the context of a consulting project, systematic is about setting goals, collecting and analyzing feedback about status of achievement of goals, and then adjusting activities to achieve the goals more effectively.

The tools and principles in this section of the Field Guide were selected because they are easy-to-understand and quick-to-apply when working with nonprofit organizations.

# How to Analyze Mental Models – How People Think

All of us have certain "filters" through which we view and analyze the world around us. The filters are formed from our long-standing belief systems, biases and patterns of thinking. Systems thinkers assert that these filters form "mental models." Two different people who have different mental models might look at the same information about an organization and come to completely different conclusions about the organization.

Many times, problems are caused by our perspectives (or mental models) and how we make conclusions based on those perspectives. Problems often can be solved by helping your client to reframe them – by taking apart the client's perspectives and helping the client to see things differently. Reframing problems can produce powerful forms of learning, especially double-loop and triple-loop learning. Techniques in this subsection will help you to understand your mental models, as well as the models of those in your client's organization.

See "Different Kinds of Learning (Loops of Learning)" on page 216 for information about double-loop and triple-loop learning.

Similar to the use of other tools that involve interaction with others, you should be sensitive as to how you can build trust, commitment and collaboration with others using the tools with you.

See "Building Trust, Commitment and Collaboration with Clients" on page 58 to review guidelines to ensure that you work with sensitivity when using the following tools.

Tools listed in this subsection include:

1.      Left-Hand Column (to Examine "Hidden" Information in Communication)

2.      Ladder of Inference (to Analyze Dynamics of Conclusions and Actions)

3.      Coaching (for Inquiry, Reflection, Actions and Learnings)

4.      Reframing Problems (to Peel Away "Layers" in Problems)

## *Left-Hand Column (Examines "Hidden" Information in Communication)*

Argyris and Schon (1974) suggested use of this tool to reveal certain assumptions that underlie conflicts that we experience, particularly during conversations with others. You can use the tool to describe what actually occurred in a conflicted conversation or what typically occurs in a conversation with a certain person.

| What was actually said | Your actual thoughts and feelings then |
|---|---|
| *Client: I would like you, as a consultant, to do some fundraising for me. I've hired two other consultants before you and neither of them knew what they were doing.* | Probably because there is no strong case for fundraising in your organization. |
| *You: Sure, I've done fundraising for years. I'd be glad to help you!* | Now I'm stuck with another project where I'm doing all the work, even writing their Strategic Plan so they qualify for fundraising! |
| *Client: I'll need you to write the grants and whatever else is needed. Just get us the funds.* | Why can't I just speak up and tell her the truth! |

The value of the left-hand column exercise is in analyzing your responses. Were they authentic? If not, why not? What were your assumptions about the other person that led to how you responded? You might use the next tool, the ladder of inference, to guide your analysis of your left-hand column information.

## Ladder of Inference (Analyzes Dynamics of Conclusions and Actions)

Argyris (1990) suggested that there is a chain, or ladder, of inferences that we make when we decide to take some action or when we form an opinion. The ladder can be used to examine how certain conclusions and actions were decided. The ladder can be useful to help us understand our thinking and the thinking of other people. Inquiry, or thoughtful questioning, is a powerful means to conduct this examination. In the following example, a sample of a useful question is associated with each step of the ladder. Note that, in most cases, the ladder is used to work backwards from a conclusion or action to understanding the process that derived that conclusion or action in the first place.

**Step 1. I observe "data" from experiences (much as a videotape might capture data).**
What information did we see? Did we consider all of the information?

**Step 2. I select "data" from what I observe (our beliefs affect what data we select).**
What information did I decide was most important from what I saw? Why?

**Step 3. I add meanings (cultural and personal).**
How did I decide what information to notice and what to ignore?

**Step 4. I make assumptions based on the meanings I added.**
What assumptions are behind the decision to notice certain information?

**Step 5. I draw conclusion(s).**
How did I form the conclusions from the information that I noticed?

**Step 6. I adopt beliefs about the world.**
What do the various conclusions mean?

**Step 7. I take actions based on my beliefs.**
How did the conclusions and meaning lead to the actions that I chose?

## *Coaching (for Inquiry, Reflection, Actions and Learning)*

Coaching is a powerful technique to work with a person, usually one-on-one, to guide and support them to reframe their problems or goals to gain more complete understanding, and then to generate personalized action planning and learning. The technique is so important in consulting that it is included in PART I as a required skill.

 See "How to Coach for Deep Problem-Solving and Learning" on page 68 for guidelines to successfully coach your clients.

## *Reframing Problems (Peels Away "Layers" in Problems)*

Quite often, finding the right problem is more important than finding the right answer. For example, it is common that new supervisors report problems with time and stress management. However, after some effective coaching and mentoring, they often realize that the reason they have time and stress problems is because they have far too much to do. They soon realize that they have too much to do because they do not know how to delegate effectively to their direct reports (to the people who report to the supervisors). They may even realize that the reason they cannot delegate effectively is because they have had little or no training in delegation. Had these supervisors taken courses in time and stress management, the courses might have created even more work for the supervisors to do, rather than addressing the root cause of the problem: they did not know how to delegate well.

Particularly with complex issues in organizations, there is a presenting priority (or set of symptoms) caused by a real (or root) problem. Recognizing the presenting priority and getting to the root causes is one of the major challenges in a consulting project.

The reframing technique can be done by using a variety of other techniques, for example, coaching (listed immediately above), "Ask 'Why' Five Times," and "What, Who, Where, When and Why?"

### "Ask 'Why' Five Times" Technique

This can be a powerful means to really dig deep into the dynamics and causes of a problem. For example, assume the original problem is "We do not have enough funds."

> Why? (#1) Because our fundraising is not successful.
>
> Why? (#2) Because we do not have a Fundraising Plan.
>
> Why? (#3) Because our Board Fundraising Committee does not know how to do a fundraising plan, and we have no Strategic Plan upon which to base a fundraising plan.
>
> Why? (#4) Because our Board has received no training and we do not believe in Strategic Planning.
>
> Why? (#5) Because we have always just "muddled along" somehow, but that approach is not working anymore.

### "What, Who, Where, When and Why?" Technique

These six questions can help people to fully examine all aspects of a current, major problem.

What? We do not have enough funds.

Who? For our Transportation Program.

Where? In all aspects of the Program, particularly for gasoline.

When? The problem shows up most near the end of the month before each month's allocation of funds to the Program.

Why? The cost of gasoline has gone up and we did not plan for that.

# How to Depict and Analyze Systems

Tools in this subsection will help you to:

1.      Identify and organize useful information about a system, especially a complex problem.

2.      Identify the influences that might be causing problems.

3.      Identify the most likely solutions to those problems in the system.

The tools in this subsection are not listed in any certain order. Rather, you should read the description of each tool and then decide if it will currently be useful to you.

As with tools in the previous subsection about examining mental models, you should be sensitive about how you use the tools in this subsection.

See "Building Trust, Commitment and Collaboration with Clients" on page 58 for guidelines to ensure that you work with sensitivity when using the following tools.

Tools listed in this subsection include:

1.      Strategic Management (for "Diagnosing" Organizations)

2.      Logic Model (to Depict Systems and Identify Relationships)

3.      Chaining Logic Models (for Aligning and Integrating Systems)

4.      SWOT Analysis (to Analyze Environments and Select Overall Strategies)

5.      Polarity Management (to Resolve Seemingly Conflicting Choices)

6.      Force-Field Analysis (to Identify and Analyze Driving Forces)

7.      Rational Problem Solving (for Identifying and Analyzing Alternatives)

8.      Upside/Downside (for Analysis of Potential Decision)

9.      "DECIDE" (to Ensure Comprehensive Decision Making)

## *Strategic Management (for "Diagnosing" Organizations)*

### Identify Root Causes

To use the strategic management process as a diagnostic tool to localize where root causes of issues might be, especially during the Discovery and Feedback phase of the collaborative consulting cycle:

1.  Have your client explain the presenting priority for you to address, such as Boards, strategic planning or fundraising.

2.  Find the priority on the table on page 158.

3.  The lower that the priority is listed on the table, the more that you should investigate the root-cause of the priority as being somewhere higher on the table. For example:

    - Problems in conducting program evaluations often are caused by poor program planning, including poor clarification of program goals and outcomes.

    - Problems in fundraising often are caused by poor financial planning, program planning and strategic planning, principally clarification of program costs, groups of clients to be served by each program and the desired outcomes for each group.

    - Problems in advertising and promotions often are caused by poor program planning, as well, such as poor identification of the specific groups of clients to be served by the program and of the specific benefits of the program to each group of clients.

    - Problems in ineffective planning and development of staff often are caused by poor strategic planning and leadership, including poor clarification of expertise needed to achieve strategic goals and also poor supervision from the Board and executives regarding how staff should be focused and organized.

    - Problems in program operations and performance often are caused by poor strategic planning, such as not having a clear organizational mission, vision and goals from which to identify programs and the needed resources to operate those programs.

    - Problems in Board operations can cause problems throughout the organization because adequate strategic planning is not conducted and implemented throughout the organization.

This hierarchy exists because activities that are included higher up in the table, such as Board operations, strategic planning and program planning, are where the overall planning often occurs. Those overall activities clarify the direction and resources needed for the success of activities included lower in the table.

Strategic management tends to focus on structures, plans, policies and practices and not so much on matters of culture and power. Consequently, the model is not powerful for identifying root causes that are formed from dysfunctional behaviors in the workplace. Examples of such behaviors include leading by intimidation and fear, making decisions based only on emotions and not data, and discouraging open discussions and sharing of information in the workplace.

## Action Plans to Address Issues

Because of the integrated relationship of the activities in the table, the table sometimes can suggest the order in which to undertake the various actions to resolve problems. You are usually better off first to attend to the actions that are placed higher up on the table. For example, if an assessment reveals symptoms of ineffective Board operations, strategic planning and fundraising in your client's organization, then you probably should ensure that your project includes actions to improve the Board operations before undertaking strategic planning. Likewise, you probably should undertake actions to improve strategic planning before actions to improve fundraising. Knowing in which order to undertake actions comes in handy, especially if your client has very limited time and resources to commit to a project. In that situation, you want to be sure that your client's limited resources are applied to the most important actions during your project.

The causal relationship described above does not always exist in every organization. However, when selecting actions to take to address problems in your client's organization, you should always conduct assessments to be sure that activities included higher up in the table are indeed being conducted effectively. That is one of the reasons why you should persuade your client to participate in a comprehensive organizational assessment, probably during the Discovery and Feedback phase, to examine the quality of all major activities in your client's organization. For example, if your client wants fundraising to be the only focus of your project, encourage your client to allow your project to include a quick assessment of the quality of their Board operations, strategic planning and program planning.

## Select Actions

This approach to selecting actions and the order in which to take them is not an exact science. You should not proceed through a project for organizational change merely by adopting the actions in the table. There is still important work to do before you finish the actions.

For example, the actions should be integrated into various action plans that specify each individual action, who will undertake that action, and deadlines to finish that action. Then all action plans should be carefully integrated into an overall plan implemented according to principles of successful organizational and systems change. The final decision on what actions to take and the order in which to take them should be decided by your client. You both should carefully follow the guidelines for collaborative consulting as described in PART IV.

## *Logic Model (to Depict Systems and Identify Relationships)*

The purpose of a logic model is to depict the major parts and processes of a system, along with their relationships.

1.  Ideally, the logic model is just one or two pages long. The level of detail should be sufficient for you to grasp the major items (inputs) that go into the system, what processes occur to those inputs, the various outputs produced by the system, and the overall benefits (or outcomes) that occur for other systems, for example, for people who participate in a program.

See "Overview of the Open System of a Nonprofit Program" on page 153 to do a logic model for a program.

See "Overview of the Open System of a Nonprofit Organization" on page 150 to do a logic model of an entire organization.

2.     For ongoing systems, include only the major, recurring processes in the system, rather than one-time processes. For example, do not include the initial activities to build the system, such as "construct the building" or "register with appropriate government authorities."

3.     Your logic model should include primarily the processes required to continue to process the inputs to produce the outputs. For example, "hold training sessions for clients" or "conduct certification assessments of clients."

4.     The size of the logic model should be such that readers can easily study the model without extensive reference and cross-comparisons between many pages.

## *Chaining Logic Models (for Aligning and Integrating Systems)*

Note that logic models can be used to depict systems that are directly integrated with each other. From that depiction, you can work to more closely align those systems. To use logic models to align systems in organizations, consider the following guidelines. Note that, in the following, the presenting priority is the area of the issue or goal that your client described to you as needing to be addressed by your project, such as Board operations, strategic planning, programs or marketing.

1.     **Always work with your client to identify directly integrated systems.**
The following guidelines should be followed with your client – your client knows at least as much as you do about which activities are directly related to other activities in their organization.

2.     **What other systems provide direct input to the domain of the presenting priority?**
For example, organizational evaluation results should provide direct input to the Board, strategic planning to program planning, strategic planning to staff planning, strategic goals to performance goals for Board committees and staff, and financial planning to fundraising activities.

See "Management Systems and Why You Should Understand Them" on page 156 for ideas of which systems might share inputs and outputs with certain other domains.

3.     **What other systems use the direct outputs from the domain?**
For example, does the domain produce program planning from strategic planning? Staff planning from strategic planning? Performance goals from strategic planning? Fundraising from financial planning?

4.     **Now develop a logic model for the presenting priority.**

See "Logic Model (to Depict Systems and Identify Relationships)" on page 423 for guidelines to develop the logic model.

5.     **Now develop a logic model for each directly integrated system.**
Again, follow the guidelines in the above step.

6.　**Now chain the logic models of the directly integrated systems.**
　　Refer to the diagram below for an idea of how to link your logic models.

Of course, the integration and alignment between systems in organizations is usually not in the complete and orderly sequence as that depicted below. However, use of the logic model for aligning systems is useful as a frame of reference during discussions with your client about which systems are directly connected.

In the following diagram, "I" represents input, "P" is process and "O" is output. The links between processes are shown by the shaded boxes. Systems in the left-hand column are for use of this example only. You should include systems that are relevant to the presenting priority of your project.

**Example of Chaining Logic Models**

| | | | | | | | | | | | |
|---|---|---|---|---|---|---|---|---|---|---|---|
| Strategic planning | O | | | | | | | | | | |
| Program planning | I | P | O | | | | | | | | |
| Financial planning | | | I | P | O | | | | | | |
| Fundraising planning | | | | | I | P | O | | | | |
| Fundraising activities | | | | | | | I | P | O | | |

## SWOT Analysis (to Analyze Environments and Select Overall Strategies)

In the following description, SWOT is an acronym for strengths, weaknesses, opportunities and threats. SWOT is a standard tool during strategic planning for organizations. However, the tool can be used for any system in an organization, as well. The SWOT analysis is useful when faced with a variety of major considerations about a complex challenge or problem for the system. The goal of the analysis is to identify strategies that build on the systems strengths to take advantage of opportunities, while shoring up weaknesses to ward off threats.

To use the tool, make a list of the opportunities that exist in the environment external to the system. Next, make a list of the threats that exist in the environment external to the system. Then make a list of the internal strengths of the system. Lastly, make a list of the internal weaknesses of the system. Then include each list in its respective place in one of the four cells in the table below. Each cell includes a term that suggests what you might do with the information in that cell, for example, invest more resources or divest (or terminate activities).

Kearns (1992, pp.3-22) provides a useful approach to using SWOT information to organize and identify major types of strategies. Kearns' approach is to develop a SWOT analysis grid, which organizes the SWOT information into four quadrants. Kearns' approach includes labeling each quadrant according to a likely strategy to take regarding the nature of the information in that quadrant, as depicted below.

**Types of Strategies from SWOT Analysis**

|  | Opportunities | Threats |
|---|---|---|
| **Strengths** | *Invest*<br>Use the strengths to take advantage of the opportunities. | *Defend*<br>Use strengths to ward off threats. |
| **Weaknesses** | *Decide*<br>Decide whether to invest resources to shore up weaknesses to take advantage of opportunities or divest areas of weakness. | *Divest*<br>Threats in this quadrant should be monitored and avoided as much as possible, without extensive investment of resources. |

The tool can be handy for planners or problem solvers when working from the various considerations described in the SWOT information and trying to decide what the organization should do in the future to address those considerations.

## Polarity Management (to Resolve Seemingly Conflicting Choices)

Johnson (1992) goes beyond asserting the common cliché that "life is full of paradoxes" – he goes to on suggest how those paradoxes, or polarities, can be managed.

### What Is a Polarity?

When attempting to solve a problem or make a major decision, it often seems as if the issue is unsolvable because all options seem desirable, but many are contradictory. For example, leaders in the organization often want organizational members to show strong, individual creativity and innovation, yet the leaders also want strong teamwork. However, the more individualistic that people are, the less likely that they can be strong team members.

The "individual versus team" matter is a polarity. The distinguishing feature of a polarity is there seems to be two "sides" to the situation and one "side" is highly dependent on, or can be affected by, the other "side." The sides are seemingly contradictory, but cannot completely exist without the presence of the other. Other examples of polarities include: expert versus collaborative consultants, centralize versus decentralize, expand market share versus increase profit (it costs money to expand market share), inhale versus exhale, right versus wrong, cost versus quality, and autocratic versus participatory.

Some matters are not polarities – there is one course of action that will not affect another, or opposite, course of action. For example, choosing to buy a house is not a polarity. If you buy the house, you have not, in turn, reduced your capability to buy the house.

Members of an organization are confronted with polarities all the time. If they see these situations as problems, they tend to focus on one "side" of the polarity to the detriment of the other. They pursue actions regarding the one side, and soon find that the lack of attention to the other side has caused an entirely new, major problem. However, if people can see the situations as polarities, they are much more likely to be able to manage, not "solve," them.

## How Are Polarities Managed?

The overall approach to manage a priority is based on the use of what Johnson calls the Polarity Map. The Map uses the following terms:

- "Left Pole" refers to the current direction that leaders choose to follow regarding a certain polarity, for example, to cultivate teamwork instead of individual initiative, decentralize rather than centralize, or pursue quality rather than cutting costs.

- "Right Pole" refers to the seemingly opposite direction, for example, to cultivate individual initiative.

- "Upside" refers to the strong advantages of following a particular course of action, for example, of cultivating teamwork, decentralizing or pursuing quality.

- "Downside" refers to the disadvantages from following a course of action to excess and/or to the exclusion of all other options, for example, disadvantages from over-emphasis on cultivating teamwork to the exclusion of any individual initiative.

### Polarity Map

|  | Left Pole | Right Pole |
|---|---|---|
| **Upside** | Left+ | Right+ |
| **Downside** | Left- | Right- |

To manage a polarity, people have to fill in all four of the Map's quadrants about the overall situation. For example:

1.  As people identify a "problem" (usually from experiencing too much of something), they fill in the symptoms of the problem in one quadrant (for example, in the "Left-" quadrant).

2.  As a "solution" to the "problem," it is natural to suggest quickly going to the opposite direction, to the upside of the other pole (or to the "Right+" quadrant). It is common then that people quickly focus all their energy and resources on achieving that "solution."

3.  However, over time, people realize that they are experiencing too much of that "solution." At that point, they are experiencing the downside of the "solution" (they are experiencing the "Right-" quadrant).

4.  Very soon, they experience this (the "Right-") as a major problem, and they suggest quickly going to the opposite direction (to the "Left+" quadrant) as the new "solution." It is common then that people quickly focus all of their energy and resources on achieving that "solution."

5.  However, over time, people realize that they are experiencing too much of that "solution." At that point, they are experiencing the downside of the "solution" (they are experiencing the "Left-" quadrant all over again).

By now, they have experienced all four quadrants and have not solved their "problem."

Benefits of using the Polarity Map include that:

1.  Once people have mapped all of the effects of each quadrant, they can anticipate and understand all aspects of the polarity, which, in turn, helps them to more effectively see the "big picture" and manage the polarity.

2.  Leaders can be much more realistic about expectations and planning. They accept that for every major action, they must consider the opposite and natural reaction down the road. They begin to think in terms of "both/and," rather than "either/or."

3.  Members of the organization begin to view challenges as polarities and not as problems that cannot be solved, so they can avoid the deep despair of "never being able to solve our problems."

4.  Members of the organization begin to hear the "complete truth" about a situation (rather than about "silver bullets" and "quick fixes") from their leaders and, in turn, develop more trust in the leaders and the organization.

## Force-Field Analysis (to Identify and Analyze Driving Forces)

The Force-Field Analysis is useful for identifying and organizing influences that will support (positive forces) and oppose (negative forces) a proposed course of action during organizational change. Consequently, it is also useful when choosing various action plans during the Action Planning, Alignment and Integration phase of consulting. The goal is to strengthen the positive forces, while removing or weakening the negative forces.

To conduct a force-field analysis, consider the following procedure.

1.  At the top of the following diagram, describe the problem or goal to be analyzed.

2.  Brainstorm a list of factors, such as people and influences, which are reasons for (in support of) the change and record each on the left-hand column. Remember that, during a brainstorming activity, the goal is to generate all ideas and not to judge them as they are being identified. They are judged after all ideas have been gathered.

3.  Brainstorm a list of factors that are reasons against (that oppose or would be obstacles to) the change and record each on the right-hand column.

4.  When all of the supporting and opposing forces have been identified, analyze the situation by answering the following questions.

a) Is each force real? Does it really exist?

b) How strong, or important, is each force?

c) Which opposing force can be removed or weakened and which supporting force can be strengthened?

d) What is the timing on changing those forces that can or should be changed (for example, go faster or go slower)?

e) Which change to the forces would quickly provoke overall organizational change?

f) Which change to the forces would cultivate organizational change more slowly?

g) What resources are needed to make the changes to the supporting and opposing forces?

h) How can we get and apply those resources soon?

5. Some people might assign a weight, or score, to each final supporting and opposing force, for example, "1" is weakest and "4" is strongest. Then they strengthen the supporting forces with the highest scores and weaken the opposing forces that have the highest scores.

## Force-Field Analysis Grid

Description of proposed change

| Supporting Forces | Opposing Forces |
|---|---|
|  |  |

## *Rational Problem Solving (for Identifying and Analyzing Alternatives)*

Some people prefer to take a comprehensive, "linear" (step-by-step) approach to analyzing problems. The following procedure will help you in that regard. Do not be intimidated by the length of the list of guidelines. After you have practiced them a few times, they will become second nature to you – enough that you can deepen and enrich them to suit your own needs and nature.

1.  **Define the problem.**

    This is often where people struggle. They react to what they think the problem is. Instead, seek to understand more about why you think there is a problem.

    *Defining the problem: (with input from yourself and others)*

    Ask yourself and others, the following questions:

    a)  What can you *see* that causes you to think there is a problem?

    b)  Where is it happening?

    c)  How is it happening?

    d)  When is it happening?

    e)  With whom is it happening? (HINT: Do not jump to "Who is causing the problem?" When we are stressed, blaming is often one of our first reactions. To be an effective consultant, you need to address issues more than people.)

    f)  Write down a five-sentence description of the problem in terms of "The following should be happening, but is not ..." or "The following is happening and should not be: ..." As much as possible, be specific in your description, including what is happening, where, how, with whom and why.

    *Define complex problems:*

    If the problem still seems overwhelming, break it down by repeating steps a-e until you have descriptions of several related problems.

    *Verify your understanding of the problems:*

    It helps a great deal to verify your problem analysis by conferring with a peer or someone else.

    *Prioritize the problems:*

    If you discover that you are looking at several related problems, prioritize which ones you should address first.

    Note the difference between "important" and "urgent" problems. Often, what we consider to be important problems to consider are really just urgent problems. Important problems deserve more attention. For example, if you are continually answering "urgent" phone calls, you have probably got a more "important" problem – to design a system that screens and prioritizes your phone calls.

    *Understand your role in the problem:*

Your role in the problem can greatly influence how you perceive the role of others. For example, if you are stressed out, it will probably look like others are, too. Or, you may resort too quickly to blaming and reprimanding others. If you feel guilty about your role in the problem, you may ignore the accountabilities of others.

2.  **Look at potential causes.**
    It is amazing how often you do not know what you do not know about your client's organization. Therefore, in this phase, it is critical to get input from other people in the organization who might have noticed the problem and are affected by it. It is often useful to seek advice from a peer or your supervisor to verify your impression of the problem.

    a)  Collect input from other individuals one at a time (at least at first). Otherwise, people tend to be inhibited about offering their impressions of the real causes of problems.

    b)  Write down your opinions and what you have heard from others.

    c)  Write down a description of the cause of the problem in terms of what is happening, where, when, how, with whom and why.

3.  **Identify alternative approaches for resolution.**
    At this point, it is useful to keep others involved unless you are facing a personal and/or employee performance problem. Brainstorm solutions to the problem. Simply put, brainstorming is collecting as many ideas as possible, and then screening them to find the best idea. It is critical when collecting the ideas to not pass any judgment on the ideas – just write them down as you hear them.

4.  **Select an approach.**
    When selecting the best approach, consider:

    a)  Which approach is the most likely to solve the problem for the long term?

    b)  Which approach is the most realistic to accomplish for now? Do you have the resources? Are they affordable? Do you have enough time to implement the approach?

    c)  What is the extent of risk associated with each alternative?

5.  **Plan the implementation of the best alternative.**

    a)  Carefully consider "What will the situation look like when the problem is solved?"

    b)  What steps should be taken to implement the best alternative to solving the problem? What systems or processes should be changed in your organization? Do not resort to solutions where someone is "just going to try harder."

    c)  How will you know whether or not the steps are being followed? These are your indicators of the success of your plan.

    d)  What resources will you need in terms of people, money and facilities?

    e)  How much time will you need to implement the solution? Write a schedule that includes the start and stop times, and when you expect to see certain indicators of success.

    f)  Who will primarily be responsible for ensuring implementation of the plan?

    g)  Write down the answers to the above questions and consider this as your action plan.

    h)  Communicate the plan to those who will be involved in implementing it.

6. **Monitor implementation of the plan.**
   Monitor the indicators of success:

   a) Are you seeing what you would expect from the indicators?

   b) Will the plan be completed according to schedule?

   c) If the plan is not being followed as expected, consider: Was the plan realistic? Are there sufficient resources to accomplish the plan on schedule? Should more priority be placed on various aspects of the plan? Should the plan be changed?

7. **Verify if the problem has been resolved or not.**
   One of the best ways to verify if a problem has been solved is to resume normal operations in the organization. Still, you should consider:

   a) What changes should be made to avoid this type of problem in the future?

   b) Lastly, consider "What did you learn from this problem solving?" Consider new knowledge, understanding and/or skills.

   c) Write a brief memo that highlights the success of the problem solving effort and what you learned as a result. Share it with your clients and peers.

## *"Upside / Downside" (for Analysis of a Potential Decision)*

This is a simple technique to decide whether to implement a strategy, or course of action. The procedure includes:

1. Describe the proposed course of action, or strategy, to the group of people charged with deciding whether or not to follow the course of action. (The strategy may have been suggested by the group members themselves.)

2. Discuss the course of action among members of the group.

3. Write, or present, a description of the action for all members and ask if any member believes they do not understand the description.

4. Then identify and list the "upside," or possible benefits or results, from following the course of action.

   Consider possible effects such as changes in:

   a) Resources (in the environment, facilities, funding, human resources)

   b) Learning (enhanced knowledge, skills and capabilities)

   c) Conditions (standard of living, happiness)

   Consider possible effects on:

   a) People served by the organization (clients, or customers)

   b) Other stakeholders of the organization (employees, Board members, funders, community leaders, collaborators)

5.  Then identify and list the "downside," or possible ill effects or results, from following the course of action. Address the same areas of possible change (resources, learning, conditions) and who might be affected by the changes (clients, other stakeholders).

6.  Once all upsides and downsides have been identified then "validate" each by asking:

    a) Is it real?

    b) How strong, or important, is it?

    c) Which downside can be removed or de-emphasized and which upside can be retained or emphasized?

7.  Some people might assign a weight, or score, to each upside and downside, for example, "1" is the weakest upside and "4" is strongest upside and "-1" is the least important downside and "-4" is the most important downside. Then calculate a total for the upsides and total for downsides, and then make a decision about the proposed course of action by comparing the two totals.

## *"DECIDE" (to Ensure Comprehensive Decision Making)*

This handy acronym (a word formed from abbreviations taken from a phrase) can help group members ensure that they take a comprehensive approach to making their decision, considering the perspectives of all key stakeholders in the situation.

- D – What is the dilemma or decision that must be made?

- E – What have been the effects, or results, of the dilemma on others?

- C – Who should be consulted – who has special expertise or knowledge that should be involved in making the decision?

- I – Who else should be involved in making the decision?

- D – What should be the final decision – what is the course of action that should be taken?

- E – What will be the final effect, or result, of the decision on the dilemma?

# Changing Systems

Guidelines in this section are about changing major systems, including organizational systems and major problems within those systems. The guidelines will be useful, especially as you progress through the various phases of the collaborative consulting cycle. This is true whether you are an external or internal consultant.

> Before using the information in this section, be sure that you have gained the general knowledge in the section, "Understanding Change and Capacity Building."

## Important Principles for Changing Systems

Experts in systems theory have identified numerous principles about how the systems of organizations work and how to solve problems in those organizations. It is not within the scope of this guide to explain all of those principles. However, some of the most important principles are listed below. Keep these principles in mind when thinking about how to address challenges in nonprofit organizations. One of the best descriptions of systems principles is in Senge (1990) and in Kaufmann (1984). The following principles are adapted from those publications.

A summary of the following principles is depicted in a table at the end of this subsection.

### The System's Overall Behavior Depends on the Entire Structure

Too often in organizations (and in management training programs), we think we can break up the system and only have to deal with its parts or with various topics apart from other topics. Systems theory reminds us that if you break up an elephant, you do not have a bunch of little elephants. If you hire a professional fundraiser to improve fundraising activities without examining the effectiveness and integration of the Board of Directors and the Strategic Plan, the nonprofit may be no better off than before the fundraiser was hired.

### A Circular Relationship Exists Between the Overall System and its Parts

Ever notice how an organization seems to experience the same kinds of problems over and over again? The problems seem to cycle through the organization. Over time, members of the organization come to recognize the pattern of events in the cycle, rather than the just the events themselves. Parents notice this as they mature as parents. Over time, they recognize the various phases their children go through and consider these phases when dealing with the specific behaviors of their children.

### Structures Determine Behaviors, Which Determine Events

For example, when a new supervisor confronts a problem in the workplace, they focus mostly on the major event and the behaviors associated with that event. Let us look at the example of two employees, Tom and Sally, who keep arguing with each other. New supervisors often try to handle the problem by simply telling Tom and Sally not to argue. On the other hand, the wise supervisors would probably consider the structures, or systems, in the organization that might be causing Tom and Sally to argue. Tom and Sally might not be clear on what their roles and responsibilities are in the organization. They may have conflicting roles and responsibilities because the nonprofit has no clear action plans associated with its overall Strategic Plan.  Or, Tom and Sally might be lacking the resources required to effectively carry out their jobs because there is no effective employee performance management system that includes training and development.  Rarely is the problem simply that Tom and Sally like to argue with each other.

## There Is No Blame

When issues recur in an organization, it is usually the fault of a dysfunctional process or structure in the organization, rather than the fault of the people struggling to operate with that dysfunctional process or structure.  For example, one of the ways that ineffective leaders try to lead their people is by using fear and blame.  They threaten employees that the organization will shut down if the employees do not do a much better job.  Then, if the organization does not do much better, they blame the employees even more.  Soon the fear and blame no longer motivate employees.  Too often, the leaders cannot change their ways and, as a result, the employees leave.  These leaders need to recognize that the organizational problem is probably not caused by some amazing coincidence that all of their employees are inept, but rather by larger problems in the organization itself.  For example, there may be no demand for the organization's services, prices might be too high, or methods to deliver services might be poorly designed.

## Problems Are Often Solved One Level Above the Problem

In our example with Tom and Sally, assuming Tom and Sally are reasonably mature adults, the wise supervisors would probably realize that any long-lasting change in the situation must involve the supervisors of both Tom and Sally, not just Tom and Sally themselves.  This principle is one of the reasons that many problems in nonprofits are addressed at the top levels of a nonprofit.

## Person Reporting the Problem Is Often a Part of the Problem

Wise supervisors have learned first to look at themselves before they make conclusions about other peoples' problems or behaviors.  These supervisors realize that if they are not competently leading and managing themselves, they likely cannot effectively lead and manage others.  A common example of this type of situation is when supervisors are feeling burned out, they often believe that everyone else in the organization feels that way too, so the supervisors conclude that the entire organization has a problem with burnout.

## Problems Usually Lie in the Relationships Between Parts

One of the best examples of nonprofit problems associated with this principle is in regard to strategic planning.  If the planning did not address integration of strategic goals and strategies or if the action planning did not address integration of plans, all kinds of problems can ensue.  For example, employees might have conflicting roles, budget allocations are sporadic and inconsistent, and programs are less efficient.  Another example is when a program is not getting adequate administrative support but other programs are, then the overall problem is often in the conflicting demands placed on the administrative support staff from all of the various programs.

## Long-Lasting Change Results from Changes to Structures

For example, new supervisors often try to change the performance of their employees merely by preaching at them.  This rarely works for the long-term.  Wise supervisors have learned that to effect long-lasting change among their employees, they need to establish clear roles and goals for their employees, ensure their employees understand their roles and goals, and then monitor employees' progress toward those goals. This principle is also one of the reasons that long-lasting changes in a nonprofit involves changes or updates to the nonprofit's strategic plan – the changes must be integrated into the various structures resulting from the strategic plan.

## Today's Problems Are Yesterday's Solutions

Many times we fail to see the larger ramifications of our favorite, quick-fix solutions. Often, those quick-fix solutions just make things worse. For example, if we do not know how to manage money wisely in our nonprofit organization, it will not do much good to just focus on getting more money from fundraising. Sooner or later, funders will realize that their money is not being well spent and so they will quit providing money to the organization. Hopefully, consultants and clients soon focus less on fundraising and more, for example, on effective market research to identify client's true needs and how those needs can be met. They might focus on more effective program evaluations to ensure that programs are really meeting the needs of clients, resulting in much stronger grant proposals and, thus, more effective fundraising.

## Harder You Push, the Harder the System Pushes Back

When the parts of a system come together naturally to find their own way of operating, it can be extremely difficult to change that system merely by pushing at the organization to change. For example, it usually does little good to tell burned out employees or even members of the Board of Directors to just "suck it up" and do a better job. Their performance will just get worse. They will feel more frustration, anger and despair. Rather than coming at them with dire warnings about the future of the nonprofit, first listen to the employees or members of the Board to hear their side of the story. With this approach, you and your clients are much more likely to recognize the condition of burnout, what caused the condition and how it can be addressed.

## Behavior Grows Better Before It Grows Worse

Usually, quick fixes (rather than real fixes) to the symptoms (rather than to the real causes) of a problem will make things better, but only for a while. For example, if employees often seem confused about what they are doing and why, it might make them temporarily feel good if their supervisors provide short, specific lists of tasks to achieve. However, it is likely that things will soon get even worse when employees realize that they are being treated like machines, attending only to the "to do" lists. Wise supervisors soon realize that the short-term fixes are not working and will take the time required to effectively plan, clarify roles and delegate with their employees.

## The Easy Way Out Usually Leads Back In

Doing what is familiar is easy and comfortable. That is why, when we realize that our organization or program is really struggling, we often resort to doing what we were already doing. We just do it harder. This principle is often hardest for new leaders to learn. A new supervisor may seek to get rid of an employee, rather than work with that employee to improve their performance, when first encountering an employee performance problem. Often, the employee leaves, only to be replaced by another employee who soon has the same problems. Eventually, the supervisor learns that the employee has not received effective training, does not have adequate resources to do the job, or is doing a job simply too much for one person to do. Unfortunately, the organization has already spent a great deal of time and money in lost productivity and recruitment of new employees.

Perhaps H. L. Mencken said it best, "For every difficult and complex problem, there is an obvious solution that is simple, easy and wrong."

## *Faster Is Slower*

For example, if leaders do not take the time and energy required to develop and implement effective plans, it might seem that they have even more time to attend to the day-to-day matters in their organizations. However, they will soon realize that they seem to be attending to the same problems over and over again. They will feel that if they do not work even harder, they will soon be overwhelmed. Hopefully, they will realize that they have to take the time to work smarter, rather than harder. They will begin to plan and to delegate. This principle does not mean that they should not ever make decisions and act quickly – it means that most of those quick decisions should be guided from plans, policies and practices in the organization.

The following table depicts a summary of the systems principles for change.

## Table VII:1 – Summary of System Principles

The following principles are adapted from Peter Senge's *The Fifth Discipline* (Doubleday, 1990) and Draper Kaufmann's *Systems 1: An Introduction to Systems Thinking* (Future Systems, Inc., 1984). There are many principles derived from systems thinking. However, the following are some of the most relevant when working to produce significant change in nonprofit organizations.

1. The system's overall behavior depends on the entire structure.

2. A circle relationship exists between the overall system and its parts.

3. Structures determine behaviors, which determine events.

4. There is no blame.

5. Problems are often solved one level above the problem.

6. The person with the problem is often part of the problem.

7. Problems usually lie in the relationships between the parts of a system.

8. Long-lasting change results from a change in structures.

9. Today's problems are yesterday's solutions.

10. The harder you push, the harder the system pushes back.

11. Behavior grows better before it grows worse.

12. The easy way out usually leads back in.

13. Faster is slower.

# Guidelines for Successful Organizational Change

## Relationship Between Organizational Change and Capacity Building

It is the author's assertion that the principles to accomplish successful capacity building – especially when building a significant portion of an organization – are also the principles to accomplish successful organizational change. Backer (2000) suggests eight core-competencies of effective capacity building in nonprofits. He suggests that capacity building activities be comprehensive, customized, competence-based, timely, peer-connected, assessment-based, readiness-based and contextualized. These eight core-competencies are integrated into numerous other guidelines in the paragraphs throughout this subsection about accomplishing successful organizational change.

The guidelines in this subsection are organized into the following subtopics:

1.    Nature of Overall Organizational Change Process

2.    Your Role as Consultant and Change Agent

3.    Core Requirements for Your Client

4.    Core Areas of Focus of Change Process

5.    Core Components of Change Plans

Guidelines in this subsection are intended to impart further, general knowledge about organizational change. The guidelines in this subsection are not organized in the particular sequence to be followed when working to address problems or achieve goals with your client during a project. That sequence is in PART IV about the collaborative consulting cycle.

## Consider Sharing These Guidelines with Your Clients

One of the most meaningful activities that you can do with your client early on in your project is to help your client to understand the nature of organizational change. The following paragraphs in this subsection provide principles and guidelines about the nature of change in organizations. You might copy this subsection and provide it to your client. Your client will likely have questions about the following information, such as questions about various terms, interpretation of various guidelines, and how to follow the guidelines. The resulting discussion between you and your client can be a meaningful opportunity to further develop collaboration, trust and commitment.

Because others might read the information in the following paragraphs, it is important here to suggest certain definitions for terms. "Change model" refers to an overall, coherent and integrated set of guidelines about how to carry out change in an organization. The terms "change effort" and "change process" are used to mean the overall general set of activities to define and carry out the change. "Project plan" includes the documented specifications about how to conduct activities in the change effort. "Action plans" are the various specific activities that are specified in the overall project plan.

(Permission is hereby granted by the author and publisher for the purchaser of this Field Guide to copy information from the 10 pages in this subsection, "Guidelines for Successful Change," to provide the information to the purchaser's clients or to use within the purchaser's organization. Include reference to the author, Dr. Carter McNamara, and the book title.)

A summary of the following principles is depicted in a table at the end of this subsection.

## Nature of the Overall Organizational Change Process

Before you initiate a change process, it will be helpful for you to get a feel for the nature of the process. Guidelines in the following paragraphs will be helpful to you in that regard.

1.   **A change process is a "journey" that you take with your client.**
     The change process rarely occurs in a predictable, step-by-step fashion. Instead, there are usually surprises along the way. For example, various action plans get changed, or there is different emphasis on different aspects of the process. Therefore, it often helps to view the process as a journey, rather than as an implementation of a specific sequence of specific procedures.

2.   **Each change process with each client is different – it is customized.**
     Much as friendships are each unique, change processes are, as well. Experienced consultants have learned to consider the context-sensitive features of each client's organization when developing project plans. Rarely can one project plan be implemented in exactly the same way among various different organizations.

 See "Context-Sensitive Features – What Makes Each Nonprofit Unique" on page 144 to learn more about how each organization is unique.

3.   **A change process rarely is an "aha!"**
     During the process, participants often realize major accomplishments and learning by reflecting back on what has occurred so far in the process and in their organization. That is why it is important to build in regular "check in" periods into your plan so participants in the process can capture their learning and celebrate their accomplishments.

4.   **A change process usually takes longer than you think.**
     Experts assert that successful change requires a change to the culture of the organization. Cultural change can be like changing someone's personality – it is not done overnight. That is why it is important to sustain momentum in your project, building in some quick successes and ensuring that all participants are always aware of the project plan and the status of its implementation.

## Your Role as a Consultant and a Change Agent

It is not uncommon for consultants to carefully think about how their clients can successfully go through the change process, but to completely forget about how they can get through it themselves. The following paragraphs address the most important aspects of guiding yourself during a change process with your client.

1.   **Manage your time and stress.**
     This is probably the most important guideline for you to follow because if you become stressed out, your perspective on everything else suffers.

2.  **Recognize the effect of your own nature on others in the change process.**
    Your nature (your biases, style, expertise, etc.) is an "instrument of change" during the project so you should know how to use that instrument, including how it might affect others during the change process.

3.  **Adhere to your personal values and ethics.**
    If you lose your moral compass during a project, your perspective on everything else suffers, especially during a complex and dynamic change process.

4.  **Although change is often unpredictable, have at least one change model in mind.**
    Even if you do not implement the model completely, the model can serve as a common frame of reference for communication between you and your client.

     See "Various Organizational Change Models" on page 188 for more information about change models.

5.  **Build trust, commitment and collaboration with your client.**
    Skills in multiculturalism, authenticity, communication, coaching and in managing expectations will be particularly useful to you.

6.  **Get some ongoing, "outside" feedback.**
    Get a mentor or join a group of consultants to get their ongoing, fresh perspectives. Otherwise, you can get too close to your client's situation and get lost in it yourself.

7.  **Maintain sufficient skills in your primary areas of service.**
    You can follow every other guideline for successful change, but they all will be useless unless you follow this guideline, as well. You must be able to conduct effective training, coaching and facilitation in your primary areas of expertise.

8.  **Have at least basic understanding of a range of consulting services.**
    For example, be aware of other sources of further assistance for your clients. Also, know when to ask for help in a project. That way, you can directly, or indirectly, provide a comprehensive and competence-based array of services.

9.  **Do not try to control change, but instead to guide it during the project.**
    Plans will change as you and your client continue to learn and take actions during the project. Let the plans change, but change them systematically and then communicate those changes to relevant stakeholders in the project.

## Core Requirements for Your Client

Obviously, your client will need to do their part if your project is to be successful. However, there are certain core requirements that they must meet. Those requirements are described in the following paragraphs.

1.  **Your client must have the resources to implement the plan for change.**
    Far too often, the plan results in your client having to do even more than they are doing now, so the change effort ends up failing because your client becomes overwhelmed. Usually, for clients to successfully participate in a change effort, they either have to a) give up doing some of their current activities to find the time and energy to conduct the new activities in

the project plan, and/or b) get more resources to conduct those new activities. This overall situation has to be taken into account in the early phases of the project planning.

> See "Collaborative Planning for Relevant, Realistic and Flexible Plans" on page 316 for guidelines to ensure that your client makes these considerations when developing plans for the project.

2. **Your client needs to be ready for the change process.**
   It is critical in the early phases of the project to assess the readiness of your client. You can assess readiness by asking your client about, for example, if they have the resources for the project, what obstacles might they foresee, if there are any other people who might be uncomfortable with the project, if your client is open to other perspectives than theirs about the project, or if your client has used a consultant before and how that project worked out. Ultimately, it is a "judgment call" on your part – and your client's – as to whether your client is ready for the project or not.

> See "Assess Client Readiness for the Project" on page 245 for useful guidelines to be sure your client is ready.

3. **Top leadership in your client's organization must support the project.**
   This assertion has become conventional wisdom in literature about organizational change. Still, many projects still do not enjoy strong, visible support from top leadership. Visible support could be provided, for example, in the form of speeches and memorandum about the need for the project, and in participation in the project. Some experienced consultants ask for the signatures of the Board President and Chief Executive Officer on a consulting contract as means to verify top leadership's support of the project.

4. **Your client must take ownership of the change process.**
   Inexperienced consultants sometimes compensate for their initial insecurities by doing the vast majority of work in the change process. While that approach might quickly generate various results in the process, for example, plans and reports, that approach rarely generates the kind of ownership and participation from your client that is necessary to successfully change their organization and learn from that change. The collaborative approach to consulting explained throughout this Field Guide usually produces that kind of ownership.

5. **Your client must trust you, and you must trust your client.**
   Without this firm foundation of trust, both you and your client will expend a great deal of energy in clarifying – and verifying the truth of – what each of you is saying. Mistrust cultivates conflict and conflict cultivates poor communication – and the two issues create a vicious cycle. The way to cultivate trust is for you and your client to participate authentically with each other – to be as direct and honest with each other, as possible, in the here-and-now of the project.

> See "Building Trust, Commitment and Collaboration with Clients" on page 58 for numerous guidelines to help ensure that your client trusts you.

## Core Areas of Focus of the Change Process

Inexperienced consultants often target their project plans only on the specific problems and/or goals that their client prefers to address during the project. However, for your plans to be successful, you should consider all of the important areas of focus. Those areas are described in the following paragraphs.

1. **Ensure project activities are focused on organizational performance.**
   As mentioned in the section, "Nonprofit Organizational Performance," in PART III, an organization can successfully meet goals, but if those goals are not directly aligned with meeting certain needs in the community, it could be argued that the organization is not really performing at all. Therefore, when establishing project goals with your client, always tactfully ask how those goals are directly aligned with meeting certain needs in the community. Otherwise, the organization might not improve its effectiveness even if project goals are achieved. Or, more performance-based activities might interrupt the project.

2. **Integrate project goals into the context of overall organizational goals.**
   One of the most successful approaches to ensuring that project goals are relevant and realistic is to align those goals with overall organizational goals, for example, with strategic goals. That approach helps to ensure that the organization's resources are efficiently used and that project goals are more likely to be performance-based.

3. **Focus on "success" for the project – define "success" early in the project.**
   "Success" can mean many things to many different people. For example, success might be achieving project goals, not exceeding the budget or schedule, or maintaining a strong relationship with clients. Whatever "success" is to the project, ensure that project activities are focused on achieving the conditions of that success.

   See "How to Define Project Success" on page 99 for options and guidelines to clearly define project success.

4. **Focus on activities that cause the symptoms of the problem.**
   For projects that are designed to solve problems in your client's organization (as opposed to achieving more forward-looking, developmental goals), ensure that you identify both the presenting problems and the real causes of those issues. Project plans should be focused on the real causes of issues.

   See "Phase 3: Discovery and Feedback" on page 258 for guidelines to help you identify presenting versus real issues by conducting a thorough analysis of your client's issues and goals.

5. **Focus on major organizational parts and their relationships.**
   Major problems and goals in an organization are seldom completely addressed by attending to only one part of the organization, for example, only to Boards, programs, the Chief Executive Role, other staff, marketing, finances, fundraising or evaluations. When identifying action plans during a project, consider any effect on each major part of the organization and especially how plans will affect relationships between the parts.

See "Analyzing Systems" on page 417 for tools and guidelines to analyze systems.

6. **Focus on changing structures, not on changing personalities.**
When considering action plans, focus primarily on changing plans, policies, roles, procedures and processes, rather than primarily on changing peoples' personalities. While this suggestion might sound obvious, it is surprising how often people try to cultivate change primarily by preaching at people and evoking them to change.

7. **Focus on the first 20% of effort that generates the first 80% of results.**
In most complex things in life, there is indeed that 20% of effort that seems to make the biggest difference. Far too often, we dwell on the remaining 80% of detail that generates only 20% of results, so over time, we become tired, frustrated and distrusting of our efforts. Instead, it helps to focus primarily on the 20% of activities that leverages the most results. You can identify those activities by first conducting a practical comprehensive organizational assessment in your projects.

8. **Build from strengths at least as much as – if not more than – from weaknesses.**
That approach can help you ensure that action plans remain realistic and that participants maintain strong buy-in during the change process. The approach is useful, particularly with stressed-out personnel who desperately need something to feel good about in the project. One of the most notable breakthroughs in organizational development is Appreciative Inquiry (AI). The major principle of AI is, rather than dwelling on what has not worked in the past, to instead identify what has worked in the past and use those strengths to achieve a compelling vision for the future.

 See "Another Perspective – Appreciative Inquiry (AI)" on page 27 for information about AI.

9. **Do not damage program activities that currently provide badly needed services.**
Although that is a rather obvious suggestion, it is surprising how often personnel can quickly get focused mostly on implementing project plans to the detriment of all else, including the programs that currently are effective. Therefore, early in the project, work with your client to identify what activities are off limits to the project, including any programs that are currently successful.

10. **Focus on getting some quick successes in the project.**
Quick successes help to ensure credibility for the project, enthusiasm among participants for project plans, and momentum for ongoing project activities. Examples of quick successes might include development of various plans, completion of planning meetings, generation of major reports, or identification of useful learning.

11. **Consider current grant requirements.**
Nonprofits make certain promises to donors when they donate resources to the nonprofits. Usually those promises are specified in terms of certain grant requirements, such as outcomes that must be achieved and methods used to achieve those outcomes. During change efforts, those requirements still must be met unless permission is provided otherwise from the donor.

12.  **Schedule the project's actions to occur on a timely basis.**
    Activities should not occur too slowly, so as to be obsolete by the time they are conducted.
    Nor should they occur so fast that they cause an array of other problems. One of the best
    ways to ensure that actions occur on a timely basis is to work collaboratively with your
    client to develop and implement plans.

> See "Collaborative Planning for Relevant, Realistic and
> Flexible Plans" on for guidelines to ensure that your client
> works collaboratively with you during planning.

13.  **Integrate results throughout the organization.**
    One of the most challenging aspects of any change process is to ensure that the change effort
    accomplishes long-lasting results in the organization. Meeting that challenge means that
    project plans must focus at least as much on implementation and follow-through as on
    developing the plans. Therefore, results of the change effort should be integrated throughout
    the organization, by updating structures, organizational goals and strategies, policies and
    procedures, and roles and responsibilities.

> See "Phase 5: Implementation and Change Management" on
> page 349 for guidelines to integrate results throughout your
> client's organization.

14.  **Focus on accountabilities.**
    In project plans, include specific deliverables (tangible results) to be produced by your client
    during the project. If a deliverable is not produced when scheduled, immediately discuss the
    situation with your client. Note that inexperienced consultants sometimes struggle with that
    practice because they want their client to like them at least as much – if not more than – they
    want their client to learn and accomplish successful change. Experienced consultants have
    learned that a) it is their client who must continue to do the work in their organization if a
    project is to be successful and b) the moment that a client backs off from doing that work,
    the consultant and client need to authentically revisit the client's ownership in the project.

15.  **Focus on the process as much as on the final results.**
    When focusing only on achieving the desired final results, you can forget other critically
    important aspects of the change process, such as the quality of your relationship with your
    client. Also, you can become too rigid about considering necessary changes to the project
    plans. If you and your client work authentically in a highly collaborative process focused on
    continued action and learning, the results that really are meant to occur will occur.

16.  **Focus on learning during the change process.**
    Learnings form the basis from which we verify what is working and what is not during a
    project. Remember that a major goal of your consulting activity should be for your clients to
    learn how to solve more of their own problems. Therefore, be sure to integrate opportunities
    for learning into your project plans.

> See "Develop a Learning Plan to Capture Learning During the
> Project" on page 334 for guidelines to develop and use a
> Learning Plan.

## Core Components in Change Management Plans

1. **Train your client about organizational change.**
   Many consultants do not understand the nature and requirements of organizational change. Far more clients do not have that understanding, as well. Consequently, you need to help your client to understand the realities of a change effort. Consider sharing this subsection's guidelines for change with your clients.

2. **Include an integrated set of activities in your project plan.**
   The most powerful project plans are those that include an integrated set of actions. Depending on the needs and preferences of your client, strive to go beyond providing a written report or a simple, one-size-fits-all training. Instead, include assessments, customized trainings, ongoing one-on-one coaching, facilitation of an overall change process, opportunities for participants to learn from each other in peer networks, opportunities for participants to reflect on their own learning, and more assessments.

3. **Develop and communicate a written change management plan.**
   The plan should be developed collaboratively with your client. Document the plan and have your client review and approve it. Ensure that it is systematic – that it includes overall goals, methods to achieve the goals, and methods to assess whether or not the goals are being achieved. Share the plan with all key stakeholders as identified by your client.

4. **Conduct assessments as benchmarks for change.**
   In the middle of complex and dynamic change, you and your client need some consistent "stakes in the ground" – some aspects of the project that are, at least for now, considered to be specific and stable. Assessments, or measures of the quality of various activities, are useful during a project as means to measure the progress of a project, as well as a reference point around which you and your client can discuss the project. This Field Guide suggests use of assessments at various times during the collaborative consulting cycle.

    See "Best Methods to Collect Data" on page 276 for guidelines about when and how to use assessments.

5. **Plan for key roles during the change and identify the roles during the process.**
   During the change process, attempt to identify:

   a) The initiator of the change

   b) A champion (who provides enthusiasm and motivation during change)

   c) Various change agents (people responsible to guide the change) at different times

   d) The sponsor of the change (official coordinator of the change)

    See "Major Roles During Change and Capacity Building" on page 190 for information about the major roles during change.

6. **Produce written action plans with indicators and timelines.**
   Work with your client to produce action plans that specify who is going to be doing what and by when, including what resources each person will need. Resources are usually people,

445

facilities, money and supplies. Sometimes clients are reluctant to get to this level of detail because this is when they realize that they need to make specific commitments of their own time and resources. That level of commitment may be one of the reasons that your client is struggling in the first place. So you might need to coach your client through making the commitment of time and resources to the project. It also helps at this point to remind your client that plans are guidelines – they can be changed if needed.

7.  **Manage expectations between you and your client**.
    You can do this by collaboratively documenting the project plan, associated action plans and the status of implementation. Use strong communication skills, especially listening skills, to ensure that you and your client are really hearing each other. Successfully managing expectations may be one of your most important accomplishments during the project because it ensures that expectations are realistic and that your clients believe that they are being heard.

    See "How to Keep It Real – Managing for Realistic Expectations" on page 76 for guidelines to manage expectations.

8.  **Acknowledge accomplishments**.
    This component is often forgotten, yet it is one of the most important for ensuring realistic expectations, strong participation and sustained momentum during a project. The approach by which accomplishments are acknowledged, or even celebrated, should be according to the nature of your client's organization. One of the best ways to identify that approach is simply to ask your clients for their ideas.

    See "How to Help Your Client Appreciate Accomplishments" on page 77 for guidelines to help your client acknowledge accomplishments.

9.  **Specify how the project plan and action plans can be changed systematically**.
    As mentioned many times in this Field Guide, plans rarely are implemented as originally designed. It is permissible to change plans, but they should be changed in a systematic manner.

    See "Systematically Adjust Plans When Really Needed" on page 359 for guidelines to systematically change plans.

## Table VII:2 – Summary of Principles for Successful Change

### Nature of Overall Organizational Change Process

- A change process is a "journey" that you take with your client.
- Each change process with each client is different – it is highly customized.
- A change process rarely is an "aha!" experience.
- A change process usually takes longer than you think.

### Your Role as Consultant and Change Agent

- Manage your time and stress.
- Recognize the effect of your own nature on others during the change process.
- Adhere to your personal values and ethics.
- Although change is often unpredictable, have at least one change model in mind.
- Build trust, commitment and collaboration with your client.
- Get some ongoing, "outside" feedback on your project's plans and conclusions.
- Maintain sufficient skills in your primary areas of service.
- Have at least basic understanding of a range of consulting services.
- Do not try to control change, but instead to guide it during the project.

### Core Requirements for Your Client

- Your client must have the resources to implement the plan for change.
- Your client needs to be ready for the change process.
- Top leadership in your client's organization must support the project.
- Your client must take ownership in the change process.
- Your client must trust you, and you must trust your client.

### Core Areas of Focus for the Change Process

- Ensure project activities are focused on overall organizational goals.
- Integrate project goals into the context of overall organizational goals.
- Focus on "success" for the project – define "success" early in the project.
- Focus on activities that cause the symptoms of the problems.
- Focus on major organizational parts and their relationships.
- Focus on changing structures, not on changing personalities.
- Focus primarily on the first 20% of effort that generates 80% of results.
- Build from strengths at least as much as – if not more than – from weaknesses.
- Do not damage program activities that currently provide badly needed services.
- Focus on getting some quick successes in the project.
- Consider current grant requirements – those have to be met.
- Schedule the project's actions to occur on a timely basis.
- Integrate results throughout organization.
- Focus on accountabilities – have specific people responsible for specific actions.
- Focus on the process as much as on the final results.
- Focus on learning during the change process.

### Core Components in Change Plans

- Train your client about the basics of organizational change.
- Include an integrated set of activities in your project plan.
- Develop and communicate a written change management plan.
- Conduct assessments as benchmarks for change.
- Plan for key roles during the change and identify the roles during the process.
- Produce written action plans with indicators and timelines.
- Manage expectations with your client.
- Acknowledge accomplishments.
- Specify how the project plan and action plans can be changed systematically.

# How to Respond When All Else Fails

There are times when, regardless of the particular tool used to solve various problems, the overall situation still seems stuck. The following tools will help you to stand back, take a fresh look at the overall situation, and decide what to do next. This is true for both external or internal consultants.

## "Sanity Solution"

The Sanity Solution is useful after all other options seem to have been considered, yet the overall situation still seems completely stuck. In any situation like this, there are five courses of action to pursue. While the courses of action may seem quite obvious, it often helps a great deal in the midst of all of the confusion and frustration to remind people of those courses of action – to stay sane.

1.  **Get more resources to do what you want to do.**
    If it seems impossible to accomplish certain tasks by a certain deadline, get more resources to help you do the tasks.

2.  **Get more time to do what you want to do.**
    If you cannot get more resources, expand the deadlines to do the tasks.

3.  **Decrease the scope of what you want to do.**
    If you cannot expand the deadline, reduce the size of the tasks to be accomplished.

4.  **Some combination of the above.**
    Many times, the solution involves some combination of the above.

5.  **Do nothing, but accept that doing nothing is acceptable.**
    Often, this course of action requires use of the Monkey Trap.

## "Monkey Trap"

In situations where people seem to be stuck, it often helps to resort to simple, straightforward approaches to help them get unstuck and move forward. For example, the following story can be quite powerful in helping people to realize that they are stuck and that they should simply let go of what they have been doing that has them so stuck. Letting go can be every bit as hard – even harder – than continuing to "bang your head against a brick wall." In those situations, it helps to remember the Monkey Trap.

It is rumored that in one or more tribes in Africa, members catch monkeys by using this procedure. They build a small box made out of bamboo. They cut a small hole in the side of the box, barely big enough for a monkey to insert their hand. They put a tied-up bundle of several bananas in the box and place the box in a visible place with no people around. Eventually a monkey smells the bananas, approaches the box, puts a hand through the hole and grabs the bundle, but because of the size of the bundle, it cannot pull it back out of the hole. The monkey stands there, trying over and over again to pull the bundle out of the hole, but cannot. A member of the tribe walks up to the monkey, grabs it and kills it. The monkey was caught simply because it refused to let go.

The morals of the story are:

1.  It is often a lot easier to just let go than to work harder and harder with no success.

2.  Sometimes, it can kill you if you will not "just let go."

448

# APPENDICES

A: Glossary

B: Resources for Nonprofits and Consultants

C: Useful Forms During Consulting

D: Bibliography

# Appendix A: Glossary

**Action plan**

Specification of how a specific action is to be achieved, for example, in a Change Management Plan. Includes listing of objective(s) that, when accomplished in total, accomplish the overall action. For each objective, specifies position responsible to accomplish the objective, time to start, time to stop, and who is responsible to monitor accomplishment of the objective.

**Action Planning, Alignment and Integration (fourth consulting phase)**

Consultant and client develop actions (that were identified during Discovery and Feedback) into action plans. Also develop Evaluation Plan, Learning Plan, Recognition and Motivation Plan, and Communications Plan. All plans are integrated into an overall Change Management Plan.

**Action research**

Well-established process for identifying and addressing complex issues in organizations. Many variations of the process exist, usually based on original stages of start-up, entry, diagnosis, implementation and evaluation. Also applicable as model for organizational change. Developed by Kurt Lewin, founder of social psychology, 50 years ago.

**Adoption and Evaluation (sixth consulting phase)**

Consultant and client decide whether the presenting priority in the organization has been successfully addressed and whether client's organization has adopted necessary new systems. Includes evaluation of quality of final results from project.

**Alignment**

Relationships between subsystems in an overall system. Organizations seek optimum alignment, resulting in maximum performance of the overall organization.

**Appreciative inquiry (AI)**

Philosophy, and associated theories, models and techniques, based on the belief that "problems" are social constructions – that they are created, in large part, by the perceptions that they exist. AI-based practices focus on the wishes and strengths of members in the organization to achieve its vision and goals.

**Assessment**

Systematic collection of data, followed by analysis to generate findings and conclusions. More recently, assessments are often associated with recommendations. Thus, the terms evaluation and assessment are often used interchangeably.

**Authenticity**

Capacity of a person to express themselves in an honest and direct manner based in the here-and-now.

**Best practices**

Management practices that are widely recognized as standard and effective for achieving desired results in organizations. Examples include well-known practices, such as Board training, strategic planning and employee performance evaluations.

**Board of Directors**

Group of people legally charged to govern a corporation, whether for-profit or nonprofit.

**Business development**

Activities to expand the impact and/or revenues of an organization. Includes researching the environment to identify all opportunities to provide services, conducting a feasibility study of each likely opportunity, and developing a business plan for each of the most likely opportunities.

**Business planning**

Activities to clarify the need for a product or service in the community, specific groups of people having that need, how the product or service meets each group's particular needs, resources needed to develop and provide the product or service, how the resources will be organized and managed, costs to obtain and support use of the resources, and how communications between the organization and community will be coordinated. Information is often organized into subsections of a business plan, such as description of the product or service, marketing plan, management plan and financial plan. Well-done, complete grant proposals often resemble a business plan.

**Capacity building**

Activities to help a nonprofit enhance its effectiveness.

**Change agent**

Are various perspectives on this role. For example, could be the person internal to the organization who leads the change in the organization by setting direction and influencing others to follow that direction. Also, could be the person external to the organization who provides ongoing expertise and guidance to those internal to the organization in order to change their organization.

**Change management plan (CMP)**

Documented description of the organization's presenting priority and action plans to address the priority. Can also include: 1) Evaluation Plan to assess the progress toward the addressing priority, 2) Communications Plan to ensure all key personnel are aware of the CMP, 3) Recognition and Motivation Plan to ensure members of the organization are motivated to implement the CMP, and 4) Learning Plan to recognize and utilize all important learning from implementing the CMP.

**Change model**

Organized body of theory and guidelines (and sometimes tools) that provides guidance to analyze organizations and suggests actions for change (thereby sometimes acting as an organizational diagnostic model). Can also provide guidance for making adjustments to actions and how to sustain change. Examples include the action research process, Business Process Re-engineering and Future Search Conference.

**Charitable nonprofit**

Organization that has attained status from the appropriate government agency to enable it to receive donations, such that donors can deduct their donations from their tax liabilities.

**Chief Executive Officer**

Singular organizational position responsible to implement the policies and plans of the Board of Directors, and to lead and manage all other staff members. In nonprofits, commonly referred to as the Executive Director.

**Client Start-Up (first consulting phase)**

Client first realizes the presenting priority (problems to be solved or goals to be achieved) in their organization. Client begins thinking about how to address the priority, for example, by seeking funding or bringing in an external consultant.

**Client**

Person or group who approves, works with, and/or is affected by, the consultant's activities in an organization. Are several types: 1) official client hires, pays, makes major decisions, ultimately decides if the project was successful, and is usually the same throughout the project; 2) direct clients directly work with the consultant at various times, can be different people, and are always the consultant's current priority for effective collaboration; and 3) indirect clients are indirectly and ultimately affected by the consultant's activities in the organization.

**Coaching (personal and professional)**

Using a variety of tools (assessments, deep listening, inquiry, action planning, etc.) to guide and support another individual or group to identify their current priorities, take actions to address those priorities, and learn from reflections on those actions. There are different types of coaching, for example, "being" and performance coaching, and also applications of coaching, such as life, business and executive.

**Collaborative consulting cycle**

Highly integrated set of collaborative consulting activities intended to address the presenting priority in an organization. Includes seven phases: Client Start-Up; Engagement and Agreement; Discovery and Feedback; Action Planning, Alignment and Integration; Implementation and Change Management; Adoption and Evaluation; and Project Termination.

**Collaborative consulting**

Philosophy of consulting in which the consultant and client work in partnership to address the presenting priority in the client's organization. Philosophy asserts that, the more collaborative the consulting activities, then the more trust, commitment and collaboration gained from the client and, thus, the more long lasting and successful the results of the consulting activities in the client's organization.

**Communications Plan**

Documented description of how a Change Management Plan will be communicated to key personnel inside and outside of the organization.

**Consultant**

Block (2000) explains that a consultant is someone trying to change another person or organization, but who has no direct control over that person.

### Consulting

Activities carried out by a consultant to help a client address their presenting priority in their organization. Activities can be in various forms, for example, provision of resources, trainings, coaching or facilitation. Often conducted in various phases that generally conform to phases of the action research process.

### Content (facilitation)

Information, materials and other resources that group members are working on in their group. In contrast to process, which includes information, materials and other resources that are directly in regard to how a group of people function together.

### Context-sensitive features

Certain aspects of an organization that make it unique, including especially its culture, life cycle, size, source and style of top-level leadership, structure and strategies, and rate of change in the external environment.

### Culture

Personality of an organization as defined by the aggregate of values, assumptions, opinions, behaviors, etc., by which members act in the organization. Is a context-sensitive feature of an organization that makes it unique from other organizations.

### Discovery and Feedback (third consulting phase)

Consultant and client further examine the presenting priority. Includes systematic data collection and analysis to fully examine the presenting priority and generate recommendations to address issues. Ends with carefully planned activities to share (or feed back) the results of the discovery to others in the organization.

### Domain

Focus of the performance management system, for example, an individual position, team, project, cross-functional process, function, program or the entire organization.

### Engagement and Agreement (second consulting phase)

Usually the first time the consultant and client meet. Overall goals are for both to understand each other's nature and needs, articulate how each prefers to work, begin exploring the presenting priority in the client's organization, assess the readiness of the client to begin a consulting project, decide if there is a suitable match between both of them, and then decide next steps, such as how a formal agreement can be established.

### Environment

All systems, materials and information that exist outside of the boundaries of a system. To be effective, systems exchange and address ongoing feedback with their environment.

### Ethics

Simply put, ethics involves learning what is right or wrong, and then doing the right thing. Ethics includes the fundamental ground rules by which we live our lives. A code of ethics is an articulated set of values or principles by which a person or group should act.

### Evaluation

Systematic collection and analysis of data to make a decision. Includes generation of findings and recommendations to address findings.

**Evaluation (formative)**

Evaluation of the quality of activities while those activities are being conducted.  Primarily intended to improve the quality of those activities while underway.

**Evaluation (summative)**

Evaluation of the quality of final results after activities have been finished.  Primarily intended to determine if the desired results have been achieved or not.

**Evaluation Plan**

Documented description of how the results of a project will be evaluated (summative evaluation).  Can also include description of how project activities will be evaluated while underway (formative evaluation).  Identifies what information is needed, how it will be collected, who will collect it and when.

**Executive Director**

Title commonly used for the Chief Executive Officer of a nonprofit organization.

**External consultant**

Someone considered not to be an official, ongoing member of the organization.  The one-time relationship of the consultant to the organization is determined usually by a project's contract or Letter of Agreement.  If the consultant is paid (rather than volunteering), payment is on the basis of a particular project that specifies certain desired results and deliverables from the consultant.  Payroll taxes are not withheld from the person's paycheck – the person pays their own payroll taxes.

**Facilitating**

Helping a group to decide what results they want to achieve together, how they want to achieve them and then helping the group to achieve them.  Styles range from highly directive to indirect.

**Feedback**

Information provided to, received by, or exchanged between systems and useful to enhancing the performance of one or more systems.

**Financial management**

Activities to ensure the organization's finances are effectively accounted for, legally allocated, at minimum risk and utilized in an optimum manner.  Includes operating according to fiscal policies and procedures, bookkeeping to monitor and record transactions, generating and analyzing financial statements, and actions to improve financial management.

**Founder's Syndrome**

Exists when an organization operates more according to the personality of someone in the organization (not always the founder) than to its mission.

**Function (nonprofit)**

Highly integrated set of ongoing management activities.  For example, Board operations, programs, staffing, marketing, financial management, fundraising and evaluations.

**Fundraising**

Activities to solicit and report about funds from donors, including individuals, foundations, corporations and/or government. Includes identifying fundraising targets (total monies to be raised during a certain period), researching prospective donors, soliciting each donor (via grants, events, etc.), recognition to donors, and managing grant documents and requirements.

**Implementation and Change Management (fifth consulting phase)**

Consultant and client guide and support implementation of the Change Management Plan. Focus is on implementation according to principles of successful organizational change. Consultant and client use a variety of tools to monitor status of implementation. Ensuring ongoing motivation and momentum is of primary importance.

**Indicators**

Measures of performance that suggest the extent of progress toward achieving certain desired results.

**Inputs**

Tangible or intangible resources used by various processes in a system to produce outputs and outcomes from the system. Types of inputs are people, money, equipment, facilities, supplies, ideas and time.

**Internal consultant**

Someone considered to be an official, often ongoing member of the organization. The relationship of the consultant to the organization is determined usually by a job description and various personnel policies. If the person is paid (rather than volunteering), payment is on the basis on their ongoing official roles in the organization. Payroll taxes are withheld from the person's paychecks. Successful internal consultants for change often use a highly collaborative and facilitative approach – the same style required by internal leaders to successfully guide change. Therefore, leaders can also sometimes be considered internal consultants.

**Intervention**

An activity introduced into a system to address a current problem or achieve a goal for that system, for example, forms of capacity building for an organization, such as training, coaching or strategic planning.

**Leader (nonprofit)**

Person who conducts leadership activities or has that capacity in a nonprofit organization. Anyone in the organization can be a leader. Commonly refers to official roles of top-level influence, such as Board Chair, Chief Executive Officer or Program Director. Leader can act as internal change agent if working to guide change internally.

**Leadership**

Activities or capacity to establish direction and influence a domain to follow that direction. Type of skills required depends on the domain of leadership, for example, leading self, other individuals, other groups, an organization, a community or a society. Can also refer to leadership traits or leadership roles.

**Learning Plan**

Documented description of how learning will be recognized and utilized during implementation of the Change Management Plan.

**Learning**

Enhanced or enhancing knowledge, behaviors, skills, attitudes, conditions or values.

**Life cycle**

Stage of development of a system. There are various perspectives on the types and numbers of stages, for example, stages of start-up, growth and maturity, with stagnation or development between each of those three stages.

**Logic model**

Graphic depiction of a system. Includes depiction of the system's inputs, processes, outputs and outcomes.

**Management support organization**

A nonprofit organization whose mission is to help other nonprofits become more effective.

**Management system**

Systematic activities in managing a particular system. Includes inputs to the system, planning, developing, operating, evaluating and outputs from system. For example, each function (Boards, strategic planning, marketing, etc.) has its own management system.

**Management**

Traditionally, refers to the activities involved in the four general practices: planning, organizing, leading and coordinating. The four functions recur throughout the organization and are highly integrated.

**Marketing**

Activities to establish and maintain a beneficial and ongoing relationship between an organization and certain groups of external stakeholders. "Inbound" marketing includes researching the external environment to: 1) identify the specific types of needs of each specific group of clients, 2) how to meet each of those needs, 3) what value (prices, fees, etc.) needs to be obtained in return for meeting those needs, 4) what collaborators exist and 5) what competitors exist. "Outbound" marketing includes: 6) advertising, 7) promotions and 8) public relations to enlighten stakeholders about products, services and the organization.

**Measures**

Objective information that provides specific information, such as indicators toward achievement of results. Typically expressed in terms of time, quantity, quality or cost. Results are a form of measures.

**Members (of the organization)**

This Field Guide considers members of an organization to include members of the Board of Directors and staff. Staff members include paid and volunteer members as well as the Chief Executive Officer, if the Board chooses to use that role.

**Nonprofit organization**

Organization that exists primarily to meet a community need, rather than primarily to generate a profit. An informal nonprofit has not been incorporated and usually exists as a short-term, informal gathering of people to meet a short-term, specific need in the community. A chartered, or incorporated, nonprofit has filed with the appropriate government agency to be its own legal entity. A tax-exempt nonprofit has attained status from the appropriate government agency that allows the nonprofit to refrain from paying certain federal, state (provincial in Canada) and/or local taxes. A charitable nonprofit has attained status from the appropriate government agency to enable it to receive donations, thereby, allowing donors to reduce their tax liabilities by the amount of their donations.

### Nonprofit service provider

Organization that provides ongoing services to nonprofit organizations, for example, for-profit consulting firms, management support organizations, associations and training centers.

### Open systems

Viewpoint that healthy systems regularly exchange feedback with, and are influenced by, their external environments (environments outside the boundaries of the systems). Includes the concept of equifinality, that there is more than one way to accomplish the same or similar result in a system. Thus, there is no one right way to, for example, lead, manage and guide change in an organization.

### Organization Development (OD)

Field dedicated to expanding the knowledge and effectiveness of people to accomplish more successful organizational change and performance. Different people often have different perspectives on the field, depending on their particular values and skills.

### Organizational change

Nature of activities to accomplish significant change and development in an organization.

### Organizational development

(See organizational change.)

### Organizational diagnostic model

Are differing opinions. Some people suggest that models should come without bias or suggested solutions, and should be used to accomplish an objective, unfolding understanding of organizations. Others believe that models should suggest what types of practices should be occurring in the organization, the order in which those practices should be occurring, and standards of performance for the various practices.

### Organizational effectiveness

Success of an organization in working toward its mission and achieving its goals in a highly effective and efficient manner.

### Outcomes

Changes in the external environment as a result of a system's activities. Can be used to measure the performance of the system. In nonprofits, typically refers to changes in participants from participating in a program, including changes to their: 1) knowledge (short-term outcomes); 2) behaviors (intermediate outcomes); and 3) attitudes, values, conditions, etc. (long-term outcomes). In contrast to outputs, which can measure changes internal to the system.

### Outputs

Tangible results produced by a system. Can often be used to measure quantitative changes internal to a system. Often described by using numbers, such as the number of graduates produced by a certain program. In contrast to outcomes, which measures changes external to the system.

**Performance appraisal**

Assessment of extent and quality of a system's progress toward achieving certain desired results, along with whether certain performance standards were met or not.

**Performance development plan**

Conveys how the conclusion was made that a change in performance was desired and also how that change will be accomplished, whether remedial or developmental. Includes identification of specific standards and/or desired results, what actions are to be taken and by whom in order to improve performance, and when performance will be assessed again and how.

**Performance management**

Activities to select results to be achieved by a system, monitor indicators toward achieving those results, reinforce behaviors where results are being effectively achieved, and improve performance where results are not being effectively achieved. In contrast to "busyness" where activities, although frequent, are not directly in regard to achieving desired results.

**Polarity**

A situation in which there seems to be two "sides" and one "side" is highly dependent on, or can be affected by, the other "side." The sides are seemingly contradictory, but cannot completely exist without the presence, of the other. Examples include: inhale versus exhale, cost versus quality and decentralize versus centralize.

**Presenting priority**

A current major priority in the client's organization which causes the client to seek assistance to address the priority. Also referred to as a presenting problem.

**Process (cross-functional)**

Organizational activities that span more than one major subsystem in an organization. For example, processes of information technology and quality management.

**Process (facilitation)**

Information, materials and other resources directly in regard to how a group of people function together. In contrast to content, which is information, materials and others resources in regard to what members are working on in their group.

**Processes (system)**

Activities to manipulate the system's inputs to achieve the overall desired results (outputs and outcomes) of the system.

**Program (nonprofit)**

Set of highly integrated activities intended to meet a specific need in the community. Nonprofits usually provide major services in the form of programs.

**Program evaluation**

Systematically collecting and analyzing information about a program to make a decision about the program. Common forms are process, goals-based and outcomes-based.

**Program planning**

> Activities to define results (goals and outcomes) for a program, resources needed to achieve those results, how those resources will be obtained and supported, who will obtain the resources and by when, and how the resources will be organized and managed.

**Project plan**

> Documented description of the results to be achieved by a project, along with methods to achieve those results, resources needed to use the methods, roles and responsibilities of the consultant and client during the project, budget for the project, and schedule for the project.

**Project Termination (seventh consulting phase)**

> Consultant and client formally terminate the consulting project and relationship. Both reflect on project achievements and learning.

**Recognition and Motivation Plan**

> Documented description of how leaders in the organization will ensure that members of the organization are motivated and sustain momentum to implement the Change Management Plan.

**Resistance (individual and group)**

> Emotional response in reaction to a perceived threat from current or intended change. Can be direct or indirect. Direct resistance is the person's authentic (direct, honest and open) expression about the perceived threat and why they are not going to support the change. Indirect resistance is when the person does not authentically express their concern about why they will not support the change. Usually, resistance is indirect and, therefore, can be difficult for the consultant and client to recognize and address.

**Resource development**

> Activities to obtain resources and make them ready for utilization by the organization, for example, regarding people, funding, facilities and materials.

**Results**

> Overall accomplishments desired from the performance of the domain. Are measures of products, services or changes (outcomes) for an internal or external customer. Often expressed in terms of cost, quality, quantity, time or learning.

**Rewards**

> Various forms of reinforcement intended to guide and/or reinforce a system's performance toward achieving desired results. Rewards in employee performance management might include merit increases, promotions, certificates of appreciation and letters of commendation.

**SMART**

> An acronym for Specific, Measurable, Achievable, Relevant and Time-bound. Often used to suggest the nature of useful goals and objectives.

**Staff**

> Members of a nonprofit organization other than the Board of Directors. Includes the Chief Executive Officer. Can be paid or volunteer.

**Stakeholder**

Person or group of people who have an interest in, or are affected by, the nonprofit now and/or in the near future.

**Standard**

Specifies how well a desired result should be, or was, achieved by a system. For example, "meets expectations" or "exceeds expectations."

**Standards of excellence**

Principles that are widely recognized as standard and effective for guiding management practices toward achieving desired results in organizations.

**Strategic management**

Systematic implementation of a Strategic Plan, including monitoring status of implementation and making adjustments to implementation and/or the Plan, as necessary.

**Strategic planning**

Major activity carried out on a regular basis to clarify the organization's purpose (mission), desired results (vision, goals and objectives), when the results are to be achieved, and by whom. Sometimes specifies the overall nature (values) in how results are to be achieved.

**Structures**

Plans, policies, positions, procedures, etc., that configure and guide the overall relationships, integration and performance of systems in an organization.

**Subsystem**

System that is part of another overall system, where the part has its own inputs, processes and outputs, which share feedback with the larger, overall system. For example, a nonprofit program in an overall nonprofit organization.

**Supervision**

Activities by a supervisor to oversee the progress and productivity of people who report directly to the supervisor. Includes activities of employee performance management, such as staffing analysis, specification of duties and responsibilities (job description), recruitment and selection of employees, assignment of goals, feedback on achievement of goals, rewarding achievement of goals and addressing performance problems.

**Supervisor**

Position in an organization that is responsible for supervision of people who report directly to the supervisor.

**System**

A collection of resources and activities aligned and integrated to accomplish an overall goal. Includes inputs, processes and outputs to achieve the goal. An automobile engine is a system. A pile of sand is not a system.

**Systematic**

In the nature of a system; a methodological approach to have goal(s), monitor feedback regarding achievement of goal(s), and make necessary adjustments to more effectively achieve the goal(s).

**Systems theory**

Field which studies systems from the perspective of the whole system, its various subsystems and the recurring patterns in the relationships between the subsystems. Has spawned a manner of thinking (systems thinking) that has produced principles and tools for understanding and changing systems.

**Systems thinking**

Approach to analyze and understand systems by identifying the overall goals of the system, its various subsystems, recurring structures and patterns in the relationships among the subsystems, and, in particular, the quality of those relationships and how they might be better integrated and aligned.

**Tax-exempt nonprofit**

Organization that has attained status from the appropriate government agency that allows the organization to avoid paying certain federal, state/provincial and/or local taxes.

**Team building**

Activities to form and develop a small group of people to effectively work toward a common purpose and achieve specific goals. At a minimum, includes clarifying the group's purpose and goals, leadership roles, means of communication, and how members will make decisions and solve problems.

**Teamwork**

Activities among team members to effectively achieve the results desired from the team.

**Training**

Traditionally, activities to convey specific information to help an individual or group to more effectively do a current or future task or job.

**Turnaround (of nonprofit organization)**

Outcome from a project for change where the organization previously experienced issues throughout most or all of the organization and now, as a result of the project, has resolved most or all of the issues and is experiencing strong performance.

**Vision for change**

Description of an organization and its clients at some point in the future. Often used as guiding and motivational tool during change. Strategic vision depicts a realistic state that will be achieved by implementing the Change Management Plan. Grand vision depicts an ideal state, often at a time farther out than the time of the strategic vision.

**Whole systems thinking**

Approaches to examine an entire system and how to address all major issues and goals in the system. The positive effect of those solutions leverages improvement throughout the system.

# Appendix B:
# Resources for Nonprofits and Consultants

## Free Management Library<sup>SM</sup>

The Library includes extensive free materials about personal, professional and organizational development. The Library includes over 675 topics that are organized into the following popular categories. The list of topics is located at http://www.managementhelp.org/ on the Web.

| Advertising and Promotion | Benefits and Compensation | Boards of Directors |
|---|---|---|
| Career Development | Chief Executive Role | Communication (Interprsnl) |
| Communication (Writing) | Computers, Internet & Web | Consultants (using) |
| Coordinating Activities | Creativity and Innovation | Crisis Management |
| Customer Satisfaction | Customer Service | E-Commerce |
| Employee Performance | Employee Wellness Programs | Ethics - Practical Toolkit |
| Evaluations (many kinds) | Facilities Management | Finances (For-Profit) |
| Finances (Nonprofit) | Fundraising (Nonprofit) | General Resources |
| Group Performance | Group Skills | Guiding Skills |
| Human Resources Mgmnt | Insurance (Business) | Interpersonal Skills |
| Interviewing (all kinds) | Jobs | Leadership (Introduction) |
| Leadership Development | Legal Information | Management (Introduction) |
| Management Development | Marketing | Operations Management |
| Organizational Alliances | Organizational Change | Org'l Communication |
| Organizational Performance | Organizations (Introduction) | Organizing (many kinds) |
| Performance Management | Personal Development | Personal Productivity |
| Personal Wellness | Planning (many kinds) | Policies (Personnel) |
| Product Selection & Dev. | Program Management | Project Management |
| Public and Media Relations | Quality Management | Research Methods |
| Risk Management | Sales | Social Entrepreneurship |
| Staffing | Starting an Organization | Supervision (Introduction) |
| Supervisory Development | Systems Thinking | Taxation |
| Training Basics | Volunteers | ---------------- |

# Free Nonprofit Micro-eMBA<sup>SM</sup> Organizational Program

This self-directed, on-line training program includes 12 highly integrated courses that can be taken for free by anyone, anywhere at any time. At the end of the program, each learner will have all of the basic systems and processes needed to start and operate a nonprofit. Learners are encouraged to work with their Boards of Directors while going through the program. During the program, participants share plans, policies and procedures.

Any of the 12 courses in the program can be taken separately. To see the courses and their learning objectives, go to the "Course Catalog" located at http://www.managementhelp.org/np_progs/org_dev.htm on the Web.

Courses include the following

1.      Preparatory Workshop

2.      Starting and Understanding Your Nonprofit

3.      Overview of Role of Chief Executive

4.      Basic Skills in Management and Leadership

5.      Building and Maintaining an Effective Board of Directors

6.      Developing Your Strategic Plan

7.      Designing and Marketing Your Programs

8.      Managing Your Finances and Taxes

9.      Developing Your Fundraising Plan

10.     Staffing and Supervision of Employees and Volunteers

11.     Evaluating Your Programs

12.     Organizational "Fitness Test"

# Professional Organizations

Note that many of the following organizations have local chapters in various states.

1.      Association of Management Consultant Firms
        National organization to foster understanding of management consulting, provide a forum
        for confronting common challenges, expand the knowledge base and champion ethics
        http://www.amcf.org

2.    Alliance for Nonprofit Management
      National organization that provides information, research and forums to enhance nonprofit
      effectiveness, and includes nonprofits and nonprofit service providers
      http://www.allianceonline.org

3.    Organization Development Institute
      International organization for professional Organization Development practitioners – the
      only one that suggests specific levels of professionalism among practitioners
      http://www.odinstitute.org/

4.    National Organizational Network
      National organization that develops, supports and inspires practitioners and enhances the
      body of knowledge in human organization and systems development
      http://www.odnetwork.org/

5.    American Society for Training and Development
      National organization for professionals in training and development
      http://www.astd.org

6.    International Association of Facilitators
      National organization for facilitators of a wide variety of applications, for example, strategic
      planning, action planning or general meeting management
      http://www.iaf-world.org/

7.    International Society for Performance Improvement
      National organization focused on models, tools and techniques to improve performance of
      organizations, processes and individuals
      http://www.ispi.org/

## Sources of Nonprofit Consultants and Mentors

1.    In the USA, contact your Secretary of State and/or state's Attorney General's office and ask
      for a list of resources.  In Canada, contact the appropriate provincial agency.

2.    Executive Service Corps (ESC) provides experienced consultation in the areas of technical
      and management.

3.    National Council of Nonprofit Associations (NCNA) has chapters in almost all of the states.

4.    Contact the local volunteer recruitment organization in your community and ask for
      assistance.

5.    Look in the Yellow Pages of your local telephone directory for professional associations.
      Look for networks or associations of organization development practitioners, facilitators or
      trainers.

6.    Look in the Yellow Pages of your local telephone directory under the categories
      "Consultant" and "Volunteering."

7.   Contact local large corporations. They often have community service programs and can provide a wide range of management and technical expertise. Speak to the head of the Human Resources Department.

8.   Call a local university or college and speak to someone in the college of Human Resources, Training and Development, or Business Administration.

9.   Ask other nonprofits (particularly those that have similar services and number of staff) or current clients for ideas, contacts and references.

10.  Ask a retired business person (from a for-profit or nonprofit organization). They have extensive expertise in professional and organizational development.

# Web Sites and On-Line Forums

There are many web sites and on-line forums about organizational development, organizational change and nonprofits. A comprehensive listing would be overwhelming. In the following major sites, you can pose questions, get answers and get references to other useful Web sites and forums.

1.   Free Management Library web site (see Appendix B)
     One of the world's largest collections of well-organized, free, on-line resources about organization, management and business development
     http://www.managementhelp.org

2.   TRDEV on-line forum
     Free, on-line forum about training and development
     http://groups.yahoo.com/group/trdev/

3.   HRNET on-line forum
     Free, on-line forum about human resource management
     http://groups.yahoo.com/group/HRNET

4.   Appreciative Inquiry (AI) Commons web site
     Free, comprehensive repository of information about AI
     http://appreciativeinquiry.case.edu/

5.   Charity Channel forums
     Provides a wide variety of on-line forums about many nonprofit topics (fee-based service)
     http://www.charitychannel.com

# Appendix C:  Useful Forms During Consulting

Checklist to Assess Client Readiness for Change

Sample Proposal for Organizational Change

Sample Contract Form

Organizational Assessment Tool

Planning the Research

To download a copy of the worksheets in this Appendix, point your Web browser to the following Web address (note that it might take a while to download the worksheets, depending on the speed of your browser).

http://www.authenticityconsulting.com/pubs/CN-gdes/worksheets.doc

Save the document to your computer's disk, for example, use the "Save As" command in your browser and name the file "worksheets."

The author and the publisher hereby grant permission for the purchaser of this guide to reproduce the contents of Appendix C for use with the purchaser's clients or within the purchaser's organization.

# Checklist to Assess Client's Readiness for Change

Before you and your nonprofit client start your project for organizational change, you both should determine whether your client's organization is really ready for that change. This is a critical determination to make. Below are several questions to guide you and your client now. Next to each question, indicate whether you and/or your client believe your client's organization is really ready. The final determination is up to you and your client. If both of you conclude that the organization is not yet ready, use the considerations in the right-hand column to determine how your client might get ready and when you might be able to begin your project. This checklist will be useful to you whether you are an external or internal consultant.

| Readiness Questions | Yes – Ready | Not Ready | Considerations If Not Ready |
|---|---|---|---|
| 1. Does your client have sufficient funds budgeted for the project? | | | How can your client get funds in time to start a project soon? |
| 2. Does your client have the time to participate in a major project for organizational change? | | | How can your client find the time to participate in a project like this? |
| 3. Is your client open to other perspectives than theirs about the project? | | | How can your client become more open to other perspectives? |
| 4. Is your client open to hearing specifically about what might be their own role in any issues found in the organization? | | | How can your client become more open to hearing about their own role? |
| 5. Has your client had success using consultants before? | | | If difficulties were experienced, what were they? How can your project avoid those experiences? |

**Checklist to Assess Nonprofit Client Readiness for Change (cont.)**

| Readiness Questions | Yes – Ready | Not Ready | Considerations If Not Ready |
|---|---|---|---|
| 6. Were all important people in attendance at your initial meeting(s) with your client? | | | If there were important people missing, who were they? How will they get involved in the project? |
| 7. Can you, the consultant, be assured access to necessary people and organizational activities for the project? | | | If not, how will you get access to those people? |
| 8. Are all important people comfortable with the project? | | | If there are people who would be uncomfortable, what should be done? |
| 9. Do you, the consultant, feel that your client is really ready for a project for major organizational change? | | | Are there any "red flags," or feelings of concern on your part? If there are, what are they? How can they be addressed? |
| 10. Does your client feel that their organization is really ready for a project for major organizational change? | | | Are there any "red flags" or feelings of concern on their part? If there are, what are they? How can they be addressed? |

If you have any checks in the "Not Ready" column for any of the 10 items, consider addressing the questions in the right-hand column for that item.

Considering creating an action plan based on the answers to questions in the right-hand column. Work with key individuals to execute that plan and, afterwards, conduct a reassessment about readiness to begin a project for change.

# Sample Proposal for Organizational Development Services

*This sample proposal might be a useful reference for you and your client as you both specify and communicate a project plan for change. Information in the proposal will be useful to external and internal consultants. In this example, the organizational development and change activities are conducted in the overall context of development and implementation of a Strategic Plan. Ongoing coaching during the project guides the successful organizational change and learning that results during, and shortly after, implementing the Strategic Plan. Of course, the final content of your proposal depends on the preferences of your client and you.*

*Note that many consultants do not include estimated numbers of hours for project activities in their proposals, as in this sample. These consultants base their consulting fees on the project's overall value to the client, rather than on the number of hours required in the project. These consultants believe that information about the number of hours in the project detracts clients from focusing on the total value of the project.*

## Background

The consultant, OD Bob, met with the client contact, Ed Executive Director of the Transitioning Nonprofit (TN), on July 1, 2010 regarding a possible organizational development project. Also in attendance at that meeting were two Board members who, together with Ed, comprised the Search Committee. During the meeting, Ed described TN's current challenges, which included the need for fundraising, strategic planning and outcomes evaluation. Ed explained that TN had experienced recurring cash shortages, declining number and amounts of grants from donors, and recurring conflicts among members of the Board and staff. Ed added that things seemed to be getting worse.

OD Bob described how an overall systematic approach to organizational development would be the most effective approach to addressing TN's major problems. OD Bob added that the organizational development activities would best be conducted in the overall context of short-term, internally strategic planning, including the development and implementation of the Strategic Plan.

After some discussion, participants agreed that a systematic approach to overall organizational development would be highly useful to TN. Ed asked OD Bob to provide a proposal that described more specifics on how OD Bob might work with TN. This proposal itemizes OD Bob's proposed project and includes: outcomes, overall activities and deliverables, work plan, evaluation plan, schedule, roles and responsibilities of the consultant and client, costs and payment terms. The proposal also includes description of OD Bob's qualifications as a consultant, along with reference to relevant clients whom Ed could contact regarding the quality of OD Bob's work.

## Project Outcomes

The following outcomes are typically achieved from implementation of a realistic, relevant and flexible Strategic Plan with focus primarily on addressing internal priorities:

1.      Effective Board governance, including oversight and operations.

2.      Clear delineation and coordination of Board and staff roles.

3.      Common vision and goals for all leaders in the organization.

4.      Strong focus and evaluation regarding specific program outcomes.

5. Enhanced credibility and image among stakeholders.

6. Stronger marketing, including research, advertising and promotions.

7. More stable and consistent revenue streams.

8. Overall, more proactive direction-setting, decision-making and problem-solving.

## Project Activities and Deliverables

1. Organizational assessment and development planning, including initial assessment and recommendations, resulting in a written Assessment Report and an Organizational Development Plan to address issues described in the Report.

2. Board development, including engagement, staffing and organization of members, along with comprehensive, step-by-step guidelines and materials for all critical and ongoing Board activities, resulting in a written Board Development Plan.

3. Strategic planning, including customizing planning process, identification and/or clarification of all critical issues and specific strategies to address each issue, resulting in a written relevant, realistic and flexible Strategic Plan.

4. Program outcomes evaluation planning, including clarification of each program's outcomes, outcome targets, indicators, information needed to measure progress toward indicators and how that information can be collected in a highly practical fashion. Activities result in an Outcomes Evaluation Plan for each program.

5. Leadership and supervisory development, including identifying performance goals for each position, clarifying roles and organization, and customizing employee performance management system, along with comprehensive, step-by-step guidelines and materials for all critical leadership and supervisory activities, resulting in an Organization Chart, a Staffing Plan, job descriptions and an updated handbook of Personnel Policies.

## Project Work Plan

### Ongoing Coaching for Change Management and Learning

Coaching will be focused on the successful implementation and evaluation of the Strategic Plan, resulting in an overall successful organizational development and change effort. Learning will be identified, documented and shared on an ongoing basis during the project.

1. Half-hour coaching sessions with Chief Executive Officer every two weeks for approximately 7 months.

2. Monthly, half-hour coaching sessions with Board Chair for 7 months.

### Phase #1: Organizational Assessment and Development Planning

1. Review organizational information, for example, history, programs and current activities.

2. Coordinate quick, comprehensive, practical organizational assessment of all internal functions, preferably with input from key Board and staff members, and then produce written Organizational Assessment Report.

3. Provide written Organizational Development Plan that addresses issues described in the Organizational Assessment Report.

## Phase #2:  Develop "Plan for Plan" for Strategic Plan

Plan-for-Plan will specify parameters for developing the Strategic Plan, and will address at least the following priorities.

1.  Orient Board members about strategic planning, its purpose and their role in the planning.

2.  Focus the Strategic Plan for a one-year period for the development of internal systems to address the issues described in the Organizational Assessment Report.

3.  Establish a Planning Committee to oversee development of Strategic Plan.  Ideally, the Committee is comprised of Board Chair, Chairs of committees, Chief Executive Officer and key staff members.

4.  Analyze how members of Board and staff can realistically take part in strategic planning, and then refine a three-month schedule of planning activities to develop and approve a Strategic Plan document.

5.  Establish a Stakeholder Team to provide stakeholder input to the planning and provide an external reference to monitor successful implementation of the Strategic Plan.

Shortly after this phase, various groups will be assigned homework to identify strategic goals and strategies.

## Phase #3:  Identification of Strategic Goals and Objectives

Based on the issues described in the Organizational Assessment Report, goals in the Strategic Plan might pertain to following areas.  Note that achievement of all of the strategic goals will not necessarily be done within the four-month time period in which the Strategic Plan document will be developed and approved.  Also note that planners might modify the following list during planning.

1.  Board development, working from an approved "Board Development Plan," managed by the Board Governance Committee.

2.  Facilities planning, focused on facilities requirements, available facilities, potential costs and plans for maintenance, resulting in an approved "Facilities Plan," managed by the Facilities Committee.

3.  Establishing financial policies and procedures, especially regarding zero-based and balanced budgeting, program-based budgeting, and amounts of cash reserves per year, resulting in an approved "Fiscal Policies and Procedures," managed by the Finance Committee.

4.  Strategic fundraising, including identifying fundraising targets for donations from individuals, foundations, corporations and government; along with which donors will be approached by whom, how and when; resulting in an approved "Resource Development Plan," managed by the Fundraising Committee.

5.  Program analysis and evaluation planning, focused on clarifying program outcomes, outcome targets, indicators, methods of data collection and analysis and reporting, resulting in an approved "Evaluation Plan" for each program, managed by the Programs Committee.

6.  Staffing analysis, including identifying and organizing expertise needed to implement the Strategic Plan and desired programs, modification of job descriptions, analysis of employee performance management and compensation systems, resulting in approved up-to-date job descriptions, employee performance management practices (in Personnel Handbook), and compensation practices (in Personnel Handbook), managed by the Personnel Committee.

7.   Sustained public relations to key stakeholders, to convey the "transformed" Transitioning Nonprofit, resulting in a public relations campaign, managed by the Marketing Committee.

Shortly after this phase, various groups will be assigned homework to identify action plans.

### Phase #4: Action Plans to Implement Strategic Plan

1.   Action plans, in the Strategic Plan, will specify for each strategic goal:

   a)   Objectives

   b)   Responsibilities

   c)   Deadlines for completion

2.   Action plans will also include:

   a)   Staffing plans

   b)   Operating budget

3.   Action plans will also include development of a one-year schedule during which the Strategic Plan will be implemented, with provision of status reports to the Board and Stakeholder Team.

Shortly after this phase, various groups will be assigned homework to begin drafting the Strategic Plan document.

### Phase #5: Development and Approval of Strategic Plan Document

Includes:

1.   Drafting Strategic Plan document

2.   Review by Board and Stakeholder Team

3.   Approval by Board of Directors

## Approaches to Evaluating Project

### Focus of Evaluation Plan(s)

Evaluation planning should be based on the project's goals and outcomes. After the goals and outcomes have been finalized, the consultant and client will work together to establish the focus of each Evaluation Plan. Plan(s) could focus on:

1.   Project activities, as those activities occur (a formative, process evaluation).

2.   Project deliverables (proposed deliverables are listed in the above section, "Project Activities and Deliverables").

3.   Outcomes achieved by the project (the proposed outcomes are listed in the above section, "Project Outcomes").

### Contents of Evaluation Plan(s)

The consultant and client will work together to design the content of each Evaluation Plan, which will include evaluation questions, information needed to answer each question, and methods to gather and analyze that information.

## *Proposed Project Schedule to Develop Strategic Plan*

### Approximate Time Required to Produce Strategic Plan Document

**Week of…**

| Phase | Aug 4 | Aug 11 | Aug 18 | Aug 29 | Sep 1 | Sep 8 | Sep 15 | Sep 22 | Sep 29 | Oct 6 | Oct 13 | Oct 20 | Oct 27 | Nov 3 | Nov 10 |
|---|---|---|---|---|---|---|---|---|---|---|---|---|---|---|---|
| 1. Organizational assessment and report | ▓ | ▓ | ▓ | ▓ | ▓ | ▓ | | | | | | | | | |
| 2. "Plan for Plan" | | | | | | ▓ | | | | | | | | | |
| 3. Identify goals and strategies | | | | | | ▓ | ▓ | ▓ | ▓ | | | | | | |
| 4. Develop action plans and resource needs | | | | | | | | ▓ | ▓ | ▓ | ▓ | | | | |
| 5. Draft, review and approve Strategic Plan | | | | | | | | | | ▓ | ▓ | ▓ | ▓ | ▓ | ▓ |

(Time is in hours. Board meeting time is included. Travel time is not included. "ED" refers to the Executive Director.)

| Activity | Executive Director and Other Senior Staff | Each Project Team Member | Each Board Member (addition to Project Team) | Consultant |
|---|---|---|---|---|
| Preparation | 0 | 0 | 0 | 5 |
| Phase 1: Organizational Assessment (6-week period) | 5 for ED | 2 | 1 | 5 |
| Phase 2: Plan for Plan (1-week period) | 5 for ED | 3 | 2 | 5 |
| Phase 3: Goals & Objectives (4-week period) | 15 for ED 15 for other | 10 | 8 | 30 |
| Phase 4: Action and Resource Planning (4-week period) | 10 for ED 10 for other | 3 | 4 | 20 |
| Phase 5: Approve Plan (6-week period) | 5 for ED 5 for other | 2 | 5 | 20 |
| Total Hours Required | 40 for ED 30 for other | 20 | 20 | 85 |

## Approximate Time to Completely Instill New Systems

The focus of this project is to instill new systems as a foundation to bring about change, such that the outcomes of the project are achieved. However, the long-term health of the organization depends on how well those new systems are fully integrated and utilized on a regular basis throughout the organization. Complete change often involves changing the culture of the organization – realistically, that can take a year or more. The amount of time to make those new systems an automatic part of operations for the client depends primarily on the leadership and amount of resources that the client can apply to the change effort, and on whether any unexpected major events occur during that effort.

The overall organizational development activities in this project will occur during a seven-month period, including a three-month period of coaching that follows the four-month development of the Strategic Plan document. The coaching will be focused on successfully managing organizational change during that seven-month period. Approximate time for coaching sessions is:

| Activity | Executive Director | Board Chair | Each Board Member (addition to Project Team) | Consultant |
|---|---|---|---|---|
| Ongoing Coaching (biweekly with ED; monthly with Board Chair; for 7 months) | 15 for ED | 7 for Board Chair | NA | 22 |

## *Roles and Responsibilities*

### Consultant

1.    Provide prompt response to client communication.

2.    Provide ongoing coaching to Chief Executive Officer and Board Chair as mutually scheduled during the seven-month period.

3.    Administer organizational assessment; analyze results and generate written Organizational Assessment Report and Organizational Development Plan.

4.    Generate written Board Development Plan.

5.    Facilitate strategic planning process, including customization and development.

6.    Review draft of Strategic Plan document.

7.    Facilitate staffing analysis, including roles and structures, and review of Staffing Plan.

8.    Facilitate development of employee performance management system.

9.    Provide complete step-by-step guidelines and materials for organizational assessment, all aspects of strategic planning, staffing analysis, roles and structures, and employee performance management.

10.    Generate written status reports shortly after end of all phases of project.

11.    Regularly reflect, document and share learning from the project with the client and members of the client's organization.

## Client

1.   Provide prompt response to consultant communication.

2.   Provide adequate organizational information for consultant to understand the organization.

3.   Finish organizational assessment.

4.   Board Chair participates in monthly half-hour coaching sessions for 7 months.

5.   Chief Executive Officer participates in biweekly half-hour coaching sessions for 7 months.

6.   Board and staff coordinate and participate in meetings as planned, including Board training and strategic planning sessions.

7.   Promptly finish actions as necessary between meetings, including preparation for upcoming meetings and actions identified from the meetings.

8.   Board forms Planning Committee to oversee development of Strategic Plan, including review of status of activities and written reports from consultant.

9.   Generate written Strategic Plan, organizational chart, Staffing Plan, job descriptions and arrange for expert review and development of updated personnel policies.

10.  Regularly reflect, document and share learning from the project with the consultant and members of the client's organization.

## *Proposed Costs and Payment Terms*

### Costs

| Fees: | Cost |
|---|---|
| Ongoing coaching for seven months | |
| Phase 1: Organizational Assessment | |
| Phase 2: "Plan for Plan" | |
| Phase 3: Identify goals and objectives | |
| Phase 4: Action and resource planning | |
| Phase 5: Finalize Strategic Plan | |
| **Total Fees:** | |
| | |
| **Materials and Expenses:** | |
| Travel expenses (estimated[1]) for four round trips | |
| Session materials | |
| **Total Estimated Materials and Expenses:** | |
| | |
| **Total Estimated Project Cost** | |

### Payment Terms

- $ XXX invoiced to client upon signing contract (equal to fees for Phase 1).
- $ XXX invoiced after Phase 2.
- $ XXX invoiced after Phase 3.
- $ XXX invoiced after Phase 4.
- $ XXX invoiced after Phase 5.
- $ XXX invoiced at end of seven-month period (this fee for coaching after the Strategic Plan has been approved).
- Materials and expenses invoiced within two weeks of incurring them; copies of receipts attached to invoice.
- Payments due from client within 30 days of receiving invoice from consultant.

## *Qualifications of Consultant*

*[In this section, you should insert information, such as your resume, information about your company and a listing of references to past clients.]*

---

[1] Travel costs will be reimbursed based on actual incurred costs.

# Sample Basic Contract Form for Consulting Services

*Especially for external consultants, here is a three-page basic contract form that you might customize for your consulting services. Use of this form assumes that you had initially submitted a proposal and project plan to your client and that your client wants to hire you because of the content of your proposal.*

*The following contract form should not be interpreted as legal advice from this author.*

This agreement is made by and between [*insert name and address of your client's organization*], hereby referred to as "the client," and [*insert name and address of your consulting organization*], hereby referred to as "the consultant."

1.  **Consultation Services.** The client hereby employs the consultant to provide services in the areas of [*insert overall type of consulting services that you are providing*]. Services are itemized in the attached proposal from the consultant to client, dated [*insert date of the proposal that was accepted by your client*].

2.  **Terms of Agreement.** This agreement will begin at the date of contract signing and will end [*insert the date that your services will end*]. Either party may cancel this agreement on thirty (30) days notice to the other party in writing, by certified mail or personal delivery. Any outstanding fees will be paid to the consultant by the client within ten (10) days after cancellation.

3.  **Key Organizational Representatives.** [*Insert name of person who will be your official contact in the project*] will represent the client during the project. [*Insert your name*] will represent the consultant.

4.  **Place Where Services Will Be Rendered.** The consultant will deliver services on or near the client's facilities in [*insert description of the city or other location*]. All other services will be provided via telephone or e-mail between the consultant's and client's offices.

5.  **Contract Costs.** Professional fees for this project can total up to [*insert the total that was included in your proposal*] as specified in the attached proposal. Costs for materials and expenses can total up to [*insert the total that was included in your proposal*]. Any additional work or travel that the client may require of the consultant that falls outside the bounds of the proposal will require an additional contract.

6.  **Payment to Consultant.** The client will remit payment for the professional fees within two weeks of invoicing according to the following schedule (materials and travel expenses will be invoiced within two weeks of incurring expenses).

| Amounts | Payment Terms |
| --- | --- |
| [*insert any partial payments to be made*] | Invoiced upon signing the contract |
| [*insert any partial payments to be made*] | [*insert description of the project phase or deliverable that is associated with that partial payment.*] |

7.      **Ownership of Intellectual Property.** The consultant will retain the ownership of any intellectual property (workbooks, presentations materials, etc.) that it brought to the project. Property created during the project and specific to the client's organization will be considered "work for hire" and owned by the client.

8.      **Independent Contractor.** Both the client and the consultant agree that the consultant will act as an independent contractor in the performance of its duties under this contract. Accordingly, the consultant shall be responsible for payment of all taxes including Federal and State taxes arising out of the consultant's activities in accordance with this contract, including by way of illustration but not limitation, Federal and State income taxes, and any other taxes or business license fees as required.

9.      **Confidential Information.** The consultant agrees to keep in confidence any proprietary information to which it is given access. It is of utmost importance that the consultant keep confidential any of the following categories of information from all persons outside of the client organization, including:

- Weaknesses or criticisms of the client that are revealed in interviews or other methods of gathering of facts.

- Ideas for potential new programs or revisions to the client's existing programs.

- Fundraising strategies, specific institutional or individual targets for fundraising, grant proposals and fundraising letters.

10.     **Signatures.** Both the client and the consultant agree to the above contract.

CLIENT:                                                      DATE:

_____            _____
*[Insert your name]*

BOARD CHAIR or WITNESS FOR CLIENT:        DATE:

_____            _____

CONSULTANT:                                              DATE:

_____            _____
*[Insert your name]*

WITNESS FOR CONSULTANT:                      DATE:

_____            _____

# Organizational Assessment Tool with Best Practices

The following assessment tool might be used to get a concise "snapshot" of the completeness and quality of standard practices conducted in a nonprofit organization.

 For guidelines to conduct research and collect data, see the sections in PART VI.

## Description

*Note that the following checklist, or assessment tool, originally developed by the Greater Twin Cities United Way of Minnesota (USA), has been slightly modified by the author to make it relevant to nonprofit organizations in Canada, as well as the United States.*

The following checklist is a resource developed by staff and volunteers of the Greater Twin Cities United Way for internal use by nonprofit organizations. Management can use the checklist to identify their organization's administrative strengths and weaknesses. It is believed that widespread use of the checklist ultimately results in a more effective and efficient nonprofit community. The checklist is not intended to be used as a tool for external evaluation, or by grant makers in making funding decisions. This tool will be used to assist nonprofit organizations to gain a better understanding of their management needs and/or make improvements to management operations.

This checklist includes the following topics:

- How to Use the Tool

- Disclaimers

- Legal Indicators

- Governance (Board) Indicators

- Human Resources Indicators

- Planning Indicators

- Financial Indicators

- Fundraising Indicators

## How to Use the Tool

Five of the above-listed topics include a variety of indicators for that topic. Each of the many indicators in this tool suggests a management practice needed to have a healthy, well-managed organization. Since it is a self-assessment tool, organizations should evaluate themselves honestly against each indicator and use the response to change or strengthen its operations.

## Ratings of Each Indicator

Each indicator is rated based on its importance to the operation and effectiveness of the organization. Thus, the ratings could be interpreted as representing "best practices." The ratings are:

1.  **E** – Indicators marked with an "E" are essential or basic requirements to the operations of all organizations. Organizations that do not meet the terms of these indicators could be placing their organizations in jeopardy.

2.  **R** – Indicators marked with an "R" are recommended as standard practices for effective organizations.

3.  **A** – Indicators marked with an "A" can enhance and strengthen operations.

## Possible Responses to Each Indicator

Organizations can respond in one of three ways to each indicator used:

1.  **Met** – Each indicator marked as "Met" indicates that the organization has met the terms of that indicator. However, the organization should review this indicator again in the future to be sure that their management remains healthy in view of the many internal and external changes, which constantly occur in all organizations.

2.  **Needs work** – Each indicator marked as "Needs Work" indicates that work is yet to be done towards meeting the terms of that indicator. The organization is aware of the terms for that indicator, and is working towards meeting those terms.

3.  **N/A** – An indicator marked as "N/A" can indicate several conditions, including:
    - the indicator is not applicable to the management operations of this organization.
    - the organization is not sure of the need to meet the requirements of this indicator.
    - the organization has not met, nor is working on this indicator presently, but may address it in the future.

## Analysis of Responses to Indicators

All responses to indicators should be reviewed carefully to see if they could improve management operations. Indicators checked "N/A" due to uncertain applicability to the organization must be further reviewed to determine if they should become a part of "doing business." If the assessors simply do not know what the indicator means, further information may be needed to accurately assess the feasibility of its application. Indicators marked "N/A" because they have not been met but that apply to the organization, may require immediate attention. Technical assistance, consulting or training may be required to implement these indicators.

The indicators in this checklist should be informative and thought provoking. The checklist can be used to achieve not only a beginning level of good management, but improve existing management to provide the organization with greater stability, reliability and success. It is particularly useful if an organization is experiencing management problems, to help pinpoint any weaknesses so action can be taken or assistance sought to improve the organization's health. All organizations should use the checklist to re-assess themselves periodically to ensure compliance with established rules and regulations, and to continue improving administrative health through the indicator's helpful suggestions.

## *Disclaimer*

As advised throughout this Field Guide, you should be careful when selecting and applying assessment tools so as not to convey that the tool is somehow a pre-determined, standard "solution" to your client's issues. Information gleaned from assessments should be informed by your knowledge of organizations and causes of issues in them. The assessment tools should be selected in collaboration with your client and according to the nature and needs of your client's organization.

This checklist is designed to provide accurate and authoritative information regarding the topics covered. Legal requirements and non-legal administrative practice standards reflected herein are susceptible to change due to new legislation, regulatory and judicial pronouncements, and updated and evolving guidelines. The checklist may be utilized only with the understanding that the provision of this checklist does not constitute the rendering of legal, tax or other professional services.

If the organization requires professional assistance on these or other legal, governance or management issues, please contact your own professional advisors.

## *Legal Activities*

| Rating * | Indicator | Met | Needs Work | N/A |
|---|---|---|---|---|
| E | 1. All relevant legal filings are current and have been made according to the laws and regulations of the nonprofit's country. (For example, in the USA, requirements might include: Annual Registration, Articles of Incorporation with all amendments, Change of Corporate Name, Change of Corporate Address.) | | | |
| E | 2. The organization is registered with and has filed its annual report with the appropriate governmental agency. (For example, in the USA, the report might be filed with the state's Attorney General's office.) | | | |
| E | 3. For organizations operating on a tax-exempt basis, the organization has filed the necessary government form to obtain tax-exempt status. (For example, in the USA, the IRS form 1023 was filed and the IRS provided a letter of determination. If the Form 1023 was either filed after 7/15/87 or was in the organization's possession on this date, it is made available for public inspection.) | | | |
| E | 4. Tax reports are filed on a regular basis. (For example, for tax-exempt organizations in the USA, the IRS form 990 and 990T for unrelated business income, if required, have been filed and copies of the 990 are available to the public.) | | | |
| E | 5. Federal and state (or provincial) payroll tax withholding payments are current. (This requirement applies to organizations with employees.) | | | |
| E | 6. Quarterly and annual payroll report filings are current. (This requirement applies to organizations with employees.) | | | |
| E | 7. If the organization has qualified employee health and/or welfare and/or retirement benefit plans, they meet with all the federal and state/provincial laws. (For example, in the USA, COBRA; initial IRS registration; plan documents; annual filings of the 5500 C/R with copies available to employees.) This requirement applies to organizations with employees. | | | |
| E | 8. Organization acknowledges and discloses to their Board and auditor any lawsuits or pending legislation which may have a significant impact on the organization's finances and/or operating effectiveness. | | | |
| E | 9. When the Board of Directors makes decisions, a quorum is present and minutes are maintained. | | | |
| E | 10. If the organization is subject to sales tax, federal, state/provincial and/or city, filings and payments are current. | | | |
| E | 11. Organizations that participate in grassroots or direct lobbying have complied with all necessary filings and government regulations. | | | |
| E | 12. Organizations that conduct charitable gambling have complied with government regulations. | | | |
| E | 13. Organizations with employees represented by a union must have copies of the union contracts on file. | | | |
| E | 14. Organizations that operate in a fiscal or host-organization relationship with another organization or group have a written agreement on file. | | | |
| Indicators ratings: E=essential; R=recommended; A=additional to strengthen organizational activities | | | | |

## *Governance*

| Rating * | Indicator | Met | Needs Work | N/A |
|---|---|---|---|---|
| E | 1. The roles of the Board and the Chief Executive Officer are defined and respected, with the Chief Executive Officer delegated as the manager of the organization's operations and the Board focused on policy and planning. | | | |
| R | 2. The Chief Executive Officer is recruited, selected and employed by the Board of Directors. The Board provides clearly written expectations and qualifications for the position, as well as reasonable compensation. | | | |
| R | 3. The Board of Directors acts as governing trustees of the organization on behalf of the community at large and contributors, while carrying out the organization's mission and goals. To fully meet this goal, the Board of Directors must actively participate in the planning process (as outlined in planning sections of this checklist). | | | |
| R | 4. The Board's nominating process ensures that the Board remains appropriately diverse with respect to gender, ethnicity, culture, economic status, disabilities, and skills and/or expertise. | | | |
| E | 5. The Board members receive regular training and information about their responsibilities. | | | |
| E | 6. New Board members are oriented to the organization, including the organization's mission, bylaws, policies and programs, as well as their roles and responsibilities as Board members. | | | |
| A | 7. Board organization is documented with a description of the Board and Board committee responsibilities. | | | |
| A | 8. Each Board member has, and is familiar with, the Board operations manual. | | | |
| E | 9. If the organization has any related party transactions between Board members or their families, they are disclosed to the Board of Directors (in the USA, the Internal Revenue Service and the auditor). | | | |
| E | 10. The organization has at least the minimum number of members on the Board of Directors as required by their bylaws or federal and state/provincial statute. | | | |
| R | 11. If the organization has adopted bylaws, they conform to state/provincial statutes and have been reviewed by legal counsel. | | | |
| R | 12. The bylaws should include, at a minimum: a) how and when notices for Board meetings are made; b) how members are elected/appointed by the Board; c) what the terms of office are for officers/members; d) how Board members are rotated; e) how ineffective Board members are removed from the Board; and f) a stated number of Board members to make up a quorum which is required for all policy decisions. | | | |
| R | 13. The Board of Directors reviews the bylaws at least yearly. | | | |
| A | 14. The Board has a process for handling urgent matters between meetings. | | | |
| E | 15. Board members serve without payment unless the agency has a policy identifying reimbursable out-of-pocket expenses. | | | |
| R | 16. The organization maintains a conflict-of-interest and Board attendance policy and all Board members and executive staff review and sign the policies to acknowledge compliance with the policies. | | | |
| R | 17. The Board has and implements an annual calendar of Board activities. The Board also achieves at least a quorum of Board members in each meeting. | | | |

## *Governance (Cont.)*

| Rating * | Indicator | Met | Needs Work | N/A |
|---|---|---|---|---|
| A | 18. Meetings have written agendas, and materials relating to significant decisions are given to the Board in advance of the meeting. | | | |
| A | 19. The Board has a written policy prohibiting employees and members of employees' immediate families from serving as Board Chair or Treasurer. | | | |
| Indicators ratings: E=essential; R=recommended; A=additional to strengthen organizational activities | | | | |

## Human Resources – Staff and Volunteers

### Staff

| Rating * | Indicator | Met | Needs Work | N/A |
|---|---|---|---|---|
| E | 1. The organization has a written personnel handbook/policy that is regularly reviewed and updated, and at a minimum: a) describes the recruitment, hiring, termination and standard work rules for all staff; b) and maintains compliance with government employment laws and regulations. (For example, in the USA, this includes Fair Labor Standards Act, Equal Employment Opportunity Act, Americans with Disabilities Act, Occupational Health and Safety Act, Family Leave Act, Affirmative Action Plan if required, etc.) | | | |
| R | 2. The organization follows nondiscriminatory hiring practices. | | | |
| R | 3. The organization provides a copy of or access to the written personnel policy to all members of the Board, the Chief Executive Officer and all staff members. All staff members acknowledge in writing that they have read and understand the personnel handbook/policies. | | | |
| R | 4. The organization has job descriptions including qualifications, duties, reporting relationships and key indicators of performance. | | | |
| R | 5. The organization's Board of Directors conducts an annual review/evaluation of its Chief Executive Officer in relationship to a previously determined set of performance expectations. | | | |
| R | 6. The Chief Executive Officer's salary is set by the Board of Directors in a reasonable process and is in compliance with the organization's compensation plan. | | | |
| R | 7. The organization requires employee performance appraisals to be conducted and documented at least annually. | | | |
| A | 8. The organization has a compensation plan, and a periodic review of salary ranges and benefits is conducted. | | | |
| A | 9. The organization has a timely process for filling vacant positions to prevent an interruption of program services or disruption to organization operations. | | | |
| A | 10. The organization has a process for reviewing and responding to ideas, suggestions, comments and perceptions from all staff members. | | | |
| A | 11. The organization provides opportunities for employees' professional development and training within their job skill area and also in such areas as cultural sensitivity and personal development. | | | |
| A | 12. The organization maintains contemporaneous records documenting staff time in program allocations. | | | |
| Indicators ratings: E=essential; R=recommended; A=additional to strengthen organizational activities | | | | |

## *Human Resources – Staff and Volunteers (Cont.)*

### Volunteer HR Management

| Rating * | Indicator | Met | Needs Work | N/A |
|---|---|---|---|---|
| E | 13. The organization has clearly defined the roles that volunteers have within the organization. | | | |
| E | 14. Job descriptions exist for all volunteer positions in the organization. | | | |
| R | 15. The organization has a well-defined and communicated volunteer management plan that includes, at a minimum: a) a recruitment policy, b) a description of all volunteer jobs, c) an application and interview process, d) possible stipend and reimbursement policies, e) a statement of which staff has supervisory responsibilities over what volunteers, and f) any other volunteer personnel policy information. | | | |
| E | 16. The organization follows a recruitment policy that does not discriminate, but respects, encourages and represents the diversity of the community. | | | |
| E | 17. The organization provides appropriate training and orientation to assist the volunteer in the performance of their activities. Volunteers are offered training with staff in, for example, cultural sensitivity. | | | |
| E | 18. The organization ensures background checks and liability insurance to ensure low-risk utilization of volunteers' skills. | | | |
| R | 19. The organization is respectful of the volunteer's abilities and time commitment and has various job duties to meet these needs. Jobs should not be given to volunteers simply because the jobs are considered inferior for paid staff. | | | |
| R | 20. The organization does volunteer performance appraisals periodically and communicates to the volunteers how well they are doing, or where additional attention is needed. At the same time, volunteers are requested to review and evaluate their involvement in the organization and the people they work with and suggest areas for improvement. | | | |
| R | 21. The organization does some type of volunteer recognition or commendation periodically and staff continuously demonstrates their appreciation towards the volunteers and their efforts. | | | |
| A | 22. The organization has a process for reviewing and responding to ideas, suggestions, comments and perceptions from volunteers. | | | |
| A | 23. The organization provides opportunities for program participants to volunteer. | | | |
| A | 24. The organization maintains contemporaneous records documenting volunteer time in program allocations. Financial records can be maintained for the volunteer time spent on programs and recorded as in-kind contributions. | | | |
| Indicators ratings: E=essential; R=recommended; A=additional to strengthen organizational activities | | | | |

## Planning (Strategic and Programs)

### Strategic Planning

| Rating * | Indicator | Met | Needs Work | N/A |
|---|---|---|---|---|
| E | 1. The organization's purpose and activities meet community needs. | | | |
| R | 2. The organization frequently evaluates, by soliciting community input, whether its mission and activities provide benefit to the community. | | | |
| R | 3. The organization has a values statement that is reflected in the agency's activities and is communicated by its constituents. | | | |
| A | 4. The values statement includes standards of ethical behavior and respect for other's interests. | | | |
| E | 5. The organization has a clear, meaningful written mission statement which reflects its purpose, values and people served. | | | |
| R | 6. The Board and staff periodically review the mission statement and modify it to reflect changes in the environment. | | | |
| E | 7. The Board and staff develop and adopt a written Strategic Plan to achieve its mission. | | | |
| A | 8. Board, staff, service recipients, volunteers, key constituents and general members of the community participate in the planning process. | | | |
| E | 9. The plan was developed after researching the internal and external environments. | | | |
| R | 10. The plan identifies changing community needs. | | | |
| R | 11. The planning process identifies the critical issues facing the organization (including the agency's strengths, weaknesses, opportunities and threats). | | | |
| R | 12. The plan sets goals and measurable objectives that address these critical issues. | | | |
| E | 13. The plan integrates all the organization's activities around a focused mission. | | | |
| R | 14. The plan prioritizes the agency goals and develops timelines for their accomplishment. | | | |
| A | 15. The plan establishes an evaluation process and performance indicators to measure the progress toward the achievement of goals and objectives. | | | |
| R | 16. Through work plans, human and financial resources are allocated to ensure the accomplishment of the goals in a timely fashion. | | | |
| A | 17. The plan is communicated to all stakeholders of the agency – service recipients, Board, staff, volunteers and the general community. | | | |
| Indicators ratings: E=essential; R=recommended; A=additional to strengthen organizational activities | | | | |

## *Planning (Cont.)*

### Planning Regarding the Organization's Programs

| Rating * | Indicator | Met | Needs Work | N/A |
|---|---|---|---|---|
| E | 1. Programs are congruent with the agency's mission and Strategic Plan. | | | |
| A | 2. The organization actively informs the public about its programs and services. | | | |
| A | 3. Clients and potential clients have the opportunity to participate in program development. | | | |
| R | 4. Sufficient resources are allocated to ensure each program can achieve the established goals and objectives for each program. | | | |
| R | 5. Staff has sufficient training and skill level to produce the program. | | | |
| A | 6. Programs within the organization are integrated to provide more complete services to clients. | | | |
| R | 7. Each program has performance indicators to insure that attainment or goals can be measured. | | | |
| R | 8. Performance indicators are reviewed annually. | | | |
| A | 9. The agency networks and/or collaborates with other organizations to produce the most comprehensive and effective services to clients. | | | |
| Indicators ratings: E=essential; R=recommended; A=additional to strengthen organizational activities | | | | |

### Planning Regarding the Organization's Evaluations

| Rating * | Indicator | Met | Needs Work | N/A |
|---|---|---|---|---|
| R | 1. Every year, the organization evaluates its activities to determine progress toward goal accomplishment. | | | |
| A | 2. Stakeholders are involved in the evaluation process. | | | |
| R | 3. The evaluation includes a review of organizational programs and systems to insure that they comply with the organization's mission, values and goals. | | | |
| R | 4. The results of the evaluation are reflected in the revised plan. | | | |
| A | 5. Periodically, the organization conducts a comprehensive evaluation of its programs. This evaluation measures program outcomes. | | | |
| Indicators ratings: E=essential; R=recommended; A=additional to strengthen organizational activities | | | | |

## *Financial Activities*

| Rating * | Indicator | Met | Needs Work | N/A |
|---|---|---|---|---|
| E | 1. The organization follows accounting practices which conform to generally accepted accounting standards. | | | |
| E | 2. The organization has systems in place to provide the appropriate information needed by staff and Board to make sound financial decisions and to fulfill government requirements (for example, in the USA, the Internal Revenue Service). | | | |
| R | 3. The organization prepares timely financial statements including the balance sheet, income statement and cash flow statement which are clearly stated and useful for the Board and staff. (Note that these statements might be referred to by different names in various countries.) | | | |
| R | 4. The organization prepares financial statements on a budget-versus-actual and/or comparative basis to achieve a better understanding of their finances. | | | |
| E | 5. The organization develops an annual comprehensive operating budget which includes costs for all programs, management and fundraising and all sources of funding. This budget is reviewed and approved by the Board of Directors. | | | |
| R | 6. The organization monitors unit costs of programs and services through the documentation of staff time and direct expenses and use of a process for allocation of management, general and fundraising expenses. | | | |
| E | 7. The organization prepares cash flow projections. | | | |
| R | 8. The organization periodically forecasts year-end revenues and expenses to assist in making sound management decisions during the year. | | | |
| E | 9. The organization reconciles all cash accounts monthly. | | | |
| E | 10. The organization has a review process to monitor that they are receiving appropriate and accurate financial information whether from a contracted service or internal processing. | | | |
| E | 11. If the organization has billable contracts or other service income, procedures are established for the periodic billing, follow-up and collection of all accounts, and the documentation that substantiates all billings. | | | |
| E | 12. Government contracts, purchase of service agreements and grant agreements are in writing and are reviewed by a staff member of the organization to monitor compliance with all stated conditions. | | | |
| E | 13. Payroll is prepared following appropriate federal and state/provincial regulations and organizational policy. | | | |
| E | 14. Persons employed on a contract basis meet all federal and state/provincial requirements for this form of employment. (In the USA, disbursement records are kept so 1099's can be issued at year end.) | | | |
| E | 15. Organizations that purchase and sell merchandise take periodic inventories to monitor the inventory against theft, to reconcile general ledger inventory information and to maintain an adequate inventory level. | | | |
| R | 16. The organization has a written fiscal policy and procedures manual and follows it. | | | |
| E | 17. The organization has documented a set of internal controls, including handling of cash and deposits, statement reconciliation, approval over spending and disbursements. | | | |

## Financial Activities (Cont.)

| Rating * | Indicator | Met | Needs Work | N/A |
|---|---|---|---|---|
| E | 18. The organization has a policy identifying authorized check signers and the number of signatures required on checks in excess of specified dollar amounts. | | | |
| E | 19. All expenses of the organization are approved by a designated person before payment is made. | | | |
| R | 20. The organization has a written policy related to investments. | | | |
| R | 21. Capital needs are reviewed at least annually and priorities established. | | | |
| R | 22. The organization has established a plan identifying actions to take in the event of a reduction or loss in funding. | | | |
| R | 23. The organization has established, or is actively trying to develop, a reserve of funds to cover at least three months of operating expenses. | | | |
| E | 24. The organization has suitable insurance coverage which is periodically reviewed to ensure the appropriate levels and types of coverage are in place. | | | |
| E | 25. Employees, Board members and volunteers who handle cash and investments are bonded to help assure the safeguarding of assets. | | | |
| E | 26. The organization files forms in regard to tax-exempt and/or tax-deductible (charity) status on a timely basis. | | | |
| R | 27. The organization reviews income annually to determine and report unrelated business income to the necessary government agency (for example, to the IRS in the USA). | | | |
| R | 28. The organization has an annual, independent audit of their financial statements, prepared by a certified public accountant. | | | |
| R | 29. In addition to the audit, the auditor prepares a management letter containing recommendations for improvements in the financial operations of the organization. | | | |
| R | 30. The Board of Directors, or an appropriate committee, is responsible for soliciting bids, interviewing auditors and hiring an auditor for the organization. | | | |
| E | 31. The Board of Directors, or an appropriate committee, reviews and approves the audit report and management letter and with staff input and support, institutes any necessary changes. | | | |
| E | 32. The audit, or an organization-prepared annual report which includes financial statements, is made available to service recipients, volunteers, contributors, funders and other interested parties. | | | |
| A | 33. Training is made available for Board and appropriate staff on relevant accounting topics and all appropriate persons are encouraged to participate in various training opportunities. | | | |
| Indicators ratings: E=essential; R=recommended; A=additional to strengthen organizational activities | | | | |

## Fundraising Activities

### General Fundraising

| Rating * | Indicator | Met | Needs Work | N/A |
|---|---|---|---|---|
| E | 1. Funds are raised in an ethical manner for activities consistent with the organization's mission and plans. | | | |
| E | 2. The Board of Directors and organization staff are knowledgeable about the fundraising process and the roles in the organization. | | | |
| E | 3. The organization's Board of Directors has established a committee charged with developing, evaluating and reviewing fundraising policies, practices and goals. | | | |
| E | 4. The committee is actively involved in the fundraising process and works to involve others in these activities. | | | |
| R | 5. The Board of Directors, Chief Executive Officer and committee supports and participates in the total fundraising process, including project identification, cultivation, solicitation and recognition. Each Board member contributes financially and/or in-kind to the organization. | | | |
| R | 6. The fundraising program is staffed and funded at a level consistent with fundraising expectations. | | | |
| A | 7. There is direct communication and relationship between information services and marketing to assist in the fundraising needs and efforts. | | | |
| E | 8. The organization is accountable to donors and other key constituencies and demonstrates their stewardship through annual reports. | | | |
| Indicators ratings: E=essential; R=recommended; A=additional to strengthen organizational activities | | | | |

## *Fundraising (Cont.)*

### Using an Outside Fundraiser

| Rating * | Indicator | Met | Needs Work | N/A |
|---|---|---|---|---|
| A | 9. The organization meets the nonprofit standards of the state/provincial charities review council, if one exists. | | | |
| R | 10. If the organization chooses to use outside professional fundraisers, several competitive bids are solicited. Each prospective outside fundraiser's background and references are checked. | | | |
| E | 11. The organization makes legal, mutually agreed upon, signed statements with outside professional fundraisers, outlining each parties' responsibilities and duties, specifying how the contributed funds will be physically handled, and guaranteeing that the fees to be paid are reasonable and fair. | | | |
| E | 12. The organization has verified that the contracted fundraiser is registered as a professional fundraiser with the appropriate government agency and all filings necessary have been made before the work commences. | | | |
| E | 13. The fundraising committee or appropriate representatives from the Board of Directors reviews all prospective proposals with the outside professional fundraiser and reviews and accepts all agreements before they are signed. | | | |
| R | 14. If the outside professional fundraiser plans to contact potential donors directly, the organization reviews the fundraising materials (e.g., public service announcements, print or broadcast advertisements, telemarketing scripts, pledge statements, brochures, letters, etc.) to verify their accuracy and to ensure that the public disclosure requirements have been met. | | | |
| E | 15. The organization properly reports all required information regarding use of outside professional fundraisers, amount of funds raised and the related fundraising expenses as required by federal and state/provincial governments. The gross amount of funds raised by the contracted fundraiser is reported on the organization's financial statement. The fees and costs of the campaign must be reported on the statement of functional expenses. | | | |
| Indicators ratings: E=essential; R=recommended; A=additional to strengthen organizational activities | | | | |

# Planning the Research

The section, "Phase 3: Discovery and Feedback," in PART IV, includes guidelines to finish these worksheets.

---

**Name of Client's Organization**

---

**Date**

---

**Nature of consulting project (project, process, program, etc., for which research is conducted)**

---

**Domain(s) of presenting priority:**
(Is for an individual position, team, project, process, function, program or organization – for example, Boards, strategic planning, fundraising, teamwork, financial management, fundraising, information technology, quality improvement, programs, evaluations or marketing.)

---

Be sure to copy and finish this worksheet for each research question.

**Research Questions and Data Collection**

**Research question:**

| Data to collect | Source(s) of data | Data collection method(s) |
|---|---|---|
| | | |
| | | |
| | | |
| | | |
| | | |

## Planning the Research (Cont.)

**Timing of data collection**

**Context-sensitive considerations**

**Who will conduct the research**

**Field-test research plans**

**How you will prepare people**

# Appendix D:  Bibliography

There is a vast amount of publications about activities required to help a nonprofit organization to improve its effectiveness.  The following publications will help to get you started.  The bibliographies in many of these publications will likely direct you to other useful publications.

## *Citations*

The following publications were cited in the body of this Field Guide.

Argyris, Chris and Schon, Donald, *Theory and Practice* (Jossey-Bass, 1974).

Argyris, Chris, *Overcoming Organizational Defenses* (Prentice Hall, 1990).

Backer, Thomas, *Strengthening Nonprofits: Capacity Building and Philanthropy* (Human Interaction Research Institute, 2000).

Beckhard, Richard, *Organization Development: Strategies and Models* (Addison-Wesley, 1969) p. 9.

Block, Peter, *Flawless Consulting* (Jossey-Bass, 2000).

Blumenthal, Barbara, *Investing in Capacity Building: A Guide to High-Impact Approaches* (The Foundation Center, 2003).

Bolman, Lee and Deal, Terrance, *Reframing Organizations* (Jossey-Bass Publishers, 1991).

Connolly, Paul and York, Peter, *Building the Capacity of Capacity Builders* (Conservation Company, 2003).

Cooperrider, David and Whitney, Diana, *A Positive Revolution for Change: Appreciative Inquiry* (paper, 2000) http://appreciativeinquiry.cwru.edu/uploads/whatisai.pdf.

Cummings, Thomas, and Worley, Chris, *Organization Development and Change*, Sixth Edition (West Publishing, 1997) p. 2.

Daft, Richard, *Organizational Theory and Design* (West Publishing, 1992).

Goldman, Daniel, *Emotional Intelligence* (Bantam Books, 1997).

Herman, Robert D. and Renz, David, *Nonprofit Organizational Effectiveness: Practical Implications of Research on an Elusive Concept,* An Occasional Paper Issued by the Midwest Center for Nonprofit Leadership, 2002.

Horton, Thomas, *Delegation and Team Building: No Solo Acts Please,* Management Review, September, 1992, pp. 58-61.

Ingram, Richard, *Ten Basic Responsibilities of Nonprofit Boards* (BoardSource, 2002).

Johnson, Barry, *Polarity Management: Identifying and Managing Unsolvable Problems* (HRD Press, Inc., 1992).

Jung, Carl, *Psychological Types* (Pantheon Books, 1923).

Kaufmann, Draper, *Systems 1: An Introduction to Systems Thinking* (Future Systems, Inc., 1984).

Kearns, Kevin, *Comparative Advantage to Damage Control: Clarifying Strategic Issues Using SWOT Analysis,* Nonprofit Management and Leadership, Volume 3 Number 1, Fall 1992, pp. 3-22.

Kirkpatrick, Donald, *Evaluating Training Programs: The Four Levels* (Berrett-Koehler, 1994).

Letts, Christine, and Ryan, William and Grossman, Allen, *High Performance Nonprofit Organizations: Managing Upstream for Greater Impact* (Wiley, 1998).

Lewin, Richard, *Field Theory in Social Science* (Harper and Row, 1951).

McNamara, Carter, *Field Guide to Designing, Marketing and Evaluating Nonprofit Programs* (Authenticity Consulting, LLC, 2002).

McNamara, Carter, *Field Guide to Developing and Operating Your Nonprofit Board of Directors* (Authenticity Consulting, LLC, 2002).

McNamara, Carter, *Field Guide to Leadership and Supervision of Nonprofit Staff* (Authenticity Consulting, LLC, 2002).

McNamara, Carter, *Field Guide to Nonprofit Strategic Planning and Facilitation* (Authenticity Consulting, LLC, 2003).

Neilsen, Eric, *Becoming an OD Practitioner* (Prentice-Hall, 1984), pp. 2-3.

Patton, Michael, *Developmental Evaluation,* Evaluation Practice, Vol 15, No. 3, pp. 311-319, October, 1994.

Patton, Michael, *Qualitative Evaluation and Research Methods,* 3rd edition, (Sage, 1990).

Patton, Michael, *Utilization-Focused Evaluation Methods* (Sage Publications, 1986).

Quinn, Robert and Cameron, Kim, *Organizational Life Cycles and Some Shifting Criteria of Effectiveness,* Management Science, 29, Institute for Operations Research and the Management Sciences, 1983, pp. 31-51.

Schein, Edgar, *Process Consultation: Its Role in Organizational Development,* Vol 1, (Addison Wesley, 1988).

Schon, Donald, *Theory in Practice* (Jossey-Bass, 1974).

Senge, Peter, et al, *The Fifth Discipline Fieldbook* (Doubleday, 1994).

Senge, Peter, *The Fifth Discipline* (Doubleday, 1990).

Simon, Judith Sharken, *5 Life Stages of Nonprofit Organizations* (Amherst H. Wilder Foundation, 2001).

Strickland, Bill, *Genius at Work* (an interview with Bill Strickland, CEO of Manchester Craftsmen's Guide and the Bidwell Training Center).

Swanson, Richard, *Performance Improvement Theory and Practice*, Advances in Developing Human Resources, Number 1, 1999.

Terry, Robert, *Authentic Leadership: Courage in Action* (Jossey-Bass Publishers, 1993).

Watermann, Robert and Peters, Tom, *In Search of Excellence* (Warner, 1982).

Weisbord, Marvin, *Productive Workplaces* (Jossey-Bass Publishers,1987).

Whyte, William Foote, *Participatory Action Research* (Sage, 1991).

## *Recommended Readings – an Annotated List*

Various categories of readings are included below. The following readings are by no means all of the important works in each category. However, the listed works will provide you a strong start to understanding information in that particular category. Also the bibliographies of many of the works listed below will help you to find related works from which you can continue to develop your knowledge about the particular category. Some of the following were also listed in the previous list of Citations.

### Boards of Directors

*Building Better Boards,* David A. Nadler (Editor), Jossey-Bass, 2005.

> This book describes how Boards can become high-performing teams. Lists the influences that have the greatest effects on Board success and principles to improve Boards. Although the book is based on research with organizations that have many resources, the principles still apply to small- and medium-sized nonprofits.

*Exploring the Puzzle of Board Design: What's Your Type,* David Renz, Nonprofit Quarterly, Winter 2004, Vol 11, Issue 4. (Also at http://www.nonprofitquarterly.org/section/655.html)

> The article reminds consultants that there is no one right design for Boards. The article clearly conveys the wide range of types, or personalities, of Board of Directors and how to categorize them. Includes a well-designed graph for discerning the type of any governing Board.

*Field Guide to Developing and Operating Your Nonprofit Board of Directors,* Carter McNamara, Authenticity Consulting, LLC, Minneapolis, MN, 2003.

> This guidebook explains how to start a Board and nonprofit organization, or to fix a struggling Board. It also explains all of the activities required for effective Board operations, such as staffing, meetings, decisions and self-evaluation.

*The Strategic Board: The Step-by-Step Guide to High-Impact Governance,* Mark Light, Wiley, 2001.

> Includes broad guidelines for achieving effective governance, such as establishing clear vision and values for strong leadership, effective delegation through clarity of roles and responsibilities, and translating Board decisions throughout the organization via clear management plans and measures.

### Capacity Building

*Building Capacity in Nonprofit Organizations*, edited by Carol J. De Vita, Urban Institute Press, 2001.

> Written especially for foundations considering capacity building programs, but relevant to all providers. Depicts overall framework for nonprofit capacity building. Suggests eight aspects of effective capacity building programs and describes continuum of capacity building services. Free at http://www.urban.org/UploadedPDF/building_capacity.PDF

*Building for Impact: The Future of Effectiveness for Nonprofits and Foundations*, Grantmakers for Effective Organizations, 2002.

Report on the 2002 National Conference of grantmakers that highlights expected trends in philanthropy, suggesting more priority on nonprofit performance. Offers four possible scenarios that grantmakers might follow in the future. Challenges grantmakers to focus on their own organizational effectiveness for capacity building. Free at http://www.geofunders.org/_uploads/documents/live/conference%20report.pdf

*Building the Capacity of Capacity Builders*, Conservation Company, June 2003.

Provides overview of nonprofit capacity builders, suggests four key capacities for effective nonprofit organizations: leadership, adaptive, managerial and technical. Includes recommendations for capacity builders to improve services. Free at http://www.tccgrp.com/pdfs/buildingthecapacityofcapacitybuilders.pdf

*Echoes from the Field: Proven Capacity Building Principles for Nonprofits*, Environmental Support Center and Innovation Network, Inc., 2002.

Suggests nine principles of effective capacity building. An excellent read for those who want to understand the broad context of capacity building and the realities of providing capacity building programs. Free at http://www.envsc.org/bestpractices.pdf

*Effective Capacity Building in Nonprofit Organizations*, Venture Philanthropy Partners, 2001.

Suggests seven overall elements of nonprofit capacity building. Describes lessons-learned from nonprofits that have engaged in successful capacity building efforts. Provides comprehensive assessment instrument to assess organizational effectiveness according to the seven elements. Free at http://vppartners.org/learning/reports/capacity/capacity.html

*Lessons from the Street: Capacity Building and Replication,* Milton S. Eisenhower Foundation.

Based on street-level experience from 1990 to 2000 in offering technical assistance and training for capacity building, especially with grassroots organizations in inner cities. Offers top ten lessons and recommendations for funders regarding assistance and replication of programs. Free at http://www.eisenhowerfoundation.org/aboutus/publications/lessons_intro.html

*Mapping Nonprofit Capacity Builders: A Study by LaSalle University's Nonprofit Center*, Kathryn Szabat and Laura Otten (1999?).

Overview of research to identify "the universe of capacity builders ..." Mentions capacity builders by general characteristics and reports results of research, with percentage of capacity builders in various categories. This is an interesting perusal for those wanting a quick impression of the world of capacity builders. Free at http://www.np-org-dev.com/survey.doc

*Reflections on Capacity Building,* The California Wellness Foundation.

Lists numerous lessons-learned from TCWF's implementation of capacity building services. Reflections and lessons-learned are numerous and meaningful for funders providing capacity building services. Free at http://www.tcwf.org/reflections/2001/april/index.htm

*Results of an Inquiry into Capacity Building Programs for Nonprofits*, by Susan Doherty and Stephen Meyer of Communities for Action.

> Describes organizational capacity and why it is important. Explains why capacity building does not happen naturally and offers seven overall elements that work for capacity building efforts. Brief overviews of major areas of capacity building. Free at http://www.effectivecommunities.com/ECP_CapacityBuildingInquiry.pdf

*Strengthening Nonprofit Organizations: A Funder's Guide to Capacity Building*, by Carol Lukas, Amherst H. Wilder Foundation.

> Describes types of capacity building services. Provides straightforward explanation of process for funders to consider offering capacity building programs and adds general strategic process for funders to identify which capacity building services to offer.

## Consulting

*Consultants Calling*, Geoffrey M., Jossey-Bass, 1990.

> Does an excellent job helping readers closely examine why they want to be a consultant. Includes numerous guidelines to set up a practice, understand organizations and clients, maintain balance and boundaries, and more.

*Consulting for Dummies*, Bob Nelson and Peter Economy, IDG Books, 1997.

> Highly readable resource that touches on the most important aspects of setting up and marketing a consulting business. The *Dummies* series is well-known for being easy to reference and well-designed.

*Consulting With Nonprofits: A Practitioners Guide*, Carol Lukas, Amherst H. Wilder Foundation, 1998.

> Easy-to-read, general overview of one perspective on stages of consulting to nonprofits, including the "artistry" of working with others and the business and marketing of consulting with nonprofits.

*Flawless Consulting: Guide to Getting Your Expertise Used,* Second Edition, Peter Block, Jossey-Bass Publishers, 2000.

> Block's break-through book first heralded in the innovative approach of collaborative consulting. His book is probably the most referenced general resource when first training consultants to conduct collaborative and effective consulting projects.

*How to Succeed as an Independent Consultant,* Herman Holtz, Third Edition, Wiley, 1993.

> This well-known resource goes into more depth than most other consulting books about the roles of a consultant, starting a business, writing proposals and contracts and reports, etc.

*Jumping the Job Track,* Peter C. Brown, Crown, 1994.

> Comprehensive guidelines for considering changing jobs to consulting, including conducting a skills inventory, thinking about your markets, setting up shop, etc. Includes many real-life examples.

## Facilitation and Groups (General)

*Facilitation,* T. Bentley, McGraw-Hill, 1994.

> Provides a somewhat philosophical overview of facilitating, particularly about indirect facilitation. Readers would be best to review this book after having first reviewed more basic books on facilitation, such as Clarke's book listed below.

*Process Consultation: Its Role in Organization Development*, E. Schein, Addison Wesley Publishing Company, 1969.

> This is a seminal work in group dynamics and facilitation. Process consultation is widely considered to be the foundation for group dynamics and effective facilitation. This is a must-read for facilitators for organizational change.

*Technology of Participation: Group Facilitation Methods,* Institute of Cultural Affairs, 1994.

> Provided in the Institute for Cultural Affairs' ToP facilitation workshop. Provides a straightforward overview of facilitating discussions, workshops and action planning techniques, especially for multi-cultural organizations.

*The Skilled Facilitator: Practical Wisdom for Developing Effective Groups*, R. M. Schwartz, Jossey-Bass Publishers, 1994.

> Provides a comprehensive and useful overview of facilitation. It is somewhat academic, that is, research-oriented with theories, models and concepts. Readers might read this after reading a more basic, straightforward book, such as Clarke's, below.

*Who, Me Lead a Group?*, J. I. Clarke, Winston Press, Inc, 1984.

> Beginning facilitators might read this straightforward book first to get an understanding of different types of meetings and then how to lead them.

## Financial Management

*Bookkeeping Basics: What Every Nonprofit Bookkeeper Needs to Know,* Debra L. Ruegg and Lisa M. Venkatrathnam, Amherst H. Wilder Foundation, 2003.

> The book explains important practices and procedures in bookkeeping and the overall bookkeeping cycle, generating the most important nonprofit financial statements, and how to establish the most important financial controls in a nonprofit organization.

*Streetsmart Financial Basics for Nonprofit Managers,* Thomas A. McLaughlin, John Wiley and Sons, 1995.

> The book describes how to make management decisions based on financial information. The book includes numerous, easy-to-reference diagrams, along with numerous examples. Includes on-line copies of useful checklists and worksheets.

## Fundraising

*Fundraising Basics: A Complete Guide, Second Edition,* Barbara L. Ciconte and Jeanne Jacob, Jones and Bartlett, 2001.

This book explains the basics of fundraising, including critical foundations for successful fundraising, types of fundraising, how to plan your fundraising activities, and trends in fundraising. Includes fundraising on the Internet. Includes case studies and real-life examples.

*Fundraising for Dummies, Second Edition,* John Mutz and Katherine Murray, Jossey-Bass, 2000.

This book describes the most important basic considerations and activities to plan and conduct your fundraising. Includes how to get the Board engaged in fundraising, and how to research major donors and write grants. Similar to other *Dummies* books, this book includes a lot of handy tips and conventional wisdom.

*Raise More Money: The Best of the Grassroots Fundraising Journal,* Kim Klein and Stephanie Roth, Jossey-Bass, 2001.

This book combines the best advice from Klein's seminal publications on grassroots fundraising. The advice is always specific and easy-to-apply. This is a must-read for anyone working with small- to medium-sized nonprofit organizations. The advice still applies to nonprofits of any size.

## Leadership and Supervision (includes staffing and volunteers)

*Executive Director's Survival Guide,* Mim Carlson and Margaret Donohoe, Jossey-Bass, 2003.

This book was written for the Chief Executive Officer who wants to understand all aspects of the role and develop into a wise and effective leader. Includes guidelines to avoid burnout, identify organizational effectiveness, lead organizational change and work effectively with the Board.

*Executive Leadership in Nonprofit Organizations: New Strategies for Shaping Executive-Board Dynamics,* Robert D. Herman and Richard D. Heimovics, Jossey-Bass, 1991.

The is one of the first publications to suggest that, although theory and law assert that the Board governs the organization, the quality of the working relationship between the Board and Chief Executive Officer is one of the most important determinants of the effectiveness of the organization.

*Field Guide to Leadership and Supervision for Nonprofit Staff,* Carter McNamara, Authenticity Consulting, LLC, Minneapolis, MN, 2002.

This guidebook provides complete, step-by-step guidelines to conduct the most essential activities in successful leadership and supervision in a nonprofit organization. Includes Board and staff roles, leading yourself, analyzing staff roles, recruiting and selecting staff, training and organizing staff, meeting management, performance management and how to avoid Founder's Syndrome.

## Marketing (including advertising and promotions)

*Field Guide to Nonprofit Program Design, Marketing and Evaluation,* Carter McNamara, Authenticity Consulting, LLC, Minneapolis, MN, 2003.

> There are few resources about program planning, so this book is unique. It addresses the activities of program design, marketing and evaluation as they should be – as activities that are highly integrated with each other. This guidebook includes complete step-by-step guidelines and on-line worksheets to successfully conduct activities on an ongoing basis.

*Successful Marketing Strategies For Nonprofit Organizations*, Barry J. McLeish, Wiley, 1995.

> The author argues that marketing is not just an activity, but should be an orientation among all management. Guidelines describe how to develop a strategic marketing plan from analyzing the external and internal environments of the nonprofit and then producing a plan that best fits both environments.

*Workbook for Nonprofit Organizations: Volume 1 Develop the Plan*, Gary J. Stern, Amherst H. Wilder Foundation, 1990

> This book explains the theory and importance of marketing in nonprofits. It describes a five-step process to develop a marketing plan: establishing goals, positioning the nonprofit, doing a marketing audit, developing the plan, and associating a promotions campaign. Includes worksheets.

## Organizational Development and Change (including Appreciative Inquiry)

*Appreciative Inquiry: Change at the Speed of Imagination,* Jane M. Watkins and Bernhard J. Mohr, Jossey-Bass, 2001.

> Appreciative Inquiry (AI) has become a prominent movement in organizational change and development. It offers a truly new paradigm in how we see organizations and its members, and as a result, how we plan and change organizations. There are numerous resources on AI, but this book is one of the most well-organized and understandable, replete with various models to apply AI and even how to explain AI to other people.

*Changing the Essence*, Richard Beckhard and Wendy Pritchard, Jossey-Bass, Inc., 1992.

> This is one of the seminal works on organizational change and written by the "father" of the field of Organization Development. It includes a comprehensive and strategic overview of key considerations in achieving successful organizational change.

*Making Sense of Life's Changes*, William Bridges, Addison Wesley, 1980.

> Bridge's book provides an excellent overview of the psychological and sociological aspects and considerations for successful organizational change. His book, combined with Block's (in the "Consulting" section in this Appendix) and Beckhard's (above), comprise a comprehensive "toolkit" for conducting successful organizational change.

*Organizational Culture and Leadership*, 3rd Edition, Edgar H. Schein, Jossey-Bass, 2004.

> Seminal work on the subject. Defines culture, levels and dimensions, key issues to manage during change, relationship between leadership and culture, and how leaders create organizational cultures.

*Organization Development and Change,* Seventh Edition, Thomas G. Cummings and Christopher G. Worley, South-Western Educational Publishing, 2000.

This is a classic, up-to-date text on the field and practices of Organization Development (OD).  Includes history, movements and major research findings.  It is a must-read for the reader serious about becoming a professional in the field of Organization Development.

*Power of Appreciative Inquiry: Practical Guide to Positive Change,* Diana Whitney and Amanda Trosten-Bloom, Berrett Koehler, 2002.

This is a comprehensive, yet practical, book about AI.  It provides numerous approaches to AI across a wide variety of organizations, and includes case studies for the approaches, as well.

*Practicing Organization Development: A Guide for Consultants,* William J. Rothwell, Roland Sullivan and Gary N. McLean, Jossey-Bass, 1995.

This book is focused on guidelines and other advice for the practitioners who seek "how to" resources to conduct successful organizational development projects.

*Reframing Organizations,* Lee Bolman and Terrence Deal, Jossey-Bass, 1991.

This book has been a wonderful gift to organizational consultants because it reminds them that different people can have quite different perspectives on the same organization.  Those different perspectives can result in widely varying interpretations and suggestions about organizational change.

*The 5 Life Stages of Nonprofit Organizations,* Judith Sharken Simon, Amherst H. Wilder Foundation, 2001.

Provides a highly understandable and meaningful overview of life stages of nonprofits and includes a comprehensive, yet practical, life-stage assessment tool with examples, analysis and advice.

## Program Evaluation

*Evaluation of Capacity Building: Lessons from the Field*, Deborah Linnell, Alliance for Nonprofit Management, 2003.

Describes results of research among a variety of capacity builders, along with descriptions of the general activities of each builder and what they are doing to evaluate their particular programs.  Numerous lessons-learned are conveyed, as well as suggestions for further research.

*Field Guide to Nonprofit Program Design, Marketing and Evaluation,* Carter McNamara, Authenticity Consulting, LLC, Minneapolis, MN, 2003.

There are few resources about program planning, so this book is unique.  It addresses the activities of program design, marketing and evaluation as they should be – as activities that are highly integrated with each other.  This guidebook includes complete step-by-step guidelines and on-line worksheets to successfully conduct activities on an ongoing basis.

*Qualitative Evaluation and Research Methods,* Michael Quinn Patton, Sage Publications, 1990.

Provides comprehensive overview of qualitative research and data collection methods, many of which can be used in practical approaches to market research and program evaluation.

## Program Planning and Design

*Field Guide to Nonprofit Program Design, Marketing and Evaluation,* Carter McNamara, Authenticity Consulting, LLC, Minneapolis, MN, 2003.

There are few resources about program planning, so this book is unique. It addresses the activities of program design, marketing and evaluation as they should be – as activities that are highly integrated with each other. This guidebook includes complete step-by-step guidelines and on-line worksheets to successfully conduct activities on an ongoing basis.

*Designing and Planning Programs for Nonprofit and Government Organizations*, Edward J. Pawlak, Robert D. Vinter, Jossey-Bass, 2004.

Books focuses on nonprofit and government organizations. Suggests step-by-step activities for major phases, including planning, implementation and program operations. Ideally suited to large organizations with complex programs and systems.

## Strategic Planning

*Field Guide to Nonprofit Strategic Planning and Facilitation*, Carter McNamara, Authenticity Consulting, LLC, Minneapolis, Minnesota, 2003.

Comprehensive, step-by-step guidebook to facilitate a Strategic Plan that is relevant, realistic and flexible. Includes a variety of planning models that can be used and guidelines to select which model is best. Also includes on-line tools that can be downloaded for each planner.

*Five Most Important Questions You Will Ever Ask About Your Nonprofit Organization: Participant's Workbook*, Peter F. Drucker Foundation, Jossey-Bass Publishers, 1993.

Top-level workbook guides organizations through answering five key strategic questions: What is our business (mission)? Who is our customer? What does the customer consider value? What have been our results? What is our Plan?

*Strategic Management: Formulation, Implementation, and Control*, Fourth Edition, John A. Pearce II and Richard B. Robinson, Jr., Irwin Publishing, 1991.

Explains the strategic planning process in the overall context of strategic management. Explains complete strategic management cycle, primarily for large for-profit corporations. Much of the information applies to nonprofits, including processes that nonprofits tend not to do, but should.

*Strategic Planning for Public and Nonprofit Organizations,* John Bryson, Jossey-Bass Publishers, 1995.

Provides an extensive, well-organized and in-depth explanation of a 10-step strategic planning cycle that can be used in planning with organizations ranging from small to large. This book is often referred to as the seminal source of strategic planning expertise for nonprofit organizations.

*Strategic Planning Workbook for Nonprofit Organizations,* Revised and Updated, Bryan Barry, Wilder Foundation, St. Paul, MN, 1997 (651-642-4022).

Well-organized and readable, top-level workbook provides guidelines and worksheets to conduct strategic planning for a variety of types, sizes and designs of nonprofit and public organizations.

## Systems Thinking, Chaos Theory and Tools

*Chaos Theory Tamed*, Garnett P. Williams, Taylor and Francis, 1997.

> Intermediate-level, yet accessible, read on chaos theory, including the mathematical and physics backgrounds underlying its dynamics. Uninitiated reader might best be suited to first read "Complexity Theory and Organization Science" listed below.

*Complexity Theory and Organization Science*, A Journal of the Institute of Management, Anderson, Phillip, Sciences, 1999, v. 10, 3, May/June.

> Explains core premises of chaos theory and how premises apply, especially to strategic management. Describes several strategic planning approaches that rapidly collect feedback from participants and can quickly adapt to feedback from external and internal environments.

*Fifth Discipline*, Peter Senge, Currency/Doubleday, 1990.

> Senge's book is the seminal work in systems thinking and tools. It provides an understandable and cogent explanation of systems theory, its relevance to organizational and management development, and presents various tools to analyze and change systems.

*Fifth Discipline Field Book*, Peter Senge, et al, Currency/Doubleday, 1994.

> This resource is rich with models, tools and techniques to analyze and change systems. The book is a compendium of resources contributed by various practitioners and is well designed for ease of reference.

*Leadership and the New Science: Learning About Organization from an Orderly Universe*, Margaret J. Wheatley, Berrett-Koehler, 1992.

> This is a seminal work on self-organizing systems. Introduces the concept and explains how social and organizational systems resemble natural, biological systems. Self-organizing systems are major concept in understanding chaos theory.

*Systems 1: An Introduction to Systems Thinking*, Draper L. Kauffman, Jr., edited by Stephen. A. Carlton, from The Innovative Learning Series by Futures Systems, Inc., 1980, Stephen A. Carlton, Publisher, Minneapolis, MN, (612) 920-0060.

> This handy booklet presents a concise overview of principles of systems thinking. The principles can be used to analyze systems and suggest approaches to successfully change systems, as well.

# Index

## *Authenticity Consulting Titles Specific to Nonprofits*

### Field Guide to Developing, Operating and Restoring Your Nonprofit Board

This guide will help your Board to be highly effectively in all of the most important aspects of governance, including strategic planning, programs, marketing, staffing, finances, fundraising, evaluations, transparency, sustainability and lobbying. It includes guidelines to detect and fix broken Boards; select the best Board model for the nonprofit to implement; define how much the Board members should be involved in management, depending on the Board model; decide whether to use committees or not, and if so, which ones; establish specific, appropriate goals for Board committees; conduct comprehensive succession planning of the CEO position; ensure legal compliance to the Sarbanes-Oxley act; and ensure highly ethical behavior of Board members. Comprehensive guidelines and materials are written in an easy-to-implement style, resulting in a highly practical resource that can be referenced at any time during the life of a Board and organization.

296 pp, softcover, revised 2008    Item #7110, ISBN 978-1-933719-05-4 / 1-933719-05-2        $32

### Field Guide to Nonprofit Strategic Planning and Facilitation

The guide provides step-by-step instructions and worksheets to customize and implement a comprehensive nonprofit strategic plan – that is relevant, realistic and flexible for the nonprofit organization. The guide describes the most useful traditional and holistic approaches to strategic planning. It also includes the most important tools and techniques to facilitate strategic planning in an approach that ensures strong participation and ownership among all of the planners. Emphasis is as much on implementation and follow-through of the plan as on developing the plan document. Hardcopy and online worksheets help you to collect and organize all of the results of their planning process.

284 pp, softcover, revised 2007    Item #7120, ISBN 978-1-933719-06-1 / 1-933179-06-0        $32

### Field Guide to Leadership and Supervision for Nonprofit Staff

Top-level executives, middle managers and entry-level supervisors in nonprofit organizations need the "nuts and bolts" for carrying out effective leadership and supervision, particularly in organizations with limited resources. This guide includes topics often forgotten in nonprofit publications, including: time and stress management, staffing, organizing, team building, setting goals, giving feedback, avoiding Founder's Syndrome, and much more. It also includes guidelines to ensure a strong working relationship between the Chief Executive Officer and the Board.

303 pp, softcover, revised 2008    Item #7130, ISBN 978-1-933719-07-8 / 1-933179-07-9        $32

### Field Guide to Nonprofit Program Design, Marketing and Evaluation

Nonprofits have long needed a clear, concise – and completely practical – guidebook about all aspects of designing, marketing and evaluating nonprofit programs. Now they have such a resource. This guide can be used to evolve strategic goals into well-designed programs that are guaranteed to meet the needs of clients, develop credible nonprofit business plans and fundraising proposals, ensure focused and effective marketing, evaluate the effectiveness and efficiencies of current programs in delivery of services to clients, evaluate program performance against goals and outcomes, and understand how a program really works in order to improve or duplicate the program.

252 pp, softcover, revised 2006    Item #7170, ISBN 978-1-933719-08-5 / 1-933719-08-7        $32

## *Titles Specific to Nonprofits - continued*

### Field Guide to Consulting and Organizational Development With Nonprofits

This highly practical book combines the tools and techniques of the field of Organization Development with the power of systems thinking and principles for successful change in nonprofits. The book also addresses many of the problems with traditional approaches to consulting and leading. The result is a proven, time-tested roadmap for consultants and leaders to accomplish significant change in nonprofits. You can use this book to accomplish change in small or large nonprofit organizations, for instance organizations that

    1) have a variety of complex issues,
    2) must ensure a strong foundation from which to develop further,
    3) must evolve to the next life cycle,
    4) need a complete "turnaround,"
    5) must address Founder's Syndrome or
    6) want to achieve an exciting grand goal.

517 pp, softcover, 2005     Item #7180, ISBN  978-1-933719-00-9 / 1-933719-00-1          $58

## *Additional Titles for Business, Government and General Use*

### Field Guide to Leadership and Supervision in Business

Top-level executives, middle managers and entry-level supervisors in organizations need the "nuts and bolts" for carrying out effective leadership and supervision, particularly in organizations with limited resources. This guide includes topics often forgotten in trendy publications, including: time and stress management, staffing, organizing, team building, setting goals, giving feedback, and much more. It also provides guidance for Boards and business leaders to work together effectively.

262 pp, softcover, revised 2010       Item #7430, ISBN 1-933719-27-3 / 978-1-933719-27-6          $32

### Field Guide to Consulting and Organizational Development

This highly practical book combines the tools and techniques of the field of Organization Development with the power of systems thinking and principles for successful change in for-profits and government agencies. The book also addresses many of the problems with traditional approaches to consulting and leading. The result is a proven, time-tested roadmap for consultants and leaders to accomplish significant change. You can use this book to accomplish change in small or large organizations, whether the organization is dealing with a variety of complex issues or striving to achieve goals for the future.

499 pp, softcover, 2006     Item #7480, ISBN  978-1-933719-20-7 / 1-933719-20-6          $58

## Additional Titles About Action Learning and Peer Coaching Groups

### Authenticity Circles Program Developer's Guide

Step-by-step guidelines to design, build, manage and troubleshoot an Action Learning-based, peer coaching group program. The program can be used by consultants or an organization's leaders for training enrichment, problem solving, support and networking among peers.

127 pp, comb-bound, 2002      Item #7730, ISBN 978-1-933719-10-8 / 1-933719-10-9      $26

### Authenticity Circles Facilitator's Guide

This Guide describes how to organize, facilitate and evaluate peer coaching groups. Groups can be facilitated by an external facilitator or groups can self-facilitate themselves. It can also be used to recruit, develop and support facilitators of peer coaching groups. The Guide includes appendices with worksheets for the facilitator's use and a handy Circles Quick Reference tool.

114 pp, comb-bound, 2002      Item #7720, ISBN 978-1-933719-11-5 / 1-933719-11-7      $22

### Authenticity Circles Member's Guide and Journal

This Guide provides step-by-step guidelines for group members to get the most out of their Action Learning-based, peer coaching groups, including how to select goals to be coached on, how to get coached and how to coach others. The Guide includes a journal of worksheets to capture the learning of the group members and a handy Circles Quick Reference tool.

110 pp, comb-bound, 2004      Item #7710, ISBN 978-1-933719-12-2 / 1-933719-12-5      $16

## Coming in 2010 – Watch our website for news!

**Field Guide to Strategic Planning and Facilitation** - *For business now too!*

## To order

To get your copies of these and other useful publications, contact us:

Online:      www.authenticityconsulting.com/pubs.htm

Phone:      800.971.2250 toll-free in North America  or  +1.763.971.8890  direct

Mail:      Authenticity Consulting, LLC
4008 Lake Drive Avenue North
Minneapolis, MN  55422-1508  USA